QUI
TRANSTULIT
SUSTINET
CONN
CUT.

I0837048

Engraved by J. G. Kellogg.

John Winthrop

Eng[d] for Hollister's History of Connecticut.

THE HISTORY OF CONNECTICUT,

FROM THE

FIRST SETTLEMENT OF THE COLONY.

BY G. H. HOLLISTER.

In Two Volumes:

VOL. I.

"I wish [this task] had fallen into some better hands, that might have performed it to the life. I shall only draw the curtain and open my little casement, that so others of larger hearts and abilities may let in a bigger light; that so at least some small glimmering may be left to posterity what difficulties and obstructions their forefathers met with in first settling these desert parts of America."—*Mason's History of the Pequot War.*

SECOND EDITION, ENLARGED AND IMPROVED.

HARTFORD:
PRINTED BY CASE, TIFFANY & CO.
1857.

R. H. HOBBS,
Stereotyper, Hartford, Ct.

CASE, TIFFANY & CO.,
Printers, Hartford, Conn.

TO

THE HONORABLE I. W. STUART,

OF THE CHARTER OAK PLACE,

HARTFORD.

THESE VOLUMES ARE RESPECTFULLY INSCRIBED BY

THE AUTHOR.

PREFACE TO THE SECOND EDITION.

In committing to the press the second edition of the History of Connecticut, I take the opportunity to express my gratification to the public for the very liberal patronage hitherto bestowed upon the work. The task of preparing these volumes was not commenced with any idea of pecuniary profit, but rather with a view of filling a void which seemed to exist in the historic annals of my native State. The valuable researches of my predecessor, Dr. Trumbull, terminated several years anterior to the American Revolution; from which time onward, Connecticut was without any written history whatever. My main object in undertaking the work, (as I stated in the preface to the first edition,) was to turn the attention of the descendants of the Connecticut emigrants from the present to the glorious past; to remind them of the sacrifices, the toils, the sufferings of their fathers' fathers; and to awaken, though it be with a momentary breath, the coals that once glowed like the vestal fire day and night upon the altar of Freedom. Those who read these pages, will find that they little need to be ashamed of their origin, and that it can be said of them as truly and in a higher sense than the fifth Henry could say to his troops on the day of battle, that "their blood is fet from fathers of war-proof." Indeed, no State since the fall of Lacedæmon has ever, in the history of the world, waged so many wars in the same number of years, with equal success, or voluntarily borne such heavy burdens, as Connecticut. If I have failed to prove these facts, I am sure they are capable of proof when some author more worthy of the theme, shall address his energies to the task. Meanwhile, I humbly commend my labors to my brothers who still remain upon the soil of the State, and to those who, in regions far remote, yet turn their eyes with a fond regard toward the green hills and soft valleys where lie the bones of the men who felled the forest and planted the vine.

The second edition has been carefully revised, and a series of biographical sketches have been added to the first volume. Three new indexes have also been added at the close of each volume, viz.: an Alphabetical Index of Names, an Alphabetical Index of Subjects, and an Index of Questions. For purposes of reference, these indexes will add much to the value of the work, and, I hope, will serve to render it still more acceptable to those for whom it is particularly designed. The *subject*, at least, will commend itself to all the sons and daughters of Connecticut, wherever in the providence of God their lot may be cast. To their special care and keeping I commit these results of my labors. The stranger and general reader will not reasonably expect to find, in a mere local history, that comprehensive arrangement and perspicuity of detail so essential in the history of races and of nations. The territorial limits of the commonwealth of which I have written, are so contracted that the area is scarcely observable on the map of our common country; while her entire population is less than that of the single city of New York. With a feeling of filial love, I have here sought to follow her varied fortunes, from the day when a little band of Englishmen, on the borders of our "great river," first broke the silence of the primeval wilderness. The subsequent settlement and growth of her towns; the struggles and privations of her pioneers; her wars with the Indians, the Dutch, the French, and, finally, with the mother country; her civil history; the progress of liberty, religion and education within her limits; the gradual development of her resources—all these I have sought candidly and truthfully, to portray. With what success, the reader must judge.

CONTENTS.

CHAPTER I.

CHAPTER II.

CHAPTER III.

CHAPTER VI.

CHAPTER VII.

CHAPTER VIII.

CHAPTER IX.

CHAPTER X.

CHAPTER XI.

CHAPTER XII.

CHAPTER XIII.

HISTORY

OF

CONNECTICUT.

CHAPTER I.

SETTLEMENT OF THE CONNECTICUT RIVER VALLEY.

SOME time during the year 1631, an Indian Sachem visited the governors of the Massachusetts and Plymouth colonies in the guise of a suppliant. He said his name was Wah-qui-ma-cut. He described the country occupied by his own and kindred tribes as a rich, beautiful valley, abounding in corn and game, and divided by a river called "Connecticut," which he represented as surpassing all other streams, as well in its size and in the purity of its waters, as in the excellence and variety of the fish that swam in it, and the number of the otter and beaver that might be found along its banks. He begged that each of the colonies would send Englishmen to make settlements in this valley. He even offered to give the new emigrants eighty beaver skins annually, and supply them with corn, as an inducement to make the trial; and proposed that two men should first be delegated to view the country, and make report to the governors, before any steps should be taken towards a removal there.

The governor of the Massachusetts received him courteously, but declined to entertain his proposition. Governor Winslow, of Plymouth, without directly acceding to it, was unable wholly to dismiss it from his mind; and not long after went himself to spy out the riches of this Indian Paradise.* He found it in primitive loveliness. All that his eye rested on was wild and coy, as if no foot save that of the savage

* Morton's Memorial, 395; Brodhead, i. 210, 233; Trumbull, i. 30.

had trodden there since the dawn of creation. So Winslow doubtless thought, for he named himself the "discoverer" of the River and the Valley.

Governor Winslow must have made a very favorable report of the country, for we find during the following year other explorers, from Plymouth, searching the Connecticut river up and down; and, as early as October, 1633, they had, under the sanction of the colony, established a trading house near the mouth of the Tunxis river in Windsor, and were already carrying on a successful traffic in furs with the Indians, in defiance of the Dutch, from Manhattan, who just before had erected a house called "Good Hope," at Hartford,* but six miles below, and who vowed vengeance against the English traders, who had encroached upon the rights of the "original discoverers of *The Fresh River*." William Holmes was the man who had been selected by the Governor of Plymouth to build the trading house at Windsor. With the frame of this house fitted, and all the materials requisite for completing it, Holmes, with his commission in his pocket, set sail for the mouth of the Connecticut. He passed up the river without meeting with any resistance, until he arrived at the Dutch fort at Hartford. This fortification was not very formidable, having only two small pieces of ordnance; but, such as it was, its little garrison bristled with opposition at sight of the ill-omened sail, stood gallantly by their guns, and commanded Holmes "to strike his colors, or they would fire upon him."† But Holmes was not a man to be intimi-

* Brodhead, (in his "History of the State of New York," vol. i. p. 238,) states that this Dutch trading house was projected in 1623, but was not built until 1633, when the new director general, Van Twiller, "dispatched John Van Curler, one of his commissaries, with six others, to finish the long-projected fort on the Connecticut river, and to obtain a formal Indian deed for the tracts of land formerly selected." Through the negotiations of Van Curler, the Dutch claimed to have purchased a tract of land of the Pequots, as conquerors, "with the good-will and assent of Sequeen." A few years afterwards, however, (July 2, 1640,) Sequasson, son of Sequeen, testified before the court at Hartford, "that he never sold any ground to the Dutch, neither was at any time conquered by the Pequots, nor paid any tribute to them."

† Bradford, in Hutchinson, vol. ii. p. 435; Brodhead, vol. ii. p. 241.

dated by words. He had, he said, a commission from the governor to go up the river, and he should go. A fierce replication from the Dutch followed; but, whether their guns had no powder and ball in them, or whether they thought it best to save their ammunition against a time of greater need, they suffered the English to sail by, and erect their trading house, and surround it with palisades, before they made any further attempt to restrain them. But Holmes soon found difficulties beginning to thicken around him. The sachems of the river tribes had been driven away from their territories by the Pequots, and Holmes, after bringing them back in his vessel, had purchased of them such land as he found requisite for carrying out his enterprise. Enraged that their old masters were restored by the English to their former dominion, the petty chiefs along the river incited the Indians to acts of violence against the traders.

Meanwhile, the news of Holmes' expedition reached the ears of the Dutch governor, Wouter Van Twiller, at Fort Amsterdam. Astonished at the presumption of the intruders, his excellency immediately sent a detachment of troops to the infested district, with instructions to drive the English traders from the river. It is probable that this company was joined by allies from "Good Hope," for when it presented itself without the palisades at the mouth of the Tunxis, its ranks numbered full seventy armed men, under spread banners, inflamed with a noble ardor, that boded no good to Holmes and his men. But all this martial array, so near his gates, though attended with the promise of utter annihilation unless he acceded to their terms, like the threats at "Good Hope," produced an effect the very reverse of what had been intended. The fur trader and his men stood on the defensive. It was obvious there must be bloodshed before the colors of the States General could be displayed inside of the palisades—an awkward situation for an invading army, from which it was prudently extricated by a parley, and a well-timed retreat.*

* De Vries' Voyages, p. 150; Winthrop, vol. i. pp. 123, 148, 153, 386; Brodhead, Vol. i. p. 242.

Thus ended the exploits of Wouter Van Twiller and the garrison at "Good Hope," against the Plymouth traders, leaving the latter in the bloodless and peaceful possession of the soil, to contend, as best they might, with the rigors of impending winter, and to abide their time for the coming on of the calamities that awaited them, of which I am to speak in their order.

Sometime before Winslow discovered the Connecticut river and the lands adjacent, the country—possibly from the representations of Indian runners, who had enlarged upon its beauties at Boston and Plymouth, or perhaps from that love of the marvelous that causes men to desire most earnestly whatever is unexplored and untried—had been sought after with no ordinary solicitude by men of no vulgar rank. In the course of the year 1630, the famous Plymouth Company, the mother corporation that gave life to all the New England grants, conveyed the whole territory of what was subsequently called the colony of Connecticut, and much more, to Robert Earl of Warwick; and the better opinion is, that this grant was, during the same year, confirmed to him by a patent from Charles I. But as no trace can be found of any such patent, it has been doubted if it ever had an existence.* On the 19th of March of the next year, Robert of Warwick executed under his hand and seal the grant since known as the old patent of Connecticut, wherein he conveyed the same territory to Viscount Say and Seal, Robert Lord Brooke, John Hampden, Pym, Sir Richard Saltonstall, and others, whose names still shed a mild light over the clouds of revolution that darkened the sunset of the most graceful, yet erring, of all the monarchs that have ever sat upon the throne of England. Men they were, who may well be said to have been as free from the incendiary spirit that sought to unsettle the old order of the British constitution, as their souls were abhorrent of the oppressive acts of the Court of High Commission. One of them, the muse of Gray has named as the

* As the validity of the patent granted by the Earl of Warwick to Lord Say and Seal and his associates, seems never to have been called in question, it is reasonable to infer that he was vested with full power to grant such a patent.

poet's ideal of the patriot; and another, even Milton, who condescended to flatter no one, could not forbear to write, "with honor may I name him, the Lord Brooke." Such were the original grantees of the soil now known—may it ever be!—as Connecticut. Such were the illustrious men, who looked to the seclusion of her shades for a retreat for themselves and their friends from the grasp of a too stringent political and ecclesiastical domination. But, before the new proprietors could find time to take possession of their purchase, it was pre-occupied, as we have seen, by the Dutch and the fur traders from New Plymouth.

By this time, such numbers had come over from England, and planted themselves in the vicinity of Boston, that the people at Watertown, Dorchester, and Newtown, (Cambridge,) began to find themselves crowded into such close neighborhoods, that they had neither land enough fit for culture, nor pastures for their cattle.* Especially they were in want of meadow lands. They began to cast about them for a more ample domain; and, from the rumors that reached them from time to time of the rich intervals that lay on either bank of the Connecticut, described in such glowing terms by all who brought tidings of their luxuriance, what meadows so likely to make glad their flocks and herds, and what fields promised to yield a more grateful recompense to the toil of the planter? They dwelt upon these pictures until they could no longer banish them from their minds. They hesitated, they debated with one another, whether they should a second time face the exposures that must meet them in a wilderness. But the motives for a removal were too strong to be resisted, and, besides, as their history has since proved, they were strangers to fear. They resolved to go. But would they be allowed to go? At first, the General Court of Massachusetts consented to it; yet, when it was made known that these adventurers proposed to plant a new colony upon the Connecticut river, their enterprise was stoutly opposed. In September, when the court

* Trumbull, vol. i. p. 58.

again met, the matter gave rise to a hot debate. The Houses were divided.* There appeared in the field two champions of no ordinary character. In 1630, the Rev. Thomas Hooker, for some time a minister of the Established Church at Chelmsford, in the county of Essex, "was silenced for non-conformity." Forty-seven conforming clergymen presented a petition in his behalf to the Bishop of London, wherein they vouched for the soundness of his doctrines and the purity of his life. But their efforts proved unavailing, and to save himself from the severities likely to follow his recusancy, he fled to Holland. As, in later days, Bolingbroke and Chesterfield attended upon the preaching of Whitefield, and Montague and Mackintosh upon that of Robert Hall, so did the Earl of Warwick, and other men of note, often go many miles to yield themselves up to the fascinations of Hooker's eloquence. It is not to be wondered at, that the whole body of his parishioners, from whom he had been so suddenly torn, felt the keenest anguish at the separation, and that a large proportion of them, with the expectation that their pastor would follow them, embarked soon after for America. Many personal friends and admirers of his genius, who had never been connected with him by so delicate a tie, were of the same party. A few came over at first, and commenced a plantation at Weymouth. Afterwards, a larger number arrived in the year 1632, and, with the former, all established themselves at Newtown. At their earnest solicitation, to come over and place himself at their head, Hooker finally sailed for America, with Samuel Stone, his assistant, and arrived in Massachusetts on the 4th of September, 1633. He had been in Massachusetts, therefore, only a year, when this interesting question, of the propriety of allowing the petitioners to found a new colony, came up for a second discussion. Hooker, who had already made up his mind to be of the emigrating party should the petition be granted, advocated the cause of the people. Most of the other ministers, at the head of whom

* Winthrop, (Savage's Ed.,) i. p. 168.

was the famous John Cotton, strongly opposed the project. Hooker argued their want of room in which to expand themselves. It was a vital error, he said, that so many towns should be crowded into so small a space. They had neither land to till nor for pasturage. The people were poor. They were unable, so long as they remained as they were, to support their own ministers, much less to give any thing in aid of others, who should afterwards come over from England in a destitute condition. He set eloquently before them the advantages of the country whither it was proposed to remove; the importance of the river, in a military and political point of view; the close neighborhood of the Dutch at Manhattan; the fact, that they had already a trading house in the richest part of the country; and the urgent need there was that immediate possession should be secured.* We may well believe, too, that he did not omit to set forth in bright colors, the facilities presented by a large and navigable stream for commerce; the rich furs supplied by that stream and its many tributaries, in its flow of hundreds of miles through a wild region, accessible, indeed, through the medium of savages, but long to remain unexplored by civilized men.

On the other hand, Cotton, the most learned and persuasive of the clergy, urged the weakness of Massachusetts; that its principal poverty was a poverty of men, to subdue and cultivate a wilderness large enough to support many times their number, and to make a successful stand against the tribes of savages that lurked in its solitudes; that those who had sought to leave the colony in this defenseless state, had taken a solemn oath to promote the interests of the Massachusetts, and that they would violate their consciences, were they to desert the commonwealth in its infancy, and while it might well be said to be struggling for existence. Finally, let the case be as it might with those who remained, those who should go would be exposed to the horrors of war, both with the Dutch and Indians; that it

* Savage's Winthrop, vol. i. p. 167; Trumbull, vol. i. p. 58.

would be in a measure a suicidal act, and that it was the part of benevolence, rather than of tyranny, that the General Court should interpose and prevent a calamity so terrible.

The whole colony was thrown into a state of intense excitement by this discussion. Hooker's powerful eloquence, poured, as it was, into the popular current, carried along with it, as might have been expected, a majority of the representatives. The vote of the assistants was against the application, and so, as a matter of course, it was lost.* In looking back upon this debate, in which those who took a part and felt an interest have all been dead for nearly two centuries, and in looking over those vast regions, washed by the great lakes, the Pacific, and the gulf of Mexico, divided by magnificent rivers—regions teeming now with the posterity, as well of those who advocated, as of those who opposed an emigration to the valley of the Connecticut—the large views and noble liberality of Hooker, exhibited on that occasion, assume the dignity of a sublime prophecy, as if he must have seen in his mind's eye the millions that were one day to inhabit them.

The fate of the application in the General Court gave a temporary check to the plans of Hooker and his friends; but it was far from being satisfactory to the petitioners, and some there were who secretly set it at defiance, and resolved to remove at all hazards. A number of the inhabitants of Watertown, during the fall of the same year, set out for the interdicted country; and, arriving in season to construct temporary houses in which to pass the winter,† made, it is believed, at Pyquaug, (Wethersfield,) the first settlement on the Connecticut river.

In May of the following year, the old application of Hooker and his friends was renewed, and leave to remove reluctantly granted by the General Court, with the proviso, that those who emigrated should still "continue under the jurisdiction of Massachusetts."‡

---

* Savage's Winthrop, i. p. 168.

† Trumbull, vol. i. p. 59.

‡ Savage's Winthrop, vol. i. p. 191.

During the summer of the same year, several of the people belonging to the congregation of the Rev. Mr. Wareham, of Dorchester, removed to a point on the river near the Plymouth trading house, and, much to the alarm of Holmes and those whom he represented, prepared to lay the foundations of the town of Windsor.* The whole of that season, the Watertown settlers, in little parties of a few families, continued to make additions to the gallant little company of pioneers at Wethersfield. The planters at Newtown were getting ready, also, to remove to Hartford the next spring. Thus passed the eventful summer of 1635, in bustling preparation, until, in the middle of October, when the trees were half stripped of their leaves, and the chestnuts and acorns were dropping from the boughs in the lovely autumn weather, sixty persons, among whom were women and little children, set out on their tedious march to the new settlements. They took along with them such movable property as they could, including their horses, cattle, and swine. A slow, wearisome journey they made of it. They were delayed by so many obstacles, that frosts and snows were pressing hard upon them before they reached the eastern bank of the Connecticut. And so much time was spent in making rafts, and crossing the river with their cattle, that they were not ready for winter when it came. Most of them settled in Hartford.

In the fall of the same year, came over to America John Winthrop, the younger, a commissioned agent of Viscount Say and Seal, and the other noblemen, knights, and gentlemen, named in the original patent of the colony,† with instructions to repair immediately to the mouth of the Connecticut river with fifty men, and commence the building of a strong fortification, and houses as well for the garrison as for gentlemen, expected to arrive in the course of the next year. The fort was to be built upon a very large scale, to embrace within its inclosure "houses suitable for the reception of men of quality," to be erected as soon as practicable. Win-

* Savage's Winthrop, i. p. 198; Trumbull, vol. i. p. 60.

† Ib. vol. i. pp. 202, 203.

throp was directed to take possession of a suitable tract of land, near the fort, containing from a thousand to fifteen hundred acres, that was to be reserved for the use of the fortification. He was constituted by this commission, "Governor of the river Connecticut," for the space of a year after his arrival there.

When Governor Winthrop arrived in Massachusetts, he heard rumors that the Dutch were preparing to anticipate him in the erection of a fort at the place named in his commission. He waited only to collect about twenty men, and sent them by sea to take possession of the mouth of the river, and to erect embankments, and to plant their cannon there with all dispatch. They had much need of haste; for, scarcely had they begun to make themselves ready for defence, when a Dutch sail from Manhattan was seen making for the mouth of the river. The current of the Connecticut, at this place, pressed close upon the western bank; and here, upon a bluff that juts out boldly into the deep water, almost upon the very line where the river loses itself in the sea, Winthrop's men had hastily thrown up their embankments and mounted their guns. When the Dutch had approached near enough to the land to see the new fortress, with the English colors floating above it, they withdrew without any show of resistance, leaving the governor's forces in quiet possession of the key to the treasures of a country that had for some time tempted their cupidity, but was henceforth to be forever locked against them.

I have already alluded to the severity of that memorable winter. The garrison at Saybrook suffered severely; but it was reserved to the three settlements further up the valley to encounter all the horrors of a winter in the wilderness.

By the middle of November, the river was frozen completely over. The personal effects of the settlers, such as they could not well carry with them in their journey through the woods, had been forwarded by sea; but the vessels that bore this precious lading, of beds, clothing, and provisions, for delicate women and little children, were either wrecked upon that coast, even in this age of improved navigation, so fatal to mariners, or forced to put back again into Boston harbor. By the first of December, the pangs of famine began to be added to the numbing influences of cold. With a frugal hand, the father of the household measured out the stinted dole of bread and meat to his offspring, until both bread and meat were gone. Corn was bought, in small quantities, of the Indians; but these simple-minded creatures, with their usual improvidence, had but too little to spare. Finally, in small parties, the inhabitants of the three settlements, regardless of all other enemies, fled, pallid with fear, from the agonies of starvation. Some crossed the river upon the ice, and, committing themselves to the pathless snows, waded back to the Massachusetts.* Seventy persons were induced to go down to the fort at Saybrook, with the hope of meeting the vessels that should have brought their provisions from Boston. But they looked in vain for the frail ships, that had proved unable to withstand the rocks and shoals whither the blasts that sweep the New England coast at that tempestuous season of the year had driven them. They went aboard a small vessel of sixty tons burden, which they found twenty miles above the fort, hoping to be able to sail in her to Massachusetts. But they saw that she was fast anchored in the ice, and it was two days before they could get her under way. With much difficulty, they reached Boston, after a dangerous voyage of many days. But of the few that remained, the condition was still worse. When they had spent their small stock of food, and could get no more from the Indians, the more hardy of them betook themselves to the woods, to hunt the bear and the deer; and, when this resource failed them, they dug up acorns from beneath the snow, and ground-nuts from the banks of the streams. Many of their cattle died, and those that survived, like their owners, were sickly and drooping. Add to all this bodily suffering, the consciousness of utter helplessness. They were alone. The Indians, though kind to them, were kind only from motives

* Savage's Winthrop, i. 207.

of interest or fear. How long would they remain so, was a question asked doubtingly, and answered by an apprehensive glance of the eye. The vast forest, a familiar home to the savage, was to them frowning and bewildering. Besides, there was something terrific in the consciousness, that the very forces of nature, but a few weeks before so genial and smiling, were banded together to crush them. Still, they hoped and struggled on. In their darkest hours, they never forgot the promise, that seed-time and harvest shall not fail.

At last, the winds began to lull, the snow crumbled and slowly melted away, and a few scattered birds began to give token that April and the bursting buds were close at hand.

The Connecticut settlements were nominally under the rule of the mother country; but they really, from the first, governed themselves. For three or four years, their courts consisted of magistrates, to a number not exceeding six, and from nine to twelve committee men, each town sending an equal number. On the 14th of January, 1638–9, it was ordered that, in future, there should be two general courts in each year, viz.: on the first Thursdays of April and September—the first to be called a court of election, on which occasion seven magistrates should be chosen, the governor to be elected from among them. It was further ordered, that the towns of Hartford, Wethersfield, and Windsor, should be entitled to four deputies each; and that the number to be elected in such towns as might subsequently be admitted to the jurisdiction, should be determined upon according to their population.* The special or particular courts, holden in the interim, were variously constituted—sometimes a jury being substituted for the deputies—three or more of the magistrates being always present—the governor, deputy governor, or a moderator, presiding.† The general courts were invested with all the legislative and judicial functions of the colony, including the power of

* Notwithstanding these provisions of the glorious constitution, (which was adopted at the preceding date,) the "committees" continued to attend the court until April, 1640, when "deputies" were substituted.

† Vide J. Hammond Trumbull's "Colonial Records."

making treaties, a power much exercised in alliances with the Indians.

On the 26th of April, 1636, the first court was held in the colony. It met at Newtown (soon after named *Hartford.*) Roger Ludlow, Esq., of whose liberal views and far-sighted policy, as a statesman, it will be our pleasure by and by to treat, was a member. At this court, it was ordered, among other excellent regulations, that the inhabitants should not sell arms and ammunition to the Indians.

With the first springing of the green grass, and the unfolding of the leaves, so that their cattle could subsist in the woods, those who fled from the plantations in the winter, now hastened to return. Others came with them, and others still followed them, in little groups, through the whole month of May.

About the beginning of June, the first soft, warm month of the New England year, Mr. Hooker, with his assistant, Mr. Stone, and followed by about one hundred men, women, and children, set out upon the long-contemplated journey. Over mountains, through swamps, across rivers, fording, or upon rafts, with the compass to point out their irregular way, slowly they moved westward; now in the open spaces of the forest, where the sun looked in; now under the shades of the old trees; now struggling through the entanglement of bushes and vines—driving their flocks and herds before them—the strong supporting the weak, the old caring for the young, with hearts cheerful as the month, slowly they moved on. Mrs. Hooker was ill, and was borne gently upon a litter.* A stately, well-ordered journey it was, for gentlemen of fortune and rank were of the company, and ladies who had been delicately bred, and who had known little of toil or hardship until now. But they endured it with the sweet alacrity that belongs alone to woman, high-toned and gentle, when summoned, by a voice whose call can not be resisted, to lay aside the trappings of ease, and to step from a position that she once adorned, to a level that her presence ennobles.

* Winthrop, i. 223; Trumbull, i. 64, 65.

The howl of the wolf, his stealthy step among the rustling leaves, the sighing of the pines, the roar of the mountain torrent, losing itself in echoes sent back from rock and hill, the smoking ruins of the Indian council fire—all forcing upon the mind the oppressive sense of solitariness and danger, the more dreaded because unseen—all these, the wife, the mother, the daughter, encountered, with a calm trust that they should one day see the wilderness blossom as the rose.

At the end of about two weeks, they reached the land almost fabulous to them—so long had hope and fancy been shaping to their minds pictures of an ideal loveliness—the valley of the Connecticut. It lay at their feet, beneath the shadow of the low-browed hills, that tossed the foliage of their trees in billows, heaving for miles away to the east and west, as the breath of June touched them with life. It lay, holding its silvery river in its embrace, like a strong bow half bent in the hands of the swarthy hunter, who still called himself lord of its rich acres.

Let us, in imagination, stand by the side of those wanderers, now in sight of a resting-place, and look with them on their new home. What glorious oaks pierce yonder hill-sides with their rugged roots, that, with the lapse of centuries, seem never to grow old! What clumps of tulip-trees, each shooting high into the air its cluster of quaint-fashioned leaves and yellow flowers! More than one of those smooth trunks might be hollowed to form as large a canoe as any in sight, that ripples over the eddies of the river, or is tied by its cord to the trees that grow by the cove. In the thatch grass at your feet, some Indian fishermen, with hempen nets or hooks of bone, are dragging ashore a score or two of yellow salmon; and near by, at the entrance of that wigwam, where the smoke rises so faintly, a few squaws are kindling a fire of drift wood to broil a meal for their lazy lords, that they will eat in approving silence. There are some fields of hemp growing; and further on is a clearing in the woods, though here and there a scattered tree with its rough bark has escaped the fire that felled its companions, where you may see maize, and beans, and squashes, struggling with the grass that taxes the strength of the squaws to keep it down. Who ever saw such patriarchal elms, with such gracefully spreading branches, that droop till they dip their leaves in the brim of the river? At intervals, up and down the valley, are the log huts erected by their friends who preceded them, that rest in the eye of these tired travelers more lovingly than the pleasant manor houses and cottages that they have left behind them. Here these men shall found a city, the capital of a State that shall not be unknown to fame, that shall extend itself under the influences of mild laws, equally administered, contending bravely for its rights, sometimes for its existence, on fields of battle, against wild savages, against the armies of France; and she confesses with tears, yet not with shame, that the most bloody conflict, in the course of two centuries, to be recorded by her historian, was with the children of the country from which her founders fled, contending for principles planted, by Hooker and such as he, ineradicably in the soil.

CHAPTER II.

CONNECTICUT A WILDERNESS. THE PEQUOT WAR AND ITS CAUSES.

THE difficulties that were to be encountered by the English in making settlements in Connecticut, can hardly be estimated by us who now occupy the same territory. We have our sea-ports, our cities, our villages, swarming with a thriving population. The steam engine is hurrying us from one great business centre to another with astonishing velocity, dragging in its train the products of our varied industry, and bringing back those of all nations in return. We have our banks and other corporations, that represent the accumulated earnings both of the dead and living; our city mansions, our hospitable country houses, surrounded by their well-tilled acres, where the ploughshare, as it glides along, is scarcely obstructed by the roots of the forest trees, that once lay coiled like serpents beneath the sod.

Forest trees, standing alone, or in the scattered patches of our woodlands, we have still remaining, though constantly decreasing in number and size, and gradually withdrawing from our habitations to the tops of mountains or the beds of streams, where yet they may be safe for a little while, until the necessities of some newly-built furnace or manufactory shall follow them even there.

How different is the Connecticut of to-day from that of the first half of the seventeenth century! With the exception of the clearings made by the Indians, by burning over the bent grass and dry leaves in the fall or spring, for the purposes of hunting or of their meagre tillage, the whole country was covered with primitive trees. The oak, the chestnut, the pine in all its varieties, the walnut, the cedar, the wild cherry, the maple,—these, with other sturdy trees that thrive in high or temperate latitudes, here shot up and grew luxuriantly, extending over the rough country and the smooth for hundreds of miles,—trees of no puny growth, for they fed on the decayed trunks of other trees, their predecessors, and on the leaves that annually fell and slowly mouldered above their roots. Every year their season of growth was brief, for then, as now, summer came late, and did not tarry long; yet they grew with wonderful rapidity, usurping to themselves all the richness of the soil. Many of them, especially oaks, pines, and elms, attained a vast size, for they stood in such close neighborhood that their branches intertwined and screened each other from the ice and snows that loaded them, and the winds that buffeted them in vain. Not broken, as our thin woods are in modern times, from exposure to the fierceness of the elements, they kept their vigor and grew for many ages. They sheltered a great variety of wild animals—for game, the moose, the deer, the bear; along the streams, the otter, the beaver, and many other fur-producing animals, that requited well the labors of the trapper. There were not a few of the destructive order. Wolves, in thousands, infested the new settlements. They killed the cattle, they stole and carried off the sheep, and did what they could by their unearthly howlings at night, to add to the horrors that thickened on the skirts of the wilderness. It will be a part of our task to call to the reader's mind the many statutes that our ancestors passed to regulate those unruly citizens—how they kept watch and ward to defend against them—how they set bounties upon the heads and ears of those who offended by coming within a given number of miles of their settlements, and how these depredators proved, after all, incorrigible, and with their fellow malefactors, the bears and catamounts, could only be brought into subjection by totally exterminating the whole race, the innocent with the guilty. Wild-fowl also abounded in the woods. Turkeys, more swift-footed than the Indian runners themselves, and of a size almost incredible, were nearly as numerous as the fallen logs beneath which they hatched their young. Pigeons innumerable might be seen on the wing constantly in the spring and autumn days, or startled in the midsummer from the thicket where they had built their nests. In the lakes and rivers were plenty of wild geese, and the whole duck family in all its varieties.* All the little creeks and inlets of Long Island sound, sent ashore their treasures of lobsters, oysters, and other shellfish of all sorts, that now supply the tables of the inhabitants, as well of those who dwell inland, as of those who inhabit the sea-shore.

Within the limits of Connecticut, as its boundaries are now fixed, were probably from twelve to fifteen thousand† Indians, broken into many clans or tribes, speaking different dialects, that had a common basis, so that the individuals belonging to one tribe could understand the words spoken by those of another. All their gestures, too, and ordinary modes of life—their rules of war and of peace, their traditionary laws, their gods, their heaven and hell, had a common origin. They were quite unequally distributed in different parts of the commonwealth. Those who lived on either bank of the Connecticut, and were hence called river Indians, were nearly all within the old limits of Windsor, Hartford, Wethersfield, and Middletown. There were ten sovereignties of them in Windsor alone, who could muster, it was said, an aggregate of two thousand bowmen. Hartford swarmed with them. We shall name only a few of the tribes now, reserving a more particular notice of them when we come to treat of the places where they lived, as, each in its order of time, we gather the new plantations or towns into the constantly enlarging circle reclaimed by our fathers from the solitudes of nature.

We must not omit, however, to make allusion to the Indians called Pequots and Mohegans, who occupied a large tract of country, about thirty miles square, extending from

---

* Hoyt's Indian Wars.

† The number has been variously estimated by different historians, some placing it as high as twenty thousand, while Mr. Deforest, in his "History of the Connecticut Indians," estimates the number at from six to seven thousand only. A careful investigation of all the accessible authorities, leads us to the conclusion that the number stated in our text can not be far from the truth.

the Connecticut river, on the west, to the Narragansett country, on the east, and from the sea-coast, on the south, to the northern boundary line of the colony—making up the whole of the counties of New London and Windham, with a large part of Tolland county. Though usually treated of by historians as separate tribes, yet they do not appear to have been so, except that Uncas, the Mohegan chief, who was too ambitious, himself, to favor the aspiring views of Sassacus, the head sachem of the Pequots, thought it best, from motives of policy, to take the part of the English settlers, in order that he might find in them an ally against the burdensome power of his superior chieftain. Uncas was a rebel chief, who was glad to avail himself of such aid as he could find, and the more powerful the better, against his master. Why he has received the laudations of so many writers, it is not easy to see, unless, in their love of the treason that helped them to crush a troublesome enemy, they have learned also to cherish the memory of the traitor. For ourselves, we set a much lower estimate upon the character of this Indian, than upon that of the Pequot chief, who fought the English to the last hour of his life, and scorned to ask quarter of those to whom he had himself denied it. As the event proved, Uncas was doubtless the shrewder politician of the two; and was too cunning, after witnessing the prowess of his new allies, ever to think of deserting them. Uncas, both by his father's and mother's side, was descended from the royal Pequot line, and he also married a daughter of a Pequot chief; so that he is entitled to whatever honor can be derived from rejoicing over the downfall of the family and the nation from which he sprung.

Sassacus was the most intractable and proud of all the New England Indians. He is described as having excelled all the other men of his tribe in courage and address as a warrior, as much as that tribe surpassed all the neighboring ones in its haughty claims to dominion. Sassacus had twenty-six sachems under him, when the English settlers first came to the Connecticut river. His most familiar haunts were in the present towns of Groton and New London. He had two harbors, one at the mouth of the Pequot river, (now called the Thames,) and the other at the mouth of the river Mistick. He had also two principal forts. The larger one occupied the summit of a high hill, that looks off upon the indented line of the shore and the quiet waters of that part of the Atlantic that is shut away from the main by the low sandy barrier of Long Island—a little archipelago, as viewed from this eminence, containing in its bosom a cluster of islands as lovely as any that lie in the embraces of the ocean. Here, in such rude state as savages know how to put on, lived Sassacus, keeping watch over his fishing-coast and hunting-grounds, administering justice after the rude manner of his ancestors, punishing rebels, bringing home the scalps of conquered chiefs, and sending his haughty messengers for hundreds of miles, into far off regions, whose inhabitants trembled at the terrors of his name. In the expressive language of those who feared him, he was "all one god." Here, by the copious spring that still bubbles up to the lips of him who goes thither to read the lost memorials of a nation now extinct, he had gathered the grim trophies of his savage grandeur; here, were his treasures of wampum, his armory of war clubs, and bows, and arrows pointed with bone or flint.

A few miles to the eastward of this fort, and having a pleasant lookout upon the adjacent country, and his harbor at the mouth of the river Mistick, was the other fort just named.

I have been thus minute in regard to this sachem and his tribe, because their fate is first in the order of events to be set forth in this work. But, before proceeding to the details of a story not so pleasant to dwell upon as to induce us to hasten our steps, let us premise a few words in reference to the personal appearance, character, and habits, of the Connecticut Indians.

They were almost without exception athletic, well-developed men, tall, graceful in their movements, with not very regular features, high cheek-bones, thin lips, black eyes, and coarse hair of the same color. They dressed in a fantastic, yet very becoming manner, in the skins of wild beasts, the warriors having an eye to the picturesque and the terrible, seeking to make themselves as frightful as possible when they went forth to make war. The women wore petticoats of skins about the loins, extending belôw the knees. The chiefs wore belts of wampum, some of them very costly and beautiful, and of a variety of colors. When dressed for a war council, they were decorated with great care and magnificence.

The Indian was roving and untamable in his disposition. He set a high value upon demeanor. Possessed of the most intense curiosity, he habitually hid it beneath the mask of a stony indifference. He was proud, beyond all other men, both by nature and education. He has been called cowardly in his mode of warfare.* But when it is recollected how puny were his offensive weapons, how slight those of defense, how little his dress protected his person, and how deadly were the guns of the English, we ought not to form hasty conclusions adverse to his valor. The Indians were not wanting in intellectual endowments. They had little sympathy with external nature, and yet they were from necessity keen observers of all natural phenomena. They had a rude, wild gift of eloquence, highly impassioned, abounding in metaphors sometimes extravagant, always bold and striking. In all their allusions to the glory of their ancestors, and the places where their bones had been laid, they spoke with a delicate simplicity, that formed a striking contrast with the frigid selfishness that is stamped as indelibly upon the Indian character as it is written legibly in his face. They were too good tactitians to be trustworthy as friends. As enemies, they were

* From the frequent taunts made by the Indians to the inmates of the fortification at Saybrook, we may infer that they regarded it as the perfection of cowardice to fight from behind the walls of a fort. "Come out here, and fight like men," was their summons to the English; yet, no sooner was the call complied with, than the wily savages flew to the thicket for shelter, and there, skulking behind trees, or beneath the tall underbrush, sent forth the swift messengers of death upon their enemies. Self-protection was the object in both cases, though different means were used to attain the end.

implacable, and seldom suffered the embers of an old feud to go out in their bosoms. They schooled themselves to endure tortures, the most excruciating that can rack the human frame, with a grim composure of countenance, or smilingly courted still keener agonies by menacing gestures, scornful distortions of the lip, and the most insulting way of rolling the eye-balls in the presence of their tormentors. The most complex tortures known to the traditionary code of the Indian, called forth from the victim no confession of their efficacy. Limb after limb might be torn from him, his face mutilated, his tongue plucked out by the roots, his body scorched in the hot breath of the flames that wreathed around the stake, still, like the images of stone that embodied his rude ideal of a creating intelligence, he preserved his scornfulness of look, until his spirit left the shriveled body for such a heaven as the traditions of his people had promised to the warrior whose brown cheek had never paled with fear.

The male Indians did little manual labor. They spent their time in hunting, fishing, contriving wars and executing them, or, when leisure was allowed for indulgence, in a dull round of animal enjoyments. They had no regular division of time, ate no regular meals, and had no hours set apart for social enjoyment. While her lord lay under the shade of a tree within sight of the cornfield, and snored away the hours of a summer afternoon, the squaw turned up the sods, and drew the dark, rich loam around the maize; or, not far off, in the mortar that had been worn ages before in some earth-fast rock, her stone pestle fell in regular strokes upon th shining kernels that she had raised the year before, and laid carefully aside, to furnish the requisite supply of "samp," that constituted the staple of the Indian's food. As might be inferred from their habits, the squaws were strong ana hardy, and more capable of enduring fatigue than the men, though their figures were not so slender and graceful. Of household furniture they had little. A few cooking vessels of wood and stone, a knife made of shell or a species of reed, made up nearly the whole inventory. They had stone axes too, and chisels. Their most delicate manufactures were weapons of war. Of these, they had a good variety, and they were often wrought by the warriors themselves. The most graceful, as well as the most complex, appear to have been the bow and arrow. The bow was made of ash, oak, walnut, but especially of the sassafras, the most elastic and fragrant of all the kinds of wood known to them. Their bow strings were made of hemp, or of the sinews of the deer. The swamps supplied them with an abundance of reeds for arrows, and some of them were carefully wrought of wood. They were all loaded with a piece of flint stone, or bone, sharpened to a point, and shaped like a spearhead, that steadied their flight, and made them, in the hands of such good marksmen as the Indians were, formidable weapons.* They had, also, a prominent weapon, the well-known tomahawk—a name terrible to us from associations of horrible cruelty connected with its use in all wars waged by them against the English. This weapon was made of various materials, and was of various forms of construction. It was either a short, strong club of hard wood, with one of its ends fitted to the hand, and the other in the form of a large knob of deer's horn; or else it was a hatchet of stone, with a grooved neck for the reception of the little stick that was twisted around it as a handle. This weapon the warriors managed with a great deal of skill, and threw to a considerable distance with fatal dexterity and force. They made spears, too, several feet long, with heads of stone like their arrows.†

Lastly, as connected with the science of war, they had some skill in the manufacture of canoes. In Connecticut, these do not appear to have been made of bark, but of the vast trunks of trees. The pine and whitewood, or tulip-tree, were usually selected. Some of these trees shot upward seventy or eighty feet, straight as an arrow, before sending out a limb. As fire was the main agent in felling the tree and hollowing it, the task of making a canoe must have been almost as formidable as our own ship-building.

* Trumbull, i. 47, 48. † Deforest's History of the Indians of Conn. p. 6.

Like many other pagan nations, the Indian deities represented the abstract idea of force—illimitable, indeterminate force. They worshiped the elements. The waters, whether rolling between the banks of rivers, or tossing, white capped, upon the shores of the sea; the fire, the lightning, the thunder, the wind—nature in all her rude forms—every phenomenon that seemed to bespeak a power superior to their own, they deemed worthy of homage, but propably not so much as gods as the symbols of gods. Of these deities, there were two of especial note. The first was called Kitchtan, or Kritchtan, and was believed to be the benevolent or "good god," who cared for them in this world, and received the souls of the good and brave when they died. He was the Great Spirit of the Indian's heaven. He lived in a lovely land, far away to the sweet south-west, beyond the hills where the haze of the Indian summer rested like a dim dream, inhabiting hunting grounds where the deer and the moose awaited his children; a land of plenty, a land of rest from labor and freedom from care, where the warrior could sate himself in the enjoyment of those animal pleasures that could alone make up the Indian's heaven. To this land they made ready to go. The young brave had it in his eye when he went forth to battle; the old chief spoke of it to his children when he laid himself down upon his mat to die. There they were to meet to part no more.

But the deity who received most of their offerings, was Hobbomocko, the representative of the principle of evil.* Love him they could not, for not one of his attributes was lovely; but, true to the instincts of the savage, they feared him, and, therefore, from motives of policy, they worshiped him. It has been thought that they sacrificed human victims to him. At any rate, they set apart a large share of their most valuable property for the festal days consecrated to him, and burned it with well-dissembled pleasure, in the hope of deluding him into the belief that they revered and honored him. These ceremonies were usually connected with some great

* Trumbull, i. 43.

public event or threatened public calamity,* and were conducted by a class of men set apart for that purpose—a kind of priesthood, who were called Powaws. At these solemnities, they danced in rings around great fires, and made a variety of such hideous noises that the English pioneers regarded with aversion and horror these unholy rites, where they had good reason to believe the devil presided.

The government of the Indians was an hereditary monarchy, in theory absolute, and virtually so, where the chief, like Sassacus, was a man of great prowess in war, and superior wisdom in council.† But in all cases he was surrounded by an aristocracy, who claimed a right to be consulted in matters of public importance. This aristocracy was made up of men selected from the wisest and bravest of the tribe, who constituted not only the privy councilors, but also the body-guard of the monarch. From childhood they were inured to hardships and fatigue, fed upon coarse fare, and made to drink decoctions of bitter roots and herbs, that they might be the "more acceptable to Hobbomocko." They were called Paniese. They, in common with the Powaws, exalted themselves in the estimation of the lower orders, by visions and revelations of a spiritual kind, and by interviews with Hobbomocko, face to face. These they related to the credulous multitude in the most extravagant language, enforced by the wildest gestures.

When Winslow and his handful of Plymouth men first made the acquaintance of the powerful Massasoit, and when, at a later day, the chiefs that lived in the neighborhood of Boston walked into the new settlement to sate their curiosity, by looking upon the humble state of the governor of Massachusetts, it seemed a pleasant thing to them that this little company of pale-faced men had come among them. It broke up for a while the monotony of savage life, and, besides, it promised to the politic sachem the advantages of a lucrative traffic. It gratified, too, his vanity, that court should be paid to him by men of such strange attire, and of wealth to

* Mather's Magnalia, iii. 192. † Trumbull, i. 51.

him so boundless. Even after he had learned how fatal to the moose and the deer, the wolf and the bear, were the weapons of the English planter, still it did not occur to him that the same weapons could be turned upon him with the like destructive effects; and after he had learned that guns were more deadly in war than bows and arrows, his mind was directed rather to the injury they might do to his enemies than intimidated by the anticipation that they might one day be turned against himself. Hence, each chief courted an alliance with the new race, never once dreaming that a few farmers, who busied themselves with tasks fit, in his estimation, only for women, would soon get possession of the choicest lands that had been transmitted through a long line of Indian kings, and, finally, rising up as one man, would sweep whole tribes from the earth, and blot out their proudest names from remembrance. Uncas was doubtless leagued with the Connecticut river sachems in urging the English to make settlements there. He felt that he had nothing to lose, and much to gain, by calling to his aid new men and a new mode of warfare, well adapted to strike terror into the minds of his enemies.

Scarcely had the first log cabin been built by the pioneers in the valley of the Connecticut, when the high-spirited Sassacus, forecasting the growth and fruitfulness of resources incident to the English race, began to devise means for their destruction. An Indian runner would carry news through the woods at the rate of eighty, and sometimes an hundred, miles a day, and the nimble couriers of this ambitious chieftain were seen flying in every direction. They represented the white men as rapidly advancing, driving the Indian as the fire drives the deer, when it sweeps over a hunting-ground—that one or the other of these races must give place. They advocated a war of extermination, as absolute as was destined to overtake them.

Sassacus also sent out little depredating parties, who lay in ambush near the new settlements, and committed sad ravages upon the inhabitants. They stole cattle from them.

They shot arrows, from their secret lurking-places, at the farmer when he went into his field in the morning, or buried the stone hatchet in the forehead of his wife, and dashed out the brains of his little children, when they were left unprotected at home.

In the year **1634**, two traders, Captain Stone and Captain Norton, came up the Connecticut river with the design of trafficking with the Dutch at Hartford. They hired Indian pilots to direct them, as they were ignorant of the channel. Two of the crew were sent forward to Dutch Point, with those pilots. Faithless guides they proved to be, for they murdered both the Englishmen at night while they slept.*

There were twelve Indians on board Stone's vessel, and while it was anchored near shore at night, and while Stone was asleep in his cabin, they stole upon him and murdered him, hiding his body beneath some rubbish. They then made an attack upon the crew, with little resistance, and killed them all except Norton, who betook himself to the cook room, and fought desperately, and with such address, that it seemed for a long time doubtful how the battle would end; when, at last, his powder, that had been put in an open vessel, took fire, and so blinded and mutilated him that he was disabled and slain. The booty that resulted from this treacherous skirmish was shared between the Pequots and the western Nihanticks. Sassacus and Ninigret, the sachems of these tribes, doubtless had a secret agency in the business, as they partook of the plunder.

Soon after this outrage, unprovoked, so far as can now be known, the deep-seated hostility that existed between the Narragansetts and Pequots began to exhibit itself. The Narragansetts had already dug up the hatchet, and were sending out their runners against their old enemy, Sassacus. They were making preparations for a general war. The Dutch, too, had paid an old debt of revenge for some injuries done to them, by killing a Pequot sachem, together with some

* Trumbull, i. 70; Winthrop, i. 146; Miss Caulkins' Hist. New London, 27, 28; Mass. Hist. Collections, viii. 130, new series.

of his warriors, and taking others captive. Sassacus and his paniese began to be alarmed. What was to be done? There was much need of a good ally. At last, it was resolved by the Pequots to send a messenger to the English in the Massachusetts, with the view of making a league, offensive and defensive, with them. In November of the same year, the Pequot courier presented himself before the governor at Boston, and made proposals for a treaty. But the governor, not satisfied with the credentials of the ambassador, and, doubting his rank, put himself upon his dignity as the representative of the people, and told him frankly that he did not like his quality, and that the Pequots must send men of more weight and consequence, or he could not treat with them. The messenger, rather humbled, one would think, in being the bearer of his own disgrace at a foreign court, seems to have done his errand faithfully, for in due time two ministers plenipotentiary appeared, armed with an acceptable present, and of a gravity of character suitable to the business in hand. His excellency said he was not averse to peace, but that there were some old scores to be settled between the two powers. He charged the Pequots with the murder of Captain Stone and his crew, and said that the perpetrators of it must be given up to him for punishment. The ambassadors made answer, that Stone was any thing but what he should have been; that he had abused the Indians, and tempted them to kill him. They further urged, that their nation was not responsible for this murder, as they had neither plotted nor sanctioned it; that it was the work of one of the inferior chiefs, who acted without authority from his master, and that he had already been slain by the Dutch. Finally, they alleged, that only two of the authors of this crime survived, and they promised to use their influence with Sassacus to induce him to deliver them up to justice. They begged the English to send a vessel with cloths to trade with them, and proposed to give them whatever title they had to the lands on the Connecticut river, if they would send men to live there. They also promised to give to their new ally four hundred fathom of wampum, forty beaver skins, and thirty otter skins.

The treaty was at last established between the two powers, with the usual solemnities, much after the terms proposed by the Pequots.

How much sincerity there was on the part of the Indians in making these overtures, it is difficult to say. If honest at the time, their habitual fickleness and love of excitement prevented them from enjoying the blessings of an alliance that had cost them so much trouble in the making, and was liable to misconstructions of every sort, as well from the old jealousies that beset it on every side, as from the different character, habits, and languages of the contracting parties.

The next year, while Mr. John Oldham was trafficking with the Indians off Block Island, a large number of them made an attack upon him while on board his pinnace, and killed him. John Gallop, who was engaged in the same traffic not long after, sailing near enough to Oldham's vessel to see that her deck was swarming with Indians, readily divined what had happened. He bore down upon the pinnace, and, with one man and two boys, (his whole crew,) gave them such showers of duck shot that he soon drove them under hatches. He then stood off, and, with crowded canvass and a brisk sail, ran down upon the pinnace, striking her quarter with such violence that he nearly overset her. Six of the Indians, under the terrors inspired by this new mode of warfare, plunged overboard and were drowned. He repeated this experiment, again striking the pinnace with such force that he bored her with his anchor, and might have had trouble in disentangling himself from her had not the terrified savages allowed him to have it all his own way. A third time he bore down upon her with such address, that several more of the savages leapt into the sea. Gallop then boarded her and took two prisoners, one of whom he bound and threw overboard.* Two or three others, who had taken refuge below and armed themselves, could not be driven from

* Miss Caulkins' Hist. New London, 29.

their retreat. Oldham's dead body was found on board, the head split in half, and the trunk and limbs brutally mangled. It lay hidden under a fishing net.* Gallop had no difficulty in recognizing the remains, and exclaimed, as he washed the blood from the ghastly features of the murdered man, "Oh, brother Oldham, is it thou? I am resolved to avenge thee!"† Mutilated as was the dead body, Gallop committed it to the sea with reverent hands. After these simple obsequies were over, they stripped the pinnace of her rigging and whatever lading the Indians had left on board, and proceeded to tow her into port; but the wind rose as the sun went down, and they were obliged to cut her adrift.

There is little reason to doubt that Oldham was the victim of unprovoked, premeditated murder. He was from Dorchester, and was a respectable trader. The Block Island and Narragansett Indians executed this plot, which was contrived, as was supposed, by several of the Narragansetts. Whether the Pequots helped to plan the murder, was never distinctly proved; but it is most probable that they did, as they secreted and protected several of the conspirators, who took refuge among them.

Had it been known to our ancestors, as it is known to us, how little power the great sachems had to control the conduct of their petty chiefs, perhaps some of the darkest annals of our colony might never have been penned. Canonicus, the wise and noble sachem of the Narragansetts, disclaimed any knowledge of this murder, and felt keenly the suspicion that rested upon his tribe. He took the most stringent measures to find out the authors of it.

The governor, "by the advice of the magistrates and ministers" of Massachusetts, resolved that the Block Island Indians should be chastised. To execute this rash penalty, ninety men were sent under the command of John Endicott. Endicott was ordered to sail for Block Island, and put to death all the men on it, take the women and children prisoners,

---

* Savage's Winthrop, i. 226; History of Boston, by S. G. Drake, Esq., p. 198.

† History of Boston, by Drake, 199.

and carry them to Boston.* This was to avenge the death of Oldham. Having done this, he was directed to sail for Pequot harbor, demand of the Pequots the murderers of Captain Stone, (whose death that tribe had already atoned for, as they supposed, by executing such terms of the late treaty as they could,) and one thousand fathom of wampum, as well as some Pequot children as hostages. If the Pequots failed to meet these demands, he was to use force.

Endicott repaired to Block Island, and arrived there on the last day of August. The surf rolled so high that he could scarcely land his men. Indian warriors, to the number of sixty, met him on the beach. But, in spite of the surf and the natives, he at length got his troops ashore. The island, called by the Indians Manisses, or the Island of the Little God, was mostly covered with small sand hills, that were overgrown with dwarf oaks. To the shelter afforded by this forbidding screen, the Indians betook themselves, firing their arrows behind them as they fled. There were two large plantations upon the island, with about sixty wigwams. The Indians had on these plantations two hundred acres of corn, a part of it piled in heaps and a part still standing. In two days, Endicott hunted out and killed fourteen Indians, destroyed the corn, staved in the canoes, and burned every wigwam that he could find.† He then set sail for the Pequot country. On his way he stopped at Saybrook, and reported to Gardiner, who commanded at the fort, what he had done. Gardiner, who thought the Narragansetts, and not the Block Island Indians, were guilty of the murder of Oldham, complained bitterly of this rash step. "You come hither," said he, "to raise these wasps about my ears, and then you will take wing and flee away."‡ This metaphor, as is often the case with figurative language, embodied a sad truth, that was but too well understood in Connecticut not long after.

The Massachusetts leader lost no time in reaching Pequot harbor. The Pequots were taken by surprise by this visit.

---

* Drake's History of Boston, 201. † Drake, 202.

‡ Savage's Winthrop, i. 231, 232; Trumbull, i. 73.

They came cautiously down to the shore, and there learned from the invader the nature of his errand. This landing-place was on the eastern side of the harbor, and the ascent that the English toiled to gain, has since been consecrated by the blood of Ledyard and his brave compatriots, who have given to fort Griswold a fame that will outlast the monument that towers above the spot.* At length they reached a cultivated country, where the humble habitations of the natives rose out of the cornfields that stretched along the hill-sides, and looked off upon the harbor and river that bore the name of the Pequot, and afforded many a stealthy glimpse of the sea-shore.

Endicott had, from his first arrival, told the Indians that he must have the heads of the men who had killed Stone, or else, said he, "we will fight." He also demanded an interview with Sassacus. He was told that the chief was at Long Island and could not be seen.† He then asked to see the sachem who was next in rank; and after much delay, and not until the English had reached the high land, whence they could see the Indian huts, were they told that the chief of whom they were in search, was found. Endicott ordered a halt, and here the cunning savages kept him in parley for four hours, while they could find time to remove their women and children to a safe hiding place, and secrete their most valuable personal property. When this was done, the nimble-footed warriors began to retire, leaving the English leader in such ill humor with himself for having been outwitted, that he ordered the drum to beat and the troops to advance upon them. The savages let fly their arrows at a safe distance from behind the rocks and trees. Endicott now advanced upon the deserted wigwams, and burnt them to ashes. Then he destroyed the corn that was growing, and dug up that which had been buried in the earth by the Indians. He spent the whole day in this work of destruction, and at night re-embarked with his men.‡

---

* Miss Caulkins' New London, 31. † Savage's Winthrop, i. 232.

‡ Drake, 202. This learned antiquarian and historian is free to acknowledge

The next day they landed on the west side of the river, upon the site of the town of New London, and burned and desolated the country in a similar manner. They then sailed for Narragansett bay, leaving the twenty men who had joined the expedition at Saybrook fort to return at their leisure. Gardiner had furnished these men, though he was opposed to the enterprise. He had also provided them with bags to be filled with corn. "Sirs," said he, after entering his protest against the enterprise, "Sirs, seeing you will go, I pray you, if you don't load your barks with Pequots, load them with corn."

Pursuant to this advice, soon after Endicott had sailed, the men furnished by Gardiner went ashore and filled their bags with corn. They were on a second visit to the corn-fields, and had filled their bags again, when they were startled by frightful yells. The owners of the property had caught them in the very act, and their arrows sped so nimbly among the plunderers, that they were forced to drop their sacks and stand on the defensive. This they did so boldly, that the Indians, who fought in their usual irregular way, were soon checked. Yet the attack was so often renewed, that the English did not reach their shallops again until nearly night.

Thus ended this unlucky expedition of John Endicott; but it was followed by a long train of unhappy events. The wasps were indeed stirred up, and their sting was poisonous and deadly. The first attack was made upon the Saybrook fort, whither the corn had been transported. Perhaps the Pequots reasoned as the ministers and magistrates of Massachusetts had done, that they who shared the plunder were responsible for the bloodshed.

Early in October, as five men belonging to the garrison were carrying home hay from the meadows, the Pequots concealed themselves in the tall grass, surrounded them, and took one Butterfield prisoner. The rest escaped. Butterfield was

---

the impolicy as well as the injustice of Endicott's expedition. He did not cripple the enemy in the least, but only served to exasperate them, and arouse in their bosoms the most implacable hatred toward the English.

roasted alive, with the most brutal tortures. During the same month, one Tilly, the master of a small vessel, was taken captive by the Pequots, as he was sailing down the Connecticut river. He had anchored his craft about three miles above the fort, and imprudently gone ashore in a canoe with a single attendant to shoot wild-fowl. The first discharge of his gun was a signal for a large body of Pequots, who lurked in the woods, to rush upon him. They took Tilly alive and killed his attendant. They then set themselves to the task of destroying Tilly by piecemeal. The captive knew enough of their war customs to be aware that any show of submission on his part would be treated with scorn. He therefore remained passive, as an Indian brave would have done in his situation. First they cut off his hands. He made no complaint. Then, in their barbarous way, they amputated his feet. Not a groan escaped him. Thus they continued to follow him up with their most ingenious modes of torture, until he died. Even in death, his features showed no traces of pain. His admiring tormentors left his remains with the merited eulogy that he was a "stout man."*

Nothing could exceed the activity of these Indians, now that they were thoroughly aroused. They lurked in the lowlands that surrounded the fort like a malaria. They stole up and down the river by night and day, watching for victims. A house had been built for the uses of the garrison about two miles from the fort, and six men were now sent to guard it. Three of them went out upon the same errand that had cost Tilly his life, when one hundred Pequots rose against them and took two of them. The other escaped, wounded with two arrows. Success finally made them so bold that they destroyed all the store-houses connected with the fort, burned up the haystacks, killed the cows, and ruined all the property belonging to the garrison that was not within the range of their guns. The fort was literally besieged through the entire winter.†

In February, the court met at Newtown, and ordered that

* Trumbull, i. 57; Savage's Winthrop, i. 238. † Winthrop.

letters should be sent to the governor of Massachusetts, deprecating the evils resulting from Endicott's expedition, and calling on the governor for men to help prosecute the war with vigor. Soon after, Captain Mason was sent with twenty men to reinforce the garrison at Saybrook.

Lieutenant Gardiner went out one day in March, with about a dozen men, to burn the marshes. The Indians lay in wait for him, as he passed a narrow neck of land, killed three of his men, and mortally wounded another. Gardiner himself was also wounded. They pursued him to the very walls of the fort, and, surrounding it in great numbers, mocked the fugitives, imitating the dying groans and prayers of the English whom they had taken captive and tortured, and challenging the garrison to leave the fort and come out and fight like men. They said they could kill Englishmen "all one flies." Nothing but grape shot could quiet them.*

Soon after, the Pequots in canoes boarded a shallop as she was sailing down the river. She had three men on board. The Englishmen made a bold defence, but in vain. One of them was shot through the head with an arrow, and fell overboard. The Indians took the other two and killed them. They then split their bodies in twain, and suspended them all by their necks over the water, upon the branches of trees, hideous spectacles, to be gazed at by the English as they passed up and down the river.

The Indians united the keenest sarcasm with a power of imitation and grimace unrivaled even among children. They would put on the clothes of Englishmen whom they had roasted alive, and present themselves in little bands on the lawn in front of the fort, where they would enact over again the horrible drama, kneeling down and praying with the fervent voice and agonized gestures of the sufferers, and utter lamentations and cries indicative of the most unspeakable anguish. This theatrical entertainment was usually ended with insults offered to Gardiner in broken English, or with

* Trumbull, i. 76.

peals of demoniac laughter. Then they would take to their heels and run into the woods.

About this time, Thomas Stanton, who could speak the Indian language so well that he often acted as interpreter for the colonies, arrived in a vessel at Saybrook. While waiting at the fort for a fair wind, a few Indians were seen to come down one day to a hill within musket range of the palisades, and hide themselves behind the trees. Gardiner ordered that the cannon should be pointed at the place where they lurked, and fired off when he waved his hat. Three of the savages soon rose and cautiously advanced towards the fort under pretense of a parley. Gardiner, willing, perhaps, to amuse his guest, walked out with him a little way, that they might come within speaking distance of the Indians. When the Englishmen had reached the stump of a large tree they stopped. "Who are you?" asked the Indians. Stanton, replying to them in their own language, said, "That is the Lieutenant," and added that his own name was Thomas Stanton. The Indians replied, "It is false; we saw the Lieutenant the other day shot full of arrows." But as soon as Gardiner spoke they saw their mistake, for one of the Indians knew him well. They then cunningly asked, "Will you fight with the Nihanticks? The Nihanticks are your friends, and we have come to trade with you." "We do not know one Indian from another," replied Stanton, "and we will trade with none of them." "Have you had fighting enough?" asked the Indians. "We do not know that yet," returned the interpreter. "Is it your custom to kill women and children?" rejoined the other party to the dialogue. "That you shall see hereafter."

A long pause ensued, when one of the Indians said, with a haughty air, "We are Pequots; and have killed Englishmen, and can kill them as mosquitoes: and we will go to Connecticut, and kill men, women, and children, and carry away the horses, cows, and hogs." Gardiner then replied, with that good-natured irony so common with him, "No, no; if you kill all the English there, it will do you no good. English women are lazy, and can't do your work. The horses and cows will spoil your corn-fields. The hogs will root up your clam banks. You will be completely undone. But look here at our fort. Here are twenty pieces of trucking-cloth, and hoes, and hatchets; you had better kill us and get these things, before you trouble yourselves to go up to Connecticut."*

The Indians, enraged at this taunt, and unable to answer it, betook themselves to the thicket. They had scarcely reached it, when Gardiner gave the signal that was followed by a discharge of grape, that did the Indians little harm beyond the fright that it gave them.

In April, they went as far as Wethersfield, and waylaid the farmers as they went into the fields to labor. They killed six men and two women, and took captive two maidens,† who were long and anxiously sought after, and were finally safely restored to their friends by the Dutch. They owed their lives to the wife of Mononotto, a chief second only to Sassacus. She protected them with a faithfulness and delicacy, that were honorably requited when it came her turn to be a prisoner. At Wethersfield, also, they killed twenty cows, and destroyed other property to a large amount.

Not long after, John Underhill, who had served under Endicott in his attack upon the Pequots the year before, was sent from Massachusetts with twenty men, to reinforce the garrison at Saybrook. When he reached the fort, Mason and his men returned to Hartford.

With such an enemy hanging about the skirts of their three infant settlements—an enemy, growing every hour more daring and reckless—it was evident that some decisive steps must be taken at once.

In the midst of these calamities the General Court met at Hartford, on the 1st of May, 1637. This court represented the little republic of less than three hundred souls. An excited session it was, and one fraught with doubts and teeming

* Gardiner. Mass. Hist. Col. xxxiii. 144, 146; Mass. Hist. Col. xxxvi. 11.

† Mass. Hist. Col. viii. 132, new series; Trumbull, i. 77.

with weighty considerations. There is little evidence left us that there was a single faint heart in this company of fifteen picked men—six magistrates, and nine committee-men—who had in their hands the fate of Connecticut. Little evidence of fear, indeed, is to be found in the records of this body, for the first written memorial that we have of their doings, is in the following concise words: "It is ordered that there shall be an offensive war against the Pequot, and there shall be ninety men levied out of the three plantations of Hartford, Wethersfield, and Windsor;"* a declaration of war of a phraseology so unmistakable in its simplicity, that we would joyfully recommend it to the legislative bodies of our own day—words that the reader will not be surprised to find employed by a body, including the names of Ludlow, Steele, Talcott, and Sherman. Of these troops, Hartford was to furnish forty-two, Windsor thirty, and Wethersfield eighteen. It was a short session, for long speeches were not then in fashion in any of the American colonies, where a sound head and a ready hand were in better request than nimble tongues. After providing for the munitions and supplies requisite to carry on the war, the court adjourned.

The little commonwealth was united as one man in the cause, and the preparations went forward with such promptness, that in about a week after the war was resolved upon, the troops were ready to set sail.

It was on Wednesday, the 10th of May, that the heroic army embarked at Hartford, in "a pink, a pinnace, and a shallop,"† a hundred and sixty men;—the ninety English levied from the plantations, and seventy Mohegan Indians, under the command of Uncas,—and set sail for the mouth of the river. The renowned John Mason was Captain of the army, and Samuel Stone, scarcely less known to fame for his battles in a different field of strife, was its chaplain, or spiritual guide.

The water was so shallow at this season of the year, that

* J. Hammond Trumbull's Colonial Records, i. 9.

† Mason's "History of the Pequot War."

the vessels several times ran aground in dropping down the river. This delay was so irksome to the Indians, that they begged to be set ashore, to which Mason consented, on their promising to meet the English at Saybrook. It was not until the 15th of May, that Mason and his men arrived at Saybrook, having spent five days in sailing about fifty miles. Uncas kept his word, and joined the English at Saybrook fort. He had fought one battle during his absence, and killed seven hostile Indians. The report of this skirmish was verified by Captain John Underhill, who came with Uncas, when he rejoined the English troops. Underhill also tendered to Mason his services, with nineteen men, for the expedition, if Lieutenant Gardiner, who as we have seen commanded at Saybrook fort, would consent to it. Gardiner as readily granted him and his men leave to go. Mason was delighted with this new ally, and at once resolved to send back twenty of his own troops to protect, during his absence, the almost defenceless towns upon the river.* In his recent expedition, Uncas, in addition to the seven Indians that he had killed, had also taken one prisoner. Unluckily for the captive, he was known to be a spy. He had affected great friendship for the English, and had lived with the garrison at the fort long enough to acquire their language. He then communicated to Sassacus their most secret counsels. Besides, he had been present at the horrid murders perpetrated by the Pequots at Saybrook. Uncas claimed the right to execute this Indian after the custom of his tribe. Never was justice meted out to a wretch with a more lavish hand. He was torn limb from limb, and roasted in a fire kindled for that purpose, and then passed around the council-ring, and eaten by Uncas and his Mohegans with a relish equaled only by the demonstrations of joy with which they threw the bones into the fire when they had completed their meal.†

Mason now began to be aware how critical was the task he had undertaken. From Wednesday, when he arrived at the mouth of the Connecticut river, until the next Friday,

* Mason; Drake 207; Brodhead, i. 271. † Trumbull, i. 80.

his little fleet lay wind-bound near the fort, and within sight of the Pequot runners and spies who kept watch along the river. Mason's commission instructed him to sail directly for Pequot harbor, land his men there, and attack the enemy on their own ground. But the keen soldier saw at a glance the peril of obeying such orders. Had he not been kept so long at Saybrook, the case might have been different. But eight days had elapsed since he set sail from Hartford, and he well knew that a Pequot runner, could carry the news from the mouth of the Connecticut to that of the Thames in an hour, and that the shore would be lined with savages to meet them on their arrival. Besides, the shore was wild and rough, with rocks and trees that afforded a safe screen to the Indians. He also knew from the poor girls who had been taken captive at Wethersfield, and who had just been brought safely back to Saybrook by the Dutch, that the Pequots had sixteen guns in their possession, and had learned how to use them. The Pequot warriors, too, he was aware, many times outnumbered his own, and were swift of foot, and having the advantage of a favorable position on land, could offer a formidable opposition to the English, who were more slow in their movements. The Pequots, too, could choose their ground, as their harbor was the only place within many miles where the English could land. Lastly, he saw, that if he could fall upon the enemy in the rear, and when they were not prepared for an attack, they would fall an easy prey into his hands.

Mason summoned a council of war, and assigned boldly these reasons, among others, why it was necessary to depart from the letter of the commission, and land at some other point than the one named in it. He said, in such an emergency, their necessities must be their masters. He urged the propriety of sailing past the Pequot country, as far as Narragansett bay, and, there landing his army, march through the Narragansett country, under the protection of the old hereditary enemies of the Pequots, steal upon them in the night and crush them.

This advice, backed as it was by such cogent reasoning, the other members of the council did not dare to second. The grim authority of the court haunted their minds like a spectre. They were law-abiding men. How should they dare traverse the written will of the republic? They saw the overwhelming force of Mason's arguments—they foresaw the death that awaited them, if they pursued the line marked out by the commission, yet those iron-hearted men, in the strong language of Mason, "were at a stand, and could not judge it meet to sail to Narragansett." What was to be done? A breeze might spring up at any moment, and then they must set sail. They had clearly no time to waste in debate. At last Mason remembers that these men, though they honor the authority of written laws, do so only because those laws are supposed to express the will of God. Is not Mr. Stone, one of the chosen servants of God, on board one of his vessels? What so fitting as to consult the chaplain?

Accordingly, Mason had an interview with Mr. Stone, and begged him "to commend their condition to the Lord that night," and ask advice of Him.

The next morning, the chaplain came ashore, and told Captain Mason "he had done as he had desired, and was fully satisfied to sail for Narragansett." The council was again called, the case again stated, and with one consent they agreed to sail for Narragansett bay.* It was on Friday morning that they set sail, and arrived in port on Saturday evening. But the wind blew with such violence from the north-west, that they could not effect a landing until Tuesday at sunset; at which time Captain Mason landed and marched up to the residence of Miantinomoh, the chief sachem of the Narragansetts. Mason told the sachem, that he had not an opportunity to acquaint him beforehand of his coming armed into his country; yet he doubted not the object would be approved by him, as the English had come to avenge the wrongs and injuries they had received from the common enemy, the Pequots. Miantinomoh expressed himself pleased with the

* Mason's Narrative.

design of Mason, but thought his numbers were too few to deal with the enemy, who were, as he said, "very great captains, and men skillful in war."*

During the night, an Indian runner came into the camp with a letter from Captain Patrick, who had been sent from Massachusetts with a small body of men to assist Connecticut in prosecuting the war, informing Mason that he had reached Providence with the Massachusetts forces, and begging him to remain where he was until they could unite. But the Connecticut troops were worn with fatigue and impatient to return home; and it was finally resolved that they would not wait for their Massachusetts allies, but would march for the Pequot country the next morning. The Narragansett Indians entertained such a dread of the Pequots that they could not believe the English to be in earnest.

It was on Wednesday, the 24th of May, that the little army of seventy-seven Englishmen, sixty Mohegans and Connecticut river Indians, and about two hundred Narragansetts, began their march for the Pequot forts. They went that day about twenty miles, when they reached the eastern Nihantick, a country that bordered on the Pequot territory. Here was the seat of one of the Narragansett sachems, and here he had a fort. But he refused to treat with the English, or let them enter his palisades to pass the night. Mason, having good cause to think from their behavior, that these Indians were in league with the Pequots, set a strong guard about their fort, and would not allow one of them to escape from it during the night.† But the conduct of the Nihanticks, was attributable to suspicion and fear, rather than to any alliance with the Pequots, as the event proved; for when they saw, the next morning, that the English were reinforced by a large party of Narragansetts, sent on by Miantinomoh, they took heart, and, forming a circle, declared that they, too, would fight the Pequots, and boasted with their usual bravado how many they would kill; so that when Mason resumed his march on Thursday, he had about five hundred Indian war-

* Mason's Narrative. † Ib.

riors in his train. The day was very sultry and oppressive, and some of the men fainted from heat, and the exhaustion that followed from a want of suitable provisions. After marching about twelve miles to a ford in the Pawcatuck river, the old fishing-ground of the Pequots,* the army made a halt and rested a while. The Narragansett Indians, had, from the first arrival of Mason among them, looked with ill-concealed contempt upon the scanty numbers and supposed weakness of the English. They had more than once hinted that Mason and his men had not the courage to fight the Pequots, and that whatever skill and firmness there was in the army, was confined to their own ranks. But, now that they had come into the country of Sassacus, and found that they were within a few miles of his principal fortress, the expedition seemed no longer to be a pleasant jest to them, but an earnest reality, that grew more and more fearful with every step that lessened the distance between them and the chief, who was more terrible to their imaginations than Hobbomocko himself. Mason at last called Uncas to him, and asked him what he had to expect from the Indians. The chief replied, that the Narragansetts would all drop off, but that he and his Mohegans would never leave the English. "For which expression and some other *speeches* of his," says Mason, "I shall never forget him."

After dining upon such coarse fare as was to be had, they marched about three miles to a field just planted with Indian corn. Here they made another halt and held a council, for it was thought that they drew near the enemy. The Indians now told them, for the first time, that the Pequots had two forts, and that they were "almost" impregnable. Nothing daunted by this intelligence, the council resolved to attack both these fortresses at once. But, on further inquiry, it appeared that the principal fort, where Sassacus resided, was too remote to be reached before midnight, so they were compelled to abandon this plan, and attack the smaller one at Mistick.

* Johnson's Wonder-Working Providence, Mass. Hist. Coll. xxiv, p. 47.

The prediction of Uncas, with regard to the Narragansetts, was soon verified. Indeed, all the Indians, who had at first marched in the van, fell into the rear; and soon not a Narragansett was to be seen. Wequash, a petty chief who had revolted from Sassacus, was the guide upon whom Mason most relied, and he proved worthy of trust. They marched on in silence until about an hour after sunset, when they reached a small swamp between two hills. Here, supposing that they were near the fort, "they pitched their little camp" between two high rocks, ever since known as "Porter's Rocks." It was a clear night, with a shining moon. Mason set his guards, and stationed his sentinels at a great distance from the camp, to prevent the possibility of a surprise. Then the tired soldiers, with no tents to shelter them from the dew, laid themselves down under the open sky and slept. "The rocks were our pillows," says the heroic leader of the expedition, "yet rest was pleasant." Mistick fort was farther off from the camp than they had been led to suppose. It was so near, however, that the sentries heard the enemy singing there till midnight, a wild strain of joy and exultation, they afterwards found it to have been, in commemoration of the supposed flight of Mason and his men—for they had watched their vessels a few days before, when they sailed eastward, and rationally enough concluded that they dared not meet the dreaded Pequot in battle. This night of festivity was their last.

About two hours before day, the men were roused up and commanded to make themselves ready for battle. The moon still shone full in their faces as they were summoned to prayer. They now set forward with alacrity. The fort proved to be about two miles off. A long way it seemed over the level though stony ground, and the officers began at last to fear that they had been led upon the wrong track, when they came at length to a second field of corn, newly planted, at the base of a high hill. Here they halted, and "gave the word for some of the Indians to come up." At first not an Indian was to be seen; but finally, Uncas and Wequash the guide showed themselves. "Where is the fort?" demanded Mason. "On the top of that hill," was the answer. "Where are the rest of the Indians?" asked the fearless soldier. The answer was, what he probably anticipated, "Behind, and very much afraid." "Tell them," said Mason, "not to fly, but to stand as far off as they please, and see whether Englishmen will fight."

There were two entrances to the fort, one on the north-eastern side, the other on the west. It was decided that Mason should lead on and force open the former, while Underhill, who brought up the rear, was to pass around and go in at the western gate.

Mason had approached within about a rod of the fort, when he heard a dog bark, and almost in a breath, this alarm was followed up by the voice of an Indian, crying, "Owanux! Owanux!"—Englishmen, Englishmen! No time was to be lost. He called up his forces with all haste, and fired upon the enemy through the palisades. The Pequots, who had spent the night in singing and dancing, were now in a deep sleep. The entrance near which Mason stood, was blocked up with bushes about breast high. Over this frail obstruction he leaped, sword in hand, shouting to his men to follow him. But Seely, his lieutenant, found it more easy to remove the bushes than to force the men over them. When he had done so, he also entered, followed by sixteen soldiers. It had been determined to destroy the enemy with the sword, and thus save the corn and other valuables that were stored in the wigwams. With this view, the captain, seeing no Indians, entered one of these wigwams. Here he found many warriors who crowded hard upon him, and beset him with great violence; but they were so amazed at the strange apparition that had so suddenly thrust itself upon them, that they could make but a feeble resistance. Mason was soon joined by William Hayden, who, as he entered the wigwam through the breach that had been made by his impetuous captain, stumbled against the dead body of a Pequot, whom Mason had slain, and fell. Some of the Indians now fled from the wigwam; others, still stupefied with sleep, crept under mats and skins to hide themselves.

The palisades embraced an area of about twenty acres—a space sufficient to afford room for a large Indian village. There were more than seventy houses in this space, with lanes or streets passing between them. Mason, still intent on destroying the Pequots, and at the same time saving their property, now left the wigwam, and passed down one of these streets, driving the crowd of Indians that thronged it before him from one end of it to the other. At the lower extremity of this lane stood a little company of Englishmen, who, having effected an entrance from the west, met the Indians as they fled from Mason, and killed about half a dozen of them. The captain now faced about, and went back the whole length of the lane, to the spot where he had entered the fort. He was exhausted, and quite out of breath, and had become satisfied that this was not the way to exterminate the Indians, who now swarmed from the wigwams like bees from a hive. Two of his soldiers stood near him, close to the palisades, with their useless swords pointed to the ground. Their dejected faces told him that they felt as he did, that the task was a hopeless one. "We shall never kill them in this way," said the captain; and then added, with the same laconic brevity, "*We must burn them!*" With these words the decree of the council of war to save the booty of the enemy was annulled; for, stepping into the wigwam where he had before forced an entrance, he snatched a fire-brand in his hand, and instantly returning, applied it to the light mats that formed the covering of their rude tenements. Almost in an instant, the little village was wrapped in flames, and the frightened Pequots fled in dismay from the roofs that had just before sheltered them. Such was their terror, that many of them took refuge from the English in the flames, and perished there. Some climbed the palisades, where they afforded but too fair a mark for the muskets of their enemies, who could see to take a dead aim in the light of the ghastly conflagration. Others fled from the beds of mats or skins, where they had sought a temporary concealment, and were arrested by the hand of death in the midst of their flight. Others, still, warping up to the windward, whence the fire sped with such fatal velocity, fell flat upon the ground and plied their destroyers with arrows. But their hands were so palsied with fear, that the feathered messengers either flew wide of their aim or fell with spent force upon the ground. A few, of still stouter heart, rushed forth with the tomahawk, to engage the invaders of their homes in a hand to hand combat. But they were nearly all, to the number of about forty, cut in pieces by the sword. The vast volume of flame, the lurid light reflected on the dark background of the horizon, the crack of the muskets, the yell of the Indians who fought, and of those who sought vainly to fly, the wail of women and children as they writhed in the flames, and the exulting cries of the Narragansetts and Mohegans without the fort, formed a contrast, awful and sublime, with the quiet glories of the peaceful May morning, that was just then breaking over the woods and the ocean.

Seventy wigwams were burned to ashes, and probably not less than five hundred men, women, and children were destroyed.* The property, too, shared the same fate. The long-cherished wampum-belt, with the beads of blue, purple, and white, the war-club, the eagle plume, the tufted scalps, trophies of many a victory—helped only to swell the blaze that consumed alike the young warrior and the superannuated counselor, the squaw, and the little child that clung helplessly to her bosom. Of all who were in the fort, only seven were taken captive, and about the same number escaped.

Notwithstanding their victory, the English forces were in no very enviable situation. Two of their men lay dead on the field, and about twenty had been wounded. The surgeon had been left at Narragansett bay with the vessels, and by

---

* As to the number of the Pequots who perished on that memorable morning, authorities widely differ. Mason, the chief actor in the transaction, (whose narrative of the expedition we have generally followed,) says "six or seven hundred as some of them confessed;" Winthrop puts the number at about three hundred. Brodhead, at six hundred. Trumbull, at five or six hundred. Underhill, at four hundred, &c.

some misunderstanding had not arrived to attend upon such as needed his services. Nearly all the provisions, and other comforts required by men exhausted and wounded, were also on board the vessels. Without provisions, one quarter of his men disabled, in the midst of a country unknown to him, but familiar to his enemies, within a short distance of the fort of Sassacus, who had around him hundreds of fierce warriors, his ships far away, and his powder and ball almost spent, Mason found much to test the skill of a leader, and to call forth his courage.

While debating what measures should be adopted, it was with delight that he saw his little vessels, their sails filled with the welcome gale that blew from the north-east, gliding into Pequot harbor. The fainting soldiers hailed them with joy, as if they had been angels sent to deliver them.

By this time, the news of the destruction that had fallen upon his tribe at Mistick, heralded, no doubt, not only by the handful of men who had escaped from the fort, and by the clouds of smoke that floated from the fatal scene, but by the dismal cries that attended this exterminating sacrifice, had reached the fort of Sassacus, and three hundred warriors came rushing towards the English with the determination to avenge themselves for an injury not yet half revealed to them. Mason led out a file of his best marksmen, who soon gave the Pequots a check. Seeing that they could not stand his fire, he commenced his march toward Pequot harbor. Of the twenty wounded men, four or five were so disabled that it was necessary to employ about twenty other men to carry them; so that he had but about forty men who could engage in battle, until he succeeded in hiring some Indians to take charge of the wounded. They had marched about a quarter of a mile, when the Pequot warriors, who had withdrawn out of the range of their muskets, reached the spot where, not two hours before, their fort had sheltered so much that was sacred to them. When they came to the top of the hill, venerable to them from so many associations connected with the history and glory of their tribe—when they saw the smoking palisades, the flames of their wigwams, not yet extinguished, the blackened bodies that lay scattered where death had overtaken them—in their grief and rage, they stamped upon the ground, tore the hair from their heads, and then rushed madly down the hill, as if they would have swept the enemy from the face of the earth. Captain Underhill, with a file of the bravest men, was ordered to defend the rear. This he did with such efficiency that the Indians were soon compelled to fall back. Yet such was their resolve to have their revenge upon the English that, during their march for the next six miles, they pursued them, sometimes hanging on their rear, sometimes hidden behind trees or rocks in front, discharging their arrows in secret, at others, making desperate attacks, that could be repelled only by the too deadly use of the musket. They fought at fearful odds, as was evinced by the dead bodies of their warriors picked up by the Mohegans who followed in their train, while not an Englishman was injured during the whole line of their march. At last, wearied with a pursuit that only brought harm to themselves, they abandoned it, and left the English to continue their march unmolested, with their colors flying, to Pequot harbor. Here they were received on board their vessels with many demonstrations of joy.

In about three weeks from the day when the army embarked at Hartford, to go upon this uncertain and dangerous enterprise, they returned to their homes, where the kindest congratulations awaited them.

CHAPTER III.

PROSECUTION OF THE PEQUOT WAR.

THE Pequots, who had gone out to view the scene of the fatal conflagration at Mistick, and who had sought in vain to avenge it upon the heads of its authors, now returned to the principal fort, and told to Sassacus the details of the dismal story, as they had been able to gather it from the too certain indications that still remained. Their reverence for him, no longer kept them aloof from him. From having been his most abject servants, they now became his accusers. They charged it upon his arrogance and ambition, that his subjects had revolted and had called in to aid their rebellion, such terrible allies as the English were, with weapons that resembled the thunder and the lightning, who went upon the sea, and who made use of fire to execute their wrath. They said the ruin of the whole tribe would soon follow. They said that he merited death, and they would kill him. Indeed, it is probable that they would have done so, had not the counselors of the chief interposed with mild words to calm the excited passions of the warriors. They consented to spare his life, but the spell of his influence over them was broken forever. He had ceased to be "all one god," from the moment that it became known how inadequate he was to protect his people from the English. A consultation was now held of the most solemn character. What should be done? Should they remain in the fort, and be exposed to the fate that had awaited their brothers at Mistick, or should they imitate the example of their enemies, and commit this their old retreat, and its royal wigwams and high palisades, to the flames, and then seek the fastnesses of the rocks and cedar swamps for a last refuge? It was with a bitter struggle that they finally resolved to burn the fort, and thus help to blot out the Pequot name. They burned it to ashes with their own hands, and in little companies, as they could best agree to assort themselves, they fled into the most inaccessible hiding-places. Sassacus, Mononotto, and about eighty of his friends and braves, making up the proudest of the tribe, who preferred to die rather than desert their chief in his misfortune, set their faces toward the west, and fled for their lives.

Meanwhile Roger Williams, always the good angel of those who persecuted him, sent an Indian runner to Boston with the tidings that Connecticut had gained a victory over the Pequots at Mistick.

The governor and council of the Massachusetts, resolved to follow up Mason's success, sent forward with all haste one hundred and twenty men, under the command of Mr. Stoughton, with instructions to prosecute the war, even to the destruction of the Pequot name. The famous Mr. Wilson of Boston went with the army as chaplain. They reached Pequot harbor late in June, and soon found a party of the Indians, where they had secreted themselves in a swamp. They took eighty captives there—fifty women and children, whom they spared, and thirty men, every one of whom they killed with the exception of the sachems, whom they saved on their promising to conduct them to Sassacus.

In June, the Connecticut court met at Hartford, and ordered that forty men should be raised, and put under the command of Mason, to carry on the war.* The wise Ludlow, and several of the principal gentlemen of the colony, went along with the party as advisers, for by this time the court had learned the folly of tying up Mason by the terms of a commission. They soon joined the Massachusetts men, under Stoughton, at Pequot harbor. A council of war was held, and it was resolved to follow Sassacus in his flight toward Hudson river. They soon found traces of the enemy. It was evident from the close proximity to one another of the rendezvous, where the Pequots spent the night, that they marched at a slow pace, and had their women, children, and movable property with them. The smoke that arose from

* J. H. Trumbull's Colonial Records, i. 10,

their fires, the prints of their fingers in the woods, where they had dug up the earth to search for roots to quell the cravings of hunger, and the marks that the tides had not obliterated where they had searched for clams in the wet sea-sand, rendered it no difficult task to pursue them. But the Pequots were scattered into so many parties, that it was impossible for the English to tell from these doubtful signs whether they were on the trail of Sassacus or of some petty chief. At last, in this perplexity, they summoned the sachems taken by Stoughton at Pequot harbor, who had been spared under the promise of pointing out the trail of the great chief, and called upon them to redeem their pledge. But they refused to give information against him, and were put to death.* The place where this too summary execution took place was within the limits of the present town of Guilford, where the land, rising into a bluff, affords a grateful elevation for the sea-breezes that have long tempted the lovers of cool summer nights and good cheer to take up a temporary abode. It still bears the name of "Sachem's Head." A part of the army, guided by Uncas and some of his Indians, marched along the shore within sight of the vessels, that hovered as near them as the nature of the coast would allow. When they reached Quinnipiack, now New Haven, they saw a great smoke curling up through the trees, and hoped to find the fugitives near at hand. But the fires, they soon found, had been kindled by the Connecticut river Indians.

Here was a good harbor, and as the march through the woods had proved toilsome, and had resulted in nothing, the English all went on board the vessels. Here they stayed several days, in doubt what they would do, and waiting for the return of a Pequot, who had been sent forward to spy out the enemy. At last he returned, and reported that Sas-

* Drake, in his History of Boston, p. 216, names Mononotto as one of the sachems beheaded at this time. Trumbull, however, mentions him as one of the survivors of the "swamp fight," which took place several days after; adding, that he was one of the twenty who fled to the Mohawks, all of whom were slain by the Mohawks, "except Mononotto, who was wounded, but made his escape."

sacus and his party, were secreted in a swamp a few miles to the westward.

The English were soon on the trail. They found the swamp without difficulty. It was situated within the limits of the old town of Fairfield. In this swamp were hidden about eighty Pequot warriors, with their women and children, and about two hundred other Indians. A dismal, miry bog it was, covered with tangled bushes. Dangerous as it was, Lieutenant Davenport rushed into it with his men, eager to encounter the Pequots.

The sharp arrows of the enemy flew from places that hid the archers, wounding the soldiers who, in their haste to retreat, only sunk deeper in the mire. The Indians, made bold by this adventure, pressed hard upon them, and would have carried off their scalps, had it not been for the timely aid of some other Englishmen, who waded into the swamp, sword in hand, drove back the Pequots, and drew their disabled friends from the mud that had threatened to swallow them up. The swamp was now surrounded, and a skirmish followed that proved so destructive to the savages, that the Fairfield Indians begged for quarter. They said, what was probably true, that they were thère only by accident, and had never done the English any harm—and that they only wished for the privilege of withdrawing from the swamp, and leaving the Pequots to fight it out.

Thomas Stanton, who knew their language, was sent into the swamp with instructions to offer life to all the Indians who had shed no English blood. When the Sachem of the Fairfield Indians learned the terms proposed by Stanton, he came out of the swamp followed by little parties of men, women, and children. He and his Indians, he said, had shed no English blood. But the Pequot warriors, made up of choice men, and burning with rage against the enemy who had destroyed their tribe and driven them from their old haunts, fought with such desperate bravery, that the English were glad to confine themselves to the border of the swamp.

There now sprang up a controversy among the officers,

as to the best mode of annihilating this little handful of Pequots. Some advised that they should plunge into the swamp, and there fight them. But the experiment of Davenport discouraged others from so foolhardy a course. Others suggested that they should cut down the swamp with the hatchets that they had brought with them; others, that they should surround it with palisades. Neither of these propositions was adopted. They finally hit upon a plan that was more easily executed. They cut down the bushes that grew upon a little neck of firm upland, that almost divided the swamp into two parts. In this way, they so lessened the area occupied by the Pequots that, by stationing men twelve feet apart, it could all be surrounded by the troops. This was done, and the sentinels all stationed, before nightfall. Thus keeping watch on the borders of the morass, wet, cold, and weary, the soldiers passed the night under arms. Just before day, a dense fog arose, that shrouded them in almost total darkness. A friendly mist it proved to the Pequots, for it doubtless saved the lives of many of them. At a favorable moment they rushed upon the English. Captain Patrick's quarters were first attacked, but he drove them back more than once. Their yells, more terrible from the darkness that engulfed the scene of the conflict, were so unearthly and appalling, the attack was so sudden and so well sustained, that, but for the timely interference of a party sent by Mason to relieve him, Patrick would doubtless have been driven from his station or cut in pieces. The siege had by this time given place to a hand-to-hand fight. As Mason was himself marching up to aid Patrick, the Pequots rushed upon him from the thicket. He drove them back with severe loss. They did not resume the attack upon the man who had recently given them such fearful proofs of his prowess; but turned upon Patrick, broke through his ranks, and fled. About sixty of the Pequot warriors escaped. Twenty lay dead upon the field. One hundred and eighty were taken prisoners. Most of the property that this fugitive remnant of the tribe had attempted to carry with them, fell into the hands of the

English. Hatchets of stone, beautiful wampum-belts, polished bows, and feathered arrows, with the utensils employed by the women in their rude domestic labors, became at once, as did the women themselves, the property of the conquerors. The captives and the booty were divided between Massachusetts and Connecticut. Some were sent by Massachusetts to the West Indies, and there, as slaves, dragged out a wretched, yet brief existence. Among the captives taken in this battle, was the wife of Mononotto and her children. With much dignity, she begged them to save her honor inviolate and to spare her life and that of her offspring. She had been kind to the girls who had been taken from Wethersfield, and for this she and her little ones were recommended, not in vain, to the mercy of the governor of Massachusetts.*

Those who fell to the colony of Connecticut found their condition more tolerable. Some of them, it is true, spent their days in servitude; yet its rigors softened as the horrors of the war faded from the recollections of the English. Sassacus seems not to have been present at this battle. Foiled and discomfited at every turn, he fled far to the westward, and sought a refuge among the enemies of his tribe, the Mohawks. But he looked in vain for protection at their hands. He had defied them in his prosperity, and in his evil days they avenged themselves. They beheaded him, and sent his scalp as a trophy to Connecticut. A lock of his black, glossy hair was carried to Boston in the fall of the same year, as a witness that the proud sachem of the Pequots was no more!

On the 21st of September, Uncas and Miantinomoh, with the remaining Pequots, met the magistrates of Connecticut at Hartford. About two hundred of the vanquished tribe still survived. A treaty was then entered into between Connecticut, the Mohegans, and the Narragansetts. By its terms, there was to be perpetual peace between these two tribes and

* The scene of this famous "swamp fight" lies on the borders of Long Island sound, about three miles from Greenfield Hill, in the town of Fairfield. President Dwight, (who celebrated the battle in his poem, "Greenfield Hill,") states, in the preface of that work, that the "swamp" was at that time a beautiful field.

the English. If the subjects of either tribe did wrong to those of the other, the injured party promised not to take summary justice into its own hands, but to appeal to the English. Then, with imposing ceremonials, the magistrates divided the remnant of the Pequots among the Narragansetts and Mohegans. To Uncas, their favorite, they gave one hundred, to Miantinomoh eighty, and twenty to Ninigret. These poor creatures, thus given over to their enemies and subjected to their bitterest taunts, were to be called Pequots no more, nor were they ever to dwell again in their old haunts, or pay their wonted visits to the burial-places of their dead, or meet on festal days to revive the traditions of their people around the embers of the council fire.

The thoughtful reader may feel disposed to ask us, if we can justify the story that we have told with such painful minuteness. We answer, that such a war should never have been begun. The expedition of Endicott, the primary cause of this war, was ill advised, and carried on in defiance of the wishes of Connecticut. But, after the horrid murders that were committed by the Pequots, the sequel of this unhappy affair, Connecticut was compelled to take the field. The war was then one of extermination, for the enraged Pequot would give no quarter to the English. Some lineaments of the campaign are harsh and repulsive. Most gladly would we soften them with more delicate tints. But the features of truth have often a sharp, stern outline, as had the characters of those unflinching men, the fathers of New England, who struck down their enemies as they felled their forest trees, aiming at every blow of the axe at the annihilation of the wilderness. The roots of the brave old woods they could not at once destroy. A few years sent up a new growth, with fresh leaves, to wave in the breath of summer, and ripen beneath the August sun. But no new race of men sprung up to fill the places of the crushed and desolate Pequots. Let the reader decide the question of guilt or innocence as best he may; but let him not forget to weigh against the fate of the Indians the atrocities that they had perpetrated, and the horror inspired by their war-whoops as they mingled at night with the howl of the wolf around the farmer's dwelling. Let him also bear in mind how much the last two centuries have done to modify the rules of war and the social and political relations of the world. In this way he will be able to adjust the scales between the contending parties, in a struggle not so much for dominion as for a national existence.

CHAPTER IV.

THE FIRST AMERICAN CONSTITUTION.

Civil liberty, as Christian nations understand the term, seems to have had its seeds first sown with a liberal hand in England. But England, with all her health and vigor, borrowed from the feudalism of the continent, during the early and middle ages, many a constitutional taint, that showed itself in the blood of the state, and sometimes threatened it with a speedy dissolution. The struggle between the villein and his lord—the oppressive power of the great barons—their disregard of the interests of the lower orders—their bloody wars, waged to make and unmake kings—kept her in a state of almost perpetual unrest for centuries. There, too, the religious sentiment, long meditating the mild studies of the scholar and the doctrines of the Prince of Peace, in the depths of the cloister, was roused by the blast of the clarion to follow the wildest of priests and the most romantic of kings to the wars of the Holy Sepulchre, and often kindled to acts of violence at home that have left marks still visible in every part of the island.

But, by slow degrees, often repulsed, and still gathering its forces anew, popular constitutional liberty gained ground. By a union of the people with the crown, the barons were subdued, and the kingly prerogative itself was at length confined to fixed channels. Sometimes, indeed, swollen by the strong passions of some imperious monarch like Henry VIII., it broke over its banks, and spread a temporary desolation among the people; but the waters soon subsided into their calm and regular flow. But Henry VIII. was an exception to all rules. It is not often that a nation is governed by a monarch of such scholastic attainments, such intellectual endowments, such a strong and marked individuality, and such an imperious will. Never did a prince come to the throne with more flattering anticipations. A handsome person, a bold and gallant manner, a full exchequer, an undoubted title, all contributed to swell the popular shouts that hailed him king. With all these advantages, Henry was almost totally devoid of moral culture. He was also the victim of the most insatiate passions. It is idle to call him a Protestant, in any such sense as the term was understood in his day, or in that of his daughter Elizabeth. So far was he from being so, that he himself wrote what he called a refutation of Luther's tenets, in Latin, for which he was honored by Leo X. with the title of "Defender of the Faith." Nor is there any reason to suppose that he would have ever broken away from the Roman see, had he not been enraged at the excommunication that followed a public disclosure of his secret marriage with Anne Boleyn. All that he then did was to declare himself the "Head of the English Church." Still he adhered as closely as ever to the theological tenets of the Roman Catholic Church. He executed Sir Thomas More and Bishop Fisher, because they refused to take the oath of supremacy to him, and at the same time caused hundreds of reformers to be burned at the stake. The cruel and barbarous destruction of the religious houses, and the confiscation of monastic property, in 1538, the expunging of the sainted name of Thomas á Becket, from the calendar, and the burning of his bones to ashes, were acts of violence leveled not against the Roman Catholic religion, but against those who dared to dispute his own ecclesiastical supremacy. His alliance with Catherine Howard brought him still more immediately under the control of the Catholic party, and while the new queen retained his favor a fearful persecution was waged against the Protestants.

If he ever was a Protestant, it was while under the brief dominion of Catherine Parr, his sixth wife, whose heart was touched, though she dared not openly avow it, with the dawning beams of the Reformation. Even this secretly-cherished preference had well-nigh proved her ruin. That the king afterwards forsook his old friends, does not evince, that I am able to discover, any change in his religious tenets.

All this while, the quick leaven of the Reformation was working in the minds of the English people. While the monarch was busy in freeing himself from the burden of one queen, only to become entangled in the toils of another, whose glory, alas, was to be equally evanescent; while he was writing that darling word "supremacy," in characters red with the blood of bishops and statesmen adhering to their old allegiance, mingled, too, with that of reformers, whose pure souls were breathed forth in prayer, that the sickle might quickly be thrust in by other hands, since to them it was denied to reap the whitened harvest field—all this while, a large portion of his subjects, in the words of an English writer second to none, were "casting off the rags of their old vices," and were reading the Bible diligently to find the spirit and the form of the primitive church; the spirit first, after that the form; the weightier matters of the law, after these, tithes of mint and cummin. By this party I mean not the Puritans alone, but rather the Reformation party, embracing the high-born and the lowly of every rank and name, who dared for themselves to search the Scriptures, and apply to the exposition of them the light of conscience and reason. This party was never able to make head against the self-willed monarch, but it grew in secret, and waited for his death with such patience as a fiery zeal is able to command.

With his death, this large party, made up of those who afterwards fell in with the established order of things under Edward VI., as well as of the Puritans, who fled from the pursuit of bloody Mary into Germany and Switzerland, dared to assert its claims to royal notice, and those claims were for a brief space in part allowed. During the mild reign of Edward much was accomplished. Articles of faith were compiled, that in later years served as the basis of a more complete and perfect system. In this reign, too, Cranmer and Ridley were associated with other divines to frame a liturgy, not in Latin, but in the vernacular tongue. The first part of the homilies also, boldly setting forth the doctrines of Christianity, and defining with more certainty the then unsettled landmarks of the Protestant faith, were published under the same monarch.

But the mild reign of Edward and the fierce persecutions of Mary soon passed away. On the accession of Elizabeth to the throne, this large liberal party, that I have called the Reformation party, became severed, never to be united again. The queen, retaining in her mind too keen a remembrance of her own dangers and sufferings during her father's and sister's reign, ever to commit herself cordially to the arms of the Roman Catholic Church, yet wedded by the very stateliness of her character to its venerable forms of prayer, its lofty chants, its respect paid to externals, and the hold that it had upon the imagination, dating as it did from a remote antiquity, was ready to adopt some middle ground between the two extremes of the national mind—some safe ground where the more conservative elements of the state might blend themselves with the loyalty still inherent in the hearts of the lower orders—some sacred ground, fit for a shrine, where the sentiment of religion and that of patriotism might dwell together under the protecting shadow of the throne.

Where was this ground of union? The queen was proud—for when was pride absent from the house of Tudor? Yet in her, the loftiest pride was united with that sturdy sense, that keen, intuitive vision, that characterized her noble family, and enabled them to measure the English people, and judge with such accuracy how far they might push the royal prerogative, and note the line of foam that marked the dangerous proximity of popular breakers. Besides, stern as she was, she was not deaf to the voice of those softer monitions that in perilous times whisper of weakness and danger in the ear of woman. Proud as she was, therefore, she had much need to consult her wisest subjects. I can not impugn the motives of this high-toned woman, placed as she was upon the verge of that fearful revolution whose swift wheels were stayed until her eyes were closed in death—I can not blame her that she was not endowed with a prophetic vision; nor did the Puritans, whom she subjected to the rigors of a legislation for which she was to a degree responsible, though they complained of her severity, ever speak of her in terms of disrespect. She took counsel of the most profound scholars and revered prelates, as well as of that circle of glorious statesmen and philosophers that have made her name and era forever illustrious. Doubtless, she felt an honest solicitude to place the church upon its original basis, and doubtless many of her advisers offered up earnest prayers that they might be led in the right way. She, and those who acted under her, did much for Christianity and the Protestant faith—more than had been effected under any monarch who had gone before her. She believed that the church and state were united in holy bonds. Had she contented herself with suppressing factions; could she have distinguished between those who hated and those who sought to reform the abuses of the established church—abuses not inherent in the church, but resulting from its alliance with the state, that have since been gradually acknowledged and reformed—she might have saved herself many cares, and her people many deep wrongs.

Conformity, even in points that had long been carefully evaded, a most rigid, punctilious conformity, was required.* Many of the most learned of the clergy,† alarmed at the disregard paid to the rights of individual conscience, fled in dismay from their places, to avoid the most severe penalties. Some flew to foreign lands; others took refuge in the forests and caverns, where it was a crime not only for them to preach, but for the people to listen. In 1583, a Court of High Commission was established, to search out and suppress nonconformities, clothed with powers the most revolting to the spirit of men brought up under the philosophic rule of the common law of England, pronounced by Lord Coke to be the "perfection of human reason." Under this anomaly, so foreign to the British constitution that Burleigh did not

* Neal's Puritans, i. 396. † Hallam's England, i. 270.

scruple to liken it to the Spanish inquisition,* such outrages were practiced as would scarcely be credible, did not the blood of its victims cry out to us from the ground. Two men were hanged for distributing Brown's tract on the right of a free pulpit.† Ten years after that, Barrow and Greenwood were hanged at Tyburn for non-conformity.‡ These violent coercive measures quickened the growth of Puritanism. At first comprising but a handful of obscure men, in a few years it numbered many thousands, and not a few names that have since made the world echo with their renown.

The union of England and Scotland, under James I., was hailed by the Puritans as the harbinger of religious liberty. But the king soon took more decided grounds against them than his predecessor had done. The number of clergymen who were "silenced, imprisoned, or exiled," in a single year, has been estimated as high as three hundred.|| Mad with the doctrine that attributed to kings a divine right, impatient of all opposition, this weak monarch evinced his hatred toward this now large and respectable portion of his subjects, by acts of severity, and language unworthy of a king.§ It is idle to attempt to deny these facts, authenticated as they are by vast treasuries of English record evidence. No less idle is it to reiterate the charge, equally false, that Episcopacy is wholly responsible for them. When will a day at last dawn upon us, of a light pure enough to dispel the mists of prejudice and bigotry that hang over the history of civil and religious liberty in England? The puritans were the progressive party. They were impatient of the old order of things, just as the members of the established church under Elizabeth had themselves a few years before been opposed to the order of things then existing. Both these parties were in their turn persecuted. Each in its turn was denominated radical and incen-

* Hallam's England, i. 271–273; Strype's Whitgift, 157.

† Strype's Annals, iii. 186; Fuller's Church History, b. ix. 169.

‡ Strype's Whitgift, 414; Neal's Puritans, i. 526, 527.

|| Calderwood, Neal, &c.

§ Barlow's Sum and Substance of the Conf. at Hampden Court, 83.

diary; and each persecution, though inflamed by religious zeal, was essentially political. The English mind, as a whole, was not then prepared for entire freedom of conscience. Those who were in power were timid and solicitous. They deemed every step taken by the popular party as an encroachment upon their own limits, that they were called upon to check, or allow themselves ultimately to be supplanted. It was a struggle between conservatism, fortifying and defending herself, and progress, advancing to drive her from her position. The outrages committed against the puritans in the reigns of Elizabeth, James, and Charles I., on the one hand, and the shocking vindication of them on the other, by the iron-handed protector—a vindication revolting, as well from the blood that stained its grim features, as from the insults so shamelessly offered to the most ancient monuments of British glory, and the destruction of the most sacred temples and shrines—evince alike the wild fermentation out of which civil and religious liberty were at last to come. Both these parties, when dominant, were overbearing and cruel; when in the minority, were sadly oppressed. Each was partly right and partly wrong; and those writers furnish but a poor commentary upon human progress, and wretched evidence of that freedom of conscience which is the boast of our age, who at this day can find in any party of the sixteenth or seventeenth centuries an expression of their ideal, either of loveliness or perfection.

The puritans then were driven to the alternative of giving up their own mode of worship, and taking oaths that were repugnant to their views of right; they must renounce all political honors and emoluments, all prospects of social advancement for themselves and for their children who held to the same belief, and remain in England the scoff of those who found it popular to deride them; or they must cast about them for a retreat, not straightened and accessible like the forests and caves of their native island, where in vain they had sought to hide themselves, but remote and open for the employment of their faculties as well as for the exercise of their religious rites. Some of them fled to Germany, some to Holland, and lingered there till this species of self exile became too painful to be borne. Then, one after another, surrounded by his little flock, many a clergyman, who had been nursed in the bosom of Oxford or Cambridge, who had long sat under the bowers of the manse and eaten of the fruits that grew upon the pleasant glebe, who had quickened his steps as he walked, when the sweet tones of his church bell warned him that the child waited at the font to be signed with the mystic sign, made ready to go to a wild, remote country, where he might be free from oaths save such as he should prescribe for himself, where he might pray and worship by no formularies save such as he might choose.

Right or wrong, this was the leading motive. But other motives doubtless operated with greater or less force upon many of the emigrants. The mind of the old world was then turned toward the new. The various rumors that were rife in England with regard to the illimitable extent of this territory, washed by the waves of the Atlantic and the South Sea, as they vaguely denominated the Pacific ocean, from its very vastness, took a strong hold of the imagination; and these puritans, stern and practical as they were, did not escape the contagion. There were also stories of exciting adventure to stimulate the desires of the young—visions of wealth, from rich acres tamed to the possession and uses of man, or from the furs of wild animals, floated in the dreams of the prudent and money-loving. To deny that the puritans alone were free from the promptings of motives such as these, is to claim for them what they never arrogated to themselves. They were modest men, too earnest in the belief that they were sinners, ever to affix to themselves the attributes of God.

After their arrival here, they sought (why should they not?) to avail themselves of the resources of nature. Hence, urged by no necessity, but simply to better their condition, the fathers of Connecticut left the Massachusetts for the alluvial meadows where they finally established themselves.

I have thought it best to premise thus much upon the

causes that led to the settlement of Connecticut, before introducing to the reader's notice her first written constitution, that was adopted at a general convention of all the planters at Hartford, on the 14th of January, 1639.

We read in treatises upon elementary law, of a time antecedent to all law, when men are theoretically said to have met together and surrendered a part of their rights for a more secure enjoyment of the remainder. Hence, we are told, human governments date their origin. This dream of the enthusiast as applied to ages past, in Connecticut for the first time upon the American soil became a recorded verity. Here, at least, we are permitted to look on and see the foundations of a political structure laid. We can count the workmen, and we have become familiar with the features of the master builders. We see that they are most of them men of a new type. Bold men they are, who have cut loose from old associations, old prejudices, old forms; men who will take the opinions of no man, unless he can back them up with strong reasons; clear-sighted, sinewy men, in whom the intellect and the moral nature predominate over the more delicate traits that mark an advanced stage of social life. Such men as these will not, however, in their zeal to cast off old dominions, be solicitous to free themselves and their posterity from all restraint; for no people are less given up to the sway of unbridled passions. Indeed, they have made it a main part of their business in life to subdue their passions. Laws, therefore, they must and will have, and laws that, whatever else they lack, will not want the merit of being fresh and original.

As it has been, and still is, a much debated question, what kind of men they were—some having over praised, and others rashly blamed them—let us, without bigotry, try if we can not look at them through a medium that shall render them to us in all their essential characteristics as they were. That medium is afforded us by the written constitution that they made of their own free will for their own government. This is said to give the best portrait of any people; though in a nation that has been long maturing, the compromise between the past and present, written upon almost every page of its history, can not have failed in some degree to make the likeness dim. Yet, of such a people as we are describing, who may be said to have no past—who live not so much in the present as in the future, and who forge as with one stroke the constitution that is to be a basis of their laws—are we not provided with a mirror that reflects every lineament with the true disposition of light and shade? If it is a stern, it is yet a truthful mirror. It flatters neither those who made it nor those blear-eyed maskers, who, forgetful of their own distorted visages, look in askance, and are able to see nothing to admire in the sober, bright-eyed faces of their fathers who gaze down upon them from the olden time.

The preamble of this constitution begins by reciting the fact that its authors are, "under Almighty God," inhabitants and residents of Windsor, Hartford, and Wethersfield, upon "the river Connecticut." It also states that, in consonance with the word of God, in order to maintain the peace and union of such a people, it is necessary that "there should be an orderly and decent government established" that shall "dispose of the affairs of *the people* at all seasons." "We do therefore," say they, "associate and conjoin ourselves to be as one public state or commonwealth." They add, further, that the first object aimed at by them, is to preserve the liberty and the purity of the gospel and the discipline of their own churches; and, in the second place, to govern their *civil affairs,* by such rules as their written constitution and the laws enacted under its authority shall prescribe. To provide for these two objects, the liberty of the gospel, as they understood it, and the regulation of their own civil affairs, they sought to embody in the form of distinct decrees, substantially the following provisions:

1. That there shall be every year two general assemblies or courts, one on the second Thursday of April, the other on the second Thursday of September: that the one held in April, shall be called the Court of Election, wherein shall be

annually chosen the magistrates, (one of whom shall be the governor,) and other public officers, who are to administer justice according to the laws here established; and where there are no laws provided, to do it in accordance with the laws of God; and that these rulers shall be elected by all the freemen within the limits of the commonwealth, who have been admitted inhabitants of the towns where they severally live, and who have taken the oath of fidelity to the new state; and that they shall all meet at one place to hold this election.

2. It is provided that after the voters have all met and are ready to proceed to an election, the first officer to be chosen shall be a governor, and after him a body of magistrates and other officers. Every voter is to bring in, to those appointed to receive it, a piece of paper with the name of him whom he would have for governor written upon it, and he that has the greatest number of papers with his name written upon them, was to be governor for that year. The other magistrates were elected in the following manner. The names of all the candidates were first given to the secretary for the time being, and written down by him, in the order in which they were given; the secretary was then to read the list over aloud and severally nominate each person whose name was so written down, in its order, in a distinct voice, so that all the citizen voters could hear it. As each name was read, they were to vote by ballot, either for or against it, as they liked; those who voted in favor of the nominee, did it by writing his name upon the ballot—those who voted against him, simply gave in a blank ballot; and those only were elected whose names were written upon a majority of all the paper ballots handed in under each nomination. These papers were to be received and counted by sworn officers, appointed by the court for that purpose. Six magistrates, besides the governor, were to be elected in this way. If they failed to elect so many by a majority vote, then the requisite number was to be filled up, by taking the names of those who had received the highest number of votes.

3. The men thus to be nominated and balloted for were to be propounded at some general court, held before the court of election, the deputies of each town having the privilege of nominating any two whom they chose. Other nominations might be made by the court.

4. No person could be chosen governor oftener than once in two years. It was requisite that this officer should be a member of an approved congregation, and that he should be taken from the magistrates of the commonwealth. But no qualification was required in a candidate for the magistracy, except that he should be chosen from the freemen. Both governor and magistrates were required to take a solemn oath of office.

5. To this court of election the several towns were to send their deputies, and after the elections were over, the court was to proceed, as at other courts, to make laws, or do whatever was necessary to further the interests of the commonwealth.

6. These two regular courts were to be convened by the governor himself, or by his secretary, by sending out a warrant to the constables of every town, a month at least before the day of session. In times of danger or public exigency, the governor and a majority of the magistrates, might order the secretary to summon a court, with fourteen days notice, or even less, if the case required it, taking care to state their reasons for so doing to the deputies when they met. If, on the other hand, the governor should neglect to call the regular courts, or, with the major part of the magistrates, should fail to convene such special ones as were needed, then the freemen, or a major part of them, were required to petition them to do it. If this did not serve, then the freemen, or a majority of them, were clothed with the power to order the constables to summon the court—after which they might meet, choose a moderator, and do any act that it was lawful for the regular courts to do.

7. On receiving the warrants for these general courts, the constables of each town were to give immediate notice to the

freemen, either at a public gathering or by going from house to house, that at a given place and time they should meet to elect deputies to the General Court, about to convene, and "to agitate the affairs of the commonwealth." These deputies were to be chosen by vote of the electors of the town who had taken the oath of fidelity; and no man not a freeman was eligible to the office of deputy. The deputies were to be chosen by a major vote of all the freemen present, who were to make their choice by written paper ballots—each voter giving in as many papers as there were deputies to be chosen, with a single name written on each paper. The names of the deputies when chosen were indorsed by the constables, on the back of their respective warrants, and returned into court.

8. The three towns of the commonwealth were each to have the privilege of sending four deputies to the General Court. If other towns were afterwards added to the jurisdiction, the number of their deputies was to be fixed by the court. The deputies represented the towns, and could bind them by their votes in all legislative matters.

9. The deputies had power to meet after they were chosen, and before the session of the General Court, to consult for the public good, and to examine whether those who had been returned as members of their own body, were legally elected. If they found any who were not so elected, they might seclude them from their assembly, and return their names to the court, with their reasons for so doing. The court, on finding these reasons valid, could issue orders for a new election, and impose a fine upon such men as had falsely thrust themselves upon the towns as candidates.

10. Every regular general court was to consist of the governor and at least four other magistrates, with the major part of the deputies chosen from the several towns. But if any court happened to be called by the freemen, through the default of the governor and magistrates, that court was to consist of a majority of the freemen present, or their deputies, and a *moderator*, chosen by them. In the General Court was lodged

the "*supreme power* of the *commonwealth.*" In this court, the governor or moderator had power to command liberty of speech, to silence all disorders, and to put all questions that were to be made the subject of legislative action, but not to vote himself, unless the court was equally divided, when he was to give the casting vote. But he could not adjourn or dissolve the court without the major vote of the members. Taxes also were to be ordered by the court; and when they had agreed on the sum to be raised, a committee was to be appointed of an equal number of men from each town to decide what part of that sum each town should pay.*

This first written constitution of the new world was simple in its terms, comprehensive in its policy, methodical in its arrangement, beautiful in its adaptation of parts to a whole, of means to an end. Compare it with any of the constitutions of the old world then existing. I say nothing of those libels upon human nature, the so-called constitutions of the continent of Europe—compare it reverently, as children speak of a father's roof, with that venerated structure, the British constitution. How complex is the architecture of the latter! here exhibiting the clumsy handiwork of the Saxon, there, the more graceful touch of later conquerors; the whole colossal pile, magnificent with turrets and towers, and decorated with armorial devices and inscriptions, written in a language not only dead, but never native to the island; all eloquent, indeed, with the spirit of ages past, yet haunted with the cry of suffering humanity, and the clanking of chains that come up from its subterranean dungeons. Mark, too, the rifts and seams in its gray walls—traces of convulsion and revolution. Proud as it is, its very splendor shows the marks of a barbarous age. Its tapestry speaks a language dissonant to the ears of freemen. It tells of exclusive privileges, of divine rights, not in the people, but in the king, of primogeniture, of conformities, of prescriptions, of serfs and lords, of attainder that dries up like a leprosy the fountains of inheritable blood; and lastly, it discourses of the rights of

* J. Hammond Trumbull's Colonial Records, i. 20.

British subjects, in eloquent language, but sometimes with qualifications that startle the ears of men who have tasted the sweets of a more enlarged liberty. Such was the spirit of the British constitution and code of the seventeenth century. I do not blame it, that it was not better; perhaps it could not then have been improved without risk. Improvement in an old state, is the work of time. But I have a right to speak with pride of the more advanced freedom of our own.

The constitution of Connecticut sets out with the practical recognition of the doctrine, that all ultimate power is lodged with the people. The body of the people is the body politic. From the people flow the fountains of law and justice. The governor, and the other magistrates, the deputies themselves, are but a kind of committee, with delegated powers to act for the free planters. Elected from their number, they must spend their short official term in the discharge of the trust, and then descend to their old level of citizen voters. Here are to be no interminable parliaments. The majority of the General Court can adjourn it at will. Nor is there to be an indefinite prorogation of the legislature at the will of a single man. Let the governor and magistrates look to it. If they do not call a general court, the planters will take the matter into their own hands, and meet in a body to take care of their neglected interests.

One of the most striking features in this new, and at that time strange document, is, that it will tolerate no rotten-borough system. Every deputy, who goes to the legislature, is to go from his own town, and is to be a free planter of that town. In this way he will know what is the will of his constituents, and what their wants are.

This paper has another remarkable trait. There is to be no taxation without representation in Connecticut. The towns, too, are recognized as independent municipalities. They are the primary centres of power, older than the constitution—the makers and builders of the State. They have given up to the State a part of their corporate powers, as they received them from the free planters, that they may have a safer guarantee for the keeping of the rest. Whatever they have not given up, they hold in absolute right.

How strange, too, that, in defining so carefully and astutely the limits of the government, these constitution makers should have forgotten the king. One would not suppose, that those who indited this paper were even aware of the existence of titled majesty beyond what belonged to the King of kings. They mention no supreme power, save that of the commonwealth, which speaks and acts through the General Court.*

Such was the constitution of Connecticut. I have said it was the oldest of the American constitutions. More than this, I might say, it is the mother of them all. It has been modified in different states to suit the circumstances of the people, and the size of their respective territories; but the representative system peculiar to the American republics, was first unfolded by Ludlow, (who probably drafted the constitution of Connecticut,) and by Hooker, Haynes, Wolcott, Steele, Sherman, Stone, and the other far-sighted men of the colony, who must have advised and counseled to do, what they and all the people in the three towns met together in a mass to sanction and adopt as their own. Let me not be understood to say, that I consider the framers of this paper perfect legislators, or in all respects free from bigotry and intolerance. How could they throw off in a moment the shackles of custom and old opinion? They saw more than two centuries beyond their own era. England herself at this day has only approximated, without reaching, the elevated table-

* See Rev. Leonard Bacon's discourse on the Early Constitutional History of Connecticut, p. 5. See, also, Rev. Dr. Hawes' Centennial Address, which points out with great clearness and ability the distinct features of this document. Examine, too, Rev. Dr. Bushnell's "Historical Estimate," which should be read by all those unworthy sons of Connecticut, now residents here, who in traveling write themselves down upon the books of hotels, as citizens of Boston, or New York. Such wretches, who, in the language of Wordsworth, would "botanize upon their mother's grave," are the only specks that need to be washed off from the surface of our history. However, we have occasion to rejoice that they do not indicate the degeneracy of Connecticut, as it is believed that none of them sprung from the early families.

land of constitutional freedom, whose pure air was breathed by the earliest planters of Connecticut. Under this constitution they passed, it is true, some quaint laws, that sometimes provoke a smile, and, in those who are unmindful of the age in which they lived, sometimes a sneer. I shall speak of these laws in their order, I hope with honesty and not with too much partiality. It may be proper to say here, however, that for one law that has been passed in Connecticut of a bigoted or intolerant character, a diligent explorer into the English court records or statute books for evidences of bigotry, and revolting cruelty, could find twenty in England. "Kings have been dethroned," says Bancroft, the eloquent American historian, "recalled, dethroned again, and so many constitutions framed or formed, stifled or subverted, that memory may despair of a complete catalogue; but the people of Connecticut have found no reason to deviate essentially from the government as established by their fathers. History has ever celebrated the commanders of armies on which victory has been entailed, the heroes who have won laurels in scenes of carnage and rapine. Has it no place for the founders of states, the wise legislators who struck the rock in the wilderness, and the waters of liberty gushed forth in copious and perennial fountains?"

REV. JOHN DAVENPORT.

John Davenporte.

CHAPTER V.

FOUNDING OF NEW HAVEN COLONY.

It has been found necessary to depart a little from the order of events as they transpired, for the sake of a more distinct arrangement. Let us now return.

Although one powerful enemy had been subdued, the little commonwealth was threatened by others almost equally formidable. Early in November, the ground was hidden with snow. It fell to a great depth during the winter, and remained until late in March. A second time the people were threatened with famine. There was an alarming scarcity of corn. Mr. Pyncheon of Agawam, (now Springfield,) a gentleman of great resources and tact, was deputed by the court to negotiate with the Indians for this then indispensable staple of human food. Mr. Pyncheon contracted to furnish five hundred bushels. But this inconsiderable quantity would scarcely keep the inhabitants from starvation a week, and it was necessary to take other measures. A vessel was dispatched upon the same errand to the Narragansett bay, but it would seem with little success, for it soon became necessary to look further. A committee was finally sent to Pocomtock, (Deerfield,) where there was a large Indian village, and such large stores of corn, that all apprehensions of famine were soon at an end. Such quantities were bought there, that the natives came down the river with fifty canoes laden with it at one time.* But other troubles pressed hard upon the people. The colony, on account of the expenses of the Pequot war, was largely in debt. A further outlay of money was also needed to provide guns and magazines of powder and ball for future security. A tax of six hundred and twenty pounds†—the first ever levied in Connecti-

* Mason's History. † J. H. Trumbull's Colonial Records, i. 12.

cut—was ordered by the General Court to be immediately collected from the towns. This was done in February, 1638, and, in the March following, the court appointed John Mason commander-in-chief of the militia of Connecticut. He was directed to call out the militia of each town in the colony ten times during each year, and instruct and practice them in military affairs. For this arduous service he received a salary of forty pounds.* The eloquent Hooker was designated as most fit to deliver to him the staff of his new official rank. The ceremony, simple as it doubtless was, must have been imposing and memorable to all who witnessed it. But I will not attempt to represent a scene that has been described by one of the most eloquent of American writers in words like the following:

"Here is a scene for the painter of some future day—I see it even now before me. In the distance, and behind the huts of Hartford, waves the signal flag by which the town watch is to give notice of enemies. In the foreground stands the tall, swart form of the soldier in his armor; and before him, in sacred, apostolic beauty, the majestic Hooker. Haynes and Hopkins, with the legislature, and the hardy, toil-worn settlers and their wives and daughters, are gathered round them in close order, gazing with moistened eyes at the hand which lifts the open commission to God, and listening to the fervent prayer that the God of Israel will endue his servant, as heretofore, with courage and counsel to lead them in the days of their future peril. True, there is nothing classic in the scene. This is no crown bestowed at the Olympic games, or at a Roman triumph, and yet there is a severe, primitive sublimity in the picture, that will sometime be invested with feelings of the deepest reverence. Has not the time already come, when the people of Connecticut will gladly testify that reverence, by a monument that shall make the beautiful valley of the Yantic, where Mason sleeps, as beautifully historic, and be a mark to the eye from one of the

* J. H. Trumbull's Colonial Records, i. 15.

most ancient and loveliest, as well as most populous, towns of our ancient commonwealth?"*

Meanwhile, a new colony was preparing to plant itself in the woods of New England. On the 26th of July, 1637,† arrived in Massachusetts, the Rev. John Davenport, accompanied by Theophilus Eaton, Edward Hopkins, and a number of other gentlemen of wealth and character, with their servants and household effects. They were for the most part from London, and had been bred to mercantile and commercial pursuits. Their coming was hailed at Boston with much joy, for they were the most opulent of all the companies who had emigrated to New England.

The Massachusetts planters made strong efforts to retain these gentlemen within their own jurisdiction. If they would stay, the General Court offered them whatever place they might choose,‡ and the inhabitants of Newbury said they would give up their whole town if they would consent to occupy it. But the new emigrants had come to found a distinct colony, and therefore declined to accept these generous overtures. They were only in doubt where they should go. The pursuit of the Pequots from the mouth of the Thames westward along the coast to Fairfield, had led the English to explore that charming tract of country, with its inlets, harbors and coves, and its extended plains of rich, alluvial land, enlivened with the sparkling waters of the Housatonic, and numerous smaller streams that impart such a pleasing variety even to a level country. Those who went upon this expedition had brought back such a favorable report of the fertility of this territory, that it was resolved to make it the seat of a new colony. Accordingly, in the fall of the same year, Eaton with a few of his friends visited Connecticut, and made a careful exploration of the sea-coast and the back country adjacent to it. They finally pitched upon a place that had a good harbor, called by the Indians, Quinnipiack, as the most eligible spot whereon to found the capital city of their colony.

---

* Rev. Dr. Bushnell's Historical Estimate of Connecticut, 22, 23.

† Savage's Winthrop, i. 272; Trumbull, i. 95. ‡ Winthrop.

Here they built a temporary hut, and left a few servants in it to keep possession during the winter. The Dutch had been familiar with this locality long before, and probably from the color of the high rocks, that are visible to a great distance, had given it the name of "Red Mount."

On the 30th of the next March, the whole company set sail for Quinnipiack. They must have had a rough voyage, as they were a whole fortnight in reaching their destined harbor. They kept their first Sabbath, with services suited to the occasion, under a branching oak, large enough to give its imperfect shelter to every man, woman, and child, in the colony.* We may almost recall this simple yet imposing scene. The grim old oak, whose buds, just opened, have not yet passed from gray to green, stretching its gnarled limbs between the worshipers and the ungenial April sky, darkened at brief intervals by flitting clouds; the brown trunks of the elms, their slender boughs at last evincing signs of life; the different varieties of maple, some adorned with blossoms of pale green, others blushing in hues bright as those that flush the cheek of the young maiden; further off, the dingy cedar, with tangled grape vines coiled around its top; in the distance, a bald, red rock, bending its well-defined outline around the border of the plain; to the east of it, another of a different form rising solitary like a sentinel, a tuft of pines surmounting its seamy forehead; near by, a lively view of dancing blue waters, rocking two small ships with reefed sails—make out the more marked traits of external nature that meet the eye.

Beneath the oak, the worshiping assembly is ranged in due order. Near the trunk of the tree are the two Eatons—one in the robes of the English church, for they were not yet thrown aside in New England except in the Plymouth colony. The Rev. Mr. Prudden, Hopkins, Gregson, Gilbert, and other gentlemen—Davenport in canonicals forming the central

* Trumbull, i. 96. This oak, according to tradition, stood near the north-east corner of College and George streets, (New Haven) in the present door yard of a venerable dwelling, in which was born that staunch old divine of the puritan stamp, the Rev. Lyman Beecher, D.D.

figure—opposite them, their wives and daughters; and at a respectful distance the humbler classes, the males and females in separate groups; a sober, decent congregation of Christians, setting at naught the inclemencies of the sky, or laying them to heart as the chastening frowns of God and the hiding of his face for a season, they listen attentively, first to Davenport, as he discourses to them from the first verse of the third chapter of St. Matthew, and warns them "of the temptations of the wilderness;"* and then to Prudden, who follows his fellow-laborer with a well-chosen text from the same chapter, "The voice of one crying in the wilderness, prepare ye the way of the Lord, make his paths straight." Were they druids beneath their consecrated groves, the scene would be interesting and instructive; but Christians as they are, under whatever forms they invoke the aid of Heaven—Christians contending with a wilderness, that must ultimately fall before them, the spectacle is sublime.

They had not been long at Quinnipiack before they entered into a "plantation covenant," the language of which is, "that as in matters that concern the gathering and ordering of a church, so also in all public affairs that concern civil order, they would all of them be ordered by the rules which the Scripture held forth to them."

The spring of that year was backward and forbidding. The seed corn rotted in the ground, and the farmers were obliged to plant their fields twice, and in some instances three times, before the tardy grain sprouted and grew.† This sadly disheartened them. But it came up at last, and throve so well that they took courage. But on the first of June their prospects were again overcast. Between three and four o'clock in the afternoon of that day, the whole surface of New England was shaken by an earthquake. We are told that it came "like continued thunder," or the rattling of coach-wheels along a paved street. In some places it was so violent that it threw down the chimney-tops. Nor did it

* Bacon's "Historical Discourses," 13; Kingsley, 80; Trumbull, i. 96.

† Winthrop; Morton.

stop with the land. The ships trembled in the harbors. The islands, as well as the main land, felt the shock. The chroniclers tell us, perhaps with some exaggeration, that the earth shuddered for several minutes, and that for many days after it was unquiet and tremulous.*

In the following November, Theophilus Eaton, Mr. Davenport, and other gentlemen, made a contract with Mo-mau-gu-in in reference to a sale of lands. A very interesting document it is, being in the nature both of a deed of sale of Quinnipiack and a league or solemn treaty, offensive and defensive; the chief covenanting neither to terrify, disturb, nor injure the English, who in return agreed to protect the chief and his tribe, and see that they had lands on the east side of the harbor both for hunting and tillage. The celebrated Thomas Stanton interpreted the indenture, and it was executed with the usual formalities. On the 11th of December following, the same gentlemen bought another large tract of land lying northerly of the former purchase. This second piece of land was ten miles wide from north to south, and thirteen miles in length from east to west. It was deeded to them by Mon-to-we-se, son of the great sachem of Mat-ta-be-seck. It was a valuable territory, and has since been divided into the towns of New Haven, Branford, Wallingford, East Haven, Woodbridge, Cheshire, and North Haven.† To one who now stands upon the summit of West Rock, and looks off upon the church steeples that are visible within the limits of those towns, it seems scarcely credible that the consideration of this deed was thirteen English coats, with the reservation of the right to plant and hunt upon the granted premises. But the price was an adequate one. What could the grantors do with money? and the liberty to occupy the land for the two purposes named in the deed, comprised in the mind of an Indian, nearly all that lawyers mean by the term fee simple.

In the character of its immigrants the colony of New Haven was peculiarly fortunate. Early in the year 1639, another

* Trumbull, i. 96. † Trumbull, i. 99.

company of gentlemen of high character arrived from England. This new emigration was headed by the Rev. Henry Whitfield. Its other principal men were William Leete, afterwards governor of the colony; Samuel Desborough, (or Disbrowe,) to whom Cromwell afterwards assigned the post of lord chancellor of Scotland, at a time when he was in need of efficient men; also Robert Kitchel and William Chittenden, both men of high character.

On the 4th of June, 1639, the free planters of Quinnipiack met for the first time to form a civil and religious organization. They had no spacious hall, as now, where they might assemble and discuss affairs of state. The best shelter from the sun that the humble architecture of the place could then afford its population, was "Mr. Newman's barn"—Robert Newman's, probably—a locality doubly consecrated, for here, within a few feet of the spot where the planters of Quinnipiack first convened to found a commonwealth, lived and died Noah Webster, the first philologist of modern times.* A grave matter was pending, and Mr. Davenport brought the minds of the planters to a suitable frame, by preaching to them from the words of Solomon: "Wisdom hath builded her house, she hath hewn out her seven pillars." It was a pungent and weighty discourse, in the sentiments of which Theophilus Eaton probably concurred, as he appears to have had a good understanding with his pastor upon all topics. The preacher expressed himself very explicitly in reference to the divine origin of government, and argued that the church and the civil polity were inseparable. Davenport claimed that the church ought to be supported by seven pillars or members of eminent piety, and that the other members should be added to the seven pillars.

* For the discovery of the location of this primitive hall of legislation, the public are indebted to the researches of the Rev. Leonard Bacon, D.D., whose eloquent "Historical Discourses, on the completion of two hundred years from the beginning of the first church in New Haven," have brought to light many interesting facts in the early history of the New Haven colony, which were before either wholly unknown or entirely misapprehended.

A series of resolutions were adopted at this meeting, of which I subjoin a copy.

I. That the scriptures hold forth a perfect rule for the direction and government of all men in all duties which they perform to God and men, as well in families and commonwealth, as in matters of the church.

II. That, as in matters which concerned the gathering and ordering of a church, so likewise of all public offices which concern civil order, as the choice of magistrates and officers, making and repealing laws, dividing allotments of inheritance, and all things of like nature, they would all be governed by those rules which the Scripture held forth to them.

III. That all those who had desired to be received as free planters, had settled in the plantation with a purpose, resolution, and desire, that they might be admitted into church fellowship according to Christ.

IV. That all the free planters held themselves bound to establish such civil order as might best conduce to the securing of the purity and peace of the ordinance to themselves and their posterity according to God.

V. That church members only should be free burgesses; and that they only should choose magistrates among themselves, to have power of transacting all the public civil affairs of the plantation; of making and repealing laws, dividing inheritances, deciding of differences that may arise, and doing all things and businesses of like nature.

That civil officers might be chosen, and government proceed according to these resolutions, it was necessary that a church should be formed. Without this there could be neither freemen nor magistrates. Mr. Davenport, therefore, proceeded to make proposals relative to the formation of it, in such a manner that no blemish might be left on the "beginnings of church work." It was then resolved to this effect:

VI. That twelve men should be chosen, that their fitness for the foundation work might be tried, and that it should be in the power of those twelve men to choose seven to begin the church.*

Under this constitution, so original and unique in some of its provisions, that I have been able to find no other previously existing to which I might compare it, the colony of New Haven was organized and continued to flourish for many years. The seven pillars were Theophilus Eaton, Esquire, Mr. John Davenport, Robert Newman, Mathew Gilbert, Thomas Fugill, John Punderson, and Jeremiah Dixon. It has attracted much attention, and many severe remarks have been made, arraigning it for bigotry and intolerance. That it was not erected upon that basis of universal freedom peculiar at that early day to the constitution of Connecticut, and that some of its terms are harsh and jar upon the ears of men who, in the nineteenth century, have been reared under a system of government where the church and the state, though on terms of friendly intercourse, have no forced or arbitrary connection, can not be denied. The government organized under this constitution has been called a theocracy, but with what propriety the term has been applied to it, I am unable to see. The free planters, without reference to church membership, and before their church was instituted, met together, debated earnestly the principles that were to be embodied in their constitution, and then voted with one consent that "church members only should be free burgesses, and that they only should choose magistrates among themselves, to have power of transacting all the public civil affairs of the plantation." This is not a claim set up by the church, to rule the people by virtue of a divine right. As yet, they have no church. But the planters themselves designate, of their own choice, for reasons that they deem valid, a body or class of men whom they choose, out of which all officers of civil trust shall be elected. Nor are the interests of the church and state in any way blended. No church officer, as such, has any civil power. But we are told that these men were surely fanatics in one respect; that they adopted the

* Trumbull, i. 104, 105.

laws of God as laid down in his revealed word. The reader will remember that the people of New Haven were fourteen months deliberating what kind of constitution they would form. They were still more slow and cautious in coming to a conclusion what should be the temper and spirit of the laws passed under it. And in order that no act of legislation might be passed with unseemly haste, they decided to adopt the laws of Moses until they could form others more applicable to the state and condition of their people. What outrage did they perpetrate under these laws? What injustice did they practice either toward the wild tribes of savages that surrounded them, or toward their own citizens? What was the practical working of their system? Let their schools, where learning, elastic and free as the air of the north, yet substantial and well-grounded as the hills on whose summits that air lingers to sport with the cheek of health that meets it there—let that fair city, laid out in squares by its first founders, as if they were prescient of the beauty that was to adorn its forehead like a chaplet of unfading flowers, long after the green mounds should be leveled and the monuments thrown down that claimed for the leaders of the colony "the passing tribute of a sigh"—let these, and the good order that still springs up and grows upon the spot as if it were indigenous there like the leaves of the shade trees that make the city a bower, yet grows not old and fades like them—answer for the spirit and the practical workings of the constitution and laws of their commonwealth. "By their fruits ye shall know them." Bigotry, superstition, intolerance, are words of weighty significance in the mouths of wise, dispassionate men, when applied to the history of civil and religious liberty in England and America. But when adopted as the catch-words of a party, ecclesiastical or political, and hurled like thunderbolts from army to army of the combatants to blast and shatter their adversaries, what are they but the implements of a blind destruction, at sight of which reason retires from the field, and Christian charity shudders as she turns away her face? It is my purpose to avoid the application of those words as much as possible in delineating the various parties and classes of people representing different interests in Connecticut, both before and since the American revolution. The laws of the colony of New Haven I shall treat of, when I come to express my views of the jurisprudence of Connecticut.

Having thus established itself at home upon safe foundations, the colony of New Haven began to send out liberal swarms from the metropolitan hive. On the 12th of February, 1639, Wepowage (Milford) was purchased,* and Menunkatuck (Guilford,) in September of that year. Both towns were settled according to the New Haven plan. The Rev. Peter Prudden led the way in the settlement of Milford. The "seven pillars" of the Milford church were, Peter Prudden, William Fowler, Edmund Tapp, Zechariah Whitman, Thomas Buckingham, Thomas Welch, and John Astwood. Milford was an independent commonwealth until 1643, when it became merged in the colony of New Haven.† Their civil institutions did not differ essentially from those of New Haven. The planters of Milford were most of them from the counties of Essex, Hereford, and York, in England. A part of them came first to New Haven; a still larger part followed Mr. Prudden from Wethersfield, where he preached for a little while in the course of the year 1638. Among the principal gentlemen who came from Wethersfield to Milford, were Robert Treat, Esq., afterwards governor of Connecticut, and renowned both as a civilian and soldier, and John Sherman, a venerable name, of whom I shall by and by give a more extended sketch. There were fifty-four heads of families, and more than two hundred persons in all, who first went to Milford.‡ A more substantial company of emigrants never followed a clergyman into the wild woods of America, than the fathers of Milford. Guided by Thomas Tibbals, they went through the forest from New Haven to Wepowage. An Indian trail was their only path. The territory at that time was occupied with the Paugussett Indians, of whose

---

* Lambert's Hist., New Haven Colony, 85. † Lambert. ‡ Ib. 90.

sachem, Ansantawae, the land in the centre of the township was purchased by these pioneers. This was a numerous and powerful tribe, and occupied a region extending some sixteen or eighteen miles along the coast, and reaching at least twelve miles into the interior.* My limits forbid that I should at present do more than make this brief allusion to the heroic little commonwealth at Milford.

The first settlers at Guilford were a large proportion of them gentlemen. The rest were known as yeomen. Both gentlemen and yeomen were almost all planters. There were so few mechanics among them that they could scarcely find carpenters to build their houses; not a blacksmith was to be found among them, and it was with difficulty that they finally procured one. The early citizens of Guilford, almost without exception, emigrated from Surry and Kent. Mr. Henry Whitfield, their clergyman, was of an old English family, and had preached with eminent success at Oakley in Surry. He was a friend of Mr. Fenwick of Saybrook. An intimacy also existed between him and Desborough. Desborough was the first magistrate of Guilford. Indeed, he appears to have been born to good fortune. Some more minute account of him may not only interest the reader, but serve to correct some errors into which several of our antiquaries have fallen, who appear to have mistaken him for John, his elder brother, who was a brother-in-law of Cromwell, and a major-general. Samuel Desborough was the third surviving son of James Desborough, Esquire, and was born at Ellisley, on the third of November, 1619. After his return to England in 1650 he was immediately sent to Scotland to enter upon the discharge of some public trust under the government, at the instance of his brother John, and of Oliver Cromwell, who was then a general in the army. He was soon after chosen a member of Parliament to represent the city of Edinburgh. On the 4th of May 1655, at a council held at Whitehall, Oliver Cromwell, then Lord Protector, appointed him one of the nine councilors for the kingdom of Scotland. In 1656

* Deforest, 50.

he was elected a member of parliament for the sheriffdom of Midlothian. He manifested such singular ability in the discharge of these several official functions, and became such a favorite of the Protector, that on the 16th of September, 1657, was made keeper of the great seal of Scotland. He continued lord chancellor of Scotland during the remainder of Cromwell's life, and during the brief reign of his son Richard, and after the restoration, when the royal proclamation made at Breda, reached him, he thankfully availed himself of the clemency so graciously tendered him, and signed his submission to king Charles II. on the 21st of May, 1660.

He was ever after treated by the king with kindness and delicacy. None of his ample estate resulting from a lucrative office was confiscated. He retired to his seat at Elsworth where he continued to reside in a munificent and hospitable manner until his death, which happened on the 10th of December, 1690. On the south side of the communion rails in the chancel of the venerable old church at Elsworth, is a black marble slab with a simple inscription commemorative of the virtues of Samuel Desborough, lord chancellor of Scotland. On the north side of the communion rails in the same chancel is a corresponding memorial informing the reader that Rose Pennyer, the wife, who was proud to share his noonday honors and his later fortunes, is resting by his side.

There are still extant a portrait of Lord Desborough, and an excellent miniature. The latter is by Cooper. Both represent him in middle life. The face is oval, with whiskers, a small lock extending beneath the lower lip. The features are very handsome and engaging; the eye bright and piercing; and the whole countenance, expressive of that good sense, discriminating judgment, moral courage, and quick zeal tempered by discretion and experience that constituted the best traits of his marked and commanding character.* Such was Desborough, magistrate of Guilford. In naming the principal gentlemen of Guilford, we should not forget to speak

* Noble's "House of Cromwell," vol. ii. pp. 295, 296.

in this place of William Leete, Esq. He emigrated from Cambridge, where he was for some time register of the Bishop's Court. He had been bred to the law in England. When Desborough left the peaceful magistracy at Guilford to mingle in the stormy civil wars that convulsed England, Leete became his successor. He played an important part in the history of the colony at a later day—so we leave him for the present. Rev. Mr. John Hoadly, also, was one of the first planters of Guilford.* The town was at first independent of New Haven colony, and had its own constitution and code of laws for several years.

The year 1639 was fruitful in the birth of new plantations, and Connecticut did her part toward peopling what might then with propriety be called "the west." The reader will remember that Ludlow, the great lawyer and statesman of the colony, had accompanied as a counselor the little army that followed the remnant of the Pequots to Sasco swamp, where they made their last unavailing stand against the allied powers of Massachusetts and Connecticut. Ludlow, who was not only a good lawyer and an enthusiastic lover of liberty, but a man whose love of adventure fitted him for pioneer life and whose exuberant imagination asked for ampler room in which to expand itself, fixed his sagacious eye on the rich plains of Un-quo-wa, (Fairfield,) and saw at a glance their natural advantages. Indeed, he saw every thing at a glance. His mind intuitively recognized the relations of things the most abstract as well as those connected with the common affairs of life. He had that gift of insight and love of moral beauty that forms a principal element in the

*Rev. Mr. John Hoadly, was born January, 1616–17, and came to New England, 1639, where he married July 14, 1642, Mrs. Sarah Bushnell whom he accidentally met with on his passage to this country. He was one of the "Seven Pillars" of the first church in Guilford. In 1653, he returned to England and became chaplain to Cromwell's Garrison at Edinburgh Castle. He had several children born in Guilford, among whom was Rev. Samuel Hoadly, born September 30, 1643, who was the father of the celebrated liberal Bishop Benjamin Hoadly of Winchester, in the time of George I. and II., and of John Hoadly, Archbishop of Armagh. See article prefixed to Bishop Hoadly's works, Vol. I., fol. Lond. 1773.

mind of a great poet like Milton. His views upon government more nearly resemble Milton's than those of any other writer upon constitutional liberty of the seventeenth century. Ludlow, such as I have represented him, could not long remain without the excitement of another removal, and selected Fairfield as his point of destination. He was an inhabitant of Windsor, and took with him eight or ten families, his neighbors and admirers. This handful of adventurers was soon joined by a party from Watertown, Massachusetts, and not long after another accession was made to its numbers from Concord. Under the auspices of Ludlow, the plantation soon grew into a large town, and became, as it has ever since remained, a part of Connecticut. The township was honorably purchased of the Indians.

Within the range of the same year, those parts of Stratford called Cupheag and Pughquonnuck were purchased, and settlements commenced there under the superintendence of Mr. Fairchild, who was the first magistrate of the town. John and William Curtis and Samuel Hawley came from Roxbury, Massachusetts, and Joseph Judson was from Concord. These were the earliest planters and principal gentlemen of Stratford. Afterwards, a few heads of families arrived from Boston, and Samuel Wells from Wethersfield with three sons. The first clergyman of Stratford was Mr. Adam Blackman, who had preached with eminent success, first at Leicester and then in Derbyshire, England. He was a gentleman of such pleasant manners and so many winning traits of character, that many of his parishioners followed him to America. He had been a clergyman of the church of England. "Entreat us not to leave thee," said his weeping flock, as they gathered about him, "for whither thou goest we will go, thy people shall be our people, and thy God our God." This beautiful town bordering on the Housatonic river and Long Island sound, and commanding a pleasant view of each, has been the scene of many stirring adventures and thrilling incidents, and is hallowed as the residence of men whose names are "of the treasures" not only of the State but of the nation. It is too early in the order of events to mention them.

CHAPTER VI.

COLONEL FENWICK ESTABLISHES A GOVERNMENT AT SAYBROOK.

While the people of Connecticut and New Haven were thus enlarging their boundaries, there sprang up at the mouth of Connecticut river a new commonwealth, independent of them both; indeed, with rights paramount to theirs, even to the very soil that they occupied, had its proprietors chosen to assert them—for those proprietors, the Lord Say and Seal, the Lord Brooke, and others, it will be remembered, had a paper title to a vast region, embracing much more than the territory now called Connecticut. This new commonwealth was established by Colonel George Fenwick, who, with his wife, sometimes known as Lady Fenwick and sometimes as the Lady Alice Boteler, together with the other members of his household, arrived about midsummer of the year 1639.* Colonel Fenwick had in his charge two ships, and was accompanied by several gentlemen of high respectability, who, with their attendants, aided in laying the foundations of Saybrook—for so they named the settlement in honor of two of its principal patrons and proprietors. Colonel Fenwick was one of the original patentees, and acted in their behalf. There had been a garrison kept up at the fort since its first erection by Mr. Winthrop, in 1635,† but no civil government was organized until the arrival of Colonel Fenwick and his company. Among the first proprietors of this town were Captain John Mason, Thomas Tracy, Lyon Gardiner, who was the commander of the fort, and Thomas Leffingwell. The Rev. Thomas Peters was the first clergyman there. Upon its early records, also, appear the names of Huntington, Baldwin, Backus, Hyde, Bliss, Whittlesey, Waterman, and Dudley. Houses had been built under the superintendence of Winthrop for gentlemen of quality in connection with the fort,

---

* Trumbull, i. 110. † Savage's Winthrop, i. 207, 208.

so that Colonel Fenwick experienced less of hardship and privation in carrying out his enterprise than was usual with the founders of new settlements. Saybrook, as I have said, owed no allegiance to Connecticut. She had her own independent government, which was administered by Colonel Fenwick until the year 1644, when it fell into the hands of Connecticut.

In the meantime, the citizens of Wethersfield had become involved in a quarrel with Sowheag, the great sachem of Mattabesett, (Middletown,) that threatened the colony with another Indian war. Sowheag was originally not only the proprietor of the present towns of Middletown and Chatham, but his jurisdiction extended into Pyquag, (Wethersfield.)* The inhabitants of Wethersfield—who had never forgotten the murders committed by the Indians in the spring of 1637, and the theft and abduction of the two maidens, of whose fate they were so long kept in doubt—had at last found out that the Pyquag Indians, under their old chief Sowheag, had aided the Pequots in perpetrating those outrages. This was the original cause of the quarrel. Sowheag protected the guilty Indians, and carried himself haughtily towards the planters of Wethersfield, who complained of his conduct, and insisted that he should give up the murderers. The court decided, after giving all the matters in dispute a grave hearing, that the Wethersfield people had been the aggressors, and therefore that they should forgive Sowheag, and continue on terms of friendship with him. Mr. Samuel Stone and Mr. Goodwin were appointed a committee to bring about a reconciliation. But these discreet gentlemen could effect nothing. The planters were willing to listen to fair terms; but Sowheag not only refused to deliver up the murderers to justice, but also added new insults and injuries to the old. In this state of affairs, the court determined to send one hundred men to Mattabesett to take the murderers by force, and dispatched a messenger to New Haven to inform the authorities there of the proposed expedition. This project did not receive any

* Rev. Dr. Field's Centennial Address at Middletown.

countenance at New Haven.* The governor and his council agreed to the proposition, that the delinquents ought to be punished, but did not like that mode of doing it. They dreaded, they said, to be involved in an Indian war. They had hitherto kept aloof from all troubles with the Indians, and meant to do so as long as they could. They regarded war as a horrible calamity. Connecticut followed the advice of New Haven, and wisely abandoned the enterprise.

War, however, was resolved on in another quarter. The Pequots had agreed, at the close of the campaign that resulted in the overthrow of their tribe and the partition of the wretched remnant that survived among the three rival chiefs who were eager for the spoils, that they would never again organize themselves as a distinct people, would never resort to their old haunts, rebuild their wigwams, range the hunting grounds, or plant the fields that had been taken from them. This agreement they had violated by taking possession of Pawcatuck, a part of the prohibited country, erecting some huts there, and planting some fields with corn. The court therefore sent Mason with forty Englishmen, with instructions to "drive them off, burn their wigwams, and bring away their corn."† Uncas, with one hundred Indians and twenty canoes, went with the English leader. On his arrival at Pawcatuck, Mason fell in with three Pequots, and sent them forward to inform their friends of his coming, and to advise them to leave the place peaceably. Whether the couriers did their errand is doubtful, for when Mason had landed his men and surrounded the little village, the Indians were so taken by surprise that they had no time to carry off their treasures or their corn. They fled in hot haste, leaving their old men to the mercy of their enemies, who did them no harm. Uncas had a little skirmish with about fifty of the warriors, that resulted in the injury of neither party, but served to amuse the English who stood still and witnessed it. Seven persons

* See J. H. Trumbull's Colonial Records, i. 31, 32.

† For some particulars of the doings of the court at this time, and the causes that led to this second expedition against the Pequots, see J. H. Trumbull, i. 31, 32.

were taken, whose lives were spared at the intercession of a Narragansett sachem. Mason and his men spent the night on board their vessel that was anchored in the little creek. As soon as it was light, they were surprised to see on the shore not far off about three hundred armed Indians. The soldiers were ordered under arms. The sight of the Englishmen so terrified the Indians, that some of them fled, and others hid themselves behind the rocks and trees. In a minute not an Indian was to be seen. Mason now called to them. "I desire to speak to you," said he, in a loud voice. In an instant numbers of them rose up and timidly showed themselves. Mason proceeded to say, that the Pequots had broken their covenant. He was interrupted by the Indians, who replied with much energy, "The Pequots are good men, and we will fight for them, and protect them." "It is not far to the head of the creek," resumed Mason; "I will meet you there, and we will try what we can do at fighting." "We will not fight with Englishmen for they are spirits; but we will fight with Uncas," replied the sons of the forest.

The Indians were near by the whole day, while the English were destroying the wigwams and carrying on board the rich harvest of corn that they found there, but they did not dare to interpose. The corn, kettles, trays, mats, wampum, and other treasures, filled the vessel and fifty canoes. Thirty of these canoes were taken from the Indians.*

In August of this year, the first steps were taken toward "a general confederation of the colonies for mutual offense and defense." The General Court of Connecticut appointed the deputy governor, Roger Ludlow, Mr. Thomas Wells, and Mr. Hooker, a committee to repair to Saybrook and consult with Colonel Fenwick on this important matter.† Colonel Fenwick "was in favor of a union of all the New England colonies." This proposed union was to guard the English settlements against the Dutch at New Netherlands, (New York,) who were rapidly increasing in wealth and numbers, and whose new governor, William Kieft, had forbidden the

* See Mason's History; also Trumbull, i. 113. † Colonial Records.

English to carry on their trade at "Good Hope," and had made a solemn protest against the occupation of Quinnipiack by the English. This proposal, to organize a general confederation, was the first breaking up of the fallow ground wherein to sow the seeds of that great confederation of the thirteen colonies, which, more than a century and a quarter later, gave such a fatal blow to the British dominion upon this continent, and laid the foundations of an empire that will soon have no boundaries more circumscribed than the polar ice of the Arctic on the north, and upon the east, south, and west, the tides of those oceans, gulfs, and seas, that in their ceaseless ebb and flow so fitly represent the inexhaustible energies of the greatest republic of the world.

This year, also, on the 10th of October, the General Court incorporated all the towns in the commonwealth, and authorized them to manage their own internal affairs.* This amounted to little more than a recognition of rights previously existing, but was highly important, as it defined the limits of the local jurisdictions by instituting a local tribunal in each town. This tribunal consisted of a body of men not less than three nor more than seven—one of whom was to be called a moderator. They were called "principal men," and were to be chosen by the votes of the respective towns. A majority of these "principal men," including the moderator, who was only to have a casting vote, was to constitute a municipal court in each town. This court brought justice home to the door of every man in the colony. It had jurisdiction of all matters of trespass or debt where the matter in demand did not exceed forty shillings. It held its stated sessions once every two months.

At this session, our admirable system of recording all conveyances of land was instituted. "The towns," say the court, "shall each of them provide a ledger book with an index or alphabet unto the same; also shall choose one who shall be a town clerk or register, who shall, before the General Court in April, next, record every man's house and land

* J. H. Trumbull, i. 36, 37.

already granted." It is made the duty of the owners of lands, under heavy penalties, to present to the town clerk a description of their real estate for record. "The like to be done for all land hereafter granted and measured to any; and all bargains or mortgages of lands whatsoever shall be accounted as of no value until they be recorded."

This excellent safeguard against fraudulent conveyances has with some modifications continued to exist in Connecticut from that day to the present. It is one of those monuments of legislative wisdom erected by our fathers, of which there are so many still standing. A legal provision, in order to endure the test of time, must embody a principle and teach some great moral lesson. It must be a commentary at once upon the necessities that compel man to conform to the rules of civil society, based as they are upon eternal justice and equity, while it is no less a commentary upon that corrupt heart and those unruly passions that are perpetually inciting him to violate those rules.

At this session, also, the dead were remembered as well as the living; and provision was made for taking an inventory of the estate of deceased persons, carrying into effect their wills either written or nuncupative, if they left any; or, if they died intestate, to see that a proper administration was had of their effects, and an equitable distribution made to the heirs. Wills and all proceedings in the settlement of estates were to be recorded. If no kindred of the deceased could be found having inheritable blood, then his estate was to escheat to the commonwealth, care being taken to register a perfect inventory of his property, so that if legal representatives should ever appear, they might receive what justly belonged to them.

I merely allude to these great landmarks of our jurisprudence as historical facts, that will be treated of at length elsewhere.

It proved to be no easy matter for the colonies of Connecticut and New Haven to get the Indian title to their lands. There were so many original elements among the different

Indian tribes, that in some instances it became necessary, for the sake of peace, to purchase the lands several times over. The colony of Connecticut bought of Uncas the whole Mohegan country, and was obliged to pay for it many times in the troubles and quarrels that were thrown upon them by their connection with that restless chief. The inhabitants of the towns, too, were obliged, when they made their settlements, to pay Uncas for the same land.

In 1640, the commonwealth bought Waranoke, (Westfield,) and began a settlement there. The same year, Roger Ludlow purchased of the Indians that part of Norwalk that lies between the Saugatuck and Norwalk rivers. Captain Patrick bought the central part of the town, and a few hardy men with their families soon removed thither. The western part of the town was not purchased until 1651.*

Greenwich was bought about the same time in behalf of the colony of New Haven. But through the address of the indefatigable governor of New Netherlands, the inhabitants were induced to put themselves under his protection—who with much solemnity proceeded to incorporate the new town.† If his Dutch excellency was guilty of any treachery, as the New England writers of that day charged upon him, he was well requited for it. The Indians drove off the planters of Greenwich. Indeed, no settlement could ever thrive there until Connecticut procured her charter and took the plantation under her protecting wing.

Connecticut further extended her limits by making a purchase of a large tract of land upon Long Island. This territory extended from the eastern boundary of Oyster Bay to the western line of Holmes' Bay. It was a large and valuable tract, embracing the whole northern portion of the island between the limits above described. The eager planters hastened to occupy it.

New Haven was not to be outstripped by her older sister in this work of planting new towns. Some of her most en-

* History of Norwalk.

† De Vries, 152; Brodhead, i. 294, 296; Trumbull, i. 118.

terprising planters were therefore not long in securing the title to Rippowams, which they bought honorably of two principal chiefs, Ponus and Toquanske. This grant contained the entire town of Stamford. Richard Denton was their first minister. New Haven also took a still more adventurous flight when, soon after, she sent men under Captain Turner to buy lands on both sides of Delaware Bay, and followed up the negotiation by sending fifty families to take immediate possession.* New Haven further prosecuted the work of colonization by obtaining a deed from the Corchaug Indians of the eastern extremity of Long Island. The Indian name of the place was Yennicock, which the English changed to that of Southold. This plantation was commenced under the direction of the Rev. John Youngs of Hingham, in Norfolk, who arrived in New Haven that summer with his parishioners, and, after reorganizing his church after the plan of that colony, soon set sail for Long Island, and commenced a settlement. Some of the leading planters were William Wells, Jeremiah Vaill, and Matthias Corwin.

Of all the towns belonging to Connecticut, Wethersfield seems from the first to have been most involved in difficulties, civil and ecclesiastical. The settlement had been commenced by a high-spirited and very excitable people, impatient of control, delighting in the most daring enterprises, and stimulated rather than alarmed at the dangers that beset them. Did the Pequots make a fierce incursion into the settlement, murder and scalp a part of their freeholders, and carry off their fair maidens? So far from striking terror into the hearts of those who remained, it only stirred them up to a resistance so determined and obstinate, not only against the Pequots, but against the chief upon the Connecticut river, who was thought to have harbored the delinquents, that the authority of the General Court commanding them to forgive the suspected sachem and take him into their confidence, availed so little, that, but for the timely interposition of New Haven the colony would have again been involved in war.

* New Haven Colony Records.

Their conduct in leaving the jurisdiction of the Massachusetts, in opposition to the decision of the General Court, had elicited the remark from their friends at Cambridge, "that it was the opportunity of seizing a brave piece of meadow," that led them with such precipitate haste to seek the valley of the Connecticut—a remark not entirely disinterested, we may infer from the fact, that these very neighbors had an eye upon that same brave piece of meadow-land. This restlessness of the citizens of Wethersfield, so much spoken of by our early writers, was attributable, among other causes, to the fact, that they left Massachusetts without a clergyman to lead them.

We have seen how the settlement of Hartford was begun. Windsor had a similar origin, being led into pleasant pastures, and to lie down by the still waters, under the mild authority of the Rev. John Wareham, that melancholy shepherd, whose desponding eye, lenient and gentle towards the faults of others, was yet so stern and austere when turned upon his own, that he did not dare at all times to partake of the bread and wine that he administered at the sacrament, fearing, in the beautiful words of his biographer, that the seals of the covenant were not for him. Aside from the salutary influence of Mr. Wareham upon the people of Windsor, he was seconded by a large number of gentlemen, at the head of whom stood Henry Wolcott and Roger Ludlow, Esquires, and Captain John Mason. That the reader may see of what choice materials the population of this town was composed, I may add to these, the names of Whitefield, Eggleston, Holcombe, Marshall, Pomeroy, Strong, Tudor, Parkham, Buckland, Palmer, Terry, Watson, Phelps, Griswold, Moore, Hurlbut, Williams, Denslow, Loomis, and Thornton. The Ellsworths arrived there at a later day. The other early towns in Connecticut and New Haven colonies had the same advantage. But Wethersfield was without this balance-wheel to steady her motions. Her people had left Mr. Phillips behind them in Watertown, and in the hurry to emigrate, (who that ever saw the Naubuc meadows, and the fields of Nayaug, or drank of the healing waters of the pools of Neipsic, can blame them for it?) that they forgot their discipline, and for awhile broke their ranks, in the eager pursuit of treasures so dazzling to the eye. Hence, the unhappy troubles and strifes during the first few years after they established themselves there. Hence, too, it fell out that scarcely a new plantation was made in the colony, for a long time, that did not receive some of its most opulent and best planters from the discontented of Wethersfield. The clergymen and more influential members of the church, both of Hartford and Windsor, did what they could to tranquilize those differences. At last, in 1641, the Rev. Mr. Davenport, and other gentlemen, from New Haven, were called in as advisers. Mr. Davenport, who seems to have had a quick knowledge of the governing motives of men, and a happy facility in giving good advice in difficult emergencies, proposed that the contending parties, as they could not well be reconciled, should separate; and that one of them should go away, and make a new settlement by themselves. At first this council did not avail, for they could not decide which party should go. The church at Watertown, Mass., now took them in hand, but without much better success. At length, as matters were all the while growing worse, Mr. Andrew Ward, Mr. Robert Coe, and twenty other planters, with their families, followed the advice of Mr. Davenport, and removed to Stamford, thus placing themselves under the protection of New Haven colony. Among those gentlemen who removed were the Rev. Richard Denton, Matthew Mitchel, Thurston Raynor, Richard Law, and Richard Gildersleeve. Among the principal gentlemen of Wethersfield, who remained or soon after arrived, were the names of Welles, Wyllys, Talcott, Goodrich, Hollister, Wright, Kimberly, Kilbourn, Hale, Treat, Belden, Deming, Smith, and Bacon. Most of these proprietors owned land on the eastern bank of the Connecticut, in that part of the town now embraced within the boundaries of Glastenbury; and several of them built upon those estates and removed there long before the incorporation of the last mentioned town. Almost all of these families, before 1700, intermarried, and from their blood have sprung many of the brightest ornaments of Connecticut.*

The Dutch and English had so many difficulties during the years 1641 and 1642, and the Indians assumed such a hostile attitude towards our colonies, that in 1643 the old proposition for a confederation of the New England colonies was renewed on the part of Connecticut, and pressed with great earnestness.† Indeed, she had for several years previous annually appointed delegates to go to Massachusetts to urge forward this project that appeared to be of such vital importance to all the colonies, especially to the weaker ones.

Massachusetts, from her independent resources and comparatively dense population, was not so much exposed as the other colonies to foreign invasion. She therefore felt less anxiety to form an alliance that might impose upon her some unpleasant burdens. But Connecticut and New Haven, with their towns scattered along the coast, planted remote upon Delaware Bay and Long Island, where the Dutch, the Swedes, and the Indians had an easy access to them, were warned early by their critical situation, to adopt some permanent measures for self-protection. Massachusetts claimed a part of the Pequot country by right of conquest. She also claimed Springfield and Westfield, which towns it was insisted belonged to the jurisdiction of Connecticut. By delaying to comply with the urgent request of Connecticut in reference to the desired confederation, this powerful colony hoped the more readily to bring her weaker sister to admit both these claims.

But clouds now gathered darkly over all the colonies. In May, four of them, Connecticut, New Haven, Saybrook, and Plymouth, all sent commissioners to Boston. Connecticut selected Governor Haynes and Edward Hopkins; New

* See Rev. Dr. Chapin's History, in which the genealogies of nearly all those families are fully given.

† Colony Records.

Haven chose Governor Eaton and Mr. Gregson; Governor Winslow and Mr. Collier represented Plymouth; Col. Fenwick went in behalf of Saybrook; and Massachusetts confided her interests to the care of Governor Winthrop, Dudley, Bradstreet, associated with Hawthorne, Gibbons, and Tyng—a body of men whom I name with pride, as worthy to represent the American Colonies in their first association against foreign encroachment; worthy, too, to prefigure and typify that other body of men who, at a later day, affixed their names to a paper which was at once a protest against the tyranny of proscription, and a memorial of the rights of man, that will gradually extend its benign dominion, until, of the strong holds of despotic power, whether American, European, or Asiatic, there shall not be left one stone upon another that is not thrown down.

These articles of confederation commence by stating the object of all the colonies in removing to America, and then proceed to name them "The United Colonies of New England." They go on to declare, that they do jointly and severally enter into a firm and perpetual league of friendship and amity, offense and defense, mutual aid and service.*

The distinct sovereign jurisdiction of each contracting power is not only provided for, but it is expressly stated, that no two colonies shall be united in one, nor any other colony be received into the confederacy, without the consent of the whole. Each colony, without reference to size, is to send two commissioners, and no more. These commissioners are to meet once every year. They are clothed with power to make war and peace, laws and rules for the protection and regulation of the confederacy. In case there should be a war offensive or defensive, involving the interests of the whole, or any one of the allied powers, the expense was to be borne according to the number of the male inhabitants in each colony, between the ages of sixteen and sixty years. When any member of the confederation was invaded, all the

* For a copy of the articles of confederation, see Hazard's State Papers, vol. ii. first article.

others were bound to send troops to its assistance—Massachusetts, one hundred; each of the others, forty-five men. Before more could be demanded, there must be a special meeting of the commissioners.

In this New England Congress, the vote of six commissioners upon any measure was binding upon the whole body. If those who voted for it were less than six, and yet constituted a majority, the matter should be referred to the General Court of each colony, and should not be binding, unless the courts unanimously ratified it. It was provided, too, that all servants running from their masters, and all criminals flying from justice, from one colony to another, should, upon demand and proper evidence of their character as fugitives, be returned—the servants to their masters, the accused to the colonies whence they fled.

From this brief synopsis of these articles of confederation, it will be seen how analagous they are to the articles of confederation of the thirteen colonies, as well as to the present Constitution of the United States of America.

The new government was soon put in requisition. The Pequots and Narragansetts, as will be remembered, had been enemies long before the Pequot war. After the overthrow of Sassacus, and the division of the little remnant of his people among the Narragansetts, the Nihanticks and Mohegans, the two most powerful tribes who shared the spoils, soon began to entertain the most vindictive feelings towards each other. Miantinomoh represented the Narragansetts, and Uncas the Mohegans. Whether Miantinomoh was angry at the unequal distribution of the Pequots, or whether his more open and generous nature was goaded to acts of violent recrimination by the arts of his more subtle antagonist, or whether the Narragansett sachem had become tired of the monotony of peace, and sought an occasion to practice himself and his warriors in the old pastime, that made life so full of pleasant incident to them, I am unable to say.

One cause of this ill blood was probably the attack made by Uncas upon Sequasson, a Connecticut river sachem, who was a kinsman of Miantinomoh. It appears that Uncas had killed several of Sequasson's warriors, and burned his wigwams; and that the haughty Narragansett took up the quarrel, and determined to punish Uncas for these acts of violence. Whatever may have been the cause of Miantinomoh's hostile feelings towards Uncas, and whether they were justifiable or not, it is certain that the Narragansett chief violated the very condition on which he had received his share of the Pequots—that of maintaining perpetual peace with all the contracting parties—and had commenced open hostilities against Uncas. At the same time it was believed, that he used all his eloquence and address to incite a general insurrection of the Indians against the English. It was thought, too, that the Indians were employed in preparing guns and ammunition, and were making a general preparation for war. The people of Connecticut thought themselves obliged again to keep watch and ward every night, from sunset to sunrise, in all their towns.

Connecticut sent letters to the Court at Boston, asking for one hundred men to be sent to Saybrook Fort, to be ready for any emergency. But the Court of Massachusetts was not satisfied that it was necessary to take such a step, and declined complying with the request.

Miantinomoh made no declaration of war against Uncas. His preparations were all secret. He collected a choice army of not less than six hundred warriors, and stealthily set forth for the Mohegan country. It was hot summer weather, when some of the enemy might be expected to linger in the shade, to protect their squaws, while they were in the fields taking care of the growing corn, others to be found loitering under the shadows of the rocks that overhung the Yantic, and leisurely drawing up the speckled trout from its dark pools. The invading chief knew the habits of the Indians too well, not to be aware that this was a season of indolent repose to them, and that then, if ever, Uncas would be found off his guard. He must have known, too, the Mohegan retreats, and places of resort, almost as well as they did themselves. He intended, therefore, to steal upon Uncas slily, and take him by surprise.

But whatever faults the Mohegan sachem had, a neglect to see after his own interests certainly did not constitute one of them. His spies were on duty night and day. A party of them, probably stationed upon a high hill within the present limits of Norwich, discovered the Narragansetts as they were crossing a ford in the Shetucket river, near where it unites itself with the Quinnebaug. This post was called Wawekus Hill, and a path led from it to the Little Plain, a spot hallowed as the burial place of the Mohegan sachems. I follow the account of Miss Caulkins, as I find it in her history of Norwich. "A cleft or ravine from this spot, once the bed of a rivulet, came out directly by the Indian landing-place at the foot of Yantic Falls, whence a canoe could glide in a few minutes to Shantok Point, five miles below, where Uncas had a fort. In this way the intelligence may have been communicated to the sachem with great rapidity."

In whatever way the presence of this hostile force in his territory was detected and disclosed to Uncas, the chief lost no time in arming himself. Nor did he merely stand on the defensive. With about four hundred warriors, he was soon on the march to meet the enemy. He was not long in ascertaining that Miantinomoh had crossed the fords of the Yantic with his men, and that he was in hot pursuit of him. He was a mile and a half from the Yantic on the "Great Plain," when he received this intelligence. Immediately he drew up his warriors on a little eminence, and hastily informed them of his plan of conducting the battle.

The Narragansetts were soon visible upon a neighboring hill, pressing on to meet him. Uncas sent forward a courier to demand a parley with Miantinomoh. He assented to it, and the two chiefs at once stepped forth to meet each other upon the plain, between the two armies, while Narragansetts and Mohegans alike stood still and awaited the result of the interview. As Uncas had sought the parley, so was he the first to open it.

"You have some stout men with you," said he to his adversary, with well-dissembled magnanimity; "so have I with me. It is a pity that such brave warriors should be killed in a private quarrel between you and me. Come like a man, as you profess to be, and let us fight it out. If you kill me, my men shall be yours; if I kill you, your men shall be mine."

"My men came to fight, and they shall fight," replied the haughty sachem of the Narragansetts. Uncas instantly fell flat upon the ground, a signal well understood by his warriors, who in a breath discharged a whole flight of arrows into the ranks of the Narragansetts, who afforded the fairest possible mark for them, standing as they did in a listening attitude, with their eyes fixed upon the two sachems. Before the astonished Narragansetts could rally to defend themselves, the Mohegans, with Uncas at their head, gave the war-whoop, and rushed furiously upon them with their tomahawks.*

In such a confused state of mind, a successful resistance was impossible. The out-witted invaders fled toward the fords of the Yantic. Their lamentations mingled wildly with the victorious shouts of the Mohegans, who pursued them across the Yantic, and, like greyhounds running with the game in sight, followed them as they sped over hills, covered with prickly bushes, along dangerous precipices, and across sharp ledges of rock, in their flight towards the fords of the Shetucket. Some of the Narragansetts were driven down these precipices and impaled as they fell upon the jagged corners of the rocks that bristled upon their sides. Others were shattered to atoms in the ravines below.

Miantinomoh had on a corselet of mail that he had procured of the English, and, encumbered by its weight, he ran with difficulty. It was probably a part of Uncas' stratagem

* Trumbull, i. 131; Miss Caulkins' History of Norwich, 16.

to take him alive. He was accordingly singled out by two swift-footed Mohegan captains, who followed him remorselessly until they finally came up with him near the river, and impeded his progress by throwing themselves against him. It was a desperate wager that he ran for, and, out of breath as he was, he rallied and resumed his flight only to be checked again and again by his tormentors, who were seeking to pander to the vanity of their chief by keeping the royal game at bay until he should arrive and claim the honors of the chase.

As soon as Uncas came up and laid his hand on his shoulder, the flying sachem stopped, and without attempting to offer resistance, when he knew it would be hopeless, sat quietly down upon the ground, and looked his conqueror calmly in the face ; he did not deign to utter a single word.

Uncas gave the whoop of victory. His warriors gathered around him, eager to look upon the features and figure of the noble captive, whose scornful eye regarded them with a frigid apathy.

The battle, if it could be called one, was over. In the short space of twenty minutes, thirty Narragansett warriors had been slain, and besides Miantinomoh, many prisoners had been taken, among whom were his brother and two sons of his uncle, the venerable Canonicus. Uncas affected surprise at the conduct of his prisoner. "Had you taken me," said he, "I should have besought you for my life." Miantinomoh made no reply.

Uncas now returned to his fort with his captives, whom he treated with kindness. The chief of so powerful a tribe was not an easy prize to keep, and Uncas hastened to Hartford, and committed him into the hands of the English. Samuel Gorton, of Rhode Island, had urged him to this step, hoping in this way to spare the prisoner's life. Uncas agreed to be governed by the decision of the English in the disposition to be made of the sachem, who was accordingly lodged in jail at Hartford until the Commissioners of the united colonies should meet in September, at Boston.

At last the day came when the question was discussed whether Miantinomoh should be put to death. The charges adduced against him were these; that he had killed a Pequot who had testified against him in reference to his treatment of Uncas; that he had again and again tried to take the life of Uncas by assassination and poison; that he had broken his league in making war upon the Mohegans without first taking his appeal to the English; and lastly, that he had conceived the horrible design of cutting off at a blow the whole English population, and had hired Mohawks and Indians of other tribes to assist him in its execution.*

That Uncas imposed upon the too ready credulity of the commissioners by acting upon their fears in this delicate matter, and that several of these charges were sustained by the most wicked perjury, I cannot doubt. The story in most of its details, I believe to have been a Mohegan fabrication and backed up by the testimony of Mohegan witnesses. It seems that the commissioners questioned its truth, and hesitated to act upon it. At last it was referred to five principal clergymen of the several colonies, who, after a solemn, and I doubt not an honest debate, advised that sentence of death should be passed upon the accused. The commissioners followed this unfortunate advice, and deputed Uncas—a delightful privilege, and a good reward he no doubt esteemed it, of all his exertions in the premises—to execute the sentence. Uncas repaired to Hartford, took the captive into his custody, and, accompanied by a file of English soldiers, who were sent to protect him from the vengeance of the Narragansetts, proceeded to execute the warrant. Two other Englishmen were also sent to remain by the prisoner, and see that no barbarities were practiced at the execution. Uncas took Miantinomoh, and led him to the place where he had been taken. When they had reached the fatal spot, the brother of Uncas, who was

* Winthrop appears to give full credit to the testimony of the Mohegans, especially in regard to a conspiracy against the English, and adds that "he was a turbulent and proud spirit, and would never be at rest."

marching behind Miantinomoh, split his head with a hatchet and killed him at a blow.

Notwithstanding the presence of the two Englishmen, Uncas cut a piece from the shoulder of his fallen enemy, and ate it in savage exultation. "It was the sweetest meat he ever ate," he said, and added complacently, that "it made his heart strong."

Where the chief of the Narragansetts was taken captive, where he was killed, there, too, they dug his grave. The place is still memorable as the "Sachem's Plain." A tumulus of stones was heaped high above the mound, by the pious hands of his tribe, who, year after year, made their pilgrimages to the grave. Regularly they came in September, and celebrated the anniversary of their chief's death, adding each a stone to the pile, with lamentations and gestures expressive of the deepest sorrow.

Such was the death, and such the obsequies of the sachem of the Narragansetts.

Two oak trees also, long after marked the spot; but even these stern memorials are gone, as well as the stones.* But the memory of the dead still lives, and a modern granite monument fixes the locality where a great wrong was done, under the sanction of a judicial decision. Had the commissioners, honest men as they were, viewed this act in the sober light of history, it never would have been perpetrated. Says the historian of Norwich, whose keen sense of right will not allow her to sanction this deed, "The sentence of Miantinomoh is one of the most flagrant acts of injustice that stands recorded against the English settlers. He had shown many acts of kindness towards the whites; in all his intercourse with them he had evinced a noble and magnanimous spirit, and only seven years before his death,

* Miss Caulkins, in her "History of Norwich," to which I have before adverted, says: "A citizen of Norwich, still living, N. S. Shipman, Esq., remembers this tumulus in his youth, a conspicuous object, standing large and high, between two solitary oak trees, about sixteen rods east of the old Providence road."

had received into the bosom of his country, Mason and his little band of soldiers from Hartford, and greatly assisted them in their conquest of the Pequots." For myself, were it possible, I would gladly come to a different conclusion, and whatever human fears, exercised at a time when their dominion was most to be excused, whatever the evil influences of false or prejudiced testimony may do towards palliating the decree, I shall joyfully take into the account, to qualify but never to justify it.

CHAPTER VII.

PROGRESS OF SETTLEMENT. TROUBLES WITH THE DUTCH AND INDIANS.

The relations existing between the English colonies and the Dutch of New Netherlands, were never of a very amicable character. I do not propose to follow the example either of the Connecticut or New York historians, in complaining of the motives or conduct of either party. I can only say, that the claims set up by each, being inconsistent with those of the other, and the blood of different nations flowing in their veins, it was not to be expected that they should entertain amicable feelings towards each other. It must be admitted, that the Dutch navigators first visited the coast of Connecticut and Long Island. Adrian Block, a spirited, daring adventurer, in a little yacht, named the Restless, that he had built on the bank of the Hudson river, as early as 1614,* ventured to pass through Hell Gate, and sailed as far eastward as Cape Cod. He probably did not sail very near the main-land, until he had left New Haven to the westward of him, as he has left us no traces from which we can infer that he touched upon the coast of western Connecticut. He was, probably, the first European discoverer of Montauk Point, to which, he gave the name of Fisher's Hook, and of the little cluster of brilliants, sparkling upon the bosom of Long Island Sound—that inland sea, that annually drifts its smooth pebbles and pearly sands upon the Southern line of Connecticut. One of these he called Fisher's Island;† another he named after himself, and it still bears the name of

* O'Callaghan's New Netherlands, p. 72.

† The historian of Long Island, (Thompson, p. 248,) states that this island was originally called Vischer's Island, and was probably so named by Block, from one of his companions. In the absence of any *positive* evidence on that point, the probabilities seem altogether to favor the generally received opinion, that the island was named from the chief occupation of its aboriginal inhabitants, or, from the quantities of fish with which the adjacent waters abounded.

Block Island. He probably entered most of the principal harbors, and explored, to a greater or less distance, most of the navigable streams of the main-land. After that, for several years, the Dutch traders frequented the coast and islands, and carried on a brisk trade, with the Indians, in furs. In 1632, they bought of the natives, the neck of land at the mouth of the Connecticut river, afterwards, and still known as Saybrook, to which they gave the name of Kievit's Hook, from the number of birds, called by the Dutch, Kieveet, and by the English, Peeweet, that they saw hovering about the spot.* On the 8th of June, 1633, they bought of the Indians, the place known as Dutch Point, near Hartford.† The English, who soon after arrived, disputed their right to these places, and had covered the whole territory with their paper titles, before the Dutch took possession. In addition to this, as the Cabots had discovered the main-land to the east of the Connecticut coast, the English claimed, that this discovery took in all the Continent, to the "South Seas." It is foreign to my purpose to enter into a discussion, as to the rights of these claimants. One thing is certain, the English, claiming by right of discovery, by grant from their monarch, and by subsequent purchase of the Indians, took, and have ever since kept possession of most of the country then the subject of dispute; and, as the Dutch and English have since been to a good degree, united in blood as well as in civil and social relations, in New York, it seems to me narrow and provincial, to spend much time, at this late day, in vexing anew the question of original proprietorship.

In 1643, a war broke out between the Dutch and the Indians, that for awhile allayed all disputes between the Dutch and English. It fell out in the following manner: The government of New Amsterdam had not been as careful as the colonies of Connecticut and New Haven, in enacting and enforcing sumptuary laws, and had allowed traders to sell the Indians strong liquors, more than was prudent, as the event

---

* O'Callaghan, p. 149.

† This was the *claim* of the Dutch, and I am willing to concede it.

proved; for an Indian, who had been subjected to the pernicious influences of this traffic, in a fit of intoxication, killed one of the Dutch who belonged to the jurisdiction of New Amsterdam. The Dutch demanded that the murderer should be given up to them for punishment, but he was not to be found. The injured party now applied to the governor at New Amsterdam; but the governor did not think it prudent to interfere. About this time, the Mohawks fell upon the Indians, who lived near the Dutch settlements, and killed about thirty of them. Others fled to the Dutch authorities for protection. Marine, the Dutch captain, obtained leave of the governor to kill as many of these Indians as he could. His commission certainly proved to be no farce in his hands, for he acted under it with such zeal as to make an indiscriminate slaughter of seventy or eighty men, women, and children, at one stroke. The enraged Indians rallied to avenge themselves for this wholesale slaughter. In the spring of 1643, the Indians began to retaliate. They set fire to the store-houses of their adversaries, drove their cattle into the barns, and then burned up both barns and cattle. The Indians upon Long Island joined those upon the main-land, and destroyed a great amount of property.

In this situation, the Dutch governor applied to Captain Underhill, of Stamford, for assistance, which so enraged Marine, that he pointed his pistol at his Excellency, and would have shot him but for the interference of a friend. One of Marine's tenants leveled his gun, loaded with ball, and deliberately discharged it at the governor, but missed him. A sentinel immediately avenged this rash act, by shooting the tenant dead upon the spot.

The Dutch do not appear to have liked a war with the Indians as well as their executive functionary had anticipated. Indeed, so indignant were they at the conduct of the governor, that he was obliged to keep a guard of fifty Englishmen constantly about him, to protect his person from the violence of his subjects. During the summer and fall, the Indians killed fifteen men of the Dutch, and for a time almost broke up all the settlements between Stamford and New York. The horrors of this destructive war were felt for many miles along the coast.*

The unfortunate Mrs. Hutchinson, who, when banished from Massachusetts for her religious opinions and factious conduct, had fled to Rhode Island, where she seems to have been as persuasive and bewitching as ever before, in 1642, and after the death of her husband, became tired of the sceptre of authority that she wielded over a very submissive people, and, as other monarchs had done before her, abdicated, and retired with her family and a few servants to a place between New Haven and New York—a remote refuge in the heart of the deep woods. Here, this mother of the Communitarian school of politics, that has made so much progress in America, surrounded by savages whom her bold heart scorned to fear, and whose friendship she cultivated with a faithfulness and assiduity deserving of a better fate, had erected her dwelling and begun to clear a few fields beyond the supposed jurisdiction of the English. Perhaps this ambitious woman intended to establish here a new empire, more transcendental than Plato's fancied Arcadia—a spiritual superstructure upon temporal foundations, that was to lift its fantastic battlements high into mid-heaven. More probably, however, shocked with the illiberality of the age, she meant to avert forever her visionary eye from what she considered the tyranny of her fellow-countrymen, and in retirement fix its abstracted gaze upon the wild speculations of an ideal philosophy. But an evil hand was upon her wherever she went. The children of the forest understood her divine mission no better than the General Court of Massachusetts. They stole upon her settlement, murdered her, together with Mr. Collins, her son-in-law, and all her children who were with her, except a single daughter, who was carried into captivity. Her servants, and several of her neighbors, eighteen persons in all, shared her tragical fate.†

* Savage's Winthrop, ii. 117.

† Winthrop; also Hildreth, i. 288; Trumbull, i. 139.

The Indians kept on killing the Dutch, and burning their houses after this unhappy affair, as before, and even extended their depredations from the main-land to Long Island.

The Dutch governor, in alarm, solicited the colony of New Haven to send troops to assist him, but owing to the construction put upon the articles of confederation, it was thought necessary to confine the action of the colony in behalf of the applicants, to the furnishing of such provisions as could be spared to them.

This war lasted for several years. Underhill was the fast friend of the Dutch government, and commanded the Dutch forces, with such men as he himself could furnish. But for him and his army of little more than one hundred men, the Dutch settlements must have been annihilated. He killed, before the close of the war, between four hundred and five hundred Indians.* The people of Stamford at last began to be alarmed at the contagious effect produced by this protracted struggle upon the Indians, who lived within their own borders. They wrote to the authorities at New Haven, begging for protection, and added that if their houses should be burned, on account of the remissness of the other plantations, the negligent parties ought to sustain the loss.†

The year 1644 was an eventful one. The Narragansetts appeared to be making ready to avenge the death of Miantinomoh. England, too, was now in a state of civil war.

These troubles at home, and in the mother country, filled the minds of the colonists with forebodings. They appointed days of fasting and prayer to avert the impending calamities. The Indians of western Connecticut, who had at first conducted themselves with so much leniency towards the English planters, now showed all the treachery and cruelty of their nature, by committing the most unprovoked murders, as well of women and children as of men. Early in the year they wantonly killed a man, belonging to Massachusetts, between Fairfield and Stamford. The murder was

* Belknap, i. 50. † New Haven Colonial Records.

soon made known, and the Indians promised that the author of it should be brought into Fairfield, and delivered up to justice, if Mr. Ludlow would appoint men to take him into custody. Mr. Ludlow sent a company of ten men for this purpose, but when the Indians came with the prisoner, within sight of the village, they set him at liberty, and he fled. Mr. Ludlow, with a view of striking terror into the minds of the Indians, took about a dozen of them captive, one of whom was a chief. This enraged the savages so much, that they assembled in such numbers as to induce Mr. Ludlow to write to New Haven for advice. The Court counseled him to retain the captives, and prepared to send twenty men to his assistance. Meanwhile, four of the sachems visited the village, and promised to deliver up the murderer within a month, if the English would restore their friends. Accordingly they were set at liberty. A little while afterwards, an Indian went into a dwelling in Stamford, and, seizing a lathing hammer, which he found at hand, commenced a brutal attack upon the mistress of the house. With this deadly instrument he struck her a violent blow upon her head, as, in obedience to the instincts of a mother, she stooped over the cradle to take up her infant child. She fell senseless. He then struck her twice with the edge of the instrument, which penetrated her skull. After that he plundered the house, and fled into the woods. The poor woman was restored to her senses long enough to give an intelligible account of the transaction, and to describe the dress and personal appearance of the Indian. But this return of reason was temporary, and, although her wounds were healed, she soon fell into a state of blank idiocy. This outrage was followed up by others. The Indians refused to have any conference with the English, but, deserting their wigwams and corn, they assembled near the town, armed with guns, and threatened to destroy the whole settlement. In this critical condition, the towns of Fairfield and Stamford applied to New Haven and Connecticut for assistance. The wretch who had worse than murdered the woman at Stamford, was finally delivered up to justice. He was taken to New Haven, and executed. "He sat erect and motionless, until his head was severed from his body."*

Wethersfield was the fruitful mother of many towns. Her difficulties still continued, and by this time another company of the disaffected was ready to leave her borders. William Swaine was at the head of the party. They had long been ready to remove, and only waited until they could obtain a favorable place for a settlement. A few miles east of New Haven was a place, called by the Indians, Totoket, which had been purchased of the inhabitants as early as 1638, and in 1640 granted to Mr. Samuel Eaton, on condition that he would found a settlement there. That gentleman failed to comply with the stipulations of the grant, and in 1644 the same territory was conveyed to Mr. Swaine and his friends, who, on their part, agreed to remove there and establish a town that was to be under the jurisdiction of New Haven. Soon after this conveyance was made, the Rev. Abraham Pierson, of South Hampton, upon Long Island, with a part of his congregation, sailed for Totoket Harbor, and made common cause with Mr. Swaine's party. To this delightful town, overlooking two clusters of lilliputian islands, and fanned by cool sea-breezes, the inhabitants gave the solid English name of Branford.†

On the 5th of September, 1644, the commissioners of the United Colonies met at Hartford. A claim was set up by those who represented Massachusetts, that they had a right of precedence in subscribing all treaties and other documents requiring the signatures of that body, as they, in behalf of their colony, had first signed the articles of confederation. After some debate, this claim was denied as a right, but yielded through courtesy. All the other commissioners were to follow in the order in which they had signed those articles.‡

From north to south, the Indians were, during the year

* New Haven Colony Records; Winthrop, Trumbull, &c.

† Barber's Conn. His. Coll., p. 198. ‡ Journal of the Commissioners.

1644, unusually troublesome. In Virginia, whole settlements were annihilated. In some villages the inhabitants were all murdered at one fell stroke. It was believed that the New England Indians, and those tribes living farther south, were combined to destroy the whole white population. The Narragansetts were particularly restive. They encroached alike upon Connecticut and Massachusetts. The old quarrel between the Narragansetts and Mohegans waxed hot and threatening. It was necessary to take some steps to quell it. The commissioners, therefore, sent their old interpreter, Thomas Stanton, with Mr. Willet, to visit the sachems of both these nations, and inform them that the commissioners were then in session at Hartford, and if they would appear before that body, and state their grievances, an impartial hearing should be had; and that all proper steps should be taken to reconcile their differences. These gentlemen were instructed to offer the sachems of the two tribes, or those who might go in their stead, a safe passage to and from Hartford, and to enjoin on them and their people to keep the peace, not only during these negotiations, but after they had returned to their respective countries.

The Narragansetts sent one of their principal chiefs, and Uncas went in behalf of the Mohegans. One principal theme of complaint alleged, on the part of the Narragansetts was, that Uncas had taken a ransom for Miantinomoh, and after his death, had refused to return it. This Uncas stoutly denied under oath. Other evidence was heard, both in support of the charge and in behalf of the defense. The hearing resulted in favor of Uncas.

The Narragansett deputation agreed to abide by the decision, and to make no war upon Uncas, until after the next year's planting-time—and after that, before commencing hostilities, that they would give the governors of Massachusetts and Connecticut thirty days notice. This stipulation was to be binding also upon the Nihanticks, as well as upon their own tribe.*

* See Trumbull, I. 145, 146.

About this time, four sachems from Monhausett, upon Long Island, came over in canoes with their companions, and humbly waited upon the commissioners with a petition. They stated that they and the other Indians upon the island, had paid tribute to the English ever since the Pequot war, and that they had never done any harm, either to the English or the Dutch, but were the friends of both. They begged that they might have a certificate given them of this friendly relationship, and that the United Colonies would take them under their protection. The commissioners gave them the certificate, and assured them of protection, as long as they remained at peace with the English, and kept aloof from all the quarrels with the Indians. With this certificate—a cabalistic charm to them—the simple-hearted tributaries took their leave, deeply impressed with the superiority of the English.

During the same session, the claim of Massachusetts to a part of the Pequot country was renewed. Col. Fenwick interposed in behalf of himself and those whose interests he represented, and begged that the consideration of this matter might be postponed, until the Lord Say and Seal, and the other noblemen, knights, and gentlemen, who were named as grantees in the Warwick patent, and, who claimed this very territory, could have an opportunity to be heard. The commissioners decided that a convenient time ought to be given to those noble claimants to plead their title to the land in controversy.

Massachusetts, also, renewed her claim to Westfield, while Col. Fenwick, on the other hand, insisted that it was the property of the same grantees. It was finally decreed that Westfield, with all its houses and lands, should be under the jurisdiction of Massachusetts, until it was proved to which colony the plantation belonged; and that all lands, not exceeding two thousands acres, should belong to the purchasers.

South Hampton, upon Long Island, was this year taken under the jurisdiction of Connecticut. This town had been settled in 1640 by about one hundred families from Lynn.*

* Trumbull, i. 148.

When the General Court of Connecticut met in the preceding April, a committee was appointed to treat with Col. Fenwick in relation to a purchase of "Saybrook Fort, and of all guns, buildings, and lands in the colony, which he and the lords and gentlemen interested in the Patent of Connecticut might claim." On the 5th of December, 1644, the negotiation was completed by articles of agreement, signed by Col. Fenwick and the committee appointed by the General Court of Connecticut. On the part of himself and the other grantees, Col. Fenwick made over to Connecticut, the fort at Saybrook and its appurtenances; also all the lands on the Connecticut river! Such lands as were not sold, were to be given out by a committee of five, of whom Col. Fenwick was to be one. Col. Fenwick also agreed that all the lands from Narragansett river to Saybrook fort should fall under the jurisdiction of Connecticut, if it should come into his power so to dispose of it. On the other hand, the committee who represented Connecticut, agreed that Col. Fenwick should enjoy all the houses belonging to the fort for a period of ten years, and that a duty should be paid to him for a like term on corn, biscuit, bacon, and cattle, which should be exported from the mouth of the river. The General Court ratified this agreement in February, 1645, and passed an act to regulate the duty stipulated in the articles of agreement.* Provision was also made that a memorandum of the landing of each cargo passing beyond the river's mouth should be made of all commodities, subject to this duty, and delivered to Col. Fenwick, as a basis, from which to determine how much tribute was due him. This was the first tariff ever sanctioned by the people of Connecticut.

The duty was as follows:

1st. Each bushel of corn of all sorts, or meal, that shall pass out of the river's mouth, shall pay two pence per bushel.

2d. Every hundred biscuit that shall in like manner pass out of the river's mouth, shall pay sixpence.

3d. Each milch cow, and mare, of three years or upwards,

* J. H. Trumbull's Colonial Records, i. 119, &c.

within any of the towns or farms upon the river, shall pay twelve pence per annum, during the aforesaid term.

4th. Each hog or sow, that is killed by any particular person, within the limits of the river and the jurisdiction aforesaid, to be improved either for his own particular use, or to make market of, shall in like manner, pay twelve pence per annum.

5th. Each hogshead of beaver, traded within the limits of the river, shall pay two pence. Only, it is provided, that in case the general trade with the Indians, now in agitation, proceed, this tax upon beaver, mentioned in this, and the foregoing articles, shall fail.

It proved to be no insignificant sum that the colony paid for this purchase, and has been estimated at sixteen hundred pounds sterling.*

The General Court now took vigorous measures to put this important fortification in good repair. A tax of two hundred pounds was levied on the towns for this purpose. The Court also addressed a letter to Col. Fenwick, soliciting him to act as the agent of the colony, and sail for England, with a view of procuring an enlargement of the patent, "and to furnish other advantages for the country."

In the midst of these stirring events, died George Wyllys, Esquire, third governor of Connecticut, who, had there been left no written memorial of his worth, could not have failed of a traditionary fame more enviable, though less glaring, than that of the proudest military conqueror. He came of an old and honorable family, and was, before he left England, the possessor of an elegant mansion and a valuable estate in land, situated in Knapton, in the county of Warwick. Few English gentlemen had less occasion to become an adventurer; none had less cause to seek his fortune in the trackless labyrinths of the American woods. His birth, his wealth, his intellectual endowments, enriched by the most refined culture, entitled him, in the best of English neighborhoods, to the confidence and friendship of that order of Eng-

* See Trumbull, i. 150.

lish nobility, whom Burke has signalized as the "best society in the world." So that, whatever may be said of others, it cannot truthfully be said of Wyllys, that he sought to better his fortunes by emigration. He knew well, that as the world understands the term, he could not improve his condition, and that to change it, was to make it worse. His eye was not to be dazzled with the surfaces of things. With the earnestness that characterizes all noble natures, he sought after the truth, and, by the gradually increasing light of religious liberty, saw in that early dawn, the shadows of superstition beginning to grow pale and dim. He loved the traditions, the institutions, the customs, immemorial as the green old oaks and flowering hedges of his native island. Yet, like John Hampden, Herbert Pelham and Sir Harry Vane, though he lingered over the past with a loving step, his gaze was still fixed on the future. He was one of the few men of that harsh, intolerant age, whose large natures—incapable of bigotry, whether lurking under the folds of the surplice, or haunting the secret chambers of the conventicle—soared above the poisonous atmosphere of political strifes, and panted for a liberty, religious and civil, that should strike its roots in a deep, fresh soil, and bear those "golden apples" that in later years, requiting the culture of such hands as his, were to blush upon the branches of the Hesperian tree. Perhaps, too, he foresaw, and was not unwilling to avoid for himself and his children, the baleful fires of that bloody conflict, so soon to light up the English coast—the struggle between the old and the new, between prerogative and progress, of which all Europe was to "ring from side to side"—a struggle destructive as the whirlwind, yet tending to purify the moral atmosphere, as all great convulsions of the elements are said to vitalize the air.

In 1636, Mr. Wyllys sent over his steward, William Gibbons, with twenty men, to purchase and prepare for him, in Hartford, an estate suitable to his rank, erect a house, and make preparations for the reception of himself and his family. Two years after this, he bade adieu to the home of his childhood, and sailed for America. He arrived in Connecticut early enough to give to the framers of the Constitution of 1639, the benefit of his sound judgment and elevated views, and was elected a magistrate annually under it, from the time when the freemen adopted it by acclamation, to the day of his death. In 1641, he was elected deputy governor, and in 1642 he was made governor of Connecticut.

He led a calm, pure life, far enough elevated above the level of his contemporaries to point them where to look for the ideal of human excellence, yet near enough to stretch forth a benevolent hand to those whose vision was less keen, and whose feeble steps faltered as they ascended the rugged hill. Peace to his venerable dust, which, without a monument, sleeps near that of Hooker, in the old cemetry of Hartford, guarded by the piety of the thousands who inhabit the city, and who have succeeded to the noblest inheritance in the world—a spotless public life.

The Charter Oak Place, where he lived and died, with all its thrilling historical associations, has none that should tempt the lover of the heroic past more eagerly to visit its shades, than that it was the home of Wyllys.

In the summer of 1645, the Narragansett Indians again violated their treaty with the English, in commencing hostilities against Uncas.* They went into the heart of the Mohegan country, and attacked Uncas at his fort. They killed his men and threatened to annihilate both him and his tribe. So bent were they on the destruction of their old enemies, that Connecticut and New Haven were obliged to send each a detachment of soldiers, to keep the Mohegan country from being overrun by the invaders.

Governor Winthrop, in alarm, called a meeting of the commissioners to convene at Boston, on the 28th of June. As soon as that body had assembled, they sent couriers into

* See Bancroft, i. 211, who claims that the "temporary truce" had expired when the Narragansetts marched after Uncas. The action of the commissioners, however, seems to forbid such a conclusion.

the territories of the contending tribes, proposing that their sachems should repair to Boston, and refer their causes of quarrel to the decision of the commissioners, as had been done before. The sachems at first seemed disposed to listen favorably to the proposal, but at last declared they would neither go nor send. The Narragansett chiefs were highly excited. They insulted the messengers, and said very rough things of the English. One of them said "he would kill their cattle and pile them in heaps, and that an Englishman should no sooner step beyond his door than the Indians would kill him; that whoever began war he would continue it, and nothing would satisfy him but the head of Uncas."

Affairs now assumed such a threatening attitude, that Roger Williams, who was usually the apologist of the Indians and especially of the Narragansetts, wrote to the commissioners, that an Indian war was impending. After a careful consultation, the commissioners made a formal proclamation of war, and ordered that three hundred men should be forthwith levied, and placed under the command of Maj. Edward Gibbons. Capt. Mason had the immediate command of the Connecticut and New Haven forces. Humphrey Atherton, with forty men, was sent forward with all haste to meet Mason at Mohegan, and place himself under his direction, the better to defend Uncas until the whole army should unite their strength under Maj. Gibbons.

Gibbons was ordered not only to protect Uncas, but to invade the country of the Narragansetts and Nihanticks, and cut off their supplies. He was authorized, however, to offer them peace, and to make a treaty with them, should they be disposed to fall in with any reasonable proposals. If they were disposed to fight, he was to give them battle. If they would neither fight nor come to any amicable terms, but on the other hand fled before him, he was ordered to build forts in the territory of both these hostile tribes, and there accumulate the corn belonging to them gathered from far and near.*

* Records of the Commissioners.

Before hostilities had been decided upon by the English, the Narragansetts had sent a present to governor Winthrop at Boston, asking for peace with the colonies, but begging the privilege of fighting with Uncas, and avenging the death of Miantinomoh. The governor did not accept this present, but allowed it to be left in his keeping. The commissioners sent it back with a message to Canonicus, Pessacus, and the other sachems of the Narragansetts and Nihanticks, that they would not accept their gift, nor permit them to be at peace until they had atoned for their past offenses, and given pledges for their future good behavior. The messengers who were entrusted with this delicate commission soon returned to Boston, with tidings that Pessacus, the great war-chief of the Narragansetts, and other sachems, were coming to treat with the commissioners for a peace.

The Indian ambassadors, with Pessacus at their head, soon arrived at Boston, in great state, attended by a large retinue, and presented themselves before the commmissioners. They denied that they had been guilty of violating their faith in breaking the most solemn treaties, and urged their old claim of the ransom alleged to have been taken by Uncas, with astonishing pertinacity, if it was indeed a false claim. They offered to bind themselves again, to refrain from waging war with their hated enemy, until the next planting-time.

The commissioners assured them that it was idle to talk of such a thing—that they would be trifled with no longer—that the time had come for an ultimate decision, either for lasting peace or bloody war, and it was better that they should at once understand each other. They said it was useless for the Indians to pretend that they had kept faith with the colonies, as proofs of their perfidy were too glaring and abundant to be truthfully met, and that falsehoods could stand them in stead no longer.

The Indians finally acknowledged their treachery in reference to the treaties, and one of the principal chiefs took a stick, and humbly presented it to the commissioners, as a symbol of submission, and a token that he only waited for the English to dictate the terms of a new treaty, at their own discretion.

The commissioners decided that the new treaty should be substantially upon the following terms: that the Indians should pay to them two hundred fathom of white wampum; restore to Uncas all the captives and canoes that they had taken from him; that they would maintain perpetual peace with the English, and with all their allies, and that they would give hostages for the faithful performance of all these stipulations. With much reluctance the Indians finally signed the articles embracing these conditions.* But fear impelled them to do it, as they knew that English troops were now in the country, and ready to enforce even more stringent demands.

As early as 1640, some of the most enterprising citizens of Hartford commenced a settlement at a place about ten miles west of the city, upon the alluvial meadows of the Tunxis river. They gave to their little neighborhood the name of the brimming river, that swept past their log-houses, and enlivened the long summer days, as it wound through the meadows, where haymakers kept it company. It was not incorporated until 1645, when it was called Farmington. Almost all the inhabitants were planters. The township was not far from fifteen miles square.† This territory has been, from time to time, divided between the mother town and its offshoots. Out of it have sprung the towns of Southington, Berlin, Bristol, Burlington and Avon. The pioneers who purchased this tract of the original proprietors, the Tunxis Indians, and begun the plantation, were among the best families of Hartford, and their descendants have maintained to an unusual degree their marked traits of character.

In 1646, when the commissioners of the united colonies met at New Haven, the old difficulties between the colonies of New Haven and Connecticut on the one part, and the Dutch at New Amsterdam on the other, were presented to their consideration. It appears that the Dutch governor,

* Bancroft, i. 313. † Pease and Niles' Gazetteer.

Kieft, had written a spirited letter to governor Eaton, of New Haven, in which he took occasion to reassert the claims of the States General to the coast of Connecticut in very positive terms. He charged the English with violating ancient treaties existing between the two nations, under which they respectively claimed, and with having acted in defiance as well of the law of nations as of natural justice. He called them "breakers of the peace, and disturbers of the public tranquillity," and threatened them with war if they did not give up the places belonging to his jurisdiction that they had usurped, and make amends for the losses that his government had sustained on account of their encroachments.

Governor Eaton made answer that the colony of New Haven had never dispossessed the Dutch of any of their lands, or disturbed them in the enjoyment of any of their rights. He ended by proposing to leave all differences to be arbitrated by unbiased men, either in Europe or America.

Connecticut also made complaint against the Dutch of Good Hope, charging them with acting in opposition to the authorities of the colony, and especially in harboring an Indian woman, who was both a fugitive from justice and a runaway servant of one of the citizens of Hartford.*

The commissioners of the united colonies, in reference to these alleged wrongs, wrote a letter to governor Kieft, not much calculated I should think, to conciliate him. This letter recites at length all the claims of the two colonies, Connecticut and New Haven, and alludes in no very gentle terms, to the behavior of the dignitary to whom it was addressed. It is never pleasant to be told of one's faults, and the aversion that we all feel to it, is much enhanced when the censor

---

* For a more particular account of this controversy, the reader is referred to page 253, of that beautiful work entitled "Hartford in the Olden Time," by SCAEVA—an author who seems first to have entertained the thought that our local histories could be invested with some other interest than that of frigid details, and who never forgets what the Greeks taught the world, that a muse presides over history as well as song. His work is substantially a history of Connecticut, during the first few years of her existence.

is supposed to be our enemy. This epistle certainly lacked one characteristic of a modern diplomatic paper. It could not be said to say one thing and mean another.

Another letter was ordered to be written and sent to the same functionary, complaining that the Dutch traders were badly in arrears in their accounts with the English, and refused to pay, and that he had aided his subjects in withholding payment.

At the purport of these two letters, his excellency of New Netherlands was greatly incensed. He met all the charges contained in them with a flat denial, couched in the very strongest terms that he could frame, which he embraced in two corresponding documents, and sent to New Haven by the messenger who had been employed by the commissioners. The affair of the Indian woman appeared to inflame him most, for he honored that with a special traverse. With regard to the other allegations, he contented himself with saying that they were untrue, and that he would submit them to the arbitrament of nobody in Europe or America. The mildest thing that he would do, unless he met with better treatment from the English, was to avenge himself by an appeal to arms. In his excited state of mind, he used a very bold figure of speech, likening the commissioners to "eagles that soar aloft and despise the little fly." He denied the right of the English to any part of the coast of Connecticut, and especially to New Haven, the very name of which he ignored, adhering to the old Dutch name of "Red Mount." "We protest," he said in conclusion, "against all your commissioners met at *Red Mount*, as against breakers of the common league, and also infringers of the rights of the lords, the states, our superiors, in that you have dared without our express and special consent, to hold your general meeting within the limits of New Netherlands."*

To these letters the commissioners made a very curt reply, the substance of which was, that the exaggerated strain of his correspondence was no more than was to be expected from him.

* Letter of Kieft on the Records of the United Colonies.

The Connecticut river Indians, this year, were unusually troublesome. Sequasson, one of their chiefs, conceived the design of murdering governor Haynes, governor Hopkins, and Mr. Whiting, one of the magistrates. He hired a Waranoke Indian to execute the plot. The consideration to be paid was a number of wampum-girdles. But after he had received the price of blood, he went deliberately to Hartford, and betrayed his employer. The Windsor Indians at about the same time did the inhabitants of Windsor much damage, by burning up large quantities of their personal property. The magistrates issued a warrant, and arrested the Indian whom they supposed to be the author of this mischief, but the Indians rescued him from the hands of the officers with violence.*

The commissioners in session at New Haven, sent a message to Sequasson, citing him to appear before them, and make answer to the charges against him. But the cunning savage thought it best to keep out of harm's way. The Indians were subject to strange paroxysms of mischief, that would break out suddenly and take possession of them like physical diseases. In reading the best authenticated accounts of their behavior, the descriptions that we meet with in the New Testament of those who were under the influence of devils, are constantly forced upon the mind. On such occasions, their passions led them whithersoever they would.

The Mohawks, now that the Pequots were exterminated, had the field to themselves, and spent their time in waging war with the eastern tribes, and collecting tribute from them. They had sagacity enough to keep on friendly terms with the English, and confined their depredations to the Indians. Their tax-gatherers were so punctual in their annual visitations, that those who paid them tribute knew when to expect them. They knew, too, that an armed force usually followed these leeches, to see that none of the subjects departed from their allegiance.

---

* Trumbull, i. 158, 159.

Some years after Milford was settled by the English, a company of Mohawks came within the borders of the town, and secreted themselves in a swamp, where they awaited an opportunity of making an attack upon the Milford Indians. Some Englishmen saw the Mohawks, and were friendly enough to inform their swarthy neighbors of their danger. They immediately rallied in great numbers, raised the war-whoop, and rushing suddenly upon the Mohawks, gained a complete victory. Among the prisoners was a stout Mohawk warrior, whom the conquerors decided to kill by famine and torture. They stripped him naked, and having tied him to a stake, left him in the tall grass of the salt meadows, to be eaten up by the mosquitoes. An Englishman, named Hine, who found the poor wretch in this deplorable condition, shocked at this barbarous mode of torture, cut the thongs from his limbs, and set him at liberty. He then invited him to his house, gave him food, and helped him to escape. This kind act was never forgotten by the Mohawks. They treated the English of Milford ever after with marked civility, and did many kind and friendly acts, that testified their gratitude towards their deliverer and his family.*

It has been said that the principal inhabitants of New Haven were originally engaged in commerce and merchandise. They soon found that the unpeopled wastes of New England offered little opportunity for them to pursue their old occupations. The estates that they had brought with them, declined in value, and left them disappointed and comparatively helpless. Their settlement at Delaware had proved a heavy burden to them. Besides, they had long waited in vain for the arrival of certain wealthy gentlemen, who had given them assurance that they would soon join them and share their enterprise. At length, despairing of any such relief, and conscious that some new steps must be taken to retrieve their sinking fortunes, some of their most enterprising merchants united their resources to build a ship, of one hundred and fifty tons burden, and fit her out for England. They

---

* Lambert.

freighted her with furs, corn, and plate, almost all their little stock of merchantable wealth. She had also seventy souls on board, including Gregson, Lamberton, and some other men of note in the colony.

It was in the stark month of January, and the harbor was frozen over so firmly that the citizens were obliged to cut a way for her through the ice, with saws, for three miles, before she was free to float in the water. Mr. Davenport, and many others who were to stay behind, went out upon the ice and bade her adieu. As he stretched his hands towards heaven in prayer, the reverend man said, doubtingly, "Lord, if it be thy pleasure to bury these our friends, in the bottom of the sea, they are thine—save them!"

They watched her gallant sails and trembling keel, till their eyes were blinded with tears. Ships arrived one after another from England, but they brought no tidings to the people of New Haven, of the bark that bore from their sight so much that was dear to them. Months passed, each dropping its heavy plummet deeper than its predecessor, into the abyss of mystery and gloom that shrouded the fate of the ship. At last inquiries ceased to be whispered by the wife, the father, the friend; and the heart spoke its agonized meaning only in the quivering lip and the fixed eye. Still they waited for tidings, and perhaps beneath the calm exterior of despair, there trembled a pulse of hope, but this too, died. Then succeeded another long period of silence.

In November, 1647, those who embarked in the ill-starred vessel were treated as deceased persons, and their estates went through the due course of administration. Not quite two years and a half after the missing ship sailed, one pleasant afternoon in June, as the sunbeams lit up the clouds that still lingered—the lurid curtains of a thunder storm that had spent its volleys in the heavens—there was seen on the level line of the horizon, hovering over the harbor, the figure of a three-masted ship. Shadowy at first, and without shroud or tackle, but gradually taking on a fearful distinctness, until her full sails swelled in the summer breeze; and on her upper deck there stood the semblance of a man, a solitary form. Though the wind blew from the north, she made her course bravely against it for a full half hour, until the little children ran and cried as she drew near, "There's a brave ship." The weird bark was the exact counterpart of the lost one. For many minutes she remained, until the anxious and the curious were assembled, to welcome her home. And there upon her deck, its left hand pressed against its side, and its right hand grasping a sword, stood the mournful shape, pointing silently towards the sea. Finally, a cloud of smoke arose, faint at first, but darkening as it wreathed its sombre folds around the Phantom Ship and the armed spectre, till both were swallowed up from mortal sight!

It has not come down to us what was the name of the vessel. It is a wild legend, and is not without a strange interest. The reader must settle for himself the question, whether it is fabulous or true.*

During the year 1649, the chiefs of the Narragansetts and Nihanticks were again cited to appear before the commissioners at Boston, to answer for not having kept their last treaty with the English. Ninigret obeyed the summons, but Pessacus sent in an excuse. He would be very glad to go to Boston, but he was too unwell to undertake such a journey. He further pleaded the terms of the late treaty were very hard upon his tribe, and that they could not comply with them. He claimed that they were void, too, from having been obtained by duress, while he was in Boston, and an armed force of Englishmen marching against his defenseless country. However, he sent two deputies to represent him, and prepared to be bound by whatever Ninigret should stipulate. Ninigret pleaded the cause of the two nations with great dignity and eloquence, and the parties at last agreed upon terms of adjustment satisfactory to all concerned.

The tax levied upon the towns soon after the purchase of

* The Rev. James Pierpont, of New Haven, who was a firm believer in the miraculous nature of the apparition, wrote an interesting account of it at the request of Cotton Mather, who published it in his Magnalia.

Saybrook fort, was not raised by the inhabitants of Springfield. The General Court of Massachusetts denied the right of Connecticut to tax this town, as it was claimed to be within the jurisdiction of Massachusetts. The commissioners refused at first to make any order in the matter, as it was a very delicate one, and had not been particularly referred to them by one of the claimants, but suggested that the money to be expended upon the fort was for the benefit of all the towns upon the river. After the action of the General Court of Massachusetts, and after the resolutions had been passed, the commissioners, upon a full hearing, decided the question as well as they could by ordering, that inasmuch as Springfield enjoyed the benefit of the fort, she "should pay the impost of two pence per bushel for corn, and a penny on the pound for beaver;" but that the parties disputing the right to lay the impost, might have the privilege afterwards to show reasons against it.

During this very session, John Winthrop, of Pequot, (now New London,) laid claim to the whole country of the Western Nihanticks, embracing a large part of the present town of Lyme, by virtue both of a deed of purchase and a deed of gift from the Indians. Mr. Winthrop did not pretend that he had any paper title, but offered abundant evidence of a fair transfer by parol. To these claims, the commissioners who represented Connecticut made answer, that Mr. Winthrop's pretended purchase was without date, had no fixed boundaries, and that, for aught that appeared, the grantor had himself no title to the granted premises; that the contract was a parol one, and that at the best it was but a vague, loose way of transferring an estate in lands; while on the other hand, Connecticut owned the territory by right of conquest. The decision was, at the request of Connecticut, postponed to a later day, and the claim was never afterwards presented by Mr. Winthrop.

Not far from this time—at what precise date is not known, but probably during the year 1648—died at Saybrook the Lady Alice Boteler, since and still known as Lady Fenwick.* She was a daughter of Sir Edward Apsley, and married, first, Sir John Boteler, and after his death became the wife of Col. George Fenwick, with whom she sailed for America. Not only is the date of her decease unknown, but not a circumstance alluding to so interesting a fact has come down to us. Near the remains of the old fort, probably within its limits as it was first built, and close upon the river-bank, where the plaintive murmurs of the Connecticut blend with the heavy moanings of the sea—upon supporters that seem to stoop with the weight of their burden—rests a table of grey sandstone, bearing a scroll without an inscription or a name. Yet to me, as I looked upon it, without a tree to droop over it in summer, or screen it from the fierce winter winds—without a flower to symbolize the beauty and loveliness of the high-born sleeper—no epitaph could have spoken with such eloquence as the silence of the monument and the desolation of the spot. It spoke to me, as it may have done to others, of the crowning excellence and glory of a woman's love, who could give up the attractions of her proud English home, the peerless circles wherein she moved and constituted a chief fascination, to follow her husband to this

* Lady Fenwick was a daughter of Sir Edward Apsley, of Thackham. Sir Edward married Eliza, daughter of Edward Elmes, of Lyford, in the county of Northampton, and had children, (1,) Elizabeth, who married Sir Albert Norton knight, and secretary of state; (2,) Edward, living at Thackham in 1634, mentioned in Col. Fenwick's will as the "Uncle" of his daughters; (3,) Alice, who married, first, Sir John Boteler, and afterwards George Fenwick; and (4,) Ann, who married Matthew Caldecott, of Sherington, in the county of Sussex. Sir John Boteler, Lady Fenwick's first husband, was the eldest son of Sir Oliver Boteler, of Teston, who was knighted by James 1st, in 1604. Sir John died in his father's life time. Sir John's younger brother, William, inherited Sir Oliver's estate, and was created a baronet by Charles 1st, in 1641. He espoused the cause of the king in the civil war, and was killed at Cropedy Bridge in June, 1644. The wife of Col. Fenwick appears always to have retained the name and title given her by her first husband. The receipt given for her monument in 1679, describes it as the "Tomb Stone of the Lady Alice Boteler, late of Saybrook." (See Saybrook Records.) I am indebted to the accomplished editor of the "Colonial Records of Connecticut" for the facts above recited, as I am for many other favors of a like character. I shall add nothing to his reputation, though I shall do myself a great pleasure, when I say, that I do not think there is a more accurate and at the same time philosophical antiquarian in New England.

desolate peninsula, where the humble houses of wood within the inclosure of the fort, opened their forbidding doors with a grim welcome that must have chilled her heart. Here she lingered in obscurity till she died. Perhaps when her husband was away at Hartford, or Boston, as he often was, attending to the interests of Connecticut, as she looked off upon the blue waters, her eye was dimmed with tears of disappointment as she in vain sought the long expected sail that was to waft that noble coterie of lords and ladies, knights, and gentlemen, to Saybrook, whither they had promised to flee from the civic strifes that beset them at home. But that sail was only seen in her dreams, and the towers of the new city that was to have sprung up under the plastic touch of the patentees of Connecticut, were lost with the other fantasies of the night in the glimmering moon-beams that fell upon her startled eyelids through the frosted window-panes. She died in her place of voluntary exile. Two hundred years have rolled away. The shrill cry of the plover now as then pierces the ear as it flies over the spot. But the rude fort, with its walls of wood and earth, is gone. The Connecticut swarms with vessels of every description, filled with a free population that need no cannon at the mouth of the river, as in that iron age, to guard them from violence. How much can be learned from an old, solitary tomb! The dead need no monument, but are themseves a monument of the "dead old time." Their names, when uttered, are vital as their ashes shall be on the morning of the resurrection. But let not the sons of a state, in whose bosom sleeps the dust of Alice Apsley, forget that the forbidding aspect of her tomb, though it dishonors not her, disgraces them; and if she has left no other claim upon their affectionate remembrance, let them bear in mind that she was at least the wife of Fenwick!

CHAPTER VIII.

FOUNDING OF NEW LONDON.

As early as the spring of 1646, under the auspices of the General Court of Massachusetts, Mr. John Winthrop, jun., and a few others, had already begun to plant the fields lying upon Pequot Harbor, and found a settlement there. Mr. Thomas Peters,* a clergyman, was associated with Mr. Winthrop, and these two gentlemen were entrusted with the authority of framing a form of civil government, and administering it, until further orders.† This territory was for a long time debated ground, as has been before stated: Connecticut claiming both by virtue of a grant and by right of conquest, and Massachusetts asserting a right to it as her share of the conquered country of the Pequots. Mr. Peters did not stay long enough in the new settlement to lend much aid to his associate, for in the fall of 1646 he embarked for England, and never returned to America. Mr. Winthrop did not remove his family from Boston until the fall of 1646, when he sailed with his wife and a part of his children, to the country over which he claimed jurisdiction. His brother, Dean Winthrop, accompanied him. They had a very rough and tedious passage. They spent that winter upon Fisher's Island. In the spring of 1647, Mr. Winthrop built a house upon the main-land at Pequot, and removed his whole family thither. The place was also called Nameaugs. This was the first beginning of the now flourishing city of New London. Although the plantation was commenced under the protection of Massachusetts, yet after the action of the commissioners upon the question of jurisdiction in July 1647, the

* This gentleman was a brother of the celebrated Hugh Peters, and was himself one of the ejected Puritan divines of Cornwall, England. He appears to have been for some time chaplain to Mr. Fenwick, and to the garrison at Saybrook.

† New London Records. See Miss Caulkins' History, p. 45.

dominion over it was conceded to belong to Connecticut; and in the following September, the court gave Mr. Winthrop a commission "to execute justice" according to the laws of Connecticut, "and the rules of righteousness." *

At the session of the General Court in May 1649, John Winthrop, Esquire, with Thomas Minor and Samuel Lathrop as assistants, were authorized to hold a court in the town, with jurisdiction over "all differences among the inhabitants under the value of forty shillings."† To encourage the enterprise of the first settlers of New London, and to induce new adventurers to take up their abode there, the court at the same session granted the inhabitants exemption from taxation for the period of three years. The court also advised that the town should be called "Fair Harbor." But the planters claimed the privilege of naming the place, and finally, after some changes and debates, hit upon the name of New London, which was sanctioned by the General Court.

The old subject of alarm and debate, the perfidy of the Narragansett and Nihantick Indians, could not long remain quiet. These Indians were resolved not to pay the wampum that they had agreed again and again to do, and had hired the Pocomtocks and Mohawks to unite with them in exterminating the hated Mohegans. The Narragansetts and Nihanticks secreted their women and children in swamps, and raised an army of eight hundred warriors, who were to meet their allies, the Mohawks and the Pocomtocks, in or near the Mohegan country. The governor and council sent a deputation, at the head of whom was Thomas Stanton, to Pocomtock. When they arrived there they found the Indians of the place in arms and awaiting the arrival of the Mohawks.‡ The Indians confessed their error, but said they had been hired by the Narragansetts. It was represented to Stanton, that the Mohawks had four hundred guns, and plenty of ammunition. This must have been a

* J. Hammond Trumbull, Colonial Records, i. 157. † Ib. i. 186.
‡ Trumbull, i. 171.

very exaggerated account of their resources. It is not likely that the whole tribe were possessed of one-fourth part that number of guns. Stanton told the Indians that they must not march into the Mohegan territory, and that the English would defend Uncas against all his enemies, and would avenge all his wrongs. This well-timed threat had the effect to keep the Pocomtocks at home, and as the Mohawks (if indeed they had ever intended to aid in the enterprise,) were detained in their own country by some troubles that they had with the French, the Narragansetts dared not take it upon themselves to chastise the Mohegans, and so the affair was dropped for awhile. But the Narragansetts did not by any means remain idle. They made depredations upon the people of Rhode Island, broke into their houses, stole their goods, and insulted the planters in every conceivable way. At Warwick they killed an hundred cattle, and threatened the inhabitants with the most cruel violence. In their perplexity and alarm, the authorities of Rhode Island applied to the commissioners to be admitted into the confederacy. That grave body, then in session at Plymouth, made answer in substance, that the whole region occupied by the petitioners was included in the Plymouth patent, and of right ought to be under the jurisdiction of that colony; that if the people of Rhode Island would consent to relinquish their claims to an independent existence, and be merged in the colony of New Plymouth, their interests would be tenderly cared for; but they refused to treat with them as a distinct commonwealth.* However, the commissioners sent a new deputation to the Narragansetts and Nihanticks, complaining among other things of the outrages that they had committed in Rhode Island, whose people had never wronged them, and warning the sachems to keep their men under better discipline.

During the same session, the old affair of the impost for the repair of the fort at Saybrook came up for further discussion. Massachusetts complained of the former decision

* Records of the United Colonies.

of the commissioners, and the General Court of that colony had appointed a committee to draw up an answer in writing to the arguments and reasons of Governor Hopkins in behalf of Connecticut at the previous session. Whatever the merits of the case might be, this answer was certainly a very able one. It alleged that Springfield was under no more obligation to pay for the repairs of the fort, than any other town not within the limits of Connecticut; that if that town derived any benefit from the fort, it was an incidental one, and was no greater than that resulting from the same source to any of the towns of New Haven colony that lay along the coast. It urged that New Haven or Stamford might with as much propriety be taxed for this object as Springfield; and added, that the former decision of the commissioners ought to be reviewed, as it was carried by the votes of the members from New Haven colony, who were interested parties; and also because it was induced in part by the alleged provisions of the Connecticut patent, a document which was not produced, as it ought to have been if any claim of title was set up under it.*

The committee in behalf of Massachusetts appear to have thought it advisable to let it be known how powerful their commonwealth was, and how little dependent it was upon the other colonies, for in connection with this argument they took occasion to intimate that Massachusetts could do as she liked about complying with the order of the commissioners in this matter without any breach of faith, and complained of the inequality of the representation in a body where such small powers as New Haven and New Plymouth had an equal vote with Massachusetts. The committee also said that this impost was a bone of contention that was likely "to interrupt their happy union and brotherly love." They greatly feared that unless this stumbling-block could be removed, they might be tempted "to help themselves in some other way."

In behalf of Connecticut, Roger Ludlow and governor

* See Trumbull, i. 172, 173.

Hopkins replied, that the arguments and proofs that had been the basis of the order at the former session, had not been met by any thing that was set forth in the remonstrance of Massachusetts, and that they were indeed unanswerable. After alluding briefly to what had been said in relation to the old claims of Massachusetts in 1638, with regard to the exemption from impost of the plantations under their alleged jurisdiction, and the change of circumstances which ten years had brought about,—and after disposing summarily of the question of a priority of right so strongly urged by the other party, they go on to speak with some sensitiveness of the charge made against the commissioners of founding their decree, either in whole or in part, upon the supposed contents of the Connecticut patent, a paper that they had never seen. These gentlemen argued that such a charge was unreasonable, and without foundation. That a copy of this patent was certainly brought forward at the time the confederation was established; that its contents were publicly known, and that the gentlemen of Massachusetts were the last persons in the world who could plead ignorance of the fact that it had recently been owned by the committee of parliament, and that it had as much vitality and power over the territory embraced within the boundaries named in it, as had the patents of Massachusetts and Plymouth over their own. To make good what they said, they backed it up by producing a copy of the Connecticut patent which governor Hopkins, who had compared it with the original, offered to make oath to as authentic.

In regard to the appeal made by Massachusetts to the sympathies and fears of the commissioners, that the impost was inexpedient and threatened the existence of the amicable relations and brotherly love that had so long bound the four colonies together, they answered with a very delicate severity, that it was the wish of Connecticut, that in all the doings of the confederation, "*truth* and *peace* might embrace each other"—that it was impossible for them to see how the setting forth of the claims of truth and righteousness could be the means of breaking up the subsisting relations of peace and brotherly love.

Upon a full hearing, the commissioners again decided in favor of Connecticut.

Previous to this, on the 27th of May, 1647, his Excellency, Peter Stuyvesant, governor of New Netherlands, arrived at Manhattan and entered upon the duties of his office.* The commissioners, in the name of the united colonies of New England, hastened to address to him a congratulatory letter upon his accession to the government. In this letter they also took occasion to inform him that the Dutch traders had been in the habit of selling firearms and ammunition to the Indians, and sometimes within the boundaries of the English plantations, and begged him to put an end to this ill-judged and dangerous traffic. They also made complaint of the imposts laid by the Dutch, which they said, fettered the freedom of trade. The letter also complained of seizures made by the Dutch of English vessels and goods.

His Excellency of New Netherlands made no answer to these complaints, and it will appear from what followed that he gave very little heed to them. Perhaps he thought, though I am not aware that he has left us any record of his reflections on this subject, that congratulation and remonstrance might have afforded materials for two distinct communications. Be that as it may, he evidently disregarded the complaints, for in the year 1648 he caused a vessel belonging to Mr. Westerhouse, a Dutch merchant and planter of New Haven, to be seized while she was riding at anchor in the harbor.† Westerhouse stated his grievance to the commissioners, who espoused his cause as that of the united colonies, and at once wrote a letter to governor Stuyvesant, expressing in the strongest terms their horror of this insult offered to the English colonies, and wrong done to an innocent private citizen. They again took occasion to "protest against the claim of the Dutch to all the lands, rivers, and streams from Cape Henlopen to Cape Cod," while they re-

* See Brodhead, i. 433. † Trumbull, i. 175; Brodhead, i. 496.

iterated the oft-assailed right of the united colonies to all these plantations and domains held by the double title of grant from the British crown, and of purchase from the Indians, the native proprietors of the soil.

The seizure of this ship from one of their own harbors they represented to be an atrocious and unparalleled outrage, which they neither could nor would suffer to pass without some redress. They thought the letters that he had written to them and to the governors of Massachusetts and New Haven, were couched in a phraseology so mysterious and equivocal that it was impossible to understand them. They begged him to be less oracular and more explicit. They insisted upon the necessity of a meeting between him and them for the purpose of coming to a more full understanding. Until there was some such adjustment, they said the Dutch merchants and marines should enjoy no privileges in the New England harbors or plantations, either of anchoring, searching or seizing, more than the English did at Manhattan; and if upon search they should find arms or ammunition on board any Dutch ship, which were designed to be sold to the Indians within the borders of the united colonies, they would seize them "until further inquiry and satisfaction should be made." The epistle closed in a very high tone, from which the governor of New Netherlands might readily infer that unless he saw the error of his ways, it would soon be necessary for him to vindicate them by force of arms.*

The murder of Mr. John Whitmore, in 1648, at Stamford, and the discovery of an old murder of Mr. Cope and a part of his crew upon Long Island, both of which were committed by the Indians, occasioned much uneasiness in the colonies of Connecticut and New Haven.

In the year 1647, the old fort at Saybrook, built by Gardiner, under the direction of Winthrop, by some unfortunate accident took fire and was burned to ashes. In May, 1649, the General Court ordered "that there shall be a dwelling-house erected at Saybrook about the middle of the new fort,

* Record of the United Colonies.

at the charge and for the service of the commonwealth."* The building of a new fort was also prosecuted with vigor.

During the same year, 1649, the Indians upon Long Island committed at Southold some terrible murders. The Narragansetts and Nihanticks were by no means inactive. They had remained quiet as long as they could restrain their diabolical passions; but at last their hatred of Uncas broke forth. They had been thwarted so often in their attempts to make war upon the Mohegan chief, that they now determined to assassinate him. With this view they confided their secret to a trusty Indian, who undertook, for a reward, to accomplish the murder. The assassin went on board a vessel in the Thames, where Uncas was, and stabbed him in the breast. He meant without doubt to kill him, and for a long time it was thought that the chief would die of the wound. But he at last recovered, and that too in due time to present himself before the commissioners, exhibit his scars, tell over again his old story about the Mohawks, reiterate his complaints against his enemies, whom he meekly represented as thirsting for innocent blood, and beg that as he had never deserted the English in times of peril, they would requite his friendly services by extending to him their protection. All that he appeared to want was justice, and he certainly had much occasion to congratulate himself upon his good luck, that his prayers in this respect were not answered. However, it cannot be denied that he told the truth when he said that he had always been faithful to the English. Ninigret was cited to appear and clear himself of the charge preferred against him by Uncas, that he and Pessacus had hired the assassin. It is probable that this charge was substantially true, as the wretched murderer himself, we are told, gave the same account of the matter. At any rate, it was thought by the commissioners that the Nihantick sachem made but a meagre defense. He was dismissed with the assurance that unless he immediately liquidated the old arrearages, the English would leave him to his fate.

---

* J. H. Trumbull, i. 187.

About this time the colonies were thrown into a convulsion by a rumor, the author of which it is not difficult to divine, that a son or brother of Sassacus was negotiating an alliance with Ninigret, and was about to marry his daughter, and that the Narragansetts and Nihanticks were contriving to gather up the scattered Pequots, and place them under the dominion of this bugbear chief. This story is so shallow and incredible to us of the present day, that it seems astonishing that it should have gained any credence. But the crafty politician who devised it was a shrewd judge of character, and knew that the very word Pequot had not ceased to be terrible to the English. This fabrication was intended to have a double edge. Uncas knew that the Pequots who had been assigned to his keeping had more than two years before been induced by his tyranny to revolt from him, and set up for themselves. He also knew these Indians had in 1647, presented to the English a memorial, such as they were able to frame, against his outrageous treatment of them, which recited a list of exactions and cruelties; and he also knew that he was guilty of all that they charged upon him. The English, slow to believe their favorite and ally to be such an unprincipled wretch as he was represented, were at last, upon frequent repetition of the accusation, beginning to lose confidence in him. What so likely, in this pressing exigency, to divert the attention of the English from himself and fix it where he most desired it to remain, as an appeal to the fears of his allies, by putting in circulation this well-contrived story of the anticipated alliance of the Pequots, his accusers, with the Nihanticks and Narragansetts, who were his old enemies? It would serve the double purpose of lulling the growing suspicions against himself, and increasing those already existing against his rivals. The prospects held out to him by this story were so flattering that he could not resist them.

Meanwhile his evil deeds were sent forth upon every wind. The insulted Pequots repeated their charges in the ears of the English, until their frigid incredulity gradually dissolved. The Pequots affirmed that since they had been put under his protection, he had exacted from them payments of wampum forty several times. They farther asserted that upon the death of one of his children, the hypocritical father made his squaw presents to comfort her, and compelled them to give her wampum by way of adding to this extraordinary consolation. Whereupon Uncas expressed great satisfaction, and gave his word that he would ever after treat them with the same consideration as if they were of Mohegan blood; and that, in violation of this promise, he had cheated them and wronged them in a variety of ways. One of the Pequot sachems in particular, insisted that Uncas had taken away his wife from him and conducted towards her as if she had been his own. Others testified that he had wounded and tortured some of the Pequots, and robbed the whole of them. This memorial was presented in behalf of more than sixty Pequots. Uncas of course denied all the allegations set forth in it, but they were so thoroughly substantiated that the commissioners could not help believing them. They rebuked Uncas, ordered him to give up the wife of the chief whom he had stolen, make the Pequots good for all the damages he had done them, and pay a fine of one hundred fathom of wampum. He was also directed to take back his abused subjects without inflicting any punishment upon them for complaining of his cruelties towards them. But the poor creatures refused to comply with this order, although they were obedient to the English in all other respects. Year after year, as the commissioners met, they presented their humble petition, in which they feelingly alluded to their condition as a conquered people, and owned that their tribe had met a just fate; but they begged to be delivered from the rapacity and overbearing insolence of Uncas. They said that whatever might have been the fault of their tribe, they at least had killed no Englishmen, and that Wequash, the guide, who had led Mason to the fort, had given them his word that if they would fly from the Pequot country, and do the colonies no injury, they should be safe from harm.

These plaintive supplications at last had the effect to mitigate the condition of the petitioners. This relief was in part due to the interposition of Mr. Winthrop, who knew Uncas too well to take his part. There was never any cordiality between that gentleman and the Mohegan chief.

This year, (1649,) the affair of the impost was again brought before the commissioners, and decided as before in favor of Connecticut. The members from Massachusetts then produced an order of their General Court, imposing a duty upon "all goods belonging to any of the inhabitants of Plymouth, Connecticut or New Haven, imported within the castle, or exported from any part of the bay." This was done by way of retaliating upon Connecticut, and upon the other colonies, for voting in behalf of the Connecticut impost. It was an act which the historians of Massachusetts have never attempted to justify, and was unworthy of the high character of that noble colony—a character so steadily sustained from that day to the present.

On the 5th of September, 1650, the commissioners again met at Hartford. Governor Hopkins of Connecticut presided. There was no want of topics to occupy their attention. The Narragansetts still neglected to produce the wampum that they had long been obligated to pay. The gallant Captain Humphrey Atherton, of Massachusetts, was sent with twenty men under his command to enforce the payment. He was authorized, if the arrearages were not paid, to seize upon such property as he could find to an amount equal in value to the sum due, or to take possession of the person of Pessacus or of his children, and bring them away as hostages, to insure the final liquidation of this troublesome account. With such a liberal commission, Atherton, with his handful of men, marched into the heart of the Narragansett country. He had no difficulty in procuring an interview with Pessacus, but the sachem immediately began to practice his old arts of diplomacy. He advanced a number of propositions with provisional clauses and conditions involved, which, in the language of the logicians, he proceeded to argue in a circle, arriving at the same point whence he started, without stating any thing in an explicit manner. He kept the English aloof from his person during this oration, evidently "talking against time," while his warriors were gathering around him in formidable numbers. The high-spirited Atherton, who probably never knew what fear was, could control his temper no longer. He marched to the door of the chief's wigwam, and there leaving his men, rushed into his presence, and in a very unparliamentary way, it must be admitted, seized his majesty of Narragansett by the hair, in the midst of his oration, and dragging him forth from the circle of his attendants, pointed a loaded pistol at his head, and told him he would blow his brains out if he dared to offer the least resistance. Arrested, probably, in the very flush of some lofty metaphor, like a falcon struck down by an arrow while in the swiftest turnings of his airy flight, the chief in astonishment and alarm ended the negotiations at once, by counting out the wampum which he had sworn that he was not possessed of, and paying it over to Atherton, who thereupon set him at liberty.*

Taking leave of Pessacus, the English ambassador hastened to pay a visit to Ninigret. He was not long in finding him. As he came on business, and not for the sake of enjoying the luxuries of Indian hospitality, Atherton proceeded at once to state to the Nihantick sachem the object of his mission, and to tell him some very wholesome though unwelcome truths. He charged upon him the intended alliance of his family with the Pequot chief, and with his manœuvres to possess himself of the conquered country. In the course of the conversation he demanded of him where the proposed bridegroom was to be found, and what number of warriors he had with him. He insisted on having direct answers to all his questions, as he said he wanted to make a faithful report of all that passed between them, to the commissioners. What information he gleaned in regard to the alliance, I am unable to say. His visit was not without its effect, and served the

* Trumbull, i. 188.

purpose for which it was intended, that of intimidating the Nihanticks.

This expedition of Atherton is one of the boldest enterprises recorded in our annals. It has also the merit of being entirely bloodless; and has such a happy mixture in it of tragedy and comedy, that it leaves a very pleasant effect upon the mind. The conduct of Atherton gives us, in a few bold, dashing strokes, a complete portraiture of his character.

All this time affairs were getting worse between the confederacy of New England and Peter Stuyvesant, governor of New Netherlands. At last, the Dutch governor with a view of bringing about some arrangement between the contending powers, both in reference to commerce and jurisdiction, thought it advisable to accept the invitation sometime before tendered him by the commissioners, and take a journey to Hartford, where that body was then in session. He arrived at Hartford on the 11th of September, 1650. He came in a style befitting his rank. He was invited, as he had often been before, to attend the meetings of the commissioners. With much stateliness he declined to accept the invitation, and expressed a wish that the business should be transacted through the medium of written correspondence. This formality of putting upon paper what could be so much more readily expressed by oral conference, did not accord with the practical usages adopted by the other party; but as his Excellency was inflexible, they thought it best to yield the point as one of mere etiquette.

The Dutch governor having prevailed as to the *manner* of conducting the negotiation, he may have thought he should succeed equally well as to the *matter*.

He commenced this diplomatic correspondence by a state paper that struck at the root of the controversy at once. He complained of the encroachments of the English upon the rights of the West India company, and of the injuries done to the Dutch, especially by the colonies of Connecticut and New Haven. He asserted that the Dutch had an unquestionable title to all the lands upon the Connecticut river, having bought them of the aboriginal proprietors, before the English, or any other power had laid claim to them. He demanded a surrender of those lands, and a suitable remuneration for the use of them. He entered his protest against the act, which excluded the Dutch from the English colonies for the purposes of trade. He spoke with indignation of the custom, which he said prevailed among the English traffickers, of selling goods to the Indians at such ruinously low prices, that other nations could not compete with them. He expressed a willingness to come to some understanding in relation to the boundaries of the respective claimants. Worse than all, and most likely to widen the breach between the English and his government, he dated this unlucky letter at New Netherlands. The commissioners could with difficulty suppress their contempt at his arrogant pretensions. They replied that they would not treat with him unless he dated his epistles at some other place than New Netherlands. In answer to this objection, he said, that if they would not date at Hartford, he would not date at New Netherlands. He suggested, by way of compromise, that they should both date at Connecticut. The English made answer that he might date at Connecticut if he liked, but as for themselves they should date at Hartford. Very reluctantly governor Stuyvesant was compelled to give way. He found that the English were as fastidious and captious as he in relation to forms, when those forms might be afterwards converted into substantive evidence as descriptive of a part of the territory in dispute, and as an acknowledgment either of title or jurisdiction.

Having settled this preliminary question, the English were not backward in stating their title to Connecticut, by possession, purchase, and discovery. They added, that the honorable West India company had set up so many claims, and couched them in terms so ambiguous, that the commissioners were not well advised either as to the extent of country that the Dutch supposed themselves entitled to, or as to the title by which it was held. After a great deal of mutual accusation and recrimination, involving a minute recital of all the quarrels by sea and land that had sprung up between the two powers, it was agreed that the whole matter, including the boundary question, should be submitted to arbitration. Several days were spent, and numerous and tedious were the letters that passed between them, before they came to this result.

The commissioners chose Bradstreet of Boston, and Prince of Plymouth; and his Excellency of New Amsterdam, chose Thomas Willet and George Baxter, as arbitrators, with full power to settle all differences.*

On the 19th of September, the arbitrators made and published an award, that appears to have been as satisfactory to the parties concerned as could have been anticipated. It is a state paper of very great ability and conciseness. It very adroitly states at the outset, that most of the alleged grievances complained of by Connecticut and New Haven colonies, had happened during the administration of governor Kieft, the predecessor of governor Stuyvesant, and that they postpone a hearing upon all these questions until the Dutch governor can find time to prepare his answer.

They pass over the controversy growing out of the seizure of Mr. Westerhouse's vessel in a manner equally acceptable to governor Stuyvesant, by finding that the affair happened partly through a mistake of his secretary, and partly through the default of Westerhouse in trading at New Haven without a license; and that the seizure was by no means ordered or made by way of asserting title in the Dutch to New Haven. It was then awarded that the cölony of New Haven should rest satisfied with this explanation, and not claim any remuneration for the same.

Having thus bestowed the shell of the nut, these worthy gentlemen proceeded to dispose of the boundary question, which was the kernel, in the following words:

"I. That upon Long Island, a line run from the westermost part of Oyster Bay, and so a straight and direct line to

---

* Records of the United Colonies.

the sea, shall be the bounds betwixt the English and Dutch there, the easterly to belong to the English, and the westermost to the Dutch.

"II. The bounds upon the main to begin at the west side of Greenwich bay, being about four miles from Stamford, and so to run a northerly line, twenty miles up into the country, and after, as it shall be agreed, by the two governments of the Dutch and New Haven, provided the said line come not within ten miles of Hudson's river. And it is agreed, that the Dutch shall not, at any time hereafter, build any house or habitation within six miles of the said line; the inhabitants of Greenwich to remain (till further consideration thereof be had,) under the government of the Dutch.

"III. The Dutch shall hold and enjoy all the lands in Hartford that they are actually possessed of, known and set out by certain marks and bounds, and all the remainder of the said land, on both sides of Connecticut river, to be and remain to the English there.

"And it is agreed, that the aforesaid bounds and limits, both upon the island and main, shall be observed and kept inviolable, both by the English of the united colonies, and all the Dutch nation, without any encroachment or molestation, until a full and final determination be agreed upon in Europe, by the mutual consent of the two states of England and Holland.

"And in testimony of our joint consent to the several foregoing conclusions, we have hereunto set our hands this 19th day of September, Anno Domini, 1650.

Simon Bradstreet,
Thomas Prince,
Thomas Willet,
George Baxter."

In the month of June, 1650, the General Court of Connecticut granted to Nathan Ely, Richard Olmsted, and other inhabitants of Hartford, liberty to remove to Norwalk and commence a plantation there, provided "they attend a due payment of their proportions in all the public charges, with a ready observation of the other wholesome orders of the country."*

As early as 1640, Roger Ludlow had purchased of the Indians the eastern part of the town. Captain Patrick had also procured the title to the central part of it. The better evidence appears to be, that a few bold planters had taken possession soon after these grants were made, and had continued to retain it until the arrival of the company under Mr. Ely and Mr. Olmsted. Of this fact, however, there is no record proof.

Although leave was granted to the petitioners in 1650, they did not remove to Norwalk until 1651. The western part of the town was deeded to them by Runkinheage, on the 15th of February. It is quite probable from the date of this instrument, that the whole company removed in January, or the early part of February, and it is not unlikely that the tradition is true, that a part of them spent the entire winter there. As appears by a contract made by Roger Ludlow, Esquire, with this company, under date of June 19, 1650, the principal families, aside from the two gentlemen already mentioned, bore the names of Webb, Richards, Marvin, Seymour, Spencer, Hales, Roscoe, Graves, Holloway, and Church. By this agreement the company became bound to mow the grass on the meadows, and stack the hay in the summer of 1650, and as early as the spring of 1651 to break up the ground in Norwalk, preparatory to planting during the next summer. This agreement gives additional authority to the legend that a portion of the inhabitants spent the winter of 1650 on the spot. The Indians would probably have burned up the haystacks before spring, had not some of the farmers been there to guard them. It is very probable, too, that the hay was most of it fed out to the cattle during that winter. This contract with Ludlow was of the nature of a quit-claim deed of that gentleman's original purchase for the consideration of fifteen pounds, the same price that he had paid for it ten years before, with the interest from the date of his purchase,

* J. H. Trumbull, i. 210.

and a reservation of a convenient lot, to be laid out for Mr. Ludlow's sons. The name of this charming place, with its rich lands, its excellent harbor, its unrivaled fishing-grounds, and its most attractive river, was derived from the tribe of Indians who inhabited it — the Norwalks, or Norwakes. No town in Connecticut has more salubrious sea-breezes or a climate more healthful and invigorating. The Rev. Thomas Hanford, the first clergyman, began to preach there in 1652, soon after which a church was formed and he was ordained as its regular pastor.*

Some time during the year 1651, the place called Mattabesett began to be inhabited by the English. This settlement had long been in contemplation, probably some time before October, 1646, as we find by our record of the doings of the General Court, that on the 30th of that month a gentleman, bearing the name of Phelps, was designated to "join a committee for the planting of Mattabesett." The committee made very slow progress in the settlement of the place, but it is quite probable that a few hardy men, who stood less in awe of Sowheag than the other Englishmen did, soon after this began to remove into the immediate neighborhood of that formidable sachem; and that little parties dropped down the river in boats from Hartford and Wethersfield, from time to time, until the fall of 1650, when the number of planters who had established themselves there, seemed to call upon the General Court for their order bearing date the 11th of September, that "Mattabesett should be a town," and should proceed to make choice of a constable.

Owing to the want of early records, some obscurity hangs over the birth and infancy of this town. It is certain that in the fall of 1652, it was represented in the General Court, and that in the fall of 1653, its name of Mattabesett was changed to that of Middletown, which it has since kept with honorable distinction. It is not surprising that a fierce tribe of Indians should for so long a time have kept the inhabitants

* The Rev. Edwin Hall, D. D., of Norwalk, is the author of a valuable History of that town, published in 1847. It comprises 320 pages.

of Hartford and Wethersfield, as well as those who ultimately came from Massachusetts, from occupying this interesting part of the valley of the Connecticut. Indeed, the external features of the scene, as presented to the eye of those who passed up and down the river, must have been less inviting to men who looked rather for rich lands than for beautiful scenery, especially when contrasted with the plains that opened up their perspective of grass-lands, lengthened interminably by the over-arching elms that lured the eager sight on either bank, a few miles further up the valley. The pioneers were not tourists in search of the diversified and the picturesque in nature, and therefore as they sailed down they must have turned a cold shoulder to the apparently wet lands, covered with wild bushes that lay above the site of the present city, and it could not have occurred to the most prophetic mind of all the voyagers, that the cliffs of red sandstone rising above the water that had been fretting their base for so many obscure ages, could contain quarries of such inexhaustible wealth, so soon to be developed by their descendants. Below the city, too, where the swift stream, with frowning evergreens fringing its dark borders, could be twice spanned by the flight of the Indian's arrow, as, speeding on its errand of mischief, it skimmed the surface of the compressed current, selecting its victims from the pinnace or the shallop, the sun-browned traffickers must have shuddered at the sight of the very shades that now tempt the leisure-loving on a summer's day to lean over the sides of the boat and look back with a kindly regret. But when once the keen English farmer had ventured to go ashore and ascend the hills that command the rich and variegated landscape, he could not long remain in ignorance of the abundance that had been poured from the full horn of plenty on every side.

The Indians at Mattabesett were very numerous. A good deal of trouble was expected to result from their being so near the English settlement, but they were much more docile than their white neighbors anticipated. The tribe had a reservation on the western bank of the Connecticut, in the place called Newfield. Here was an old burial-ground. A cemetery it has been very properly called, for these Indians indulged enough in the refinements of external mourning to erect monuments over the graves of their dead. On the eastern bank of the river was another reservation. At a place called Indian Hill was a graveyard with rude stones and inscriptions after the manner of the English. Here, in a sitting posture, with his blanket wrapped about his shoulders, the vessel containing the food prepared by his friends, that was to sustain him upon his long journey, resting upon his knee, the warrior's skeleton may still be found blackened with the mouldering earth. Ghastly the exhumed skull frowns upon the obtruding sunlight for a moment, and then slowly crumbles beneath the corroding influences of the upper air, to which it has been so rudely exposed!*

The settlement at Delaware was too remote to be anything other than a burden to the colony of New Haven. In the spring of 1651, fifty men from New Haven and Totoket hired a vessel and with their effects sailed for Delaware bay. They went provided with a commission from governor Eaton, and with two letters, one from him and the other from the governor of Massachusetts—both addressed to governor Stuyvesant, informing him that these adventurers were about to settle their own lands, and would not encroach upon the rights of the Dutch. When Governor Stuyvesant had read these letters, he was very much enraged. He seized the messengers who delivered them to him, and put them under guard. At the same time, under pretence of making some inquiries, he sent to the master of the vessel to come ashore, and as soon as he could get him within his reach, he caused him to be arrested. He also got possession of the commission of the company by some feint, and refused to deliver it up to the owners. He forced all who came on shore to sign a paper, in which they promised very solemnly that they would

* For a more full account of the early history of Middletown, and the adjacent towns, the reader is referred to the Rev. Dr. Field's statistics of Middlesex County, and to his centennial address at Middletown, in 1850.

not pursue their voyage, but with all speed of wind and wave would hasten back to New Haven. He dismissed them with direful threats of confiscation of goods, and imprisonment in Holland, if he ever caught them attempting to make a settlement at Delaware.

On the 14th of September, the commissioners met at New Haven. It was not very long before Jasper Crane and William Tuttle, smarting under the summary proceedings to which they had been subjected at New Amsterdam, presented their petition in behalf of themselves and others, calling fervently for redress. It was a very inflammable document, setting forth the character of Governor Stuyvesant in a light that he could hardly have contemplated with equanimity. It spoke of his subjects, too, in terms of great severity. It ended with a stirring appeal to the commissioners for protection and vindication.

The commissioners lost no time in writing to Governor Stuyvesant a letter, charging him with breaking his faith, so solemnly plighted at Hartford. They told him, among other salutary truths, that his interference with the planters who had sailed for Delaware, was insupportable, and that the New England colonies had as good a right to Manhattan as the Dutch had to these Delaware lands.

At this same session, it was resolved that if the petitioners should begin a plantation at Delaware, numbering one hundred and fifty good men, well armed, within twelve months, they would uphold them in the enterprise, and defend them from all opposition, whether from the Dutch or Swedes.

While at New Haven the commissioners were also waited upon by a deputation that must have been the fruitful theme of conversation at New Haven for many days,—two French gentlemen, M. Godfroy and Gabriel Druillets, agents of M. D'Aillebout, governor of Canada. These gentlemen presented three commissions, one from their governor, another from the council of New France, and a third addressed to M. Druillets himself, giving him authority to teach to the Indians the doctrines of Christianity. They appeared in behalf of the French in Canada, and in hehalf of the christianized Indians of Acadie, whom they represented to be suffering, on account of their religion, the hardships and cruelties of a bloody persecution, waged against them by the Mohawks. A holy war, they denominated it, that was designed, in violation of the most solemn treaties, to quench in blood the last spark of the Christian faith upon the western continent. M. Druillets was an orator of a very graceful and persuasive address. He used all the arguments at his command to induce the colonies to declare war against the Six Nations. If they were opposed to involving themselves in a war with the Indians, he begged that they would allow volunteers to go from any of the New England colonies, with a "free passage by land or water to the Mohawk country," and that the converted Indians might be taken under the protection of New England. He held out the prospect of a free trade to be established upon a permanant basis between the French and English colonies, as a fair requital for the favors, if they should be granted.

With becoming politeness the commissioners, for many good reasons, declined to add to all the evils then impending over them, the burden of a new war.

On the 30th of June, 1652, the General Court of Connecticut met to adopt measures for the defense of the colony against the Dutch. A war had already broken out between England and Holland. It was ordered, that the cannon at Saybrook should be mounted upon carriages, and that all the families in the neighborhood should be brought within the inclosure of the fort. The Indians in the vicinity of all the plantations were required to evince signs of their friendship to the English, by delivering up their arms to the governor and magistrates.

Some time in March it became rumored abroad that Governor Stuyvesant had concerted a plan with Ninigret to exterminate the English in all the colonies, and that the sachem of the Nihanticks had been spending the winter with his ally, at Manhadoes, and had been sent home in a Dutch sloop in very great state, and with a large supply of guns and ammunition. The sole evidence to support this charge, was the testimony of Indians, who came to Hartford and other towns, and made oath to the existence of the plot. Nine sachems sent in their affidavits to Stamford, to the same effect.* The story, without foundation as it was, and originating in the malice and cunning of some one who had a motive for giving it currency, could not fail to alarm the English. A meeting of the Congress was called on the 19th of April, and the commissioners proceeded to hear the allegations. They were presented in such an adroit manner, and backed up by such an army of Indian witnesses, that six of the commissioners were satisfied of the existence of the conspiracy. Those who represented Massachusetts were so remote from the supposed scene of the tragedy, and were so conscious of the strength of their colony, that they could look at the evidence more calmly, and were convinced that the charges against the Dutch and Indians were without foundation. It was resolved to send letters to the Dutch governor before war was declared.

When Governor Stuyvesant heard of this attack upon his character, he was highly incensed. His conduct on the occasion was, however, dignified and becoming. He hastened to write letters to the Congress, in which he denied that he was guilty of the outrageous wickedness attributed to him. His sensibilities were so shocked at the reflection that his character could be thus misrepresented, that he generously offered to send a messenger, or go in person to Boston, if it was desired, to establish his innocence; or if the Congress would send a committee to Manhadoes, he would undertake to give the colonies the most satisfactory proofs of his integrity and honor. At the same time he expressed his astonishment that the English could give credit to such accusations, coming from such corrupt sources.

The suggestion of Stuyvesant was adopted, and a committee was sent with plenary power to investigate the matter.

* Trumbull, i. 203.

This committee was made up of Francis Newman of New Haven, John Leverett, afterwards governor of Massachusetts, and William Davis.* They repaired to Manhattan, and presented themselves for the discharge of their duties. Owing, perhaps, to the unpleasant tone of the letters sent to Manhattan in reply to the exculpatory communications of Stuyvesant, as well as owing to the offensive nature of their mission, these gentlemen were not received with much cordiality. The governor refused to answer any questions except such as should be approved by men of his own appointing, and chose two who had especially incurred the dislike of the English at Hartford. One of these men had been put under bonds while there, for his misdemeanors. At this, the agents of the Congress were offended, and remonstrated against the insult offered to the colonies and the king. Both parties were evidently in no very dispassionate mood. The governor remained inexorable as to the mode of transacting the business, and the agents, after demanding satisfaction for all past injuries and indemnity against all future wrongs, took a very haughty leave of a host who appears to have been glad to be rid of them.

On their way home, the English agents spent some time in gathering additional proof of the guilt of the Dutch governor; and when they arrived, they were in a favorable mood to make an alarming report of the treatment that they had received at his hands. Letters soon after arrived in Hartford and New Haven, giving the additional intelligence that Stuyvesant had also hired the Mohawks to join in this execrable measure. Again Stuyvesant remonstrated and at the same time, in a fit of exasperation, asserted his old claims of jurisdiction to New Haven and Connecticut.

The commissioners, with the exception of Bradstreet, were now all in favor of a declaration of war. That gentleman represented the wishes of the General Court of Massachusetts. His opposition led to a harsh debate, and finally to a committee of conference between the Congress and the Gen-

* Hutchinson, i. 166; Trumbull, i. 203.

eral Court, which brought about a reference of the whole matter to the elders. That learned body very judiciously advised the colonies to "forbear the use of the sword," but to be in readiness for defense.* This decision did not satisfy the Congress. Again they resolved on war. Massachusetts still remained firm in her opposition.

On the 30th of May, the Rev. Mr. Norris, of Salem, sent a memorial to the Congress, calling loudly for the war.† It is a paper of great ability and eloquence. After presenting a vivid picture of the condition of the Dutch and English nations, then in a state of war at home, and warning the Congress against the loss of respect among the Indians, by pursuing such a vacillating policy, he alludes to the situation of these colonies now exposed to danger, who have "sent their moan" to the Congress, and called for their assistance, which, if they should refuse, the "curse of the angel of the Lord against Moses would come upon them."

Still the General Court of Massachusetts continued inexorable and passed a resolve that no determination of the Congress could induce the colony to unite with the others in an offensive war with the Dutch, which should appear to the General Court to be unjust. This resolution led to a written controversy between Massachusetts and the other colonies, which might have ended in the dissolution of the union, but for the interference of Cromwell, who took the part of the weaker colonies without any reference to the supposed conspiracy, as it best suited his stern policy to do. Massachusetts was thus compelled to yield. The ships of the Protector were already on their passage to America, to reduce the pride of the governor of New Netherlands.

I have already stated it to be my belief that the story of the plot against the English was a sheer fabrication. Who was its author, I am of course unable to say. The fact that the Mohawks were made parties to it, and that it resulted in a declaration of war against Ninigret, enables me to draw an inference that certainly exonerates the English from any

---

* Hutchinson, i. 167; Trumbull, i. 207. † Records of the United Colonies.

blame, unless it be in the exercise of too large a measure of credulity in a matter that appeared to them to threaten their very existence. As regards the conduct of Massachusetts in ignoring the resolves of a confederacy which she was solemnly pledged to support, I will only quote the language of her own historian, who dismisses this topic with the remark that, "where states in alliance are greatly disproportioned in strength and importance, power often prevails over right."* This is a very happy blending of the elements of praise and blame in a simple sentence, and expresses all that need be said upon a subject that certainly gave occasion for much just censure on both sides.

---

* Hutchinson, i. 168.

CHAPTER IX.

THE DEPARTURE OF LUDLOW. DEATH OF HAYNES, WOLCOTT AND EATON.

The alarm excited by the charges against the Dutch and Indians resulted in some unhappy contentions. Stamford and Fairfield were in a state of excitement bordering on phrensy. They complained that the war was not prosecuted by the Congress, and that Connecticut and New Haven neglected to lend a helping hand to them at a time when their enemies were pressing upon them. These little settlements, so near the Dutch jurisdiction, with the remembrance still alive of bloody Indian depredations so recently brought to their very doors, had much reason to be anxious when they reflected upon their situation, in a remote and solitary region, where they might be murdered, and their houses burned to ashes, long before the news could be carried to New Haven. Having demanded troops to protect her, and not receiving them from the government of New Haven, Stamford finally lost all patience and threatened to free herself from the expensive taxes of a colony that either could not or would not defend her, and place herself under the immediate protection of England. It was not until the deputy governor, in company with Mr. Newman, paid them a visit, and read to them an order of the committee of Parliament, calling upon all the towns to obey their respective colonial governments, that they were induced to yield.*

The citizens of Fairfield held a town meeting, and with one consent determined to raise troops independently of Connecticut, and carry on the war themselves. They appointed Roger Ludlow commander-in-chief.† As the year 1654 may, for the purposes of historical narrative, be considered as the year of his civil death, I cannot omit this occasion

* Trumbull, i. 214. † Trumbull; Brodhead, i. 565; Allen, 548.

of making a brief allusion to the character and to the personal history of this remarkable man, as far as I am able to gather it from the scattered shreds that are left of his impulsive career. He was a lawyer of good family, and resided in Dorchester, in the county of Dorsetshire, in the southern part of England. On the 10th of February, 1630, he was chosen an assistant by the General Court of Massachusetts. In May, following, he sailed from Plymouth for America, in the Mary and John, and entered upon the discharge of his official duties at the first Assistant Court, held at Charlestown in August of the same year. He continued to occupy this place for four years. In 1634 he was chosen deputy governor of the province, and hoped to have been raised to the rank of governor, but was disappointed by the jealousy of the deputies, who appear to have taken offense at some impolitic remarks made by him, probably in relation to their growing strength and to the frequency of elections. To show him how well they could vindicate themselves, and perhaps to reciprocate his good advice by giving him a practical lesson upon exercising the Christain virtue of humility, they elected John Haynes governor. Ludlow protested against this appointment in terms of severity. He alleged that the election was void for the reason that the deputies had agreed upon their candidate before they left their respective towns. By way of requital for making such an accusation, which was in all probability true, and as a further proof of the popular power, he was left out of the magistracy for that year. He had not learned the art, so common in our age, of telling the people precisely what he did not believe to be true.

Discouraged at this decided expression of the popular displeasure, he removed to Connecticut during the summer or fall of the year 1635, and established himself at Windsor. Here he continued under the gentle ministrations of Mr. Wareham, and soon became one of the most conspicuous men in the colony. In the summer of 1637, he was sent by the General Court as one of the advisers of the Connecticut forces in the second stage of the Pequot war.* He was probably the first lawyer who ever came into the colony, and one of the most gifted who have ever lived in it.

I have already incidentally alluded to the part that he took in framing the constitution of 1639. I cannot help regarding it as mainly his work. The phraseology is his: it breathes his spirit. It must have been substantially the offspring of some one mind, that pierced like an eagle through the clouds that shrouded the seventeenth century, and sought the pure region of right reason, shining none the less brightly, that, like the rolling spheres of light, it is expressed in distinct forms. I have compared this paper with those written by Milton, expressive of his views of government and of liberty. In the political writings of the great poet I can see the marks of unbounded genius, vast imagination and prophetic hopes, lighting up the dim horizon with the golden promises of dawn. But I find there no well-digested system of republicanism. He deals alone with the absolute. His republic would befit only a nation of Miltons. His laws are fit only to govern those who are capable of being a law unto themselves. But Ludlow views the concrete and the abstract both at once. He is a man of systems—such systems as can alone be placed in the hands of frail men to protect them against their worst enemies—their own lawless passions.

On the 11th of April, 1639, he was chosen deputy governor of the commonwealth, and was the first who ever held that office in Connecticut.† John Haynes, whose elevation to the place of governor in Massachusetts, in 1635, was the cause of Ludlow's removing from that province, was elected governor of Connecticut at the same time that Ludlow was made deputy governor. This unlucky coincidence must have been galling to the pride of an ambitious man, and whether it induced him, when considered in connection with his former defeat, to regard Haynes as his evil genius, or whether he intended to found a new colony, rather than a

* J. H. Trumbull, i. 10. † J. H. Trumbull, i. 27.

town, in a place that seemed remote enough for such a purpose, I cannot positively aver; yet had he been placed at the head of the magistracy, I have no doubt that he would have remained longer at Windsor. Still it would have been only a brief sojourn. This enthusiastic, restless man could not have been tempted to tarry long in any one place even could he have been rewarded with a diadem. It was not alone the stirring of that emulation, that, like the love of fame, belongs to all noble minds—not alone the "trophies of Miltiades," that drove sleep from his pillow; but rather the bright visions that throbbed in the pulses of the adventurer, and called him, not for the love of earthly goods, but to give zest to the faculties and room for the free tides of a restless nature to ebb and flow without restraint—that led him to venture forth again into the wilderness. He had already visited Unquowa, and his eye had made such a pleasant acquaintance with its fields and streams, that he could not long hesitate whither to betake himself. After his removal to Fairfield, he still continued to perform important services for Connecticut, and in 1646 he was appointed by the General Court to reduce her crude and ill-defined laws to a system.* This he did as well as it could be done when we consider the scanty materials that were furnished him for such a structure. The code was published at Cambridge in 1673.† He was several times a commissioner for the colony in the New England Congress. His connection with the Congress appears to have been the remote cause of his sudden though voluntary exile. Why the conduct of the citizens of Fairfield, in arming either to defend themselves or to go in pursuit of a dreaded enemy, who was every day expected to invade their settlement, should have been looked upon by Connecticut as an act worthy of animadversion, when the General Court itself admitted the existence of the dangerous emergency that induced them to take the step, I am unable to say. It is certain that no sedition was in their hearts.

* J. H. Trumbull, i. 138, 154. † Allen's Biog. Dic., 548.

Angry they doubtless were, and Ludlow not the least, for he had an "infirmity of temper" that often visited him—angry and grieved that they had been left by the government in such a defenseless condition; but they only took up arms in obedience to the instinct of self-preservation, that is, according to the common law of England, a divine voice, paramount in its authority to all earthly jurisdictions. Yet their conduct was treated as reprehensible and seditious, and Robert Bassett and John Chapman were charged with "fomenting insurrections," and were treated as the leaders of the project. Ludlow must have known that these accusations were aimed at him, as he was the principal man of the town. He felt that he had, without any moral guilt, incurred the displeasure of the colony, and that unless he should make some humiliating concessions, his behavior would not be likely to escape public censure. It was quite evident that his popularity had already reached its meridian. Proud and sensitive to a high degree, he brooded over the change that had taken place in his prospects, as well for promotion as for usefulness, and at last came to the conclusion, not without many keen regrets, to leave the colony where he had held so conspicuous a place for nineteen eventful years.

On the 26th of April, 1654, he embarked at New Haven, with his family and effects, for Virginia, where he passed in obscurity the remainder of his days.*

I have been thus minute in treating of him, because I felt called upon to do justice to the memory of a great man, whose faults were better understood than his virtues by his contemporaries, and who is almost a mythological character, except as his name still keeps the brief paragraph allotted to it in the records that load the shelves of the antiquary. He seems indeed himself to have courted oblivion, for he carried away with him the entire records of the town that he had planted, and of which he was the register at the time of his romantic flight, as if to blot out every trace of his irregular

* I am indebted for some of the facts set forth in this sketch, to the Hon. James Savage, LL. D., President of the Massachusetts Historical Society.

footprints from the soil of Connecticut. But his fame, like that of all other men of genius, who have labored in the cause of the people, rests upon no such frail foundation; for genius builds its own imperishable temple, whose worshipers are the millions of "freemen whom the truth makes free."*

Just before the departure of Ludlow from the colony, died his Excellency, John Haynes, while in the midst of his official term. He was as unlike Ludlow as one man could well be dissimilar to another. He was a native of the county of Essex, in England, and was of good lineage. He was the owner of Copford Hall, an elegant seat that afforded an annual income of one thousand pounds sterling. He was an ardent admirer of Hooker, and, regardless of all social and pecuniary considerations, accompanied him to America. As I have already stated, he was made governor of Massachusetts in 1635. The next year he was succeeded by Sir Henry Vane, and in the month of June, went with that large party who traversed the glades and thickets of the primitive forest in quest of the valley of the Connecticut. He had the honor of being the first governor of the little commonwealth, an office that he held every alternate year until his death. He was a gentleman of stately deportment, graceful manners and great stability of character.† With less intellectual acumen than Ludlow, and without any of his genius, he was yet greatly superior to that wandering and whimsical man in all the attributes that commanded the popular suffrages. Haynes was one of the best representatives of the republicanism of that day, which Coleridge has so justly called a "religious and moral aristocracy." He was one of the best examples of the Puritan class or party. Ludlow on the other

* The family name of Ludlow is an ancient one in England, and from it probably the famous castle of Ludlow received its name. Ludlow is celebrated as the place where Butler wrote a portion of Hudibras, and there were deposited some of the remains of Sir Henry Sidney.

† See Trumbull, i. 216, &c.; Mather's Magnalia, ii. 17; Hutchinson, i. 39, 43, 55; Holmes, i. 303.

hand, belonged to no party, but was himself the prototype of a different order of republicanism that has at last diffused itself like the air over the surface of the continent.

The question of the Dutch and Indian war still agitated the colonies. About the time of Ludlow's removal, one Manning, master of a small armed vessel, was arrested by the authorities of New Haven colony, for carrying on a contraband trade with the Dutch at Manhattan. While Manning's trial was going on at New Haven, his men took possession of his ship, and in defiance of the government sailed out of Milford harbor, where she had been riding at anchor. The gallant people of Milford armed and manned a vessel, and gave the fugitive such a chase that they came in sight of her before she reached Manhattan, and pressed so hard upon her that her crew betook themselves to their boat, and left her adrift to fall an easy prey into the hands of her pursurers, who brought her back into the harbor, where she was condemned with her cargo as a lawful prize.

A few days after, Major Sedgwick and Captain Leverett arrived in Boston with a fleet, sent over by the Lord Protector at the request of Connecticut and New Haven, to carry on the war with the Dutch.* On the 8th of June, governor Eaton received a letter from Cromwell, informing him that he had sent the fleet for the assistance of the colonies. Major Sedgwick and Captain Leverett also sent letters, asking that each of the governments would send commissioners to consult with them as to the objects of the expedition. Connecticut and New Haven both sent commissioners, and such was the zeal of Connecticut that she authorized Mason and Cullick, whom she chose to represent her in this important embassy, to engage in her behalf two hundred soldiers, and, rather than that the enterprise should fail, even five hundred if necessary.†

In Massachusetts the old opposition to the war remained unshaken. On the 8th of June, the General Court convened in a state of considerable excitement. They would vote to

* Brodhead, i. 582, 583. † J. H. Trumbull, i. 260.

raise neither men nor money for the war. Still they resolved that Sedgwick and Leverett might enrol five hundred volunteers in Massachusetts if they could.* The commissioners decided that an army of about eight hundred men would be sufficient to reduce the Dutch to subjection.† The ships were to furnish two hundred, three hundred volunteers were to be raised, if they could be, in Massachusetts; Connecticut was to send two hundred, and New Haven one hundred and thirty-three. All this bustle and preparation was nipped in its first beginnings by the news—not very grateful to Connecticut and New Haven—that England and Holland were again at peace.

Major Sedgwick employed this fleet and the Massachusetts volunteers to drive the French from Penobscot, St. John's, and the adjacent coasts. It is needless to say that he would not have dared to do it had he not acted under secret instructions from Cromwell.‡

---

* Hazard, i. 587, 589; Hutchinson, i. 169. † Records of the United Colonies.

‡ The following letter from the renowned geologist, Professor Adam Sedgwick, of Cambridge University, England, addressed to General Charles F. Sedgwick, of Sharon, Connecticut, contains much valuable information relative to the family of Major General Robert Sedgwick, who is the ancestor of all the Sedgwicks in New England. This letter cannot fail to interest the public. It is intrinsically a gem, aside from the great name of its author.

"CAMBRIDGE, FEB. 26, 1837.

"SIR;

"After an absence from the University of several months I returned to my chambers yesterday, and found your letter on my study table. I first supposed that it might have been there some time, but on looking at the date, I was greatly surprised that it had reached me in a little more than three weeks after it had been committed to the post on the other side of the Atlantic. Of your patriarch, Robert Sedgwick, I have often heard, as the active part he took during the protectorate, made him, in some measure, an historical character; and about the same time there were one or two Puritan divines of considerable note and of the same name; but whether or no they were relations of his, I am not able to inform you. The clan was settled from very early times, among the mountains which form the borders of Lancashire, Yorkshire, and Westmoreland, and I believe every family in this island of the name of Sedgwick can trace its descent from ancestors who were settled among those mountains. The name among the country people in the valleys in the north of England, is pronounced *Sigswick*, and the oldest spelling of it that I can find is *Siggeswick;* at least it is so written

Owing to the steady opposition of Massachusetts, the war that had been previously declared against Ninigret had not been pursued; and that Indian had become so much em-

in many of our old parish records that go back to the reign of Henry VIII. It is good German, and means the *village of victory*, probably designating some place of successful broil, where our rude Saxon or Danish ancestors first settled in the country and drove the old Celtic tribes out of it, or into the remoter recesses of the Cambrian mountains, where we meet with many Celtic names at this day. But in the valleys where the Sedgwicks are chiefly found, the names are almost exclusively Saxon or Danish. Ours, therefore, in very early days was a true border clan. The name of Sedgwick was, I believe, a corruption given like many others through a wish to explain the meaning of a name, (Siggeswick,) the real import of which was quite forgotten. The word *Sedge* is not known in the northern dialects of our island, and the plant itself does not exist among our valleys, but a branch of our clan settled in the low, marshy regions of Lincolnshire, and seems to have first adopted the more modern spelling, and at the same time began to use a bundle of sedge (with the leaves drooping like the ears of a corn sheaf,) as the family crest. This branch was never numerous, and is, I believe, now almost extinct. Indeed the Sedgwicks never seem, (at least in England,) to flourish away from their native mountains. If you remove them to the low country, they droop and die away in a few generations. A still older crest, and one which suits the history of the race, is an eagle with spread wings. Within my memory, eagles existed among the higher mountains, visible from my native valley. The arms most commonly borne by the Sedgwicks, are composed of a red Greek cross, with five bells attached to the bars. I am too ignorant of heraldic terms to describe the shield correctly—I believe, however, that this is the shield of the historical branch, and that there is another shield belonging to the *Siggeswicks* of the mountains, with a different quartering, but I have it not before me and do not remember it sufficiently well to give any account of it. All the border clans, and ours among the rest, suffered greatly during the wars of York and Lancaster. After the Reformation they seem generally to have leaned to the Puritanical side, and many of them, your ancestor among the rest, served in Cromwell's army. From the Reformation to the latter half of the last century, our border country enjoyed great prosperity. The valleys were subdivided into small properties; each head of a family lived on his own estate, and such a thing as a rented farm hardly existed in the whole country, which was filled with a race of happy, independent yeomanry. This was the exact condition of your clansmen in this part of England. They were kept in a kind of humble affluence, by the manufactory of their wool, which was produced in great abundance by the vast flocks of sheep which were fed on the neighboring mountains. I myself, remember two or three old men of the last century, who in their younger days had been in the yearly habit of riding up to London to negotiate the sale of stockings, knit by the hands of the lasses of our own smiling valleys. The changes of manners, and the progress of machinery, destroyed, root and branch, this source of rural wealth; and a dismal change has now taken place in the social and moral aspect of the land of your fathers.

boldened by the pacific demeanor of the English towards him, that he continued to follow up the interdicted hostilities against the Long Island Indians, with renewed vigor. These Indians were allies of Connecticut, and he well knew that the faith of the colony was pledged to defend them.

Connecticut now sent Major Mason with a small number of men, and with a supply of ammunition, as a present to the sachem of Montauket, which he was not to use to injure Ninigret, but simply to defend himself.* New Haven, also, sent Lieutenant Seely with men to join Mason at Saybrook, and aid him in encouraging and defending the Montauket Indians.†

In September, the Congress met at Hartford and soon sent messengers to Ninigret, commanding him forthwith to appear before them. Ninigret sent back a very argumentative and elaborate answer, the purport of which was, "that he would neither go to Hartford nor send an ambassador there to treat with the Congress, and that he owed no tribute on account of the Pequots."‡ The commissioners ordered forty horsemen and two hundred and fifty foot soldiers,§ to be raised and sent into his country to bring him to a better frame of mind. The Congress nominated three gentlemen, Major Gibbons, Major Denison, and Ninigret's old acquaintance,

---

It is now a very poor country, a great portion of the old yeomanry, (provincially called *statesmen*,) has been swept away. Most of the family estates (some of which had descended from father to son for two or three hundred years,) have been sold to strangers. The evil has, I hope, reached its crisis, and the country may improve, but it seems morally impossible that it should ever again assume the happy Arcadian character which it had before the changes that undermined its whole social system.

I have now told you all I can compress into one sheet, of the land of your fathers' fathers, of the ancestors of that pilgrim from whom my transatlantic cousins are descended. A few families have survived the shock; mine among the rest. And I have a brother in the valley of Dent, who now enjoys a property which our family has had ever since the Reformation. I fear you will think this information very trifling—such as it is, it is very much at your service. Believe me, Sir, your very faithful servant, A. SEDGWICK."

* J. H. Trumbull, i. 295.

† New Haven Colonial Records.

‡ See Holmes' Annals, i. 301.

§ Records United Colonies; Hutchinson i. 172; Trumbull, i. 223.

Captain Humphrey Atherton, leaving it to the discretion of Massachusetts to select any one of them to take the chief command. All these nominees were gallant and skillful officers, who would soon have brought the refractory chief to terms. But for reasons best known to the General Court of Massachusetts, they were all rejected, and Major Willard was appointed. Willard had orders from the Congress to move forward by the 13th of October, march directly to Ninigret's quarters, and demand of him the Pequots who had been entrusted to his care, and the unpaid tribute. In case of a refusal, he was to take both Pequots and tribute by violent means. He was farther instructed to demand of the Nihantick sachem to desist from waging the war with the Montauket Indians. Should Ninigret fail to comply with this order, force was to be employed to bring him to subjection. Willard either acted under secret instructions from Massachusetts, or he was not possessed of the courage becoming the leader of such an enterprise. On arriving at the principal village of the Nihanticks, he found it deserted. The corn and other valuables had been left in the care of a few old men, squaws and children, and Ninigret had taken refuge in a swamp about fifteen miles distant from the village. Without going in search of the fugitive chief, or so much as making known to him the object of this apparently friendly visit, the heroic Willard brought back his army without any awkward accident of bloodshed or harsh words to qualify the pleasure that he must have felt in the wearing of laurels so innocently won. About one hundred Pequots, who had suffered every thing but death from the cruelties practiced upon them by Ninigret, took advantage of his absence and followed the army to Connecticut, where they put themselves under the protection of the English.*

The Congress did not receive Major Willard with much cordiality. It was in vain that he attempted to excuse his inertness by professing not to understand his instructions. The disappointed commissioners coldly replied—"while the

* Holmes, i. 301, 302; Hutchinson, i. 172.

army was in the Narragansett country, Ninigret had his mouth in the dust." If Willard acted under private instructions from Massachusetts, as governor Hutchinson would seem to intimate, that colony departed for once from her usual frank and open manner, to do what was wholly unworthy of her.

The attempt on the part of Connecticut to defend the Long Island Indians, was honorable and necessary to the preservation of her faith. Besides, it was both impolitic and unjust, irrespective of the existing treaty, to allow Ninigret, upon false pretexts, to wage a war with those defenseless Indians. The fact that he had drawn over to his interests the Wampanoags, was of itself, as Massachusetts learned to her cost at a later day, no inconsiderable cause for alarm. But it is quite time that this old quarrel was forgotten, and I feel no disposition to revive any discussion in relation to it.

The refugee Pequots begged so earnestly to be taken under the protection of the English, that their prayer was at last granted, and they had lands assigned them on the Pawcatuck and Mistick rivers. They were allowed the privilege of hunting on that tract of wild forest land lying west of the Mistick, and were placed under the direction of an Indian governor, who ruled them according to a code specially provided for them.

Ninigret was now more haughty than ever, and kept the whole eastern portion of Long Island in commotion by his boisterous manner of prosecuting the war against the Montaukets. The inhabitants of East Hampton and SouthHampton especially complained to the Congress of his reckless behavior towards them. The Rev. Mr. James, minister of the former place, and Captain Tapping of the latter, both wrote urgent letters, calling for interference. In obedience to this call, an armed vessel, under the command of Captain John Youngs, was stationed in the road between Neanticut and Long Island to watch the movements of Ninigret.* Youngs was authorized to draft men from Saybrook and New Lon-

* Trumbull, i. 225.

don, if he needed them. Should Ninigret attempt to cross the Sound, Youngs was ordered to stave in his canoes, and to kill him, and as many of his warriors as he could. The most thorough measures were taken at the same time to protect both the Indians and the English upon Long Island.

This sanguinary order resulted in no harm to Ninigret, except that he was obliged to stay at home, and abide his time for falling upon his enemies. This he did not soon find an opportunity to do, as Connecticut and New Haven at their own expense continued to keep the armed vessel for still another year cruising along his coast. It was a very unpleasant constraint upon his movements and power to do mischief, but he was obliged to submit with as good grace as he could.

It is a very trite observation, and has been found true in human experience, with nations as with individuals, that calamities journey not alone; but by some subtle law of affinity, are grouped together, and sustain each to the other a mournful yet instructive relationship. So was it with Connecticut during this interesting period of her history.

Before the grief occasioned by the departure of Ludlow and the death of Haynes was assuaged, she was called to mourn the loss of still another eminent citizen. In the 78th year of his age, but with a judgment unclouded, and his usefulness unimpaired, the venerable Henry Wolcott, one of the principal magistrates and advisers of the colony, quickly followed his friend and comrade to the grave. I cannot help making a brief mention of him, and yet were I to speak at any considerable length of all the bright examples of patriotism and exalted worth that have borne the name of Wolcott in Connecticut, I should find this work extending itself beyond the limits that I had marked out for it.

Henry Wolcott, Esquire, the ancestor of all the Wolcotts of this state, was of a very ancient family, and the owner of a large estate in Somersetshire.* He was born in Tolland on the 6th of December 1578, and was the son and heir of John Wolcott of Golden Manor. The manor-house is still standing, and is of very great antiquity and extent. It was originally a splendid mansion, designed, as well for the purposes of defense against the excesses of a lawless age, as for a permanent family residence. It is still richly ornamented with carved-work, and if left to itself unassailed by the hand of violence, it will stand for ages. The familiar motto of the family arms, borrowed from the Roman poet, is still to be seen upon the walls of the manor-house, its bold words informing us that the family who have adopted it as their text of life were "accustomed to swear in the words of

---

* Through the researches of Mr. Somerby, of Boston, in the herald's office, among the subsidy rolls, wills, and parish records of England, the genealogy of Henry Wolcott, Esquire, (the emigrant,) has been traced, through fifteen generations, back to Sir John Wolcott, knight, as follows:

1. Jeran Wolcott, (son of Sir John,) of Wolcott, who married Anna, daughter of John Mynde, of Shropshire.
2. Roger Wolcott, of Wolcott, who married Edith, daughter of Sir Wm. Donnes, knight.
3. Sir Philip Wolcott, of Wolcott, knight, who married Julian, daughter of John Herle.
4. John Wolcott, of Wolcott, who married Alice, daughter of David Lloyd, Esq.
5. Sir John Wolcott, of Wolcott, knight, A.D. 1382.
6. Thomas Wolcott.
7. John Wolcott.
8. John Wolcott, of Wolcott, who married Matilda, daughter of Sir Richard Cornwall, of Bereford, knight.
9. Roger Wolcott, of Wolcott, Esq., who married Margaret, daughter of David Lloyd, Esq.
10. William Wolcott, settled in Tolland, Somersetshire.
11. William Wolcott, who married Elizabeth. His will is dated A.D., 1500.
12. Thomas Wolcott, who was living in Tolland in 1552.
13. Thomas Wolcott, who married Alice. Will dated Nov. 4, 1572.
14. John Wolcott, of Golden Manor, in Tolland. Will proved, Nov. 10, 1623.
15. Henry Wolcott, (the emigrant,) who conveyed the manor house to his son Henry.

no master."* It is alike in keeping with the independent spirit of an English gentleman of the middle ages, and with that of a Puritan of the 17th century who spurned the dictation of ecclesiastical dominion.

In his early life Henry Wolcott lived after the manner of the landed gentry, at an era when the term "country squire" was synonymous with whatever was bold, athletic, and hardy in the steeple-chasing, hospitable days of "merry England." But as years stole on, and the principles of the Reformation, making little progress at first, began to invade not only the wrestling-ring of the yeoman, and the counting-room of the merchant, but the hall of the country gentleman, Wolcott, among others, was led to direct his thoughts to more serious topics, than the pastimes that had engrossed his earlier manhood. While meditations respecting a future state of being occupied his mind, a religious teacher, Mr. Edward Elton, became his guide, and led him to that clear understanding of the doctrines of Christianity, and those firm convictions of its truth that remained with him to the day of his death. Of an ardent temperament and lively sensibilities, and seeing much that needed to be reformed in the severities practiced upon so many of the best subjects of the realm, he soon became identified with the Puritan party, sold a large estate in lands, including the manor-house, for which he received about eight thousand pounds sterling, probably much less than its value, and made preparations to spend the remainder of his days in America. In 1628 he visited New England to examine the country, and returned.

* "Nullius addictus jurare in verba magistri." In relation to the Wolcott coat of arms, the following anecdote may not be without interest to such as are curious in matters of heraldry. John Wolcott, of Wolcott, who lived in the reign of Henry the Fifth, and who married Matilda, daughter of Sir Richard Cornwall, of Bereford, knight, assumed for his arms, the three chess rooks, instead of the crow, with the "fleurs de lis," borne by his ancestors. It is recorded of him in the old family pedigree, that "playinge at the chesse with Henry the Fifth, kinge of England, he gave hym (the king) the checke matte with the rourke; whereupon the kinge changed his coate of arms, which was the crowe and fleur de leues, and gave him the rourke for a remembrance."

His sympathetic nature could not fail to attach itself inseparably to the self-accusing though charitable and delicate Wareham, and he sailed with him for the new world in the same ship, and arrived in Massachusetts in May, 1630. Roger Ludlow was of the same party. Wolcott remained in Dorchester until 1636, when he removed to Windsor upon the Connecticut river. He was, as most of our best early inhabitants were, a planter, and was the principal one in Windsor. He was a member of the General Court of Connecticut in 1639.

In 1643 he was chosen into the magistracy, and continued to be one of its most safe and immovable pillars till his death in 1655.* His monument of imperishable sandstone, built by the same hands that fashioned the one that stands over the Fenwick tomb at Saybrook, has been always a shrine to tempt towards it the feet of his numerous descendants, who have piously guarded it, and lovingly adorned it, for two hundred years. Time has spared, and the gray moss has not obliterated, the quaint and simple epitaph, whose plain lettering tells us that it is the resting place of "Henry Wolcott, some time a magistrate of this jurisdiction."

The colony of New Haven was regarded by Cromwell with singular favor. The Protector had brought Jamaica within the power of the British government, and entertained the hope that he should be able to people it with the inhabitants of New England, who, he thought, might be induced to leave a sterile region in exchange for the prodigal fruits and genial atmosphere of a more tropical clime. With this view, in 1656, he wrote letters to his friends in New Haven, wherein he adroitly appealed to their sense of religious duty, telling them, in the phraseology of the day, that they had "as clear a call" to remove to that island, as they formerly had for leaving their native land for New England. These letters were laid before the Court by Governor Eaton, and their contents made the subject of earnest debates. After a careful discussion, the court resolved that, much as they re-

* Trumbull, i. 226, 227.

garded the love that his highness bore them, "yet for divers reasons they could not conclude that God called them at present to remove thither."*

This year, from representations previously made at New Haven, that the people of Greenwich lived in a disorderly and riotous way, sold intoxicating liquors to the Indians, received and harbored servants who had fled from their masters, and joined persons unlawfully in marriage, the General Court of that colony resolved to assert their jurisdiction over the town and bring its citizens to a more orderly manner of demeaning themselves. In May, the General Court sent a letter, calling upon those living at Greenwich to submit to its authority. They returned an answer couched in very spirited language, declaring that New Haven had no right to set up such a claim, and that they never would submit to it unless compelled to do so by parliament. But when the spirit of such men as Eaton and Davenport pervades a legislative body, it is not easily driven from any position that has been deliberately taken. The General Court passed a resolve, that unless the recusants should appear in open court, and make a formal submission by the 25th of June, Richard Crabbe and some others who were most stubborn in their opposition, should be arrested and punished according to law. This had the effect intended; Crabbe and others, who were not ready for martyrdom, yielded with as good grace as they could.†

The Indians in Connecticut, who had been kept in check for some time, now found it impossible any longer to restrain their bad passions. With the exception of an occasional outbreak of malice, and the constant flow of falsehood and subtlety that could hardly be expected to rest even during the hours of sleep, Uncas had been very exemplary in his conduct for a long time. But as one extreme is said to lead to another, he suddenly made amends for his good behavior by an outrageous and unprovoked attack upon the Podunk Indians at Hartford. He embroiled the whole Indian popu-

* New Haven Colonial Records. † Trumbull, i. 229.

lation wherever he could exert any influence, setting one tribe in opposition to another, by circulating every kind of scandal and gossip, and representing the different sachems as speaking such haughty and impious words concerning their neighbors, as best suited his plans. He taunted the Narragansetts with the loss of Miantinomoh, whom he had himself murdered, and challenged them to fight. He even proved false to the interests of the Montauket sachem, and espoused the cause of his old enemy, Ninigret. The Congress had enough to do to quench the flames of discontent lighted up in so many places at once by this Indian. They obliged him to make restitution to the tribes that he had wronged, so far as they were able to follow the sly trail of his mischief. There was nothing that Uncas disliked so much as to make an honorable restitution. It humbled his pride; and what was worse, it made an appeal to the most grasping and confirmed avarice. The English knew his weak points of character almost as well as he knew theirs, and were generally able to bring him to a temporary state of quiesence—but keep him quiet they never could for any considerable period of time.

The colony of New Haven, on the 7th of January 1657, sustained an irreparable loss in the death of Theophilus Eaton, who had been its principal patron, and who had held the place of governor from the first establishment of the colonial government until he died. He was the son of an English clergyman, and was born at Stony Stratford, in Oxfordshire. He was bred a merchant, and was carefully educated. He was for several years the agent of the East Land or Baltic Company, and discharged his trust with such ability that he received from that corporation the highest expressions of confidence, and many rich presents. He was also for some time an ambassador of the king, at the court of Denmark. On his return home, he established himself as a merchant in the metropolis, where he continued to add to his wealth, until his removal to America in 1637.

At New Haven he attempted to carry on his old pursuits,

but soon abandoned them for agriculture. His public duties occupied a large portion of his time. As a judge he was impartial, clear-sighted, and inflexible. His magisterial presence was calm and majestic, as well from an easy and graceful bearing, the result of a native manliness, and an extended acquaintance with the world, as from a commanding figure, and a very handsome, open countenance. He possessed the qualities of a good statesman, and, ingenuous as he was, he was still eminently fitted to be a diplomatist. In private life, strict and severe in the discharge of all his religious duties, he was yet a model of affability and gentlemanly courtesy. He managed his large household with systematic regularity. He cared for the moral and religious culture of the humblest servants beneath his roof, and although he lost no suitable occasion to inculcate a lesson, he did it with such well-timed delicacy, that they regarded it as an act of affectionate condescension, rather than as a rebuke, when he chid them for a fault. He was one of the few men who know how to employ an ample fortune munificently, and yet for the benefit of themselves, and of society.

His death was very sudden and unexpected. He had not been known to be ill, when, on the evening of the 7th of January, he entered the apartment of his invalid wife to bid her a kindly good night; "Methinks you look sad," said Mrs. Eaton, inquiringly. "The differences in the church at Hartford make me sad," replied the good man. Thinking it a fair opportunity to press upon his mind a topic that she had much at heart, this lady (who was a daughter of Bishop Morton, and was ill-satisfied with her husband's abode in a neighborhood so uncongenial to her,) resumed with much warmth, "Let us even go back to our native country." "I shall die here," said the governor, and immediately left the room. These were the last words he ever addressed to her. About midnight a deep groan was heard in his bed-chamber. A member of his household, who slept near by, rushed anxiously into the room to inquire the cause. "I am very ill," said the dying man, and instantly expired.*

His funeral was deferred until the 11th of the month, and took place, as the secretary tells us with a minuteness that evinces the keenness of the public sorrow, and the importance of the event, at "about two o'clock in the afternoon." His death was deeply felt in all the colonies, but the heaviest blow fell upon New Haven, where he had so long shed such a benign example. His great wealth, his unbounded hospitality, his christian virtues, his honesty and his fearlessness, have still a traditionary fame in the city that was laid out under his eye, and beautified by his hand.

Almost at the same time, died Edward Hopkins, Esquire, son-in-law of Eaton, for several years governor of Connecticut. Like Eaton he also was a wealthy London merchant, and from the same causes of discontent left England under the guidance of the strong-willed, bold-hearted Davenport. Hopkins was not pleased with the mode of government established at New Haven, and soon took up his abode at Hartford, where he was chosen a magistrate in 1639. The next year he was elected governor of Connecticut, and continued to serve in that capacity every alternate year until 1654. Soon after this, he sailed for England, where his merits were acknowledged with equal readiness, for he was successively chosen warden of the English fléet, commissioner of the admiralty and navy, and a member of parliament. He was chiefly eminent for his solid understanding, his integrity, and for the mild exercise of the Christian charities. Though he left Connecticut, and did not lay his bones in her soil, yet it is evident that his heart was never alienated from her, for in his will he gave nearly all that part of his property still remaining in New England to trustees, to dispose of it for the "breeding up of hopeful youths in a way of learning." The trustees very judiciously gave the legacy, amounting to about one thousand pounds

* Mather's Magnalia, ii. 29; Bacon's Hist. Dis., 110.

sterling, to aid in the support of two grammar schools, one at Hartford, and the other at New Haven. He also gave five hundred pounds out of his estate in England to charitable purposes, but in such equivocal language that it was finally made the subject of a decree in chancery. It was held to belong to Harvard College, and the Grammar School at Cambridge in Massachusetts.*

As early as 1649, William Chesebrough, of Rehoboth, commenced a settlement upon that tract of land lying between the Mistick and Pawcatuck rivers. Thomas Stanton, the interpreter, also, about the same time went there, and was the first Englishman who settled upon the bank of the Pawcatuck. He did not remove his family to the place until some time after he had been himself established there as a trader with the Indians. This tract of land was called Pequot, and was considered as a part of New London. Chesebrough was a blacksmith, and went there under the authority of Massachusetts. The fear that this worker in metals would aid the savages in repairing their fire-arms, and provide them with other sharp and deadly weapons, added to the jealousy excited in the General Court of Connecticut; and the fact that the stranger had come to take possession in the name of another jurisdiction, did not at all conduce to Chesebrough's peace of mind. Scarcely had he built his little hut on the bank of the cove that lies a little to the eastward of Stonington Point, and begun to engage in the traffic with the Indians of Long Island, and perhaps of the main-land, when his operations were interrupted by the constable of Pequot, ordering him in the name of the magistrates of Connecticut to desist. Chesebrough refused to comply with the order, as he claimed to belong to the jurisdiction of Massachusetts. Not long after this, he was commanded to leave the territory or appear before the court and defend himself. The alarmed pioneer accordingly in March 1651, presented himself before the General Court at Hartford. He made a very able defense. He acknowledged

* Trumbull, i. 232, 233; Holmes' Annals, i. 309, &c.

that he had been a blacksmith, but asserted that he had recently become a farmer, and had sold all the tools that he formerly used in carrying on his trade, and had not reserved enough "to repair a gun lock or make a screw pin." He represented that he had intended to settle in Pequot with the other planters, but that he could not suit himself so well there as he could upon the salt marsh at Pawcatuck, where he could find an immediate support for his cattle. He declared that he did not go there to live alone because he was a heretic or a heathen; and that he believed in the truth as it was taught in the New England churches. He did not expect when he went there, to live a great while alone, for he supposed others would soon follow him.

His arguments did not satisfy the court, yet upon his giving bonds for his good behavior, and with the assurance that he would get a respectable company to live with him before the next winter, they suffered him to remain.* Historians have conspired with the court to wrong him.

Thomas Minor in 1653 became an inhabitant of Pawcatuck. In 1657 the General Court appointed a committee, at the head of which was John Winthrop, Esquire, to meet at New London, and compare the differences between that plantation, and the people of Mistick and Pawcatuck.† By this it appears that considerable accessions had already been made to the population of the disputed settlement. In 1658 several families removed there. Captain George Denison, Thomas Shaw, and two men of the name of Palmer, were among the early planters.

In 1658 the commissioners decided that the river Mistick should be the boundary line between the two jurisdictions of Massachusetts and Connecticut. Thus Pawcatuck became a Massachusetts town, and took the name of Southerton. It was known by that name, and continued under the government of Massachusetts until after the royal charter of Charles II. was granted to us, when it became a part of Connecticut. In 1665 the General Court decreed that the

* Trumbull, i. 235; Caulkins' New London, 99, 100. † J. H. Trumbull, i. 300.

place should be called Mistick, in commemoration of Mason's victory. In May 1666, by a like order, the name of the town was again changed to that of Stonington, which it has ever since continued to bear.* It has been the rugged nurse of some of the most gallant and heroic men, who have done honor to the State during the French and Indian wars, and during the more bitter and sanguinary struggles that belong to a later day. The sons of Stonington, like those of New London, have for several generations gone down to the sea in ships, and done business on the great waters.

The names of Welles and Webster, at the election of 1660, no longer appear in the roll of the magistracy. During the year, one had dropped "like ripe fruit seasonably gathered," into the silent grave. The other had sought a home in Massachusetts, where he died in 1665. Thomas Welles and John Webster, venerable names, both governors of Connecticut, whose virtues are still perpetuated in those who inherit their blood. The dust of Welles rests with that of Wyllys, in the old cemetery at Hartford. His grave is without a stone to mark the spot.

Some time during the year 1657, while the old feud between the Narragansetts and Mohegans still raged with unabated fury, Pessacus advanced suddenly upon the country of his enemy, shut up Uncas in his fort, and kept him there in a state of siege until his situation seemed hopeless. Hopeless it might have been to any other Indian, but Uncas was too fruitful in expedients ever to despair. He contrived, as a last resort, to send runners to Saybrook fort to inform the garrison of his critical situation. He bade them tell the English that famine and the sword were impending over him and the whole Mohegan tribe, and that the most fatal consequences would result to the English, should their old friends be destroyed. The wily politician had hit a very sensitive nerve. Thomas Leffingwell, an ensign at the fort, on learning this piece of intelligence, immediately loaded a canoe with provisions, paddled it from the mouth of the Con-

* Caulkins' New London, 104, 106, &c.

necticut to that of the Thames, and, under the friendly screen of night, passed up the river, and supplied the famishing Mohegans with food. Thus recruited the beleaguered chief made such a sudden and furious attack upon the panic-stricken Narragansetts, that he drove them through the woods, and down the rocks with the most complete and terrible slaughter.

We are told, though I know not upon what authority, that for this daring exploit of Leffingwell, resulting in the salvation of the Mohegan tribe, Uncas gave to his deliverer a deed of nearly the whole of the present town of Norwich. However this might be, and it is not unlikely, it is quite certain that in June, 1659, Uncas went to Saybrook, and there gave to the English company, that was probably formed as early as 1653, for the settlement of a town on the head waters of the Pequot river, a deed of a tract of land at Mohegan, nine miles square. Nothing was said in the conveyance about any old debts of gratitude to be canceled; and the consideration of the deed was not love and affection, but seventy good pounds. This was the second time that the prudent vendor had sold it to the English, and taken the money for it, unless he had also in a fit of gratitude deeded it to Leffingwell. Major Mason was at the head of the company formed at Saybrook for the founding of a new town. There were thirty-five members of this company, who signed its articles of association, and thirty-eight original settlers. A few hardy men spent the winter of 1659 in temporary huts on the new purchase.

In the spring of 1660, the Rev. James Fitch, Major Mason, Mr. Huntington, Gifford, and the other members of the association, embracing the principal part of Mr. Fitch's church and congregation, removed to the fair plain lying in the folds of the swift Yantic, where, by the practice of their proverbial industry, the settlers were soon surrounded by the delights of home. The first inhabitants were men of rare merit, and of good family, as may be seen by their names that have been honorable in the state. Among them

I may mention Tracy, Griswold, Smith, Allyn, Howard, Hyde, Waterman, Backus, Bliss, Reynolds, Caulkins, and Reed. These are not all, but the genealogist and town historian have preceded me. The high, sharp ledges of rocks that left their sombre shadows on the vale, or sometimes hid their sternest features behind the trees that shook their quivering leaves above the river, and its then copious tributaries, while they lent their romantic beauty to the town, served also to screen it from the winter winds, as the Mohegan chief and his bronzed warriors protected its inhabitants from the Nihanticks and the Narragansetts.

CHAPTER X.

THE CHARTER.

We have now reached a point in our journey where we may pause for a while and take a brief retrospect.

With the year 1603 closed the reign of Elizabeth. The remainder of the first quarter of the seventeenth century was occupied by the bigot king, James Stuart.* The next quarter of a century we behold signalized at different periods by the most whimsical tyranny and reckless violation of the faith plighted over and over again, on the part of king Charles I., and by acts of violence, the natural consequence of such behavior, on the part of the people, consummated by that awful spectacle then unknown in the civilized world, and followed as a precedent but once from that day to the present—that of a maddened and misguided people sitting in judgment upon the life of their sovereign. Then follow the few stern years of Cromwell's dominion, from whom Say and Seal, whose aid Charles had tried in vain to buy with the lure of tempting offices, turned away his face with equal pride and greater loathing—a dominion that can be regarded by the right minded as useful only in the same sense that destructive earthquakes are, that throw down the walls of cities, or fires that consume their old and tottering edifices, and thus make way for more solid masonwork, and more graceful and useful structures.

This brings us—for why should we stop to speak of the imbecile protectorate of Richard, or the deep and secret game played by Monk, that led the way with such caution to a new state of things—this brings us to the long desired restoration.

* James I. reigned from A. D. 1603 to 1625; Charles I., his successor, occupied the throne from 1625 to 1649, having been beheaded on the 30th of January of the last named year.

These first sixty years of the century were teeming with events of the most momentous consideration in their bearing upon the future destinies of mankind. No wonder, that amid such convulsions at home, revolutions chasing one another as wave follows wave to the shore, the English government should have lost sight of that handful of men who, year after year, under the shade of the mighty forest trees, stole away from the provincial government at Boston, and set up a new jurisdiction for themselves on the Connecticut river and along the sea-shore, as well of Long Island as of the main-land. Nor is it a thing to excite our surprise, that the planters of Connecticut, who sometimes turned their eyes from their absorbing employments—the taming of wild nature or wilder men—to steal a hurried glance at the dusty arena where England struggled for the freedom that she finally won, should have come at last almost to forget their allegiance to the mother country, and should have half imagined that in the recesses of their retirement they were beyond the ken of British statesmanship and out of the pale of British authority.

It is not likely that the framers of the constitution of 1639 ever entertained the idea of maintaining a government independent of the crown, although they did not think it necessary or expedient to take upon themselves the voluntary acknowledgment of a jurisdiction that was sure to thrust itself upon them as soon as they could desire to bear its burdens. It is possible, too, that they kept themselves in abeyance for the time when England, bowed down by her calamities, could no longer stretch her shortened sceptre across three thousand miles of ocean.

Let these planters have reasoned as they might, the restoration of 1660, which brought tranquillity to England and enabled the king to look abroad upon the outer borders of his empire, soon taught them to reflect upon the growing importance of Connecticut, which could not fail to tempt the cupidity of a monarch whose extravagant habits and empty exchequer called loudly for subsidies. Besides, they were in the midst of dangers: the Dutch on one side, the Indians on the other, and the powerful colony of Massachusetts not far off, of whose growing importance they had always entertained such suspicions as weak states must invariably harbor against those that are more powerful. The king had suffered all the hardships of proscription and exile, and was now, at the commencement of his reign, most anxious to please all classes of his subjects. He was a Stuart, and with increasing prosperity his love of prerogative, the ruling passion of his father and grandfather, might grow upon him and tempt him to trench upon their liberties. What time so favorable as the present?

Accordingly on the 14th of March 1661, while the good-natured king yet bore his honors with a modest face, the General Court of Connecticut determined to make a formal avowal of their allegiance to the crown, and apply for a charter. A very humble and graceful acknowledgment they made of it. They now very sedulously called the commonwealth that they represented, a colony, and avowed that all its inhabitants were the king's faithful subjects. The court also made an appropriation of five hundred pounds to prosecute the petition with energy.*

In May the Court again met, when a petition to his most gracious majesty was presented by governor Winthrop for their consideration, and was cordially approved. But in order that no form of respect might be wanting, and no reason that could be assigned might be left out of the paper, or fail to have its proper weight from being imperfectly stated, the deputy governor, Mr. Wyllys, Mr. Allyn, Mr. Wareham, Mr. Stone, Mr. Hooker, Mr. Whiting, and the Secretary, were associated with the governor as a committee to amend and still further perfect it. These gentlemen were also authorized to write letters to such noblemen and other eminent persons as they should see fit, with the design of procuring aid in bringing the application to a favorable issue. The

* Colonial Records, i. 361.

Court appointed governor Winthrop the agent of the colony, to repair to England and present the petition to the king, and to see after the general interests of Connecticut. He was particularly instructed how to proceed in the business, and was especially directed to procure, if possible, the aid of Lord Say and Seal, and the other still surviving proprietors under the old patent.*

With such a committee and such a *man* as Winthrop at its head, it is not surprising that a very strong case was made out, and stated in the petition with uncommon ability. How the lands had been purchased of the Indians at infinite labor and cost, or won from them as the prize of victories gained by the colonists at the hazard of their lives, and how they had subdivided the territory thus obtained and reduced it to a state of culture that made it, with the increased population that then inhabited it, a most valuable addition to the resources of the king's empire, were all stated with such fullness and force that they could not fail to attract the royal notice, seasoned as they were with the insinuating language of homage and flattery.

At the same time a letter was written to Lord Say and Seal, who, notwithstanding his dislike of Charles I. and Cromwell, had become reconciled to Charles II. and was known to possess the king's confidence, reminding his lordship, by an indirect allusion, of the project that he had himself once entertained of emigrating to America, and of the influence that he had exerted upon the colonists, in holding out such inducements as his presence and patronage would be to them, to remove thither to prepare the way for his coming. They further informed him at what a dear rate they had purchased of Colonel Fenwick the fort and lands that he had sold to them under a threat that, if they refused to buy upon his own terms, he would transfer his title to the Dutch; and that they paid the exorbitant price of sixteen hundred pounds for what they thus bought, because they were under such restraints as placed it out of their power

* Colonial Records, i. 368, 369.

to make the contract upon any terms that were more favorable. They called to the mind of his lordship their weakness and their exposed situation, with the powerful and grasping colony of Massachusetts on their northern border, and how impossible it was for Connecticut to settle her boundary lines either upon the north or upon the west without the limitations and authority of a charter. They begged him to assist governor Winthrop in the enterprise that they had so much at heart.*

Thus commissioned and instructed, the agent of the colony set sail in August for England, to execute the important trust that had been confided to him. When he arrived in England, he made immediate application to Lord Say and Seal to aid him in gaining a favorable hearing of the king. That venerable nobleman was at that time unable to go up to London on account of a severe attack of the gout, that prostrated his powers and unfitted him to attend to his duties at court. Yet, true as he ever had been to his old friends in Connecticut, for whom he always manifested the highest regard, not more on account of their religious sentiments than because he was himself at heart a republican, he wrote an urgent letter to the earl of Manchester, then Lord Chamberlain, the most spotless character of that corrupt age, whose sympathies for the people of New England corresponded with his own, desiring him to lend his powerful influence to the application. Lord Say and Seal was the only nobleman then surviving who had been a grantee in the original patent. His letter to Winthrop, bearing date December 11, 1661, evinces the kindest and most delicate interest in the welfare of the colony.†

Say and Seal had kept aloof from public life during the protectorate, which he abhorred more than he shrunk from the tyranny of Charles I., and had remained for a long time in haughty retirement at the isle of Lundy, where he lived more in the style of a king than of a subject. But he became

* For a copy of this letter see Trumbull, i. 513, 514.

† This letter may be found in Trumbull, i. 515.

at last tired of his magnificent obscurity and, like many others who had struggled to free England from a galling yoke, had become sated with the horrors of war, and weary of the delays, the inefficiency and the bigotry of the parliament. With these views he had not been idle in lending his powerful aid to the efforts of Monk and Clarendon, in bringing back the exiled king. Nor was Charles unmindful of the part that his noble subject had taken in the train of complicated circumstances that led to the restoration. He rewarded him for his fidelity by making him Lord privy Seal.* The interposition of such an ally in behalf of Connecticut, seconded by the efforts of the Lord Chamberlain, could not fail to have weight with the easy, vacillating monarch, who, in his best estate, though obstinate, had never possessed an independent will, and who had already begun to commit the care of his kingdom to his ministers, while he yielded himself up a too ready victim to the soft dalliance of courtly pleasures.† Connecticut was also exceedingly fortunate in the choice of her agent. Not another man in New England was so well fitted as Winthrop to bring this delicate mission to a successful result. His naturally flexible and graceful mind had been cultivated by a careful education at Cambridge and Dublin, and his manners, in addition to the sparkling endowments of nature, had been fashioned by the then rare accomplishment of an European tour, with abundant leisure to observe and study the elegant refinements of the higher circles in the various countries that he visited, and with the noble self-control to abstain from indulging in their vices.‡ Besides, he had made himself familiar with the new world as well as with the old. Its streams, unfettered by commerce, save that of the canoe with its light freight of skins, winding through woods that had already become the theme of many an enchanting fable; the habits of the wild men who frequented those woods; their laws, their modes of subsistence, of waging war, of making treaties, and their in-

* Camden's Imperial Hist. Eng., ii. 216; Trumbull, i. 248.

† See Wade's British Chronology, 220, 221. ‡ Brancroft; Allen.

tercourse with the English; the game that abounded there; the noisome serpents that startled the traveler from his lonely trail with hiss or rattle—all afforded an inexhaustible field whence an ingenious mind could extract, in details of anecdote and adventure, the honey of discourse; and who was more likely to listen with a pleased ear to the agreeable narrator of such wonders, than the boyish, fun-loving king? who more likely than Winthrop to cause the full, flashing eye of Charles Stuart to dance with merriment second only to that which flowed from the exhilaration of the wine-cup, or cause it to dilate sometimes with a pleased sympathy such as could merge for a moment the ambition of mistress Palmer in a softer passion, or tame to a feebler fluttering the gentle heart of Nelly Gwynne.*

An English gentleman, however accomplished, who had lacked the interesting experience that afforded Winthrop the opportunity to excite the curiosity and play upon the imagination of his sovereign, might have failed, as a man of unrefined manners, however well his memory might have been stored with facts relating to American life, certainly would have done; for the monarch had inherited not a little of his father's fastidious refinement, though it was gradually soiled and finally lost in the debaucheries of a later day.

With all these happy advantages, Winthrop might perhaps have failed in accomplishing his purpose but for a simple appeal to the filial piety of the king. He had in his keeping a ring of rare value, that had been presented to his grandfather by the unhappy Charles I. This ring, as if to set the seal to the favorable impression that he had made, he humbly proffered to his royal master. The king's heart melted at the sight of this touching memorial that brought to his mind the dark hours and sorrowful fate of the noble donor, who had most need of such a loyalty as that gift betokened. With a gracefulness that rendered his munificence doubly wel-

* The influence of these artful courtesans over the opinions and acts of Charles II. was often observable in public affairs. See Camden's Imperial Hist. of England, ii. 221; Wade, 229.

come, he accepted the ring and granted the prayer of the colony.*

On the 23d of April, 1662, letters patent under the great seal received the royal signature, giving to the petitioners the most ample privileges.† They confirmed in the patentees the title and jurisdiction of the whole tract of land granted to the earl of Warwick in free and common socage, and to their successors, forever. The names of the patentees in the charter were John Winthrop, John Mason, Samuel Wyllys, Henry Clarke, Matthew Allen, John Tapping, Nathan Gold, Richard Treat, Richard Lord, Henry Wolcott, John Talcott, Daniel Clarke, John Ogden, Thomas Wells, Obadiah Bruen, John Clarke, Anthony Hawkins, John Deming, and Matthew Canfield—nineteen in all—to whom, together with all the other freemen of Connecticut then existing, and who might afterwards be admitted electors or freemen to the end of time, were given the irrevocable privileges of being "one body corporate and politic in fact and name, by the name of the governor and company of the English colony of Connecticut in New England in America, and that by the same name they and their successors should have perpetual succession."

By these letters patent they are made persons in law, may plead and be impleaded, defend and be defended, in all suits whatsoever; may purchase, possess, lease, grant, demise and sell, lands, tenements, and goods in the same unrestricted manner as any of the king's subjects or corporations in England. They are annually to hold two general assemblies—one on the second Thursday in May, and the other on the second Thursday in October—to consist of the governor, deputy governor, and twelve assistants, with the more popular element of two deputies from every town or city.

The company or colonial corporation thus constituted, might choose a common seal, establish courts for the administering of justice, make freemen, appoint officers, enact laws, impose fines, assemble the inhabitants in martial array for the common defence, and exercise martial law in all necessary

* Trumbull, i. 248. † A copy of the charter is to be found in the appendix (B.)

emergencies. It is especially provided that all the subjects of the king within the colony shall enjoy all the privileges of free and natural subjects of the realm of England, and that the charter shall be construed most favorably for the benefit of the corporation. John Winthrop is named in it as the first governor, and John Mason deputy governor, and the other patentees whose names are mentioned are to be the first magistrates. All these appointees are to hold their offices until the people shall elect new ones in their places.

Such, in its substance and main features, was the charter granted by Charles II. to the colony of Connecticut. Although it bore date the 23d of April, yet as nothing was known of it in Connecticut until several months afterwards, the regular routine of the government meanwhile went on under the old constitution. In May, the freemen met as usual, and held their election. Although the deepest anxiety must have pervaded the public mind in reference to the probable fate of Winthrop's mission, yet we find no traces of it upon our colonial records. The Court proceeds with its usual calmness and sobriety to provide for the domestic economy of the inhabitants, and to relieve the burdens that appeared to fall too heavily upon the weaker towns.

The defenses of the colony were not forgotten, and effectual measures were taken to perfect its military organization. The distribution of the Bible among widows and children was at the same session made the subject of legislation.*

At the General Court held on the 22d of July, the same silence is observed as to the petition. The king is not even incidentally mentioned. The people never made any confessions of loyalty unless they considered themselves likely to reap some benefit from the humiliation.

---

* On page 381 of J. H. Trumbull's Colonial Records will be found an order of the General Court directing that the Bible sent to Goodwife Williams shall be delivered to Goodwife Harrison, "who engageth to this Court to give unto ye children of ye said Williams a bushel of wheat apiece as they shall come out of their time; and John Not doth engage to give each of ye children two shillings a piece as they come out of their time, to buy them Bibles."

At what precise time the charter arrived in Connecticut is not known. Doubtless it must have been early in September, as it appears that it was publicly shown to the New England Congress convened at Boston, on the 4th of September.*

The commissioners must have opened their eyes wide when "his majesty's letters patent under the broad seal of England were presented and read."

On the 9th day of October, it was publicly read to the assembled freemen of Connecticut, and was declared to belong to them and their successors. The freemen immediately bore testimony of their gratitude to the king for this mark of his favor, and to the value that they placed upon it, by appointing Mr. Wyllys, Captain Talcott and Lieutenant Allen a committee to take it into their custody, under the solemnities of an oath administered to them by the General Assembly, binding them faithfully to keep this palladium of the rights of the people. At this session, the General Assembly confirmed the old tenures of office and ratified all the laws of the colony that were not inconsistent with the charter.†

At the same session, also, the General Assembly began to show a bolder front than ever before, in asserting the claims of Connecticut to jurisdiction over territories before that time claimed by other colonies. Notice was given to the inhabitants of Westchester that they were embraced within the boundaries of Connecticut, and that they would be expected to conduct themselves as peaceable subjects. It was also resolved, that the people of Mistick and Pawcatuck should abstain from the exercise of all authority by virtue of any commission from any other colony, and that they should manage their affairs and elect their town officers in accordance with the laws of Connecticut.

The news that the charter had arrived, and the very liberal terms of it, flew upon the wings of the wind. As Winthrop probably anticipated, it gave much additional impor-

* See J. H. Trumbull, i. 384. (note.)

† Colonial Records, i. 384, 385.

tance to Connecticut. Here was an invaluable, sacred grant, defining the rights of the colony and placing them beyond the grasp of the royal prerogative. The people of Connecticut, whatever might be the fate of the other colonies, had the king's written pledge, under the broad seal of England, to vouch for them that they were entitled to all the rights and immunities of Englishmen. One after another, deputations from the remote border towns, upon Long Island and upon the main-land, came flocking to Hartford to tender their persons and property to the General Assembly, and praying to be admitted upon equal terms of citizenship. Whether these ambassadors represented the whole population of their respective towns, or only petitioned in behalf of themselves, they were graciously received. A large portion of the inhabitants of Stamford and Greenwich begged to be made participators of the privileges conferred by the charter. A majority of the people of Southold, and some of the principal men of Guilford, were among the applicants. The clemency and generosity of the king were upon every tongue in the colony. All the towns upon Long Island were compelled to submit. A Court was instituted at Southold, at which the magistrates of South and East Hampton were members.* Of course the territory embraced in the charter included the entire colony of New Haven. Accordingly a committee was sent to New Haven to treat with the government there for an amicable union. Matthew Allyn, Samuel Wyllys, Stone, the chaplain of the Pequot expedition, and Thomas Hooker, were the gentlemen selected for this important and delicate embassy.†

The committee repaired to New Haven with becoming dispatch, and held a long and earnest conference with the authorities and principal gentlemen there. They urged a friendly union under the patent on some fair terms. It was too mighty a matter to be disposed of at a single interview, and besides it was thought necessary that the proposition should be communicated to the freemen before any ultimate action

* Thompson's Hist. Long Island. † Colonial Records, i. 388.

was taken. The committee therefore presented the authorities of New Haven with a copy of the charter, accompanied by a very plausible and somewhat stately declaration, wherein they were careful to speak in terms of the greatest commendation of the privileges granted by the "large and ample patent," which they describe not as having been artfully procured by the colony of Connecticut, but as having come to their hand. The declaration informs New Haven that the king has united the two colonies into one body politic, and reminds the freemen to whom it is made, that they are equally interested with the people of Connecticut in all the provisions of the royal patent, inviting them to a happy and peaceable union—"that inconveniences and dangers may be prevented, peace and truth strengthened and established, through *our* suitable subjection to the terms of the patent, and the blessing of God upon us therein."

It is not certain who was the author of this paper. The conciliatory, half-reproachful reply I have no doubt was framed by Leete, whose gentle nature never showed the decision and strength that lay hidden beneath its surface until all persuasive measures were exhausted.*

The time had now arrived when the freemen of New Haven were called upon to arouse themselves. On the 4th of November they convened to consult upon the best measures to be adopted. Excited and indignant as they were, they manifested a calm dignity that was never exhibited, I pre-

* The reply of the authorities of New Haven was as follows: "We have received and perused your writings, and heard the copy read of his majesty's letters patent to Connecticut colony; wherein, though we do not find the colony of New Haven expressly included, yet to show our desire that matters may be issued in the conserving of peace and amity, with righteousness between them and us, we shall communicate your writing, and a copy of the patent, to our freemen, and afterwards, with convenient speed, return their answer. Only we desire, that the issuing of matters may be respited, until we may receive fuller information from Mr. Winthrop, or satisfaction otherwise; and that in the meantime, this colony may remain distinct, entire, and uninterrupted, as heretofore; which we hope you will see cause lovingly to consent unto; and signify the same to us with convenient speed."

sume, under like circumstances in any State of ancient Greece. Governor Leete produced the declaration of the Connecticut committee and the copy of the charter that they had left. The strange patent, that had thus suddenly disposed of their government and political existence, without giving them a premonition of the fate that awaited them, was read aloud in the hearing of the freemen; and then, to allow them time for consideration, the Court took a recess for an hour and a half to meet again at the beat of the drum.

At the sound of this primitive summons, the Court again assembled. Davenport—the venerable father of the colony that had been thus summarily passed over into other hands—Davenport, the man who was second to no other in New England for straight-froward honesty and moral courage—was the first to break the ominous silence. He rose up calmly, as his custom was, and though grown gray in the hard services of his calling, and bowed under the weight of recent bereavements, neither his hand nor his voice could have betrayed a sign of weakness, when he unfolded the paper containing his carefully written views and reasons upon this vital matter, and prefaced his reading with the characteristic remark, that "according to the occasion he would discharge the duty of his place." He did nobly discharge that duty. In his distinct and impressive way, he read to them "his own thoughts which he had set down in writing, and which he said he desired should remain his own until his hearers should be fully satisfied with them."

When he had read the paper, he committed it to the keeping of the assembly and retired. Governor Leete prudently forbore to participate in the discussion. The debate was long and earnest, and after it was ended it was agreed that a committee made up of Mr. Law of Stamford, and the magistrates and elders, should draw up an answer to the declaration of Connecticut, that was to embrace and enlarge upon the following distinct propositions:

I. The wrong and sin of Connecticut in thus attempting to rob them of their independence and colonial existence.

II. The propriety of suspending all further proceedings until Mr. Winthrop should return, or until they should otherwise obtain further information and satisfaction.

III. That New Haven could of right do nothing without first consulting the other confederated colonies.*

The committee was directed to present in their answer whatever arguments they could against the union, and if these should fail to bring about the intended result, they were ordered to prepare an address to the king, praying for relief. The document drawn up by this committee in obedience to the instructions of the freemen of New Haven, has such salient points and such a marked individuality, that no one can doubt that Davenport was the author of it.† There is a concealed and galling irony in the document that must have been intolerably provoking, while the facts as well as the deductions from them, are indeed unanswerable. The committee say in substance, that whatever may be the purport of the charter, they have looked in vain to find in it any clause that prohibits the continuance of a distinct colonial government on the part of New Haven. The fact that not one of the patentees named in it belonged to New Haven, was to their minds strong corroborative evidence that neither they who petitioned for the patent, nor his majesty who granted it, intended that she should be embraced in it or affected by it, and that for aught that appeared in the charter they were still left at liberty to petition for the same privileges that had been so recently bestowed upon Connecticut. "Yet," say the committee, "if it shall appear (after due and

* The words of the reply are not here given literally, but only in substance as found upon the New Haven Colonial Records.

† Davenport was remarkable in that age of verbiage, for his terse, direct manner of expressing his thoughts in writing. There is a manliness and patrician bearing in this comprehensive state paper, that stamps its authorship upon it as with a seal. Whoever supposes that John Davenport can be set lightly aside by the flippant charge of narrow-mindedness and bigotry, had better study the history of those times more faithfully, before he presumes to put his crude views upon paper. There was indeed a *mote* in the eye of the old pioneer clergyman, but alas! for the *beam* in that of the critic.

full information of our State,) to have been his majesty's pleasure so to unite us as you understand the patent, we must submit according to God." The solemn covenants entered into under the confederation are then again alluded to, and the request urgently made, that New Haven may go on discharging the functions of a distinct colonial government, until "either by the honored Mr. Winthrop, by the other confederates, or from his majesty," they may learn what construction should be given to the patent.

The implied charge of a breach of faith contained in the following language is exceedingly severe. "This occasion [is] given before any conviction tendered or publication of the patent among us, or so much as a treaty with us in a christian, neighborly way. No pretense for our dissolution of government, till then, could rationally be imagined. Such carriage may seem to be against the advice and mind of his majesty in the patent, as also of your honored governor, and to cast reflection upon him."

This letter bore date the 5th of November, 1662. Connecticut made no reply to it, and in this she acted wisely, for no human ingenuity could have framed a successful answer to its stern truthfulness.

On the 11th of March, 1663, the General Assembly met, and in a very pacific tone proceeded to appoint a committee to treat with New Haven in relation to the terms of the union. Deputy governor Mason was at the head of this committee. They proceeded to New Haven and attempted to hit upon some amicable mode of adjusting the difficulties. But the hot haste that the General Assembly had manifested in getting possession of Southold, Stamford and other towns belonging to New Haven, and establishing a government there, and the protection and fellowship that had been promised by Connecticut to the disaffected at Guilford, had inflicted a deep wound upon the colonial independence of New Haven, that nothing save a full and honorable restitution could be expected to heal.

In this crisis of affairs governor Leete called a special session of the General Court to commence on the 6th of May. When the freemen were convened, they were asked if it was their pleasure, on account of relations existing between them and Connecticut, to make any alteration in respect to the time or manner of holding their election? With one consent they answered "No." Had the negative been uttered by the lips of John Davenport himself, it could not have been more resolute. They further resolved, that a remonstrance against the doings of the encroaching colony should be drawn up and sent to the General Assembly of Connecticut. This was accordingly done. This able paper, reciting the causes that induced the people of the colony to establish themselves in New England, and also giving a history of the wrongs that they had recently suffered at the hands of their sister colony, protesting against those wrongs, and calling for redress, is also the composition of Davenport. It contains some passages of powerful and eloquent appeal, that my limits will not allow me to quote, nor indeed ought they to be presented in a fragmentary form.

While these disorderly proceedings were going on in America, the agent of New Haven, sent to his majesty to petition for his interference, arrived in England. Winthrop was still there, and when the state of things in the two colonies was made known to him, he undertook to be the surety of Connecticut, that New Haven should suffer no further wrong at her hands, and that if the union was to take place at all, it should be a voluntary one. In pursuance of this pledge, Winthrop, on the 3d of March, 1663, wrote a letter to the deputy governor and company of Connecticut, informing them of the purport of the arrangement that he had made with the agent of New Haven, and further stating that before he prayed out the charter, he had given the people of New Haven his assurance that their interests should in no way be compromised by the step that Connecticut was about to take. These pledges of his, made while he was acting as their agent, and in a manner speaking in their behalf, he earnestly begged them not to violate, but to abstain from all violence and from all encroachments upon the rights and territory of their sister colony. He dexterously intimated that the blame of what they had already done, was to be imputed rather to his own negligence in not making those engagements known to them, than to any wanton usurpation on their part. He added, that if the General Assembly would wait until his return, he hoped to bring about the desired union by some amicable adjustment.*

What strange infatuation had taken possession of Connecticut, I am unable to say. The General Assembly in July following laid claim to Westchester, and sent out a magistrate from Connecticut with authority to lead the voters to a choice of officers, and to administer the proper oaths when chosen. The chartered colony also stretched out her hand over the Narragansett country, and appointed rulers over the inhabitants of Wickford. Disregarding the wishes of the governor thus decidedly expressed, and in defiance of the remonstrance of the freemen of New Haven and their earnest appeal to the king, she followed up the contemplated union in the same hasty way in which it had been begun.

On the 19th of August, another session of the General Assembly was summoned, and a new committee appointed to treat not alone with New Haven, but also with Milford, Guilford, and Branford, upon the terms of the union. If the committee failed to negotiate the matter amicably, they were instructed to read the charter publicly at New Haven, and proclaim to the people there that Connecticut could not fail to resent their attempts to maintain a separate jurisdiction, as it was clear that they were included within the limits of the patent; and that the General Assembly must insist that New Haven, Milford, Guilford, Branford and Stamford surrender themselves to the jurisdiction of Connecticut. This committee, like the preceding one, effected nothing.

In September, the Congress met at Boston, and the New Haven commissioners were received and acknowledged

* See Gov. Winthrop's letter in Trumbull. i. 520, 521.

as the representatives of an independent colony. At this session New Haven prepared a complaint against Connecticut, involving a complete history of all proceedings under the charter that related to New Haven. Governor Winthrop, who had now returned from England, and Mr. John Talcott, in behalf of Connecticut, defended her course with such arguments as they could adduce. They said the complainants had no just grounds of accusation against the chartered colony, as she had never done them any wrong, and had always proposed a friendly settlement of the controversy by treaty.

That this claim of Winthrop was at war with the matter contained in his own letter of the 3d of March, and not strictly in accordance with the facts in the case, I suppose nobody would attempt at this day to deny. However, I am unwilling that such a character as this great patriot has transmitted to posterity, should be thought to have left upon its surface a stain of dissimulation. He was anxious to conciliate the applicants, and in attempting to persuade them that they were unreasonable in their complaints, he only employed the ordinary privileges of the advocate, and stated the views that his too partial mind had adopted, with such eloquence and force as was natural to him. Besides, he may have arrived at different conclusions, on finding himself in the neighborhood of the excited people whom it was his duty, as far as he rightfully could, to justify and defend in the face of the whole world, from those that had been the basis of the letter that he had written from England, and of the assurances that he had then given to the agent of New Haven.

The debate was very earnest and absorbing. Governor Leete and Benjamin Fenn—the one cautious and courtly, the other blunt and bold—resolutely met the arguments of the Connecticut commissioners, and did not find it a difficult task to procure a decree that the distinct colonial existence of New Haven should remain inviolate, that no encroachments should be made upon her jurisdiction, and that her power should continue entire, as one of the confederates, "until such time as in an orderly way it shall be otherwise disposed of." No other decision could have been anticipated from the Congress, for the jealousy of Massachusetts and of the other associated colonies against Connecticut, since it had first been made known that she had become invested with privileges unknown to themselves, knew no bounds. Aside from the just claims of New Haven, how was it to be borne by the metropolitan colony of Massachusetts, who had always patronized Connecticut as her younger and portionless sister, that she should presume all at once to give herself such matronly airs, and place herself upon a royal matrimonial alliance that afforded such a striking contrast to her Arcadian manners and humble childhood?

Governor Stuyvesant, likewise indignant at the grasping ambition of Connecticut evinced by extending her jurisdiction over Westchester and the towns adjacent, appeared at Boston and complained of the encroachments made by her upon his territories. Winthrop and Talcott begged that, as no demand had been made upon the General Assembly and consequently they were not instructed how to make answer to his complaint, that the consideration of the affair might be postponed until the next meeting of the Congress. The matter was accordingly deferred.

On the 8th of October, the General Assembly of Connecticut again convened to consider and discuss the difficulties that were impending. An act was passed, wherein the assembly declare their dissatisfaction with the plantations of New Haven, Milford, Guilford, Stamford and Branford, because they persist in maintaining a government distinct from that authorized by the charter. A committee was at the same session again appointed to treat with those towns, and debate the matters in dispute. "If," say the assembly, "they can *rationally* make it appear that they have such power, and that we have wronged them according to their complaints, we shall be ready to attend them with due satisfaction."*

It will be observed that this diplomatic piece of legislation is very far from recognizing even pretended jurisdiction on

* Colonial Records, i. 415.

the part of New Haven, as a separate colony. On the other hand, the plantations are individually spoken of, and severally treated as independent of each other, and as constituting integral portions of Connecticut under the charter.

At a special session in March, Thomas Pell was authorized in behalf of the colony and with the design of securing possession and title to all the lands included within the boundaries of the patent, to buy of the Indians all that large tract lying between Westchester and Hudson's river, and "the waters which make the Manhadoes an island."* The General Assembly also lent a willing ear to the petitions of those plantations that were situated upon the western extremity of Long Island, and took them under the protection of Connecticut, for the charter included the adjoining islands within her limits. It was also resolved that Hammonasset should be a town. During the same month, twelve planters, most of them from Hartford, Windsor and Guilford, took up their abode there. Out of respect to Mr. Griswold, one of the principal proprietors of the town, it was afterwards named Killingworth, a corruption of the historical name of Kenilworth, the birthplace of the Griswolds of Connecticut.

Meanwhile New Haven continued to struggle against her fate. On the 22d of October, her General Court convened, and Governor Leete hastened to present to the freemen the details of all that had passed, and to take their advice. The members of the Court reviewed the behavior of Connecticut towards them, the rights of government that she persisted in asserting over them, the disturbances that she fomented in the several towns, by giving encouragement to malcontents and by sowing the seeds of sedition broadcast within their borders—and with unyielding courage resolved "that no treaty be made by this colony with Connecticut before such acts of power exerted by them upon any of our towns, be revoked or recalled, according to the honorable Mr. Winthrop's letter urging the same, the commissioners' determination and our frequent desires." With one consent they resolved to petition

* Colonial Records, i. 418; Brodhead, i. 733.

the king for a bill of exemption from the government of Connecticut, and voted to raise three hundred pounds by a tax to carry out this object. They took another step of a very decided character, that could hardly fail to hasten the crisis. They ordered that in all the towns belonging to their jurisdiction, the proper authorities should issue warrants to attach the personal estate of those who had refused or should thereafter refuse to pay the taxes by law imposed upon them. In these gloomy circumstances they also sought the divine aid, and appointed a day of fasting and prayer throughout the colony.

I have said that the doom of this little republic was impending. How could it well be otherwise? A powerful colony in the field against her, clad in the impenetrable panoply of the royal charter, reflecting far and wide a baleful light that struck blind for a time even the proud eye of the colony upon the Bay, and frightened little Plymouth "from her propriety;" an empty treasury, and rebellion springing up in the midst of her own plantations—how could it be otherwise? A more wretched state of confusion and enmity can hardly be imagined. The moment that the tax-gatherers of New Haven attempted to put in force the decree of her General Court, and attach the property of those who refused to do their part towards defraying the expenses of the government, the recusants fled to Connecticut for protection, and were received by her with open arms. The government was so poor that it could not even pay the ordinary salaries to its officers.

When the officers began to collect the taxes by force, civil war was the immediate result.

John Rossiter and his son, of Guilford, who had refused to submit to the authorities at New Haven and who had been punished with some severity for their offenses, now fled to Hartford for redress. They readily procured two magistrates, a constable, and some private volunteers from Connecticut, who, armed with muskets, repaired to Guilford and arrived there on the evening of the 30th of December. In the night they fired off their guns in the town and alarmed the inhabitants to such a degree that governor Leete was obliged to send messengers to Branford and New Haven for assistance. Both these towns, startled from their sleep in the dead of the night by this executive summons, immediately sent forward an armed force for the relief of Guilford. Governor Leete and the magistrates conducted the affair with such prudence that no injury resulted from this violence. The Connecticut officers, who had come out upon this nocturnal errand, contented themselves with remonstrating against the conduct of the authorities of New Haven, in laying taxes upon those who had placed themselves under the protection of Connecticut. They desired that the matter might be postponed for further consideration.*

On the 7th of January 1664, governor Leete called a special court at New Haven. He opened the session by stating to the Court what troubles had grown out of the order for the distraining of taxes, and with what earnestness the magistrates from Connecticut had called upon New Haven to refrain from the exercise of this authority, which, they claimed, was in violation of the rights of the citizens of Connecticut. The governor asked the Court carefully to consider this demand. They made answer that it had proved idle to attempt to make treaties with Connecticut, and that they were resolved to carry on no further negotiations with her, until she should have restored to New Haven the citizens that she had unlawfully seduced from their allegiance, and still continued to protect.

Mr. Davenport and Mr. Street were appointed a committee to make a new statement of the grievances of New Haven and transmit it in writing to Connecticut. These gentlemen entered with alacrity upon the discharge of this duty. The result was, a paper in the nature of a remonstrance of singular ability. It was called "The New Haven Case Stated," and is written in Davenport's best manner. In all our New England colonial papers, I have not found a more

* Trumbull, i. 263.

touching and eloquent narrative, nor have I ever seen a more convincing argument. Unlike it predecessors from the same vigorous pen, it is free from sarcastic allusions and has a mournful strain of accusation, such as we might suppose a martyr at the stake would address to his persecutors. It has a vitality and force that is indeed refreshing to one whose eye has been long exposed to the dull pages of records and state documents of the seventeenth century, whose blinding words, like clouds of sand, seem to sweep along over an interminable desert.* This paper, however, produced no change in the policy of Connecticut.

On the 12th of May 1664, the General Assembly convened, and again asserted their claims to Long Island and appointed officers at Hempstead, Jamaica, Newtown, Oyster Bay, Flushing, and all the towns upon the western extremity of the Island.†

In the same month the freemen met at New Haven and held a general election. They reäppointed Leete governor; William Jones was made deputy governor. These gentlemen were also chosen commissioners to the Congress next to convene at Hartford. The usual number of magistrates was elected, but two of them, Mr. Treat and Mr. Nash, declined to accept the place, for they foresaw that the downfall of New Haven was at hand. So depressed were the hearts of the freemen, that no business appears to have been done at this Court, as it left no records of its proceedings.

On the 12th of March 1664, the duke of York obtained a patent of a vast tract of country lying to the north of New England as it was then defined; and what was more alarming still to New Haven, including "all that island or islands commonly called by the general name or names of Meitowax, or Long Island, situate and being towards the west of Cape Cod and the narrow Nighgansets, abutting up-

* This state paper may be found entire in the Appendix to this volume, marked (D.) A portion of it has been published before by the author of "Historical Discourses."

† Colonial Records, i. 428. 429.

on the main-land, between the two rivers there called or known by the several names of Connecticut and Hudson's river, and all the lands from the west side of Connecticut river to the east side of Delaware Bay." Massachusetts and Plymouth, too, had much occasion to be alarmed, for Nantucket, Martha's Vineyard, and all the islands contiguous to them, that studded the main ocean, were embraced in the patent.

Thus was the whole territory of New Haven with a large part of Connecticut granted out to this royal subject.

The duke lost no time in taking possession of his new estate. Doubtless a main object of this patent was the reduction of New Netherlands, and an armed fleet soon sailed for the American coast, under the command of Colonel Richard Nichols, who was instructed to bring all the Dutch settlements on the continent to subjection. He was further authorized, in conjunction with Sir Robert Carr, George Cartwright and Samuel Maverick, Esquires, to visit the New England colonies and to hear and determine all controversies that existed between them.*

On the 23d of July, Nichols arrived in Boston harbor. He made known to the colonies his errand and in the name of the king, called upon New England to raise troops to assist in reducing New Netherlands. He also dispatched letters to Governor Winthrop of Connecticut, inviting him to meet him at the western extremity of Long Island for consultation. Accompanying the commission of Nichols and others, came a very gracious letter from the king, bearing date, Whitehall, April 23, 1664, and addressed to the governor and company of Connecticut. Whether it can be fairly inferred from the tenor of this letter, that opposition to the union on the part of New Haven had been anticipated, as an event likely to happen, at the time when the Connecticut patent was granted, I leave it for the reader to decide. At any rate, the first

* See Brodhead, i. 726, 735, 736; Hutchinson, i. 211; Trumbull, i. 266. This commission may be found at length in Hutchinson, i. App. XV. and in Hazard, ii. 638, 639.

15

sentence of the royal letter seems calculated to inspire confidence rather than terror in the hearts of those to whom it was written. It begins as follows:

"CHARLES, R.

"Trusty and well beloved we greet you well, having, according to the resolution we declared to Mr. John Winthrop *at the time* when we renewed your charter, now sent these persons of known abilities and affections to us—that is to say, Colonel Richard Nichols, Sir Robert Carr, Knight, George Cartwright, Esq., and Samuel Maverick, Esq., our commissioners, to visit those our several colonies and plantations in New England, to the end that we may be the better informed of the state and welfare of our good subjects, whose prosperity is very dear to us. We can make no question but that they shall find that reception from you which may testify your respect to us from whom they are sent for your good."*

Whatever construction governor Winthrop may have given to this document, he readily complied with the request of Colonel Nichols, and, in company with several of the magistrates and principal gentlemen of Connecticut, soon joined him at the place designated.

The time had now arrived when the dominion of the Dutch in America was about to be extinguished forever. On the 20th of August, with a formidable English fleet and armament to give weight to the summons, Colonel Nichols demanded the surrender of the town and forts upon the island of Manhadoes. Governor Stuyvesant was by no means prepared to obey this summons, and unable as he was in the disordered state of his province, to make a successful stand against the invaders, he was still resolved not to yield without giving the British commander a taste of his well known skill in diplomacy. Instead, therefore, of lowering the Dutch colors, his excellency drew up a formidable statement, and I believe a truthful one, of the title of the States General to the country then in their possession in America.

* See Appendix, where this entire letter may be found marked (C.)

With the stately politeness that marks all his official correspondence, he said that he had no doubt that had the king of England been aware of the claims of the Dutch, he never would have taken such measures to extinguish them. In conclusion, he assured the British commissioners "that he should not submit to his demands, nor fear any evils but such as God in his Providence should inflict upon him."

Colonel Nichols had offered to the inhabitants the most perfect protection of life, liberty, and property, provided the town and fort were surrendered as he demanded. The burgomasters explained to the people the terms proposed by Nichols. This did not satisfy them. They insisted on seeing the document itself. Stuyvesant went in person and explained to the assembled burghers the impropriety of exhibiting it to the public. It would be disapproved of, he said, in the Fatherland; it would discourage the people. But the citizens prevailed, and finally procured a sight of the paper.

Colonel Nichols now wrote a second letter to Winthrop, begging him to wait upon Stuyvesant and assure him that if he would surrender, the most liberal provisions should be made for the Dutch. The terms of his proposal were fully detailed in this second letter. Provided with so favorable a chart to guide his negotiations, Winthrop, under a flag of truce, repaired to the city, and, presenting his letter to Stuyvesant outside of the fort, begged him to surrender. Stuyvesant refused, but, retiring within the fort, he opened the letter and then read it in presence of the burgomasters, who asked that its contents might be made public. Stuyvesant declined to comply with the request. The burgomasters grew loud and clamorous, and at last, Stuyvesant, in a fit of passion, tore the letter in pieces. The enraged citizens now left their work at the palisades, and flew to the Stadt Huys. A committee was chosen from their number to wait upon Stuyvesant and demand the letter. "The letter!" shouted the burgomasters. "The letter, the letter!" reiterated the mob. Nothing else would pacify them. Stuyvesant was obliged at last to gather up the fragments of the mutilated paper, and give a copy of it to the burgomasters for their inspection.

When it was found on what favorable terms the capitulation was proposed, solicitations poured in upon Stuyvesant from all quarters, begging him to surrender. Still he kept his ground. At last Nichols ordered Capt. Hyde, who commanded the squadron, to reduce the fort. Two of the ships now landed their forces. The others sailed in front of the fort, and anchored close at hand. The undaunted Stuyvesant, while they were passing the fortification, stood upon one of its angles and watched them. A guard with a lighted match in hand, stood near by, waiting the orders of the governor, who with difficulty could be dissuaded from commencing an attack that must have resulted in the total discomfiture of the garrison and in much bloodshed. He finally left the fort and went into the city to oppose the landing of the English troops. He now, as a last resort, sent a deputation to Nichols, with a letter, in which he said, that although he felt it to be his duty to "stand the storm," yet he was willing to try what arrangement could be made. "To-morrow," said Nichols, "I will speak with you at Manhattan." "Friends will be welcome, if they come in a friendly manner," replied the ambassadors. "I shall come with ships and soldiers," was the stern answer—"raise the white flag of peace at the fort, and then something may be considered."

Thus beset by his friends and pressed by his enemies, the brave Peter Stuyvesant was compelled to capitulate; and yet, said he, in answer to the supplications of the women and children who thronged about him, "I would much rather be carried out dead."*

Thus was the Dutch power in America annihilated. I suppose no good man, who knows the facts, will be likely to attempt a justification of this aggressive war, condemned by Camden, and acknowledged by Clarendon to have been commenced "without a shadow of justice."

* Trumbull, i. 266, 268; Holmes, i. 334; Brodhead, i. 738, 741; Smith's Hist. of N. York, p. 10, 12, 14, 22, &c.

Scarcely had the royal commissioners sailed out of Boston harbor for New Amsterdam, when Mr. Whiting of Connecticut, who was at Boston during their stay at that port, hastened to New Haven to inform the authorities there how loftily the king's functionaries carried themselves, in what danger the colonies all were, and urging the people of New Haven to throw themselves into the arms of Connecticut without delay, to assist her in defending the liberties and boundaries named in the charter.

Governor Leete, on the 11th of August, called a General Court, and laid open to the freemen the intelligence thus received. A long and serious debate ensued. It was quite obvious that the magistrates and leading gentlemen were most of them disposed to yield, if not to the solicitations of Connecticut, at least to the urgent necessities that pressed upon them. But the people generally were still averse to the union. It was finally resolved "that if Connecticut should come and *assert her claim,* they would submit until the meeting of the commissioners of the united colonies."

On the 1st of September, the New England Congress convened at Hartford. The commissioners from New Haven took their seats in that body for the last time. After a careful hearing, the Congress decided that "although the Court did not approve of the manner in which Connecticut had proceeded, yet they earnestly pressed a speedy and amicable union of the two colonies."

In conformity with the advice of the Congress, governor Leete, on the 14th of the same month, called another General Court. He placed before them the reasons urged by Connecticut, and the advice of the united colonies. The struggle was protracted and bitter. The principal opposition came from New Haven and Branford,* where Davenport and Pierson held an almost absolute sway over the inhabitants, and especially over the members of the churches, who

* The Rev. Mr. Pierson of Branford, and almost his entire congregation, were so dissatisfied with the union, that they soon removed to Newark, New Jersey. Hubbard, c. 41; Holmes, i. 338; Hazard, ii. 520.

were determined to keep the hem of their garments pure from the anticipated stains of the democracy in Connecticut, that allowed men to enjoy the rights of voters and hold any offices of trust without the qualification of church membership. Nor could the uncompromising Davenport reflect without tears that the city laid out by himself and Eaton, his bosom friend, and adorned as the capital of a prosperous republic, should thus be shorn of its metropolitan honors and degraded into a provincial town.

Davenport had been the father of the state, and it was like the blotting out of his own existence were he to consent that the insignia of republican authority should be carried from the sacred spot where he had first deposited them. Besides he had committed himself against this measure, and Davenport was one of those men who will die rather than be driven from a position when once they have taken it. He held the church in his hand, and the members of the church constituted the state. Desperately he disputed the ground, inch by inch, against those who contended for the union, and again succeeded in preventing a vote in favor of the measure.

Connecticut now appears to have begun to be thoroughly alarmed for herself. The duke of York's claim threatened, notwithstanding the loyalty of Connecticut, to dismember her territory, and the duke and dutchess of Hamilton were in the act of prosecuting their claims to an old grant, that appeared likely to interfere with the colony. This matter was also referred to the royal commissioners. Besides, the discussions in the New Haven plantations were like an epidemic, that they might not always be able to confine within such narrow boundaries. The wise men of the colony, had therefore as much as they could well do to keep the little vessel afloat with the most skillful pilotage. But they were equal to the emergency.

In October, the General Assembly, with a liberality as bland as if it had welled up from the heart of the colony, voted to make the king's commissioners a present of five hundred bushels of corn. At the same time, they appointed a committee of men of great ability to settle the boundaries between the colony and the duke of York, and another to agree upon the lines that were to divide them from Massachusetts and Rhode Island. They also charged these committees to give up no part of the lands included in the charter limits.* A third committee of three gentlemen, at the head of whom was the Hon. Samuel Sherman, was appointed, with instructions to repair to New Haven, and, "in his majesty's name to require the inhabitants of New Haven, Milford, Branford, Guilford and Stamford, to submit to the government established by his majesty's previous grant to this colony, and to receive their answer." This committee was further ordered by the General Assembly to declare all the freemen in these towns free of the corporation of Connecticut, and to admit such others as they should find qualified, and administer the freeman's oath to them. They were directed also to proclaim in the hearing of the people there, that the General Assembly had clothed Leete, Jones, Gilbert, Treat, Law, Fenn, and Crane, with the authority of magistrates.†

The committee faithfully executed the trust. Whatever alarm may have pervaded the public mind in Connecticut as to the boundary question, I do not think that Winthrop could have labored under any very oppressive apprehensions in regard to it. He had rendered important services to the king and the duke of York by his presence and councils at Manhattan, and had been instrumental in bringing about without bloodshed, an achievment that was even then understood to contribute much to the power of the British sceptre; although no human foresight could at that time have had any thing more than an imperfect glimpse of that peerless city that was, within the next century and three quarters, to rise up like a glorious vision upon the brink of the little river whose waters, in the simple language of the General Assembly of Connecticut, "make Manhadoes an island." Besides, Winthrop knew the nature of the king, and perhaps was by this time not without some knowedge—for he read character

* Colonial Records, i. 435. † Colonial Records, i. 437.

with an intuitive keenness—of the views and intentions of Nichols and the other commissioners upon the boundary question. He had also, too, a thorough knowledge of the coast, and too practical a turn of mind, not to be aware that it was better for Connecticut to give up her claim to Long Island and Delaware, and have an unbroken domain upon the sea-shore, with fixed limits, and of sufficient size to be active without being unwieldy, than to divide her energies to maintain a feeble authority over a small and scattered population. Hence, I am not sure that he was much averse to the decision of the commissioners, when, on the 30th of November, they declared it to be as follows:

"That the southern bounds of his majesty's colony of Connecticut, is the sea, and that Long Island is to be under the government of his royal highness, the duke of York, as is expressed by plain words in the said patents respectively. We also order and declare, that the creek or river called Mamaroneck, which is reputed to be about twelve miles to the east of Westchester, and a line drawn from the east point or side, where the fresh water falls into the salt, at high-water mark, north northwest, to the line of Massachusetts, be the western bounds of the said colony; and the plantations lying westward of that creek, and line so drawn, to be under his royal highness' government; and all plantations lying eastward of that creek and line, to be under the government of Connecticut."*

This decision put an end to the long struggle between Connecticut and New Haven.

On the 13th of December, the freemen of New Haven, held their last General Court. It was very thinly attended, but it adopted with one consent the following resolutions:

"1. That, by this act or vote, we be not understood to justify Connecticut's former actings, nor any thing disorderly done by their people, on such accounts.

"2. That, by it, we be not apprehended to have any hand in breaking or dissolving the confederation.

* Trumbull, i. 273.

"3. Yet, in loyalty to the king's majesty, when an authentic copy of the determination of his majesty's commissioners is published, to be recorded with us, if thereby it shall appear to our committee, that we are, by his majesty's authority, now put under Connecticut patent, we shall submit, by a necessity brought upon us, by the means of Connecticut aforesaid: but with a *salve jure* of our former rights and claims, as a people, who have not yet been heard in point of plea."*

Thus the colony of New Haven, having drawn the folds of her mantle about her, as if to prepare herself to die with the dignity that became her, found, with a pleased surprise, that union was not annihilation, and in the arms of her elder sister, whom she learned at last both to forgive and to love, "lay down to pleasant dreams."

* Trumbull, i. 274.

CHAPTER XI.

THE REGICIDES.

The restoration of Charles II. was the result of a compromise between all the factions that had participated in the struggles that preceded it. Indeed, some of the most distinguished opposers of the tyranny of Charles I., and some of the most faithful adherents of Cromwell, were indispensable agents in hastening a result that filled England with jubilee and awakened as lively anticipations as had ever swelled the bosom of a nation.

Desirous of gaining the favor of all parties, Charles had promised to be forgiving to all who were disposed to return to their allegiance, and at Breda had proffered an indemnity to all criminals save those whom the parliament should except.* As far as his fickle nature was capable of gratitude, he certainly entertained it towards those who had aided in his return. The presbyterians as well as the royalists were admitted into his counsels and had their share of the gifts that were at his disposal. He created Annesly, earl of Anglesey; Ashley Cooper, lord Ashley; and Denzil Hollis, lord Hollis. He also made the good earl of Manchester his lord chamberlain; lord Say, his privy seal; and stretched his liberality so far as to appoint two presbyterian clergymen, Calamy and Baxter, to the place of chaplains to the king. He created Montague, earl of Sandwich; his friend Monk, duke of Albemarle; Sir William Maurice, secretary of state; Sir Edward Hyde, earl of Clarendon, lord chancellor and prime minister. He raised Ormond from the rank of a mar-

* For a full account of the restoration and of the character of Charles II., consult Camden's "Imperial History of England," chapters vi and vii. This noble work is so difficult to be had, that few but the learned can have access to it. Whoever among our American publishers has the courage to furnish the public with a cheap edition of it, will be doubly paid—in the consciousness of having done a benevolent act, and in the pleasant personal experience of having added to his pecuniary resources.

EZRA STILES, S.T.D, LL.D.

President of Yale College from 1777 to 1795.

quis to that of a duke, and made him steward of the household; while the earl of Southampton was appointed high treasurer.*

Policy, doubtless, held with gratitude a divided empire in the king's breast; but he is entitled to the credit of following good advice at first, whatever may have been the follies and debaucheries that afterwards made his court so shamefully eminent.

The commons were disposed to have past offences forgotten, but the lords were not so easily pacified. In relation to the unhappy men who had sat in judgment upon the king's father, and who were called then, as they still are, regicides, the lords were especially intolerant, and encouraged the king to except every one of them from the general pardon. Thus advised, the willing monarch, almost as soon as he had seated himself firmly upon the throne of his ancestors, issued a proclamation announcing that such of the judges of Charles I. as did not within fourteen days, surrender themselves up as prisoners, should *receive no pardon.* Of course great alarm was awakened in the hearts of the regicides and of their friends by this announcement. Nineteen delivered themselves up, and awaited the event with the deepest anxiety. Others fled, and were fortunate enough to elude pursuit and escape beyond the seas; and others were arrested in their flight. Ten of these unhappy men, whose worst crime—if they were guilty of any—was, that they partook too deeply of the same maddening cup that turned even the philosophic brain of Milton, were executed, and the remains of some of the principal actors in that too fearful tragedy, were treated with profane indignities, such as have not since that day disgraced the name of English freedom.† Two of these, Edward Whalley and William Goffe, arrived in Boston in July, 1660. John Dixwell came afterwards.

---

* Camden's Imperial Hist. of Eng., 216.

† The judges who were executed were Harrison, Scot, Scrope, Jones, Clements, and Carew; besides Cook, the solicitor; Hugh Peters, the chaplain; and Hacker and Axtell, who commanded the guard. The bones of Cromwell, Bradshaw, Ireton and Pride, were dug up, hanged at Tyburn, and then buried beneath the gallows! Camden, p. 217; Wade, p. 222.

As it was not known at that time what disposition would be made of them, and as it was believed that they would be embraced in the general act of indemnity, they were treated by Governor Endicott and the other principal gentlemen of Boston, with all the marks of respect that were thought to belong to men who had filled high places in the government, and whose venerable features and soldierly bearing comported so well with their high reputation, as eminent civilians and military leaders. They were constantly entertained at the houses of the more opulent, and from the curiosity that their presence awakened in the public mind, all their movements were watched with a lively interest. They soon went to Cambridge, where they stayed until February. While there, they openly attended upon public worship on the Sabbath and on other days, and made no effort to diguise from the people who and what they were.

As soon, however, as it was made known in Boston in what light the king looked upon the official conduct of these men, and that they were regarded as traitors, a large share of those who had claimed to be their friends, avoided them as if they had been infected with some contagious disease.

Finding the indulgence and favor of the authorities of Massachusetts thus suddenly turned into loyalty, and learning that instead of caressing them, Endicott had called a court of magistrates to apprehend them and deliver them over to the executioner, they took advantage of the friendly disposition manifested towards them by some of the magistrates and fled out of the jurisdiction of that colony, and sought a refuge in New Haven among the old and tried adherents of Oliver Cromwell. They passed through Hartford on their way and arrived in New Haven on the 27th of March 1661, where they were received by Davenport with open arms. Davenport entertained them at his house with the most kindly hospitality. They here found themselves among congenial spirits, and went fearlessly from house to house and discoursed freely of the thrilling incidents that had been crowded into their lives, and could be reproduced at will, divested of their more forbidding outlines, as the painter can choose the colors that best represent to his eye the image that floats, soul-like, in the atmosphere of his mental vision. The sieges of strong castles, the busy scenes and earnest fears that lent their haggard expression to the fires that lit up the camp of civil war; the awful details of the battle of Dunbar, that seem still to speak in the tides of the German ocean as they dash against the rocky coast; the imprisonment of Charles I. at Hampton court; his escape from the hands of Whalley; his subsequent captivity; his uncompromising silence when brought to trial by his subjects; his heroic death; the stern and vigorous policy that followed that event; in short, all the doublings and windings of a self-deluding ambition, exemplified in the life of Cromwell, from the humble pleasures of agriculture to the magnificent funeral in Westminster Abbey, afforded them an inexhaustible theme for conversation and reflection. They were grave, sedate men, and bore themselves with a noble self-control and a manly cheerfulness that bespoke no secret upbraidings of conscience. It does not appear that they ever felt any such accusations or entertained a doubt as to the part that they had taken in the transactions that preceded or followed the king's death.

Meanwhile the royal mandate reached Massachusetts, requiring the governor to arrest the fugitives. With this requisition, came a detailed account of the death of ten of the regicides, and of the disposition of the court towards those who entertained the survivors who were excluded from the act of indemnity. The governor and magistrates began to be seriously alarmed. They had already made a feigned search for the exiles, and failed to find them, as it was expected that they would do when they began. But now they thought it best to evince their loyalty in earnest. They therefore responded to the requisition by giving to two zealous young royalists, Thomas Kellond and Thomas Kirk, a commission in the nature of a special deputation, authorizing them to go through the colonies as far as Manhattan, and search for Whalley and Goffe with diligence.* If they found them they were ordered to arrest them. Armed with this paper, and stimulated with the prospects of promotion that they counted on as certain to crown their success, these ambitious pursuivants eagerly started in quest of the alluring game.

They hastened to Hartford and waited upon Governor Winthrop, who, as they afterwards made report, nobly entertained them; and, as he knew that the judges were not within his jurisdiction, he very readily gave a warrant to Kellond and Kirk to apprehend them within the limits of Connecticut. Winthrop appeared to be quite earnest in the cause, but he assured them that "the colonels made no stay in Connecticut, but went directly to New Haven."

The pursuers took leave of the governor and repaired to the colony of New Haven with all dispatch. The next day they reached Guilford, where they stopped to provide themselves with a new warrant; for deputy Governor Leete resided there, who was then the acting governor.

They soon made Leete acquainted with the object of their visit, and informed him that they had good cause to believe that Whalley and Goffe were then at New Haven. They begged him to give them a warrant similar to that furnished them by Governor Winthrop, and to provide them with horses to speed them upon their journey and men to help them to make the arrest. The governor appeared to be much surprised at this request. He had not seen the colonels, he said, in nine weeks, and he did not believe they were at New Haven. He took the papers from the hands of the pursuivants and began to read them aloud, in a tone so alarmingly audible that their loyalty was shocked,

---

* This is the form of the statement made by Stiles, Trumbull, and other authorities, and the mandate from the king unquestionably ordered the arrest of the fugitives wherever they might be found. The governor and council of Massachusetts, however, evidently had no authority to commission Kellond and Kirk to extend their researches beyond their own jurisdiction. That this was so understood by the pursuivants themselves, is evinced by their applying to the governors of Connecticut and New Haven for powers to enable them to prosecute the object of their mission in those colonies.

and they were obliged to interrupt him, and let him know that "it was convenient to be more private in such concernments as that was." He delayed to furnish them with horses in season, so that they could pursue their journey that night. The next day was the Sabbath, and they were obliged to wait in Guilford until Monday morning, the 13th, at daybreak,*

If the account that they afterwards gave of the matter is true, (and they gave it under oath,) an Indian was sent to New Haven in the night, and no difficulty was found in procuring a horse for one John Meigs, who set out for New Haven long before day, and heralded their approach with most untimely haste. Governor Leete positively refused to issue any warrant or send men to assist in making the arrest, until he had consulted the magistrates. In order to do this, it was necessary that he should go to New Haven. A wearisome Sunday the pursuers must have made of it. It is quite likely that the Indian spoken of in their report to Governor Endicott was sent off on Saturday evening to give the alarm to Mr. Davenport, who on Sunday would have a favorable opportunity to inform the people and put them on their guard. Indeed, this accords so well with the statement of Stiles that I can not entertain much doubt that such was the fact.†

---

* See Stiles, Trumbull, and Bacon.

† The more I read President Stiles' History of the three judges, the more I am induced to trust myself to him as an authority. His diligence in searching out details and traditionary evidence is almost without a parallel, and I find that most of his conclusions stand the severest test. He tells us that "about the time the pursuers came to New Haven, and perhaps *a little before*, and to prepare the minds of the people for their reception, the Rev. Mr. Davenport preached publicly from Isaiah xvi. 3, 4." Now if the report of Kellond and Kirk is correct, that they reached Guilford on the 11th and New Haven on the 13th, and if the 12th was Sunday, which, as Dr. Bacon says, is "found to be true by actual calculation," what time could have been more suitable than that 12th of May for the preaching of such a discourse? The pursuivants must therefore have spent two nights and one day at Guilford, and to make sure that Mr. Davenport had notice of their coming, Meigs, the second messenger, was probably sent off before daybreak on Monday morning.

At beat of drum the worshipers assembled as usual to listen to the teachings of their patriarch. The alarming intelligence that the pursuers were near, was probably whispered at the outer door of the meeting-house, in the ears of some of the principal men, if indeed it did not interrupt for a moment the grave tranquillity of the puritan Sabbath as it circulated among the people as they met. However, they would soon become composed—hushed, indeed, as statues long before the presence of the Supreme God was invoked. From what we know of the earnest character of the auditory, we may safely conclude that the silence of death reigned throughout the humble edifice, and that all eyes were fastened upon the face of the speaker—all ears thrilled to the tones of his voice, as he gave out his text from the XVIth chapter of Isaiah, verses 3 and 4: "Take counsel, execute judgment, make thy shadow as the night in the midst of noon-day; hide the outcasts, bewray not him that wandereth. Let mine outcasts dwell with thee; Moab, be thou a covert to them from the face of the spoiler."

I have not found upon the pages of history, a better example of moral courage thwarting the purposes of vindictive power, than the one afforded by this brave old clergyman upon the remote confines of the British empire calling upon the subjects of that empire who were gathered around him, to resist for the sake of mercy, the vengeance of their king.

Kellond and Kirk, as early on Monday morning as they found it practicable, rode into New Haven. They were not received with much cordiality by the inhabitants. In momentary expectation of the arrival of Governor Leete, they were obliged to wait about two hours before his excellency came. They then again pressed their demand for a warrant, as they said they had received information that convinced them that the regicides were still in New Haven. The governor said he did not believe they were in New Haven. The young gentlemen then begged that he would empower them to arrest the judges or order others to do it. Leete replied, that "he could not and would not make them magistrates." They then said if he would enable them to do it, they would themselves make search in two houses where they had reason to suppose that the regicides lay hid. The governor then told them that he could take no steps in the matter until he had called the freemen together.

The pursuivants were very much exasperated, and set before him in a strong light the dangers that he was bringing upon himself and upon the colony of New Haven by his delay. They further told him, that they did not doubt, from his reluctance to aid in the arrest, he was willing that the traitors should escape. This remark seemed to make an impression upon him, for he soon after convened the magistrates and remained in consultation with them—so weighty was the business—for a period of five or six hours. The council at length came to the conclusion that it was necessary to call a general court. Again the pursuers remonstrated. They reminded the governor how striking was the contrast between his conduct and that of the governors of Massachusetts and Connecticut, who, with the alacrity of faithful subjects, had hastened to issue their warrants in obedience to the king's mandate; they warned him against the horrible crime of aiding and abetting traitors and regicides, and ended by putting to him the pertinent question, "whether he would obey the king or no in this affair." "We honor his majesty," replied Leete, "but we have tender consciences." Enraged at this answer, the young men told him that they believed he knew where the outlaws were. This remark, implying a charge of high treason, led the governor and magistrates into another long consultation, that lasted two or three hours.

In the evening, Leete came to the head of the stairs of the little inn where the applicants lodged, and taking one of them by the hand, told him with the greatest simplicity of manner, that "he wished he had been a plowman, and had never been in office, since he found it so weighty."

"Will you own his majesty or no?" asked the pursuivants.

"We would first know whether his majesty would own us," was the guarded answer.

Thus baffled by the authorities and overawed by the people, Kellond and Kirk hastened out of the colony of New Haven without having dared to search a solitary house. They repaired to Manhadoes, where Stuyvesant received them with great politeness, and promised to aid them in arresting the fugitives if they could be found in his jurisdiction. Soon after, they went back to Boston *

Let us now return to the exiles. It is quite probable that they were at the house of Mr. Davenport until Saturday night, (the 11th of May,) when the Indian messenger arrived from Guilford, for it appears that they fled from the town that night, and spent at least a part of it at a mill situated in the woods two miles north-west of New Haven. Here they lay concealed until the 13th, when Mr. Jones with Burrill and Sperry visited them, and, probably while those protracted consultations were going on at New Haven between the governor and the magistrates, conducted them to the house of Sperry, still another mile farther off from New Haven. They here provided them a place that has ever since been called "Hatchet Harbor," where they lodged two nights, and on the 15th of the month† went to a cave upon the mountain called by them Providence Hill, but since known as West Rock, as the cave that sheltered the regicides still bears the name of "Judges' Cave." Upon the very summit of this mountain, and towering about twenty feet above it, on a base not more than forty feet square, stood an irregular cluster of pillars of trap-rock like a clump of trees. They had been upheaved in some strong convulsion of nature, and seemed very properly to typify the fiery billows of revolution that had drifted those sorrow-stricken men to take refuge from the strength of the returning surf by clinging to their gray sides. These rocks, at some distance from

* A copy of the official report of Kellond and Kirk may be found in Stiles' History of the Judges, pp. 52, 56. It bears date "Boston, May 29, 1661."

† This is the date as given in Goffe's Journal; see Stiles, p. 77.

each other upon the ground, slanted inwards towards a common center at the top, thus forming an irregular chamber, that could, by closing the outer apertures with the boughs of trees, be made habitable but not comfortable for two or three persons.* In this forbidding spot, with no companions but the wild animals, whose voices startled them from their sleep at night, and surrounded by such forest trees as could find a footing in the barren soil, they lived until the 11th of June.† Sperry sometimes carried them food himself, and sometimes sent one of his sons, who left it upon the stump of a tree that was pointed out to him, and who, with the superstitious wonder of childhood, in vain demanded of his father why the basins that he had carried there filled with provisions were found empty at his next visit, and why he was sent upon this mysterious errand.

"There is somebody at work in the woods who wants the food," was the unsatisfactory reply.

This desolate mountain was, as I have said, the haunt of wild beasts. One night, as the regicides lay in bed, they saw a panther or catamount thrust its head into the mouth of the cave. Its blazing eyeballs and unearthly cry so frightened the inmates, that one of them fled down the mountain to Sperry's house, where he gave the alarm. This intruder, terrible to men who had proved themselves to possess true courage when man meets man upon the battle-field, drove them from the cave.‡

It is impossible that I should follow these outlawed men in all their painful wanderings to elude the vigilance of their pursuers. Tradition still points out many places along the coast where they lingered, sometimes for a night and sometimes for a longer period, as best accorded with their real or fancied security. Sometimes they appear to have been alarmed for the safety of those who had protected them, and rather than bring them into difficulty, they resolved more

* An engraved view of the "Judges' Caves" may be found in Barber's Hist. Coll. of Conn., p. 151.

† Goffe's Journal. ‡ Stiles, p. 75.

than once to surrender themselves, and would have done so but for the solicitations of those in whose behalf they proposed to make the sacrifice.

Some time between the 11th of June, when they left the cave, and the 20th of the same month, they went to Guilford with a view of delivering themselves up to Governor Leete. The walls of the cellar are still standing, and may be expected to last another hundred years, where tradition informs us that they lodged, unseen by the governor though fed from his table, while the negotiations relative to their submission were going on. It appears that they desired to yield themselves up in order to save Mr. Davenport, who resisted it with his usual fearlessness and magnanimity. Endicott, who had dared to cut the cross from the king's banner, quailed before the royal mandate. Davenport alone remained,

> "Like Teneriffe or Atlas, unremoved."

While at Guilford, the regicides also lodged at the house of Mr. Rossiter.

From their various retreats in the woods they repaired to the house of a Mr. Tompkins in Milford. In this house they remained in the most perfect concealment for two years. They had a private room devoted to them, and did not so much as venture to walk out into the orchard. The honorable Robert Treat, Benjamin Fenn, and the clergyman, Mr. Roger Newton, were in the secret, often visited them, and afforded them such consolation and support as their forlorn situation demanded. The manly, sympathetic nature of Robert Treat needed only to know that they were friendless and sorrowful. A single grasp of his hand, a glance at his gallant face, was enough to assure the regicides that their secrets were safely lodged with him.

We are not to infer from the solitude and the dangers that all the while threatened the regicides, that they were the victims of moping melancholy. On the other hand, though they behaved with a dignity worthy of their former position, they beguiled the time not only with pleasant conversation, but often with that gamesome merriment that is so strangely allied to misery. During their stay at Milford, there was brought over from England a ballad written by some hair-brained cavalier rhymer, placing the regicides in such a ludicrous light that a loyalist might be excused for laughing or a puritan for biting his lip at the recital of it. This ballad, a girl who was an inmate of Mr. Tompkins' family, or who was in the habit of visiting the house, had committed to memory and had learned to sing it, which she happened to do in the chamber above the room occupied by the judges. They were so delighted with the song that they used to beg their host to have it repeated by the young ladies of the family, who little knew what an interested auditory had been provided for them.*

On the arrival of the commissioners in 1664, and when it became known that they were charged among other things with the arrest of the judges, their friends were again alarmed for their safety, and it was thought best that they should leave Milford for some new place of concealment. Accordingly, on the 13th of October, 1664, they set out for Hadley, then a frontier town in Massachusetts, a hundred miles from Milford, and so remote from Boston, Hartford and New Haven, that it did not seem probable that their presence in such a place would be suspected. They traveled only by night, and lay still during the day in some shady nook in the woods, or by the bank of a brook where the murmuring of the water invited them to repose. These stopping-places they called Harbors. The locality of one of them is still pointed out at the now flourishing village of Meriden, that yet retains the name of Pilgrim's Harbor. They reached Hadley in safety, and there they were secreted in the house of the Rev. John Russell, in a secret chamber, probably until they died. They kept a diary of the most minute events that transpired, probably more to amuse themselves than for any historical purpose. This journal was in

* See Stiles, whose facts and dates I have generally followed in tracing the history of the judges after their arrival in New England.

the handwriting of Goffe. Indeed, Whalley became infirm not long after his removal to Hadley, and from what I can glean from the tender expressions in regard to him that I find in Goffe's letters, I have no doubt that he became demented some time before his death, that is supposed to have happened in the year 1678.

Noble tells us that the Whalleys are of great antiquity. They were a very proud family, and were royalists. Upon the breaking out of the civil wars, Edward Whalley, who had been brought up to merchandise, in opposition to the wishes of his family took up arms in behalf of the people. At the battle of Naseby, in 1645, he fought with unparalleled bravery. He charged and defeated two divisions of Langdale's horse, supported as they were by that fiery cavalier, Prince Rupert, who commanded the reserve. For his heroic bravery on that occasion, he was made by the parliament a colonel of horse. He also commanded the horse at the siege of Bristol, when Prince Rupert surrendered up the city.* He was never popular with the more fanatical of the Independents, who hated him for his aristocratic bearing, and envied him for his success. At the head of his accusers was that wolfish radical, Hugh Peters, who charged him with being a Presbyterian—a compliment that Whalley threatened to reciprocate by caning him.†

When Charles I. fell into Cromwell's hands, he committed him to the keeping of Whalley,‡ who was charged by some of the more zealous loyalists with severity towards his royal prisoner. But this falsehood the king had the generosity to deny in a letter written to Whalley after his escape.

While Charles was still in custody at Hampton Court, Captain Sayers waited on his majesty to give back the ensigns of the order of the garter that had belonged to the Prince of Orange. Whalley felt it to be his duty to interpose to prevent a private interview, when the king, in a fit of rage, pushed him away with both his hands. But this

* Noble's "House of Cromwell," ii, 143, 144; Camden.

† Noble, ii. 144. ‡ Carlyle, i. 234, 235.

passion was only momentary. Indeed, the gallantry and courtly demeanor of Whalley could not fail to win upon the affections of the king.

At the terrible battle of Dunbar, Whalley, with Monk, commanded the foot forces, and had two horses shot under him.*

In 1656 he was created a lord, and appears to have plumed himself not a little upon his accession to a dignity that was much ridiculed by the king's faction. Colonel Ashfield, who knew that Whalley's principles would not allow him to engage in a duel, and who was aware of the keenness of his sensibilities and the suddenness of his temper, took occasion to speak in the hearing of the new dignitary in slighting and very pointed terms of Cromwell's House of Lords. Whalley was so angry that he threatened to treat him as he had proposed to deal with Peters, and doubtless would have been as good as his word had the insult been repeated.† With the exception of a hot temper and those lively bubbles of vanity that float upon the surface of almost every sparkling character, there was not a more noble nature in the world than that of Edward Whalley. His talents as a civilian were highly respectable; as a soldier, he was almost unrivaled in that age of military renown.

He married a sister of Sir George Middleton, that bitter enemy of Charles I. and ardent friend of Charles II. Their daughter married General Goffe, and became the mother of a numerous family.

Major General William Goffe was a son of the Rev. Stephen Goffe, rector of Stanmar, in Sussex. Like Whalley, he drew his sword against the king in the civil wars, and threw away the scabbard. He very early distinguished himself, and was first made a quarter-master, then a colonel of foot, and afterwards a general. He commanded Cromwell's regiment at the battle of Dunbar, as appears from the following extract from one of Cromwell's dispatches:—"For my own regiment, under command of Lieut. Col. Goffe, and my Major White, did come seasonably in, and, at the push

* Carlyle, ii. 471. † Noble, ii. 153.

of the pike, did repel the stoutest regiment the enemy had there."* He was elected a member of parliament; he aided in the accusation of the eleven members; he sat in judgment upon the king, and signed the warrant for his execution. He also helped White in the difficult task of purging the parliament of those members who could not be made to subserve the purposes of Cromwell, and for this he received the appointment of major-general. To crown his honors he was created a member of Cromwell's House of Lords. He remained faithful to the interests of the protectorate after the death of Oliver, and signed the order for proclaiming Richard as his successor. Monk knew his uncompromising nature, and would not admit him into his secrets or treat with him as the emissary of the army. His great popularity, his boldness, his courage, his comprehensive intellect, the colossal proportions of his character, above all, his disinterestedness, made him a dangerous neighbor to royalty, and especially to the house of Stuart.†

Some of the letters written by Mrs. Goffe to her husband are very beautiful, and evince a delicacy of sentiment and a depth of affection that reflect honor upon the character of both. She wrote under an assumed name, and Goffe addressed her as "Mother Goldsmith." In one of these letters she writes:—"My dear, I know you are confident of my affection, yet give me leave to tell thee, thou art as dear to me as a husband can be to a wife, and if I knew any thing that I could do to make thee happy, I should do it, if the Lord would permit, though to the loss of my life."

I do not know, in all the range of female correspondence, a more wife-like and transparent sentiment, nor one more charmingly expressed. Crowns compress the brows of those who wear them into wrinkles, and the fruit of ambition but too often blisters the tongue of him who eats it, but the love of such a woman is immortal and holy as the amaranth that blooms in paradise. Now listen to the wife and mother both in one.

---

* Carlyle, i. 470. † Stiles, 15.

"Frederick, with such of the dear babes as can speak, present their humble duty to thee, talk much of thee, and long to see thee."*

When we consider that these letters were written with the full consciousness that they whom God had joined together would never again look upon each other's faces, they assume a hallowed character, as if they were the fond, unavailing words of a survivor, muttered half in hope and half in resignation over the ashes of the dead.

"Let us comfort ourselves with this," says this noble English matron, "though we shall never meet in this world again, yet I hope, through grace, we shall meet in heaven."†

This lady and Mrs. Godolphin, of a lineage scarcely better,—for the Middletons were a noble family, and Mrs. Goffe's ancestor, Sir Henry Cromwell,‡ entertained kings in almost royal state at Hinchinbrook,—are among the few women whose names have come down to us from the days of the second Charles, whom we regard with honor and reverence as giving promise then of that change in the social condition of their sex that is the boast of our age; a change that has added a new link, and one of the brightest, in the chain of evidence that establishes the efficacy and vitality of the Christian faith.

I shall give a brief sketch of the other regicide who availed himself of our hospitality, and then I shall leave this interesting topic to be handled with more minuteness by some writer who has greater ability to treat of it, and more leisure for the task.

---

* Noble, i. p. 624. † Noble, i. 425.

‡ The story that was circulated during the civil wars, and long afterwards, that the Cromwells were of low descent, was one of the most shameless falsehoods that ever gained credit with the world. The ignorance or bigotry of that man who could believe such a thing in this age, ought to make him a conspicuous object. In verification of this remark, the reader is referred to the Rev. Mark Noble's "House of Cromwell," a work written by a gentleman allied in feeling and in faith to the Church of England, whose minister he was, and who was not likely to lavish praise upon that family where it was not due. Why Carlyle has spoken in such unkind terms of this author I can not say. Noble has at least the merit of writing English.

Colonel John Dixwell, of the priory of Folkstone, in the county of Kent, belonged to the landed gentry of England, and was possessed of a manor and several other estates of value. He was the uncle and guardian of Sir Basil Dixwell. He was not one of those discontented spirits who desire political changes for the chances of promotion, but could make his election whether he would live upon his estates and pass his time in the elegant pursuit of letters, that offered so many attractions to a gentleman of his tastes, or whether he would engage in more stirring scenes. He preferred action to repose, and took up arms in the popular cause. He soon distinguished himself, and was an officer in the army before and during the protectorate. He bore the rank of Colonel. He was a member of parliament for Kent, sheriff of that county, and in 1649 was one of the king's judges.

At the Restoration he is supposed to have left England, but whither he fled, and what ministering angels supplied him with food, are secrets that have long since passed into oblivion. As appears by an entry made in the lost journal of Goffe, he visited his brother regicides, during their residence at Hadley, in February, 1665. Hutchinson informs us that he lived at Hadley for several years. This may be correct, but his granddaughter, Mrs. Caruthers, always believed that he only remained there six weeks. Thence he again wandered we know not whither, and secreted himself we know not where, until, under the assumed name of James Davids, he took up his abode at New Haven. What year he first came to New Haven is not known; but it must have been before 1672, for he assisted in the settlement of Mr. Ling's estate in 1673, and he had boarded in Ling's family for some time previous to the decease of his host. It was generally understood by the inhabitants that Davids was not the name of the retiring and quiet stranger who had thus come among them, but they seem to have preferred to remain in ignorance upon a subject that might have given trouble both to him and to themselves. He was known to Governor Jones, Mr. Street, Mr. Bishop, and a few other gentlemen who could safely be trusted with the secret; but to none so intimately as to the Rev. James Pierpont, who became the settled minister at New Haven in 1685. Between these two congenial spirits there existed the most faithful friendship, until it was terminated by the death of Dixwell. Their lots joined, and they were in the habit of meeting at the fence and holding long and secret interviews together, until we are told that there was a worn footpath leading from their respective houses to the place of conference. The attention of Mrs. Pierpont was arrested by this growing and secret intimacy, and she could not forbear asking her husband what he saw in that old man, that should make him so attractive. "He is a very knowing and learned man," Mr. Pierpont would reply.

While Sir Edmund Andross was in America, he visited Connecticut several times upon an errand not very welcome to the people; and probably in the course of the year 1686 he spent a Sunday at New Haven and attended public worship. Sir Edmund was a soldier, and had an extensive knowledge of the world. His practiced eye rested upon the erect figure and high features of the regicide, with an earnest gaze. His curiosity was awakened. There was in the venerable man before him, a presence and bearing that spoke of other scenes than those that then surrounded him. Not only did he appear to possess sterling traits of character, but it was evident that he had been a soldier. When the services were over, Sir Edmund made inquiry after this mysterious man. "Who is he, and what is his occupation?" he asked of one of the worshipers.

"He is a merchant who resides in town."

Sir Edmund Andross shook his head—"*I know that he is not a merchant,*" replied he, peremptorily.

Mr. Davids was not present at the afternoon service!

It would give me pleasure to trace more in detail the habits of Colonel Dixwell, and to speak more fully of his intercourse with his reverend friend, who was worthy to be the confidant of such an exile, and who was present to support him with his countenance and strength in his last hour.

He died in March, 1689, in the 82d year of his age. His remains rest in New Haven, and are in the keeping of those who honor his memory. Where are the graves of Whalley and Goffe? Do they, too, slumber in the same soil? Or are the bones of Whalley still at Hadley, and did Goffe wander away and die in a southern clime?

I believe that they all sleep together, but I will leave the antiquarian to settle this delicate question, if indeed he can add any thing to what Stiles* has written. I must bid adieu to the Regicides.

* I will here put upon record a little anecdote told me by a venerable graduate of Yale College, that may serve to illustrate at once the manners of President Stiles, and the reverence with which he was regarded by the students. "I knew him well," said my informant, "and honored him, for I hardly dared to love him. He was small in stature, but when he came up the chapel aisle, and bowed to the right and left as we all stood up to receive him, he filled up the space so that you could not put an eighteen-pence between him and the pews!"

CHAPTER XII.

KING PHILIP'S WAR.

When Colonel Nichols found himself master of the Dutch settlement, he entered upon the duties of his government and took up his abode in New York. The other commissioners proceeded to Boston and prosecuted their labors with vigor. They first made known their instructions to the general court, and gave them a statement of what would be required of them, that could not fail to surprise them, as it contained many things inconsistent with the provisions of the charter of that colony. They also insisted on a greater degree of toleration in ecclesiastical matters than the court was willing to concede.* The commissioners also set at defiance all the known rules of making contracts with the Indians, and went so far as to declare that the deed obtained by the people of Rhode Island was void for some trifling informality. They further decided that Atherton's deed of the large tract that he had bought in the Narragansett country, east of Pawcatuck river, was invalid, as there was no specified sum named in it as a consideration. These peremptory gentlemen also held courts in Warwick and Southerton, and attempted to make a new province independent of the colonies. This anomalous dependency upon the crown, instituted without a shadow of authority, was named by them the "King's Province." It embraced the entire Narragansett country, and extended westward to the Pawcatuck river, and northward to the southern line of Massachusetts.†

---

* Among the propositions made by the commissioners to the Plymouth jurisdiction was this:—"That all men and women of orthodox opinions, *competent estates*, knowledge, civil lives and not scandalous, may be admitted to the sacrament of the Lord's Supper, and their children to baptism." Hutchinson, i. 214.

† Trumbull, i. 315.

When they had made an end of this extraordinary mission to the Narragansett country, they returned to Boston, and in defiance of the Massachusetts charter, proceeded to exercise a jurisdiction there over all matters that did not accord with their views. The general court remonstrated against such arbitrary conduct, and thereby so offended the commissioners that they represented the colony to the king in a very unfavorable light.*

Connecticut, on the other hand, with her boundary lines, as she thought, forever settled, and her old troubles with New Haven and the Dutch brought to a close, and enjoying a large measure of the king's favor, went forward with smiling prospects to perfect her civil organization, and to plant new germs of population and strength in the unoccupied portions of her domain.

At the general assembly held in May 1666, it was enacted that the towns upon the river, from the north bounds of Windsor, with Farmington, to Thirty Mile Island, should be a county to be called the county of Hartford; that the country from Pawcatuck river with Norwich, to the west bounds of Hammonassett, should constitute another county, to be called New London; and that the large territory from the eastern bounds of Stratford to the western boundary of the colony, should be known as the county of Fairfield.†

For about three years a settlement had been made on the eastern bank of the Connecticut opposite Saybrook, before it was thought large enough for incorporation. But in the spring of 1667, when the general assembly met, the settlement had grown so rapidly that it was deemed best to incorporate it. It received the name of Lyme,‡ and has been the seat of the Griswolds and many other families of distinction from that day to this.

As early as May 1662, a purchase had been made of the Indians of a large tract of land called Thirty Mile Island—a valuable township lying on either bank of the Connecticut

* See Hutchinson, i. 228, 229. † Colonial Records, ii. 34, 35.
‡ Colonial Records, ii. 60.

river, about thirty miles from its mouth. The original proprietors were twenty-eight in number, and they began their settlement on the west side of the river. The plantation had grown rapidly. At the October session of the general assembly, 1668, it was incorporated under the name of Haddam.* It included the present town of East Haddam, then known by its Indian name of Machemoodus.† The first settlers, for the most part, were from Hartford, Wethersfield and Windsor. The lands that border the river are not alluvial, like those of Hartford and Glastenbury, but they are very productive, the prevailing soil being a dry, gravelly loam. There are large tracts of forest trees still standing in this town, and it presents some of the most picturesque views of the Connecticut that are to be found in its whole course. At the time of the first settlement of the town, it afforded excellent hunting and fishing ground.

In April 1644, liberty had been granted by the general court of Connecticut to Governor Hopkins and Governor Haynes to sell the district lying upon the Tunxis river called Massacoe, to such of the inhabitants of Windsor as they should select. In 1647, a new method was adopted towards instituting a plantation there, as the former one had not accomplished the object. The court therefore resolved that this same tract should be purchased by the "country," and a committee should sell it at their discretion to the planters of Windsor. This plan resulted favorably, and although the plantation was at first treated as a part of the old town of Windsor, it was so thriving and grew up to be so vigorous and hardy, that it was in May 1670, incorporated, and took the name of Simsbury.‡

As the same session, the place called "New Haven village" was made a town and received and still retains the name of Wallingford.§ The lands embraced in it had been bought by Eaton and Davenport of the Indians in 1638. The settlement was projected in 1669. It was at first a part

* Colonial Records, ii. 97. † Trumbull, i. 317. ‡ Colonial Records, ii. 127.
§ Ib. ii. 127.

of New Haven, as Simsbury was of Windsor. The Rev. Samuel Street was the first minister there; and we are told that Mr. Davenport was present and assisted in laying the foundation of the church, and, standing at the foot of the eminence where the village looks off so pleasantly upon the then fair range of woods and streams, preached a characteristic discourse from the words of Isaiah :—"My beloved hath a vineyard in a very fruitful hill."*

For about twenty years, the citizens of New Haven had been trying to establish a plantation at Paugasset, on the Naugatuck river. About the year 1653, Governor Goodyear, in company with several other gentlemen of New Haven, bought a large tract of land there of the Indians. A few feeble beginnings were made the next year towards a settlement upon this purchase; and at the October session of the general court of New Haven colony, in 1655, the inhabitants of the place presented their application to be made a town. The court granted their petition, gave them the privilege of purchasing a still larger tract, and relieved them from the burden of taxation. Richard Baldwin, at the same session of the court, was appointed moderator to call meetings and conduct the affairs of the town. But this piece of legislation was very displeasing to Mr. Prudden and the other citizens of Milford, for Paugasset had been a part of that town since it was first settled, and they looked upon the act of incorporation as a dismemberment of their own territory, and an encroachment upon their municipal jurisdiction. They therefore remonstrated against the doings of the court at its next session, and induced that body to reconsider its vote, at least so far as to order that Paugasset should remain a part of Milford, unless the respective parties should mutually consent to have the act of incorporation go into effect.†

In 1657 and 1659, a further purchase was made of the chief sagamores We-ta-na-mow and Ras-ke-nu-te, and the purchase was afterwards confirmed by the chief sachem,

* Lambert, 83; Barber's Hist. Coll. 253. † Trumbull, i. 321.

Okenuck. Some of the principal planters were Edmund Wooster, Edward Riggs, Richard Baldwin, Samuel Hopkins, Thomas Langdon and Francis French.*

Thus stood affairs with Paugasset, when in 1671 the inhabitants preferred a petition to the general assembly of Connecticut, the burden of which was their old prayer for town privileges. This oracle also responded somewhat equivocally, by determining that their southern bounds should be the north line of Milford, and that they might stretch their limits twelve miles northward, to a place called "the notch," and that as soon as they could swell their numbers to thirty, they should be incorporated.†

For four years more, the people of this little settlement held their peace, and then, in May of the year 1675, they renewed their application. They represented that they then had twelve families, and *should soon* have eleven more; that they had provided a minister, built a house for him, and made all the arrangements for permanent religious worship. This last appeal was irresistible. The general assembly forthwith gave them an independent existence, and called them Derby.‡ When we think of the feeble infancy of this eldest of inland towns in the valley of the Naugatuck, and see the thousands that now inhabit them, and listen to the hum of their spindles, the rattle of their looms, with all the myriad voices that industry and enterprise blend in a perpetual song of development and progress along the whole course of that swift mountain stream, the change seems indeed astonishing, and in any other country and with any other population in the world, would have been impossible.

A dispute of an ecclesiastical character, that will find a place in a subsequent chapter of this work, broke out in the church at Stratford, that ultimately led to the settlement of another plantation still further inland. This was the then celebrated controversy between the Rev. Mr. Chauncey and the Rev. Mr. Walker and their respective parties. It began in 1664, and was agitated before the general assembly for about

* Trumbull, i. 322. † Colonial Records, ii. 148. ‡ Ib. ii. 248, 249.

eight years. Governor Winthrop, following the good advice of Mr. Davenport to the people of Wethersfield, with a view of putting an end to this unhappy affair, proposed to Mr. Walker that he and his people should remove out of the limits of Stratford and found a new plantation by themselves, in some convenient place that they might choose. If this plan should be adopted, he himself offered to lend his influence to procure a grant of land and privileges of incorporation for a town.

In pursuance of this promise, we find that on the 9th of May 1672, there was granted to "Mr. Samuel Sherman, Lieut. William Curtis, Ensign Joseph Judson, and John Minor, themselves and associates, liberty to erect a plantation at Pomperaug.* There were a few reasonable restrictions in this grant, that I need not name in this connection. It was too late in the season for the planters who proposed to emigrate, to entertain the thought of breaking up the soil of the contemplated purchase, and planting it with corn to any great extent, yet they at once set about the task of making ready to go the next spring; and some of the most active men set out forthwith for the place, and planted a few acres of Indian corn, which they harvested in the fall, and placed in cribs made of logs. But they derived little benefit from it, for the Indians and the wild beasts ate it up during the winter.†

Early the next spring, fifteen planters of Mr. Walker's party set out with their families for the valley of the Pomperaug. They were told to follow the Pootatuck or Great River—now known as the Housatonick—"till they came to a large river flowing into it from the north. They were to follow up this stream about eight miles, when they would reach a large open plain." Upon this plain they were to stop and commence the foundations of their future town, away from the other settlements, alone in the wilderness.

With bold hearts they began their journey, but when they came to the mouth of the Pomperaug, the volume of water

* Colonial Records, ii. 177. † Cothren's Hist. of Woodbury, 35.

that it added to the deep current of the Housatonick—that main artery of Western Massachusetts and Connecticut—looked so scanty to them, that they passed it by, though not without some misgivings, and continued on until they came to the mouth of the Shepaug. The size of this stream did not satisfy them much better, but they ventured to trust themselves to it, and followed it up till they became bewildered in the gorges and mountains of the present town of Roxbury. They now saw their mistake and hastened to repair it. They resolved not to retrace their steps, but to take an easterly course, and make the best of their way to the stream that they had passed. They journeyed over the densely wooded hills until they came to a fair swelling ridge of rich forest land, now called Good Hill, that looked down upon a delightful valley threaded by a bright river, and already half subdued into good plow and meadow land by the Indians, who for generations had been preparing the way for the race before whose more systematic husbandry they were to vanish like the dew.

At sight of such a goodly land, whose acres they were so soon to part out among themselves and their fellow adventurers, the little company fell upon their knees and blessed God that their lines had fallen to them in such pleasant places. They encamped on the hill that night, and the next day they explored the valley with earnest diligence to find out the best locality where they might build their log cabins, and gather about them the first rude comforts of pioneer life. At evening they encamped under a white oak tree, far down the river, in the present town of Southbury. The locality still retains the name of White Oak, in commemoration of the event; and tradition, true to the fathers of Woodbury, still points out the spot where they slept, though the oak that they rested under has long since mouldered like them into the soft, warm earth of the valley.

All the large territory of this venerable town—the oldest in Litchfield county—was amicably purchased of the Indians. It was a very extensive region, fifteen miles in length from north to south, and ten miles in width. It had a good variety of hill and valley lands and was watered by many lively streams, that for the most part helped to make up the two large branches of the Pootatuck river that I have before alluded to.

The settlers, soon after their arrival, formed a constitution,* and signed it by a committee in due form. Their friends soon followed them, and in 1674, the plantation was incorporated under the name of Woodbury.† The township then embraced all the territory now included in the towns of Washington, Southbury, Bethlem, Roxbury, and a part of Oxford and Middlebury. These different sections were first set off and incorporated as ecclesiastical societies; but as they gradually increased in population, they were ultimately, one after another, invested with "town privileges."

I have mentioned the settlement of these several towns in this chapter, not only to preserve the chronological order of events, but because they were obliged to devote their infancy to the prevention of the sanguinary struggle that I now proceed to narrate.

It had been thought that for several years Philip, chief sachem of the Wampanoags, had used all his address to incite a general insurrection of the Indians for the purpose of exterminating the English. That jealousies were exciting in his breast against his white neighbors, of a deeply-rooted growth, is certainly true; it is also true that he kept under arms and paid frequent visits to the tribes that owed allegiance to him. This greatly alarmed the English colonies. A little while before the war broke out, the governor of Massachusetts sent an ambassador to him to demand of him

* For a copy of this constitution, and for a more minute account of the settlement of this fine old town, I must refer the reader to Cothren's "History of Ancient Woodbury,"—a work that will remain a monument of the learning and untiring perseverence of the author, as long as there shall continue to exist upon this continent a single antiquarian library that tells a true tale of the sufferings and privations of the earlier if not better days of Connecticut.

† Col. Rec., ii. 227.

why he would make war with the English, and requested him to enter into a treaty with them. "Your governor," said Philip to the messenger, "is but a subject of King Charles of England. I shall not treat with a subject. I shall treat of peace only with the king, my brother. When he comes, I am ready." If he entertained any design of making an attack upon the colonies, he evidently wished to conceal it until he had ripened his plans. The causes of this fierce war were many, and of slow but certain operation. The immediate occasion of it was as sudden as the eruption of a volcano.

Efforts had long been made by the authorities of Massachusetts, to subdue the savageness of the Indians by converting them to Christianity. No one can read the details of the life of Eliot, the Indian apostle on the main-land, or the still more touching story of the apostles of the isles, young Mayhew, whose missionary zeal was quenched in the billows of the Atlantic, and his aged father, who, by inverting the order of nature, took the place of his lost child, and taught the love and doctrines of Jesus to the tribes that would lend an ear to him, not without effect, until he was ninety-two years old; and not feel a deep reverence for the religion that can lead its teachers voluntarily to take upon themselves such sacrifices. Nor will any one deny, who has dispassionately conned over those labors of love, that they had much to do in keeping the Indians who were the recipients of them, in proper subjection. But with the exception of the few villages in the vicinity of Boston, and the Indians inhabiting Cape Cod, Martha's Vineyard and Nantucket, the influence of the Christian teacher could hardly be said to exert any control over the aboriginal mind.* Even those Indians were kept in check by the indefinable charm of the missionary's life and character, rather than by any effect wrought in their own hearts by the doctrines that he attempted to inculcate.

Beyond this narrow limit, the most benighted idolatry reigned throughout all the tribes of New England. The

* Bancroft, ii. 97; Mayhew's Indian Convert, &c.

Narragansetts were inflexible in their adherence to their old religion, and Philip with scorn rejected the gospel faith, as cowardly and unworthy of an Indian chief whose hereditary glory could only flourish amid the desolation of war. Besides, his father, Massasoit, for whom he appears to have cherished a deep filial regard—Massasoit, who had been the first to welcome the houseless exiles of Plymouth to the new world, and who had entertained Winslow and his retinue with such munificent hospitality in his royal wigwam at Pohansket—had strictly enjoined upon his sons never to allow the pride of the warriors of his tribe to be tamed by what he believed to be the enervating spirit of Christianity.*

What a change had taken place in the condition of the Wampanoags since the first arrival of the English! Then, all the wide expanse, extending for miles along the coast, with its bays, creeks, coves, and inlets abounding in fish, as well as the undulating wilderness that stretched away to the very fountains of the rivers, those avenues that led from one hunting-glade or cornfield to another, were his realm and inheritance. By gradual encroachments during his life time and the brief reign of Wamsutta, his elder son, cove, cornfield, forest and stream, had passed into the hands of the English, until, finally, upon the accession of Philip, two small tracts of land made up the only territory that the tribe could safely call its own, and presume to retain in its exclusive possession without fear of molestation. Other fields, once their own, they could still wander over, but wherever they went in the summer, they saw the black mould where once their eyes rested upon the green turf; the unsightly stump and tree-top, in place of the mighty oak and shapely pine; and the hated village, with its stone chimneys and curling wreaths of smoke, like a moving panorama ever advancing to meet them.

Can it be thought strange that all those changes that had come over the familiar features of nature, should have been so many tokens of jealousy to her sons? Once her luxuriant

* Bancroft, ii, 99.

beauty soothed their rugged natures to short intervals of repose. Now that she smiled on others with an altered mein, and averted her eyes from them, the very sight of her seemed only to inflame them with envy and madness.

When once the Indians began to hate their white neighbors, every event seemed to hasten the catastrophe. They were cited to appear before the authorities at Boston and Plymouth; they were subjected to the prejudices of an English jury, and scorned to appear and defend themselves before courts that must have been more than human if they had in all cases done them exact justice. But I am aware that the causes of this war have passed under the review of the best writers of New England, and I shall prudently retire from a field where there is little left to be gleaned.

Philip had already been ordered to give up his English weapons, and had been from time to time compelled to submit to a series of interferences and examinations that could not fail to arouse the indignation of an Indian sachem. He was also obliged to pay tribute to those whom he regarded as his inferiors.* Nor was it a mere nominal tribute that might serve as an acknowledgment of fealty to a sovereign power, but a heavy burden that enfeebled him and helped to enrich those who exacted it.

In a moment of passion, whether instigated by their chief or not I can not say, a few of his tribe waylaid the informer who had betrayed their interests, and killed him. One act of violence led to another, and the English, perhaps in no better spirit than the perpetrators of the first deed of blood, seized them, empannelled a jury, made up partly of Indians who were friendly to the English, and were doubtless known to be so, or their services would not have been put in requisition; and, after a hasty trial that hardly served the demands of decency, found them guilty and hung them.†

This was early in June 1675, and on the 24th of that month, this act, so rash and unnecessary that few will now

* Bancroft, ii. 100.

† Drake's Book of the Indians, b. iii, 23; Trumbull, i. 327.

attempt to justify it, resulted in the barbarous murder of at least eight of the English at Swansey.*

It would seem that this bloody recrimination was not the work of Philip, for he expressed the deepest regret when he heard the sad tidings that he must have felt to be the mutterings of the distant thunder that heralded the coming of the destructive storm, for which, if he had anticipated it as a future event, he was not then prepared.† Well might he deplore the prospects that this untimely quarrel held out to him. Many of the New England tribes were fast friends of the English, as well in Connecticut as in Massachusetts. Some of them were bound to them by self-interest, others by fear. Even the Narragansetts, that large nation so closely allied to his own people by blood, although Canonchet, their chief, with his warriors, had not forgotten the death of his father, Miantinomoh, were kept in awe by the success and growing power of the friends of Uncas. He could not avoid looking at the relative resources of those who were to mix in the strife. He must have seen the painful contrast between himself and his few hundred warriors, together with such allies as could be induced for the sake of vengeance to espouse a desperate cause, spending the summer in the woods and snatching the scanty means of subsistence at irregular intervals; passing the winter in lonely swamps, with magazines uncertain as the agriculture of the squaws was slender and unproductive; in forts that might easily be sought out by his enemies, and where surprise and defeat must be annihilation; I say, he must easily have seen the contrast between such an army, fighting for the most part with clubs and bows and arrows, and the formidable array that could be sent out to meet it by the united colonies of New England, who, he knew were pledged to support each other, who lived in permanent habitations, had abundance of food, were provided with the most deadly weapons, had warm clothing to screen them from the cold, and who, in all

* Drake, b. iii. 24.

† Callender's Hist. Dis. at Newport, R. I., 1738.

battles that they had waged with the native tribes, had been conquerors.

On the other hand, the English were not without apprehensions. They had always overrated the strength of the Indians, and had been kept in constant fear of some sudden surprise. In the earliest stages of their settlements, they had looked for total destruction at the hands of these half-naked savages, of whom they had a superstitious horror, such as they had of the devil, who, as they believed, loved best to dwell in deserts and solitary places, and often took the semblance of a painted savage. I do not think the emigrants were more superstitious than other Europeans of that age would have been in their situation. But there is a restless uncertainty that follows men into new and strange conditions, and often surrenders them to the dominion of ill-founded fears and false estimates of things. Hence it was that the Indian bow was seen in the sky, that the moon, when laboring under an eclipse, had still light enough left to give forth the ghostly semblance of a scalp from her darkened face.* Indeed, they had much cause for alarm. The Indians were not destitute of fire-arms, and they could handle them with the most fatal accuracy.

After it was made apparent to Philip that he could not shun the conflict, he addressed himself to it with all the earnestness and vigor of a mind naturally gifted, and now quickened into terrible activity by the force of circumstances. He sent his runners and ambassadors to every tribe that he had reason to think hostile to the English, or whose chiefs could be wrought upon by the eloquence of his orators, to unite with him. His eager allies daily poured in, ranged under their respective captains, and ready for battle; for the warriors, especially the younger ones, were tired of the long peace that had enervated their frames and relaxed their bow-strings. As they increased in numbers, they grew more and more intoxicated with the prospect of success. They flew from one settlement to another, silent as the pestilence,

* Bancroft, ii. 101.

swift as the lightning. Village after village was burned to ashes. On the 24th of June, Swansey was destroyed, and in quick succession, Taunton, Middleborough and Dartmouth lit up the fair expanse of Narragansett Bay. The English fled for their lives before their destroyers. Messengers were sent off by them, to give the alarm at Boston and Plymouth. As soon as the tidings reached the former place, the drum was beaten, and in three hours that brave old privateer, Captain Samuel Mosely, had gathered an army of one hundred and ten picked men, who were soon ready to march. The captain had about a dozen of his privateers under his command, and there were added to the effective forces of the expedition some blood-hounds, that were employed to track out the enemy in their concealment.*

A few days after that, the people of Swansey and Rehoboth sent to Boston for further aid. Accordingly, Captain Thomas Savage was appointed commander-in-chief of the expedition, who, with sixty horse and the same number of foot soldiers, marched forthwith for the camp of Philip at Mount Hope. On arriving there, the English made an attack upon him so suddenly, while he was dining, that he was obliged to run for his life. Mosely pursued him about a mile, and killed a few of his warriors. In this hasty flight, Philip lost his cap. It fell into the hands of Cornelius, a Dutchman, half soldier and half servant of Mosely, who kept it as a trophy. This was on the 29th of June. On the 1st of July, two or three more Indians were killed, and their scalps sent to Boston.† For the honor of those brave men, I wish it had never been found necessary to record an incident that seems to put the contending parties upon such an equal footing.

On the 8th of the same month, Benjamin Church and Captain Fuller, with a small company of kindred spirits, marched down to Pocasset Neck. Church had tried to dissuade the English commander from building a fort at Mount Hope Neck, as an utter waste of time. With characteristic

* See Drake's Book of the Indians, b. iii. 24. † Drake, b. iii. 26.

shrewdness he asked the question, that was then thought to be so impertinent in a volunteer who had not at that time proved his superior prowess and sagacity as he did soon after—"Why should we build a fort for nothing, to cover the people from nobody?"* It was a very significant inquiry, as it turned out that like a flock of pigeons, every Indian had left the place. He advised to pursue the Indians upon the Pocasset side. Had this advice been followed, the towns lying between Pocasset and Plymouth would have been saved from conflagration. It would be out of place, were I to record here the hot conflict that took place at Pocasset, even had it not been delineated with such minuteness by Church, whose pen was adequate to record whatever deeds of daring his sword could perform, and who, retreating backward to the boat that had saved his men from destruction, was the last man to take refuge in this ark of safety. At this battle, Philip was present and fought with great bravery. It was on this occasion that it was made known how well provided the Indians were with fire-arms, as was learned, says the lively chronicler, by their "bright guns glittering in the sun."

On the 14th of July, five people were killed at Mendon. They were probably shot dead while at their work in the field, and were as ignorant as their surviving friends of the authors of their death.

On the 2d of August, Captain Hutchinson was waylaid and killed, with several of his men, while going to treat with the Nipmucks. Captain Wheeler also had his horse shot under him, and was shot through the body, but escaped by the aid of his son, who, himself badly wounded, assisted him to mount another horse and fly.†

On the 3d of September, Captain Richard Beers was suddenly surprized while on his march with a company of thirty-six men to reinforce the garrison at Northfield; he was attacked by a large body of Indians, and after one of the most desperate struggles recorded in our annals, was

* Hist. of Philip's War, p. 6. † Captain Wheeler's Narrative, p. 1, 5.

killed with about twenty of his men.* The hill to which he fled and where he sold his life at so dear a rate, was called, in honor of the event, "Beers' Mountain."† The Indians, with a view of striking terror into the breasts of their enemies, committed shocking outrages upon the bodies of the slain. They cut off their heads and set them upon poles high in the air, and one "was found with a chain hooked into his under jaw and hung upon the bough of a tree."‡

The little garrison that Beers had been sent to relieve, suffered every extremity, and was saved only by the timely coming of Major Robert Treat, who arrived there from Connecticut two days after the battle, with one hundred soldiers, and conducted it to Hadley in safety.

By this it will be seen that Connecticut, whose soil was not invaded during the war, had nobly come up to the rescue of her sister colonies, and was found, as we shall see in the sequel, able to do them a service that they have been grateful enough to remember. Indeed, the people of Connecticut, though they looked for the approach of the enemy, and took the precaution to send troops to Stonington upon the breaking out of the war, to protect that exposed part of their frontier, bordering on the Narragansett and Nihantick country, yet almost every step that they took was in defence of the other colonies, in obedience to the articles of confederation.

The Narragansetts did not very cordially second the efforts of Philip, and yet they aided him indirectly by harboring his old men and women, and it is not unlikely that some of the more adventurous young warriors of the tribe joined in the exciting game. The chiefs, at the head of whom was Canonchet, had hitherto resisted the importunities of Philip, and refused to take any open part in the conflict. It was quite evident, however, that their sympathies were with him, and that their pretended neutrality was only preserved until they should be able to discover which scale of the trembling balance was likely to preponderate. There was another motive

* Bancroft, ii. 104; Trumbull, i. 334. † Drake, b. iii. 31.
‡ Hubbard.

than that of mere policy, for the inaction of the Narragansetts.

When the Mayflower first anchored off the coast that has since been so celebrated in song and story, the Narragansetts were the most wealthy and numerous of all the New England tribes. Even the pestilence, that had a few years before swept off such numbers of the other Indians, had passed by their wigwams and left them untouched. They lived in the south-western part of what is now Rhode Island, and all the tribes that dotted the shore along the western line of Narragansett Bay paid them tribute. Even Massasoit, the chief of the Wampanoags, was subject to them, and as a matter of course his tributaries at Shawmut and Neponsit, must in some sense have acknowledged their dominion.

The pestilence had thinned the ranks of the Wampanoag warriors to such a degree that the Narragansett sachems had easily subdued them. Hence the readiness of Massasoit and his tributaries to make an alliance with the people of Plymouth that should enable them to throw off this irksome bondage. To the alliance established between the English and Massasoit, Canonicus and Miantinomoh, though it cost them perhaps one half of their subjects, submitted in silence. The loss that the Narragansetts sustained when the Wampanoags thus achieved their independence, was hailed by Sassacus, chief sachem of the Pequots, with joy, as it weakened a powerful neighbor and rival. But Sassacus was too good a politician not to see, after watching for a little while the growth and policy of the English, that they would finally be the lords of the whole country unless they could be swept off at a single stroke. To this end he proposed to the Narragansett sachems an alliance, and offered to merge all their old quarrels in this last struggle for existence. But the Narragansetts had enjoyed a long interval of peace. Their warriors, from a disuse of their weapons and old arts, had become enervated and disinclined to them, and had turned their attention to the acquisition of wealth, and to the refinements of a more advanced stage of civilized life, than belonged to the tribes contiguous to them. The Narragansetts were then the mechanics and manufacturers of the Indians. At their principal village they made a large share of the peag that passed so current among the several nations of New England. Here, too, was manufactured pottery on a large scale, and other household utensils. Nor were they negligent of agriculture, as the supplies of corn that they furnished to those Indians who were destitute, and the vast stores that were found deposited in their humble granaries when their last hour of agony had come, bore witness.

On these accounts this ancient and generous tribe declined to connect themselves with the dangerous enterprise of Sassacus, and partly for the same cause, I doubt not, they shrunk at first from the still more adventurous designs of Philip.

Resolved to induce the Narragansetts to settle upon some fixed policy either of active alliance or of neutrality, the commissioners of the colonies came to the conclusion, immediately on the breaking out of the war, that it was best to make a treaty with them, and it was thought safest to send the army, that had gone to the relief of Swansey, forward into their country, to facilitate the negotiations by that most persuasive of all arguments, military force. Accordingly, this had been done before the fight at Pocasset Neck, and on the 15th of July, a treaty was concluded between the colonies and the six Narragansett sachems, in which it was stipulated that there should be perpetual peace between the parties, that the Narragansetts should return all goods stolen from the English, and that they should harbor neither Philip nor any of his subjects; but if any of the Wampanoags should take refuge among them, they should kill them.

On the part of the English, it was agreed that the Narragansetts should receive forty coats for Philip if they would take him and surrender him alive, and twenty for his head; for one of his warriors, two coats, and one for every head. The Indians were compelled to give hostages for the faithful performance of this harsh and forced treaty. Had they kept it long, it would have been more wonderful than that they broke it as early as they did.*

Soon after the unhappy loss of Beers and his men, it was thought best to establish a magazine at Hadley and garrison the town. At Deerfield there were three thousand bushels of wheat in the stack, and for the use of the garrison it was determined to transport it to Hadley. Captain Lathrop, with eighty-eight young men, "the flower of Essex county," was sent with teams to accomplish the work. He had loaded it in sacks and was on his way to Hadley, when, in passing through a secluded dell, and at a moment when his soldiers, without anticipating danger, were plucking and eating the ripe clusters of wild grapes that hung temptingly from the trees that shaded their path, they were attacked by a large body of Indians so suddenly and with such ferocity that, notwithstanding the desperate resistance that they made, they were nearly all cut off.† Lathrop himself was among the slain. Mosely, who was not far off with seventy men, came to the rescue. He found the woods filled with Indians. He computed their number at one thousand warriors, and so emboldened were they by their recent success, that they did not seek to hide themselves, but came out boldly and dared him to fight with them.

"Come, Mosely, come," said the insulting chiefs, "you seek Indians, you want Indians, here is Indians enough for you."

From eleven o'clock until almost night, the old privateer, aided by his daring lieutenants, Savage and Pickering, contested this bloody field with them. At last the English were compelled to retreat. With a strange mixture of savage improvidence and rage, the Indians cut open the sacks of wheat and some feather-beds that lay scattered about among the dead bodies, and strewed their contents upon the winds. Then with yells they commenced the pursuit. A woful flight it would have been, as the Indians were acquainted

* Trumbull, i. 331, 332.

† Hubbard's Narrative, 38; Bancroft, ii. 104; Trumbull, i. 334.

with all the passes of the woods, and night was setting darkly in to befriend them.*

Just at the moment when the little army seemed hurrying to an inevitable doom, again appeared that good angel, Major Treat, with one hundred Englishmen and seventy Mohegans from Connecticut. A sight of this hero—always so careless of himself, always so solicitous for others—inspired the retreating English with confidence. The tide was turned, and the Indians now sought the double covert of night and shade. They had little occasion to boast at their next war-dance, for they left ninety-six dead warriors upon the field, whose life-blood had mingled with that of their enemies to tinge the waters of the little stream that can not yet lose the name of "Bloody Brook."†

About the middle of September, the congress had ordered one thousand men to be raised for the general defense, half of whom were to be dragoons. Of these, Connecticut was ordered to raise three hundred and fifteen men for her proportion. A large part of this force was placed under the command of Major Treat, and employed in protecting the border towns in Massachusetts.‡

The Springfield Indians had for forty years kept their faith with the English, and had long withstood the solicitations of Philip. But when they saw that Northfield and Deerfield had fallen before him, and that he appeared every day to gain ground, they declared for him. Philip had resolved to attack Springfield and burn it. The Springfield Indians, therefore, on the evening before the contemplated attack upon the town, took him and three hundred of his warriors into their fort. The plot was discovered by Toto, a Windsor Indian, that very evening, and messengers were sent off in haste to inform Major Treat, who lay at Westfield with the Connecticut troops.§ The people of Springfield, however, would

---

* See Drake, b. iii. 32; I. Mather's Hist. of the War, p. 12.

† In 1835, the anniversary of the sanguinary event above referred to was held at "Bloody Brook," on which occasion an oration was delivered by his excellency Gov. Everett. ‡ Trumbull, i. 334—note. § Drake, iii. 32, 33; Trumbull, i. 335.

not believe the report, and Lieut. Cooper, who had command at Springfield, early in the morning rode out towards the Indian fort to see for himself what was the state of affairs there. The man who rode by his side was shot dead, and Cooper was mortally wounded. Although shot several times through the body, he still kept his horse, and, riding furiously to the garrison, gave the alarm.*

Philip, with his new allies, now commenced a resolute attack upon the place, and began to set fire to the buildings. Never was a people in a more hopeless condition, and never was a garrison more inadequate to the defense of a place or to protect itself from destruction, than the one that had been thus suddenly deprived of a rash but brave commander. It seemed as if nothing could avert the ruin that hung over the garrison and the town.

Meanwhile the news of Toto's disclosure reached Major Treat, and he made all haste to rescue the besieged. But for want of boats he was delayed so long in crossing the river with his army that before he reached the scene of action, the destruction of Springfield was consummated. Thirty dwelling houses, and many other buildings were already in ashes. With his usual address, Major Treat soon drove the enemy from the place, and saved the inhabitants from promiscuous slaughter. Their property he came too late to save. Major Pyncheon and Mr. Purchas lost each one thousand pounds, and the large and valuable library of Mr. Glover, the clergyman, as well as his house, was destroyed.†

On the 14th of October, the General Assembly of Connecticut met, and, in consideration of the gallant services rendered by Major Treat, gave him a public expression of thanks for his brave conduct, and appointed him commander of all the troops to be raised against the enemy.‡

The Rev. Mr. Fitch, of Norwich, had informed the Assembly that a large body of Indians was approaching that town, and had requested that troops might be sent to defend it.

* Trumbull. † Trumbull, i. 335. ‡ Colonial Records, ii. 266.

Major Treat was therefore directed to repair to Norwich at once.* This order was soon countermanded, and he was sent to the relief of Northampton. For this place he immediately set off.

Philip was now in the midst of a series of brilliant successes, that elated his spirits to a high degree, and inspired his warriors and large body of adherents with great confidence. With a body of about eight hundred warriors, he made a sudden attack upon Hadley.† So well had he contrived the assault, that every part of the place felt the shock at the same moment. But Hadley was defended by some brave officers and soldiers, who made a stand against the enemy, until the arrival of several small detachments from the neighboring garrisons. Major Treat, with his little army, hastened from Northampton and reached Hadley while the battle was yet doubtful. He opened such a deadly fire upon the Indians that they soon fled. Philip in this action sustained a severe loss, and his warriors were so disheartened by the blow that the main body of them retired to the Narragansett country. Still, little depredating parties prowled around the scattered dwellings of the frontier settlements, and did whatever harm they could to the English.‡

The intelligence given by Mr. Fitch, and coming from other sources, that the eastern border towns of Connecticut were in danger of being attacked, induced the General Assembly to take active measures for the protection of all the border towns in this colony. To this end, at the October session before alluded to, it was ordered that every county should raise sixty dragoons, well mounted, equipped and provisioned, to be ready when called to aid in the defense of the colony. Captain Avery was also placed at the head of forty Englishmen from New London, Stonington and Lyme, with as many Pequots as he should deem necessary to protect that part of the country, and to annoy the enemy at his own discretion.§

---

* Colonial Records, ii. 265. † Drake; Trumbull. ‡ Trumbull, i. 336.
§ Colonial Records, ii. 268.

Captain John Mason, worthy to bear the honored name of the hero of the Pequot war, was appointed to command another party of twenty Englishmen and the Mohegan Indians, to act with Avery, or separately from him, as was found most advisable. A company of one hundred and twenty dragoons was raised to act under the immediate command of Major Treat. It was ordered that all the towns should be fortified, and various other measures were taken to protect the weak and remote settlements.*

The persuasive arts of Philip to bring over Canonchet to his views, had by this time prevailed so far that the Narragansett chief was induced to take into his protection the Wampanoags and other tribes who sought shelter in his country. Whether Canonchet invited them, is not certainly known, but he gave them a friendly reception, and that was regarded by the colonies as a breach of the treaty that the presence of an army in his country had compelled him to sign. Besides, the congress had by this time become well satisfied that the young Narragansett warriors had violated the neutrality by actually engaging in the war, as some of them were reported to have returned home wounded. It was feared that the old Narragansett heroism was at length beginning to be roused. Of course, such a prospect could not do less than alarm the English, when they remembered that the tribe was reputed to have at least two thousand good fighting men, and one thousand muskets.† I do not believe that the Narragansetts had so many warriors, nor is it probable that they could produce a fourth part that number of fire-arms. That the English, however, believed the story, is quite certain.

Winter was fast pressing on. If these warriors should be added to those already engaged in the cause of Philip, and should be allowed to betake themselves to the woods the next summer, where they could hide themselves and waylay the English, it was feared that the horrors of war, already so bloody and devastating, would be fearfully increased. The

* Colonial Records, ii. 268. † Trumbull, i. 337.

fate of Hutchinson, Beers and Lathrop, with their parties, the desolation of villages, horrible murders, mutilations of dead bodies, unparalleled in barbarity, painful captivities, and famine worse than all, bore witness of the beginning of the struggle. What was to be its horrid end?

After some deliberation, the Congress decided to raise an army of one thousand men, to attack the Narragansetts in their principal fort in the winter. Massachusetts furnished five hundred and twenty-seven men, made up of six companies of foot and a troop of horse under command of Major Appleton. Plymouth provided one hundred and fifty-eight men, in two companies, led by Bradford and Gorham. Connecticut was to have brought into the field, as her quota, three hundred and fifteen men, but she sent three hundred Englishmen and one hundred and fifty Mohegan and Pequot Indians, in five companies, under the charge of Captains Seeley, Gallup, Mason, Watts and Marshall. This brave corps of soldiers was under the command of Major Treat. Josiah Winslow, governor of Plymouth Colony, was the commander-in-chief of the expedition.*

The utmost care was taken to provide for the wants of the troops, and after doing all that could be done to guard against the extremes of hunger, snow, cold, disease and wounds, the 2d of December was appointed to be observed as a day of fasting and prayer. Major Treat arrived with his forces at Pattyquamscot on the 17th of December, intending to have encamped in the houses that he expected to find there for his reception. But the Indians, only a day or two before, had burned all the houses and barns, and killed ten men and five women and children. He was obliged to pass the night without a roof to shelter his troops.

The next day he formed a junction with the forces from Massachusetts and Plymouth. The night of the 18th was cold and stormy, but the army was obliged to spend it in the open field, unprotected as before. On the morning of the 19th, at dawn, they began their march towards the fort

* Trumbull, i. 337.

or principal residence of the Narragansetts, that was about fifteen miles from the place where they had encamped. Mosely and Davenport, with the troops from Massachusetts, led the van, followed by Major Appleton and Captain Oliver. General Winslow, with the two Plymouth companies, marched in the center, and Major Treat brought up the rear with the Connecticut forces.*

The army marched on resolutely through the deep snow, without so much as taking any refreshment except what they snatched on the way, until about one o'clock, when they reached the fortified town of the enemy. It stood upon an eminence in the center of a vast swamp. Philip with his allies had erected palisades, and added as much as his means would permit to the natural strength of the place. But by the treachery of an Indian named Peter, who was a prisoner in the hands of the English, the fort was discovered. It is not likely that any one of the English could have found it in the immense area, half marsh, half moor, weary as they were with their march, and suffering as they did from hunger and cold. It was already one o'clock, and they had no time to lose, for night would soon overtake them, and the Indians would soon be upon them. So adroitly was the fort constructed, that it could be approached only at a single point with any chance of success, and even that avenue to it was guarded by a block-house in front, with flankers to cover a cross-fire. The island occupied by the fortification contained about four acres of ground, and is believed to have been covered, as well as the swamp that surrounded it, by primitive pine and cedar trees. This area was not only surrounded with high, strong palisades, but it was made still more formidable by a huge irregular hedge of fallen trees, about a rod in thickness. The sole entrance that appeared at all assailable was near a large tree, that had been felled in such a position as to form a bridge across a body of water that lay between the fort and the main swamp, that extended around it. This log was four or five feet above the ground.

* Hubbard's Narrative, 104.

As soon as the English army entered the swamp, they discovered an advance guard of the Indians, and immediately fired upon them. The enemy returned the fire and then retreated toward the block-house. Without waiting to form themselves, or reconnoitre the fort, the Massachusetts forces followed their officers, mounted the tree, and one by one, as many as could pass upon it, entered the fort, but were subjected to a raking fire of musketry from Philip's marksmen, who were stationed in the block-house, as well as at the points most favorable to repel them.

They were totally unable to contend against such fearful odds, and such as were not instantly killed, were driven back out of the fort. Yet the soldiers followed their gallant captains again and again over this exposed crossing-place, to make good the places of the slain, and as often the fire from the block-house and flankers, and other points of entrance, swept them away.*

As it turned out, there was a good deal more courage than prudence in this hasty attack upon the fort, for before the main body of the army could wade through the deep snow, and come up in aid of those who had attempted to force the entrance, Captains Johnson and Davenport, with many of the Massachusetts men, were beyond human help.† Major Treat, as he had brought up the rear of the whole army, was the last to reach the fatal pass. Regardless of danger, the Connecticut captains, one after another, led up their men, inspiring them with encouraging words, the last still supplying the places of those who went before them, and keeping good the numbers of undaunted hearts who fell before the increasing and murderous fire of the Indians. Three of the five Connecticut captains were killed.‡ Marshall fell dead from the fatal tree. The English had not looked for such an obstinate defence.

While this terrible slaughter of the Connecticut troops

* Holmes, ii. 376; Hutchinson, i. 271; Drake, b. iii. 34, 35; Trumbull, i. 338, 339.

† Hutchinson, i. 271. ‡ Holmes, ii. 376.

was going on, Captain Mosely forced an entrance through or over the hedge where it was weakest, and attacked the Indians in the rear—opening a fire upon their backs as they stood crowded closely together, with large muskets loaded with pistol bullets. The Indians now fled from their first position, and took refuge in their wigwams, and in every nook that afforded them a screen behind which to discharge their shot.

"They run, they run," shouted the English captains, as they cheered on their men.*

At this critical moment fell Captains Gallup and Seeley, both shot dead in front of their respective companies. About this time Mason received a wound that proved to be mortal. At last the English gained the center of the fort, and after a long and bloody conflict, put the Indians to flight. With frightful yells, they flew into the surrounding thickets, leaving the fort in the hands of the English, who, at a dear rate, had bought the victory. There were six hundred wigwams within the fort, containing ample shelter for four thousand human beings. There were also large stores of corn and immense quantities of wampum, and of those utensils that were wrought in such abundance and with such skill by the Narragansetts.†

There had been three hundred Indian warriors slain,‡ and others who were wounded died in the cold cedar swamp, whither they had taken refuge. About the same number were taken prisoners, besides three hundred women and children, who afterwards drank to the bitter dregs the cup of captivity and sorrow. Captain Church, who was present as a volunteer, begged that the fort and provisions might be spared for the shelter and supply of the enemy, and especially for the protection of the wounded. But other counsels pre-

* See Drake, b. iii. 35.

† Hutchinson, i. 272, 273; Trumbull, i. 339; Bancroft, ii. 105.

‡ Some authorities place the number as high as seven hundred. The number given above, however, is that contained in a letter in Hutchinson (i. 233,) attributed to Major Bradford, who was a participant in the fight.

vailed. The village was burned to ashes, and all the valuable stores that it contained, with the old men, women, and children, whose number history has never recorded, and whose agony, though brief, was only heard in its full significance by the ear of a mercy that is infinite.

What a commentary did that winter scene—the crackling flames melting the snow from the cedars and pines, and scorching their green leaves, the blackened bodies half consumed, the shivering English soldier whose blood was staunched more by the numbing touch of cold than by the surgeon who was himself paralyzed, the poor Indian fugitives, none the less miserable that they were savages, cowering unprotected beneath the bushes or to the leeward of the snow-drift, to shun the wrath of such a sky as belongs to New England in the dead months of the year—what a commentary upon the cruelty, the misery of war!

Six of the English captains had been killed, one had received his death-blow, and eighty of the soldiers had been either killed or mortally wounded. One hundred and fifty others, who had been injured in the action, recovered.* But the sufferings of the army might be said only to have just begun. Night was closing around them; the only screen that could have been afforded them in that desolate waste, was the comfortable fort, with its six hundred houses, that they had burned in spite of the wise admonitions of Church. They had marched fifteen miles since day-break, and fought a battle that had lasted for three full hours. It would be destructive to them were they to encamp upon the upland or upon the moor. There was then no alternative. Weary as they were, they must again take up their line of march, and spend the night as they had spent the morning, in wading through the snow.

Just as the sun was going down, they gathered up their two hundred dead and wounded men, and set out on their return-march to head quarters, a distance of about eighteen miles. It was a night never to be forgotten by those who

* Trumbull, i. 340.

survived it; a cold, stormy night. The blinding snow pursued them all the way, falling in vast quantities over the undistinguishable woods and swamps, obeying the impulses of the howling blast that ranged over the wide, desolate scene.

It was past midnight when the troops reached their destination. It would be idle for me to attempt to delineate the sufferings of the wounded soldiers. A part of them, as the night and storm advanced, became insensible. The pulses grew feebler, the cheek grew paler, and the frame, so languid and pliable at first to the grasp of those who bore it, stiffened into its final repose.

Of this army of one thousand men, at least four hundred were unfit for duty. The Connecticut troops were more disabled than the others,* partly because they had entered the fort when the fire was deadliest, and partly from their previous fatigue in marching from Stonington to Pattyquamscot, and then passing the night in the open air. Some of the soldiers were frozen to death. Of the three hundred Englishmen from our little republic, eighty were killed and wounded—twenty men in Seeley's company, an equal number in Gallup's, fourteen under the command of Watts, nine of Mason's, and fourteen of Marshall's men. Of these, about forty were either killed on the field or died of their wounds. Thus half of the loss of the fatal day, that broke the pride of Philip and laid waste the city of the Narragansetts, fell upon Connecticut.† Major Treat, who had been in the hottest part of the battle, narrowly escaped death from a bullet that passed through the rim of his hat. The thanksgivings that went up to heaven from the lips of our people, were mingled, as they always have been when our State has participated in deeds of valor, with the wailings of widowhood and the cries of orphan children. In the eloquent words employed by the General Assembly to commemorate the event,

* See Gov. Dudley's letter in Hutchinson, i. 274.

† Note in Trumbull, i. 341.

"Our mourners, over all the colony, witness for our men, that they were not unfaithful in that day."*

Under these circumstances, Major Treat thought it necessary to return home and recruit his troops.† Indeed, this was the only course that he could have adopted, unless he had intended to sacrifice one half of the remainder of his men.

The English now thought the opportunity would be favorable to establish peace with Philip, and various proposals were made. These overtures were answered by the burning of Lancaster and Medfield, and by the killing of Captains Pierce and Wadsworth.‡

In February 1676, a large number of Connecticut volunteers, belonging for the most part to New London, Norwich, and Stonington, were formed into companies under Major Palmes, Captain George Denison, Captain James Avery, and Captain John Stanton, further to prosecute the war against the Indians. With them were associated some Mohegans under Onecho, a son of Uncas, some Pequots under their chief, and about twenty Narragansetts belonging to Ninigret, who, by keeping his neutrality, doubtless saved his life. These companies ranged the Narragansett country from one end to the other in quest of the enemy. Nor did they work in vain. Canonchet, or, as he is now commonly known in history, Nanuntenoo, the son of Miantinomoh, and the chief sachem of the Narragansetts, had escaped the destruction of his principal town, and had still many brave fighting men with him. Some time in March, he had ventured down from the north to Seekonk, near the seat of Philip, to get seed-corn with which to plant the towns upon Connecticut river that had been deserted by the English. Denison, who had been ranging the woods with his party for several days in search of the enemy, came suddenly upon a trail near Blackstone river, and soon learned from a squaw whom he took captive, that Nanuntenoo was in his wigwam near the

* See note in Trumbull, i. 341. † See Hubbard's Ind. Wars, 135, 144.
‡ Holmes, ii. 378, 379.

river. Denison lost no time in taking measures to secure him. The chief was apprised of his danger, as the English approached, and ran for his life towards the river whither Catapazet, the chief who commanded Ninigret's men, himself a Narragansett, and who thought he recognized the fugitive, pursued him with all speed. Other Indians and English, who were swift-footed, followed close behind. Finding himself hard pressed, the sachem threw off first his blanket and then his silver-laced coat that had been presented to him at Boston. This garment was well known, and as there could now be no doubt of his personal identity, the pursuers took courage and ran with still greater eagerness. In the company was a Pequot who outran all his companions, and who gained so fast upon Nanuntenoo, as he was flying along the bank of the river, that the chief was compelled to plunge into the current before he had reached the ford. Even as it was, he would probably have escaped, had not his foot slipped from the smooth surface of a stone, and in falling brought his gun under water. So much time was lost by this accident, that also took away the power of defending himself, that the Pequot came upon him and seized him without difficulty.

Like his father, whose fate he must have remembered, Nanuntenoo made no resistance, and like him scorned to ask for a life that he knew was forfeit.

Robert Stanton came up, and with the forwardness of youth ventured to ask him some questions. At first the chief looked at him in silence, and then regarding his beardless face with hereditary scorn, he replied in broken English, "You too much child; no understand matters of war. Let your brother or chief come. Him I will answer." He kept his word.*

When his life was tendered him on condition that he and his nation would submit, he rejected the offer with indignation. Then they threatened him with death if he failed to fall in with their terms. He calmly replied that killing him

* Trumbull, i. 344, 345; Bancroft, ii. 106.

would not put an end to the war. Some of them taunted him with the violation of his treaty, and with the boast that he had made that "he would burn up the English in their houses, and that he would not deliver up a Wampanoag or the paring of a Wampanoag's nail." "Others," said the chief, quietly, " were as forward for the war as myself, and I desire to hear no more about it."

Denison took him to Stonington. A council of war was held, and it was decided that he must be shot. When the sentence of this court-martial of volunteers was made known to him, his only answer was, "I like it well. I shall die before my heart is soft, or I have said any thing unworthy of myself."† I find in the history of Greece and Rome no record of heroism more striking, nor a dying speech more in consonance with the philosophy of self-sustaining paganism, than the last words of Nanuntenoo. As his father was killed by Uncas, so the son of Uncas superintended the execution of the son of Miantinomoh.

Thus perished the last of a line of monarchs, the noblest among the New England nations, and thus another tribe, the best and the most cultivated as well as the most powerful that inhabited the northern Atlantic coast, was swept away. The rest of the details of Philip's war are foreign to my purpose, and I shall here take my leave of the chief of the Wampanoags.

One important feature of this war, however, remains to be delineated. At the election that took place on the 11th of May 1676, William Leete was chosen governor, and Robert Treat deputy governor. To carry on the war the Assembly voted to raise a standing army of three hundred and fifty men, who, with the friendly Indians, were to defend the country and harass the enemy.

Major John Talcott was appointed to the chief command of these forces; the Rev. Gershom Bulkley surgeon, and good Mr. James Fitch chaplain. The surgeon and chaplain were made a part of the council of war. Norwich was made

---

* Trumbull; Bancroft.

the first general rendezvous of the army, and from this place Talcott marched about the first of June with some two hundred and fifty Englishmen and two hundred Mohegans and Pequots, towards the Wabaquasset country, in quest of the enemy. But not an Indian was to be found, though they searched the woods faithfully in the old retreats of the savages. The wigwams were all deserted, and the fortifications made of the tops of trees were without a warrior to man them. At Wabaquasset, Talcott destroyed the fortress and about fifty acres of corn, and on the 5th of June marched on to the country of the Nipmucks. There he killed nineteen Indians and took thirty-five prisoners. He then marched to Brookfield, and thence to Northampton. The army suffered fearfully from fatigue and famine before it reached Northampton, and that march was long known to the people of our colony as the "long and hungry march."

On the 12th of June a furious attack was made upon Hadley by about seven hundred Indians. Talcott soon arrived and saved the garrison and the town. The Indians were driven off with such promptness that they were prevented, as is believed, from making attempts upon other towns that they had in their hearts devoted to destruction.

Some time after this the Massachusetts forces arrived and joined Talcott's troops. The army then scoured the woods upon both banks of the river, destroying the dwellings of the fugitive enemy, breaking up their fisheries, and despoiling them in every way that they deemed likely to take from them the power to do mischief. Talcott went as far as Deerfield Falls and then returned. After he had spent about three weeks in that part of Massachusetts, he departed with his army through the wilderness towards the Narragansett country. On the 1st of July he came near a large body of Indians and took four of them.

Two days after he surprised the main body of the enemy on the border of a large cedar swamp, and so skillfully did he dispose his forces and conduct the attack that he killed and took prisoners a large number. The rest fled into the swamp.

This Talcott surrounded, and after a fight of about three hours killed and took captive one hundred and seventy-one Indians. In this hard-fought battle thirty-four Indian warriors were killed, and after the action, ninety captives, who were fighting men, shared the same fate. Between forty and fifty women and children were preserved unhurt.

That same day he marched his army to Providence and made an attack upon the Indians on the Neck, and afterwards upon those at Norwich. In these two places he killed and captured sixty-seven. Thus, in a little more than a month, he had killed and taken two hundred and thirty-eight hostile Indians, and had done much in other respects to cripple the resources of Philip.

On the 5th of July, Talcott set out on his return march, and before he reached Connecticut took sixty more prisoners. If we add to the killed and those taken alive by this gallant officer, those also who had fallen into the hands of the volunteers since the 1st of April of that year, we shall find that four hundred and twenty of the Indians had been subdued by Connecticut alone, in the space of about three months. When we add to this the depredations made upon the country of Philip's allies, the destruction of the houses and growing crops, and the carrying away of their corn, beans, and other valuables that stood them in the stead of money, we shall be able to form some adequate conception of the aid rendered by our little colony to her distressed neighbors.

After his return, Major Talcott waited but a little while to recruit his men, and then stationed himself at Westfield. While there, he discovered a large party of the enemy flying towards the west. He pursued them, and on the third day, about midway between Westfield and Albany, he came up with them. They were lying upon the western bank of the Housatonick river, in a state of fancied security, without dreaming of the approach of the English.

It was late in the afternoon when Talcott became aware of his proximity to them, and he deemed it unsafe to attack them at that hour. He therefore retreated silently to a suitable distance and caused his army to pass the night under arms. As the dawn drew on he ordered his troops to form in two divisions, the one to cross the river below the Indians, and advance upon them from the west; the other to creep stealthily up to the eastern bank, and there lie in ambush until they should hear the gun that was to be fired by those who had crossed the river, as a signal that the savages were approaching within the range of their shot. When they heard this gun they were to open a deadly fire upon the Indians. This stratagem would have been attended with a fearful destruction of life had it not been partly defeated by an accident that the English could not have foreseen. A single Indian had left his fellows in a profound sleep, and had stolen down the river to catch fish. As the party upon the west bank was advancing to surprise his slumbering companions, he saw them and cried out in alarm "Owanux, Owanux!" He was instantly shot dead by an English soldier. This solitary musket shot was of course mistaken by the other party for the expected signal gun. Too hastily, therefore, for the success of the ambuscade, they arose and fired upon the startled Indians as they fled towards them. But the savages soon discovered their danger, and while the English who were coming up from the rear were too remote to do them much injury, they turned from the destructive bullets of the ambushed party, and ran along the bank of the river for their lives. Still, many of them fell victims to the enterprise. Nothing but the dense growth of the trees and bushes saved them from a total annihilation. The sachem of Quobaug (Brookfield) was killed and twenty-four other warriors. There were forty-five in all who were either killed or taken prisoners. Major Talcott in this war was second only to Major Treat in his practical, effective efforts to reduce the power of Philip and hasten his downfall.

CHAPTER XIII.

ANDROSS ATTEMPTS TO LAND AT SAYBROOK.

As a previous declaration of war had been made in England against the Dutch, that had caused much alarm in the colonies, and had induced the mother country to make common cause with the people of New England, all interference on the part of the government with our civil affairs was for a time suspended. But no sooner were friendly relations again established between the two contending powers, than the old jealousy that had so long existed in England, against our growing strength, began to be revived. Private interest and ambition also seconded the views of the government.

The Duke of York, who was by no means satisfied with the tenure by which he held his property in America, on the 29th of June, 1674, procured a new patent, granting the same territory named in the old one. He resolved to follow up his title thus acquired, by possession, and immediately gave to Major, afterwards Sir Edmund Andross, a commission to be governor of New York and all the territories in those parts.

With this paper to vouch for whatever arbitrary thing he might think proper to do, Andross sailed to New England.

The boundaries of Connecticut, that had been so carefully defined by the king's commissioners ten years before, were totally disregarded by Major Andross, and he now laid claim, by virtue of his master's new patent, to all that part of Connecticut lying west of Connecticut river.* Unless this outrageous demand should be acceded to, he threatened the colony with an invasion. The astonishment and indignation of the people of the colony, at this disregard of their own

* J. H. Trumbull's Colonial Rec., ii. 569; also see Doc. Hist. of N. York, iii. 78.

prior grant, ratified by a solemn award, knew no bounds. Although the war with Philip was impending, and the whole country was in a state of preparation for the uncertain issue, yet it was resolved by the governor and council of Connecticut, not to submit to a dismemberment of the colony.

It was soon made known at Hartford that Andross was about to land at Saybrook, and that he intended, after having taken possession of that important post, to proceed to Hartford, New Haven, and other places, until he had made himself ready to suppress the government of the people, and establish his own upon a firm footing.

As soon as the tidings reached Hartford, that Andross was approaching the coast, detachments of militia were ordered to repair to Saybrook and New London as speedily as possible.* Captain Thomas Bull was appointed to the command of the garrison at Saybrook. The preparations made to oppose his landing with a hostile force were as vigorous as those against Philip, or the armament that had been raised against the Dutch, during the war that had then just been brought to a close.

On the 9th of July, the inhabitants of Saybrook, who were ignorant as well of the intended invasion as of the measures taken by the government to resist it, saw with alarm an armed fleet in the sound, making all sail for the fort.† Thus taken by surprise, they were at first thrown into much confusion, and were undetermined what they should do. But without instructions, as they were, from Hartford, they were not long in recovering their self-possession. They determined to meet the emergency manfully, and treat the invaders as enemies.

True to themselves and the popular government that they had sworn to support, the gallant militia, who scarcely needed to be officered, rallied as one man to defend the fort. Bull with his company soon arrived, and with great alacrity aided them in completing the enterprise that had been so nobly begun.

* Holmes, i. 368; Trumbull, i. 328; Bancroft, ii. 404.

† Bancroft, ii. 403; Trumbull, i. 328.

Meanwhile, a letter that Robert Chapman had written to the governor and council at Hartford, informing them of the approach of the armed force, had received a very characteristic answer, that could leave no doubt in the mind of Captain Bull what would be expected of him. Never did a state paper issue in the name of a colonial government, that was couched in language expressive of more loyalty or tender regard for the king's honor. Indeed, the name and interest of "his majestie," if we follow the phraseology of the document, make up the principal burden, and even the people of Connecticut are lost sight of in their zeal to maintain the royal prerogative.

The letter is addressed to Mr. Chapman and to Captain Thomas Bull, and begins with the announcement that intelligence has just been received at Hartford of the arrival of two sloops of war from New York, bringing troops under Major Andross, who has been so considerate of the wants of the garrison and the town, as to pay them a visit with a view of lending them aid against the *Indians*. These gentlemen are then instructed to inform Major Andross that Connecticut has no occasion to trouble him in this matter, as she has already provided for the defense of her own territory; but to make him acquainted with the fact that Rhode Island is the seat of war, and that he is desired to repair thither without delay, "for the relief of the good people there, who are in distress."

After making this charitable provision for the protection of their neighbors, by generously proposing to make every sacrifice in their favor, the governor and council, without intimating a suspicion that the visit of Andross could have arisen from any other than the promptings of a humane desire to save the colony from destruction, go on to say that if the Major shall desire to go ashore with any of his gentlemen for refreshments, they are to be treated with all due respect.

Here, for some mysterious purpose not named in the letter, those to whom it was addressed were to make a decided stand. "And if so be those forces on board should endeavor to land at Saybrook, you are in his majesty's name to forbid their landing. Yet if they should offer to land, you are to wait their landing and to *command* them to leave their arms *on board;* and then you may give them leave to land for necessary refreshing, peaceably, but so that they return on board again in a convenient time." Then kindling into an irrepressible flame of loyalty, and again losing sight of the republic in their zeal to protect from insult the sacred banner of the British empire, they earnestly add, "and you are to keep the king's colors standing there under his majesty's lieutenant, the governor of Connecticut; and if any *other colors* be set up there, you are *not to suffer them to stand.* And in general, whatsoever shall be done or attempted in opposition to the government here established by his majesty, you are to declare against, oppose and undo the same."

Lest these general instructions should be liable to misconstruction from not being sufficiently explicit, they particularize as follows:

"If they make proclamations, you are to protest against them; if they command the people to yield obedience to them, you are to forbid it, and to command them to continue in obedience to his majesty and his government here established; and if they should endeavor to set up any thing, you may pull it down; and if they dig up any trenches, you are to fill them up; if they say they *take* possession, you are to say you *keep* possession for his majesty."

After thus giving expression to their enthusiastic love of their monarch, as well in detail as in general, their habitual caution comes to the rescue; but it will be seen from the context passage, that there lurks beneath the spirit of concealment, a terrible and deadly opposition.

"You are, in his majesty's name, required to avoid striking the *first blow;* but if they begin, then you are to *defend* yourselves."

In the whole body of this letter, not a word is said of the claims of the Duke of York, nor is it so much as intimated that the governor and council are aware of the real intentions of the invader. The postscript alone touches upon this dangerous ground. "You are to keep your instructions to yourselves, and give no copies of it. If Major Andross desire *a treaty*, let him present what he desires in that respect."*

On the 9th of July, the next day after the date of this letter, the General Assembly convened at Hartford, and proceeded forthwith to draw up a declaration, protesting in the strongest terms against the conduct of Major Andross. This paper, unlike the letter of instructions sent to Bull, is very explicit in its terms. After a preamble, reciting the horrors of Indian warfare, and the critical condition of the colony, and after alluding to the king's charter as the basis of their political existence, the remonstrants say, "We can do no less than publicly declare and protest against the said Major Edmund Andross, and these his illegal proceedings; also against all his aiders and abettors, as disturbers of the peace of his majesty's good subjects in this colony; and that his and their actions in this juncture tend to the encouragement of the heathen to proceed in the effusion of blood." They add further that, "they shall unavoidably lay at his door," whatever evil consequences may flow from his conduct, and that they will use their utmost power and endeavor, expecting therein the assistance of Almighty God, to defend the good people of this colony from the said Major Andross' attempts." After commanding all the people, in the king's name, to resist the demands of Andross, and on no account to obey him or lend him any countenance, in any proceedings contrary to

* I cannot doubt for a moment as to the authorship of this remarkable letter. Indeed, there was but one man then living in New England who could have framed it. The masterly use of language, the adroitness with which conclusions so startling are drawn from premises so innocent, its politeness, its firmness, its childlike transparency of language giving forth a light that can neither dazzle nor mislead—in a word, its exquisite diplomatic touch—betrays the hand of John Winthrop in every line. The whole letter may be found in vol. ii. of J. H. Trumbull's Colonial Records, pp. 334, 335.

the charter and the laws of the colony, the protest closes with the loyal words, "God save the king."*

This protest was approved by every member of the General Assembly, and sent off immediately by express to Saybrook, with instructions to Bull to propose to Major Andross that the matter in dispute should be referred to commissioners, to meet at any place in the colony that he might choose.†

Early on the morning of the 12th of July, Major Andross begged that he might be permitted to go on shore and have an interview with the ministers and principal officers. This request was granted, and he accordingly landed with his suite. While this was going on, the express arrived from Hartford with the protest and letter of instructions. With the blunt courtesy that was befitting a man of his straightforward nature, Captain Bull, accompanied by his officers and the principal gentlemen of the town, met the major on the beach and told him that he had just received orders to make a treaty with him, and told him of the terms.

The object of Andross in going ashore, was to intimidate the officers and the people, by reading the king's new patent to the Duke of York, and the Duke's commission to himself under that grant. He, therefore, with much haughtiness, rejected the proposal made by the General Assembly, and as he and his retinue had now come within hearing distance of Bull and his companions, he commanded his clerk to read aloud the two papers that gave him his pretended authority.

Little was Major Andross aware of the character of the man with whom he was dealing. With an authority that seemed to set at defiance both king and duke, Captain Bull addressed himself to the clerk and imperiously commanded him to forbear. Balked in his first attempt, the secretary attempted to persist in the execution of his office.

"Forbear!" reiterated the captain, in a tone that even Andross himself did not think it safe to oppose.

---

* Colonial Records, ii. 261, 262. † Trumbull, i. 330.

Major Andross, with all his faults, was not without fine traits of character, and was struck with a soldier's admiration at the coolness and intrepidity of the captain.

"What is your name?" he asked.

"My name is Bull, sir," was the prompt answer.

"Bull!" responded the governor, "It is a pity that your horns are not tipped with silver."*

The governor saw that it was idle to attempt to overawe the officers or the inhabitants, and that they would overpower him with numbers should he resort to coercion.

With this equivocal compliment to the captain, and with a bitter remark on the ingratitude of the colony and the meagerness of their protest, he took a hasty leave of them. With a politeness that could hardly have been agreeable to him, the militia of the town escorted him to his boat. In a few hours, his sloops were out of sight.†

The General Assembly regarded these proceedings of Andross not only as illegal, but as a marked insult to the colony. After having read a detailed account of what had happened at Saybrook, they sent a declaration to the several towns, under the seal of the colony and signed by its secretary, to be published to all the inhabitants. They say that "the good people of his majesty's colony of Connecticut have met with much trouble and molestation from Major Edmund Andross' challenge and attempts to surprise the main fort of said colony, which they have so rightfully obtained, so long possessed and defended against all invasions of Dutch and Indians, to the great grievance of his majesty's good subjects in these settlements, and to despoil the happy government by charter from his majesty granted to themselves, and under which they have enjoyed many halcyon days of peace and tranquillity." The declaration further informs the people that the Assembly had desired Mr. Winthrop and Mr. Richards, who were about to visit England, to carry with them a copy of all the papers relating to the

* Trumbull, i. 330. † Trumbull.

invasion of Andross, and anticipate, by a full narrative of the affair, any false statements that he might make at court to the prejudice of the colony.*

The colony, in the midst of her successes, was destined to suffer the keenest anguish. One after another, her patriarchs had departed from her borders or found a refuge in her bosom. Winthrop was now to follow them. He had been chosen a commissioner to represent her in the Congress of the United Colonies in May 1676, and, true to her interests in age as he had proved himself in his youth, he had gone to Boston early in the spring of 1676 to discharge the trust, and to lend to New England in her darkest day, the light of his counsels. There he was taken suddenly ill, and, after a brief period of sickness, died.†

It is difficult for me to consider him as an individual character, so inseparably is his bright image blended with that of the colony herself during the most doubtful and at the same time most glorious period of her existence. An ideal of humanity, setting forth upon a journey that was to involve the exploration of paths untried and wild; too full of hope long to remain distrustful of the future; too sincere a believer in the revealed will of God to doubt the comprehensiveness and unfailing resources of his providence; too intelligent and large-hearted for bigotry on the one hand; on the other, too keenly alive to the thrill of those finer fibers of the soul that can alone ennoble man's nature and elevate his reason into a faculty that may be called divine, ever to become a sceptic; a fair ideal, rather than an individual man with the frailties of our race binding him to the earth with chains, does he sometimes present himself to my contemplation. Whenever we would revive in our breasts the spirit of devotion to the cause of liberty, that better liberty setting bounds to itself that the very laws of its being will not permit it to pass; whenever we hallow with a sigh some half-forgotten memory of those early days when the sons of

* Colonial Records, ii. 263, 264.

† Mather's Magnalia, b. ii. p. 145; Holmes, i. 387.

Connecticut did not blush to own their parentage; when we see rash youth jostling gray-haired age aside, and hot impulse blinding the eyes of wisdom with the dust of his chariot-wheels as he drives swiftly past on his destructive career—then, if at no other moment, the strong bright eye, the benevolent face, with its indescribable blending of caution and enthusiasm, reveals to us the Winthrop of the old time, such as the poets and painters of a day yet to come will delineate him. But this is not my task, and I return to give a brief account of the Winthrop of history.

John Winthrop, of Connecticut, was the oldest son of the Hon. John Winthrop, governor of Massachusetts, and was born at Groton in England, in the year 1605.* He was not

* The Winthrops are said to have come from Northumberland, whence they removed into Nottinghamshire and settled in a little village which still bears the name of Winthrop, near Newark. From this place the ancestors of the American branch of the family went to London. As this has been one of the most eminent families in New England, we here insert the Winthrop genealogy in a single line.

1. Adam Winthrop, a lawyer of distinction, soon after the dissolution of the monasteries by Henry VIII., was lord of the manor of Groton, county Suffolk, where he died, and was buried Nov. 12, 1562.

2. Adam Winthrop (his son) was also bred to the law; married Anne Browne, 20 Feb. 1579. His burial appears upon the register at Groton, 29 March, 1623.

3. John Winthrop, Governor of Massachusetts, was born in Groton, 12 Jan. 1588; came to New England in 1630; died in Boston, 26 March, 1649. He married (1st) Mary, daughter of John Forth, Esq., of Great Stanbridge, Essex, who died 1615; (2d) Thomasine, daughter of Wm. Clopton, who died 1616; (3d) Margaret, daughter of Sir John Tindale, Kt., who died 1647.

4. John Winthrop, F. R. S., Governor of Connecticut, was born in Groton, 12 Feb. 1606. His first wife was Martha Fones; his second, Elizabeth Read, daughter of a widow whom the famous Hugh Peters afterwards married. He died April 5, 1676.

5. Fitz John Winthrop, F. R. S., Governor of Connecticut, was born in Ipswich, Mass., 14 March, 1639; died in Boston, 7 Nov. 1717. 5. Wait Still Winthrop (brother of Fitz John) was Chief Justice of Massachusetts; he died in Boston about 1688.

6. John Winthrop, F. R. S. (son of Wait Still,) born in New London, 26 Aug. 1681; married Anna, daughter of Gov. Joseph Dudley. He died 1 Aug. 1747.

7. John Still Winthrop, born 15 Jan. 1720; died 6 June 1776. His wife was Jane, daughter of Francis Borland, of Boston, and granddaughter of the

only the eldest son, but he was also the darling and idol of his father's heart, who educated him at Trinity College, Dublin. I am able to find in the annals of that day, nothing more lovely and confiding than the letters written by this excellent father to a son of such promise that every eye turned towards him with interest while the youth was still growing in stature and wisdom, and while his character was blossoming with sentiments that afterwards ripened into great thoughts and noble actions. Even if the elder Winthrop had not been a historical character, we should seem to know him as a kindly neighbor and friend from the charming tone of these letters. Other fathers, in writing to their absent sons, usually pen their doubts and fears, and qualify their expressions of love with those of parental solicitude. Most fathers dictate to their sons what course to pursue when absent from home, and assume a demeanor and show of patriarchal authority. But Winthrop takes a different course. He opens his whole heart to the boy as a lover would whisper his passion in the ear of his betrothed. He keeps nothing from his favorite. His large family, his many expenses, the engrossing cares of business, the anxieties that his other children give him, are all told with the charming simplicity of affection. At the same time he bids him spend freely whatever money his circumstances appear to indicate as requisite to maintain the position of a gentleman's son at a university.

"I purposed," he says in one of these letters, "to send you by this bearer such books as you wrote for; only Aristotle I can not, because your uncle Fones is not at London to buy it, and I know not whether you would have Latin or Greek. I purpose also to send you cloth for a gown and

---

Hon. T. Lindall, of Salem, Judge of the Superior Court and Speaker of the Provincial Legislature.

8. Thomas Lindall Winthrop, LL.D., Lieut. Governor of Massachusetts, was born 6 March 1760; died 22 Feb. 1841.

9. Robert Charles Winthrop, LL.D., of Boston, Speaker of the United States House of Representatives; United States Senator.

suit; but for a study gown, you had best buy some coarse Irish cloth."*

It may be interesting to the reader to know more about the history of the suit of clothes and the gown, that were both in danger of being outgrown by this college youth, who, as we shall see by the following extract from another communication, had not yet attained his full stature: "You may line your gown with some warm baize, and *wear it out*, for else you will soon *outgrow* it, and if you be not already in a frieze jerkin I wish you to get one speedily; and howsoever you clothe yourself when you *stir*, be sure you keep warm when you *study* or *sleep*. I send you no money, because you may have of your uncle what you need."†

It does not require a very lively imagination in any one who is familiar with the Winthrop portrait, to figure to himself the appearance of the future governor of Connecticut poring over the pages of Aristotle of a winter evening, protected from the cold by that warm baize lining and frieze jerkin. The youth may be fairly presumed to have followed his father's advice and worn out the gown at the elbows long before he outgrew it. The appellations, "loving son," "son John," "well beloved," and other expressions of endearment, abound in all these communications, not only during the young man's stay at the university, but down to the time when death separated them.

After he had finished his academical course with great honor, in order that nothing might be wanting to develop his faculties, young Winthrop was sent, (a rare accomplishment in those days,) to make the tour of Europe. He accordingly traveled in France, Germany, Holland, Italy and Turkey. Thus, before he had entered upon his twenty-fifth year, he was a thorough scholar, was possessed of liberal

* Savage's Winthrop, i. 404. In the Appendix to the first volume of Winthrop's History, Mr. Savage has given sixty-four family letters, nearly all of which were written by the elder John Winthrop to his son.

‡ Ib., i. 405.

views, a deep knowledge of the world in its varied aspects, and the most elegant and courtly manners.

In 1631, he sailed for the wilderness of New England,* and was chosen a magistrate of Massachusetts. He soon after went back to England, but in 1635 returned, as I have informed the reader in another place, with a commission to build a fort at the mouth of the Connecticut river, and to hold the place of governor of that river. In 1651, he was chosen into the magistracy of Connecticut. In 1657, he was elected governor of the colony, and in 1658, he was made deputy governor; in 1659 he was again placed at the head of the magistracy.†

The rest of his history I have already attempted to set forth, and can add little to what I have said. His life and character may be gathered from his state papers, his letters, his counsels and his deeds. He was one of the first chemists of his age, was an excellent physician, and as a diplomatist and statesman he had no superior in his day.

Though his bones repose in a sister colony, whither he had gone in the service of Connecticut, yet his heart was hers to its last beat. It must have taken away something from the bitterness of death, that though away from home he was not among strangers, and that friendly hands would place his remains in the same tomb with those of his honored father, to await the signal that they both believed would burst the bonds of the sepulchre, and leave them free in the enjoyment of a new intercourse, more spiritual, more pure and delightful than the old.

---

* See Mather's Magnalia, b. ii. 143; Trumbull, i. 345.

† Colonial Records.

CHAPTER XIV.

ADMINISTRATION OF ANDROSS.

At the close of Philip's War, Connecticut found herself deeply involved in debt. She had indeed kept that dangerous enemy from her borders, and her women and children had been spared the horrors of captivity, and had been kept safe from the pitiless edge of the scalping-knife. Still, she had suffered much. Her noble corps of volunteers had been kept in constant service. A large proportion of her brave men had been continually on duty at home, keeping watch and ward in their respective towns. They were obliged to build forts, to construct palisades about their settlements and around those houses that were selected on account of their position or strength, as fit places of refuge for the infirm and the old, helpless infancy and defenseless womanhood.

But heavy as was her expenditure, the republic lost no time in regaining her former independent position. For three years after the war began, her freeholders submitted to the tedious tax of eleven pence on the pound upon the grand list, besides paying all the customary town and parish rates. To discharge her public debt, an additional tax of eight pence upon the pound was now fixed for two years.* The colony, it was hoped, might repose upon her laurels now that Philip was dead and the Narragansetts were crushed to the earth.

The General Assembly determined that Connecticut should be remunerated for her services in the late war, by taking possession of that large tract of country whence the brave Denison and his volunteers had driven the subjects of Nanuntenoo—a country that Rhode Island had failed to defend. The Assembly set at defiance the decision of Nichols

* Colonial Records.

and his fellow commissioners, making the Narragansett country and Rhode Island a king's province, as it was averred that these gentlemen were not clothed with power to make such new colonies. The agreement made between Mr. Winthrop and Mr. Clark they also repudiated, as it was subsequent to the charter and completed without the authority of the colony delegated to Winthrop. Besides, it was claimed that the charter of Rhode Island recognized but one article of that agreement, and that all the other parts of it had always been disregarded by the inhabitants of Rhode Island. Many instances were speciously given, wherein it was alleged that they had invaded the property of the settlers named in those articles, driven off their cattle, burned their fences, and pulled down their houses.* That Connecticut behaved in this matter after the custom that governs powerful states in their relations with weaker ones, I have good cause to believe. Why should she be expected to form an exception to a rule that has never been violated perhaps since the foundation of civil politics in the world?

Edward Hutchinson, William Hudson, and others, claimants of a large tract of land in the Pequot and Narragansett country, also applied to the Assembly for relief against Rhode Island and found a ready response to their suit.†

Were I to go fully into the details of all the boundary questions that from time to time employed our commonwealth the first hundred and fifty years, I should fill a volume that might better be devoted to documentary history. There was doubtless blame on both sides.

Although Connecticut had made such efforts to prevent a false construction being put upon her conduct at court in the Andross affair, she did not succeed as she had hoped. Winthrop, the powerful mediator between her and the king, could no longer lend her his assistance in the hour of trial. The charmed ring had lost its spell, the eloquent voice could plead her cause no more. Enemies now began to thicken around her. Among others who had now learned her

* Trumbull, i. 353. † See J. H. Trumbull's Colonial Records, ii. 553, 589, 590.

friendless condition, was that common scourger of all the New England colonies, the dark, ill-boding man—Edward Randolph.

In 1676, he arrived in Boston and commenced a series of vexations and interferences that only ended with his death. He was in the habit of returning to England every autumn, and there pouring into the royal ear the poisonous slanders that he had so industriously distilled during the summer. In the spring he would return and pass the time in fomenting dissensions among the people, and exercising over them the tyranny that was so natural to him. His pastime was the lively one of writing letters to the king's ministers and favorites, complaining of the opposition that he found in New England to the trade and navigation laws. This ambitious man was possessed of no ordinary abilities, and was stimulated to action by an intense desire of self-aggrandizement that would never allow him to rest until he should, if possible, have built for himself a monument upon the ruins of the colonies.*

On account of the gloomy prospects of the colonies, the Congress recommended a general fast, that the people might humble themselves with prayer. In conformity with this request, Connecticut appointed the third Tuesday of November 1678, for a day of humiliation.

In May 1679, the General Assembly, with a view to prevent the people of Rhode Island, and others, from taking possession of lands in Narragansett, enacted that none of the conquered lands should be taken up or laid out into farms without special orders from the Assembly.

This question of jurisdiction began now to assume a serious aspect. In September 1679, Governor Cranston, of Rhode Island, held a court in Narragansett. The matter kept growing worse, until, on the 7th of April 1683, the king granted a commission to Edward Cranfield, Esq., lieutenant governor of New Hampshire, William Stoughton, Joseph Dudley, Edward Randolph, Samuel Shrimpton, John Fitz

* In a representation of his services to the committee of council, he boasts of having made eight voyages to New England in nine years.

Winthrop, Edward Palmes, Nathaniel Saltonstall, and John Pyncheon, jr., Esquires, or any three of them, of whom Cranfield or Randolph should constitute one, to examine into the claims as well of the crown as of all other persons and corporations, to the jurisdiction and title of a certain tract of land within his majesty's dominion of New England, called the king's province or Narragansett country.*

On the 22d of August of the same year, the commissioners met at the house of Richard Smith in the disputed territory. They cited all parties interested in the subject-matter of their commission to appear before them with their charters, deeds, and other exhibits, under which they pretended to have derived a title. These gentlemen, after a full hearing of the evidence, adjourned to Boston, where they made a report to the king, declaring that the jurisdiction of the country was in the colony of Connecticut.† The joy that attended this victory gained by Connecticut over the king and the colony of Rhode Island, was qualified by the appearance of another enemy, more formidable because more malicious.

On the 30th of June 1683, Edward Randolph had received a power of attorney from William and Anne, duke and duchess of Hamilton, and James, earl of Aran, their son, and grandson of James, marquis of Hamilton, to sue and receive their right of interest in lands, islands, houses, and tenements in New England. This representative of his betters, in the discharge of his duties under the power, hastened to appear before the commissioners at Boston, and in the name of his principals claimed title to the Narragansett country by a deed that bore date 1635. These new parties of course had a right to a full hearing, and had one at great length. Connecticut made an admirable defense, and one that was truly unanswerable. So it was afterwards found to be when investigated by the learned Trevor and that unrivaled authority, Sir Francis Pemberton. "Marquis Hamilton," says Sir

* Trumbull, i. 358.

† This report may be found in full in Trumbull, i. 359, 360.

Francis in his able opinion, "nor his heirs, or any deriving from him, have ever had possession or laid out any thing upon the premises, nor made any claim in said country, until the year 1683, which was about forty-eight years after said grant." Mr. Trevor advised that the grant to Rhode Island was not valid in law, being subsequent to the grant to Connecticut.

The colony meanwhile received letters from the king, giving information of a conspiracy against himself and his brother, the duke of York. The General Assembly replied in a very sensible and respectful manner, that they were much shocked at the tidings, and that for themselves "they prayed for kings and all men, and especially for his majesty and all in authority under him; that they feared God and honored the king."*

New complaints were now framed against the colonies, a share of which fell to Connecticut. It was reported and believed in England that the colonies favored piracy and harbored pirates, and in support of this charge it was averred that no laws had been passed in New England against that crime. A letter was written by the king's order to the governor and company, demanding that a law should be passed for the suppression of that offense, so much abhorred by all good men, and so directly in violation of the law of nations as well as of the law of England. On the 5th of July 1684, therefore, a special assembly was called and a law passed against piracy, a copy whereof was forthwith sent to the king's secretary of state.

As early as 1673, a number of the citizens of Farmington had presented their petition to the General Assembly, praying that a committee might be appointed to view Mattatuck, and make their report, whether the lands there were sufficiently fertile to maintain a plantation. The committee was sent out, and in May 1674 reported to the Assembly that Mattatuck could accommodate thirty families.† The General Assembly then appointed a second committee to super-

* Colonial Records. † Colonial Records.

intend the proposed settlement. The number of planters who owned shares in the Mattatuck lands at the commencement of this enterprise was less than thirty. In May 1686, they were invested with corporate privileges, and exchanged the aboriginal name for that of *Waterbury*. Its beginnings were not prosperous, nor were its prospects at all flattering for many years. Although the site of the town was not unpleasant, and the meadows that bordered the river were very inviting, yet the people were long pursued by a variety of calamities.

In February 1691, the town was almost destroyed by an inundation. The rain fell in such abundance that the Naugatuck rose to a great height, and swept through the valley with such terrible violence, that the soil of the meadows was torn and washed down with the current, and the whole surface of the fields was left rough and disfigured with loose stones. Many of the people, shocked at the desolation wrought by the flood, abjured their homes and fled from the town forever. In the fall of 1712, the place was almost depopulated by an epidemic, that left scarcely enough living inhabitants to attend upon the sick and minister the last rites to the dead.*

Indeed, for many years, and until the commencement of the present century, Waterbury was not thought to be a town that could offer any very strong inducements to those who were seeking a favorable situation for a permanent abode.

But a change has come over the aspect of the place, that reminds us of the transformations that we find in tales of Arabian enchantment. The river,, once so destructive to those who dwelt upon its banks, though sometimes even now in its more gamesome moods it loses its self-control and deluges the lands and houses of the inhabitants, is no longer the instrument of destruction to them, but is, notwithstanding its lively looks and the racy joyousness of its motions, their common drudge and plodding laborer in all departments of their manifold enterprises. The difference between

* Trumbull, i. 367.

the twenty-eight families at Mattatuck, flying from the meager settlement where poverty, inundation and disease threatened their extermination, and the young city of Waterbury, with its stone church towers, its rich mansions, its manufactories and its population that is now numbered by thousands, affords to a reflective mind a practical illustration scarcely equalled even upon the prairies of the west, of the self-renewing vigor and boundless exuberance of health that characterizes the blood of the old pioneers of New England. The Naugatuck valley, but a few years ago unknown, almost unexplored even by the citizens of Hartford and New Haven, is now one of the most interesting and busy thoroughfares in New England. How long it will be before the traveler who takes his seat in the train at Derby, will be able to journey its whole length to Winsted, without once losing sight of brick stores and stone manufactories standing by the stream, and graceful white houses perched upon the hill-sides on either hand, let the prophetic decide. I have only to do with the past.

The insertion of the settlement of Waterbury in this place, according to its chronological order, will not call for an excuse. Let us now return to the general history of that period.

During the latter years of the reign of Charles II. the king had become so reckless of his pledges and his faith, that he did not scruple to set the dangerous example of violating the charters that had been granted by the crown. Owing to the friendship that the king entertained for Winthrop, we have seen that Connecticut was favored by him to a degree even after the death of that great man. But no sooner had Charles demised and the sceptre passed into the hands of his bigoted brother, King James II., than Connecticut was called upon to contend against her sovereign for liberties that had been affirmed to her by the most solemn muniments known to the law of England.

The accession of James II. took place on the 6th day of February 1685, and such was his haste to violate the honor of the crown, that early in the summer of 1685 a quo warranto was issued against the governor and company of Connecticut, citing them to appear before the king, within eight days of St. Martin's, to show by what right and tenor they exercised certain powers and privileges.*

On the 6th of July 1686, the governor of Connecticut called a special assembly to take measures to procure the chartered rights of the colony. The assembly that day addressed a letter to his majesty, praying him, "to pardon their faults in government and continue them a distinct colony" The burden of their prayer was, that he would "recall the writ of quo warranto."† Never was a supplication more utterly disregarded.

On the 21st of the same month, came that old and dreaded enemy of the colonies, Edward Randolph, and brought with him two writs of quo warranto, which he delivered to Governor Treat. The day of appearance named in them was passed, long before the writs were served.

On receiving these formidable documents, accompanied with a letter from Richard Normansel, one of the sheriffs of London, Governor Treat called another special assembly, that met on the 28th of July. Mr. Whiting was immediately appointed the agent of the colony to repair to England and present its petition before the king. He was instructed to inform his majesty at what a late day the writs had arrived, so that it was impossible that the colony should have had a hearing at the time and place named in them. He was further directed to represent how great injuries the colony would sustain by a loss of its charter, and more particularly by a dismemberment of its territory. Should the agent fail in this matter, he was ordered to implore the king to continue inviolate the enjoyment of property among them, and above all that he would preserve to them their religious privileges.‡

* Chalmers, b. i. 295; Trumbull, i. 367. The articles of high misdemeanor, which were exhibited against the governor and company, are in Chalmers, b. i. 301—404. They are signed by Edmund Randolph.

† Colony Records, (MS) vol. iii. 182, 183. ‡ Colony Records.

In this state of uncertainty the affair rested, until, on the 28th of December, another writ of quo warranto was served upon the governor and company of the colony. This writ bore date the 23d of October, and required the defendants to appear before the king "within eight days of the purification of the Blessed Virgin." The American lawyer of the present day cannot help smiling at the most catholic and mystical return day mentioned in a citation wherein puritans were the parties summoned. It is not at all likely that they had informed themselves as to the time of that event, so interesting to King James, nor could they dream, even were the day of purification fairly known to them, on what one of those eight days the king would graciously attend upon them.*

The scribe might as well have said, within eight days of the time when the king's soul shall have been released from purgatory. The individuality of this monarch is stamped upon this whole proceeding.

I have hitherto in this work, attempted to speak of all dignitaries with respect; but this piece of royal jugglery, so unworthy of a man, not to say of a king, deserves all reprobation, and has not even the convenient cloak of bigotry and superstition to hide its meanness.† It is a political trick that any one of the courtly Plantaganets or blunt Tudors would have been incapable of practicing, and one that the grandfather, father, and brother of King James, would have scorned to be thought guilty of. Long before his ignominious reign, still marked in British history for its imbecility, its cruelty, its wanton violation of every principle of the constitution, and its disregard both of the forms and spirit of the law, a royal charter had been settled to be an irrevocable thing so long as its terms were kept sacredly by the grantees;

* The parties summoned might also have asked with propriety whether "within eight days" *before* or *after* the event designated, was intended by his majesty.

† See Wade, 251, 252.

and from immemorial time it had been the right of the subject to be duly cited to appear, before any right could be taken from him. Before this unoffending colony was perfidiously stabbed in the dark by the government, nearly fifty corporations in England had been robbed of their charters, through various pretexts, and so shallow and untenable that an honorable barrister might feel ashamed to stand up and show cause why they should not prevail. Even the city of London, herself a mighty empire, after going through the form of a trial, had lost her corporate privileges. The charter of Massachusetts had fallen a prey to the same rapacity, and that of Rhode Island, enjoyed for such a brief space of time, had been surrendered.* A general government had been appointed over all New England with the exception of Connecticut, and even from her, the Narragansett country, already declared to be hers by the commissioners named by King Charles II., had been recklessly taken away. This general government of New England was instituted under a commission granted during the first year of the new monarch's reign, and in it Joseph Dudley was named president of the commissioners. President Dudley, in pursuance of his official duty, thereupon on the 28th of May 1686, had sent abroad a proclamation "discharging all the inhabitants of Rhode Island and Narragansetts from obedience either to Connecticut or Rhode Island, and prohibiting all government of either in the king's province."†

The authorities of Connecticut could not fail to be alarmed at the threatening attitude of affairs. They had good cause to believe that judgment would be entered up against them, through default of appearance to defend, when no day had been named in the writ of quo warranto, yet they attempted to withstand the approaching shock, and still dared to hope that in the midst of the fallen columns of other temples, theirs might keep its place. Governor Treat, who has been much commended as a warrior by all our historical writers

---

* Callender, 47; Adams; Hutchinson. † Trumbull, i. 369.

who have treated of the period in which he lived, and who was no less preëminent as a civilian, summoned up all his resolution to meet the emergencies of that critical time. On the 26th of January 1687, and after the reception of the third writ of quo warranto, he called a special assembly to decide on the steps to be taken by the colony. But the sad representatives of the people with trembling lips begged his excellency, with the advice of his council, to do for them at discretion what they could not do for themselves, and then returned to their homes.

In March the court again met and declared by their vote that "they did not see sufficient reason to vary from the answer they gave Sir Edmund Andross to a motion of surrender in January last." A letter was ordered to be sent to Andross in the name of the court.*

In May they met regularly under the charter and made their annual choice of officers. Treat was again chosen governor. The General Assembly still refused to direct what measures should be adopted. Fear paralyzed all their energies, and despair began to cast a dark shadow over their deliberations. If they yielded up their corporate immunities, what would they get in place of them but a reckless provincial government, heavy taxes, unsettled tenures, broken obligations, religious persecutions? For, what faith could they expect him to keep with them, who only two years before had written a letter to Governor Treat† filled with fatherly promises and tender recognition of their corporate existence?

* Colony Records.

† This letter, addressed by James II. to Governor Treat, bearing date the 26th of June 1685, is one of the most bland and comforting documents to be found on file in our Department of State. It contains also a most absolute admission of the validity of the charter, and of our uniform observance of its terms. In it the king is pleased to compliment his subjects in Connecticut in very gracious language, and he promises to extend to them "his royal care and protection in the *preservation of their rights*, and in the *defense* and *security* of their persons and estates." The letter still remains, and taken with the other documentary evidences to be found in the same depository, it is a monument scarcely equalled in the annals of the world, of the perfidy and corruption of the false and grasping monarch who is to be held responsible for its contents.

On the other hand, if they resisted, how easy would it be for the tyrant to declare them traitors? With the deepest solicitude, the deputies again committed their distracted affairs to the governor and council, and adjourned.

Meanwhile, Mr. Whiting, the agent, did what he could in England to prevent a consolidation of the New England colonies, and especially to keep the colony that he represented from such a fate. But his efforts proved of no avail. Accordingly, on the 15th of January 1687, he wrote a letter to Governor Treat, informing him of the prospects that awaited Connecticut, and begging that the governor and council would send one or more of their own number, to defend the charter.

On the 15th of June, a special assembly was called to take advice as to the propriety of adopting this course, and after due consultation it was thought best not to send any more agents in a matter where so skillful a diplomatist as Whiting had failed. He was desired to continue his services "both in appearing for us and in our behalf to make answer to what shall be objected against us, and generally to do whatever shall be needful to be done for us." The governor, deputy governor, and assistants, were directed to present the thanks of the Assembly to Mr. Whiting for his services.*

President Dudley had already addressed a letter to the governor and council, advising them to resign the charter into the king's hands. Should they do so, he undertook to use his influence in behalf of the colony. They did not deem it advisable to comply with the request. Indeed, they had hardly time to do so before the old commission was broken up, and a new one granted, superseding Dudley and naming Sir Edmund Andross *governor of New England.*

Sir Edmund arrived in Boston on the 19th of December 1686,† and the next day he published his commission and took the government into his hands. Scarcely had he established himself, when he sent a letter to the governor and

* Colony Records. † Washburn's Judicial Hist. Mass., 94, 126.

company of Connecticut, acquainting them with his appointment, and informing them that he was commissioned by the king to receive their charter if they would give it up to him. He begged them, as they would give him a favorable opportunity to serve them, and as they loved and honored his majesty, not to keep it back any longer.

As this communication did not bring forward the much desired paper, Sir Edmund soon after addressed another to Governor Treat, in which he said that he had just received tidings from England that judgment had been entered upon default in the writ of quo warranto brought against the colony, and that he should soon receive the king's commands respecting them. He earnestly urged the company to anticipate any compulsory steps that might otherwise be taken, and to receive the gratitude and favor of their sovereign, by voluntarily yielding up what would else be plucked from them by force.

When this last epistle was received, the Assembly was in session, and it was forthwith submitted to them, in connection with another from Colonel Dungan of a like import. If caution is one trait of the people of Connecticut, the reader has by this time learned that the most cool and persistent courage is another that they possess in a high degree. With one voice, the Assembly decided to stand for their rights, and hold fast to the charter. Still, that caution might be duly mingled with courage, and that patience might have her perfect work upon them, they addressed a petition to the king, earnestly supplicating him to preserve those privileges that had been granted to them by his royal brother, and renewed by the kind assurances in his own gracious letter to their governor. If this, the burden of their prayers, should be denied them, they beg that they may not be separated from their old friends in Massachusetts, and that they may be placed under the government of Sir Edmund Andross.*

This alternative request, wrung as it was from the heart-agony of a suffering people, was artfully construed into a

* Colony Records.

voluntary resignation of their charter.* Thus was a supplication that had been obtained by fraud and lies, sought to be made available by a false construction too gross to deceive even the weakest mind. As well might a martyr's prayer for life uttered in the cold ears of his inquisitors, closing with the last request that, if he must die, his features may not be mutilated by the devilish enginery of torture, or his limbs be broken upon the wheel, be considered as fully granted, because, touched with some sense of womanly remorse, they had dexterously snatched the immortal jewel without shattering the perishable casket in which it had been imprisoned.

Notwithstanding the earnest appeal made to the king, to do justice to her, the little colony still clung to the charter.

In October, at the time prescribed by it, the General Assembly convened as usual, and held its regular session.

On Monday, the 31st of October 1687,† Sir Edmund Andross, attended by several of the members of his council and other gentlemen, surrounded by a body guard of about sixty soldiers, entered Hartford with a view of taking possession of the instrument that all his efforts had failed to procure from the reluctant authorities. The General Assembly was in session when he arrived. He was received by the governor and council, and by the other members of the Assembly, with all the outward marks of respect, but it was obvious that no cordial feeling of congratulation awaited him. Andross entering the legislative hall in the presence of the

* The author of "Will and Doom," (referring to the letter containing this petition of the Connecticut Assembly) says: "The letter being received at Whitehall, *the king readily granted their request of being annexed to the Bay*, pursues his quo warranto no further, but sends a commission to Sir Edmund Andross, Kt., (then governor of Massachusetts,) to take on him the government of Connecticut." The same writer subsequently says: "The charter government of Connecticut was laid aside by *their own act*, and the king's government was erected by his excellency without fraud or force, but with the *free consent* of all parties concerned." He could hardly have been acquainted with the principles of the English law, or he would have remembered that "*duress per minas* voids all contracts."

† Bulkley's "Will and Doom."

Assembly, publicly demanded the charter, and declared the government that was then acting under it to be dissolved. The Assembly, confronted as they were by this royal emissary with an armed force at his heels, neither complied with his demand to bring forth the charter, nor did they evince, by resolve or any other expression of their legislative will, a determination to abandon any right or immunity that they had acquired and held under it. Tradition, never controverted by a single respectable authority, tells us that Governor Treat remonstrated against this arbitrary proceeding, with the manliness and strong sense that characterized his whole life; that he gave a brief narrative of the early settlement of the colony, the hardships and dangers that beset the people for so many years; the Indian wars with their long train of evils. He pictured, as none but a participant in that sad drama could have done, the savages, the fire, slaughter, and captivity, that had made Philip's war "so memorable and so horrible;" and after representing in vivid colors the part that he had himself played in that and other kindred struggles, he said it was like giving up his life, now to give up the patent and privileges so dearly bought and so long enjoyed.*

Whether Sir Edmund condescended to reply to this touching appeal, we are not informed, but in some way the deliberations were protracted until evening, perhaps by the choice of Sir Edmund himself, certainly by his acquiescence, who may have seen in the lowering brows of the citizens as they thronged the hall and glanced silently upon him, a spirit that suggested to his mind the prudence of obtaining if he could a quiet submission. I have every cause to think from the previous and subsequent history of the colony, that Governor Treat, who could have had little hope of making any impression upon the heart of Andross by this oration, prolonged the debate as much as possible in pursuance of a plan of operations that had been before agreed upon, in which others less liable to the charge of treason were to be the principal

* Trumbull, i. 371.

actors. Be this as it might, the shades of evening gathered around the legislative chamber, and still the charter had not made its appearance. Lighted candles were brought in, and the eager crowd pressed more and more densely into the room, to witness the last pang of the expiring colony. We may suppose that by this time Sir Edmund had lost all patience, and, as he saw no such manifestations of violence and brutality as evince the madness of an English mob, that he would be still more peremptory in his demands. At last the governor and assistants appear to yield. The charter is brought in and laid upon the table in the midst of the Assembly.* It was then that the first lesson was given to a creature of the British crown, teaching him how wide is the difference between an English populace and a body of American freemen. In an instant, the lights were extinguished, and the room was wrapped in total darkness. Still, not a word was spoken, not a threat was breathed. The silence that pervaded the place was as profound as the darkness.

The candles were quietly re-lighted, but, strange to tell, the charter had disappeared. Sir Edmund, and we may well believe, the people's governor too, looked carefully in every nook and corner where it might be thought to be hid, but their search was in vain. All efforts to find the perpetrator of this rash and sudden act, proved equally fruitless.

"Had he melted in earth or vanished in air?"

Thus robbed of the prize while it seemed already in his grasp, Sir Edmund Andross smothered his resentment as well as he could, and proceeded to assume the reins of authority. In the following pompous words, he announced that the government of the people was at an end:

* The following entry in the Colonial Records doubtless has reference to this scene: "Sundry of the court desiring that the patent or charter might be brought into the court, the secretary sent for it and informed the governor and court that he had the charter, and showed it to the court, and the governor bid him put it in the box again and lay it on the table, *and leave the key in the box*, which he did forthwith."

"At a General Court at Hartford, October 31st, 1687, his excellency, Sir Edmund Andross, knight, and captain-general and governor of his majesty's territories and dominions in New England, by order of his majesty James the Second, King of England, Scotland, France, and Ireland, the 31st of October, 1687, took into his hands the government of the colony of Connecticut, it being by his majesty annexed to Massachusetts, and other colonies under his excellency's government.

FINIS."*

The new governor now proceeded to appoint officers throughout the colony. His council consisted of about fifty persons. Of these, Governor Treat, John Fitz Winthrop, Wait Winthrop, and John Allen, were from Connecticut. Sir Edmund, like his master, began his administration with

* Bulkley, in his "Will and Doom," gives a somewhat detailed account of the way in which Sir Edmund assumed the government, and of the humble manner in which Governor Treat made his resignation to his successor. It may be interesting to the reader, and I therefore subjoin it, in that quaint author's own language:

"Upon this notice, the governor summons the General Court to meet at Hartford about the same time, who accordingly attended (ready to receive his excellency when he came,) and held a court, and some say also voted a submission to him, though of this we are not yet well assured, and possibly they made no record of it.

"On Monday, October 31, 1687, Sir Edmund Andross, (with divers of the members of his council and other gentlemen attending him, and with his guards,) came to Hartford, where he was received with all respect and welcome congratulation that Connecticut was capable of. The troops of horse of that county conducted him honorably from the ferry through Waterfield, up to Hartford, where the trained bands of divers towns, (who had waited there some part of the week before, expecting his coming then, now again being commanded by their leaders,) united to pay him their respects at his coming.

"Being arrived at Hartford, he is greeted and caressed by the governor and assistants, (whose part it was, being the heads of the people, to be most active in what was now to be done,) and some say, though I will not confidently assert it, that the governor and one of the assistants did declare to him the vote of the General Court for their submission to him.

"However, after some treaty between his excellency and them, that evening he was the next morning waited on and conducted by the governor, deputy governor, assistants and deputies, to the court chamber, and by the governor him-

many professions of tender regard for the people. He bade his magistrates dispense justice with an even hand, and as nearly as might be in consonance with the established laws and usages of the colony. But these instructions were merely the thin disguise of his ultimate designs to plunder and oppress the people, or else, like many a greater man, he soon became intoxicated by too copious draughts from the exhilarating cup of power, and was led into excesses that were foreign from his original intentions. Doubtless the example of a bad king, whose favor he was too anxious to win, goaded him on to acts of blindness and lawlessness that had before that time known no precedent in Connecticut.

One of his first acts of tyranny, and the one of all others most likely to awaken the indignation of a people nurtured under the auspices of the constitution of 1639, was to put an end to the liberty of the press. He then proceeded to incur the displeasure of our youths and maidens by requiring all those parties who were about to form matrimonial alliances, first to give heavy bonds with sureties to the governor. In many cases, this was impossible, and amounted to an actual prohibition. He also took away from the clergy the power of joining persons in wedlock, and confined that privilege exclusively to magistrates. This was done to deprive the clergy of the perquisites resulting from the discharge of this delicate and sacred function.*

He soon made a still more radical innovation. The ministers, as the reader is now well aware, had been the patri-

self directed to the governor's seat, and being there seated, (the late governor, assistants and deputies being present, and the chamber thronged as full of people as it was capable of,) his excellency declared that his majesty had, *according to their desire*, given him a commission to come and take on him the government of Connecticut—and caused his commission to be publicly read.

"That being done, his excellency showed that it was his majesty's pleasure to make the late governor and Capt. John Allyn members of his council, and called upon them to take their oaths, which they did forthwith—and all this in that public and great assembly, *nemine contradicente*, only one man said that they first desired that they might continue as they were."

* Trumbull, i. 372.

archs of the colony, and its pioneers. They had acted the part of Moses and Aaron, and had led the people through the wilderness, and into the promised land. They had smitten the rock for the gushing forth of the waters; they had destroyed the molten images and superintended the cutting down of the groves; their prayers had aided in driving out the Canaanites, and in obedience to their voice the humble tabernacle had been set up in the midst of the tents of the people of God. Thus had the inhabitants of Connecticut been taught by their fathers to believe, and hence the reverence that followed the minister wherever he went was bred in the children that composed his flock. It was a reverence sometimes carried to an unwarrantable extent, amounting to a sacrifice of personal independence. But, unlike the reverence with which Sir Edmund bent the knee and bowed to the arbitrary will of the king, it was a sentiment that had in it little of the alloy of selfishness and none of the obsequious cowardice of adulation. It was certainly honest and earnest, and pervaded the whole atmosphere of society. The people had brought with them from England the belief that it was necessary to the well-being of a state that the clergy—and they had one of their own—should be supported by law. They had, therefore, grown up under a mild and greatly modified tithing system. With a view of striking a blow most calculated to wound them, and with no regard, certainly, for the promotion of that religious liberty now so universal in this country, Sir Edmund repealed the laws requiring citizens to pay taxes for the support of the clergy. If they resisted his will, he declared that he would take their meeting-houses from them, and that he would punish any body who should give two-pence to a non-conformist minister.

That this movement was imprudent and unstatesmanlike, to say nothing of its moral effect upon a people living in the seventeenth century, and brought up with the strictness peculiar to a Puritan education, I need not say to any reader who knows any thing of the philosophy of human government. It would of itself have destroyed all confidence between the governor and the governed, had any existed, and would, in the course of a few years, have resulted in resistance and bloodshed throughout New England.

Another measure adopted by him was, that all estates of deceased persons should be administered upon at Boston. The expenses of a journey to the capital city from the border towns of Connecticut were very burdensome, and in the case of widows and orphans, often amounted to an absolute denial of justice. The fees under his government were such as better befitted a mercantile city like London than the agricultural towns of Connecticut. It cost fifty shillings to prove a will, and other charges were in proportion.

Taxation was another sore burden. Without any legislative body whose sympathies were with the people, and who knew best what weight of oppression they would bear, without even consulting the majority of his council, Sir Edmund, with Randolph, and a few of his more congenial satellites, taxed the colonies at pleasure.

Thus heavily did the time drag on with the citizens of Connecticut, who had so long been fondled in the lap of freedom, that they felt more keenly than the other colonies the yoke of a provincial tyrant.

In 1688 the province of New York was brought under the same dominion, and shared the same degradation. Indeed her people for several administrations were subjected to the tyranny of the worst rulers.

All the charters were now gone except that of Connecticut, and the government had ceased to be operated under it. Sir Edmund, therefore, declared that the tenures by which the colonists held their lands were valueless. "An Indian deed," he would remark with a grim pleasantry befitting the simile, "an Indian deed is no better than the *scratch of a bear's paw.*" He, therefore, compelled the planters to take out new patents for their estates, and some of them were obliged to pay a fee to the authorities of fifty pounds apiece for these new titles to lands that they or their fathers had purchased of the Indians, had reclaimed from the wilds of nature, had built houses upon and spent many times their value in improving, not to speak of a possession, adverse as against the whole world, of more than half a century's duration, and to say nothing of solemn charters, pledging the honor and faith of kings, of commissioners that ratified, and of congratulatory letters that had again and again confirmed those charters. Some of the principal gentlemen refused to submit to this tyrannical swindle, and were served with "writs of intrusion," rightly enough named if applied to those who thus sought to eject from their patrimony the lords of the soil.*

Not only were their estates taken from the people, but in Massachusetts the personal liberty of the citizens was trampled on with the same recklessness. All special town meetings were prohibited. The people were imprisoned at the will of the governor and his minions, and the act of habeas corpus was as little regarded as in Turkey or Algiers. Indeed, Randolph, with the frankness of an unrestrained favorite, did not scruple to tell the persons with whom he corresponded in England, that Andross and his Council were as "arbitrary as the great Turk." In vain did petitions from his oppressed subjects in New England assail the ear of the king. Proud, bigoted, prejudiced against the applicants, and dividing his time between the cruelties of persecution and the seclusion of monastic life, he turned coldly away and left them to their fate.

It is true that most of these severe shocks of power fell upon Massachusetts and Plymouth. Connecticut had not made herself obnoxious to the government, as her sister colonies had done, and besides she had the benefit of Governor Treat's intercessions in her behalf, who, though he could not avert the rapacity of Andross and Randolph from the other colonies, was able to protect his own from many acts

* This was not done uniformly, and happened less in Connecticut than in Massachusetts. Had it been generally insisted on, the people would have resisted it by force, or been brought to a state of bankruptcy by it.

of oppression that would otherwise have driven her to despair. He was a member of Andross' Council, and through his instrumentality, the other rulers with whom his fellow-citizens came more immediately in contact, were such men as would follow as nearly in the old track of administering justice, as they could be allowed to do. But, notwithstanding his exertions, the affairs of the colony grew worse and worse; and when the summer of the year 1688 was brought to a close, Connecticut was more desponding and distrustful than she had been at the commencement of the administration. A dead torpor reigned throughout the colony.

But this darkness only heralded the dawn of a brighter day. The abdication of James put an end to the license of tyranny. On the 5th of November, William, Prince of Orange, landed in England and published his plan of conducting the affairs of his realm.* A copy of this manifesto soon arrived in Boston, and when its contents were made known to Andross, he caused the messenger who had brought it to be arrested and committed to jail "for bringing a false and traitorous libel into the country." The people bade the noble adventurer God-speed in his undertaking, and on the 18th of April, 1689, the popular indignation, so long repressed, broke forth in civil war. The people of Boston, and the towns adjoining, arose in a mass, seized Andross and the more odious members of his Council, and re-instated the old officers of the colony.

On the 9th of May, Governor Treat, Deputy Governor Bishop, and the old magistrates under the Charter, resumed the government of Connecticut. The Assembly was convened, and before the close of the same month the glad tidings reached Connecticut that William and Mary, of blessed memory, were established upon the throne of the British empire. With hearts as glad as the smiles of the summer that was opening, the General Assembly, specially called for that purpose, hailed the new king. With a truly epic magnificence, the glorious

* Wade, 261.

little colony who alone had kept her charter, told King William how the "Lord who sitteth King upon the floods, had separated his enemies from him as he divided the waters of Jordan before his chosen people." In words flattering and sweet, she also told him that it was "because the Lord loved his people, that he had exalted him to be king over them, to execute *justice and judgment.*" Her General Assembly told him further the simple story of her wrongs, the oppression of the provincial tyrant who had wantonly usurped the government of a people that had never surrendered their patent, and how they had now taken the liberty to resume the reins of government until they could learn his majesty's good pleasure. The officers who were in power at the date of the usurpation, were re-installed into their respective places.*

But, perhaps some one will ask me if I have forgotten to tell what had become of the charter, and where it lay hid during the unhappy period of Andross' usurpation? I have not indeed forgotten it; neither have I forgotten the other legend that has come down to us unchanged in its fair proportions, or in its power over the public mind—a legend more sacred than history, more veritable than a record, for it is still represented by a living witness, whose biography, were it written, would be read with an interest that could invest the life of no merely human personage.

I have already said that before Governor Wyllys came to America, he sent forward Gibbons, his steward, to prepare a place fit for his reception. We are told that while he was felling the trees upon the hill where Wyllys afterwards lived, he was waited upon by a deputation of Indians from the South

---

* Bulkley argues that the Charter Government was *extinct*, because the people of Connecticut had "voluntarily omitted their annual election, the only means to continue their government, in 1688," and that, consequently, the resumption of the government was void, "there being no Governor or Deputy Governor to summon a Court of Election, according to the Charter." This would be sound reasoning but for two facts, viz., the failure to elect the annual officers in 1688, was *not* "voluntary," and therefore did not vitiate the Charter; and as the Charter had never been surrendered, it was still in full force.

Meadow, who came up to remonstrate against the cutting down of a venerable oak that stood upon the side of the mound now consecrated to freedom. With the true eloquence of nature, the brown sons of the forest pleaded in behalf of the immemorial tree. "It has been the guide of our ancestors for centuries," said they, "as to the time of planting our corn. When the leaves are of the size of a mouse's ears, then is the time to put the seed in the ground."* At their solicitation, the tree was permitted to stand, and continued to indicate the time when the earth was ready to receive the seed corn: a vast legendary tree, that must have begun to show signs of age a hundred years before that day, in the cavity at its base that was gradually enlarging, as one generation after another of red men passed from beneath its shadow.

As soon as the lights had been extinguished in the legislative chamber, in the presence of Andross, Captain Wadsworth seized the precious charter and bore it from the midst of the Assembly. Secretly he flew with it to the friendly tree, and deposited it in the hollow of its trunk. Thus the Charter of Charles II., in imitation of the exile of its author, took refuge in an oak; and thus the king and the patent, have transmitted to the trees that respectively shadowed them, an immortal name. But how different the lesson taught by them! The one saved from his enemies the representative of the principles of despotic power; the other gave an asylum to the record that bore witness to the rights of humanity to resist that power.

But the *Charter Oak* has fallen at last! After having braved the tempests of a thousand years, and for the last two centuries cherished as a precious memorial of liberty by millions of free hearts, this venerated relic no longer stands sen-

* The legend, as well as the beautiful words, I have from the pen of Historicus, a writer, who under several names can never hide himself from his readers. The article is to be found in the Supplement to the Connecticut Courant, under date September 13, 1845.

tinel on Wyllys Hill. About one o'clock, on the stormy morning of August 21st, 1856, it fell to the earth with a giant crash, and henceforth it lives *only* in history. At noon, Mr. Stuart, the proprietor and occupant of the adjacent mansion, who had long guarded it with almost paternal care and solicitude, caused solemn dirges to be played over its remains by Colt's Armory Band; and at sun down, the various bells of the city were tolled in commemoration of the event.

CHAPTER XV.

FRONTENAC'S INVASION. ATTEMPT UPON QUEBEC.

WHILE such important changes were taking place in New England, New York also felt the shock of revolution. Jacob Leisler had taken the government of that province into his hands, and held the fort and city in behalf of King William. As the French and Indians were assuming a very threatening attitude towards the English on the Northern frontiers, Leisler wrote to Connecticut, begging her to send troops to aid in the defence of his borders. On the 13th of June, 1689, the Assembly appointed Major Gold and Captain James Fitch to go to New York and confer with Leisler on that subject, and to decide in behalf of Connecticut, how many men she should furnish.*

In accordance with the decision of this committee, the governor and council sent Captain Bull with a company to Albany, not only to defend that part of the country, but also to aid in bringing about a treaty with the Five Nations, that should secure their friendship for the English colonies. Connecticut sent another party of soldiers to protect the fort and city of New York.†

While the Indians on the northern frontier were busy in their preparations for war, the tribes within the limits of New England were not idle. They began to assemble in numbers, and again plundered the property of the English. This new

* Colony Records; O'Callaghan's Doc. Hist. New York, ii. 15, 16, 17, 18; Trumbull, i. 378.

† O'Callaghan, ii. 98. On the 10th of October the Assembly ordered the recall of the troops sent to relieve the fort in New York city, but they were directed to hold themselves in readiness to go to the relief of said fort in case of an attack.

excitement among the eastern tribes was thought to be owing to the arrogant behavior of Sir Edmund Andross towards them. To inquire into the causes of it, and if possible prevent bloodshed, a special assembly was called, and commissioners were appointed to meet those of the other colonies and consult with them as to the causes of the disturbance; and, if it should appear that the Indians had been wronged, to see that justice was done them. If, on the other hand, it should be found true that the Indians were the aggressors, then the commissioners were ordered to pledge the colony for the furnishing her proper quota of men.*

The revolution of 1688, the best landmark in British history, as it set the empire free from the chains of superstition and tyranny, as might have been expected, brought along with it the indignation of France, and involved the two nations in war. In 1689, a large number of land forces was levied, and a fine fleet was prepared for the reduction of New York. The undertaking was foiled by the incursions of the Mohawks, who now kept Canada in a state of constant distress and fear.

To inspire the French colonists with a new courage, Count Frontenac sent out several companies of French and Indians against the frontier settlements of New York and New England. As New York was the least able to defend herself, and the most exposed on account of her thin population and remote border towns, the principal part of this hostile force was directed against her. A detachment of between two hundred and three hundred Frenchmen and Indians, under the command of D'Aillebout, De Mantil and Le Moyn, was therefore dispatched from Montreal to lay waste the unprotected districts of New York. These forces were provided with food and clothing suitable for a winter campaign, and arrived at Schenectady, after a painful march of twenty-two days, on Saturday, the 8th of February, 1690. It was dead winter and they had suffered so much from fatigue, cold, and hunger, that they approached the neighborhood of this outpost

* Colony Records.

of civilization, with the anticipation that they should be obliged to surrender themselves prisoners of war to the people whom they had come to subdue. But the scouts who had preceded them, and who had spent some hours in the village without exciting any suspicions, returned to them with the intelligence that the inhabitants were not prepared for their reception, and that it would be easy to surprise the town.*

Encouraged by the tidings, they resolved to make an attack. The ferocity of the French character was exhibited on this occasion, as it was afterwards in the conflicts that followed. They found the gates open and without guard. They returned to the place about eleven o'clock at night, and, dividing their forces into little parties, surrounded every house at once, while the inmates were asleep. They were aroused from their slumbers only to fall into the embraces of a still deeper repose. While yet their heads were upon their pillows, the awful work of destruction began. The very beds were streaming with blood, and mutilated bodies were scattered upon the floors of the houses. In a few minutes the whole village was in flames, and sixty of its inhabitants were slain. The barbarities practiced upon the dead are too sickening to be reported. That infants were torn from their mothers' arms, and cast as fuel into the blaze that gleamed from the half consumed dwelling, is not the less calculated to awaken our sympathy, when we reflect that they must have perished in the snow-storm that swept hurriedly by, as if to avoid the scene of murder and atrocity that outbraved the fierceness of the elements.†

Twenty captives were secured and reserved for the gratification of savage vengeance, when it should again demand its customary food. The rest of the inhabitants of Schenectady fled in their night-clothes through that awful storm. "Twenty-five of the poor wretches who thus sought to better

---

* Brodhead; Trumbull; Smith. † Trumbull; O'Callaghan, ii. 71, 156.

their condition, lost their limbs through the sharpness of the frost."*

In the massacre—I can not call it a battle—Captain Bull's Lieutenant, one of his sergeants, and three privates were killed, and five were taken prisoners.† The Connecticut troops had little opportunity for the display of their valor on this occasion, but they did all that brave men, under a brave leader, could do in their circumstances.

As soon as the news of this midnight butchery had reached Albany the next morning, universal dismay and horror filled the hearts of the people. Some of them counseled that the place should be at once destroyed, and the whole country abandoned to the ravages of the enemy. So panic-stricken were the inhabitants, that they lost all discretion, and, disaffected as they were at the government of Leisler, they refused to keep watch and ward, or maintain any regular military discipline. This had been the case especially at Schenectady. Had they followed the advice of Bull, and held themselves in readiness for an attack, they might have successfully repelled it. They had been unable to believe that the enemy could march hundreds of miles in that forbidding season of the year, and steal upon them in the night.

The destruction of Schenectady was only a part of the tragedy. On the 18th of March, another party of French and Indians made a sudden attack upon Salmon Falls, a settlement that had been made upon the bank of the stream that divides New Hampshire from Maine. At daybreak they entered the village, and in small parties, as they had done at Schenectady, began the massacre from several points at once. The people rallied and nobly defended themselves, until they were crushed by the superior force of their invaders. Thirty-six men were killed, and fifty-four women and children were taken captive. Of course, the dwellings were burned, and the whole place laid waste.‡

The more eastern colonies were alarmed at this near approach of the enemy, and earnestly begged that Connecticut

* Trumbull, i. 380. † Trumbull, i. 380. ‡ Trumbull, i. 380, 381.

would send troops to protect their frontier. Massachusetts, especially, sent letters, asking for men to guard the upper towns upon the Connecticut river.* New York and Albany also asked the further aid of our colony, not only in the continuance of Bull and his company among them, but they prayed that fresh soldiers might be sent to reinforce them.†

It has been one of the attributes of Connecticut always to be true to her friends in the hour of peril, although in doing so she has more than once been obliged to overlook some painful negligences on their part. Consistent with herself, she now responded to the call of her neighbors, and with one voice her Assembly declared that the settlement of the French at Albany must be prevented at every risk. Two companies, each of one hundred men, were immediately sent to the relief of Albany, and at the same time other troops were dispatched for the relief of the Massachusetts settlements upon the Connecticut river.

Nor did the Assembly fail to provide against any encroachments upon their own territory, but compelled all the towns to keep a constant watch within their limits. None of the inhabitants except assistants, ministers, and the aged and infirm, were exempt from this duty, and even they were obliged to employ substitutes to discharge it for them, provided their pecuniary condition would admit of it. Thus every citizen in the colony was taught to spend his strength and wealth for the general good of the people.‡

Meanwhile the Assembly was not unmindful of the municipal wants of the republic. At the same session it was ordered that all of that part of Wethersfield lying east of the Connecticut river should be invested with the ordinary corporate privileges, and should be known and called by the name of Glastenbury.§ Thus was the oldest town in the colony, after so many moral and ecclesiastical divisions resulting in the birth of plantations near and remote, finally allowed to follow in its municipal regulations the great land-

* Holmes' Annals, i. 431; Hutchinson † Trumbull; O'Callaghan.

‡ Colonial Records, MS. § Colonial Records, MS.

mark of the valley, and divide itself for the sake of convenience into two separate jurisdictions.

I have spoken elsewhere of the beauty and fertility of the district comprising these two towns. Both of them had their birth in the midst of convulsions, threatened calamities and impending wars, and each has done its part towards the support of the fame and honor of the State.

On the 1st of May, the commissioners or Congress met at Rhode Island to consult upon the affairs of the colonies, and to decide what measures were to be adopted in order to defend the country against the French and Indians. It was finally resolved that to invade the enemy would be the best security against a further attack from them, and it was accordingly ordered that eight hundred and fifty men should be raised for the reduction of Canada. It was deemed advisable, too, in this state of affairs, to ask for the help of the mother country. Accordingly, an express was sent to England to inform the government of the condition of the colonies, and to implore that a fleet might be dispatched to engage the French by sea, while the colonies invaded them by land. England, however, was unable at that time, in her unsettled state, to render the provinces the assistance that she would gladly have done under other circumstances.*

New England and New York, undaunted by this discouraging intelligence, resolved to prosecute the enterprise alone. The plan of operations was of a bold and daring character. It was determined that about nine hundred Englishmen and more than half that number of Indians should march through the wilderness and make an attack upon Montreal, while at the same time a fleet and army of about two thousand men were to sail around to the mouth of the St. Lawrence, proceed up the river with all haste, and reduce Quebec.†

Under the direction of Jacob Milborn, who had married a daughter of Leisler, and who was to act as commissary, it was expected that New York would supply the land army with provisions and canoes to enable it to cross the navigable

* Hutchinson, i. 353; Holmes, i. 431. † Holmes, i. 432.

waters that were interposed between the east country and Montreal. The five nations, too, were counted upon as safe allies of the English, when it was remembered how remorselessly they had fought against the French.

This army was placed under the command of Major-General Fitz John Winthrop,* of Connecticut. As soon as he could get his forces in readiness, Winthrop set out for Canada, and arrived at the head of Wood Creek early in August. Instead of finding at the appointed rendezvous the warriors of the five nations assembled in readiness to carry on a war with the French, Winthrop saw to his surprize only about seventy Mohawks and Oneidas. He sent a courier to the other tribes, to know if they designed to join him. They replied, evasively, that they were not yet ready to go. This was only a polite way of informing the general that they did not mean to go at all, as the event proved. However, he advanced about one hundred miles, until he came to the borders of the lake where he had expected to find canoes in readiness to give the army a safe passage. Here also he found that this indispensable requisite was not provided. The few canoes that he found there were totally inadequate to perform such a task.† He applied to the Indians in this emergency, and besought them to build canoes enough to transport the whole army. They replied that the season for peeling the bark from the trees had already gone by, and that they could make no more canoes until the next spring. More timid, probably, than treacherous, they told General Winthrop, that in aiming a blow at such a strong place as Quebec, he "looked too high," and begged him to depart from his

* Fitz John Winthrop, son of Gov. John Winthrop, of Connecticut, became magistrate of Connecticut in 1689. In 1694 he was sent to England as agent of the colony, and discharged the duties of the appointment so satisfactorily that the Legislature made him a present of £500. He was distinguished, like his father, for his knowledge of philosophy, his skill in politics, and his piety, and was honored by being elected a member of the Royal Society. In 1698 he was elected governor of Connecticut, and held the office till his death, in 1707.

† See Secretary Allyn's letter to Lieut. Gov. Leisler in Doc. Hist. New York, vol. ii. p. 254; also Trumbull, Brodhead, and others.

first design, and make an attack upon Chambly and the border towns upon the hither bank of the St. Lawrence. Milborn had also neglected to provide suitable provisions for the subsistence of the army, so that the troops were not only kept from crossing the river, but were now beginning to be threatened with famine. A council of war was called, and it was reluctantly decided that the army must retreat to Albany.*

In the meantime, the fleet under command of Sir William Phipps, Governor of Massachusetts, having sailed from Nantasket, made haste to reach Quebec. It was made up of nearly forty vessels, the largest carrying forty-four guns and two hundred men. Owing, however, to the many delays that he experienced, the number of his vessels, the adverse winds, and the strength of the river current, Sir William did not reach Quebec until the 5th of October.†

On the 8th, he landed the troops and advanced upon the town; and on the 9th, the ships were drawn up before it and opened a full fire upon it, but did little injury to a place so formidable from its natural position.‡

Frontenac, only a few days before, had returned to Quebec, after learning that the land army which he had started in search of had retreated to Albany, and now set himself about the defense of the fortress with great ability. He opened such a deadly fire upon the English ships from his batteries that they were obliged to withdraw, and on the 11th of the month the troops were compelled again to embark. The terrible winds that beset the St. Lawrence in the autumn, and herald the approach of the dead season that binds the noblest of all our northern streams in fetters of ice, soon after scattered the vessels of the English fleet and warned Sir William to return home. Had he arrived at

* Trumbull, i. 383; O'Callaghan, ii. 289.

† Hutchinson, i. 354; Holmes; Trumbull.

‡ Trumbull, i. 384. About this time, Leisler wrote to Governor Treat, "We rejoice to understand the *victorious success* of Sir William Phipps at the eastward;"—alluding, possibly, to the capture of Port Royal a short time before.

Quebec a week earlier than he did, he would have found the town, on account of the absence of Count Frontenac, completely defenceless. But Frontenac having learned of the retreat of Winthrop, of whom he was in pursuit, hastened back to the fortress in time to save it.

Had Milborn been faithful in the discharge of the duty assigned him in the campaign, notwithstanding the timidity of the five nations and the late sailing of the fleet, it is probable that both branches of the expedition would have proved successful, and that the daring deeds that have since associated the brightest names of British history with that of Quebec, would never have been performed.

That the campaign was a failure was not the fault of Connecticut, whose valor has always been found equal to contend with every thing that dared to meet it, save the insuperable obstacles of nature.

The abuse heaped by Leisler, and by the miscreant Milborn himself, upon Winthrop and the gentlemen of Albany who were of the council of war, was even more disgraceful than the negligence or cowardice of those maligners that had been the cause of the retreat of which they complained. Several of the principal gentlemen of Albany, among whom was Robert Livingston, Esq., were obliged to fly from New York and take refuge in Hartford, where they were protected from violence.*

But Leisler's arrogance did not stop with persecuting the citizens of New York. After the main army had crossed the Hudson river, and while General Winthrop himself was on the west bank, and of course unprotected, Leisler brutally seized his person and attempted to go through the formalities of court-martialing the commander-in-chief of New England, who was in no way responsible to him, and who had been sent out more to protect the colony that he pretended to govern, than for any other cause. For several days Winthrop lay under arrest, and might have been murdered in cold blood had it not been for the timely interference of a

* See O'Callaghan; Trumbull, i. 384.

party of Mohawks, who, while the mockery of the trial was going on, crossed the river, broke through the guards that surrounded the prisoner, and bore him off in triumph.*

When we consider the character of Winthrop and Livingston, the defenseless condition of New York, and the efforts that Connecticut had made during the preceding winter to save the inhabitants of Schenectady and Albany from a doom that their recklessness seemed rather to covet than to shun, we are at a loss whether to admire more the ruffianly impudence or the heartless ingratitude of this transaction.

While Winthrop was in close confinement, the authorities of Connecticut addressed a letter to Leisler, reminding him, though in a courteous way, of the same obligations that he must have forgotten. "A prison," they say, "is not a catholicon for all state maladies, though so much used by you." In another place they add, "If your adherence to Mr. Milborn (whose spirit we have sufficient testimony of,) and other emulators of the major's honor, be greater than to ourselves and the gentlemen of the bay, you may boast of the exchange by what profit you find."†

The severity of this language appears, to us who know the history of New York for the century next succeeding the date of the letter, to be rather a prophetic warning than a threat. But I ought not to speak more at length upon this topic, lest it should be thought that I am unable to make a distinction between the profligacy of an administration and the character of the people who are oppressed by it. New York was not to blame for the madness of a tyrant.

In order that no imputation might rest upon the character of Major-General Winthrop, the General Assembly, in October following, went into a full investigation of his conduct. Evidence was heard not only from Albany, but from the New England officers who had been of the council of war; even the Indians who had participated in the affair, and who could testify as to the deficiency of canoes and provisions,

* Trumbull, i. 384; see also Doc. Hist. New York, ii. 288, 289.

† O'Callaghan, ii. 289.

were examined. Unanimously the Assembly resolved, "That the general's conduct in the expedition had been with good fidelity to his majesty's interest, and that his confinement at Albany on the account thereof, demanded a *timely vindication.*" *

A committee of two magistrates† was also appointed in the name of the Assembly, to thank General Winthrop for his services, and to assure him of their readiness on all future occasions to avail themselves of his fidelity, valor, and prudence.‡

In May 1692, Windham was incorporated. The tract of land embraced in it was a very fine one, and had been devised by Joshua, son of Uncas and sachem of the Mohegans, to John Mason, James Fitch, and twelve others, many years before.§ The territory thus given, comprised also the towns of Mansfield and Canterbury. Settlements were begun both at Windham and Mansfield in 1686. Windham has long been a town of historical importance, and was made a county seat in 1726.

The Mohawks gave Count Frontenac as much trouble as the English, and proved very destructive enemies. After he was relieved from the embarrassments attending the English expedition against Canada, he determined to embrace the earliest opportunity to subdue these Indians. With this view he collected an army of about seven hundred French and Indians, and sent it forth, well provided for the hardships

* Colonial Records, MS.

† Captain James Fitch and Captain Daniel Wetherell.

‡ Leisler wrote to Gov. Bradstreet (Sept. 15, 1690,) as follows: "I have used all arguments and means possible to reinforce for Canada; but by Major Winthrop's treachery and cowardice, with the rest of his tools, hath rendered this work altogether impracticable." "Mr. Livingston, that betrayer of the province, and arch-confederate with yourselves, being willing to have exposed us to the remaining inhabitants; however, God be thanked, we had those that made early provision against these devices."

Hutchinson, the historian of Massachusetts, justly remarks: "Winthrop's character seems to have been made a sacrifice to Leisler's vanity and madness."

§ Colonial Records, MS.

of a winter campaign similar to the one that had resulted so disastrously at Schenectady.

In the middle of January 1693, this army set out from Montreal for the Mohawk country. This warlike tribe occupied a number of fortified places called by our early records "castles." After suffering the extremest hardships, the invading army reached the first of these strongholds on the 6th of February. Here they took four or five men, and passed on to the second, where they met with the like success. Most of the Indians who ordinarily lived in it were absent. At the third, they were more fortunate. Here about forty warriors were assembled for a war-dance, preparatory to their departure upon an expedition against their enemies. They made a stout resistance, but were overpowered by numbers, after having killed thirty of the assailants. In this expedition the French took about three hundred of the five nations. Most of them were women and children.

Colonel Schuyler, of Albany, at the head of about two hundred men, pursued the French army with such energy that they were glad to retreat. His forces were more than doubled within a few days after he took the field, by the allied Indians who flocked to his standard. About the middle of February, he came to the place where the French army was encamped. Three times they commenced a deadly attack upon him and were driven back.

Schuyler was nearly destitute of provisions, and while he was waiting to be supplied with them, and with reinforcements from Albany, the enemy, taking advantage of a severe snow-storm, deserted their camp on the night of the 18th, and set off on their return for Canada. The next day, Captain Simms, with eighty men and a good supply of provisions, joined Schuyler, who immediately resumed the pursuit. He pressed so close upon the French that he would have overtaken them had they not crossed the north branch of Hudson's river upon a floating cake of ice, and thus effected their escape. As it was, he took from them most of the captives that had fallen into their hands.*

Letters soon arrived at Hartford, informing Governor Treat of the state of the western forces, and urgently calling for two hundred soldiers to repair to Albany for the defense of the king's dominions. On the 21st of February, a special Assembly was called, and one hundred and fifty men, under command of Captain John Miles, were immediately placed at the governor's disposal, to send wherever he should deem it most for his majesty's interest to order them. The next day fifty of them were on the march for Albany.†

The Assembly had scarcely adjourned, when new dispatches arrived by express from Sir William Phipps, governor of Massachusetts, asking for one hundred Englishmen and fifty Indians, to aid in protecting the eastern settlements both in Maine and Massachusetts.

On the 6th of March, another special Assembly was called, and the necessities of Massachusetts were responded to by Connecticut, by raising a company of sixty Englishmen and forty Indians, who were placed under the command of Captain William Whiting. The activity of our little colony, the alacrity with which her troops were sent to relieve the northern, eastern, and western borders of the neighboring colonies is in perfect keeping with her previous and subsequent history.

The halcyon days of our republic were destined again to be interrupted by the old question of jurisdiction. The anomalous authority of Leisler was now over in New York,‡ but his successor was no less likely to prove dangerous to the liberties of our people. On the 29th of August 1692, Colonel Benjamin Fletcher, the new governor, arrived from England with a commission that vested him with full powers

* Trumbull. † Colony Records, MS.

‡ Leisler and Milborn were executed in New York city for treason, May 16, 1691; Leisler having previously been succeeded in the office of chief magistrate of New York by Col. Henry Sloughter, who died in July of the same year. Col. Fletcher succeeded Sloughter.

to command the whole militia of Connecticut and the neighboring provinces.* This commission of course took for granted the fact that the charter had been surrendered or forfeited, a proposition not likely to be received with much favor by Governor Treat and the other authorities, nor by the excited militia who had shared so many battles, and who had withstood the landing of Sir Edmund Andross at Saybrook; and who already looked upon the Charter Oak with as much reverence as the ancient nations bordering upon the Mediterranean entertained for the shrine of their favorite oracle. As the charter had never been given up, and as the command of the militia was given by it to the colony, the General Assembly of course could do nothing less than resist this arbitrary demand. However, out of respect to the people, the question was referred to the freemen, whether they would petition the king to preserve to them the control of the militia and their other chartered rights.

At a special Assembly held on the 1st of September 1693, it was ordered that a petition should be presented to the throne in relation to this vital matter. This petition was to be presented by Maj. Gen. Fitz John Winthrop, who was made the agent of the colony for that purpose, and who was desired to repair as soon as possible to England, and use all his endeavors to keep the jurisdiction of the colonial government entire.†

He was instructed to tell the king what hardships the people had encountered in the infancy of the colony, without the help of the mother country, and what dangers still surrounded them; that if the military power should be then taken from them, placed under the command of strangers, and removed out of the limits of the colony to New York or Boston, the citizens of Connecticut would be left utterly defenseless, and their families and property would be at the mercy of their enemies; that an absent stranger would

* Trumbull, i. 390.

† Colonial Records, MS. Mr. Saltonstall was appointed to accompany Gov. Winthrop to England.

be but a poor judge of the wants of people who lived so remote from him, whose sympathies were not with them, and who could be expected to know nothing of the internal wants of the country, whose institutions he was ignorant of, and whose society was of a different texture, and had different wants from that in which he had been reared; that in case of insurrection the military power would thus be unavailable to restore the inhabitants to their wonted tranquillity; that the settlements in the colony, unlike the villages and hamlets in England, were thinly inhabited and remote from each other, rendering it necessary to put upon the military list all males who had arrived at the age of sixteen years, and thus, were the militia withdrawn to some other colony, Connecticut would be left in the keeping of magistrates, professional gentlemen, infirm old men and helpless women, who might hope in vain to be able to guard a line of sea-coast and frontier wilderness formidable enough to the people in their best estate. Winthrop was further instructed to say to the king that the entire population of the colony was satisfied with the charter government, and prayed that it might be perpetuated.

They bade him be sure to inform the king how unanimous the people were in their rejoicings over that happy event, the revolution of 1688, that had placed at the head of a new dynasty so gracious and acceptable a sovereign, and that if their prayer was granted, the militia should be, as it had before been, held at the service of the crown, to defend its honor, and the integrity of the king's empire as well in Massachusetts and New York as in Connecticut. They further instructed him to say, that in defense of his majesty's interests in the recent troubles in New York they had expended more than three thousand pounds and had freely shed their blood.*

It was also left discretionary with the agent whether he should venture to depart from the tone of supplication and assume an attitude of defense, setting up the charter and the rights vested by it in the authorities of the colony.

* Colonial Records, MS.; also Trumbull, i. 390, 392.

At the same time, an agent was sent to New York with a view of conciliating Governor Fletcher so far as could be done without compromising the claims set up under the charter. William Pitkin, Esq., was the agent designated for this mission. He was charged to pay his respects to Governor Fletcher, and treat with him, if possible, in relation to the militia. Owing to the obstinacy of Fletcher, the embassy proved to be a failure.

Finding all his efforts to get control over the militia unavailing, Governor Fletcher resolved to try coercive measures. On the 26th of October, therefore, he came to Hartford while the Assembly were in session, and in the king's name demanded at their hands the surrender of the militia, as they would answer to his majesty for their conduct. He insisted on receiving from them a direct answer whether they would or would not comply with his orders. He subscribed himself as "Lieutenant to his majesty, and commander-in-chief of the militia, and of all the forces by sea or land, and of all the forts and places of strength in the colony of Connecticut."*

With the same pompous authority he commanded that the militia should be summoned under arms in order that he might beat up for volunteers. As if they designed to smooth his path to authority, the officers complied with the order, and called the train-bands together. Up to this point everything was encouraging. But here to his surprise the Assembly took a resolute stand. A very favorable time it was for the legislature to assume a bolder front, now that the guns of the train-bands were seen to glisten in front of the Assembly House. Governor Fletcher had invoked some troublesome spirits that he might not be able to quell now that they were before him. In vain did he argue and remonstrate with the Assembly, and in vain did he expatiate upon the ample powers given him by his commission. The republican authorities either would not or could not comprehend how those powers were consistent with the charter.

* Fletcher's Letter on file.

In Fletcher's name, Colonel Bayard sent a letter into the Assembly, wherein he had carefully set down the object of his visit, and how remote it was from his intentions to interfere in any way with the civil rights of the colony. His excellency, said Bayard, will leave you as he found you, in the full enjoyment of your own. In Fletcher's name he also tendered to Governor Treat a commission authorizing him to command the militia. He insisted that he was contending for the recognition of the mere abstract right on the part of the king to control the military force, but that practically the colony would have the same authority as before. This "inherent, essential right" existing in his majesty, he said his excellency had come to see after, and that he would never set his foot out of Connecticut until it was acknowledged. He further said that he would issue his proclamation to the people, and then he should be able to distinguish the disloyal from those citizens who were peaceably disposed.*

If he had dropped the letter into the Connecticut river, it would have produced as much effect upon the flow of the current as it did upon the Assembly. They reiterated that they could not give up the command of the militia, and Governor Treat with his usual firmness, said it was impossible for him to receive a commission from the hands of Governor Fletcher. This peremptory demand on the one hand and refusal on the other, brought matters at once to an open issue.

As the train-bands were all ranged in due order, and as the senior officer, Captain Wadsworth, was walking up and down in front of the companies, Governor Fletcher advanced within hearing distance, and ordered his commission and instructions to be read. No sooner had Bayard begun to read, than Captain Wadsworth commanded that the drums should be beaten. This was done with such effect that the voice of the herald was entirely drowned in the din. "Silence!" said Gov. Fletcher, in a tone of offended authority. When the noise had subsided so that he could be heard, Bay-

* Col. Bayard's Letter on file.

ard again began to read the commission. "*Drum,* I say, *drum!*" said Captain Wadsworth, and in an instant the voice was again lost in the thunders of martial music. "Silence, silence!" shouted the provincial governor. "*Drum, drum,* I say!" repeated Wadsworth; and then, turning to Fletcher and fixing his sharp resolute eyes upon him, he said —"If I am interrupted *again,* I will make the *sun shine through you in a moment!*" The tone in which these words were spoken was unmistakable. Governor Fletcher knew that death would be the consequence, if he should attempt a third time to enforce his orders. He prudently forebore, and as he saw the people constantly pouring into Hartford and thronging about him and his suite with lowering brows and angry gestures, he retired from the field, and adopting for himself the silence that he had in vain sought to restore to the ranks of the Connecticut militia, departed for his own jurisdiction.*

* This lively episode in our history, like the hiding of the charter, rests upon tradition; but it has been transmitted through such hands and with so little variation, that its accuracy was never for a moment questioned. Such a tradition as this, is as worthy of trust as a record, and takes a much stronger hold on the imagination. The story is in perfect keeping with the traits of our people. As usual, the authorities were only passive, while the active resistance came from a less responsible source. (See Trumbull, i. 393; also Holmes, i. 449.)

CHAPTER XVI.

CONSPIRACY OF DUDLEY AND CORNBURY.

CONNECTICUT, thus set free from the presence of another provincial tyrant, kept on in her old way under the charter. She soon had an opportunity of showing her loyalty to King William, and lost no time in making amends for what the senior captain of the train-bands had done to Governor Fletcher. How then could it be presumed for a moment that Governor Treat and the Assembly had approved of such lawless conduct?

On the 7th of February 1694, a special Assembly was convened on account of a requisition that had been received from the king calling upon the colony to raise money for the defense of Albany. With much apparent alacrity, the legislature voted to comply with the demand, and accordingly a tax of one penny on the pound was laid to raise the sum of five hundred pounds.* The money was paid over into the hands of Colonel Fletcher. The magistrates were also directed to issue their warrants for the impressment of fifty bushels of wheat in each county, which was forthwith to be made into biscuit, and kept for the use of the soldiers in case of any sudden emergency.

In due time Major-General Winthrop, the agent of the colony, arrived in England and hastened to present her claims to his majesty. He drew up in writing a statement of the whole subject matter of his mission, embracing the instructions under which he acted, together with such reasons and arguments as occurred to his own mind. After a full hearing, the king's attorney and solicitor-general gave an opinion favorable to the claims set up by the agent, and on

* Colonial Records, MS.

the 19th of April 1694, his majesty in council graciously decided in accordance with the report thus made. It was determined that Connecticut should place at the disposal of Governor Fletcher, during the war, one hundred and twenty men, and that the rest of the militia of the colony should be, as they ever had been, under the control of the popular governor.* This arrangement was perfectly satisfactory to Connecticut, as it virtually recognized the existence and authority of the charter.

The aid rendered by Connecticut in the war was constant and effective. The whole amount of taxes during the continuance of hostilities, amounted to the enormous burden of about twenty pence on the pound; so that at the close of the year 1695, the colony had drawn from the pockets of the people and paid out seven thousand pounds in the defense of New York and Massachusetts. When we consider that the ratable polls in the whole jurisdiction numbered less than two thousand four hundred, and that the grand list amounted to only £137,646, we can not but admire the self-sacrificing spirit of the citizens; and especially when we remember that they submitted to this heavy drain from their resources from the most magnanimous and unselfish motives that ever actuated a people. To this £7,000 is to be added £3,000 for the untoward expedition against Canada under Winthrop.

For two years more, until the close of the war in September 1697, she submitted still further to the arbitrary demands of Fletcher, who took the ignominious revenge of harassing the governor or the assembly in every possible way, to compensate for the wound that had been inflicted on his dignity at Hartford. Again and again he sent out his expresses to the governor, representing the advance of the enemy towards some exposed place, giving false estimates of their numbers and movements, and calling for troops or other assistance that involved the necessity of convening the Assembly. After the forces thus demanded had set out

* Trumbull, i. 394, 395.

upon their march, another messenger would arrive in hot haste, informing Governor Treat that the exigency had passed by, and that he might recall his forces. In this way the governor and council were kept almost constantly on duty, and the deputies did little else than ride to and from the seat of government to attend these special assemblies. However, the inhabitants were only too happy that in this way they could neutralize the malice of a vindictive and cowardly spirit, and divert its attention from the charter.

Had the war lasted much longer, the people must have become bankrupt, as they had paid at the date of the peace of Ryswick* above alluded to, the almost ruinous sum of £12,000. But as in the case of Andross and Leisler, tyranny was destined at last to have an end.

On the 18th of June 1697, Richard, earl of Bellamont, received a commission to be governor of New York and Massachusetts. In order to maintain a good footing with the king, the Assembly at its October session appointed General Winthrop, Major Sellick and the Rev. Gurdon Saltonstall, a committee to wait upon the new functionary as soon as he should arrive in New York, and pay their respects to him in the name of the colony.† It was not until the spring of the next year that his excellency came over to America. He was very much gratified at receiving the congratulations of the committee, who were all gentlemen of good address and highly cultivated minds. His lordship pronounced Mr. Saltonstall to be the most ele-

---

* The treaty of peace was signed at Ryswick, in September 1697, between France, England, Spain, and Holland, and was proclaimed at Boston on the 10th of December following. Wade, 288; Holmes, i. 464. "And the English colonies had repose from war." Hutchinson, Smollet, Holmes, Blair.

† Colony Records. "Captain Nathan Gold to fill any vacancy that may occur in this committee."

At the same session (Oct. 1697,) the Assembly ordered, "That for the future there shall be *three* or *four*, at least, of the most able and judicious persons in each county appointed *Justices of the Peace* for the year." This is the *first* appointment of Justices of the Peace as distinct from the office of "Magistrate."

gant man whom he had seen in America, and one whose appearance most resembled that of an English nobleman.

Owing to the happy termination of the war and the promise of a new state of things, now that Fletcher was no longer in the way of their advancement, the inhabitants of Connecticut again looked forward to the future with new anticipations.

Grateful to General Winthrop for his faithfulness in the discharge of his trust in England, the people elected him governor in the place of Mr. Treat, who was now far advanced in life. Still, to show their unabated confidence in the former executive, while they relieved him of the more cumbersome burdens of office, they appointed him deputy governor.

At the October session for the year 1698, it was decided that there should be two distinct legislative houses in the General Assembly. The governor, or, in his absence, the deputy governor, and magistrates, were to constitute the upper house; while the deputies, the immediate representatives of the people, were to make up what was called the lower house. The action of these two branches of the legislature was to be independent, and no new law was to be enacted nor was any old one to be repealed or altered without the separate action and consent of both these powers. The deputies were to choose a speaker and other officers much as is now done in the house of representatives.*

This new organization first went into effect at the May session 1699. Mr. John Chester, of Wethersfield, was the first speaker of the lower house, and Captain William Whiting was the first clerk. They were both gentlemen of high character, and of great experience in public affairs.

In June 1659, Governor Winthrop had received permission from the General Court to purchase a tract of land at Quinibaug. He had also bought another valuable estate of Allups and Mashaushawit, the native proprietors, lying on either bank of the Quinibaug river. A few families had

* Colonial Records, MS.

already settled upon these lands before he obtained the title; but the population did not increase to any considerable extent until after the death of the governor. In 1689, a number of planters—a large share of whom came from Massachusetts—bought of the heirs of Governor Winthrop the northern portion of this territory, and began to plant and build upon it. The settlement gradually increased in population for about ten years, and in the spring of 1699, it became a town. In the year 1700 its name was changed from Quinibaug to Plainfield.

At the October session 1698, it was enacted that there should be a new plantation made at "Jeremy's Farm."* The settlement began in 1701, and in 1703 the land was confirmed to the planters by a patent. The Rev. John Bulkley, Samuel Gilbert, Michael Taintor, Samuel Northam, John Adams, Jonathan Kilborn, Joseph Pomeroy, and John Loomis were among the principal proprietors.

At the same session, leave was granted to certain inhabitants of Guilford to begin a plantation at a place called Cogingchaug. The settlement had a feeble infancy, although there were thirty-one original applicants who signed the petition. The two first planters who actually removed and settled upon the tract, were Caleb Seward and David Robinson. Others soon followed them. In May 1704, it was named Durham. Its population still continued small for several years. In 1707, it contained but about fifteen families. In May 1708, it was incorporated, and after that it began to thrive. Northampton, Stratford, Milford, and other old towns, lent to it, soon after its incorporation, some of their best inhabitants.

The boundary between Connecticut and New York had long been a fruitful theme of dispute and controversy. The line agreed upon by the royal commissioners in 1683, was confirmed by the king in council, March 28, 1700. The government of New York, however, being dissatisfied with

* Colony Records, MS. The town was named Colchester.

the bounds as thus determined, refused to unite with Connecticut in running the line, and designating it by proper landmarks. The General Assembly of this colony, after making repeated applications to Lord Cornbury and Governor Hunter without avail, finally appealed to the king. In consequence of this, the legislature of New York, in 1719, passed an act empowering their governor to appoint commissioners to run the line parallel to Hudson's river, to re-survey the former lines, and to erect the necessary monuments to distinguish the boundary. It was not, however, until May, 1725, that the commissioners and surveyers of the two colonies actually commenced operations. Meeting at Greenwich, and agreeing upon the manner in which they should proceed, the survey was commenced and executed in part, when, as is alleged, in consequence of some disagreement, the work was suspended, and each party made a report to its respective legislature. It was not until May, 1731, that a complete settlement of the boundary was perfected. By the bounds, as finally established, Connecticut very unwisely ceded to New York a tract of territory extending along the line of her western frontier, estimated at about sixty thousand acres—comprising some of the most fertile and beautiful lands within her ancient domain. This territory, from its peculiar shape, is still called *Oblong*. The pretended consideration for this summary sale, was the surrender to Connecticut by New York of a few additional miles of sea-coast and the lands adjacent, embracing the town of Greenwich, and perhaps a part of Stamford—both of which townships had long been recognized as belonging to this jurisdiction.

About this time the settlement of Voluntown on the extreme eastern border of the colony was commenced. The greater part of the territory comprised within the limits of the town, was granted in 1696, to the *volunteers* of the Narragansett war, from which circumstance its name is derived. The township was originally six miles square, and was surveyed out of the tract known as the "conquered land."

In 1719, the Assembly granted a large addition on the north, and incorporated the town*.

Nawbesetuck was set off from Windham in 1703, and incorporated as a distinct town by the name of Mansfield. The names of some of the early settlers were, Storrs, Fenton, Porter, Rogers, Hall, and Barrows.

A settlement had been made at Danbury as early as 1685, and eight years afterwards the township was surveyed. The town patent bears date, May 20, 1702.† The first settlers and principal proprietors were James Beebe, of Stratford, Thomas Barnum, Thomas Taylor, Francis Bushnel, James Benedict, John Hoyt, Samuel Benedict, and Judah Gregory, all of Norwalk. This fine old town has since been the scene of tragic interest, which has indissolubly linked its history and its fame with those of the State.‡

At the October session of the Assembly, 1703, it was enacted that the town of Plainfield should be divided, and that the territory on the west side of the Quinibaug river should form a distinct township by the name of Canterbury. Major James Fitch and Mr. Solomon Tracy from Norwich, Mr. Tixhall Ellsworth and Mr. Samuel Ashley from Hartford, and Messrs. John, Richard, and Joseph Woodward, William, Obadiah, and Joseph Johnson, Josiah and Samuel Cleveland, Elisha Paine, Paul Davenport, and Henry Adams, from Massachusetts, were among the principal settlers.§

In May, 1702, war was declared by England, Germany, and the Netherlands against France and Spain; of course the American colonies were soon involved in the conflict. At its October session (1703) the Assembly once more took into consideration what could be done for the common safety. A requisition, made by Governor Dudley and the General Court of Massachusetts, for one hundred men to be sent

---

* Colony Records, MS; see also Barber, 443. † Colony Records, MS.
‡ Trumbull i. 404.

§ At the October session, 1702, it was ordered that Town Clerks should "call the roll at each town meeting, and such freemen as were found to be absent should be subjected to a fine of two shillings," &c.

from Connecticut to aid them in the war with the eastern Indians, was exhibited at this session, and a committee of war was appointed, with plenary powers to send troops into Massachusetts and into the frontier towns of Connecticut. Troops were also ordered forth to defend our towns bordering on the province of New York.*

The Indians grew more and more restive during the winter. They felt the irksomeness of peace. Even the friendly Indians were ill at ease.

On the 15th of March 1704, a special Assembly was called. The civil and military officers in all the towns were ordered to take especial care of the friendly Indians, and keep them from yielding to the bribery and solicitations of the enemy. As these Indians were of little use at home and very serviceable in ranging the woods and tracking out the enemy, it was thought best to employ as many of them as could be engaged in active service. To facilitate this object, gentlemen were appointed to beat up for Indian volunteers and enlist them.†

Aside from the one hundred men sent to the eastern frontier in answer to the requisition from Massachusetts, four hundred men were raised for the protection of the county of Hampshire, and for the defense of Connecticut.

The fears of Governor Dudley of Massachusetts, and the exactions of Lord Cornbury, governor of New York and the Jerseys, kept our colony in constant employ. Lord Cornbury, as Fletcher had done before him, made demands for more money than a weary people, and almost empty treasury, would warrant. His lordship appears to have been terribly frightened, and whenever his timidity abandoned him

* At the same session, the Town Office of *Lister* was established. An act was passed, that persons convicted of selling liquors without a license, or keeping a tippling house, should be *publicly whipped* if the fines, costs, and security for good behavior, were not paid within twenty-four hours after such conviction.

† These friendly Indians were not to go beyond certain prescribed limits without a written order; they were forbidden to have any thing whatever to do with the "enemy Indians," but were to seize and deliver up such as they could capture, for which they were to receive ten pounds apiece.—Colony Records, MS.

for a brief interval, his malevolence towards Connecticut, and his ambition to unite her to his other dominions, rushed in like air into an exhausted receiver, to supply its place. Governor Dudley was very useful to Lord Cornbury in suggesting things to say to the authorities in England that would be most likely to poison the mind of Queen Anne against Connecticut, and induce her majesty to make an effort, as two of her predecessors had done, to pluck the charter out of the hands of the people.

Of these two colonial governors, Dudley was possessed of much the larger share of shrewdness and intrigue. He had been a member of Sir Edmund Andross' council,* and had shared in the bitterness of his prejudices against the colony. Besides, he was even then looking forward to the time when he should fill the executive chair in place of Andross, and was anxious to further his prospects for promotion, by showing as much zeal as possible in this shameful war waged by a king against the rights of his subjects.

This darling object of his ambition, so long entertained, Dudley pursued with the steadiness of aim that belongs to all keen-sighted, intriguing men, who lay their plans quite beneath the calm surface of society, as well-skilled anglers play their hooks in the eddies and under-currents that circle the depths of a shaded pool. With this view he had, before the death of King William, taken all possible precautionary measures against the promotion of men who were thought to be friendly to the liberties of New England. Hence, when he found that Sir Henry Ashurst had been appointed agent for Connecticut, he used all his influence to induce so good a friend of the colony as he knew him to be, not to accept the trust. He made repeated attacks upon the New England charters, and employed force as well as fraud to get possession of them or render them inoperative.

He had already attained the first object of his ambition—he was governor of Massachusetts; but this was only a single round in the ladder that he had proposed to himself to

* Hutchinson.

climb. Connecticut was fast increasing in population and wealth. From the fact that she spent her resources so freely in defense of the other colonies, she appeared to be much more opulent than she really was. How desirable to add all this rich taxable domain to the resources of a colonial exchequer! Besides, was she not arrogant and impertinent in persisting to keep her charter and pretending to exercise under it rights that had been relinquished by her neighbors? How pleasant to strip the plumage from this wild game-bird, and feast his revenge with a morsel that had eluded his appetite so long!

So industrious had Dudley been, and so adroitly had he played his game, that towards the close of William's reign he had succeeded in having a bill prepared to re-unite all the charter governments to the crown. Scarcely was Queen Anne seated upon the throne, when it was brought into parliament. This bill aimed not only at the New England charters, but also at those of East and West New Jersey, Pennsylvania, Maryland, and the Bahama and Lucay Islands, because it averred that these charters were injurious to the trade of the kingdom, discouraging to the other plantations, and tended to cut off the revenues of the crown. It went on to charge the charter governments with encouraging piracy and every mode of contraband trade, and declared "That all and singular, matters, and things, contained in any charters or letters patent, granted by the great seal of England, by any of his royal predecessors, by his present majesty, or the late queen, to any of the said plantations, or to any persons in them, should be utterly void, and of none effect. It further enacted, that all such power, authority, privileges, and jurisdictions, should be, and were re-united, annexed to, and vested in his majesty, his heirs and successors, in right of the crown of England, to all intents and purposes, as though no such charters or letters patent had been had or made."*

* Bill on file. Dudley continued in the office of Governor of Massachusetts until 1715. He had previously been President of Massachusetts and New

This blow was well understood by Sir Henry Ashurst, the agent of the colony, to be aimed mainly at Connecticut. His honorable and manly nature revolted at the injustice thus attempted to be practiced under the sanction of legislation. He therefore hastened to prefer his petition to the House of Lords, wherein he set forth the objects of the bill, and prayed that it might not have the sanction of parliament. The petition stated at full length the condition of Connecticut, and the wrong that would be practiced upon her inhabitants were the charter of Charles II. to be annulled; that her institutions were peculiar to herself; and that all the relations of her people, the very tenures by which they held their property, their religious privileges, and their social texture, were all the growth of the charter; and if that should be taken from them, they would be exposed to the most radical changes, and perhaps involved in utter ruin; that the charges of piracy and contraband trade, recited at length in the bill, whatever might be true elsewhere, could not be truthfully brought against this colony, whose people were agricultural in their habits, and whose authorities administered their offices with great simplicity and purity.

This petition finally obtained a hearing before the House of Lords. It was well presented in behalf of the colony. As at other times, the history of the people in whose behalf it was made was briefly recited; their hardships in commencing the settlement; their efforts to defend it; their long-tried loyalty; the sacrifices that they had made of time, money and life, to keep inviolate the honor of the British flag against so many enemies; and many other reasons, were urged with great earnestness.

The general effect that the bill would have upon the enterprise of the nation, the dishonor that would be brought upon the royal name, were it once understood that no faith

Hampshire; Chief Justice of Massachusetts and New York; Agent of Massachusetts in England; and Lieut. Governor of the Isle of Wight. He died in Boston, 1720, aged 72. Blake's Un. Biog. Dic.

could be put in the grants made by the crown, and the unsettled state of affairs that would prevail throughout all the business relations of the empire, were old titles thus to be torn up by the roots, were not left out of view. Beset with such powerful weapons, the bill was defeated.

Enraged at the failure of this favorite method of accomplishing his ends, Dudley now set himself to the task of playing upon the prejudices and ill-concealed ambition of Cornbury. He affected to take the part of his brother governor, and to favor his views. He assured Cornbury of his own disinterestedness and of his willingness to aid him in bringing Connecticut under his government. He was only too happy to serve his lordship in any way. Independent of personal considerations he was actuated by a sense of justice. Not only should Connecticut be joined to New York, but the southern colonies should be added to them.

Cornbury, weak man as he was, could hardly be expected to resist these flattering promises nor did the chances of success seem doubtful. He was himself a near relative of Queen Anne,* and had a circle of aristocratic friends who were allied to him by blood and who possessed the confidence of her majesty. Connecticut, also, as all the other states have done, cherished some unhappy sons, who, from disappointed political hopes or from pecuniary motives, were only waiting for sufficient vitality to fasten their poisonous fangs into the bosom that had warmed them. These malcontents,—I will not name them in my text†—could of course be made useful to Dudley in any enterprise that was likely to advance their fortunes or feed their revenge.

As Dudley had failed in one attempt upon the liberties of

* Lord Cornbury (Edward Hyde) was a son of the Earl of Carendon, and a first cousin of Queen Anne. (See Agnes Strickland's "Lives of the Queens of England," Vol. xii. p. 43.) He was a bigot in religion, and oppressive and unjust in his administration of the government. He was removed from office in 1708, and died in England in 1723. Blake's Un. Biog. Dic.

† Perhaps the most conspicuous of these ambitious and restless spirits was Major *Edward Palms*, a son-in-law of Governor Winthrop. His disaffection with the colonial government seems to have arisen mainly from the fact that,

the colony, he determined to lay the foundations of his second scheme with greater solidity. It was obvious that the bill to rob Connecticut of her charter had failed mainly from the fact that none of the specific charges named in it had been previously laid against her and substantiated by legal evidence. It was decided, therefore, to convict her authorities of mal-administration, contraband trade, piracy, and the other crimes named in the bill of abominations whose fate had cost its authors so many keen regrets.

With the aid of Cornbury, therefore, Dudley lost no time in filing his charges of complaint against the colony. False witnesses were procured to establish these charges, and all the customary modes of making evidence, were resorted to with a perseverance that evinced how resolute and unscrupulous were the principal actors in the scene. Even the blandishments of letters were brought to delight the English mind with one of the most remarkable fictions that has ever had its origin in the human brain. I need hardly say that I refer to Bulkley's "Will and Doom,"—previously alluded to —a work that has made indeed all other American histori-

---

the General Assembly decided against his application to annul the will of Gov. Winthrop. It seems that Palms had not been named in the will of the governor, as he claimed he *ought* to have been; but the Assembly declared in favor of the will because the wife of Palms had previously deceased. Palms appealed to the king in council, and proceeded to England to prosecute his case. The council, however, confirmed the decision of Connecticut. Maj. Palms died in New London, March 21, 1714, aged 78.

Nicholas Hallam, also a leader in the crusade against Connecticut, became disaffected with the colony in a similar manner. His step-father (Mr. Liveen,) had bequeathed most of his property to "the ministry of New London," and Hallam determined to break the will. The case was tried before the county court and the court of assistants, both of which decided that the will was valid. The suit was carried to England, where after a delay of more than four years, the decision of the Connecticut courts was sustained. See Caulkins' History of New London, pp. 222—228.

Palms and Hallam, excited as they were, stood ready to take sides with any one who might be brought in collision with Connecticut from whatever cause. Hence, Cornbury and Dudley found in them efficient friends; hence, too, their active sympathy in behalf of the Mohegans and their zeal for the "Mason heirs," as will hereafter appear.

cal extravagances, save Peters' "History of Connecticut," of which it was the type and herald, tame and cold.

This book had been written soon after the close of Sir Edmund Andross' administration, and was now resuscitated and sent over from New York by Lord Cornbury, with some other documentary evidence against the colony. It was received in England on the 16th of January, 1705.*

Aside from the accusations before made against the colony, the complaint alleged that it was a place of refuge for seamen, servants, malefactors, and other fugitives from justice who fled from the other colonies, that it also took under its protection young men who went there from New York and Massachusetts to avoid taxation resulting from the wars, that had thrown such heavy burdens upon all the northern colonies except Connecticut; that this colony had refused to aid in the fortification of New York and Albany, and had failed to send men to defend Massachusetts against the

* This singular work, though anonymous, is supposed to be from the pen of the Rev. Gershom Bulkley, who graduated at Harvard College in 1659; was settled in the ministry at New London from 1661 to 1666, and in Wethersfield from the latter date until 1677. He then removed to Glastenbury where he practiced medicine for over thirty years, and died in 1713. As a politician, he was opposed to the assumption of the government by the colonial authorities in 1689, after the arrest of Andross. In 1689, he published a pamphlet on the affairs of Connecticut, but no copy of it is now known to exist. (See Dr. Chapin's Hist. of Glastenbury.) "Will and Doom" was doubtless written soon after. December 15, 1692, Major Palms, Gershom Bulkley and Wm. Rosewell appended to the MS. volume their certificate, in which they say, that to their "best knowledge of things, the state of affairs in Connecticut is therein truly represented," and they "doubt not but every material passage in it may easily be proved by them." To be sure, it is not often that an author volunteers a formal certificate of the probable truth of his own work; but in this case, Mr. Bulkley may have done so for the purpose of better concealing the authorship of the volume, which was not calculated to increase his popularity in New England. The MS. was indorsed as follows, on its arrival in England: "Mr. Bulkley's 'Will and Doom,' relating to grievances and irregularities in the Province of Connecticut." "Received with Lord Cornbury's of the 6th of November 1704. Vide New York, Bundle X, 18." "Received 16 January; read 1st. February 1704–5. Entered Proprieties, fol. 126. No. 20."

Some have supposed that the book in question was written by the Rev. John Bulkley, of Colchester—but the improbability of this is apparent from the fact, that he did not graduate until 1699, and "Will and Doom" is not the work of a boy.

French and Indians.* All this time Dudley smiled blandly upon the colony that he was thus plotting to destroy, and in a letter that bore almost an even date with these infamous allegations, he thanked the General Assembly for the liberal supplies that they had bestowed upon Massachusetts, and the readiness with which they had responded to his requisitions.

I have said it was a part of the plan of operations to conciliate certain malcontents who lived in Connecticut. These men now aided Dudley in furnishing evidence against the colony, by giving currency to a ridiculous story that the General Assembly had abused Owaneco, chief of the Mohegans, and had driven his tribe from their planting grounds. Whoever knows any thing of the history of that tribe and of the sacrifices made by Connecticut to protect it from enemies that would have annihilated it long before this conspiracy was made, can judge what credit should be given to a tale that contradicts all the records that have been transmitted to us relating to the affairs of that expensive and burdensome tribe. Yet, inconsistent as was the accusation, it was penned into a petition to the queen, ostensibly in behalf of the Mohegans, but really with no other motives than avarice and revenge on the part of the applicants, representing the General Assembly in such false colors that it could not fail to deceive the ears for which it was intended, especially when presented and advocated by such men as Dudley. Had the complaint charged the colony with unkindness towards the Pequots after the strength of their tribe had been broken, and with yielding to the solicitations of Uncas, or submitting to the cruel robberies that he was allowed to perpetrate upon that suffering people; or had it

* Nothing could surpass the wicked falsehood of these two charges, unless it were the ingratitude that could allow the governors of these invaded colonies to deny the services of our troops in saving their inhabitants from the tomahawk and the ruinous taxes that our people paid with cheerfulness to answer pecuniary demands, sometimes entirely unnecessary and often greatly exaggerated—services rendered and taxes paid, as in the case of New York under Leisler's administration, in behalf of a people who either could not or would not help themselves.

charged Connecticut, in common with the rest of New England, with the guilt that often accompanies a too easy credulity, because she had lent a willing ear to Mohegan prejudices, and consented to the judicial murder of Miantinomoh; or because her fears had led her to sacrifice Nanuntenoo, there might have been some show of justice in the arraignment. But it has always been the fate of Connecticut to be put upon her deliverance for imaginary crimes, for the reason that her faults in some cases were too slight, and in others attended with too palliating circumstances to justify the malice of her enemies or afford a palpable ground of conviction.

The sympathies of the queen were touched at the supposed sufferings of the Mohegans, so wantonly inflicted by her English subjects, and, without waiting to allow Connecticut a hearing, she granted, on the 19th of July 1704, a commission to Dudley and Palms, the arch-enemies of the colony, and others, their instruments—twelve in all—to hear and try the cause of the afflicted Owaneco against Connecticut.*

Preparatory to this farcical court, on the 5th of July 1705, John Chandler, in behalf of Owaneco—whose ancestors had received the consideration-money more than twice over for all the lands that had ever gone out of their possession—and Mason, and the other claimants, in behalf of themselves, began a survey of the Mohegan country. They ran out the lines in accordance with their own claims, and having completed the perambulation, they made a map of the territory such as suited well enough the uses of a hearing before a tribunal that was understood to have pre-judged the case.

The lines as run by Chandler and his assistants had for their southern boundary a large rock in Connecticut river near Eight-Mile-Island, in Lyme, and thence took an easterly course through Lyme, New London, and Groton, to a lit-

* The Court of Commissioners consisted of the following persons, viz.:—Joseph Dudley, Esq., President, Edward Palms, Giles Sylvester, Jahleel Brenton, Nathaniel Byfield, Thomas Hooker, James Avery, John Avery, John Morgan, and Thomas Leffingwell. The other two appear to have been absent.

tle lake in the north-eastern part of Stonington, called Ah-yo-sup-suck; thence northerly, to another lake called Mah-man-suck, thence to a place called the Whetstone hills, and thence to Man-hum-squeeg, or the Whetstone country. From this last named point (if indeed it was a point) the line veered off in a south-westerly course, a distance of several miles, to the upper falls in the Quinibaug river; here, taking a new track, it darted away to the north-west through Pomfret, Ashford, Willington, and Tolland, to the Notch of Bolton mountain, and thence, "instinct with fire and nitre," the liberal-minded surveyors took wing in a southerly course, across Bolton, Hebron, and East Haddam, to the place of beginning.

Having completed his survey, his map, and all his other enginery of self-conviction—and who could judge so well as his excellency of the machinery best calculated to subdue his scruples—Governor Dudley carried his court into Connecticut, and planted it in a convenient place within the limits of Stonington.

As Connecticut had not been allowed a hearing as to the propriety of creating this special court, so did the court fail to serve her with a copy of the commission that was to try the question of title and jurisdiction to some of the most valuable lands within her boundaries;—so that she remained in ignorance till the day of the hearing, whether the commission merely authorized a court of inquiry, or whether it was to determine the title to the lands.

She therefore sent a committee to be present at the opening of the court, and find out what was the extent of its powers. If it was a court of inquiry, they were instructed to defend; if it was designed to try the title, they were commanded to enter their solemn protest in behalf of the colony, and withdraw in silence. At the same time, all the inhabitants of Connecticut who claimed any interest in the controverted lands, were forbidden to put in any plea or make any answer before the court. The names of the gentlemen composing this committee, were William Pitkin, John

Chester, Eleazer Kimberly, Esqrs., Maj. William Whiting, Mr. John Elliott, and Mr. Richard Lord.

Governor Winthrop, on the 21st of August, wrote a letter to Dudley, in which he is careful to speak of the commission as authorizing only a *preliminary* court.

When the committee had arrived at the place of trial and had learned that it was the intention of the tribunal to settle questions of title, they tendered to Dudley their written protest. After sketching, with a few hasty strokes, the folly and wantonness of the charges brought against Connecticut, the committee go on to say, "We must declare against and prohibit all such proceedings as contrary to law and to the letters patent under the great seal of England granted to this her majesty's colony." In conclusion they add, "It seems strange to us that your excellency should proceed in such a manner, without first communicating your commission to the General Assembly of this her majesty's colony."

After an *ex parte* hearing of a single day, in which the Indian, Owaneco, who probably did not care a whiff of tobacco smoke about the controversy, aside from the paltry presents that he might have expected for allowing his name to be used in it, and the other applicants, had it all their own way, and procured a judgment in their favor.*

If ever there was a piece of judicial villainy it was this, by which the property of hundreds of persons, and the jurisdiction of a colony, were disposed of without serving any notice upon the respondents by the adverse party in interest, who had caused themselves to be constituted a tribunal to sit in judgment upon their own untenable claims.

---

* The Court adjudged to Owaneco and the Mohegans a tract of land in New London, called Massapeag; and another tract in the northern part of the same town, containing about eleven hundred acres; also, a tract in Lyme, two miles in breadth and nine miles in length, together with the whole tract contained in the town of Colchester. These lands had been obtained by conquest, purchase treaty, and other lawful means, and had been settled upon by persons who held their deeds or patents from the Assembly. The court ordered Connecticut immediately to restore all these lands to Owaneco; and also prohibited all her majesty's subjects from settling upon or improving certain other large tracts, until a further hearing and determination of the case.

I have said that this Mohegan affair, as far as Dudley was interested in it, was designed to prejudice the mind of the queen against Connecticut, so that she might be the more readily induced to regard the people as outlaws, who had forfeited their charter privileges, and were entitled to no mercy at her hands. The fact that the hearing was not had until after the trial of the principal allegations against Connecticut before the queen in council, made little difference. The charge having been made, the chief mischief was accomplished, as the colony was in much the same condition that an accused person is while awaiting his trial for the commission of a crime. It is true that theoretically the law presumes him innocent till proved guilty, but no legal maxim or presumption can do away with the impression made upon the public mind even by a false accusation.*

On the 12th of February, 1705, after the last bundle of evidence that had been shipped by Cornbury from America was received in England, the trial of Connecticut for her charter, which had been postponed at the solicitation of Sir Henry Ashurst, in order that he might receive further evidence and further instructions from the General Assembly, came on before the queen in council.

Dudley had prepared his case with great address, and Cornbury had seconded him with an equal amount of industry and spite. The former had dug up from the archives of King William's reign a precedent in favor of the proposition that the crown had power to appoint a governor over Connecticut. He had also attempted to get an opinion from the then acting attorney-general favorable to his case; but

* This famous "Mohegan case," after having agitated Connecticut more than seventy years, was finally determined in favor of the colony in 1743. The lands in dispute, or some part of them, had been acquired by Major Mason, as agent of Connecticut—who, in a somewhat informal manner, surrendered them to the colony in March, 1661. (See J. H. Trumbull's Colonial Records, i. 359.) The heirs of Mason, and certain other designing persons, subsequently instituted a claim for the lands, and prosecuted it with great tenacity. The pretense that the Mohegans were oppressed or driven off by the English settlers, was simply designed for effect.

the best that he could induce the guarded functionary to do for him, was to make the statement "that *if it were* as Governor Dudley had represented, there was a *defect* in the *Government*, that the colony was not able to defend itself and in imminent danger of being possessed by the queen's enemies; and that in *such case*, the queen might send a governor for civil and military government, but not to alter the *laws* and *customs*." Nobody could find any fault with this opinion. It would have been equally tenable had he said, "if the authorities harbored pirates and carried on contraband trade," as Governor Dudley had represented, "they ought to be adjudged guilty of felony without the benefit of clergy." There is much significance in a legal opinion that is heralded with an "*if*." It implies at least that the *facts* have not yet been passed upon.

As had been the case in the Mohegan affair, so in this most vital matter, the grounds of the accusation and the arguments that would be set up by the complainants, had been kept secret from the agent of the colony. True, however, to the interests of his principals, as on former occasions he had proved himself, Sir Henry Ashurst* nobly stood his ground. He knew that this was a desperate struggle for colonial existence against injustice and oppression, and that it called for all the address of which he was master, and all the influence that he could command. He was a brother-in-law of Lord Paget, a nobleman of fine abilities and powerful connections. His lordship, whose sense of justice was outraged by the behavior of the applicants, magnanimously espoused the cause of Connecticut, and threw into the scale that he desired should preponderate, the full weight of his disinterested influence with the queen's favorites and the members of the council. He procured the professional aid of two of the best advocates in England, who met the

* This gentleman was a son of Henry Ashurst, Esq., member of parliament, and a firm friend to New England. Sir Henry had previously been the agent of Massachusetts at the Court of Great Britain; but accepted the agency of Connecticut in 1704, and continued to act in that capacity until his death in 1710.

sophistries and exposed the false statements of Dudley, Cornbury, Congreve, and the whole host of assailants, who argued the cause for an hour and a half before the council with great eloquence and force. I need not go over the grounds urged by these gentlemen, as they will suggest themselves to the reader who has had the patience to peruse the preceding chapter.

After exposing the intrigues of Dudley and his fellow conspirators, the counsel in behalf of the colony went on to say, that whatever might be the real truth in relation to the allegations, it was a sacred right extended to all British subjects by the constitution itself, that all persons and corporations should have an oportunity to be heard, before any legal proceeding against them could be the basis of a judgment. The advocates powerfully pressed upon the minds of the council the consideration, that as this necessary pre-requisite had not been complied with in relation to the governor and company of Connecticut, it would be doing them a great and unprecedented wrong to take from them their most precious rights—nay, their very political life, without giving them the opportunity of confronting their accusers. Then a well-timed allusion was made to the motives that led to the accusation, and a very striking portraiture was drawn of the overshadowing growth and noxious qualities of executive ambition in a remote part of the empire, beyond the conservative influences of her majesty's personal supervision. The patronage attending such a position as that held by Dudley, the facility of procuring witnesses who, from interested motives, could be induced to falsify their testimony, were dwelt upon as so many facts that should put the council upon their guard while the limited power of the governor of Connecticut under the charter, watched as he was by the other branches of the government and amenable to the annual suffrages of the freemen, afforded a very strong presumption in his favor, and seemed to call still more loudly for a public hearing of the evidence that might be within reach of the corporation. Waxing warm as they dwelt upon the contrast between such men as Dudley and Cornbury on the one hand, and Treat and Winthrop on the other, these gentlemen boldly urged, that in the case of a provincial governor who held during the pleasure of the crown, and who was liable to lose nothing but his office, avarice often tempted the incumbent to perpetrate the most barbarous cruelties, and that it might be found upon investigation of the evidence, that Governor Winthrop was better fitted to govern Connecticut, than Cornbury was to rule in New York, or Dudley in Massachusetts. In conclusion, they begged that a copy of the complaint might be sent to the governor and company of Connecticut, that they might prepare themselves at a future day to defend the corporation.

So reasonable was this request that the council could not fail to comply with it. It was therefore ordered that copies of the principal charges in the complaint should be made out and sent, one to the governor of Connecticut, and one to Dudley and Cornbury, the chief complainants; that Connecticut should make her answer to each allegation, and establish such answer if she could, by evidence legally taken and duly sealed with the seal of the colony. Dudley and Cornbury were in like manner to forward their proofs in proper legal form.

Nothing could have been more unsatisfactory to Dudley and Cornbury than this just decision. They saw at once that their schemes were ruined and their intrigues exposed. They saw the castles that they had built upon the crumbling foundations of calumny and lies, already beginning to topple down upon their heads. For did they not know that of all the accusations so pompously paraded in their complaint, not one of them could stand before the array of unimpeachable testimony that would be sent out against it by the outraged and insulted colony? Poor Dudley, the cunning artificer of this fraud, had need of all his fortitude to sustain him, for the General Assembly were able to prove, that instead of neglecting Massachusetts and New York in their day of peril, as he had attempted to make the queen believe, and that instead of leaving the inhabitants of those provinces without men and supplies, Connecticut had during that year and the preceding one, kept six hundred troops in constant requisition, and that two-thirds of that number had been engaged in actual service in those provinces. She could prove, too, that while her people had scarcely two thousand pounds of money in circulation in the whole colony, they had in three years expended a much greater sum in defending New York and Massachusetts. What was still more mortifying to Dudley, they had in their keeping a most flattering letter under his own hand, in which he thanked them for the generous aid that they had given him, and for their services during the war. To corroborate even his admissions against himself, they had also on file, ready to be produced, letters of commendation and thanks from the officers who had commanded in Massachusetts, and from the principal gentlemen there, all speaking the language of gratitude for services rendered by Connecticut. As to the cowardly charges of disloyalty to the government, contraband trade, harboring fugitives from justice or taxation, and that more infamous one of *piracy*, who knew better than the author of them, how vain would be the attempt to prove them, and with what triumph the evidence that was within the reach of the colony could sweep them away?

No wonder, then, that he gave up the complaint as hopeless, and set himself, as I have already detailed, to execute a commission in regard to a matter that was, before the date of the instrument, a foregone conclusion in his own mind; nor need I tell the reader, that when the proofs adduced by the governor and company arrived in England, the loyalty and honor of Connecticut shone but the brighter when placed in contrast with the wickedness of her accusers.

I need not say that Dudley and Cornbury did not forward their testimony, nor appear to prosecute their complaints;

nor is it necessary to add, that in due time a letter arrived from Sir Henry Ashurst, informing the *people* that it was the opinion of the best men in the realm that *they alone*, subject to the requisitions of the crown, had a right to command the militia of the colony and dispose of its money under *The Charter*.

Eng. by D. C. Hinman from a pencil sketch by Col. Trumbull in the possession of B. Silliman, Jr.

MAJ. GEN. ISRAEL PUTNAM.

Israel Putnam

Hollister's History of Connecticut.

CHAPTER XVII.

DEATH OF TREAT. SURRENDER OF PORT ROYAL.

Early in the year 1707, the colonies were again alarmed with rumors of another French and Indian invasion. On the 6th of February, a council of war, made up of the governor and most of his council with the principal military gentlemen of the colony, convened at Hartford. Robert Treat, then deputy governor, too infirm by reason of his great age to be present, wrote a letter and sent it in by a messenger to aid the deliberations of the council. This letter gave intelligence confirming these rumors. Major Schuyler sent in similar communications. It was thought that the Pootatuck and Owiantuck tribes had been consulted, and were ready to join with the French. As these Indians were within our borders, and in a position to expose our western frontiers to great hazard, it was ordered that Simsbury, Waterbury, Woodbury, and Danbury, should speedily be fortified. As Waterbury had not yet recovered from the effects of the floods alluded to on a former page of this work, the council promised to use their influence with the General Assembly to get the country rates of the town abated by way of encouraging the inhabitants to place their houses in a defensible condition. Two gentlemen from Woodbury, Captain John Minor, and Mr. John Sherman, were selected to remove the Pootatuck and Owiantuck Indians from the places then occupied by them, to Stratford and Fairfield, where they would be in the midst of a vigilant English population and could be more easily watched. It was ordered, further, that some of the chiefs of each tribe should be carried down to those towns, and there kept as hostages for the good behavior of their people. On the second of April, a special assembly was called on account of the receipt of letters from Governor Dudley, who proposed to send one thousand men against Acadie, and requested (he could not command) Connecticut to join her forces with those of Massachusetts in the expedition. The duplicity of Dudley towards the colony was by no means forgotten, and the recollection of it aided the Assembly, I have no doubt, in coming to a conclusion not to respond to the call. It was argued that Connecticut had not been consulted as to the propriety of taking this step, and that she was not yet sufficiently recovered from the burden of defending the county of Hampshire, to be able to assist in an enterprise where her hand and not her counsels were in request.

On the 27th of November 1707, while in the discharge of his duties as governor of the colony, died the Hon. Fitz John Winthrop, in the 69th year of his age. I have already given a history of his public life in my account of the expedition against Canada, and of his services in England in 1694, as the agent of the people to vindicate the right of the governor to command the militia. He was as zealous in defending that strong hold of popular liberty as his father, John Winthrop, had been in establishing it. Though maligned by some of the worst enemies that have ever beset a good man, he lived to see them, like Leisler and Milborn, suffer the penalties awarded to traitors, or like Dudley and Cornbury, baffled in the cross-currents of politics. He still keeps an honorable place in the gallery of our colonial governors, as a gentleman of great fidelity in all his public relations, and of unblemished private life.

To fill the vacancy occasioned by his death, Deputy Governor Treat convoked a special assembly on the 17th of December, at New Haven. It was ordered that the votes of both houses should be mixed and then sorted and counted, and that the candidate who received a majority of votes, should be declared governor. The ballot resulted in the election of the Rev. Gurdon Saltonstall, who then had charge of the church at New London. On the 1st of January

1708, he signified his acceptance of the place and took the oath of office. The regular election that took place on the 13th of the following May, confirmed the choice. At the same time, as the deputy governor, then eighty-six years old, had made known his desire to withdraw from the cares of public life, it was thought best to excuse him from further service. Nathan Gold was elected to fill his place.

As the infirmities of age soon confined Governor Treat to the narrow circle of his own neighborhood until his death, that took place about two years after his resignation, I havė thought this a proper occasion to give a slight sketch of his life and character.

Robert Treat, the third governor under the charter, and son of Richard Treat, one of the patentees named in it, was born in England, in the year 1622. At an early age he accompanied his father to America. Richard Treat—(always designated in our early colonial records, by the title of Mr. or Master,) was a gentleman of high character, and was among the first planters of Wethersfield. He held several important places of trust in the colony. Robert, from what cause it does not appear,* did not long remain with his father, but left Connecticut for Milford, during the infancy of that settlement, while yet it was a republic independent of New Haven. At the first meeting of the planters of Milford, and when Treat was only eighteen years old, he was chosen to aid in surveying and laying out the lands of the new plantation. Soon afterwards he was appointed one of the five judges that constituted the "particular court" of the Commonwealth. After Milford was joined with New Haven in 1644, he soon became known in the colony as a gentleman of good culture and marked abilities. In 1661, he was elected a magistrate and remained in the magistracy

* It is probable that Mr. Prudden, who preached in Wethersfield during a part of the year 1639, and had proved very acceptable to a part of the people there, may have induced Mr. Treat to remove to Milford, as he did some other planters. Certain it is that Treat was in Milford as early as 1639, as appears by the Milford records.

until 1664, when he declined any longer to hold office under a government that he felt to be already tottering to its fall, crushed by the weight of debts and taxes, and hemmed in by a troop of adverse circumstances that, like a beleaguering army, cut off at once all supplies and all hope. It was mainly through his influence that Milford left the jurisdiction of New Haven, and placed herself in the keeping of Connecticut. He was the only man then living in the colony of New Haven, who had at the same time the moral courage and the resolute will successfully to meet the unabated opposition of Davenport to the union, that could hardly have been effected as it was, had he failed to unite his fearless counsels with the persuasive admonitions of Winthrop.

In 1670, he was appointed major of the Connecticut troops, then the highest military officer in the colony. His gallantry and bravery—evinced throughout the whole course of Philip's war, from its first stages, in which he was again and again chiefly instrumental in saving from total destruction some of the finest border towns in Massachusetts, down to the fatal hour when, with the Connecticut troops, he passed from the rear to the van of Winslow's army, and led the forlorn hope across the bridge and in front of the block-house whence the murderous fire of Philip's sharp-shooters had more than once driven the forces of Massachusetts—are without a parallel in our history, save in the life of Mason who preceded him, or Putnam who came after him. In 1676, he was elected deputy governor, and in 1683, governor of the colony. He filled the executive office for fifteen years, when he declined any longer to act in that capacity, and Gen. Fitz John Winthrop was chosen to supply his place. There existed between Treat and John Winthrop the most cordial friendship, growing out of the admiration that each felt for the character and abilities of the other, and also on account of the part that they respectively took, the one in procuring the charter, the other in vindicating its jurisdiction and in preserving it from the violence of its enemies.

Winthrop died before the clouds that had begun to gather

in his day had darkened into the storm; Treat lived to withstand the fiercest bolts of delegated power.

Governor Treat was not only a man of high courage, but he was one of the most cautious military leaders, and possessed a quick sagacity united with a breadth of understanding that enabled him to see at a glance the most complex relations that surrounded the field of battle. Nor did he excel only as a hero: his moral courage and his inherent force of character shone with the brightest lustre in the executive chair or legislative chamber, when stimulated by the opposition and malevolence of such men as Andross. In private life he was no less esteemed. He was a planter of that hospitable order that adorned New England in an age when hospitality was accounted a virtue, and when the term gentlemen was something more than an empty title. His house was always open to the poor and friendless, and wherever he gave his hand he gave his heart. Hence, whether marching to the relief of Springfield, or extending his charities to Whalley and Goffe, while he drowned a tear of sympathy in the lively sparkle of fun and of anecdote, he was always welcome, always beloved. His quick sensibilities, his playful humor, his political wisdom, his firmness in the midst of dangers, and his deep piety, have still a traditionary fame in the neighborhood where he spent the brief portion of his time that he was allowed to devote to the culture of the domestic and social virtues. He died at Milford, in the 89th year of his age.*

---

* Governor Treat married Jane Tapp, the daughter of Edmund Tapp, Esq., of Milford, who died April 8, 1703. He then married the widow Elizabeth Bryan, who died in about three months after their union. The children of Gov. Treat were, (1.) *Jane;* (2.) ***Robert***, who settled in Milford, and was a magistrate; (3.) ***Samuel***, who graduated at Harvard College in 1669, was settled in the ministry at Eastham, Mass., and died in 1717, leaving a numerous family; (4.) ***John***, who d. young; (5.) ***Mary***, who m. Azariah Crane, in Newark, N. J.; (6.) ***Sarah***, who d. young; (7.) ***Sarah;*** (8.) ***Hannah***, m. Rev. Samuel Mather, of Windsor, Conn.; (9.) ***Joseph***, of Milford, who became a Justice of the Quorum; (10.) ***Abigail***, m. Rev. Samuel Andrew, of Milford; (11.) ***Anne***, m. Rev. Thomas Paine, of Weymouth, Mass., and became the mother of the celebrated Robert Treat Paine, a Signer of the Declaration of Independence.

His eventful life, that began in the early part of one century, and ended in the first quarter of another, was mild and tranquil at its close, beaming smilingly upon the world as a summer sunset lingers upon the horizon to light up with its warm blending of colors the vapors that herald the coming of darkness.

The refusal of Connecticut to furnish her quota of troops in answer to the call of Governor Dudley, delayed the contemplated expedition against Canada, but did not defeat it. At the May session of the General Assembly, 1709, a letter from the queen was presented and read, advising the colony of the plan of the campaign. It was resolved to reduce the French in Canada, Acadie, and Newfoundland. The contents of letters from the Earl of Sunderland, were also made known to the legislature, in which the number of troops and the amount of supplies to be provided by each of the colonies were specified. Connecticut was ordered to raise 350 men, and the other colonies lying east of Connecticut, were to provide an aggregate of 1,200 men, with transports, pilots, and provisions, for three months' service. The earl acquainted the colonies with her majesty's design to send a squadron of ships to Boston by the middle of May. This armament was expected to resume the old attempt upon Quebec. But this was not the full burden that was to be placed on the shoulders of the colony.

It was further proposed that Connecticut, New York, and New Jersey, and the southern colonies should raise 1,500 men to cross the country and take possession of Montreal. With her usual alacrity, Connecticut raised her share of the troops for the land army, and placed them under the command of Colonel Whiting. The Assembly, by a formal vote, also thanked the queen for her kind care of the colonies, in taking such active measures to remove a dangerous enemy. As early as the 20th of May, the provincial armament was ready to sail for Quebec. Francis Nicholson was placed at the head of the land army. He was directed to march as far as Wood Creek, and there await the coming of the fleet that was expected at Boston, when he was to press forward and reach Montreal, so that the attack upon that place might be made simultaneously with that upon Quebec. Not only did the colonies raise their respective quotas of men, but such was the zeal of the inhabitants to engage in the war, that many volunteer companies were raised and sent on to join the regular troops, and more than one hundred batteaux and as many birch canoes were constructed to transport the army across the lake. Three forts, several block-houses and store-houses, were built for the protection of the army and of the frontier. All these preparations only resulted in a useless expense to the colonies. The fleet, so long and anxiously waited for, did not come from England, and in the fall, after disease had thinned the ranks of his army and threatened utterly to depopulate his camp, Nicholson marched back to Albany. One quarter of those who had been placed under his command were dead. Connecticut alone lost ninety men. The colony was so straightened for means by this bootless enterprise that the Assembly was compelled to issue Bills of Credit* to the amount of eight thousand pounds. This was the first time that Connecticut ever resorted to an issue of paper money, though she has since done it more than once, not merely for her own protection, but for the salvation of the Union, for which she afterwards fought with such valor. Although the colonies were deeply disappointed at

* It may interest the reader to know the form of these Bills of Credit, and I subjoin an exact copy of one, taken from the Colonial Records :

"No. ( ) 20s.

"This Indented Bill of Twenty Shillings due from the colony of Connecticut, in New England, to the possessor thereof, shall be in value equal to money, and shall be accordingly accepted by the Treasurer, and Receivers subordinate to him, in all public payments, and for any stock at any time in the Treasury.

"Hartford, July the Twelfth, A. D., 1709.

"By order of the General Court."

In connection with this provision, it was enacted, that these bills should be issued from the treasury as money, but should be received in payments at one shilling on the pound better than money. One half only were to be signed and issued at first, and the other half were to remain unsigned, until it should be found necessary to put them in circulation.

the failure of a scheme that had thrown upon them such heavy burdens, yet their situation was too critical to allow them time to brood over the past. The French still retained their old Indian alliances, and were making all the efforts that they could to alienate from the English the waning affections of the five nations. Could the enemy but bring about this result they well knew that the whole English frontier would be in their power, and the settlements along its entire line would be again exposed to the sickening atrocities of an Indian border war. These the colonies had already experienced, and the recollection was enough to stimulate them to the most vigorous exertions.

That they might hit upon some uniform plan of operation, a congress of governors was held at Rehoboth, Massachusetts, in the beginning of October, to deliberate upon the condition of the country and advise what should be done. General Nicholson, Colonel Vetch, and other experienced military gentlemen, were invited to attend upon the Congress, and give it the benefit of their advice. The result of their deliberations was an address to the queen, setting forth the harmonious relations that subsisted between the colonies, the loyalty that prevailed among the people, and the necessity of adding the French colonies in North America to the other dominions of her empire. The address ended with a petition that her majesty would send out an armament which, with the provincial troops, would be equal to such an enterprise.

At the session of the General Assembly in October, Governor Saltonstall made known the doings of the executive convention and caused the address to be read. The legislature approved of its terms and adopted a similar one in behalf of Connecticut. Governor Saltonstall was appointed agent for the colony to present it to the queen.*

In 1708, twenty-five inhabitants of Norwalk united in purchasing of Catoonah, the chief sachem, and other Indians, a large tract of land lying between that town and Danbury.

* Colonial Records, MS.

The deed is dated on the 30th of September of that year, and at the ensuing session of the General Assembly, it was incorporated as a town by the name of Ridgefield. John Belden, Samuel Keeler, Matthew Seymour, and Matthias St. John, were among the chief proprietors and settlers.

That the queen might be more easily induced to send the aid that was so much sought for, Colonel Schuyler, one of the most wealthy gentlemen in the province of New York, whose whole heart was in the project, resolved to approach her majesty's confidence by exciting her curiosity and playing upon her imagination. At his own expense, therefore, he fitted out a vessel, and, with five Indian sachems in his charge, representing the five nations who had withstood the tempting offers of the French, he sailed for England.* He carried also an address from the Assembly of New York, begging for the interposition of the crown.

The queen readily granted an interview to Colonel Schuyler, and the swarthy deputation that had accompanied him, and the chiefs were received with such ceremonials as suited the rank of the respective parties. These children of the forest, erect and unabashed in the presence of royalty, made a very favorable impression upon the mind of the queen. In their simple, wild way, they gave her a history of the part that they had taken in the struggles with the French, and what faithful allies they had proved to her children across the water; with what readiness they had submitted to the loss of their best warriors, and with what delight they had received the intelligence that so great a sovereign as she was, was about to send ships and men to subdue the common enemy. They said that as one man they had hung up the kettle and taken up the hatchet in aid of Nicholson; but when they found that their great queen, on account of some weighty matters at home, had kept back her ships, their hearts were heavy, lest the enemy, who had before feared them, should now think that they were too weak to make war upon them. They said that the reduc-

* Bancroft, Trumbull, Brodhead.

tion of Canada was very necessary to them, as they could not occupy their hunting-grounds with any security as things then were; and intimated that, should the queen be unmindful of them, they must either quit their country and seek other places of abode, or remain neutral—neither of which alternatives would accord with their inclinations.*

This deputation, with the several addresses before alluded to, met with a gracious reception, and the applicants were led to hope that an armament would at once be sent to reduce Canada.

In July 1710, advices arrived in New England, that a fleet under the charge of Lord Shannon was soon to set sail; and in anticipation of it, Nicholson, with several armed ships and some transports, left England in the spring for the American coast.

These preparations, however, proved not to be designed for the reduction of Canada, but only to get possession of Port Royal and Nova Scotia.

On the 14th of August, a special assembly was convened on account of a letter addressed by the queen to the colony, calling for troops and supplies. In debt as she was, and suffering as her people still were from the heavy loss of life that befell the army at Wood Creek, Connecticut voted to raise three hundred men in obedience to the requisition. No time was lost in procuring vessels and sailors for the expedition, and in four weeks our quota of troops were safely transported to Boston.

By the 18th of September, the provincial fleet was ready to sail. It consisted of thirty-six ships of war and transports, under command of General Nicholson. On the 24th, the armament reached Port Royal, and landed without opposition. On the 21st of October, three small batteries of two mortars, and twenty-four cohorns, were brought to bear upon

* Smith's Hist. New York, i. 121, 123; Holmes, i. 501, 502. Trumbull, i. 437. These Indian sachems attracted great attention in England. Sir Charles Cotterel conducted them, in two coaches, to St. James's; and the Lord Chamberlain introduced them into the royal presence.

the fort, assisted by a bomb ship named the Star that proved very effective. The next day, the commander of the fort capitulated. Thus, unaided by the English fleet, Port Royal fell into the hands of the provincials with the loss of only about forty men, twenty-six of whom were drowned by the wreck of one of the transports in the service of Connecticut.

Flushed with the anticipation of new conquests, Nicholson sailed for England in the fall, to renew his solicitations for a fleet to prosecute the war. In June 1711, he again arrived in Boston with new requisitions from the queen, commanding the several colonies to raise fresh troops, and with the assurance that an English fleet was about to sail for America.

A convention of governors was convoked at New London, on account of this intelligence. Sixteen days after the arrival of Nicholson, the expected fleet made its appearance; but strange to say, it was almost totally destitute of provisions. This fact added to the suspicions before entertained by the colonies, that the object of the English government was not the reduction of Canada. It appeared doubtful whether the requisite supplies could be procured in the short space of time that would be allowed for that purpose. On the other hand, should the preparations come short of the demand, and the expedition prove unsuccessful, it was thought that the whole blame of the failure would fall upon New England. The colonies, therefore, put forth the utmost exertions to provide for the armament.

The General Assembly of Connecticut was in session when the fleet arrived at Boston, and speedily voted to raise three hundred and sixty men, to procure four months provisions for them, and a vessel to transport them to Albany. At the same time a letter was addressed to the queen, proffering the thanks of the colony for her tender care of its interests, and expressing a great deal of gratitude for all that her majesty had done, and, so far as can now be seen, for much that she had neglected to do.*

* Colonial Records, MS.

With such alacrity did the colonies address themselves to the preparation of this two-fold enterprise, that in about a month the land army and the fleet were both in readiness. On the 30th of July, the armament, consisting of fifteen men-of-war, forty transports, six store-ships, and a train of artillery, such as had never before been sent to the American coast, sailed out of Boston harbor for Canada. Aside from the naval forces, it carried a land army of seven thousand men, made up of five regiments from England and Flanders, and two regiments from Massachusetts, Rhode Island, and New Hampshire. Sir Hovenden Walker was admiral of the fleet, while the land forces were under command of Brigadier General Hill, brother to Mrs. Masham, the favorite of the queen. On the same day, General Nicholson began his march for Albany. His army consisted of four thousand men from Connecticut, New York, and New Jersey. Colonel William Whiting had the immediate command of the Connecticut forces;* Colonel Schuyler those of New York, and Colonel Ingoldsby, those of New Jersey.

Admiral Walker reached the mouth of the St. Lawrence with his fleet on the 14th of August. That he might wait for transports to come up, he put into the Bay of Gaspe on the 18th, where he lay at anchor until the 20th, when he sailed out of the bay. On the 22d, a dismal prospect presented itself. With a high south-easterly wind to contend against, without soundings, out of sight of land, and enveloped in a thick fog, the fleet appeared to be at the mercy of the elements. With the hope that the wind would drift them into the channel, the pilots advised that the ships should be brought to, with their heads to the southward. Even after this precaution was taken, the ships still drifted toward the dangerous rocks of the north shore.

Just as the admiral was going to retire for the night, the captain of his ship went below and told him in alarm that he could see land. As if not satisfied with the speed that was already hurrying the fleet to perdition, Walker gave orders

* Colonial Records, MS.

that the heads of the ships should be brought to the north. Captain Goddard, of the land army, flew to the cabin and begged the admiral to go on deck and see for himsef. Walker only laughed. As the ships drew nearer the gulf that yawned for them, Goddard again sought the cabin.

"For the Lord's sake," cried he, "come on deck, or we shall certainly be drowned. I see breakers all around us!"

Walker, with as much leisure as if he had been preparing to write one of his own stupid dispatches, put on his gown and slippers, "and coming upon deck," to use his own language, "I found what he told me was true!"

He might easily find out the truth of it by the light of the moon that just then pierced through the mists and showed the Egg Islands to the leeward, with the white waves breaking over them.

The admiral then, for the first time, opened his eyes and consented that the advice of the pilots should be followed.

Eight of the British transports were cast away, and of the seventeen hundred English officers and soldiers that were on board of them, eight hundred and eighty-four were lost. Admiral Walker, and the other principal officers, were saved, by trusting to their anchors, from being dashed against the rocks.*

As soon as the fleet could be extricated it sailed for Spanish river bay, but as the wind had shifted and blew stifly from the east, it was eight days before the entire armament arrived there. Here a council of war was held, the result of which was, that the admiral soon after weighed anchor for Portsmouth, England. Of course, General Nicholson had nothing to do but to retrace his steps.†

The failure of this third attempt to subdue the Canadas was of course charged upon the American pilots, who afterwards made oath that their advice was not followed, and, with equal propriety, upon the *tardiness* of the colonies, who

* See Hutchinson, ii. 180; also, Bancroft and Trumbull.

† Smith's New York, ii. 128, 130; Belknap's New Hampshire, i. 335; Trumbull, i. 441, 442; Hutchinson, ii. 190, 198; Holmes, i, 505.

in five weeks had raised and provisioned two armies of their own, besides providing supplies for the English fleet. Although the loss of life had fallen chiefly upon the English soldiers, the colonies still reflected with chagrin that the French flag yet floated from the heights of Quebec.

During the period covered by this chapter, several new townships were settled and organized, in addition to those already noted.

At the May session of the General Assembly, 1707, Hebron was incorporated. The settlement of this place was begun about three years previous to the above date. The first settlers of the town were William Shipman, Timothy Phelps, Caleb Jones, Samuel Filer, Stephen Post, Jacob Root, Samuel Curtis, Edward Sawyer, Joseph Youngs, and Benoni Trumbull. They were from Windsor, Saybrook, Long Island, and Northampton.*

In May of the following year, it was ordered that a township should be laid out south-east of Woodstock, eight miles in length and six in breadth. The inhabitants on this tract were vested with town privileges, and the town was named Killingly. Among the early settlers whose descendants still inhabit the vicinity, were Messrs. Joseph Cady, James Danielson, Sampson Howe, and Ephraim Warren.

Newtown, in the present county of Fairfield, was incorporated at the October session, 1711.

A tract of country formerly granted by Joshua, sachem of the Mohegans, lying north of Lebanon and west of Mansfield, was laid out about this time, and the town was incorporated by the name of Coventry at the October session, 1711.

A settlement was commenced in 1707, at a place called *Weatinoge*, on the Housatonick river. The Boardmans, Bostwicks, Gaylords, Nobles, Canfields, Camps, Hines, Bucks, Warners, &c., were among the early families who still retain

* Hebron is noted as the birth-place of many eminent men, among whom I may name, Dr. Benjamin Trumbull, the venerable Historian of Connecticut, Governor Peters, of this State, Governor Palmer, of Vermont, and Lieut. Governor Root, of New York.

an honorable position in the place. The town was incorporated and named New Milford, in October 1712. The famous Moravian missionary, Count Zinzendorf, established a mission among the Indians at this point.

Pomfret, was incorporated in 1713. Some of the lands here had been settled upon as early as 1686. Among the early proprietors were Major James Fitch, Lieutenant William Ruggles, Messrs. John Gore, John Pierpont, Benjamin Sabin, John Grosvenor, Nathan Wilson, Samuel Craft, Samuel and John Ruggles, and Joseph Griffin. Major General Israel Putnam, of the revolutionary army was a resident of this town.*

* For a more particular account of the above towns—and indeed of all the towns in the State, I take pleasure in referring the reader to Barber's "Historical Collections of Connecticut."

CHAPTER XVIII.

WAR WITH THE EASTERN INDIANS.

ALTHOUGH the Treaty of Utrecht, bearing date April 1st, 1713,* had restored peace to the European powers, yet it did not entirely put an end to the troubles existing in America. The French Jesuits, who had extended their influence into the region lying to the eastward of New England, lost no opportunity to intensify the prejudices and hatred of the Indian tribes who were under their control. On the other hand, the encroaching spirit of the English colonies, impelling their people to make new acquisitions of territory by means that could not always be justified, helped to quicken the embers of discontent into a flame.

Sebastian Ralle, the spiritual father of the Indians at Norridgewock, and who had established a large Indian church there, was accused by the English who lived on the frontiers with fermenting disturbances among the natives, and especially in relation to that most delicate matter, the tenure of their lands. Soon after Governor Shute entered upon his duties as governor of Massachusetts, he was induced, from the complaints that he heard from the eastern border settlements, to try what could be effected with the Indians there by treaty. With this view, he met the chiefs by appointment at Arrowsick Island, and after some delays succeeded in renewing the treaty of 1713.†

This settlement of their hostilities does not seem to have been acceptable to Father Ralle, who was supposed to have done what he could to render it inoperative, and to incite the

* By this treaty between Great Britain and France, the latter surrendered to the British government, the Bay and Straits of Hudson, the island of St. Christopher, Nova Scotia, and Newfoundland.

† A printed copy of this treaty is in the Library of the Massachusetts Historical Society. It bears date (as renewed) "George Town, in Arrowsick Island, Aug. 9, 1717."

Eng. by D.C.Hinman from a crayon sketch by Rembrandt Peale in the possession of Geo. Gibbs, Esq.

OLIVER WOLCOTT.

Oliv: Wolcott.

Indians to acts of violence. Whether this is true or false, it is certain that the Indians were constantly depredating upon the English settlements, and it appears to be equally so, that they acted not without provocation.

In the year 1720, a party of Indians made a sudden attack upon Canso, a settlement in Nova Scotia, killed several of the inhabitants and plundered the place. A number of Frenchmen from Cape Breton, acted in concert and carried off the booty in their vessels. A reprisal followed, and this was succeeded by other depredations. The English were said to have sustained a loss of about £20,000, which the government at Louisbourg refused to make good, on the ground that the plunderers were not French subjects.*

The troubles at Canso alarmed the people of eastern Massachusetts, and Colonel Walton, with a party of soldiers, was sent out to defend that part of the country. But as the disturbances still continued, Governor Shute, who had been in favor of an amicable settlement of these difficulties that had grown doubtless out of a disturbance of land titles during the war ending in the capture of Port Royal, now ordered Walton to inform the Indians that commissioners should be sent to determine all differences. The popular sentiment in Massachusetts was, however, opposed to a negotiation, and before the terms could be agreed on, the General Court was called and the house resolved that one hundred and fifty men should march forthwith to Norridgewock, and, sword in hand, compel the Indians there to make full restitution for all the mischief that they had done. It was also resolved that the sheriff of York county should have a warrant to arrest Father Ralle and bring him to Boston; and that if that officer could not find him, the Indians should take him and deliver him up. It was also, radically enough, determined that if the Indians should refuse to betray their friend in this way, they should themselves be apprehended and brought as prisoners to Boston for punishment.† The

* Hutchinson, ii. 217, 218; Trumbull, ii. 60.

† Hutchinson, ii. 218.

governor and council, foreseeing that this summary proceeding would end in a vexatious war, refused to concur with the house.*

Thus the matter remained unsettled, until the next year, when about two hundred Indians with two French Jesuits, came down to Georgetown, on Arrowsick Island, and left a letter for the governor, filled with bitter complaints against the English. The old subject matter of complaint, the title to their lands, was the burden of the letter. Father Ralle was understood to be the author of the charges contained in it, and was said to have filled the hearts of the Indians with resentment.

While affairs remained in this uncertain condition, the sachem of the Norridgewocks died, and a new chief succeeded him of a more pacific character. Through his influence and the advice of the old counselors, hostages were soon after sent to Boston as pledges for the future good behavior of the tribe, and as a guarranty for the liquidation of the old demands for damages. Still Ralle was thought to be active in fermenting disturbances and instigating the Indians to war. Mutual accusations followed, until at last the English were so inflamed that at a meeting of the General Court of Massachusetts, on the 27th of August, it was resolved that three hundred men should be sent to the Indian head-quarters, to demand that the Jesuits should be surrendered up to the English. This demand was to be enforced by severe penalties. The council concurred and the governor reluctantly consented. Still, as he had the Indian hostages in keeping at the castle, he issued no order for the raising of the troops. Not long after this, however, the hostages escaped, and the governor gave orders for levying the soldiers. These orders were countermanded as soon as the hostages were taken and sent back to Boston.†

In November, the General Court again met, when the house complained loudly of the governor for these delays.

* Trumbull; Hutchinson; Bancroft.

† Trumbull.

Reluctantly the council again consented that a party of soldiers should be sent to Norridgewock to enforce the demands of the court.

When this party arrived at the principal village occupied by the tribe, not an Indian was to be found. They had been apprised of the coming of the English, and had fled into the woods, with Father Ralle, the chief object of pursuit, under their protection. Although disappointed in not obtaining possession of his person, the invading party succeeded in finding his books and papers, which they seized and carried off with them.

The Indians did not forget this act of violence, and in June of the next year a party of sixty warriors with twenty canoes, dropped suddenly into Merry Meeting Bay, and took nine families prisoners. Several incursions of a like character, though wanting the horrors usually attending a savage invasion, followed at brief intervals, and still showed how restless was the spirit of revenge that prompted them. Other Englishmen were taken captive from time to time. Finally, emboldened by success, the Indians burned the village of Brunswick, near Casco Bay. This led to a formal declaration of war on the part of Massachusetts.

The Penobscots, the Cape Sable Indians, and those at St. John's, and St. Francois, now joined with the Norridgewocks, and mustered their braves for a bloody war. United as they were, they seemed likely to prove a terrible enemy. In July, they made a descent upon the coast, surprised Canso and other harbors, and seized seventeen English fishing vessels. The Indians had learned to manage a sail with skill, and could use fire-arms. They now began to kill and scalp their prisoners in cold blood. They gathered in larger numbers, too, as the war advanced. In September about five hundred of them made an attempt upon the village and fort at Arrowsick Island. The inhabitants flew from the village to the fort only to see their houses laid in ashes. It was not an easy task to defend the fort itself.*

* Holmes; Hutchinson; Trumbull.

Now that war was declared, and its terrible signals began to beacon up along the coast and river settlements, shedding a baleful light upon the fortifications that even French valor had not been able to keep from the English, the people of the eastern border forgot their hatred of Father Ralle for awhile to reflect upon their own dangers. New York, too, began to be alarmed. Governor Shute, anxious to avert the calamity that he had used his best efforts to prevent, now addressed a letter to Governor Saltonstall, asking for men and supplies to carry on the war. He was imprudent enough to suggest, that if Connecticut declined to act in the matter, a portion of her militia should be put under his command. Nothing could have been more impolitic than such an allusion. It brought the images of Joseph Dudley and Lord Cornbury in a moment before the General Assembly. Unluckily, too, Governor Burnet of New York had sent a letter seconding the request of Shute.

With great unanimity, both Houses resolved that the mischief done by a few eastern Indians, was not worthy to be dignified with the name of an invasion, and did not call for a general rally of the colonies from New Hampshire to Virginia, to defend it. With much stateliness the legislature therefore declined to render any assistance beyond that of sending a detachment of fifty men into the new county of Hampshire, and putting the border towns of Connecticut in a posture of defense.* The Assembly was by no means satisfied that the existing state of affairs was at all necessary, or that the part that Massachusetts had taken in it was lawful.

In November, the General Court of Massachusetts convened, and appointed commissioners to treat with the six nations. They were instructed to offer these Indians a premium for the scalps of the eastern Indians. The court resumed at this session the old quarrel with the governor, and finally succeeded in making him so unhappy that he embarked for England. He does not appear to have been a very astute

* Colonial Records, MS.

politician, but was certainly insulted and abused for doing what in all probability was right, in regard to a war that would not have broken out had his pacific and equitable counsels been followed.*

I pass by the details of Colonel Westbrook's expedition, the destruction of the church, castle, and village upon the Penobscot river, too like an Indian depredation to have owed its origin to a christian people, and the equally painful recital of the destruction of the village of Norridgewock, by Moulton, where only fifty of the inhabitants escaped the general massacre that resulted in the wanton murder of Father Ralle, the fruit of bigotry and revenge, and in the cruel butchery of the wife and helpless children of an Indian chief whose worst crime was, that he had killed a Mohawk while invading his dwelling; nor need I speak of the shameful maraud of John Lovell, desecrating the banks of the Penobscot, and the shores of Winnepesiaukee in quest of scalps, for every one of which, the General Court of Massachusetts had offered the the stimulating reward of one hundred pounds. I will only say, Connecticut regarded the war itself as unnecessary, and shrunk with horror from the barbarities that their too excited and deluded neighbors permitted to be perpetrated.

That she did nothing in this unhappy war beyond the defense of her own frontiers, and those of the county of Hampshire, solicited, as she was, again and again, affords an excellent illustration of the temperance of her statesmen, and the christian spirit that dictated her counsels.

The war cost her several thousand pounds, but as she acted solely on the defensive, not a single life was sacrificed in the colony.

Notwithstanding the continual excitement and alarm, and the exorbitant taxation, consequent upon these expeditions, the older towns in the colony continued to send out fresh re-

* Gov. Samuel Shute had served as lieut.-colonel under the duke of Marlborough. He arrived in Boston with his commission as governor of Massachusetts, Oct. 4, 1716; and sailed for England, Jan. 1, 1723. He died in 1742, aged 88 years.

cruits to subdue the forests and form new settlements in the more remote wilderness.

In 1706, a few pioneers had established themselves upon certain lands in Ashford; and the number of settlers had so increased, that the town was incorporated in 1714. The brave Colonel Thomas Knowlton, of revolutionary renown, was a native of Ashford.

Tolland was incorporated in 1715. It was laid out six miles square. The township was rough, and a large part of it was claimed by persons who were legatees of Uncas, the Mohegan sachem. These circumstances retarded the growth of the settlement, so that there were but twenty-eight families in the town in 1720. The names of some of the early settlers were, Stearns, Chapman, Grant, West, Carpenter, Dimock, and Aborne.

The township of Stafford, was surveyed in 1718, and the settlement began during the next spring. At the May session of the Assembly, 1719, the unsold lands in that town were ordered to be disposed of, "and the proceeds to be paid into the treasury of Yale College." The principal settlers were, Mr. Robert White and Mr. Matthew Thompson, from Europe; the Warners, from Hadley; the Blodgets, from Woborn; Cornelius Davis, from Haverhill; Daniel Colburn, from Dedham; John Pasco, from Enfield; Josiah Standish, from Preston; Benjamin Rockwell, from Windsor; and Joseph Orcutt, from Weymouth.

The settlement at Bolton, commenced in 1716, but the first town meeting was not held until 1720. In October of the last mentioned year, the town was incorporated. The first settlers were of the names of Pitkin, Talcott, Loomis, Bissell, Strong, Olcott, and Bishop.

In 1720, a few settlers took up their abode upon the "western lands," at a place called "Bantam." During the following year, several purchasers moved on to the tract from Hartford and Windsor. The town was surveyed, and laid out into sixty equal divisions or rights, three of which were reserved for public uses. The act of incorporation was passed by the General Assembly at the May session, 1724. Among the first settlers whose descendants still remain in the town, were those bearing the names of Marsh, Buel, Baldwin, Birge, Beebe, Culver, Catlin, Goodwin, Gibbs, Garrett, Griswold, Kilbourn, Mason, Phelps, Peck, Stoddard, Sanford, Smedley, Webster, and Woodruff. This town at the time, of its incorporation, took the name of Litchfield, and has since 1751, been the shire town of a large county. It has also a history of its own that will unfold itself during the progress of this work. Its future reputation could hardly have been prophesied from its humble infancy in the midst of a wilderness hardly yet subdued.

CHAPTER XIX

WAR WITH FRANCE AND SPAIN. CAPTURE OF LOUISBOURG.

THE reign of George I. was now over, and his son, one of the most able monarchs of modern times, was just beginning to evince the strong intelligence and keen love of war that was in a few years to add so much to the territory and renown of the British empire.

In the fall of 1739, it appeared obvious to the General Assembly of Connecticut, that certain differences then disturbing the amicable relations of England and Spain, must soon lead to a war between the two powers. The Assembly, therefore, took speedy measures to place the colony in an attitude of defense. It was ordered that ten cannon, with suitable ammunition, should be provided, to increase the strength of the battery at New London, and that a well armed sloop of war should be employed to guard the coast. An order was further made to supply the feeble and remote towns with the means of protecting themselves, and the militia were formed into thirteen regiments—each regiment being officered by a colonel, a lieutenant-colonel, and a major.*

War meanwhile was declared against Spain, and the ministry, glad to be rid of a clamorous and by no means insignificant opponent, and to assail the enemy in a weak point, resolved on sending Admiral Vernon upon an expedition where he would have an opportunity of making good some of his stately declarations as to the exploits that he could perform if he were but invested with the command of a few ships. The Spanish West Indies, Porto Bello, Carthagena

* At the same session (Oct., 1739,) the governor was made captain general, and the deputy governor was made lieutenant-general of the militia of Connecticut.

MAJ. GEN. DAVID WOOSTER.

Dav. Wooster

and Cuba, were to be the principal objects aimed at by the government, and requisitions were made upon the colonies to furnish troops for this exciting theatre of naval operations. The design was to raise four provincial regiments to be transported to Jamaica, where they were to be united with the main body of the British forces. The colonies were to provide all necessaries for the men thus raised by them, until they should reach this rendezvous. They were further expected to pay all the expenses of the transportation. As the House of Brunswick owed its accession to the throne, and its perpetuity, to the fact that it was understood, to be the champion of protestantism, it is quite probable that the zeal manifested by England as well as by Connecticut in this war, was in part owing to the fact that Spain was a catholic power.

In July, 1740, a special assembly was called, and measures were very readily taken to answer to his majesty's demands to help forward the "expedition against the territories of the *catholic king*, in the West Indies."*

As soon as the requisition reached the governor of Connecticut, he issued his proclamation making known the will of the crown, and calling upon those who were willing to volunteer for the service, to hold themselves in readiness. Committees were now appointed to superintend the military preparations, and to take the names of such as had decided to enlist. That every inducement might be offered to the citizens to join the expedition, the Assembly resolved that the governor and council should speedily appoint the officers for the troops, and that volunteer soldiers should have the privilege of selecting those under whom they would serve. His excellency was requested by the Assembly to issue a second proclamation, making known to the people with more particularity the will of the king, and again inviting those who were able-bodied to hand in their names to the committee in each county. That there might be no delay, the governor and committee of war were authorized

* Colonial Records, MS.

to draw on the public treasury for such sums as they should deem necessary for the outfit. A sloop of war of six hundred tons burthen was ordered to be procured for the further protection of the coast.

At the preceding session, bills of credit had been issued to the amount of £30,000; and at the July session, the issue was increased £15,000 more—making in all £45,000;* an enormous sum, when we consider the object of the war, and the limited resources of the colony.

The preparations in England were pushed forward with singular dispatch. Money was appropriated without stint to fit out a fleet and armament that should at the same time satisfy the national pride and silence the clamors of the opposition.

In October, the armament sailed from England under the command of Lord Cathcart, whose talents and great popularity added something to the good auguries that seemed to attend the enterprise. His lordship was conveyed by twenty-five ships of the line, with a corresponding number of frigates, fire-ships, bomb-ketches, tenders, hospital ships, and all the other enginery of mischief that even then attended the British flag, wherever it floated in hostile array over the ocean.

After the union of this large force, with that of Vice Admiral Vernon at Jamaica, the whole fleet amounted to twenty-nine ships of the line, and as many frigates.

There were fifteen thousand seamen. The land army, including the provincial troops, amounted to twelve thousand effective men. No fleet that could compare with it in size or perfect equipment had ever visited the West Indian seas. It is not surprising that Vernon, who had, with his few ships, as early as November, made good a part of his prophecy by taking and plundering Porto Bello and demolishing its fortifications,† should have felt his heart beat with pride when he saw himself at last at the head of such an armament. But he was doomed to bitter disappointment.

* Colonial Records, MS. † Univ. Hist. xii. 412, 416; Holmes, ii. 12.

Lord Cathcart suddenly died before the union of the fleets was fully effected. His death threw the command of the army upon General Wentworth, who proved to be little more than an instrument in the hands of Vernon.

Intoxicated with his success at Porto Bello, and inflamed with the true English hatred of France, Vernon, instead of embracing the favorable moment to take possession of Carthagena while it was in no condition to withstand his attacks, obtained a vote of the council of war to beat up against the wind to Hispaniola, with the hope of meeting with a French squadron that had been sent from Europe under the Marquis d'Autin to reinforce the Spaniards. This search ended in nothing but chagrin and disaster. The squadron that the British admiral was in quest of, was already far on its way to France, and before the fleet could again be in readiness to attack Carthagena, the garrison there had been so reinforced by the French that it amounted to four thousand men.*

After consuming two months in this romantic pastime, Vernon and Wentworth set themselves busily to the task of subduing Carthagena. They began the attack on the 10th of March, by assailing the forts and castles that guarded the harbor, and succeeded at length in demolishing them so that the admiral could effect an entrance. Wentworth now made a demonstration upon the town, but was driven back with the loss of about five hundred men. Discouraged at this rebuff, Vernon and Wentworth appear to have joined in the conclusion that it was idle to look any longer for laurels at Carthagena. About the 1st of April, therefore, the army and fleet were withdrawn, and spent some time in the pleasant recreation of beating about the islands in quest of Spanish ships. Six Spanish men of war, eight galleons and some smaller vessels were thus caught while fluttering between their respective ports.† But the assailants soon tired of such profitless amusement.

* Trumbull, ii. 267.

† Trumbull, ii. 268; see also, Holmes, ii. 15; Univ. Hist. xii. 429, 445.

In July, fired with a new passion for glory, they made an attack upon Cuba, and without much resistance appropriated to the fleet one of the fine harbors with which that noble island abounds. But misfortune followed hard upon them in the shape of a sudden and mortal disease that, in the burning tropical air, preyed frightfully upon the vitals of the army and the seamen who had been accustomed to the invigorating influences of a northern climate. The ravages of this enemy were like those of the plague, or of that more modern disease, cholera. For nearly a week, every day offered up its sacrifice of one thousand men; and at the height of the malady, during forty-eight hours, three thousand four hundred and forty men fell victims to it. Of the thousand athletic soldiers who went from New England, not one hundred returned.*

Thus ended this inglorious scheme, but the war still continued; and it was resolved that it should never be brought to an end until some treaty stipulations could be forced from Spain, that would place the southern colonies upon a safer footing and would prevent the future interruption of British trade.

Thus, year after year, war, like a slow and poisonous humor in the blood, continued to waste the vitality of the American colonies. In vain did Governor Oglethorpe of Georgia rally the brave men under his command, seconded by Virginia and the Carolinas, and countenanced by the fickle favors of the few Indians that could be induced to

---

* Though few had perished by the enemy, it was computed, on a moderate calculation, that before the arrival at Jamaica 20,000 English subjects had died since their first attack on Carthagena. To this desolating mortality the poet, Thomson refers, in his admirable description of the "Pestilence:" ["SEASONS"—SUMMER, I., 1040, 1050.]

> "Such as, of late, at Carthagena quench'd
> The British fire. You, gallant Vernon! saw
> The miserable scene, you heard the groans
> Of agonizing ships from shore to shore;
> Heard nightly plunged, amid the sullen waves,
> The frequent corse."

Admiral Vernon, who seems to have been held in high esteem by the opposition in England, died suddenly, 29th of October, 1757, aged 73.

follow him. Without the help of the mother country, and with the savages that lurked in the hideous swamps of the south, malignant as the serpents that are generated in the hot air of those latitudes, skulking upon his trail, he still did what human valor could do to deliver the south from the commercial interference and arbitrary exactions of Spain. But for want of a sufficient naval force he was unable to take possession of St. Augustine, and with the exception of two Spanish forts that he succeeded in taking, the expedition failed.*

France, meanwhile, though affecting to maintain her neutrality, did every thing that she could to assist Spain in prosecuting the war; secretly at first, and at last more openly, until, on the 4th of March, 1744, she had the frankness to make a formal declaration of war against England. Soon after England made a like announcement.†

Before the tidings of either declaration reached the shores of New England, an expedition had been prepared by Duvivoir, a French officer of some merit, who sailed from Louisbourg, and on the 13th of May, surprised and took possession of Canso.‡ He then made a similar attempt upon Annapolis, (formerly Port Royal,) and would doubtless have succeeded there also had not the place been just before reinforced by troops from Massachusetts. Louisbourg was also the central point whence there radiated a large number of French privateer ships and men-of-war, that hovered along the New England coast and seized upon our trading and fishing vessels in great numbers. It thus became impossible for the eastern colonies to carry on any maritime business whatever, without a convoy, and such a necessity involved an expense that amounted to a prohibition. The fishermen must renounce their employment, and the coasters must keep within port, or run the risk of captivity and a forfeiture of their goods and vessels.§

With one consent the people of New England resolved

* Holmes, ii. 14, 15. † March 31.

‡ Holmes, ii. 23; Hutchinson, ii. 364. § Hutchinson; Trumbull.

that Louisbourg must be taken; yet at first no one appears to have thought that it could be done without the coöperation of a naval force from England. But as the summer and fall passed away, and as winter drew on, it began to be whispered at Boston, that Louisbourg might be taken by surprise, and by New England valor alone. These intimations at last began to take some definite form, and it was believed by many that the fortress might be successfully besieged at a season of the year when the garrison was probably but poorly provisioned, and when it could not hope to be relieved by any large supplies from French ships, that would hardly venture in great numbers to commit themselves to the rough handling of the Atlantic coast winds in the stormy months. It was suggested, too, that a naval force adequate to keep off such few ships as might attempt to bring supplies for the relief of the garrison, could be found to cruise off the harbor, until the enterprise was completed.

Governor Shirley, of Massachusetts, meanwhile, did what he could to learn what was the condition of the fortress, and how long it would be likely to withstand a siege. Those who had traded at that post, and those who had been confined there as prisoners, were alike consulted for information. Shirley had also written to England, begging that armed sloops might be sent to protect Annapolis; and should these arrive in season, he hoped to avail himself of them to defend the provincial troops while they were employed in besieging Louisbourg. Commodore Warren, who was at the West Indies with a little squadron, might also reasonably be expected, either to arrive with his whole force, or to send a portion of it to the relief of New England, when once he had been made acquainted with the wants of the colonies.

The design was to send four thousand troops, in transports, to Canso, and as soon as practicable land them in Chapeaurouge Bay. This army was to be provided with cannon, mortars, and whatever else was necessary for the siege. As soon as the winds had subsided so that the small vessels that the colonies could muster might be expected to live in the coast waters of the Atlantic, a number of them were to be sent to hover near the harbor of Louisbourg, and cut off all supplies or reinforcements from the fortification. A minute calculation was made of the probable naval force of New England. It was found that the aggregate of their armed vessels could not exceed twelve, and the largest of these only mounted twenty guns. Yet with such a force it was believed that there was more than an even chance for success. If the ships from England, or those from the Indies, should arrive, the result might be regarded as almost certain.

Early in January, 1745, Governor Shirley made known this plan to the General Court. The most solemn secresy was enjoined upon all the members of the two houses.* Although most of the principal men of the colony were doubtless aware of the scheme, and although the necessity that Louisbourg should be taken, was a common topic of discourse throughout New England, yet the details of the plan, and the hurry with which it was proposed to attempt it, without the help, and even without the sanction of England, was appalling to the minds of the country representatives. With dispassionate calmness they debated the matter for several days.

By those who favored the measure it was argued, that if this fortress should remain in the hands of the French, it would be the Dunkirk of New England; that the French were already tired of attempting to compete with the colonies in fishing, and that if this stronghold was allowed to remain in their possession, it would soon be the rendezvous of a knot of pirates and privateers, who would find it easier to rifle the fishing vessels of the English than to trouble themselves with the details of a business they did not find congenial to their habits of life.

In addition to this calamity, it was quite probable that Nova Scotia, won with such toil from the dominion of

* Holmes, ii. 28; Hutchinson, ii. 366.

France, and still inhabited in part by disaffected Frenchmen, would be liable at any time to make a successful revolt, so long as the garrison at Louisbourg continued to give countenance to such a project. This reprisal, could it be effected, would of itself add at least six thousand to the number of active enemies, that were already so powerful and so unscrupulous.

Besides, it was urged that the garrison, ill-provisioned as it was, could not be expected to make a very vigorous resistance; that the walls of the fort were dilapidated, its barracks out of repair and scarcely tenantable, and its governor an old and infirm man, unused to the arts of war. If a favorable blow was to be struck, it must be done then. Such were a few of the arguments made use of by the advocates of the expedition.*

In reply, it was urged with great force, that the rumors so freely circulated, of the condition of the works and the garrison at Louisbourg, could not be safely relied on; that appearances were not to be trusted; that the garrison, though small, was made up of well disciplined soldiers, who were a match for many times their number of raw provincial troops; that the chances were as great, to say the least, that ships of war would arrive from France to relieve the fort and augment its garrison, as that armed vessels would come from England or the West Indies to protect the provincial army; and that at the best such a calculation, based upon probabilities and contingencies, was too vague and speculative to be made the basis of a military campaign, that might involve the dearest interests of the colonies. It was said that prudent men should look at both sides of the question, and estimate the chances of failure as well as those of success; that if, while the siege was in progress, there should appear off the harbor a single French man-of-war, it could put to flight the whole naval force of the colonies, small as were their crafts, and unaccustomed as their sailors were to the dangers of naval warfare. Further than this,

* Hutchinson, ii. 366, 367.

who could vouch for the coöperation of the other colonies, or even for their ability to furnish the men and the ships that were admitted by the most enthusiastic advocates of the scheme to be requisite to carry it on? More than all, who but the ruler of the wind and the storm could foresee or guard against the treacherous dangers of the deep, at a season of the year when the coast was white with breakers, and the caps of the waves towered above the masts of the little vessels that were expected to contend with them? Finally, even should the attack result favorably, would it not redound to the glory of England, while it proved a thankless labor for the colonies, which might ask in vain to be remunerated for the heavy expenses that they had incurred in the war.*

Such arguments as these prevailed, and the measure was lost in the house. In this decision the council acquiesced, and for some days the project appeared to have been forgotten.† Governor Shirley himself seemed to have been convinced of his error by the cogent reasoning of the opposition. But Shirley was a man not easily baffled. He secretly set himself at work to bring external influences to bear upon the recusant members. All at once, as if by a spontaneous movement, the merchants and other rich and influential men of Massachusetts began to petition the General Court to revive and pass the defeated measure. The petition set forth all the reasons that could be suggested in favor of the expedition. The flagging of commerce, especially the destruction of the fishing and coasting business, were the main considerations that were pressed upon the court.

A committee was appointed to investigate the matter anew, and was finally prevailed on to recommend the measure. For another day the subject was debated, and when the question was taken in the house, it was carried by a single vote.‡ Entire unanimity prevailed in both houses as soon

* Hutchinson, ii. 367, 368. † Hutchinson, ii. 368; Holmes, ii. 25.

‡ Holmes, Hutchinson, Trumbull, Bancroft.

as the determination of the court was made known, and all parties now addressed themselves with vigor to the work of preparation. Dispatches were sent to the neighboring colonies, soliciting their assistance. All the colonies, except those of New England, refused to participate in the dangers of the undertaking. It was determined that Massachusetts should raise three thousand two hundred and fifty men; that Connecticut should be required to furnish five hundred; and Rhode Island and New Hampshire, each three hundred.

As soon as this request was made known to Governor Law, he called a special session of the Assembly, which convened at Hartford on the 26th of February, and immediately voted to raise five hundred men for the service. A bounty of ten pounds was voted to each soldier who should provide himself with arms, knapsack, and blanket. These troops were divided into eight companies. Roger Wolcott, the Lieutenant Governor, was appointed commander-in-chief of the Connecticut forces; Andrew Burr, colonel; Simeon Lathrop, lieutenant-colonel; and Israel Newton, major.* It was ordered that the sloop of war, Defense, should sail as the convoy of the regiment. New London was to be the place of embarkation. The most liberal measures were taken to furnish supplies and munitions of war, under the direction of commissioners, while Jonathan Trumbull and Elisha Williams, Esquires, constituted a separate board, who were to repair to Boston and treat with the gentlemen whom they should find there representing Massachusetts or the other New England colonies, as to the general plan and details of the undertaking.† Only three days were spent in this most important matter.

The mildness of the weather, so unusual in March, made the task of getting the men together, and furnishing them with necessaries, remarkably easy.

The popularity of colonel, afterwards Sir William Pep-

* Elizur Goodrich, David Wooster, Stephen Lee, Samuel Adams, and John Dwight, were appointed captains at the same session.

† Colony Records, MS.

perell, commander-in-chief of the army, and of Roger Wolcott, the second in command, induced the better sort of people to enlist. Massachusetts and Connecticut sent out some of their best freeholders, and the ranks were filled with the sons of wealthy farmers. The merchants of the principal towns, the clergymen, and other educated gentlemen, made great sacrifices to render the armament as complete as possible. The whole naval power of New England that could be made available in this emergency, consisted of only twelve vessels, viz., the Connecticut sloop of war, another fine sloop of war belonging to Rhode Island, a privateer ship of two hundred tons burthen, a snow belonging to Newport, a new snow under the command of Captain Rouse, another commanded by Captain Smethurst, a ship under the command of Captain Snelling, a brig under Captain Fletcher, three small sloops under Captains Saunders, Donehew, and Bosch, and a ship of twenty guns, under Captain Ting, who commanded the whole force.*

All that New York could be induced to do in aid of the enterprise, was to yield a very tardy assent to the solicitations of Governor Shirley for the loan of ten eighteen-pounders.

The special assembly of Connecticut, that had been convoked by Governor Law on the 26th of February, stood adjourned until the 14th of March, when it met and appointed five more captains, whose names were James Church, Daniel Chapman, William Whiting, Robert Denison, and Andrew Ward. The Rev. Elisha Williams, who had been rector of Yale College, was selected to accompany the Connecticut troops as chaplain.†

By the 23d of March, the other Massachusetts troops were all embarked and ready to weigh anchor. The express boat from the West Indies arrived with tidings from Commodore Warren. The purport of his answer was, that he had lost one of his ships, and was thereby much disabled; and, further, he did not deem it prudent for him to intermed-

* Hutchinson, ii. 369; Trumbull, ii. 275. † Colony Records, MS.

dle in a matter that seemed to want the sanction of the British government. This discouraging information was not made known, however, by Governor Shirley to the army, and the fleet immediately sailed. About the same time the Connecticut troops and those from the two other colonies set sail.

The New Hampshire forces arrived at Canso on the 1st of April; those from Massachusetts, on the 4th, and those from Connecticut, on the 25th. The land army consisted of four thousand able bodied men, well officered and in excellent spirits.*

Scarcely had the Massachusetts express boat taken leave of Commodore Warren, when dispatches from England reached him, commanding him to sail for Boston with such ships as could be spared, to assist Governor Shirley in concerting and carrying out measures for the king's general service in America. Relieved from the restraints, that had before embarrassed his mind, Warren sent out an express to such ships as were to be found in the western seas, to join him as speedily as they could, and with joy hastened to fulfil the king's commands. On his passage he learned that the fleet had sailed for Canso, and without putting in at Boston harbor, he made all haste to reach Canso, where he arrived in the Superb, a ship of sixty guns, in company with the Lanceston and Mermaid, of forty guns each. On the same day, the Eltham, of forty guns, from Portsmouth, reached the same port. The pulses of the provincial soldiers beat quick and high, like the waves of that northern sea, when the British flag was seen floating from the mast head of those sturdy ships. Commodore Warren, after a short conference with General Pepperell, sailed for Louisbourg harbor.†

Already the few colonial ships and vessels, that had been cruising there, had rendered important services by seizing several vessels bound to Louisbourg with provisions. They had also fallen in with the Renomme, a French ship of

* The three hundred soldiers from Rhode Island did not reach Louisbourg until after its capture.

† Hutchinson.

thirty-six guns, bearing dispatches. She kept up a running fire for awhile with the cruisers, that resisted her entrance into the harbor, and then giving up the attempt as hopeless, she commenced her return voyage. As the Connecticut and Rhode Island troops, having farther to sail than those of the other colonies, were yet on their passage, the Renomme met them under convoy of their two small sloops, either one of which a single broadside of her metal might have sunk; yet, after saluting with a few coy shots at a distance, and doing some damage to the Rhode Island sloop, she prudently resumed her regular course. She must have easily divined that something besides the coasting trade had set in motion the sails that swarmed along the coast in such defiant array.

The fleet and army followed the men-of-war, and arrived safely in Chapeaurogue Bay on the 30th of April.

All this time the enemy had remained in ignorance of the attempt that was about to be made upon the garrison. Even the cruisers had not alarmed them, as they supposed them to be engaged in the old business of privateering for fishing and trading vessels. But when early on the morning of the 30th of April, they looked off from the heights that commanded the town, and saw the transports beating into the bay, their eyes were opened. The governor immediately sent out Bouladrie, with one hundred and fifty disciplined troops, to oppose the landing of the enemy. General Pepperell with much address kept him employed while he was effecting a landing at another point. This small detachment of brave men was sadly cut in pieces at the first fire. Bouladrie soon found himself a prisoner, and the remnant of his men flying, from the invaders easily effected a landing.*

Four hundred men, on the following morning, screened by the hills, marched to the north-east harbor, laying in ashes the houses and stores that they found in their way, until they had arrived within a mile of the general battery. From this

* Trumbull, ii. 279.

indiscriminate conflagration such dense volumes of smoke arose, enveloping the soldiers who kept close beneath its shadow, that the enemy, who could only be aware of the advance of the English by the line of fire and vapor that was gradually lengthened out below them, and who believed that the whole invading army was approaching, hastily threw their powder into a well and fled in dismay from the battery. With steady hands and bold hearts, this handful of undisciplined provincials moved forward, and took possession of it without the loss of a man. They soon brought the cannon that the enemy had left, to bear upon the town, but as the guns were forty-two pounders and consumed too much powder, the firing was soon discontinued.*

Thus far every thing had been easy; the labor was now to begin. The heart of the fortification was still sound and secure. In order to bring guns to bear upon the main works, it was necessary to drag them a distance of two miles, before they could make them available by means of fascine batteries. To add to the almost unsurmountable difficulties that attended this task, a deep morass that would not sustain the weight of oxen or horses, stretched like a Serbonian bog between them and the spot where it was necessary that these temporary batteries should be erected. Ignorant of the ordinary approaches of a besieging army, untaught, except in the rude way that nature teaches her hardiest sons, the provincial troops set themselves about the work with surprising energy, performing, under cover of darkness, the drudgery fit only for beasts of burden, dragging heavy forty-two pounders, mortars, and timbers over the trembling surface of the swamp, carrying shot and shells along difficult places, with the same persistency that had leveled the forests of their fields and committed them to the crackling fire, and with as little military education as they had been in the habit of employing in erecting cedar palisades around their border houses.

Under such discouraging auspices, waging against nature

* Hutchinson, ii. 374; Trumbull, ii. 277, 278; Holmes, ii. 26.

and struggling against a fortified and disciplined enemy, in less than twenty days they had erected five fascine batteries, one of which mounted five forty-two pounders.

While this almost unheard of labor was going forward on shore, the fleet was by no means inactive. While cruising off the harbor, the Vigilant, a French sixty-four gun ship, was met by the Mermaid whom she engaged. As the Mermaid was a forty-four gun ship, Captain Douglass suffered himself to be chased until he had drawn his adversary within the range of the commodore's guns. As soon as the Vigilant discovered her hopeless condition she struck her colors without firing a shot.* Her fate was decisive of the fate of Louisbourg. She was under the command of the Marquis de la Maison Forte, a very gallant officer, and had on board five hundred and sixty men, with stores that would have enabled the fort to hold out until a sufficient naval force could have arrived from France to have made it impregnable. This easy victory, while it emboldened the provincial army, discouraged the garrison and hastened the capitulation.

Just before the arrival of the Vigilant, it had been proposed that the men-of-war should anchor in the bay, and that the marines, and such of the sailors as could be spared, should go ashore and help to complete the batteries. Had this measure been adopted, the Vigilant would have entered the harbor, and the fortune of the expedition would have been changed.† But every circumstance seemed to favor the success of the invading army. Four days after the Vigilant had struck her colors, the English fleet was augmented by the arrival of two ships, the Princess Mary of sixty, and the Hector of forty guns. Shortly afterwards came the Canterbury and the Sunderland, each of sixty guns, and the Chester of fifty guns—in all, eleven men-of-war, viz., one of sixty-four, four of sixty, one of fifty, and five of forty guns.‡

* Hutchinson, ii. 374, 375.

† Hutchinson; Trumbull. ‡ Hutchinson, ii. 375, 376.

Looking off upon the waters, the garrison watched these vultures of the sea, one after another spreading their white wings along the line of the horizon, and pointing their beaks towards Chapeaurouge Bay. Already the island battery had ceased to make a regular response to the shot and shells of the besiegers, and was only heard to reply at long intervals, while the melancholy boom of its cannon, like a signal of distress, echoed ominously over the ocean.

Already the western gate of the town was shattered in pieces, and breaches had begun to be visible in the wall. The north-east battery was no longer defensible, and the circular battery of sixteen guns, the only one that could command the sea and defend the town against ships, was a ruin. Besides, they had every cause to expect that a general attack by sea and land would soon overwhelm the garrison and the town. With these necessities staring them in the face, the enemy, on the 15th of June, begged for a cessation of hostilities that the parties might agree upon some terms of capitulation. This was granted, and on the 17th of June, 1745, after a siege of forty-nine days, the city of Louisbourg, and the Island of Cape Breton, were surrendered into the hands of King George II.*

It is impossible to say what would have been the fate of the expedition had the garrison held out a little longer. The provincial army was already much in want of ammunition, greatly reduced from the hardships that it had encountered in constructing and afterwards manning the fascine batteries, and in lying upon the damp cold ground at night without tents that could protect them from the rains or even from the dews.

General Pepperell had sent off dispatches to New England for recruits, and fresh supplies of ammunition. The demand had been answered by the colonies as well as they were able, and about eight hundred men, and such munitions as could be purchased, had been sent forward. Connecticut voted to

* Bancroft, Hutchinson, Holmes, Trumbull.

raise three hundred additional troops upon the same terms that had induced the first regiment to enlist.* Still, it is doubtful whether this reinforcement could have reached Louisbourg in time to relieve the army. Nature, too, would have conspired with the enemy to make the situation of the besiegers most dismal had the capitulation been postponed for a single day.

On the 18th of June, there came on a violent and protracted storm. For ten tedious days, it rained almost without intermission. Had the soldiers been left to the frail covering of their tents, they must have been exposed to the most extreme hardships, and would perhaps have been compelled to take refuge on board the ships. But the houses of Louisbourg afforded quite a different shelter, where the weary farmers had an opportunity to look off upon the storm with nothing to interrupt their serenity, except an occasional twinge of recollection that forced too vividly upon their minds the images of their absent wives and daughters, and the neglected corn-fields that should supply them with food. The steadiness and coolness manifested by the colonial troops during this long siege, afforded a commentary upon the institutions under which they had been reared, that, had it been treasured up by the British government as a lesson, might have saved the more bitter lessons of experience that were to follow.

The intelligence of this wonderful victory reached Boston on the 3rd of July, and was received with the most marked demonstrations of joy throughout the colonies. Even those provinces that had thought the project chimerical, and had refused to join in it, now generously offered to share in the expenses incurred in prosecuting it. Pennsylvania appropriated four thousand pounds, New Jersey two thousand, and New York three thousand in money and provisions.†

Well might the capture of Louisbourg be regarded as an

---

* Colony Records, MS. † Trumbull, ii. 280.

important achievement. It was a fortress of great strength, and France had expended vast sums of money upon it, with a view of making it the stronghold of her power upon the Atlantic coast. The town was encircled by a wall about eighty feet wide, and its ramparts were thirty feet in height, and mounted with sixty-five cannon which presented no slight obstacle to the approach of a besieging army. The mouth of the harbor was commanded by the grand battery with thirty forty-two pounders, and by the island battery, with an equal number of twenty-eight pounders. There were also in the fortress, sixteen mortars, and ammunition and stores to withstand a six months' seige. The garrison was made up of six hundred regulars and thirteen hundred militia—all well trained troops.*

Thus fortified, France had not dreamed that Louisbourg could fall a prey to her old and hated rival, before she could send a fleet and armament to relieve it. Much less had it entered the imagination of her most cautious statesman or military leader, that without the firing of a shot from a British ship, and without the aid of a British engineer, an army of provincial troops, undisciplined, and not even acting in accordance with the expressed wishes of the English government, should have conceived and executed a plan that would have been thought so impracticable even in the hands of that government itself.

From the first commencement of those bloody wars between the two powers for dominion over the western hemisphere, no blow that France had received had penetrated so deeply, or inflicted such a rankling and immedicable wound.

The value of the prizes alone, amounted to about one million pounds sterling. Several rich merchantmen were taken during the siege, and to add to the mortification resulting from the loss, some of these ships were known to have been decoyed into Chapeaurouge Bay by the French flag that had been kept floating from the fort, in the vain

† Hutchinson.

hope of gathering together a sufficient number of armed vessels to relieve the garrison.*

New England not only captured Louisbourg, but for eleven months the place was entirely defended by New England men. More than five thousand colonial troops shared the honor either of capturing or of keeping possession of the fortress; and the disease that invaded the English garrison a few months after the capitulation, fell with the heaviest hand upon the colonies.†

Connecticut furnished for the undertaking about eleven hundred men. The expenses incurred in fitting out these men, and the wages that were paid them, came from the treasury of the colony. Connecticut petitioned the king to make her good for the money thus laid out, or to allow her to share in the prizes that had been taken during the expedition. Her prayer was disregarded, and she submitted to the loss in silence.‡

The effect of this enterprise upon the two nations interested in it, was what might have been readily anticipated. England, anxious to shun the burden while she claimed the glory of the victory, again resumed her old scheme—the reduction of Canada—and resolved to sweep from the western continent the last vestige of French dominion. On the other hand, France, stung to madness at the blow, determined to retrieve what she had thus ingloriously lost, and to add to her self-vindication, the consolations of revenge, by ranging the whole coast from Nova Scotia to Georgia.

---

* Holmes, ii. 27; Col. Mass. Hist. Soc., i. 4, 60; Douglass, i. 336; Belknap's Hist. N. Hamp., ii. 193, 224.

† Hutchinson.

‡ Our records contain frequent requests to the colonial agent in England, to petition for, and *receive* the money to reimburse the colony for her heavy expenses in said expedition; and in October, 1748, the agent is desired to obtain "a speedy payment of the money GRANTED *to us by Parliament*" for that purpose. It would seem, however, that the money was never received. This is more to be wondered at from the fact that £183,649, 2s, 1d, granted by Parliament for the purposes of reimbursement, arrived in Boston. It consisted of 215 chests, each containing 3,000 pieces of eight, and 100 casks of coined copper. There were 17 cart and truck loads of silver, and 10 truck loads of copper. Mass. Hist. Soc. Coll. This may have all been *designed* for Massachusetts, and used by her.

Animated by such motives, the two powers set themselves to perfect the enterprise that each had planned.

It was decided by the British government, that eight battalions of regular troops should meet at Louisbourg the forces to be raised in New England, and with a squadron under Admiral Warren, proceed up the St. Lawrence to Quebec; while another army from New York and the other colonies, as far south as Virginia, should rendezvous at Albany, and under the command of Governor St. Clair, march across the country to Montreal. No specified number of soldiers was required to be raised by any of the colonies, but it was thought best, in a cause where all were interested, to leave it to the magnanimity and emulation of each. It was, however, intimated that the proportion of troops to be furnished from the provinces, should be at least five thousand men. New England herself raised five thousand three hundred soldiers; New York and the other colonies, two thousand nine hundred. Of the number raised by New England, Connecticut furnished one thousand fighting men.* Such was the anxiety to accomplish this darling project, that the General Assembly of Connecticut was convoked immediately after the intentions of the government had been made known, and a bounty of thirty pounds was voted to every soldier who would enlist. It was also resolved, that if provisions could not be had without, they should be impressed.†

When we reflect that the members of the assembly were, by such a vote, exposing their own property to the same liabilities as that of their neighbors, and that the public sentiment would sustain such an order without compromising the popularity of the members, we see the reverence for law, and the manly spirit of self-sacrifice that has always characterized our people.

---

* The numbers of soldiers voted to be raised by the different colonies were very unequal, (as follows:)—New Hampshire, 500; Massachusetts, 3,500; Rhode Island, 300; Connecticut, 1,000; New York, 1,600; New Jersey, 500; Maryland, 300; Virginia, 100; Pennsylvania, 400.

† Colony Records, MS.

In six weeks from the time when the preparations began, our troops were ready to embark.

At the same time, a formidable armament was being prepared at Portsmouth, under the command of Richard Lestock, admiral of the blue, with transports carrying six regiments to act in concert with the colonial army; but such was the delay that attended the fitting out of the fleet, that when it was ready to sail, it was too late in the season to venture upon the Atlantic coast. It sailed to the coast of Brittany, in the hope of surprising the port of L'Orient, and taking possession of the military stores and ships of the French East India Company, but was able to do but little harm to the enemy.*

France made every exertion not to be outdone in the magnitude of her preparations. The Duke D'Anville, the leader of the enterprise, and a nobleman of high character and courage, soon sailed for the north Atlantic coast, with a fleet consisting of eleven ships of the line, thirty smaller ships and vessels, and transports, with more than three thousand land forces on board, who were to meet at Nova Scotia, with sixteen hundred French and Indians from Canada. The fleet and armament sailed from France on the 22d of June. An express was dispatched to Monsieur Conflans, who had been sent to Carthagena, with three ships of the line and a frigate, as a convoy of some trading vessels, ordered him to join the Duke at Chebucto.†

On account of adverse winds and other causes of delay, the Duke D'Anville, did not pass the Western Islands until the 3d of August. On the 24th of August, while yet three hundred leagues from Nova Scotia, one of his largest ships proved so unseaworthy that he was obliged to commit her to the flames. On the 1st of September, there came on a terrible storm, that so deranged the Mars and the Alcide, (both eighty-four gun ships,) that they were compelled to retire to the West Indies. Pestilence aided the winds; and soon after, the Ardent, another sixty-four gun ship, put back into

* Hutchinson. † Hutchinson; Trumbull; Bancroft, &c.

Brest, on account of an epidemic that prevailed among the crew.

On the 12th of September, the Duke finally reached Chebucto in the ship Northumberland, with only one ship of the line, the Renomme, and three or four transports. A single ship had arrived there before him, and the rest had been scattered, he knew not where, by the fury of the elements. Monsieur Conflans, who had, according to orders, arrived there in August, and had looked in vain, for the fleet had already sailed for France.*

Little did the colonies dream, while they were making such active preparations to invade Canada, that France was fitting out such an armament to overwhelm the whole coast. Therefore, when the fishermen who had fled from Chebucto on the appearance of Conflans, reported at Boston the arrival of a French fleet, their story gained little credence. Early in September, however, it was reported at Boston, from a source that could not be questioned, that a large French fleet had sailed for America. Soon after, there were flying rumors that a great fleet had been seen to the westward of Newfoundland. Still, it was hoped that this was the English fleet. On the 28th of September, an express boat brought intelligence that it was the French fleet. It was said to consist of fourteen ships of the line, and twenty smaller armed vessels, and that it had on board eight thousand troops.†

Ignorant of the injuries that the Duke D'Anville had sustained at sea, and believing that he had come with his entire fleet and armament, the colonies were thrown into consternation by this intelligence. They soon, however, recovered their self-possession and exerted themselves to the utmost to defend the coast. In a few days, more than six thousand of the inland militia were brought into Boston to reinforce the town. As many more were in readiness to go as soon as their presence might be required. Anxiously did the colonies await the coming of the English fleet.

* Hutchinson, ii. 383, 384. † Hutchinson, ii. 382.

The proud Duke D'Anville meanwhile looked with a vain longing for the scattered members of his fleet. After remaining for four days at Chebucto in a state of intense feverish excitement, and finding himself still in the same hopeless condition, he took leave of a world that appeared to have disappointed the hopes that made existence dear to him. Whether he died of apoplexy occasioned by chagrin, or from poison administered by his own hand, was never satisfactorily ascertained. He died in the morning, and in the afternoon of the same day, his Vice Admiral, D'Estournelle, with four ships of the line, came into port. His men were feeble and unfit for duty. After he had learned the sudden death of his superior officer, the departure of Conflans, and the loss of some of the best ships belonging to the fleet, he called a council of the officers, and proposed that they should return to France. But Monseiur de la Jonquiere, the Governor of Canada, who was on board, and the next in command, firmly opposed the proposition. Fresh air and wholesome food, he said, would soon recruit the men, and they had still force enough left to reduce Annapolis and Nova Scotia, and that there would be time enough to decide whether they should spend the winter in Canso Bay, or return home. This counsel prevailed after a debate of eight hours. Enraged at this rejection of his advice, D'Estournelle was thrown into a malignant fever, and in the delirium occasioned by the malady, he stabbed himself.*

Jonquiere, now chief in command, bent all his energies to carry out the plan that had resulted in the death of the Vice Admiral. The better to recruit his troops, he ordered them to go ashore, where the Acadians and Indians did everything in their power to relieve their sufferings. But dysenteries and fevers swept off hundreds of them. It was estimated that one-third of the Nova Scotia Indians died of the diseases communicated by the French troops.

A singular incident defeated the plan of Jonquiere. Gov-

* Belknap, N. Hamp. ii. c., 20; Adams, N. Eng. 210; Hutchinson, ii. 384; Holmes, ii. 30.

ernor Shirley, in the belief that he had received positive intelligence of the sailing of the English fleet, sent off an express to inform Admiral Lestock, at Louisbourg, of the state of affairs in America. On the 11th of October, the express-packet was captured by the French and carried into Chebucto. Her errand was made known to the French officers, and so alarmed them that it was thought advisable to sail immediately for France, without attempting to strike a blow.*

On the 15th of October, another fearful storm came on, and again the fleet was scattered. Only about one half of the army ever returned, and several of the ships were destroyed.† Thus ended in shipwreck and chagrin this haughty attempt upon the British colonies.

The capture of Louisbourg and the discomfiture of the French fleet by our army, that could not be subdued by human enemies, had thus prepared the way for the peace of Aix la Chapelle, that gave England an opportunity to recover from the effects of the rebellion that had now ended in the defeat of the Pretender, and gave her colonies liberty to throw off again the shackles of debts that they had incurred in the war.

Connecticut had been compelled to issue bills of credit to the amount of eighty thousand pounds. It was many years before she could redeem them. The existence of troubles at home, was the alleged cause of the neglect with which the British government treated the colonies at a time when they were threatened with total destruction. Thus robbed in peace, and left to the tender mercies of their enemies in times of danger, the hearts of the colonists were gradually alienated from the mother country.

* Hutchinson, ii. 384, 385.

† Hutchinson, ii. 385.

CHAPTER XX.

EARLY MANNERS AND CUSTOMS OF CONNECTICUT.

It may be a relief alike to the reader and the author to take a short leave of the more rapid current of historical narrative, and linger awhile where the waters, without losing their vitality, sleep tranquilly with the image of bank and tree resting upon their surface. When we read over a detailed account of the stirring events that make up what is ordinarily called history, we are apt to attribute to those events, and to the principal men who participated in them, an importance that does not belong to them. No one man, whatever may be his natural endowments, is so far in advance of his age, as his contemporaries believe him to be. Let us say, rather, that he is the expression, the utterance, of that deep, unconscious power that quickens the bosom and animates the features of his generation, as the wind-harp gives out to the ear the rich harmonies that before floated voiceless in the elements. The fibre of silk that you suspend in your window-frame, in the one case, and the hero, the great poet, the lawgiver who discloses new principles of civil polity, in the other, are each the accident that makes audible the musical cadences that are always waiting to be revealed to man. Hence, Shakspeare and Bacon are the voices that express the magnificent era in British history that united so much of the grandeur of the middle ages with the demonstrative, analytical power that was to follow it. Hence, Milton and Cromwell, as unlike each other as men could well be, spoke, shall I not rather say, prophesied—the one of the elevated tone of philosophy, polity, and religion, the other of the revolutionary tendencies of the century that was to build the fabric of society upon a new basis, that at the end of two hundred years still remains unshaken.

If these remarks are correct, it becomes us to turn our attention not only to the Ludlows, the Winthrops, the Wolcotts, and the Wyllyses, of Connecticut, but to those men, equally manly and bold, many of whom left homes as comfortable, though less known to history, and associations as tender as theirs, to accompany them into self-exile and submit to hardships such as are not known to our day, and magnified ten-fold by the dark uncertainties that attended them. Nor should we lose sight of those noble-hearted English women, who found in their natures room for the cultivation of the domestic virtues and for the devoutest love of God, who spurned the weaknesses that seem to add to the charms of the sex in times of peace, who met the worst dangers with calmness, and who shed no tears except for others.

In the lives of these fearless men and women who have left no marks to distinguish them beyond the few letters that designate upon the records when they were born, when they were married, and when they died; or beyond the brown slab placed over the spot where long ago their bones crumbled into the mould—a slab with its rough symbols and "shapeless sculpture"—are we to look for the courage that subdued the forest and its terrible inhabitants, the fortitude that bore up against the heavy burdens of life, the spontaneous sentiment of liberty that aroused them to resist the aggressions of the French and the insolence of Cornbury and Andross. In raising the monumental stone that is to bear the name of some great hero or statesman, let us look upon the shaft as commemorating not so much the virtues of an individual as of a whole people.

It has been thought by many who have had little opportunity or desire to form correct estimates of the people of Connecticut, that they sprung from a low and vulgar parentage. The want of monuments over the graves of most of them, the humble houses that they dwelt in, the plain clothing that they wore, and strange to tell, the fact that they almost all labored with their hands, have been seized upon as so many marks that they came from the undistinguishable crowd of English peasantry, whose fathers, from age to age, had been the lowest subjects of feudal villeiny. Never was a conclusion more hastily formed, or supported by so few facts. Indeed, all the analogies that are within our reach tend to a contrary result. The early planters of Connecticut were neither serfs nor the sons of serfs. So far from this were many of them, that they could trace their descent backward through the line of the knights and gentlemen of England, by means of the heralds' visitations, parish records, and county genealogies, to say nothing of those family pedigrees that were often transmitted, as heirlooms, from generation to generation, particularly in the line of the eldest sons, to a remote day, and some of them to that wavering horizon where history loses itself in fable. Thus it turns out upon investigation, that many a tomb that holds the dust of some pioneer whose memory is now cherished by a numerous posterity, yet cannot be distinguished from the surrounding earth, simply because no monument was placed above it to mark the spot, was entitled from the birth of its tenant, to be garnished with a coat of arms among the most honorable of those that swell the volumes of heraldry, with devices to modern republican eyes so quaint and strange.* But what had they, who had spent their lives in waging war with the formularies of the past time that appeared so irksome to them—what had men who made it a part of their education to discard the factitious distinctions of the world,—to do with the gauntleted hand, the helmeted brow, the griffins, the lions, the strawberries and the storks of the herald's college? The very fact that most of these symbols suggested to the mind the myths of paganism and idolatry, would of itself

* From actual examination it appears that more than four-fifths of the early landed proprietors of Hartford, Wethersfield, and Windsor, belonged to families that had arms granted to them in Great Britain. Other settlers in various parts of Connecticut, at an early or later day, bearing family names that appear never to have borne arms, are believed to have been descended from the landed gentry or other genteel English families, such as Chittenden, Ingersoll, Pitkin, Silliman, Lyman, Olmsted, Upson, Cullick, Treadwell.

make them objects of suspicion to many of the more strict order of puritans.

Besides, not only their religion, but their very physical condition, made it difficult for them to cherish with much care any thing that was not obviously connected with the great business of life. The ax of the planter, as its biting edge penetrated deeper and deeper into the vitals of the forest, letting in the sunbeams to scare away the deer that roamed over the parks that had no palings or gates, other than the natural barriers of river, mountain, or ocean, while it strengthened the hand of him who wielded it and carved his individuality upon the stumps of oak or pine, to remain there after he should have been laid to rest, was yet no fitting instrument to record the vanity of the past time. What had he to do with the past? The grim present was lowering upon him with all its sharp and angular realities. Indians, wild beasts, famine, cold, the diseases that lurk along the borders of new settlements, the French, the Dutch, the devil, and all the other calamities, actual or imaginary, that kept his faculties constantly stretched to their highest tension, gave him little time to look backward. Life, to a puritan, was a warfare, commencing with the dawn of his own existence, to be waged with a stout heart and steady hand until that existence should be lost in a future, boundless and eternal. Little time had he for the soft reverie and day-dreaming that belong to a stage of society that blends internal culture with easy circumstances and leisure-loving retirement. His business was to work. Other men retreated from the world to avoid its cares; he fled to the solitudes of nature to begin life anew. I do not mean to say that this was universally true. A few families from old ties, not easily sundered, binding them to the country of their birth, still kept up a communication with the past; but even in these exceptional instances it was lost in a few generations, and has only been revived within the last century, by resorting to the English repositories of such facts. I know this to be the case in all families now in New England that are able to give any accurate history of their lineage, extending beyond the first emigrants. Even the most illustrious names in our history, though readily traced in England, have been neglected to a degree that could not be accounted for by any one who should fail to keep in view the motives that actuated the emigrants, the necessities that surrounded them, the almost incredible amount of labor that they performed, and the estimate that they placed upon this life and the next.

I have said that the first English planters of Connecticut were of no vulgar origin. Many of them were poor, many of them when they sailed for America were in the more humble walks of life; but the planters, the substantial land holders, who began to plant those "three vines in the wilderness," sprung from the better classes, and a large proportion of them from the landed gentry of England. This fact is proved not only by tracing individual families, but by the very names that those founders of our republic bore. Any one who choses to look at the catalogue of good old English names that will be found at the close of this voulme, and compare it with any well arranged book of general heraldry, will see that they had either stolen their names, or that they were honorably descended. The first emigrants, it is true, brought with them many servants, but most of them were so from temporary causes, and were as unlike the stolid English laborer who then tilled, as his father and grandfather had done before him, the fields of the opulent English landholder, as the seventeenth century was unlike the twelfth.

This large infusion of the blood of the better class of English families might lead, were it philosophically considered, to an explanation of much that has been thought to be new and peculiar in our institutions and our people. I should hardly expect to be contradicted by any well informed genealogist either in England or America, were I to express my belief that there is hardly a man now living whose descent can be traced to the early planters of Connecticut, who will not be found to be derived, through one branch or another of his pedigree, from those families who helped to frame the British constitution, who elaborated by slow degrees the common law, who advocated the doctrines of both with their tongues and their pens, or defended them with their swords.

But it may not be clear to every mind how it happened that the early planters, if they were of such good descent, should have submitted to the most menial labors in an age when the gentry were, much more than now, a non-producing class. I reply that they were driven to it by the sternest necessity. They were poor; many of them had made great sacrifices to remove their families and their friends to America. Laborers were few, and they had no money to transport them in such numbers as were needed in a new country, to subdue the lands and render them habitable. Most of all, they were in want of mechanics. They needed houses to screen them from the weather, they must be provided with cloth, which they could not import, and that cloth must be made into garments. Their horses could not go afield, or from town to town unshod ; nor could their sons and daughters live without shoes. From these stern necessities they learned the dignity of labor. If they could not procure carpenters, blacksmiths, shoemakers, weavers, and clothiers, in any other manner, it was evident that they must learn these several employments themselves, and teach them to their children. They found themselves obliged to fell the trees and till the grounds, that they might have bread. The best planters, therefore, could find nothing degrading in the use of the ax or the plow. Besides, their religion and habitudes of mind taught them to look with reverence rather than with scorn upon all the useful occupations of life, as tending to help forward the human soul upon a journey, at the close of which it was to be invested with a robe of white and adorned with a crown of gold.

Some of them had anticipated this, and had learned to practise some useful art or mystery, either before leaving England, or while in Holland or Germany. Hence, Henry Wolcott, whose ancestors could be traced back as far as the reign of William the Conqueror, does not appear to have withheld his daughter's hand from Mathew Griswold, because he was a stone-cutter and made monuments for the few who chose to retain a custom that Welles, Leete, and the whole Wyllys family appear to have despised. Roger Wolcott, too, a grandson of the emigrant, and himself the first of the line of governors bearing that name, a man of letters and elevated views, was proud to labor in the field as a husbandman, and on rainy days and in the long winter evenings, to fill up the intervals of study in plying the shuttle that his bright-eyed sons and rosy-cheeked daughters might be warmly clad. Governor Webster, and Governor Welles, if they did not labor with their own hands, taught their sons to toil. Governor Leete, at the very time that he discharged the duties of chief magistrate of the colony, and while he was secreting the regicides at his house, kept a country store for the accommodation of his neighbors, and for many years earned a livelihood by keeping the records of Guilford. His sons were, it is believed, all taught to work in the field. Governor Treat was as well skilled in the mysteries of plowing a corn-field, or mowing a hay-field, as in fighting the battles of the colony, or defending her charter. His father, Richard Treat, a patentee named in the charter, and one of the first gentlemen in the colony, daily crossed the Connecticut river in a boat, and lent his strong muscles to the task of breaking up the fallow land of Glastenbury. Winthrop submitted to the severest hardships in removing from Boston to Pequot (now New London,) in going from place to place to exercise the functions of a magistrate, in acting as mediator between contending parties, in procuring land titles and defending them for himself and for others, in purchasing mines, in performing the office of physician, to say nothing of the burdens of public life. For these services he did not scruple to receive a fair compensation. If he did not labor with his hands, we may presume from what we know of his character, that it was from no fear of soiling them, but merely because his time was worth more in other departments of usefulness. Governor Law spent a portion of his time in the cultivation of his plantation.

I could multiply instances of names and individuals whose fame will not die while history has a niche still remaining for the statues of the fathers of the republic. I need only say, that high or low, through all the grades of society, labor was respectable, while idleness and vice were, as they have always been in every well regulated government, looked upon with suspicion.

Thus frugal, industrious, honest, the fathers of the colony were unconsciously laying the foundation of a structure, imperishable because built in accordance with the eternal laws of God's truth—imperishable, I mean, unless the indolence and hollow pretensions of their descendants shall dismantle its walls, and leave its solid frame-work to the injurious action of the elements. No people that hold labor in derision can maintain its position for three centuries. No servitude is so debasing, as that which nature is keeping in reserve for the descendants of a people who studiously inculcate in the minds of their children that it is better to be idle and hungry than to earn an honest livelihood by work.

Are we to infer, then, from the fact that physical labor was cherished by all classes of our ancestors with such care—are we to infer that they had no grades, no distinctions, in their social fabric? So far was this from being the case, that I have found in the records of no people worthy to be called civilized, the internal evidences of grade and rank adjusted more carefully than can be traced in the files and books of the early documentary history of our own colony. It may be interesting to the reader to know into what classes and grades society was divided.

1. The title of "*Honorable*" was entirely unknown in our colonial records until 1685, and was subsequently for many years applied only to the governor, and seldom to him. Previous to that date, however, the chief magistrate was sometimes designated as "our Worshipful Governor," and "our

Honored Governor." Similar titles were also occasionally given to the Deputy Governor.*

The next title was that of "*Esquire,*" employed very sparingly for the first century after the emigration, and having about the same signification that it had in England, in the times of Elizabeth and James I. Those who had been possessed of landed estates in England, and had been liberally educated, younger sons of the nobility, and the sons of baronets and knights, were addressed in writing by the addition of esquire, placed after the name and before or after that of the place of residence. When addressed colloquially, the title was a prefix usually abbreviated into the monosyllable, "*Squire.*" In Connecticut, this title was confined almost exclusively to the governor and deputy governor, until the union with New Haven colony was effected in 1665. The only exceptions found upon our records, are in the cases of Colonel Fenwick, of Saybrook, and John Winthrop, who was subsequently chosen governor. Indeed, it would seem that *office* of whatever grade did not necessarily make the official an esquire. Mr. Thomas Welles, was a magistrate for seventeen years, deputy governor for one year, and was chosen governor for the second time, before he was dignified with that honorable title.†

The next title to be noticed is that of "*Gentleman*" or, as it was usually abbreviated "*Gent.*" This designation, which occurs but seldom upon our early records, is essentially an English title, is placed at the end of the name, and, like esquire, either before or after the place of residence. Aside from its general application, it was used in England especially to designate that class who hold a middle rank between esquires and masters. This distinction seems to have been soon discarded in Connecticut.

* This title appears to have been first applied in Connecticut to Major Andross; and *by him* to Governor Winthrop.

† Such titles as the following sometimes occur on our records, or in letters addressed to the individuals named, and others, viz: "the Honored Major Talcott," "the Worshipful Captain John Allyn," "the Worshipful and much Honored John Winthrop," &c.

The prefix of "*Master*" (Mr.) belonged to all gentlemen, including those designated by the higher marks of rank that have been mentioned above. Master corresponds very nearly in meaning to the English word, gentleman. In Connecticut, it embraced clergymen, and planters of good family and estate who were members of the General Court; those bred up at a university, and those of sufficient education to manage the general affairs of the colony, either in a civil or ecclesiastical way, and who had been sufficiently well born. Comparatively few of the representatives from the several towns, even though they might be returned year after year, were honored with this title. To be called master, or to have one's name recorded by the secretary with that prefix, two hundred years ago, was a more certain index of the rank of the individual as respects birth, education, and good moral character, than any one of the high-sounding appellations with which many men of no merit whatever, in our day of swift locomotion, are content to cajole others in order that they may be enriched in their turn with the same spurious currency. It may be observed, by reference to our colonial records, that there were scores of men of good family and in honorable stations who still did not possess all the requisite qualities of masters. It was seldom that young men, of whatever rank, were called masters.

The appellation of "*Sir*," besides its ordinary use, was employed in a technical and limited sense to designate young gentlemen who had graduated at a university or college, but had not taken their Master's degree. It was formerly appended to the names of the members of the graduating class of Yale College, on the schemes used at the annual commencement, thus Sir Swift, Sir Wolcott, Sir Barlow, &c.

"*Goodman*," was also a term of civility, and in a certain qualified sense might be called a title. Its application predicated of him to whom it was given, a humble origin, and it comprehended the better sort of yeomen, laborers, tenants, and other dependents above the grade of servants, who owned a small estate, and who sustained a good moral character.

Our colonial records afford several instances of deputies to the General Court who were signalized by this mark of the public regard. The corresponding term as applied to the other sex, was *Goodwife*.

Military titles were considered of a very high order, as we should naturally expect to find them in a colony that was in an almost uninterrupted state of war from the time of the burning of the Pequot fort, until the close of the American revolution. These titles, therefore, abound in our early colonial records, from that of captain down to that of corporal, and usually took precedence of the ordinary terms of address. These gradations of official rank were expressed by the usual abbreviations, and were seldom omitted. Previous to 1654, the highest military office in the colony was that of captain; and previous to 1652, the only captain in the colony was John Mason, whose jurisdiction extended throughout Connecticut. Captain Mason, and especially in later years, Major Mason, when he visited the militia of the different towns, as he did at stated intervals, was gazed at by the boys and girls of the settlement with eyes of wide wonder, as a man to be reverenced, but not approached.

Those titles of an *Ecclesiastical* nature were of course held in high esteem by our Puritan fathers, both in Old England and in New England. The clerical prefix of *Reverend*, does not occur upon our colonial records until about 1670;* the members of the profession bearing the simple titles of Mr., Pastor, Teacher, or Elder. *Deacons* were regarded with reverence, and were often employed in civil as well as in ecclesiastical affairs. The title frequently occurs in the list of deputies and commissioners. In New Haven colony, where all the freemen were church members, the term or title of "*Brother*," was often used as a prefix to the names of persons appointed to civil office.

I have said that many of the principal emigrants brought over servants with them from England. Such was the scarcity of laborers that, with the exception of the clergy, nearly all

* The general term, "the Reverend Elders," occurs much earlier.

the original proprietors toiled earnestly upon their plantations, and frequently in the same field with their servants. But after the fibres of the state became more firmly knit, after the lands were partially cleared, when corn and money began to be more abundant, and after the tide of emigration, checked for awhile, had brought a liberal supply of working-men who were willing to till the fields and make new conquests over the still abounding forests, society began to assume its old English features, and distinct generic orders were formed upon a somewhat stable basis long before the revolution.

These orders were distinguished by the terms gentlemen, yeomen, merchants,* mechanics, and servants, or domestics. The lines drawn around these respective classes were not so strict as to be in the way of personal merit when it sought to rise; but were sufficiently so to characterize the several grades. By this time the name of planter had almost entirely disappeared from our records, and that of farmer had been partially substituted.

The term, Yeoman, was applied to that class of freeholders and planters who stood next in rank to gentlemen, of whose position I have spoken elsewhere. Some of the yeomen bore the title of master, and they were frequently called to discharge important public trusts. By this time, too, from the want of the guards that in England had always proved so favorable to the growth and continuance of privileged classes, very many of the descendants of the best families who emigrated to Connecticut, had glided imperceptibly from their position at that time, and had taken the middle stage. Many of the yeomen were as well born, and had as much pride of family, as the educated class. Indeed, the latter class was to a good extent made up from the yeomanry of the more cultivated sort, who could easily resume the place that their ancestors had filled with such honor.

* The early traders, especially in the small settlements and towns, of course did but a small business in that line, and were often freeholders and planters in addition. They subsequently became a distinct and very respectable class.

The last remark is true of many of the merchants and mechanics of those times.

The educated class filled the pulpit, the bench, the magistracy, the bar, and the medical profession, and constituted much the largest portion of the aristocracy, which grew more rapidly than ever before, from the time that the slave-trade first gave it nutriment, until it reached its zenith about twenty years after the close of the revolution. Many of the officers of the army, who were regarded with deep reverence by the people, were the principal pillars of the aristocracy. But the most thoroughly patrician body of men in Connecticut was the clergy, who exercised an almost unlimited authority over the inhabitants. I do not believe there ever was an aristocracy more deserving of respect, as well from the high tone of its morality as from the stateliness and general decorum that distinguished its members; nor do I believe there ever was a yeomanry more independent and manly or less the victims of envy.

This state of things continued, with such variations as belonged to the gradual development of society, down to the close of Governor Smith's administration, when the freemen voluntarily laid aside the charter that they had never surrendered to the crown.

With all this respect paid to orders and officials, growing partly out of their religious belief, that taught them to reverence all powers and dignitaries except such as they believed to be wrongfully applied, and partly out of those English prejudices that they brought with them, in favor of gentle lineage and established authorities, they were obliged to live in a very humble and simple way for many years. Their dwellings were at first mostly constructed of logs. The planters who spent the first winter in Hartford, Wethersfield, and Windsor, had no better houses than the wretched huts that colliers now use upon our mountains as a temporary shelter while they are watching their coal-pits and drawing their coal. After Hooker and Wareham, with their companies, arrived in the valley, better dwellings were constructed, and in all the old towns a few frame houses were soon reared for the more wealthy and respectable citizens. The houses of the ministers were made as elegant and comfortable as the circumstances of the people would afford. The dwellings of the governor and more wealthy magistrates and gentlemen, were some of them expensive. The house built by the Rev. Henry Whitfield, at Guilford, was of stone, with very solid and massive walls, that have withstood the action of the frosts and the other harsh influences of the climate, and will do so yet for hundreds of years, if man, that worst of all destroyers, will permit it to remain. It is the oldest house now standing in the United States, and is a fit memorial of the enduring fame of Whitfield, the founder of Guilford.* The house of Desborough was also of stone, but the walls were long ago thrown down.

Most of the buildings in the colony, however, were constructed of wood, and the better classes, after the first thirty years, lived in framed houses. These frames were made of heavy oak timbers, some of them eighteen inches in diameter. The rafters were larger than the plates, sills and beams of our modern country houses, and supported slit sticks called, in the rude architectural language of the day, "ribs," that were laid across them at regular distances, and to which long rent shingles of cedar were fastened with tough wrought nails. The sides of the building were covered with oak clapboards rent from the tree and smoothed with a shaving-knife. These outer boards lapped over each other, and were fastened to the upright and horizontal timbers by nails much larger than those now used in the roof-eaving. Within, the sides of the rooms only were plastered, while the sleepers and the upper floor were exposed to view. The floors were of oaken plank. The windows consisted of two small leaden frames set with diamond-shaped panes, secured by hinges that opened outward, and were fastened against the side of

* This venerable structure was built about the year 1640, and, on account of its impregnable walls, was sometimes used as a block-house or fort by the settlers.

the house. When closed, the two sashes formed nearly a square. The outer doors of the mansion were of double oaken planks, made as solid as a single piece of timber by nails or spikes driven into them in the angles of diamonds.* When these gates of his domestic paradise were secured at night by the heavy wooden bars that had stood throughout the day leaning against the wall, the planter and his family had little cause to fear the entrance of wild beasts or Indians, and other burglars for many years there were none in Connecticut. Indeed, after the Indians had been tamed and the wolves and bears driven farther off by the gradual destruction of their old haunts, the tenants of these humble Arcadian castles slept peacefully from one year to another without even barring or bolting their doors.

The rooms of the early habitations were seldom more than seven feet in height, so that the sturdy emigrants, and their sons, who had rather added to the stature of their fathers than substracted from it by athletic and wholesome exercise, in wood and field and camp, during the period of life when the bones are enlarging, and the muscles are assuming a hardened and fibrous texture, could hardly stand upright upon the kitchen floor without brushing the fur of their bear-skin caps against the timbers overhead.

The most indestructible part of the whole edifice was the huge stone tower that occupied the centre, rising out of the ridge, and called a chimney. Its foundations were about twelve feet square. The fire-places, as they were very properly termed, especially the ones most in use, were of such dimensions that the wood could be brought from the forest, taken from the cart, and heaped upon the ponderous andirons in great quantities. In the coldest weather, a large log of maple, oak, or walnut, was placed at the back of the fire-place, and other smaller ones laid upon it. The andirons were brought in front of this formidable battery, that was made still more durable by a log about eight inches in diameter, called a fore-stick. The smaller wood was then care-

* See Lambert, 201.

fully put on with pine knots, birch bark, or other dry fuel, in the middle. The quantity of wood consumed in a single day in the more severe winter weather, was enormous; and the ventilation caused by the keen currents of air that found a free entrance through the crevices of the building, would be terrific to a housewife of modern days. The fire was by no means small even in summer, and after the toils of the day, the family would gather around it even while the doors were wide open, and the cry of the frog from the marsh, and the whippöwill from the home-meadow, stole upon their seclusion with associations cheerful or sad as suited the temperaments and moods of the various members composing the circle.*

Conversation was sometimes startled and chilled into sudden silence, in the early and more superstitious days, by the gleam of a meteor seen through the diamond-shaped window panes or open door, as it lit up the little patch of sky that lay clear and open behind the branches of the trees. If, when the free laugh was ringing from the heart of the boys and girls at some grotesque account of adventures, old or new, a malicious screech-owl, seizing the loved opportunity when the face of the moon was veiled by a cloud, chanced to mingle his mocking merriment with theirs, what wonder if a shivering sigh bore quick witness how well they remembered that the devil was as fond as ever of his old pastimes in solitudes and desert places? I much doubt if King James I., had he been living in such extreme retirement, would not have found his teeth chattering and his hair bristling at a like signal from the father of lies. Even Sir Walter Raleigh would have knocked the ashes out of his pipe and mused; and my Lord Coke, would have forgotten for a moment, how necessary it was to his own proper development to ruin Sir Francis Bacon. In a much later age, Dr. Johnson himself might have found his hand arrested in the act of conveying to his mouth the thirteenth cup of tea, and might have been strangled in the midst of a sentence in which the oat-meal

* Lambert, 202.

cakes of Scotland, or the unfortunate Chesterfield, formed the theme of vituperation. Possibly the reader's nervous equilibrium might be shaken at a much less provocation, even in the midst of a hearty fit of laughter at the bigotry and superstition of the puritans.

There were a few houses in the colony of a more aristocratic type than the one that I have selected to represent the dwellings of the early inhabitants. Among these, I can only stop to name Governor Eaton's of New Haven, built in the form of a capital E, with its numerous windows, its stack of chimneys with their twenty-one fire-places; and that of his friend, Mr. Davenport, scarcely less imposing.*

The meals of the early planters were such as befitted Englishmen who were remote from all commercial relations, in a new country, where nature, with few exceptions, reduces all her sons to the common necessity of providing for their own sustenance. They ate and drank what she provided for them, and thanked God that it was so bountiful and so nourishing.

The breakfast of the farmers often consisted mainly of a soup made of salt meat and beans, and seasoned with savory herbs. This dish was called "bean porridge," and has long been the fruitful subject of verse. Tea and coffee they had none during the seventeenth century. Their drink was chiefly beer and cider, after their orchards were sufficiently grown to afford them such a luxury.†

The dinner was a much more substantial meal. A large Indian pudding, with an appropriate sauce, often constituted the first course; and after that, boiled beef and pork; and then wild game, with potatoes; and then succeeded turnips and other vegetables native to the climate. They had succatosh in the season of it; and in the fall, samp. Pumpkins were cooked by them into various dishes. Dinner was served at noon.

---

* The residence of Governor Eaton stood upon the north corner of Elm and Orange streets; that of Mr. Davenport was on the west side of Elm street, near State street, New Haven. The latter was built in the form of a cross.

† As early as 1654, laws were passed regulating the sale of "strong beer and cider."

At supper—afterwards called tea—they also ate very substantial food. It was almost always cold, with an occasional variation of cakes made of corn-meal, rye, or buckwheat. These cakes, however, were oftener prepared for breakfast.

Their table furniture was plain. Pewter was the more ordinary metal in use, but silver was often seen glittering upon the same table with the baser metal. Silver tankards and beakers were to be found in the houses of nearly all the wealthy planters of good family.*

The tables of the clergymen and magistrates, not excepting the governor, were furnished with similar fare to that above described, with various shades of difference in the arrangement; and the mode of serving it up, indicated more or less refinement. In after times, the tables of genteel families had more ambitious furniture and better viands, and never was food more wholesome and never did it better do its office of nourishing and strengthening the body, than during the period of New England history that preceded the revolution.

They had no wheeled carriages or wagons until the middle of the eighteenth century, and very few until the revolutionary war was closed.† The bridegroom who went to a neighboring town to be united with a partner whom he hoped to find through life a "help meet for him," whether he was gentleman or yeoman, rode on horseback, and carried her home on a pillion behind him.

The first inhabitants of Connecticut, as we have seen, were for the most part a very industrious, honest, and religious

* From an examination of the early inventories, I infer that most of the articles used for culinary and domestic use were made of pewter—such as spoons, platters, pitchers, cups, plates, pans, bottles, &c. The silver articles named in these inventories, are flaggons, beakers, tankards, spoons, cups, knee buckles, and shoe buckles. Tin and crockery are seldom spoken of. The Rev. J. B. Felt, of Boston, in his excellent work, "The Customs of New England," gives a description and history of hundreds of articles of household use, and of many other things tending to illustrate pioneer-life in New England.

† The first pleasure carriage (a chair) ever brought into Litchfield, was owned by Mr. Matthews, the English Mayor of New York, who was confined in that town as a prisoner of war in 1776.

people. They have been accused of narrow-mindedness and bigotry. To a certain extent this must be allowed to be true. Their bigotry was of the peculiar kind that often springs up suddenly in minds naturally enthusiastic and self-sacrificing. When they rebel against customs and practices so long established, they are often considered by those who are wedded to them to be a part of the moral and social constitution of man. Reformers always show their horror of the evils, real or imaginary, from which they have emancipated themselves, by going to another extreme so radical and marked as to constitute a boundary-line that may be readily seen. Indeed, such extremes are sooner or later the very badges and colors distinguishing the party that wears them. If the cavaliers wear long hair, the Cromwellians must of course be shorn. As soon as the cavaliers have discovered the bald heads of their opponents, they begin to apply unguents to their long locks and use all the stimulants that will be likely to give them, as nearly as possible, the appearance of so many Absaloms. When once it was known that many of the clergy had resolved not to conform to some part of the church ritual which they thought exceptionable, Queen Elizabeth proceeded to take measures at once to make still more stringent requisitions. Such is man's moral organization that he must correct extremes by other extremes. A similar law appears to prevail in the physical creation.

The bigotry of puritanism differed from the established bigotries of England not so much in degree as in kind. Both the great parties that divided that country were, so far as I can discover, equally intolerant, but their intolerance aimed at different things. The adherents of one abhorred a conventicle as if it had been a pestilence; those of the other, fled from the sight of the surplice as if it had been a mask of leprosy. One party, in seeking to discard the forms that it regarded as the relics of idolatry, came at last to shudder at the sight of the Cross, and in mockery quartered troops of soldiers in sacred chapels and fed the horses of the dragoons from the altars of venerable churches; the other, with a holy horror, sacrificed human victims to appease its wrath. The narrow-mindedness of the one party, drove it to spurn the elegancies of classical learning, and to turn away from Shakspeare with loathing; while that of the other, looked askance at the grandest epic in the whole treasury of letters, because it had been bequeathed to the world by a puritan.

The puritans abhorred profanity and debauchery, and hence, associating the vices of the cavaliers with the dresses that they wore, they assumed a new costume as unlike the old as their imaginations could devise; the cavaliers, in self-vindication, and to show how defiant they were of the puritans, placed their chapeaus upon their heads with a still more jaunty air, and curtailed their already short cloaks still the more.

Whoever sees anything to worship in any or all of these evidences of human imperfection, is at liberty to choose from the temple of prejudice the idol that he deems most worthy of his adoration. For my part, I can see nothing to admire in them, but much to shun. In doing so, I condemn not the cavaliers for clinging to the past, nor the puritans for breaking away from its thraldom; but rather the bad passions of our common nature that have so long resisted the influences of reason and the benign charities of the christian faith. They are to be treasured up as lessons.

The inhabitants of Connecticut, from the enjoyment of a larger liberty than could exist in Massachusetts under the administration of a more aristocratic and strictly provincial government, were thus taught to bestow upon those who differed from them a greater measure of liberality. Still they were not free from the taint of superstition. They had left England with a main design to enjoy their own religious tenets. With this view they had bought their wild lands; with this view they established a peculiar form of government. They looked with extreme jealousy upon the encroaching power of popery, and many of them regarded episcopacy as only a modified form of catholicism. As they had been at such pains to enjoy their own opinions, they knew no other rule than the characteristic one of that age, exclusiveness, or, if that would not avail, coercion. They resolved to keep out all religious sects from their limits, or, if they ventured to cross their border, to compel them to conform. They determined, too, that if it were possible the very festivals as well as modes of worship that were associated in their minds with oppression and arbitrary power, should be suppressed, and that other public days should be substituted.

The public days of the people of Connecticut were two, viz., *Fast*, and *Thanksgiving*.

The Fast was appointed at irregular intervals, usually on account of some special or threatened calamity which was designated by the General Court, or by the governor at the time of the appointment, care being always taken not to have it on Good Friday. On fast day, no food was cooked in the houses of the inhabitants, nor did the more exemplary church members eat any regular meals until after the sun went down. They had public worship on that occasion as they did on Sunday, and spent the time in self-examination, humiliation, and prayer. The sins of the people were made the burden of the minister's discourse, and most earnestly did he pray that he and his flock might be delivered from temptation.*

But the grand festival of the people, and the one in which they took the liveliest interest, was *Thanksgiving*.† For many years it was appointed only on occasions of special interest; but subsequently the legislature fixed upon November of each year, after the crops had all been gathered in, and during that shadowy and hushed season, the twilight of the year, when the veil of the Indian summer

* In Jan. 1644, it was ordered that there should be a day of fasting and humiliation observed throughout the plantations *every month*. A similar order was issued in August, 1676. The regular annual fast was not appointed until after the revolution.

† The first Thanksgiving Day ever appointed in Connecticut, was on the 18th of September, 1639.

heightened by partly concealing the beauty of the south-western hills. It is difficult to conceive at this remote day, when the fruits of their labors alone remain, while the hardships that they endured are forgotten, what happy associations clustered around this festival. After the first forty years had passed by, and it had begun to assume the character of an established institution, the hearts of the old and the young throbbed with anticipation as it drew near. The preparations for the dinner were very substantial and bountiful. It was usually celebrated at the old homestead and in the house of the patriarch of the family. It was held on Thursday, and generally late in the month. Thanksgiving week taxed the energies of the whole family. The stalled ox and the fatted calf were killed. The plumpest chickens and turkeys and geese were selected from the barn-yard, the yellowest pumpkins from the barn, and the finest potatoes and turnips from the cellar. The children of the pioneers, who were scattered throughout the colony, now turned their thoughts and faces homeward. The son who had left his father's roof in early manhood, and who longed once more to see the apple-trees that he had planted, and to receive the paternal blessing, now commenced his journey, with his wife and a whole swarm of sun-browned boys and ruddy girls. The brothers and sisters all met and all brought their children. Sometimes there were so many that the house would scarcely hold them; but the dear old grandmother, whose memory could hardly keep the constantly lengthening record of their births, and whose eye, dim with tears and age, could never see which child to love the best, welcomed each with a trembling hand and an overflowing heart.

The early part of the day was spent by the male members of the family in attendance upon public worship, where the old emigrant, with the white frost of his eightieth winter in his hair, sat more erect than he was wont, and could not, with all his humility, refrain from dividing his attention between the discourse and the long row of boys, who, in spite of the strictness of puritan discipline, waited impatienly for the "Amen," that was to set them at liberty.

On their return from the meeting-house, dinner awaited them. It may be presumed that there was not a single dyspeptic in the whole group, and that they did good justice to the viands.

After their repast, the family gathered around the blazing hickory fire, the children adding to its volume the shells of the walnuts and butternuts that they threw into it, without disturbing the conversation of their parents, who recounted each in his turn the incidents that had given variety to the year. Indian wars; the depredations of the Dutch; the plot of that wretch, Peter Stuyvesant, to exterminate the whole English population; the wolf and bear hunts; the marvelous stories of rattlesnakes; and, I must admit, sometimes still more marvelous manifestations from the spiritual world, apparitions, ghosts, visitations from the devil; the execution of Goodwife Knapp, and the scorn with which she looked upon her accusers, were fruitful themes to while away the evening. Games, too, helped to divert the attention of the children from subjects likely to disturb their sleep.

As the evening deepened, and the little ones began to nod upon their benches in the chimney corner, the old family bible was brought, and, after a portion of it had been read, the voice of the grandsire, tremulous with emotion rather than with age, was heard returning thanks to Almighty God for his infinite mercy in times past, in preserving the lives and health of the circle gathered around him, and supplicating him to keep them from temptation, and to multiply their descendants as the stars of the sky and the sands of the sea.

Such was Thanksgiving, a time-honored, venerable custom, that has gradually extended itself into the most distant part of our great republic. The occasion of it, only remembered now by the antiquarian, its more forbidding features worn away as the years have left behind them in their flight the noxious shades of superstition, its genial warmth, its hallowed domestic and historical associations, still survive in the bosom of him who can trace his descent from the fathers of Connecticut, whether his foot presses her soil, or whether on the borders of the great lakes and rivers of the west, in the vast forest, or in the billowy grass of the prairies, he joins with the voices of nature in returning thanks to the author of his being.

Though Thanksgiving was the only *general* festival, the reader is not to conclude that there were no other occasions of festivity and rejoicing among the people of Connecticut. Among the more primitive and rural portions of the population, there were husking, apple-pearing, and quilting parties; the social, neighborly gatherings around the great winter-fires; and the sleigh-rides, balls, and weddings, which were not confined to any particular class or locality.

I shall not attempt to describe a wedding-party among our ancestors. Indeed, the ceremony and its accompanying congratulations and rejoicings on the part of attendants and friends, were as varied then as now. True, the era of bride-stealing* has gone by; and the rustic serenade of horns and kettles is becoming an obsolete entertainment. Yet, amidst all the artificial forms and polite blandishments which modern taste and refinement have thrown around this most interesting ceremony, it were well to ask if there has been a corresponding advance in the motives and purposes that influence the union of heart and hand in bonds indissoluble? *Formerly*, at least, it was understood by both parties that the wife was to be "a help meet for her husband." On this point the minister who joined them was wont to be very emphatic.†

I have intimated that balls were among the amusements of the past in this colony. This, it is to be presumed, was ordinarily confined to the young people; and did not always meet with the hearty concurrence of the elder and more sedate portion of the community. The expenses attending such gatherings, were made to conform to the condition and circumstances of the people as they then were, and certain-

* A Poem, by Mrs. Emma Willard, entitled, "Bride-Stealing, a Tale of New England's Middle Ages," is preserved in Everest's "Poets of Connecticut." It gives a poetical account of one among many instances of "stealing the bride" that occurred in the early days of the colony.

† Bushnell's Discourse.

ly would not be thought extravagant in these days.* It was long the custom in Connecticut, for the young men and women of a parish to celebrate the occasion of the settlement of a new minister by a ball on the evening following the day of his ordination or installation. This was termed the "ordination ball," and was sometimes conducted with such propriety and decorum that church-members and even the new pastor would honor the ball with their presence. They ultimately came to be regarded as a scandal, and were at last suppressed by public sentiment.

The customs at funerals in different parts of New England were for many years somewhat peculiar, and were long since modified or abandoned. The distribution of gloves, rings, and scarfs at funerals prevailed to such an extent, that in 1721, the Legislature of Massachusetts passed a law against the usage. Town authorities complied with the fashion so far, that they distributed these articles at the burial of their paupers, and the expense was charged over to the town. At the funeral of the wife of Governor Belcher of Massachusetts, in 1736, more than one thousand pairs of gloves were distributed among the attendants.† In the form of an association recommended by the Continental Congress, in 1774, the articles of mourning for both sexes are specified; with the pledge that they "will discountenance the giving of gloves and scarfs at funerals." In Connecticut, or rather in certain parts of the colony, these and other practices, now obsolete, were long continued.

It has doubtless often puzzled those who are curious in such matters to shape to their imaginations what fashioned clothes their early ancestors wore, and how they looked in them. This is not an easy task, and yet something can be

* Morris, in his "Statistical Account" of Litchfield, speaks of a dance in that town in 1748, where a violin was used for the first time in the place, and adds—"The whole expense of the amusement, although the young people generally attended, did not exceed one dollar, out of which the fiddler was paid." Yet the parents and old people declared they should be "ruined by the extravagances of the youth."

† "Customs of New England."

said upon costume that may not be uninstructive to the general reader.

I have said that some of the emigrants brought with them from England silver-plate and articles of household furniture that betokened their rank in England. The same remark will apply to wearing apparel. Yet, except on public days, even the best planters must have dressed with great simplicity during the first twenty or thirty years after the colony began to be settled. I have also stated that labor was the common lot, and that even gentlemen did not shrink from it. As soon as they could, they raised their own sheep. In this way a staple material was provided for the winter clothing of males and females. The wool sheared by the hands of the planters, his sons, and servants, was, by his wife, daughters, and female domestics, spun and woven into cloth, and then cut into garments by the skillful matron for the members of her household. Flax, too, and hemp were cultivated with much care, and supplied them with materials that they were obliged to shape into garments that would serve them for the warmer months of the year.

I do not mean to assert that our fathers were indifferent in matters of dress and personal appearance. The gentry indulged in silks, velvets, and beavers, and there are still preserved many specimens of their taste in the shape of rich lace ruffles, elegant embroidery, silk and velvet caps, and costly ornaments of gold and silver.

Small-clothes were worn by our forefathers from the earliest times, and were made of sheep and deer skin, as well as of cloth.* Until within the last sixty years, boys were dressed in these stiff habiliments as soon as the attire of their childhood had been laid aside. These small-clothes underwent various modifications of fashion. They were usually fitted very closely to the person, and those men were thought to be very fortunate whose forms were such that they could wear small-clothes above the hips without appurtenances and stockings above the calf of the leg without garters.

* Felt's "Customs of New England," 137.

Shoes with silver or brass buckles were worn with the stockings or hose; and buckles of the same materials secured the small-clothes and stockings at the knee.

The coat was in partial use at the time of the emigration, but the doublet was more generally worn. The coat then in fashion came down directly in front below the knee, and was fastened to the very bottom with buttons or clasps, and sometimes with hooks and eyes. The skirts were very full, and were made to hang off from the person by being stiffened with buckram.* In 1715, and perhaps earlier, this garment was made with pockets opening from the outside, protected by ample flaps. The coat worn by wealthy gentlemen, and persons of official rank, was profusely decorated with gold lace. Instead of the broad collar of the present day, it had only a narrow hem that exposed to view the plaited stock of fine linen cambric, with its large silver buckle at the back of the neck.† The close-bodied coat, with its short waist and flexible skirts, was not introduced until 1790, or about the middle of the reign of George III. ‡

Cloaks were also used by the fathers of New England. They were of a variety of colors, but the most fashionable were red.

Hats were at first for the most part made of wool, but beaver hats soon came into use, and prevailed for many years. Of whatever material, they were high-crowned, and in the form of a sugar-loaf. The brims were so broad as to make it necessary for the wearer to hold them on firmly with the hand when the wind was blowing. This fashion continued until about 1700, with some slight changes. The graceful hat worn by Charles I., and his cavaliers, with its plume, was sometimes seen even in New England. The military cocked hat, called also the Monmouth hat, began to be worn

* Lambert's Hist. New Haven Col., 198. † Lambert, 198.

‡ The skins of animals were much used for garments among the early settlers. In the inventory of Mr. William Whiting, one of the wealthiest citizens of Connecticut, (who died in 1649,) are the following items: "two raccoon coats, one wolf skin coat, four bear skins, three moose."

in this country about the year 1670. The average width of the brim at that date was six inches. This inconvenient width probably suggested the plan of cocking it or turning it up and fastening it against the side of the crown. It was first cocked on one side only, then on the opposite side also, and in the reign of queen Elizabeth a third side was turned up—making the three-cornered cocked hats worn by gentlemen in New England from the year 1732 to 1779. Even gentlemen's sons of the age of fourteen years, wore the triangular hat. When gentlemen paid their respects to ladies, or to each other in public, they took it off, or in the language of the day, "*vailed it.*"

Watches were worn by gentlemen in New England as early as 1655; but this did not become general until about a century later.

Rings were worn as ornaments in Connecticut from the earliest times. Ear-rings and thumb-rings were also in use.*

The authorities of New England were originally opposed to the fashion of wearing long hair. In Massachusetts, long hair was made the subject of legislative enactments. But throughout New England, it is believed that laws regulating dress were not usually enforced as other statutes were. The beard was at first worn in New England by the upper classes, but gradually diminished until 1685, when it was closely shaven except in particular instances.

Wigs were worn in New England soon after the middle of the seventeenth century. They appear to have been of various colors, patterns, and dimensions, according to the taste of the wearer or the fashion of the particular era or locality. Judges, magistrates, lawyers, and gentlemen generally, were among the first to adopt the custom. Many of

* The ring presented by Charles I., to the grandfather of the elder Winthrop, was, it will be remembered, dexterously used by the son of the latter in procuring the charter of Connecticut from Charles II. In the inventory of the widow of Colonel John Livingston of New London, (1736,) are mentioned, "four gold rings, one silver ring, one stoned ring, a ring with five diamonds, a pair of stoned ear-rings, a stone drop for the neck, and a red stone for a locket." Caulkins' Hist. of New London, p. 365.

the clergy subsequently fell in with it and carried it to extremes; though others talked, preached, and prayed most earnestly for the suppression of the "unchristian habit."* To a man of commanding person and features, passed middle age, the full flowing white wig often gave a venerable and dignified appearance. Such appendages, however, when donned by young men and lads, as they frequently were, became mere caricatures of their original design. Wigs were often powdered, and fell in long luxuriant curls upon the shoulders. Of course the supply of human hair of light color, or indeed of any color, was far from being equal to the demand. Hence, horses and goats were shorn of their superfluous appendages, and the flaxen locks of children were cut off, and the hair thus obtained was washed in a peculiar kind of bleaching suds and then spread upon the grass to whiten like linen.† This singular fashion seems to have gradually died with the waning of the last century, though a few individuals retained the use of their wigs until a more modern date.

The early costume of the women of Connecticut seems to have exhibited as great a variety in style and taste as that of the other sex. Ever ready to conform to the peculiar circumstances in which Providence may have placed them, the mothers and daughters of New England cheerfully submitted to the privations incident to their condition. Here, in a primitive wilderness, with little or no society except that of men and women as earnest and self-sacrificing as themselves, we may readily infer that for many years the punctilious forms of etiquette, and the spirit of fashionable display, were almost entirely undeveloped. Still, even in what has been characterized as the "home-spun age," the matrons and maidens were not wanting either in taste or skill in fitting and perfecting their own garments. Their natural love of

* Mr. Felt says of Eliot, the celebrated apostle to the Indians—"He imagined it [the use of wigs] to be an abundant source of calamities which had befallen our land."

† Felt, 184.

neatness, order, and beauty, would of itself enable them to impart elegance and grace to the most rustic costume.

As the outward circumstances of the planters gradually improved, and the proportion of wealthy emigrants increased, the wings of commerce were proportionably extended to supply their growing wants. Many of the superfluities and luxuries of the old world were brought to our shores for such as were able and disposed to purchase them. The fashions of the father-land were in a measure revived. Silks, satins, laces, and other costly fabrics, were among the articles imported, and were in great demand among the rich and fashionable ladies of those times.

I design to speak only of some of the *peculiarities* of dress among the women of Connecticut in former times.

Trailing gowns, were more or less in use both in England and America for upwards of a century, ending some sixty years ago. These gowns were liberally set off with flounces and furbelows, with a trail from half a yard to a yard and a half in length, sweeping the floor or street when allowed to have its full course. They were, however, often "trolloped"—that is, fastened up at each side by loops; frequently however, the trail was carried by the lady upon her arm.* Among the most exclusive class, especially in England, one or two pages were employed to carry the trail. Thus the poet Cowley, remarks—"They cannot stir to the next room without a page or two to hold it up."

During the last century, "*hooped skirts*" were common. The form of them varied at different periods. In 1735, they projected all around the bottom of the skirts like a wheel; and in 1745, they were increased at the sides and lessened in front. During the latter year, a pamphlet was published in England, entitled, "The enormous abomination of the Hoop Petticoat, as the fashion now is." In 1757, after some depression, they expanded on the right and left. We are informed that they were exceedingly inconvenient for entering pew doors; in fact, they could have no ingress or egress at

* Lambert, 200.

such narrow apertures, except by taking a slight of hand advantage of their form, which was no doubt very gracefully done.*

Towering head dresses appear to have been in use in England long before the emigration. It is stated that in 1416, the state apartments were enlarged to accommodate such kinds of attire. When reformed under Edward IV., in the fifteenth century, it was a cone two or three feet high, with a silk streamer hanging down behind. Somewhat similar head dresses, though probably not so tall, and varying in shape, were worn by the ladies of Connecticut down to the period of the revolution. They consisted of muslin, crape, lawn or lace, and constituted a chief item of ornamental attire.

Other articles of female dress might be mentioned, that would be regarded as unique at the present day, but the limits of the work will not afford room for any very extended treatise upon a topic in itself so interesting.

* See "Customs of New England," pp. 168, 169.

THE OLD WHITFIELD HOUSE.

CHAPTER XXI.

THE ESTABLISHED RELIGION OF CONNECTICUT.

While the religious opinions of the early founders of the colony of Connecticut, cannot with propriety be left out of its history, still, these topics have been treated of at so great length by other authors, that I shall give in this work only a brief outline of such facts as appear to be necessary to a thorough understanding of the character of our institutions.

It has been said in a preceding chapter, that the main motive that led to the settlement of New England, was a desire on the part of the emigrants to worship God, in a way that they believed would be most acceptable to Him. The doctrines held by at least a large number of the divines, who lived and died in the faith of the established church of England, and whose writings are among the brightest ornaments of biblical literature, did not differ materially from those that formed the basis of puritan belief. There were many as strong Calvinists in the episcopal church of that period as the emigrants were.* The grand points of dispute, the wedges that split off the emigrants from the main English trunk, took their shape and edge not so much from differences in doctrine, as in the forms of church government. The English church had the arm of the nation to enforce conformity, and those puritans who could not yield to the demands made upon them, had no refuge but in flight.

The organization of the churches in Connecticut was very simple. The ministers, as has been stated in a preced-

---

* Brande (Encyclopedia, p. 88,) says—"The articles of the English church have been represented by different parties, as inclining both to Arminianism and Calvinism." Bishops Davenport, Sanderson, Hall, and the archbishops Usher and Leighton, were Calvinistic in their doctrines, though among the staunchest of episcopalians. (See Coleridge's "Aids to Reflection," pp. 208, 209.) Bishops Taylor, Whitby, Ward, and others, maintained the Arminian tenets, and wrote and preached against Calvinism.

ing chapter, were the leaders each of his own people. Most of the pastors brought their churches with them from England, and of course had a personal acquaintance with their members and with their families. This was true of Hooker, Davenport, Whitfield, Blackman, Wareham, and others of the principal divines of this colony. These captains of hundreds and captains of fifties were men of no ordinary mould. Every one of them possessed some striking traits of character, that have left their impress upon the age in which they lived; not distinctly defined to the eye of the careless observer, but to him who has familiarized himself with the figures that people the cloud-land of the past, these shepherds, standing upon the eminences whence their flocks could be seen and called by name, as they fed upon the green slopes, and cropped with the sweet nutriment, the herbs medicinally bitter that grew close by the poisonous flowers of temptation, these good shepherds, no longer shadowy, are seen through the long twilight of history to retain their characteristics of form and feature, as if they were still in the midst of those labors that ripened them for immortality. So subtle and keen is the vision of the true and faithful scholar, whose whole heart is in his work, that it can pierce beyond the curtain that darkness lets down before the eyes of other men; can penetrate through the vapors of prejudice and ignorance, as the rainbow seems to penetrate the less ethereal sphere of the storm-cloud that it illuminates. To him, and to him alone, is it given, to see as in a mirror, the great and the good pass in slow review before him, so that he shall be able to distinguish them and sketch them upon a canvass that shall be imperishable. To him they are not all to be set down in the dead and despised catalogue of fanatics. On the other hand, to him the fearless Davenport, with his noble bearing and unshaken resolution; Hooker, with his beautiful face, deep-toned voice, and hand that "could put a king in his pocket;" Wareham, whose self-accusing, shrinking eye was often averted from the battlements of the heavenly city, whither his finger pointed the way for others; Blackman, at the sound of whose farewell the sensibilities of his people gushed out in sparkling tears, as the rock that was smitten by the prophet; Whitfield, whose clear, contemplative soul resembled a mountain lake, reflecting all the objects, wild or tame, that help to form its solitary margin, yet never darken it, so as to conceal its calm depths from the dreamer who wanders there; and Stone, who alternately disputes upon points of church discipline, and prays for more copious showers of God's grace; to such a scholar, and to him alone, all these and many more who might be named as conspicuous members of the great household of faith, are seen as *individual men* setting up the standard of civil liberty, by the entrance-gate of the temple that they reared to the Most High. It is difficult to estimate the influences of such men, as the early clergymen of Connecticut, in laying the foundations of a nation like ours.

In every church organized according to the old puritan plan that prevailed from the first in Connecticut, there was a pastor, a teacher, a ruling elder, and deacons.* In some of their churches there were exceptions to this rule, growing out of the necessities or peculiar situation of the people; but the principal settlements all had a full complement of these several functionaries. If the church had only a few members and very limited resources, it was sometimes obliged to content itself with a ruling elder and deacons. The pastor, teacher, and elder were all ordained with equal solemnity.

The specific duty of the pastor was to exhort or preach to the people; or, in the language of that day, "to work upon the will and the affections." He was expected to possess the gift of eloquent speech, and to cultivate the winning graces of oratory; most of all, the sinewy, athletic strength that could make effective use of the fire and the hammer to break the flinty heart.†

* Owen's "Gospel Church," pp. 86, 116, 120, 128, 129; Hooker's "Survey," part ii. pp. 4, 20.

† Hookers Survey, part ii. pp. 19, 21; Cambridge Platform, chap. vi.

The teacher, on the other hand, was the private expounder of the divine law, the counselor whose learning, deep piety, calm judgment, and refined experience could be depended upon in doubtful matters. He had immediate charge of all complicated and knotty doctrinal questions, and difficult cases of conscience. He was the nursery teacher, who prepared the feeble reason and illuminated the darkened understanding for the school of church-fellowship. He also recalled the backsliding christian, and set his face toward Zion. If there was no teacher in any particular church, the pastor supplied the offices of advocate and counselor. *

The ruling elder represented that part of the executive power that did not fall specifically within the province of the pastor. He was a kind of vice-executive officer. His business was to keep strict watch over all the brethren and sisters, and see that they demeaned themselves in an orderly and godly manner. It was his duty to warn the careless, admonish the wayward, and to present the incorrigible before the proper tribunal for discipline. He was also to go from house to house like a ministering angel, and visit the sick and the afflicted, and pray with them. In the absence of the pastor and teacher he was also to pray with the congregation on the sabbath, and other stated days of worship, and expound the scriptures to them.

The office of deacon is frequently alluded to in the new testament,† though different denominations have differed as to the position and duties of the officer called by that title. Among the English puritans and their successors in New England, the specific duties of the deacons were, as stated by Owen, to provide for the poor of the parish, and to manage all other affairs of the church of a secular nature; such as providing for the *place* of the church assemblies; procuring and distributing the sacramental elements; "keeping, collecting, and disposing of the stock of the church, for the maintenance of its officers, and incidences, especially in the

* Owen's "True Gospel Church," 121, &c.

† Acts, vi; 1 Tim. iii. 8, 13, &c.

time of trouble or persecution."* It was furthermore the duty of these officers, according to the same author, "to acquaint the church of the present necessity of the poor; to stir up particular members of it into a free contribution according to their ability; to admonish those who are negligent herein, who give not according to their proportion; and to acquaint the elders of the church with those who persist in a neglect of their duty."†

In regard to the *qualifications* of persons for this office, those specified in 1 Tim. iii. 8, 13, were deemed requisite and indispensable. The candidate having been duly approved, was solemnly set apart by prayer and the imposition of hands, according to the directions contained in Acts vi. 6.

The *number* of deacons was not uniform, but was regulated mainly by the size of the church and congregation. Two or four were the more usual numbers; though in some of the churches there were seven—usually styled the "seven pillars," whose duties appear sometimes to have partaken of those of elders as well as of deacons.

During the first twenty years after the settlement, there was little or no difference of opinion among the ministers and churches of Connecticut, as to the requisites and terms of church-membership. The applicant was not only required to give his solemn public assent to the confession of faith, and to enter into covenant with God and His people faithfully to discharge all public and private christian duties, but he must give a minute account of his religious experience, and of the radical change that had taken place in his heart and life.

About 1655, however, a strong party began to manifest itself, who were for admitting all persons of regular life to a full communion in the churches, upon their making a general public confession of their belief in the christian religion, without any inquiry with respect to their experience, and

* "The True Nature of a Gospel Church and its Government," by Rev. John Owen, D.D., p. 184.

† Owen, 185.

were for treating all baptized persons as members of the church, upon their "owning the covenant." *

This subject was carried to the General Assembly, and that body applied to the General Courts of the several neighboring colonies for advice. The result was, a general council was called, which assembled at Boston, June 4, 1657. This council gave an elaborate answer to the twenty-one questions that had been propounded to them concerning the matters in controversy—the principal of which had special reference to church-membership and baptism.† The substance of their decision was, that it was the duty of adults, who had been baptized in infancy, "to own the covenant they made with their parents, by entering thereinto in their own persons;" that the church was obligated "to call upon them for the performance thereof;" and in case of refusal, they were liable to be censured by the church. Those "owning the covenant," and not scandalous in their lives, were allowed to have their children baptized.‡

This decision seems not to have been acceptable to the churches of Connecticut, and certainly did not end the controversy. In 1662 the General Court recommended the same measures to the churches; and many of them subsequently adopted the practice, though others opposed it steadfastly to the last.

This was the origin of what has since been known by "the half way covenant," which a hundred years later was so powerfully opposed by Edwards, Whitefield, Buel, and other eloquent "reformers" of that day.

The churches of Connecticut acted upon the belief that the bishops and presbyters were only different names for the same office, and that all pastors who were regularly devoted to the ministry of the gospel were bishops in a scriptural sense. They also held that in accordance with the early

* Trumbull, i 297, 298.

† These answers were afterwards printed in London with the title, "A Disputation concerning church members and their children."

‡ Trumbull, i. 303, 304.

practice of the church, every pastor was for the most part confined to his own church and congregation, whom he could keep under his own eye, and who might have the benefit of his personal example. This rule, however, did not prevent the pastor of one church from exchanging with his neighbor of the next settlement at convenient intervals; but even this exchange was only for the ordinary religious services. It was for some time after the emigration held to be irregular for any minister to administer the sacrament or the rite of baptism, except in his immediate jurisdiction.*

The churches of Connecticut did not look upon ordinations as constituting the essentials of the ministerial office. Ordination was nothing more than inducting the pastor elect into office, or recommending him and his spiritual labors to the blessing of his Divine Master. The form of ordination was very simple. If there was a presbytery in the church where the ceremonial was to be performed, the laying on of hands was done by them; if not, the church selected from its members a number of the most venerable and exemplary to act as elders for the occasion. This mode of ordination and these views as to its relative importance and significance, were by no means peculiar to the Connecticut churches. They were supported by the high authority of St. Augustine, St. Chrysostom, Zanch, Bucer, and even by the great Melancthon himself, an interpreter of the scriptures unsurpassed since the days of Paul for close ratiocination, and dispassionate, calm judgment.†

The Connecticut churches were congregational. In other words, they held that the right to choose and to settle its own minister, discipline its own members, and to perform all juridical functions, was vested in each individual church, and that no external organization, whether under the name of presbytery, synod, general council, or assembly, had any power to interfere with the exercise of that right. They might advise and counsel, and their opinions were held to be entitled to reverence; but they could neither command

* Hooker, Trumbull, Owen.

† Hooker's Survey.

nor compel. The individual church, through its regular channels of communication, and with the bible for its guide, was, under God, to be the ultimate arbiter of all matters arising within its own jurisdiction.* Whether they always rightly interpreted the bible, is to be settled by men who are most competent to judge of matters too mysterious and solemn for the pen of the historian. However this may be, I suppose it will not be questioned, even by their bitterest enemies, that they read it with as much avidity as any class of men ever did, and earnestly sought to follow its teachings. Indeed, the bible was the constant companion of the early inhabitants of Connecticut. The emigrant studied it by day and by night. He taught it to his children with the same constancy that supplied them with daily food, and the burden of his prayers was, that they might understand it in its deepest, most spiritual significance. The bible was the pole-star of the colony. Its precepts are written in letters of light upon our early records. Its doctrines were discussed in the field where the laborers bent over the ridges of the corn; and in the heart of the great forest, while the woodman sat in the still noon leaning against the trunk of the oak that he had felled, he pondered its precepts in secret. It was carried into the battle field by the soldier, and with an honest joy when the victory was won, its promises were read anew. Children were named from its great prophets, poets, and heroes.

At the time of the union of New Haven and Connecticut there were in the colony only seventeen hundred families, or between eight thousand and nine thousand inhabitants. To preach to this small number, the services of about twenty ministers were put in constant requisition. This would make on an average one preacher to eighty-five families. In several of the new plantations, thirty families maintained a minister; and out of the large towns, forty families was thought to be a good congregation.† When it is remember-

* Trumbull, i. 284; Cambridge Platform, ch. xvi. † Trumbull.

ed that most of these clergymen were gentlemen of uncommon powers of mind, of elegant manners, and thorough-bred scholars, in an age when scholars were rare, it will be seen that no people have valued religious instruction more than our fathers did, and that seldom if ever in the history of the world has a people been more faithfully taught. At no time since that day has there been such a class of educated gentlemen in New England as were the emigrant pastors of Connecticut. The generation of clergymen who succeeded them, were of course their' inferiors in education, as the institutions of a new country are less thorough than those of an old one.

I have said that the qualifications for church-membership caused many dissensions among the churches. As it has been thought important to give these disputes a prominence in times past, that seems not to have belonged to them originally, I am hardly at liberty to pass them by without some notice. They possess an interest to the antiquarian that the general reader has never yet found in them, and those honest men who have collected and perpetuated them in books, as they were known to be friendly to the fame of the state, have evinced, it must be admitted, not only a desire to tell the whole truth, but a noble indifference to the opinion of the world and a confidence in the greatness of those men whose characters could bear to be set in so unfavorable a light and still elicit the admiration of posterity. I doubt if there can be found in the history of any other people so many industrious proclaimers of the ecclesiastical bickerings and neighborhood, nay family quarrels, of the founders of its institutions, as have been set forth by respectable writers, who have spent their lives in trying to do honor to Connecticut in this apparently equivocal way. I say, apparently equivocal, for doubtless the time will come when such minute details of the imperfections of human nature will be regarded with more indulgence than now, as they will be seen to have indicated a transition from the dead calm of formalism, to the lively, healthful atmosphere of religious toleration, and philosophical inquiry.

The first of these controversies, as has been stated in a former chapter, originated at Wethersfield, and might never have happened had Mr. Phillips, the pastor of the first emigrants, been induced to accompany them to Connecticut. They had at first no settled minister, and for several years were in a state of confusion that was beyond the reach of their best spiritual advisers, until the sagacious Davenport suggested that as they could not live together they should separate. This good counsel led to the settlement of Stamford, and could not have been continued beyond the spring of 1641, when Mr. Coe and Mr. Ward, with their party, removed from Wethersfield. The particulars of this quarrel can hardly be known at this remote day, as no documentary memorial of it is known to exist.

In 1641, and after Prudden, Sherman, and Denton had all preached to the people, and in time had sought other and more quiet fields of labor, the Rev. Henry Smith entered upon his duties as the first regular pastor in Wethersfield. He was a gentleman of good family, and he is, aside from the interest that he excites in us as the patriarch of one of the best sustained and most accomplished families in New England, entitled to our regard as a gentleman of uncommon culture, refinement, and firmness. He probably arrived in Boston in 1637, as he and Mrs. Smith were admitted into the communion of the church at Watertown on the 5th of December, of that year.* At what precise period he removed to Connecticut, is not certainly known, but he was a resident there at the time of the division of the lots on the east side of the Connecticut river, in 1639–'40, as he received a farm of consider-

* Mr. Smith brought over from England, among other articles of value, a silver tankard with his family coat of arms, beautifully engraved upon it. This venerable piece of silver, probably two hundred and fifty years old, is still in excellent condition, and is now in the hands of his great, great, great grandson, Wm. Mather Smith, Esquire, of Sharon, the only son of His Excellency, John Cotton Smith, the last charter governor.

able size at that time, which descended to his son Samuel.* He did not find his task in Wethersfield a very easy one, as there were still left some restless spirits in his church and congregation. He was, from the beginning of his ministry, the victim of suspicions the most unfounded, and accusations the most bitter.

In **1643**, an application was made to the General Court, involving charges against him that were found on investigation to be false.† His ministry terminated with his death in **1648.**

Just before the decease of Mr. Smith, died Mr. Thomas Hooker, the pastor of the church in Hartford. No minister in New England possessed such unbounded sway over popular assemblies as did this truly wonderful man. He was born at Marshfield, in the county of Leicester, England, in the year 1586, and graduated at Emanuel College, Cambridge, at a very early age. He was soon promoted to a fellowship there, and was not long in acquiring a high reputation for learning and ability. He was called "the light of the New England churches," and well merited the appellation; for in his clear manner of setting forth the truth, his intimate acquaintance with the doctrines of the bible, his bold eloquence and the pungency of his illustrations, he had few equals and no superiors in New England. Hooker was to Connecticut what Cotton was to Massachusetts, and what Davenport was to New Haven. They were all men of such marked traits

---

* Dr. Chapin's Hist. of Glastenbury, p. 34.

† The committee appointed by the General Court to investigate these charges, reported on the 13th of April, 1643. This committee, among other things, say,—"We find also that many of those who put up their names for removal, were not induced thereunto by any dislike or engagement they have in the present quarrels, but *for want of lots* and other considerations."

On the 10th of November of the same year, the General Court ordered that—

"Mr. Chaplin, for divulging and setting his hand to a paper called a declaration, tending to the defamation of Mr. Smith, is fined £10.

"Francis Norton, for setting his hand to the said writing, is fined £5.

"John Goodridge, for setting his hand to said writing, 40s.

"Mr. Plum, for preferring a roll of grievances against Mr. Smith, and failing of proof in the prosecution thereof, is fined £10."

of character, that perhaps no one could assign to any one of them the highest place. Davenport might be compared, in his opposition to the passions of the people and in the solidity of his character, to one of those sheer promontories that the mariner sees as he sails along the New England coast, defying the storms and frowning down upon the white waves that recoil from its base; Cotton, to a limpid river flowing between steep hills that feed its current with the unfailing resources of bubbling springs gushing out of the natural fissures of the rocks, while they crowd it into a channel that allows it more depth than surface, with here and there a basin among the more lofty and retreating mountains, that expose, indeed, a broader area where the warm beams of the sun-light may bathe themselves, yet take away nothing from the boldness of the shore; Hooker, to the same river further on in its course, its volume increased by the tributaries that drain larger and wilder regions—sometimes turbid, too, with the added violence of the spring floods, having a strength and vastness of sweep always self-sustained and convincing. Hooker was not only the most attractive pulpit orator in New England, but he was equally distinguished by the fervency and pathos of his prayers, which, we are told, were like Jacob's ladder "wherein the nearer he came to the end, the nearer he drew to heaven." He was well skilled in the governing motives of men, and on that account was much consulted in matters relating to church discipline and the general management of ecclesiastical affairs. In his charities he was very munificent. His chief conflict was with himself, in striving to subdue the irregularities of a temperament naturally vehement and impetuous. In his domestic and social relations he was very happy, and few men have been more deeply loved.

In person, Hooker was tall and elegant, his features classical, his eye thoughtful yet piercing, his voice rich and of great compass, and his manner graceful and majestic. He possessed physical as well as moral courage in a high degree. Even Mason was overawed by the noble bearing of this soldier of the cross when following the little army, that was about to go in search of the Pequots, to the brink of the river that he might dismiss them with his benediction, his eye flashed as he bade them "in martial power to fight the battles of the Lord and of his people."

He died at Hartford, of a fever, on the 7th of July, 1647, in the 61st year of his age. "I am going to receive mercy," said the patriarch to a friend who stood by his bedside; then closing his eyes tranquilly, a smile playing about his lips, he took his leave of a world that satisfies least of all a soul of such boundless energies and such an ethereal mould.*

Aside from Davenport, the founder of New Haven, that place was for many years distinguished for the wisdom and ability of its clergymen. Of these Hooke, Street, and Pierpont are among the most eminent. James Pierpont was born at Roxbury, Massachusetts, in 1659, graduated at Harvard in 1681, and was ordained at New Haven in 1686. Descended from an illustrious family, and gifted to a high degree with intellectual endowments, eloquent speech, a graceful person, handsome features, and manners the most courtly and winning, he appears to have been from early youth too intently occupied with the mission of saving the souls of his fellow men, ever to think of himself. I suppose, of all the clergymen whose names belong to the early history of New England, Pierpont was the most lofty and pure in his aspirations, and of the most spiritual temper. With none of the sternness of Davenport, without the despondency of Wareham, and free from the impetuous moods that proved such thorns in the pillow of Hooker, his words, like the live coals from the altar in the hand of the angel, "touched and purified the lips" of those who listened to his teachings. His moral nature was so softly diffused over his church and people, that they appeared to lose themselves in the absorbing element, as dark forms seem sometimes in

* See Biography of Rev. Thomas Hooker, by Rev. E. W. Hooker, D.D.

pleasant summer days, to dissolve in an atmosphere of liquid light.*

* 1. ***Robert de Pierrepont***, who came to England with William the Conqueror, and possessed estates in Suffolk and Sussex, amounting to ten knights' fees—all of which he held of William, Earl of Warren.

2. ***William de Pierrepont***, son and heir, (time of William II.)

3. ***Hugh de Pierrepont***, son and heir, (time of Henry II.)

4. ***William de Pierrepont***, owner of the Lordship of Halliwell, in Lancashire.

5. ***Sir Robert de Pierrepont***, knight.

6. ***Henry de Pierrepont***, of Holbeck, Woodhouse, county of Nottingham.

7. ***Sir Henry de Pierrepont***, of Holme Pierrepont, in the right of his wife, Annora, sole daughter of Michael Manvers, Lord of Holme. He died A. D., 1291.

8. ***Sir Robert de Pierrepont***, of Holme Pierrepont, governor of New Castle, married Sarah, daughter of Sir John Hering, knight, of Derbyshire, 1308.

9. ***Henry Pierrepont***, of Holme Pierrepont, only son and heir, married Margaret, daughter of Sir Wm. Fitz Williams of Emly, knight.

10. ***Sir Edmund Pierrepont***, son and heir, knight, married Joan, only daughter of Sir John Monboucher, of Nottinghamshire, knight. He died in 1370, and was buried at Holme Pierrepont.

11. ***Sir Edmund Pierrepont***, son and heir, married Frances, daughter of Thomas Kingsman. He was knighted in 1422.

12. ***Sir Henry Pierrepont***, son and heir, married Ellen, daughter of Sir Nicholas Langford, knight.

13. ***Henry Pierrepont***, only son and heir, married Tomasin, daughter of Sir John Melton, of Ashton, Yorkshire.

14. ***Sir Francis Pierrepont***, knight, son and heir, married Margaret, daughter of John Burdon, Esq.

15. ***Sir William Pierrepont***, son and heir, married Jane, daughter of Sir Richard Empson, knight. He was knighted in 1513.

16. ***Sir George Pierrepont***, son and heir, married Winnifred, daughter of William Thwaites, of Essex. He was knighted in 1547, and died 1564.*

17. ***William Pierrepont***, of Brereton, Lancaster county, son and heir, married Elizabeth.

18. ***James Pierrepont***, who died at Ipswich, Mass.

19. ***John Pierrepont***, born in London in 1619; admitted a freeman in Massachusetts in 1652; representative in 1672; died Dec. 7, 1682. He married Thankful Stow, and had five sons, viz., Benjamin, Joseph, Ebenezer, ***James***, and John.

20. ***Rev. James Pierpont***, of New Haven, born in 1659; and died in 1714.

* Sir George Pierrepont, had a son Robert (older than William,) who was created Earl of Kingston in 1628. His lordship's last male descendant, Evelyn Pierrepont, second duke of Kingston, died in 1773 without issue, when the honors and estates *ought* to have descended to the heirs of William, who were then and still are in America. Instead of this, however, they went to the nephew of the Duke, Charles Meadows, Esq., who assumed the surname of Pierrepont, and was created Earl Manvers.

The next great controversy in order of time, and one of the most important that ever occurred in New England on account of its duration, the bitterness of feeling by which it was characterized, and the exalted character of the men who participated in it, was that which commenced in the first church in Hartford about the middle of the seventeenth century. It appears to have originated in a difference of opinion between the Rev. Samuel Stone, pastor of that church, and Mr. William Goodwin, its ruling elder, on some nice points of congregationalism. It was claimed that persons had been baptized and admitted to the church in an informal manner, and without the proper qualifications; though Dr. Mather intimates that it was difficult, even at the time of the controversy, to ascertain what were the *precise* points of variance. The dispute, however, spread like a contagion, until nearly all the churches in the colony became more or less affected by it. The local and secular affairs of societies, towns, and of the entire commonwealth, were to a great extent influenced by the all-absorbing topic of thought and conversation. The General Court frequently interposed its advice and orders, with a view to quiet the agitation, and ecclesiastical bodies as often met to consider and decide upon the merits of the controversy; but for a long time without avail. About the year 1660, in consequence of the death or removal of many of the principal belligerents, both the church and state, so long the victims of discord, were again restored to comparative good order.

Among those who were disaffected with Mr. Stone and steadfastly adhered to Elder Goodwin throughout the controversy, were Governor Webster, Mr. Cullick, Mr. Bacon, and Mr. Steele, all leading men both in the church and in the colony.*

By this time the church at Wethersfield had again become ripe for dissensions. Probably within two years after the death of Mr. Smith, but at what precise date is not known,

* Trumbull, i. 296, 301.

the Rev. John Russell was called by the church and ordained there, so far as appears, without opposition. The first part of his ministry was quiet and seemed to promise well for the future. But the Hartford controversy gradually extended into his church, and some other elements of a very combustible character, were made to feed the flame. Among other things, Mr. Russell appears to have been a witness in a law suit, and to have testified in a way that was severely animadverted upon by Lieutenant John Hollister, a prominent member of his church. Mr. Russell held the same views with Mr. Stone of Hartford in relation to church government and discipline, and without giving the offending member an opportunity to have a hearing, or even the benefit of a vote of the church, he privately excommunicated him in 1656, and afterwards refused to give his reasons for such a summary proceeding when they were demanded by Mr. Hollister.* Had Mr. Russell been anxious to test the practical workings of his plan of church government, he could hardly have chosen a more favorable subject than one of Captain Mason's military officers—a gentleman of undoubted probity, an experienced member of the General Court, and a man not likely to be outdone by Mr. Russell, in the steadiness of his purposes and the obstinacy of his resistance. Besides his own natural force of character, Hollister had married a daughter of Richard Treat, Esquire,† one of the most formidable opponents in the colony, and could bring into the quarrel an array of names that the General Court would hardly treat with contempt.

The whole town was of course thrown into a state of excitement at this unusual war waged by a clergyman against a member of his church. A petition was prepared and signed by the excommunicated member, four other male and six female members of the church, and thirty-eight others, probably all members of the society, many of whom (as will be seen by referring to the subjoined note and docu-

* Dr. Chapin's Hist. of Glastenbury, p. 35; Cothren's Hist. of Woodbury.

† Chapin, 185.

ment,*) were men of high position—praying the Court to relieve the applicants from the burden of a minister who had "taken a scandalous and grievous oath, acknowledged by

* In this singular paper, a copy of which is here given, it will be seen that the church members signed by themselves, first the individual aggrieved, followed by the other male members; then the female members, with Mrs. Treat, the wife of Richard and mother of Governor Treat, at the head, and next to her, Mrs. Hollister, her daughter, the wife of the principal applicant. These male and female names are separated with as much decency as their owners would have observed in the meeting house on the Sabbath. The remaining signers were not church members.

"To the right Worshipful, the Governor and Deputy Governor, the Worshipful Magistrates, and Deputies, assembled at Hartford in This Honored Court, your humble petitioners wish increase of all felicity. August 17th, 1658.

"We, inhabitants of Wethersfield, are necessitated to implore the aid and assistance of this Honored Court, and thereafter by right of an order made last March; for Mr. Russell, as we conceive, is not our settled and approved minister: First, He having sent us a writing, in the Spring, to provide for ourselves lest we be destitute, and we having professed, we look upon ourselves as free by answer of our committee, nor can we close with him, and are afraid to venture our souls under his ministry, he having given so great a scandal to the Gospel of our Lord Jesus Christ by such a grievous oath, acknowledged by himself to be ambiguous, rash, and sinful, and what more may be made evident. Therefore, we, your humble petitioners, humbly crave that we may not be held in bondage, but may use our liberty in procuring a minister who may be faithful in the administrations of the Gospel, and inoffensive in his conversation; otherwise, we, your humble petitioners, shall be forced to undergo whatever inconvenience or damage may come upon us or ours, for we think him altogether unfit for our comfort. And we, your humble petitioners, humbly crave your help, for we profess it lies as a heavy burden upon our consciences, and we know no rule that he should compel us to it. And if your humble petitioners find acceptance and relief, you will more engage us to all loyal subjection to you, so humbly we take our leave of you, and rest yours to be commanded.

[Members of the church.]	[Not members of the church.]	[Not members of the church.]
John Hollister.	Thomas Curtis.	John Deming, Jr.
Thomas Wright, Sr.	John Chester.	Thomas Gilbert.
John Deming, Sr.	Samuel Boardman.	Thomas Williams.
John Edwards, Sr.	Thomas Standish.	John Sadler,
Richard Smith, Sr.	John Kilbourn.	John Belden.
	Richard Treat.	Emanuel Buck.
Alice Treat.	John Nott.	Hugh Wells.
Joana Hollister.	Thomas Lord.	John Harrison.
Mary Robbins.	Thomas Wright, Jr.	Benjamin Crane.
Margaret Wright.	John Riley.	Mathias Treat.
Rebeccah Smith.	Richard Smith, Jr.	William Colefoxe.
Dorothy Edwards.	James Wright.	Philip Goffe.

himself to be ambiguous, rash, and sinful," who had himself cut asunder the ties that had bound him to the church, and who still remained " a heavy burden upon their consciences."

[Members of the church.]	[Not members of the church.]	[Not members of the church.]
	James Wakeley.	James Treat.
	Joseph Smith.	Samuel Wright.
	Michael Griswold.	Jonathan Smith.
	George Wolcott.	John Curtis.
	Thomas Wickham.	James Boswell.
	Nathaniel Graves.	Henry Crane.
	John Wadhams.	Lewis Jones.

Mr. *Hollister* was a native of Bristol, England, and emigrated to New England about the year 1642. In 1643, he was admitted a freeman at Weymouth, Massachusetts, and was a representative in the General Court of Massachusetts, at the session immediately following. In June, 1644, he was a member of the jury of a particular court held at Hartford, he having a short time previous to that date, become a resident of Wethersfield. He attended as a deputy to the General Court of Connecticut for the first time, at the September session of the last named year, a post to which he was subsequently re-elected fourteen times. In October, 1654, Mr. Hollister was appointed by the legislature a member of a committee " to press men and necessaries in each town," for the expedition to the Narragansett country against Ninigret. Three years after, he was placed on the committee with the deputy governor and magistrates, " to attend any occasions as to the state of the commonwealth in reference to the Indians." Divers other legislative and popular appointments evince the high respect with which he was regarded both by the people and by the authorities of the colony. When he first came to Connecticut he bore the prefix of "Mr.," which was superseded in 1657 by the military title of " Lieutenant." He died in 1665.

Mr. *John Deming*, Sen., was a juror of the particular court at Hartford in March 1643, and in December, 1645, was a member of the General Court from Wethersfield, an office to which he was chosen at twenty-five semi-annual elections. He was one of the patentees named in the charter of 1662. Among his descendants, who are numerous and highly respectable, I may name with honor the late Julius Deming, Esq., of Litchfield.

Thomas Wright, Sen., was descended from John Wright, Bishop of Bristol, Winchester, and Litchfield. He was a cousin of Mr. Nathaniel Wright of London, one of the assistants of the first General Court of Massachusetts, before the government was removed to Boston. He first appears in New England, at Swamscott, (now Exeter,) in company with Col. John Wheelwright, 1629. It appears by the deed given by the Sagamores to Col. Wheelwright and others, that Mr. Wright was one of his company. In 1640 he was admitted a freeman at Exeter. In 1643, Sept. 4th, his name next occurs as one of the jurors of a particular court at Hartford. For some years previous to his death, he was a deacon in the church. The descendants of Thomas Wright are very numerous. He

Meanwhile that nothing might be wanting to the success of the petition, Hollister was again returned a member of the Court,* that he might present it and advocate it with such earnestness as only an interested party could be expected to do.

At the session of the Court held on the 18th of August, 1658, Hollister presented the petition and obtained an order that Mr. Russell should give the reasons for his conduct towards "ye Lieut. Hollister." Those reasons were to be delivered to Hollister or be placed in the hands of a messenger of his who should call for them at the elder's house. In case this order should not be complied with, Messrs. Samuel Wells and Samuel Boardman were ordered "seasonably

---

was the ancestor of the Wrights of Hartford and Litchfield, and of most of the name in the Western and Middle States. There are now living, of his descendants, two senators, three members of Congress, three governors, and two judges of the supreme court.

John Edwards, Sen., was often a juror of particular courts, and was a deputy in 1643.

Captain *John Chester* was frequently a deputy and commissioner, and was one of the most eminent citizens of Wethersfield.

Samuel Boardman was a leading man in the colony for nearly thirty years; he was "custom-master," colonial grand juror, and member of the General Court.

Sergt. *John Kilbourn* emigrated from Cambridgeshire, England, with his parents in 1635, at the age of ten years. He was occasionally a deputy to the General Court, was a colonial grand juror from 1662 until the organization of the counties in 1666, and was appointed to run the boundary line between Hartford and Wethersfield, and between Middletown and Wethersfield. He died in 1703.

Richard Treat was often a deputy and magistrate, and was one of the patentees of the colony. He was the father of Governor Treat.

Sergt. *John Nott* was a juror of the particular Court at Hartford as early as 1640, and was subsequently a member of the General Court at twenty semi-annual sessions.

John Riley was on the jury of the particular court in May 1649; was on the list of freemen in Wethersfield in 1669, and in 1675 was "postman" between Hartford and Saybrook.

James Treat (a son of Richard,) was a deputy from Wethersfield in May, 1672, and at several subsequent sessions.

Henry Crane was a deputy from Killingworth in May 1675, and at other times.

* J. H. Trumbull's Colonial Records, i. 323.

to repair unto Mr. Russell in behalf of Lieutenant Hollister, and in the name of the court, desire and if need be *require* of him and the church of Wethersfield the particular charges or offences for which Mr. Hollister was censured, and having received the said charges from Mr. Russell and the church, forthwith to deliver them to Mr. Hollister for his help and conviction,"* and inasmuch as "Mr. Treat, Mr. Hollister, and John Deming, were desirous and willing to attend some regular way for the composing their differences," the Court desired the church at Wethersfield to devise some way of reconciliation between the parties, if that were possible.†

When the court met in October 1659, it was found that the same "tedious differences and troubles still existed between Mr. Russell and the lieutenant," and that some more decisive measures must be taken.

The court therefore desired the churches of Hartford and Windsor "to send two or three messengers apiece to meet in Wethersfield, on the 1st Tuesday in November 1659, to give such advice in the premises as God shall direct them unto by the light of scripture and reason." Even this expedient failed.‡

The quarrel ended with the removal of Mr. Russell to Hadley, with his adherents, where he spent the remainder of his days.§ At this remote day it is impossible to say who was most in fault in this unhappy controversy. The more charitable conclusion is the one that has been arrived at by all the authors who have written upon it, that the conduct of neither party could be justified, and that each was too rash and unforgiving in his behavior.¶ This was certainly the opinion of the General Court at the time.

* J. H. Trumbull's Colonial Records, i. 330, 331. † Ibid.

‡ J. H. Trumbull's Colonial Records, i. 342.

§ Mr. Russell was a graduate of Harvard College, and was highly esteemed by his cotemporaries for his learning and piety. It was at his house that Whalley and Goffe, two of the Judges of Charles I., were concealed for several years, and there, it is supposed, at least one of them died. Mr. Russell died Nov. 10, 1692.

¶ Vide Trumbull, Chapin, Cotton, Mather, and others.

In 1659, a violent feeling began to manifest itself in the church at Middletown against their pastor, the Rev. Mr. Stow, which resulted in his dismissal.

In October 1666, the General Court, in order "to consider some way or means to bring these ecclesiastical matters, that are in difference in the several plantations, to an issue," ordered that a synod should be called, to which all the pastors in the colony, and certain clergymen in Massachusetts, should be invited.* The ministers, however, objected to meet as a synod, and in consequence, the legislature at a subsequent session judged it expedient to alter the name of the council, and to call it an assembly of the ministers of Connecticut. The assembly met early in the summer of 1667, and, after conversing upon the subjects and appointing committees, adjourned to meet again in the fall and make their report.

In the meantime, it was ascertained that a decision was not likely to be obtained in unison with the wishes of a majority of the legislature, and an effort was commenced to prevent the re-assembling of the ecclesiastical council. This was accomplished by procuring an order from the commissioners of the united colonies, that "all questions of public concernment about matters of faith and order, should be referred to a synod or council of messengers of churches, indifferently called out of the united colonies, by an order of agreement of all the General Courts; and that the place of meeting should be at or near Boston."†

The general convention was never called, and no further attempt was made to bring the questions in dispute into a public discussion. The great point at issue between the two parties appears to have been, the conditions of church membership.

The people of Windsor had for a long time been in an unquiet state respecting the settlement of a colleague to assist Mr. Wareham in the work of the ministry, he having become advanced in years. Mr. Chauncey, who was invited

* J. H. Trumbull, ii. 53, 54.

† Trumbull, i. 357, 358.

to preach there, met with bitter opposition. The General Court finally interfered, with the hope of bringing matters to a crisis. It enacted that "all the freemen and householders in Windsor and Massacoe," should assemble at the meeting house at a given day and hour, and express their minds by ballot *for* or *against* Mr. Chauncey. The result was, eighty-six for, and fifty-five against, Mr. Chauncey. The legislature then decided that the majority might settle their favorite, and that the minority had liberty to call and settle an orthodox minister among themselves, if they thought expedient.*

The minor party thereupon immediately called Mr. Woodbridge to preach among them. Both of these ministers continued to preach in Windsor, one to the one party and the other to the other, from 1667 to 1680. Several councils were called to consider the matter. One in 1677, and another in 1680, advised that Messrs. Chauncey and Woodbridge should both leave the town, and that the two parties should unite in calling one minister—but without effect.

In October of the last mentioned year, the legislature confirmed the advice of the council, and called upon all the good people of Windsor to assist therein, "and not in the least to oppose or hinder the same, as they will answer the contrary *to their peril.*"†

The Rev. Samuel Mather was soon after called to preach in Windsor, and in 1682, he was ordained to the pastoral office over the whole town. He gave good satisfaction to all, and the affairs of the society flourished under his ministry until his death in 1726.

The fruitful topics of controversy, which had disturbed the harmony of so many churches in the colony, again began to agitate the church in Hartford. Stone and Goodwin were no more; but a like difference of opinion seems to have characterized their successors. Mr. Whiting and a part of the church zealously adhered to the opinions and practices of the congregational churches since the emigration to

* Trumbull, i. 460. † Col. Records, MS.

New England. On the other hand, Mr. Haynes and a majority of the congregation claimed to have adopted more liberal views. The difference became so great, that a division of the church was effected in 1669.* Contentions also occurred in the church in Stratford about the same time, which resulted in a division, and in the removal of one of the contending parties to Pomperaug (now Woodbury.)†

Previous to 1708, the Cambridge Platform had been the general plan of church fellowship and discipline in New England. Divers opinions had long existed as to the policy and efficacy of some of its provisions and omissions. In obedience to repeated requests and memorials, the legislature, at their May session, 1708, passed an act requiring the ministers and churches of Connecticut to meet and form an ecclesiastical constitution.‡ They accordingly assembled at Saybrook, on the 9th day of September 1708, and after due deliberation adopted the celebrated "Saybrook Platform," together with a confession of faith. A uniform standard of faith and action being thus agreed upon, a period of harmony and good feeling followed, such as had not been before experienced for many years.

The first serious ecclesiastical disturbance after the union thus effected, occurred in Guilford in 1728. Mr. Thomas Ruggles, the minister of that place, had died, and the church and society proceeded to call his son of the same name to preach for them, and finally procured his ordination and settlement, much to the dissatisfaction of a respectable minority who had opposed him from the beginning. The minority, consisting of about fifty members of the church and many others belonging to the society, separated ; they declared their dissent to the Saybrook Platform, invited a young clergyman, Mr. Edmund Ward, to preach for them, and petitioned the legislature to make them a distinct ecclesiastical society. The legislature denied their request ; whereupon they appealed to the court at New Haven to be qualified, according

* Trumbull, i. 461. † Col. Records, i. 177. ‡ Col. Records, MS.

Jonathan Edwards

to the act of William and Mary, for the ease of sober consciences, to worship by themselves. The court deferred the matter until their next meeting, in April—on which day several of the dissenters, together with Mr. Ward, appeared in court and qualified themselves according to the act of parliament and the laws of the colony.

They now renewed their request to the legislature to be freed from paying taxes to the first society, and to be made a distinct ecclesiastical body. On a full representation of the facts in the case, their first request was granted. Efforts were now renewed to effect a reconciliation between the parties, but they proved unavailing. The breach grew wider and wider, until, on the 30th of June 1731, the church under the care of Mr. Ruggles, suspended from communion forty-six of the dissenting members.

The contention continued with unabated violence until May 1733, when the friends of Mr. Ward were finally made a distinct ecclesiastical society by the legislature.*

In 1735, there began a most remarkable religious awakening under the preaching of the celebrated Jonathan Edwards, at Northampton, which has since been designated as the "great revival."† It spread into many towns in Connecticut, and the feeling and interest manifested on the great themes of religion were intense and absorbing. This appears to to have been followed by a period of great religious declension and formality until 1740; when a still more general and extraordinary revival commenced, which spread throughout New England and some of the more southern and western colonies. Childhood, manhood, old age—the learned and the ignorant—the moralist and the skeptic—men of wealth and the highest official position, as well as paupers and outcasts—were numbered among its converts. We are told that even

* Trumbull, ii. 115, 134.

† At the request of Dr. Watts and other English divines, Mr. Edwards wrote a narrative of the "great revival," which was published in London, and has since been frequently republished.

the Indians, on whom no impression could previously be made, became humble inquirers after the truth.*

Among the most zealous and efficient laborers in the work, were Whitefield, Edwards, and Tennant, from abroad; and Wheelock, Bellamy, Pomeroy, Mills, Graham, Meacham, Whitman, and Farrand, among the pastors of Connecticut. Many of the clergy of the colony, however, strenuously opposed the measures employed and the effects produced; and many of the magistrates and other leading men joined with them in denouncing the "itinerating clergy" and their converts as enthusiasts, new lights, and ranters. Laws were passed, with severe penalties, against any clergyman or exhorter who should attempt to preach in any parish or town without the express desire of the pastor or people thereof.†

It is not to be denied that many gross errors and irregularities followed in the train of this remarkable moral revolution. Many of the most enthusiastic of its subjects forsook their pastors and their usual places of worship, and followed the "itinerants" from parish to parish and from town to town. Some of the preachers and exhorters encouraged the most boisterous manifestations of feeling during the public worship, on the part of the audience, and sought to arouse them by raising their own voices to the highest key, accompanied by violent gestures and the most unnatural agitations of the body. Some claimed to know, by a divine instinct, who were christians and who were sinners; and in particular cases, took it upon themselves to declare openly that their pastors and other christian friends were hypocrites or self-deceivers. They grew pharisaical, uncharitable, censorious, bitter, self-sufficient, and finally claimed that they had been regenerated

* Trumbull, ii. 144.

† Any person not an ordained or settled minister who should attempt publicly to teach or exhort without the express desire and invitation of the pastor or a major part of the church and congregation, should be bound in the sum of one hundred pounds lawful money not to offend again.

Any foreigner or stranger not an inhabitant of the colony, whether ordained or not, who should so offend, was ordered "to be sent as a vagrant person, from constable to constable, out of the bounds of the colony."

and *could not sin.* Some of them took delight in denouncing and vilifying the established religion and its ministers, as well as the civil government and all in authority under it.*

The assembly not only passed laws against these alleged irregularities, but the several ecclesiastical bodies interposed their authority to check the innovations of the "new lights." After numerous attempts to discipline the refractory preachers, the consociations and association proceeded to suspend or expel all the "new light" pastors in the colony. The pretexts for this summary action were various. In some instances the offenders had repudiated the Saybrook platform, in others, they were charged with violating the statute which prohibited them from preaching in other parishes without the requisite consent; while in other cases they were suspected of dangerous heresies.† The trial of the Rev. Philemon Robbins of Branford, who was charged with all these offenses, commenced in 1742 was continued till 1747, and resulted in his deposition from the ministry. He, however, continued to preach to his people as before, to their general satisfaction; they increased his salary, and encouraged him by various acts of public and private liberality.

The difficulty arising out of the settlement of Mr. Whittlesey at Milford, partook largely of a personal character, and deserves little notice from the historian. It resulted in a division of the church in that town, and in the settlement of Mr. Prudden by the minority.

Mr. Noyes, pastor of the first church in New Haven, had

---

* Rev. John Owen of Groton, and Rev. Benjamin Pomeroy of Hebron, were brought before the legislature in May 1744, for scandalizing the laws and officers of the government, &c. The former made some concessions, and was dismissed on his paying the costs of prosecution; the latter was bound to keep the peace, in a bond of fifty pounds, and was made to pay the cost of prosecution, amounting to £32 : 10 : 8.

† In 1744, the Rev. Messrs. Leavenworth of Waterbury, Humphreys of Derby, and Todd of Northbury, were suspended by the consociation for assisting in the ordination of the Rev. Jonathan Lee, at Salisbury, because he and his church had adopted the Cambridge platform.

been one of the violent opposers of the religious excitement of the times. He excluded the "revival preachers" from his pulpit, and openly approved of the laws that had been passed to suppress or regulate the extravagances and alleged fanaticism that had grown out of that excitement. As a consequence, many of his parishioners became disaffected towards him; and, as they failed to secure that redress from the consociation, to which they felt themselves entitled, they withdrew, organized themselves under the "toleration act," and were formally recognized as a distinct and independent church and society by a council called for that purpose.* For several years the new church was without a pastor, but in the meantime enjoyed the ministrations of many able preachers. In 1751, an ecclesiastical council met at New Haven and installed to the pastoral office the Rev. Mr. Bird.† This is still known as the second or north church in New Haven.

The "Wallingford controversy" agitated the churches of Connecticut from 1758 to 1763, and was frequently the subject of comment long thereafter. It commenced in a spirit of hostility to the Rev. James Dana, who was called to preach in that town, and was finally settled there in opposition to a large proportion of the members of the society. It was contended by his opponents that he was not orthodox in sentiment; that he had evaded the enquiries of the committee as to his views on important doctrinal points, and finally replied impertinently; and, after his alleged ordination, it was claimed that the ordination was not valid inasmuch as it was not done in accordance with the provisions of the Saybrook platform. The members of the ordaining council were excluded from the association and were never restored. The individuals who withdrew from the church in

* The council convened at New Haven in Sept. 1751, and consisted of the Rev. Messrs. Philemon Robbins, Joseph Bellamy, Eleazer Wheelock, Samuel Hopkins and Benjamin Pomeroy, together with lay delegates from their respective churches.

† Trumbull.

Wallingford formed a new society, which was incorporated at the May session of the legislature, 1763. The Rev. Simon Waterman had become their pastor some time before that date.*

The religion of the colony was established by law at an early date. In October 1644, the General Court adopted the proposition of the united colonies relative to the support of ministers. This proposition, which was enacted as the law of the colony, provided that each individual should "voluntarily set down what he is willing to allow to that end and use;" and if any man refuse or neglect to pay his proportion, he should be rated by authority, and the amount collected by due course of law as in the case of other just debts. This principle was borrowed in part from the institutions of England, though it was greatly modified and softened in its practical application. Here, it will be seen, as in the fatherland, all adults, whatever may have been their own religious views, were obliged to contribute to the support of the established church. Instead, however, of a system of tithes, taxation was resorted to. In addition to this, the whole population was obliged to attend the regular meetings on Sundays, fasts, and thanksgiving days.

At the same time, with a liberality not at all in accordance with the example set them in England, provision was made for those who dissented from the mode of worship thus established, and "all sober, orthodox persons" who did not fall in with the usages of congregationalism, were allowed, after having made their wishes known in a public manner to the General Court, peaceably to worship in their own way.†

The practical operation of this system was much more lenient than one would infer even from the statutes them-

* Trumbull.

† In May 1669, after expressing their full approval of congregationalism, the General Court say—"Yet forasmuch as sundry persons of worth for prudence and piety amongst us are otherwise persuaded, This court doth declare that all such persons being also approved according to law as orthodox and sound in the fundamentals of the christian religion, may have allowance of their persuasion and profession in church ways or assemblies without disturbance."

selves. A sedate, calm people growing up under institutions that every individual in the republic had helped to frame, and for which he consequently felt a personal responsibility, the general desire was that there should be a sober and equable exercise of authority throughout the colony.

The difficulties growing out of a new church government, several of which have been delineated in this chapter, are just what we should have anticipated as likely to follow in the train of those struggles in the early part of the sixteenth century, when Martin Luther and his contemporaries, "wielding the hammer of the Word, wrought upon the hard metal of human unbelief, till the world rang,"* and extended down to the time when the blood, that was at once the most vital and the most conservative that then flowed in English veins, rebelled against the arbitrary exactions of the old world and warmed with the promises of the new.

Thus I have attempted, in a very humble way, to describe the beginnings of our venerable republic. The reader has seen the seeds sown by the whirlwind taking root in the desert and growing up and blossoming with hope while "winter lingered in the lap of May." Hoping that something of the fragrance of their young growth has been distilled upon the last page of this volume, I close it, only to open another that shall describe the glorious fruit that those seeds have borne.

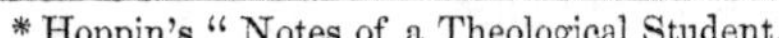

* Hoppin's " Notes of a Theological Student.

LADY FENWICK'S TOMB.

APPENDIX.

A.

PATENT OF CONNECTICUT—1631.

To all people vnto whome this present writeing shall come, Robert, earle of Warwick, sendeth greeting, in our Lord God everlasting: Know yee, that the sayd Robert, earl of Warwick, for divers Good causes & considerations him therevnto moueing, hath giuen, Granted, Bargained, sold, enfeoffed, Aliened & confirmed, & by these presents doth giue, grant, Bargain, sell, enfeoffe, Alien & confirme vnto the Right Honourable William, Viscount Say & Seale, The Right Honourable Rob't, Lord Brooke, The right honourable Lord Rich, & the Honourable Charles fines, Esq'r, Sr. Nathaniel Rich, Knight, Sr. Richard Saltonstall, Knight, Richard Knightly, Esq'r, John Pim, Esq'r, John Hamden, Esq'r, John Humphrey, Esq'r & Herbert Pelham, Esq'r, theire heires & assignes & their associates foreuer, all that part of New England in Americah, which lyes & extends it selfe from a Riuer there called Narrogancett Riuer, the space of forty leagues vpon a straight lyne neere the sea shore towards the Sowth west, west and by sowth or west, as the coast lyeth, towards Virginia, accounting Three English Miles to the league; & allso all & singuler the lands & hereditaments what soeuer, lyeing & being with in the lands afoarsayd, North & South in Lattitude & bredth, & in Length & Longitude of & with in all the bredth afoarsayd, through out the Maine lands there, from the westerne oscian to the sowth sea; & all lands & grounds, place & places, soyle, wood & woods, Grounds, hauens, portes, creeks & Rivers, waters, fishings & hereditaments what soever, lying with in the sayd space & every part & parcell thereof; & allso all Islands lying in Americah afoarsayd, in the sayd seas or either of them, on the western or eastern coasts or parts of the sayd Tracts of lands by these pr'sents mentioned to be giuen, granted, Bargained, sold, enfeoffed, aliened & confirmed; & allso all Mines, Mineralls,—(as well Royall mines of Gold & Siluer as other mines & mineralls) what euer in the sayd lands & premises, or any part thereof; & allso the several Riuers with in the sayd limits, by what Name or Names soever called or known; & all Jurisdictions, rights & Royalties, liberties, freedomes, Immunities, powers, priuiledges, franchizes, preheminencies & comodities what soever, which the said Rob't earle of Worwick, now hath or had, or might vse, exercise or injoy, in or within [the said lands and premises or within*] any part or parcell thereof, excepting & reseruing to his Ma'tia, his heirs & successors, the fift part of all Gold & Silver oare that shall be found with in the sayd premises or any part or parcell thereof: to haue & to hold the sayd part of New England in Americah which lyes &

* The portion in brackets is found only in an early copy made by Mr. John Talcott, "of that Coppy which was in Mr. Hopkins his Custody." [Towns and Lands, Vol. 1. No. 5.]

extends & is abutted as afoarsayd, and the sayd severall Riuers, & euery part & parcell thereof, & all the sayd Islands, Riuers, portes, Hauens, waters, fishings, Mines, Mineralls, Iurisdictions, powers, franchizes, Royalties, liberties, priuiledges, commodities, hereditaments & premises whatsoeuer, with the appurtenances, vnto the sayd William, Viscount Say & Seale, Robert, Lord Brooke, Robert, Lord Rich, Charles fines, Sr. Nathaniel Rich, Sr. Richard Saltonstall, Richard Knightly, John Pim, John Hamden, John Humphery & Herbert Pellam, theire heirs & assignes & their associates, to the onely proper & absolute vse & behoofe of them the sayd William, Viscount Say & Seale, Robert, Lord Brook, Robert, Lord Rich, Charles fines, Sr. Nathaniel Rich, Sr. Richard Saltonstall, Richard Knightly, John Pim, John Hamden, John Humphrey and Herbert Pelham, their heirs and assignes and their associates for evermore. In **Witness** whereof, the sayd Robert Earle of Warwick hath herevnto set his hand & seale, the Nineteenth day of March, in the Seventh yeare of the Reigne of our Soueraigne Lord Charles, by the Grace of God, King of England, Scotland, france and Jreland, Defender of the fayth, &c. Anno Dom. 1631.

ROBERT WARWICK. [*L. S.*]

Signed, Sealed & deliuered in the presence of
Walter Williams,
Thomas Howson,
Hartford, August 6, 1679.

*Vera Copia, JOHN ALLEN, Secr'y.**

B.

CHARTER OF 1662.

Charles the Second, By the Grace of God, King of England, Scotland, France and Ireland, defender of the Faith, &c.; **To** all to whome theis presents shall come, Greetinge: **Whereas**, by the severall Navigatons, discoveryes and successfull Plantatons of diverse of our loveing Subjects of this our Realme of England, Severall Lands, Islands, Places, Colonies and Plantatons have byn obtained and setled in that parte of the Continent of America called New England, and thereby the Trade and Comerce there hath byn of late yeares much increased, **And whereas,** wee have byn informed by the humble Petiton of our Trusty and welbeloved John Winthrop, John Mason, Samuell Willis, Henry Clerke, Mathew Allen, John Tappen, Nathan Gold, Richard Treate, Richard Lord, Henry Woolicott, John Talcott, Daniell Clerke, John Ogden, Thomas Wells, Obedias Brewen, John Clerke, Anthony Haukins, John Deming and Mathew Camfeild, being Persons Principally interessed in our Colony or Plantaton of Coneeticutt in New England, that the same Colony or the greatest parte thereof was purchased and obteyned for greate and valuable Con-

* Towns and Lands, Vol. 1. No. 2. The original Patent is supposed to be lost.

sideratons, And some other part thereof gained by Conquest and with much difficulty, and att the onely endeavours, expence and Charge of them and their Associats, and those vnder whome they Clayme, Subdued and improved, and thereby become a considerable enlargement and additon of our Dominions and interest there,—**Now Know yea,** that in Consideraton thereof, and in regard the said Colony is remote from other the English Plantatons in the Places aforesaid, And to the end the Affaires and Business which shall from tyme to tyme happen or arise concerning the same may bee duely Ordered and mannaged, **Wee have** thought fitt, and att the humble Petiton of the Persons aforesaid, and are graciously pleased to Create and Make them a Body Pollitique and Corporate, with the powers and Priviledges herein after mentoned; And accordingly Our will and pleasure is, and of our especiall grace, certeine knowledge and meere moton, **wee have** Ordeyned, Constituted and Declared, And by theis presents for vs, our heires and Successors, **Doe** Ordeine, Constitute and Declare That they, the said John Winthrop, John Mason, Samuell Willis, Henry Clerke, Mathew Allen, John Tappen, Nathan Gold, Richard Treate, Richard Lord, Henry Woolcot, John Talcot, Daniell Clerke, John Ogden, Thomas Wells, Obadiah Brewen, John Clerke, Anthony Hawkins, John Deming and Mathew Camfeild, and all such others as now are hereafter shall bee Admitted and made free of the Company and Society of our Collony of Conecticut in America, shall from tyme to tyme and for ever hereafter, bee one Body Corporate and Pollitique in fact and name, by the Name of Governour and Company of the English Collony of Conecticut in New England in America; And that by the same name they and their Successors shall and may have perpetuall Succession, and shall and may bee Persons able and capable in the law to Plead and bee Impleaded, to Answere and bee Answered vnto, to Defend and bee Defended in all and singuler Suits, Causes, quarrelles, Matters, Actons and things of what kind or nature soever, And alsoe to have, take, possesse, acquire and purchase lands, Tenements or herditaments, or any goods or Chattells, and the same to Lease, Graunt, Demise, Alien, bargaine, Sell and dispose of, as other our leige People of this our Realme of England, or any other Corporaton or Body Pollitique within the same may lawfully doe. **And further,** that the said Governour and Company, and their Successors shall and may for ever hereafter have a Common Seale to serve and vse for all Causes, matters, things and affaires whatsoever of them and their Successors, and the same Seale to alter, change, breake and make new from tyme to tyme att their wills and pleasures, as they shall thinke fitt. **And** further, wee will and Ordeine, and by theis presents for vs, our heires and Successors **Doe** Declare and appoint, that for the better ordering and manageing of the affaires and businesse of the said Company and their Successors, there shall bee one Governour, one Deputy Governour and Twelve Assistants, to bee from tyme to tyme Constituted, Elected and Chosen out of the Freemen of the said Company for the tyme being, in such manner and forme as hereafter in these presents is expressed; which said Officers shall apply themselves to take care for the best disposeing and Ordering of the Generall busines and affaires of and concering the lands and hereditaments herein after mentoned to bee graunted, and the Plantaton thereof and the Government of the People thereof. And for the better executon of our Royall Pleasure herein, **wee doe** for vs, our heires and Successors, Assigne, name, Constitute and appoint the aforesaid John Winthrop to bee the first and present Governour of the said Company; And the said John Mason to bee the Deputy Governour; And the said Samuell Willis, Mathew Allen, Nathan Gold, Henry Clerke, Richard Treat, John Ogden, Thomas Tappen, John Talcott. Thomas Wells, Henry Woolcot, Richard Lord and Daniell Clerke to bee the Twelve present Assistants of the said Company; to contynue in the said severall offices respectively, vntill the second Thursday which shall bee in the Moneth of October now next comeing. **And** further, wee will, and by theis presents for vs, our heires and Successors, **Doe** Ordaine and Graunt that the Governour of the said Company for the tyme being, or, in his absence by occasion of sickness, or otherwise by his leave or permission, the Deputy Governour for the tyme being, shall and may from tyme to tyme vpon all occasions give Order for the assembling of the said Company and calling them together to Consult and advise of the businesse and Affaires of the said Company, And that for ever hereafter, Twice in every yeare, That is to say on every second Thursday in October and on every second Thursday in May, or oftner, in Case it shall bee requisite. The Assistants and freemen of the said Company, or such of them (not exceeding twoe Persons from each place, Towne or Citty) whoe shall be from tyme to tyme therevnto Elected or Deputed by the maior parte of the freemen of the respective Townes, Cittyes and Places for which they shall bee soe elected or Deputed, shall have a generall meeting or Assembly, then and their to Consult and advise in and about the Affaires and businesse of the said Company; And that the Governour, or in his absence the Deputy Governour of the said Company for the tyme being, and such of the Assistants and freemen of the said Company as shall bee soe Elected or Deputed and bee present att such meeting or Assembly, or the greatest Number of them, whereof the Governour or Deputy Governour and Six of the Assistants at least (to bee Seaven) shall be called the Generall Assembly, and shall have full power and authority to alter and change their dayes and tymes of meeting or Generall Assemblies for Electing the Governour, Deputy Governour and Assistants or other Officers, or any other Courts, Assemblies or meetings, and to Choose, Nominate and appoint such and soe many other Persons as they shall thinke fitt and shall bee willing to accept the same, to bee free of the said Company and Body Politique, and them into the same, to Admitt and to Elect, and Constitute such Officers as they shall thinke fitt and requisite for the Ordering, manageing and disposeing of the Affaires of the said Governour and Company and their Successors. **And wee doe** hereby for vs, our heirs and Successors, Establish and Ordeine, that once in the yeare for ever hereafter, namely, the said Second Thursday in May, the Governour, Deputy Governour, and Assistants of the said Company and other Officers of the said Company, or such of them as the said Generall Assembly shall thinke fitt, shall bee in the said Generall Court and Assembly to bee held from that day or tyme newly Chosen for the yeare ensueing, by such greater part of the said Company for the tyme being then and there present. And if the Governour, Deputy Governour and Assistants by these presents appointed, or such as hereafter bee newly Chosen into their Roomes, or any of them, or any other the Officers to bee appointed for the said Company shall dye or bee removed from his or their severall Offices or Places before the said Generall day of Electon, whome wee doe hereby Declare for any misdemeanour or default to bee removeable by the Governour, Assistants and Company, or such greater part of them in any of the said publique Courts to bee Assembled as is aforesaid, That then and in every such Case itt shall and may bee lawfull to and for the Governour, Deputy Governour and Assistants and Company aforesaid, or such greater parte of them soe to bee Assembled as is aforesaid in any of their Assemblies to proceede to a New Electon of one or more of their Company in the Roome or place, Roomes or Places of such Governour, Deputy Governour, Assistant or other Officer or Officers soe dyeing or removed, according to their discretions; and imediately vpon and after such Electon or Electons made of such Governour, Deputy Governour, Assistant or Assistants, or any other Officer of the said Company in manner and forme aforesaid, The Authority, Office and Power before given to the former Governour, Deputy Governour or other Officer and Officers so removed, in whose stead and Place new shall be chosen, shall as to him and them and every of them respectively cease and determine. **Provided,** alsoe, and our will and pleasure is, That as well such as are by theis presents appointed to bee the present Governour, Deputy Governour and Assistants of the said Company as those that shall succeed them, and all other Officers to be appointed and Chosen as aforesaid, shall, before they vndertake the Executon of their said Offices and Places respectively, take their severall and respective Corporall Oathes for the due and faithfull performance of their dutyes in their several Offices and Places, before such Person or Persons as are by these Presents hereafter appoynted to take and receive the same; That is to say, the said John Winthrop, whoe is herein before nominated and appointed the present Governour of the said Company, shall take the said Oath before one or more of the Masters of our Court of Chancery for the tyme being, vnto which Master of Chancery **wee doe,** by theis presents, give full power and authority to Administer the said Oath to the said John Winthrop accordingly. And the said John Mason, whoe is herein before nominated and appointed the present Deputy Governour of the Company, shall take the said Oath before the said John Winthrop, or any twoe of the Assistants of the said Company, vnto whome **wee doe** by these presents, give full power and authority to Administer the said Oath to the said John Mason accordingly. **And** the said Samuell Willis, Henry Clerke, Mathew Allen, John Tappen, Nathan Gold, Richard Treate, Richard Lord, Henry Woolcott, John Talcott, Daniell Clerke, John Ogden and Thomas Welles, whoe are herein before Nominated and appointed the present Assistants of the said Company, shall take the Oath before the said John Winthrop and John Mason, or one of them, to whome **wee doe** hereby give full power and authority to Administer the same accordingly. **And** our further will and pleasure is, that all and every Governour or Deputy Governour to bee Elected and Chosen by vertue of theis presents, shall take the said Oath before two or more of the Assistants of the said Company for the tyme being, vnto whome wee doe, by theis presents, give full power and authority to give and Administer the said Oath accordingly. And the said Assistants and every of them, and all and every other Officer or

Officers to bee hereafter Chosen from tyme to tyme, to take the said Oath before the Governour or Deputy Governour for the tyme being, vnto which said Governour or Deputy Governour wee doe, by theis presents, give full power and authority to Administer the same accordingly. **And further,** of our own ample grace, certeine knowledge and meere moton **wee have** given and Graunted, and by theis presents, for vs, our heires and Successors, **Doe** give and Graunt vnto the said Governour and Company of the English Colony of Conecticut in New England in America, and to every Inhabitant there, and to every Person and Persons Tradeing thither, And to every such Person and Persons as are or shall bee free of the said Collony, full power and authority from tyme to tyme and att all tymes hereafter, to take, Ship, Transport and Carry away, for and towards the Plantaton and defence of the said Collony such of our loveing Subiects and Strangers as shall or will willingly accompany them in and to their said Collony and Plantaton; (Except such Person and Persons as are or shall bee therein restrayned by vs, our heires and Successors;) And alsoe to Ship and Transport all and all manner of goods, Chattells, Merchandizes and other things whatsoever that are or shall bee vsefull or necessary for the Inhabitants of the said Collony and may lawfully bee Transported thither; Neverthelesse, not to bee discharged of payment to vs, our heires and Successors, of the Dutyes, Customes and Subsidies which are or ought to bee paid or payable for the same. **And further,** Our will and pleasure is, and **wee doe** for vs, our heires and Successors, Ordeyne, Declare and Graunt vnto the said Governor and Company and their Successors, That all and every the Subiects of vs, our heires or Successors which shall goe to Inhabite within the said Colony, and every of their Children which shall happen to bee borne there or on the Sea in goeing thither or returneing from thence, shall have and enioye all liberties and Immunities of free and naturall Subiects within any the Dominions of vs, our heires or Successors, to all intents, Constructons and purposes watsoever, as if they and every of them were borne within the Realme of England. **And wee doe** authorise and impower the Governour, or in his absence the Deputy Governor for the tyme being, to appointe two or more of the said Assistants att any of their Courts or Assemblyes to bee held as aforesaid, to have power and authority to Administer the Oath of Supremacy and obedience to all and every Person and Persons which shall att any tyme or tymes hereafter goe or passe into the said Colony of Conecticutt, vnto which said Assistants soe to bee appointed as aforesaid, **wee doe,** by these presents, give full power and authority to Administer the said Oath accordingly. **And wee doe further,** of our especiall grace, certaine knowledge and meere moton, give and Graunt vnto the said Governor and Company of the English Colony of Conecticutt in New England in America, and their Successors, that itt shall and may bee lawfull to and for the Governor or Deputy Governor and such of the Assistants of the said Company for the tyme being as shall bee Assembled in any of the Generall Courts aforesaid, or in any Courts to bee especially Sumoned or Assembled for that purpose, or the greater parte of them, whereof the Governor or Deputy Governor and Six of the Assistants, (to bee all wayes Seaven,) to Erect and make such Judicatories for the heareing and Determining of all Actons, Causes, matters and thinges happeing within the said Colony or Plantaton and which shall bee in dispute and depending there, as they shall thinke fitt and convenient; And alsoe from tyme to tyme to Make, Ordaine and Establish All manner of wholsome and reasonable Lawes, Statutes, Ordinances, Directons and Instructons, not contrary to the lawes of this Realme of England, aswell for setling the formes and Ceremonies of Governement and Magestracy fitt and necessary for the said Plantaton and the Inhabitants there as for nameing and Stileing all sorts of Officers, both superior and inferior, which they shall find needfull for the Governement and Plantaton of the said Colony, and distinguishing and setting forth of the severall Dutyes, Powers and Lymitts of every such Office and Place, and the formes of such Oathes, not being contrary to the Lawes and Statutes of this our Realme of England, to bee Administred for the Executon of the said severall Offices and Places; As alsoe for the disposeing and Ordering of the Electon of such of the said Officers as are to bee Annually Chosen, and of such others as shall succeed in case of death or removall, and Administring the said Oath to the new Elected Officers, and Graunting necessary Comissions, and for impositon of lawfull Fines, Mulcts, Imprisonment or other Punishment vpon Offenders and Delinquents, according the Course of other Corporatons within this our Kingdome of England, and the same Lawes, fines, Mulcts and Executons to alter, change, revoke, adnull, release or Pardon, vnder their Comon Seale, As by the said Generall Assembly or the maior part of them shall bee thought fitt; And for the directing, ruleing and disposeing of all other matters and things whereby our said people, Inhabitants there, may bee soe religiously, peaceably and civilly Governed as their good life and orderly Conversaton may wynn and invite the Natives of the Country to the knowledge and obedience of the onely true God and Saviour of mankind, and the Christian faith, which in our Royall intentons and the Adventurers free profession is the onely and principall end of this Plantaton; **Willing,** Commanding and requireing, and by these presents, for vs, our heires and Successors, Ordaineing and appointeing That all such Lawes, Statutes and Ordinances, Instructons, Impositons and Directons as shall bee soe made by the Governor, Deputy Governor and Assistants, as aforesaid, and published in writeing vnder their Comon Seale, shall carefully and duely bee observed, kept, performed and putt in executon, according to the true intent and meaning of the same. **And** these our letters Patent, or the Duplicate or Exemplificaton thereof, shall bee to all and every such Officers, Superiors and inferiors, from tyme to tyme for the Putting of the same Orders, Lawes, Statutes, Ordinances, Instructons and Directons in due Executon, against vs, our heires and Successors, a sufficient warrant and discharge. **And wee doe further,** for vs, our heires and Successors, give and Graunt vnto the said Governor and Company and their Successors, by these presents, That itt shall and may bee lawfull to and for the Cheife Commanders, Governors and Officers of the said Company for the tyme being whoe shall bee resident in the parts of New England hereafter mentoned, and others inhabiting there by their leave, admittance, appointment or directon, from tyme to tyme and att all tymes hereafter, for their speciall defence and safety, to Assemble, Martiall, Array and putt in Warlike posture the Inhabitants of the said Colony, and to Commissionate, Impower and authorise such Person or Persons as they shall thinke fitt to lead and Conduct the said Inhabitants, and to encounter, expulse, repell and resist by force of Armes, as well by Sea as by land. And alsoe to kill, Slay and destroy, by all fitting wayes, enterprizes and means whatsoever, all and every such Person or Persons as shall att any tyme hereafter Attempt or enterprize the distructon, invasion, detriment or annoyance of the said Inhabitants or Plantaton, And to vse and exercise the Law Martiall in such Cases onely as occasion shall require. And to take or surprize by all wayes and meanes whatsoever, all and every such Person and Persons, with their Shipps, Armour, Ammuniton and other goods of such as shall in such hostile manner invade or attempt the defeating of the said Plantaton or the hurt of the said Company and Inhabitants; and vpon iust Causes to invade and destroy the Natives or other Enemyes of the said Colony. **Neverthelesse,** Our Will and pleasure is, And **wee doe** hereby Declare vnto all Christian Kings, Princes and States, That if any Persons which shall hereafter bee of the said Company or Plantaton, or any other, by appointment of the said Governor and Company for the tyme being, shall att any tyme or tymes hereafter Robb or Spoile by Sea or by land, and doe any hurt, violence or vnlawfull hostillity to any of the Subiects of vs, our heires or Successors, or any of the Subiects of any Prince or State beinge then in league with vs, our heires or Successors, vpon Complaint of such iniury done to any such Prince or State, or their Subiects, **wee,** our heires and Successors, will make open Proclamaton within any parts of our Realme of England fitt for that purpose, That the Person or Persons commitinge any such Robbery or Spoile, shall within the tyme lymitted by such Proclamaton, make full restituton or satisfacton of all such iniuries done or committed, Soe as the said Prince or others soe complayneing may bee fully satisfied and contented. And if the said Person or Persons whoe shall committ any such Robbery or Spoile shall not make satisfacton accordingly, within such tyme soe to bee limitted, That then itt shall and may be lawfull for vs, our heires and Successors, to putt such Person or Persons out of our Allegiance and Protecton. And that it shall and may bee lawfull and free for all Princes or others to Prosecute with hostility such Offenders and every of them, their and every of their Procurers, ayders, Abettors and Councellors in that behalfe. **Provided,** alsoe, and our expresse will and pleasure is, **And wee doe** by these presents for vs, our heires and Successors, Ordeyne and appointe that these presents shall not in any manner hinder any of our loveing Subiects whatsoever to vse and exercise the Trade of Fishinge vpon the Coast of New England in America, but they and every or any of them shall have full and free power and liberty to contynue and vse the said Trade of Fishing vpon the said Coast, in any of the Seas therevnto adioyning, or any Armes of the Seas or Salt Water Rivers where they have byn accustomed to Fish, And to build and sett vpon the wast land belonging to the said Colony of Conecticutt, such Wharfes, Stages and workehouses as shall bee necessary for the Salting, dryeing and keepeing of their Fish to bee taken or gotten vpon that Coast,—any thinge in these presents conteyned to the contrary notwithstanding. **And Knowe yee further,** That Wee, of our more abundant grace, certaine knowledge and meere moton **have** given, Graunted and Confirmed, And by theis presents, for vs, our heires and Successors, **Doe** give, Graunt and Confirme vnto the said Governor and Company and their Successors, **All** that parte of our Dominions in Newe England in America bounded on the East by Norroganсett River, comonly called Norroganсett Bay, where the said River falleth into the Sea, and on the North by the lyne of the Massachusetts Plantation, and on the South by the Sea, and in longitude as the lyne of the Massachusetts Colony, runinge from East to West; that is to say, from the said Narroganсett Bay on the East to the South Sea on the West parte, with the Islands thereunto adioyneinge, Together with all firme lands, Soyles, Grounds, Havens, Ports, Rivers, Waters, Fishings, Mynes, Myneralls, Precious Stones, Quarries, and all and singuler other Comodities, Iurisdictons, Royalties, Priviledges, Francheses, Preheminences and hereditaments whatsoever within the said Tract, Bounds, lands and Islands aforesaid, or to them or any of them belonging, **To have and to hold** the same vnto the said Governor and Company, their Successors and Assignes, for ever vpon Trust and for the vse and benefitt of themselves and their Associates, freemen of the said Colony, their heires and Assignes, **To bee holden** of vs, our heires and Successors, as of our Manor of East Greenewich, in Free and Comon Soccage, and not in Capite nor by Knights Service, **Yielding and Payinge** therefore to vs, our heires and Successors, onely the Fifth parte of all the Oare of Gold and Silver which from tyme to tyme and att all tymes hereafter shall bee there gotten, had or obteyned, in liew of all Services, Dutyes and Demaunds whatsoever, to bee to vs, our heires or Successors, therefore or thereout rendered, made or paid. **And lastly,** Wee doe for vs, our heires and Successors, Graunt to the said Governor and Company and their Successors, by these presents, that these our Letters Patent shall bee firme, good and effectuall in the lawe to all intents, Constructons and purposes whatsoever, accordinge to our true intent and meaneing herein before Declared, as shall bee Construed, reputed and adiudged most favourable on the behalfe and for the best benefitt and behoofe of the said Governor and Company and their Successors, **Although Expresse menton** of the true yearely value or certeinty of the premises, or of any of them, or of any other Guifts or Graunts by vs or by any of our Progenitors or Predecessors heretofore made to the said Governor and Company of the English Colony of Conecticutt in New England in America aforesaid in theis presents is not made, or any Statute, Act, Ordinance, Provision, Proclamaton or Restricton heretofore had, made, Enacted, Ordeyned or Provided, or any other matter, Cause or thinge whatsoever to the contrary thereof in any wise notwithstanding. **In witnes** whereof, wee have caused these our Letters to bee made Patent: **Witnes** our Selfe, att Westminster, the three and Twentieth day of Aprill, in the Fowerteenth yeare of our Reigne.

By writt of Privy Seale. **Howard.**

C.

LETTER of His Majesty CHARLES II. to CONNECTICUT, April 23rd, 1664,
CHARLES R.,

"Trusty and well beloved, we greet you well, having, according to the resolution we declared to Mr. John Winthrop *at the time* when we renewed your charter, now sent these persons of known abilities and affections to us—that is to say, Colonel Richard Nichols, Sir Robert Carr, knight, George Cartwright, Esq., and Samuel Maverick, Esq., our commissioners, to visit those our several colonies and plantations in New England, to the end that we may be the better informed of the state and welfare of our good subjects, whose prosperity is very dear to us. We can make no question but that they shall find that reception from you which may testify your respect to us from whom they are sent for your good.

"We need not tell how careful we are of your liberties and privileges, whether ecclesiastical or civil, which we will not suffer to be violated in the least degree; and that they may not be, is the principal business of our said commissioners, as likewise to take care that the bounds and jurisdictions of our colonies there, may be clearly agreed upon; that every one may enjoy what of right belongeth unto them, without strife or contention; and especially that the natives of that country, who are willing to live peaceably and neighborly with our English subjects, may receive such justice and civil treatment from them, as may make them the more in love with their religion and manners; so not doubting of your full compliance and submission to our desire, we bid you farewell. Given at our Court, at Whitehall, the 23d day of April, 1664, in the sixteenth year of our reign.

"By His Majesty's command, HENRY BENNIT."

D.

"NEW HAVEN'S CASE STATED.

"*Honored and beloved in the Lord*,—We, the General Court of New Haven colony, being sensible of the wrongs which this colony hath lately suffered by your unjust pretenses and encroachments upon our just and proper rights, have unanimously consented, though with grief of heart, being compelled thereunto, to declare unto you, and unto all whom the knowledge thereof may concern, what yourselves do or may know to be true as followeth.

"1. That the first beginners of these plantations by the sea-side in these western parts of New England, being engaged to sundry friends in London, and in other places about London (who purposed to plant some with them in the same town, and others as near to them as they might) to provide for them and themselves some convenient places by the sea-side, arrived at Boston in the Massachusetts, (having a special right in their patent, two of them being joint purchasers of it with others, and one of them a patentee, and one of the assistants chosen for the New England company in London,) where they abode all the winter following; but not finding there a place suitable to their purpose, were persuaded to view these parts, which those that viewed approved; and before their removal, finding that no English were planted in any place from the fort (called Saybrook) to the Dutch, proposed to purchase of the Indians, the natural proprietors of those lands, that whole tract of land by the sea-coast, for themselves and those that should come to them; which they also signified to their friends in Hartford in Connecticut colony, and desired that some fit men from thence might be employed in that business, at their proper cost and charges who wrote to them. Unto which letter having received a satisfactory answer, they acquainted the Court of magistrates of Massachusetts colony with their purpose to remove and the grounds of it, and with their consent began a plantation in a place situated by the sea, called by the Indians Quillipiack; which they did purchase of the Indians the true proprietors thereof, for themselves and their posterity; and have quietly possessed the same about six and twenty years; and have buried great estates in buildings, fencings, clearing the ground, and in all sorts of husbandry; without any help from Connecticut or dependence on them. And by voluntary consent among themselves, they settled a civil court and government among themselves, upon such fundamentals as were established in Massachusetts by allowance of their patent, whereof the then governor of the Bay, the Right Worshipful Mr. Winthrop, sent us a copy to improve for our best advantage. These fundamentals all the inhabitants of the said Quillipiack approved, and bound themselves to submit unto and maintain; and chose Theophilus Eaton, Esq. to be their governor, with as good right as Connecticut settled their government among themselves, and continued it above twenty years without any patent.

"2. That when the help of Mr. Eaton our governor, and some others from Quillipiack, was desired for ending of a controversy at Wethersfield, a town in Connecticut colony, it being judged necessary for peace that one party should remove their dwellings, upon equal satisfying terms proposed, the governor, magistrates, &c. of Connecticut offered for their part, that if the party that would remove should find a fit place to plant in upon the river, Connecticut would grant it to them, and the governor of Quillipiack (now called New Haven) and the rest there present, joined with him, and promised that if they should find a fit place for themselves by the sea-side, New Haven would grant it to them, which accordingly New Haven performed; and so the town of Stamford began, and became a member of New Haven colony, and so continueth unto this day. Thus in a public assembly in Connecticut, was the distinct right of Connecticut upon the river and of New Haven by the sea-side, declared, with the consent of the governor, magistrates, ministers, and better sort of the people of Connecticut at the time.

"3. That sundry other townships by the sea-side and Southold on Long Island, (being settled in their inheritances by right of purchase of their Indian proprietors,) did voluntarily join themselves to New Haven, to be all under one jurisdiction, by a firm engagement to the fundamentals formerly settled in New Haven; whereupon it was called New Haven Colony. The General Court, being thus constituted, chose the said Theophilus Eaton, Esq., a man of singular wisdom, godliness, and experience, to be the governor of New Haven Colony; and they chose a competent number of magistrates and other officers for the several towns. Mr. Eaton so well managed that great trust, that he was chosen governor every year while he lived. All this time Connecticut never questioned what was done at New Haven; nor pretended any right to it, or to any of the towns belonging to this colony; nor objected against our being a distinct colony.

"4. That when the Dutch claimed a right to New Haven, and all along the coast by the sea-side, it being reported they would set up the Prince of Orange's arms, the governor of New Haven, to prevent that, caused the king of England's arms to be fairly cut in wood, and set upon a post in the highway by the sea-side, to vindicate the right of the English, without consulting Connecticut or seeking their concurrence therein.

"5. That in the year 1643, upon weighty considerations, an union of four distinct colonies was agreed upon by all New England, (except Rhode Island,) in their several general courts, and was established by a most solemn confederation; whereby they bound themselves mutually to preserve unto each colony its entire jurisdiction within itself, respectively, and to avoid the putting of two into one by any act of their own without consent of the commissioners from the four United Colonies, which were from that time, and still are, called and known by the title of *the four United Colonies of New England.* Of these colonies, New Haven was and is one. And in this solemn confederation Connecticut joined with the rest, and with us.

"6. That in the year 1644, the general court for New Haven colony, then sitting in the town of New Haven, agreed unanimously to send to England for a patent; and in the year 1645, committed the procuring of it to Mr. Grigson, one of our magistrates, who entered upon his voyage in January that year, from New Haven, furnished with some beaver in order thereunto as we suppose. But by the providence of God, the ship and all the passengers and goods were lost at sea, in their passage towards England, to our great [grief] and the frustration of the design for the time; after which the troubles in England put a stop to our proceedings therein. This was done with the consent and desire of Connecticut to concur with New Haven therein. Whereby the difference of times, and of men's spirits in them, may be discovered. For then the magistrates of Connecticut with consent of their General Court, knowing our purposes, desired to join with New Haven in procuring the patent, for common privileges to both in their different jurisdictions, and left it to Mr. Eaton's wisdom to have the patent framed accordingly. But now they seek to procure a patent without the concurrence of New Haven; and contrary to our minds expressed before the patent was sent for, and to their own promise, and to the terms of the confederation, and without sufficient warrant from their patent, they have invaded our right, and seek to involve New Haven under Connecticut jurisdiction.

"7. That in the year 1646, when the commissioners first met at New Haven, Keift, the then Dutch governor, by letters expostulated with the commissioners, by what warrant they met at New Haven without his consent, seeing it and all the sea-coast belonged to his principals in Holland, and to the lords the States General. The answer to that letter was framed by Mr. Eaton, governor of New

Haven, and then president of the commission, approved by all the commissioners, and sent in their names with their consent to the then Dutch governor, who never replied therennto.

"8. That this colony in the reign of the late King Charles the First, received a letter from the committee of Lords and Commons for foreign plantations, then sitting at Westminster, which letter was delivered to our governor, Mr. Eaton, for freeing the several distinct colonies of New England from molestations by the appealing of troublesome spirits unto England, whereby they declared that they had dismissed all causes depending before them from New England, and that they advised all inhabitants to submit to their respective governments there established, and to acquiesce when their causes shall be there heard and determined, as it is to be seen more largely expressed in the original letter which we have, subscribed. 'Your assured friends,

'PEMBROKE,	'MANCHESTER,	'WARWICK,
'W. SAY AND SEAL,	'FR. DACRE, &c.	'DENBIGH.'

"In this order they subscribed their names with their own hands, which we have to show, and they inscribed or directed this letter—'To our worthy friends the governor and assistants of the plantations of New Haven in New England.' Whereby you may clearly see that the right honorable, the Earl of Warwick, and the Lord Viscount Say and Seal, (lately one of his majesty King Charles the Second's most honorable privy council, as also the right honorable Earl of Manchester still is,) had no purpose, after New Haven colony, situated by the sea-side, was settled to be a distinct government, that it should be put under the patent for Connecticut, whereof they had only framed a copy before any house was erected by the sea-side from the fort to the Dutch, which yet was not signed and sealed by the last king for a patent; nor had you any patent till your agent, Mr. Winthrop, procured it about two years since.

"9. That in the year 1650, when the commissioners for *the four united colonies of New England*, met at Hartford, the now Dutch governor being then and there present, Mr. Eaton the then governor of New Haven colony, complained of the Dutch governor's encroaching upon our colony of New Haven, by taking under his jurisdiction a township beyond Stamford, called Greenwich. All the commissioners, (as well for Connecticut as for the other colonies,) concluded that Greenwich and four miles beyond it belongs to New Haven jurisdiction; whereunto the Dutch governor then yielded, and restored it to New Haven colony. Thus were our bounds westward settled by consent of all.

"10. That when the honored governor of Connecticut, John Winthrop, Esq., had consented to undertake a voyage for England to procure a patent for Connecticut in the year 1661, a friend warned him by letter, not to have his hand in so unrighteous an act, as so far to extend the line of their patent, that the colony of New Haven should be involved within it. For answer thereunto, he was pleased to certify that friend, in two letters which he wrote from two several places before his departure, that no such thing was intended, but rather the contrary; and that the magistrates had agreed and expressed in the presence of some ministers, that if their line should reach us, (which they knew not, the copy being in England,) yet New Haven colony should be at liberty to join with them or not. This agreement, so attested, made us secure, who also could have procured a patent for ourselves within our own known bounds according to purchase, without doing any wrong to Connecticut in their just bounds and limits.

"11. That notwithstanding all the premises, in the year 1662, when you had received your patent under his majesty's hand and seal, contrary to your promise and solemn confederation, and to common equity, at your first general assembly, (which yet could not be called general without us, if we were under your patent, seeing none of us were by you called thereunto,) you agreed among yourselves, to treat with New Haven colony about union, by your commissioners chosen for that end within two or three days after the assembly was dissolved. But before the ending of that session, you made an unrighteous breach in our colony, by taking under your patent some of ours from Stamford, and from Guilford, and from Southold, contrary to your engagements to New Haven colony, and without our consent or knowledge. This being thus done, some sent from you to treat with us, showed some of ours your patent; which being read, they declared to yours that New Haven colony is not at all mentioned in your patent, and gave you some reasons why they believed that the king did not intend to put this colony under Connecticut without our desire or knowledge; and they added that you took a preposterous course, in first dismembering this colony, and after that treating with it about union; which is as if one man proposing to treat with another about union, first cut off from him an arm, and a leg, and an ear, then to treat with him about union. Reverend Mr. Stone also, the teacher of the Church at Hartford, was one of the committee, who being asked what he thought of this action, answered, that he would not justify it.

"12. After that conference, our committee sent, by order of the General Court, by two of our magistrates, and two of our elders, a writing containing sundry other reasons for our not joining with you; who also, finding that you persisted in your own will and way, declared to you our own resolution to appeal to his majesty to explain his true intendment and meaning in your patent, whether it was to subject this colony under it or not; being persuaded, as we still are, that it neither was nor is his royal will and pleasure to confound this colony with yours, which would destroy the so long continued and so strongly settled distinction of *the four United Colonies of New England*, without our desire or knowledge.

"13. That, accordingly, we forthwith sent our appeal to be humbly presented to his Majesty, by some friends in London, yet out of our dear and tender respect to Mr. Winthrop's peace and honor, some of us advised those friends to communicate our papers to Honored Mr. Winthrop himself, to the end that we might find out some effectual expedient, to put a good end to this uncomfortable difference between you and us,—else to present our humble address to his Majesty. Accordingly it was done; and Mr. Winthrop stopped the proceeding of our appeal, by undertaking to our friends that matters should be issued to our satisfaction, and in order thereunto that he was pleased to write a letter to Major Mason, your deputy governor, and the rest of the court of Connecticut Colony, from London, dated March 7, 1663, in these words:

"Gentlemen: I am informed by some gentlemen who are authorized to seek remedy here, that since you had the late patent there hath been injury done to the government at New Haven, and in particular at Greenwich and Stamford, in admitting several of the inhabitants there unto freedom with you, and appointing officers which hath caused division in the said towns which may prove of dangerous consequence if not kindly prevented. I do hope the sin of it is from misunderstanding and not from design of prejudice to that colony; for when I gave assurance to their friends that their rights and interests should not be disregarded or prejudiced by the patent, but if both governments would with unanimous agreement unite in one, their friends judge of advantage to both. And I must further let you know that testimony here doth affirm that I gave assurance before authority here, that it was not intended to meddle with any town or plantation that was settled under any other government. Had it been otherwise intended or declared, it had been injurious in taking out the patent, not to have inserted a proportionable number of their names in it. Now upon the whole, having had serious conference with their friends authorized by them, and with others who are friends to both, to prevent a tedious and chargeable trial and uncertain events here, I promise them to give you speedily this representation how far you are engaged. If any injury hath been done by admitting of freemen or appointing officers or other unjust intermeddling with New Haven colony, in one kind or other, without the approbation of the government, that it be forthwith recalled, and that for the future there will be no imposing in any kind upon them, nor admitting of any members without mutual consent, but that all things be acted as loving neighboring colonies as before such patent was granted, and unto this I judge you are obliged. I have engaged to their agent here that this will be by you performed, and they have thereupon forborne to give you or me any further trouble; but they do not doubt that upon future consideration there may be some right understanding between both governments, that a union of friendly joining may be established to the satisfaction of all, which at my arrival I shall endeavor (God willing,) to promote, not having more at present in the case, I rest your humble servant, JOHN WINTHROP."

The copy of this letter was sent to Mr. Leete, unsealed, with Mr. Winthrop's consent, and was written with his own hand; and the substance of this agreement between some of our friends in London is fully attested by them in their letters to some of us. Say not that Mr. Winthrop in acting in this agreement is nothing to you, for he acted therein as your public and common agent and plenipotentiary, and therefore his acting in that capacity and relation are yours in him.

"14. That after Mr. Winthrop's return, when some from you treated again with our committee about union, it was answered by our committee that we could not admit any treaty with you about that matter till we might treat as an entire colony, our members being restored to us who have been unrighteously withheld from us, whereby those parties have been many ways injurious to our government and disturbers of our peace—which is and will be a bar to any such treaty, till it be removed, for till then we cannot join with you in one government without a fellowship in your sin.

"15. That after this, nothing being done to our just satisfaction, at the last meeting of the commissioners from the four colonies of New England, at Boston, on the — day of November 1663, the commissioners from New Haven colony exhibited to the Commissioners their confederates a complaint of the great injuries done to this colony by Connecticut in the presence of your commissioners, who for answer thereunto showed what treaties they had with New Haven; but that plea was inconsiderable, though you persisting *unrighteously* in withholding our members from us, whereby our wounds remain unhealed, being kept open and continually bleeding. The result of the commissioners' debates about that complaint was in these words:

"The commissioners of Massachusetts and Plymouth, having considered the complaints exhibited by New Haven against Connecticut for infringing their power of jurisdiction, as in the complaint is more particularly expressed, together with the answer returned thereto by Connecticut commissioners, with some debates and conferences that have passed between them, do judge meet to declare that the said colony of New Haven being owned in the articles of confederation as *distinct* from Connecticut, and having been so owned by the colonies in their present meeting in all their actings, may not, by any act of violence, have their liberty of jurisdiction infringed upon by any other of the united colonies, without breach of the articles of confederation; and that where any act of power hath been exerted against their authority, that the same ought to be recalled, and their power reserved to them entire until such time as in an orderly way it shall be otherwise disposed of, and for particular grievances mentioned in the complaint, they ought to be referred to the next meeting at Hartford, &c."

"Now we suppose that when they speak of disposing of it otherwise than in an orderly way, they mean with our *free* consent, there being no other *orderly* way; by an act or power of the united colonies for disposing of the colony of New Haven, otherwise than as it is a *distinct* colony, having entire jurisdiction within itself, which our confederates were bound by their solemn confederation to preserve inviolate.

"16. That before your General Assembly in October last, 1663, our committee sent a letter unto the said assembly, whereby they did request that our members by you unjustly sent *from* us, should be restored to us according to our former frequent desires and according to Mr. Winthrop's letter and promises to authority in England, and according to justice and the conclusion of the commissioners at their last session in Boston, whereunto you returned a real negative answer, contrary to all promises, by making one ***Brown*** your constable at Stamford, who hath been sundry ways injurious to us, and hath scandalously acted in the highest degree of contempt not only against the authority of this jurisdiction, but also of the king himself, pulling down with contumelies the declaration which was sent thither by the court of magistrates for this colony in the king's name, and commanded to be set up in a public place that it might be read and obeyed by all his majesty's subjects inhabiting our town of Stamford.

"17. That thereupon at a General Court held at New Haven for this jurisdiction the 22d day of October 1663, the deputies for this General Court signified the minds of our freemen as not all satisfied with the proposals of the committee from Connecticut, but thought there should be no more treaty with them unless they first restore us to our right state again. The matter was largely debated, and this General Court considering how they of Connecticut do cast our motion in the forementioned letter and gave us no answer but that contrary thereunto as is reported, have further encouraged those of Guilford and Stamford, therefore this court did them order that no treaty be made by this colony with Connecticut before such acts of power exerted upon any of our towns, be revoked and recalled according to Hon. Mr. Winthrop's letter enjoining the same common advice and our frequent desires.

"18. That in this juncture of time we received two letters from England mentioned in the following declaration published by the court of magistrates upon that occasion in these words:

"Whereas, This colony hath received one letter under his majesty's royal hand and seal manual in red wax annexed, bearing date the 21st of June 1663, from his Royal Court at Whitehall, directed to his trusty and well beloved subjects, the governor and deputy governor and assistants of the Massachusetts, Plymouth, New Haven, and Connecticut colonies in New England; and one other letter from the Lords of his Majesty's most Hon. Privy Council, bearing date the 24th of June in the year aforesaid, superscribed for his majesty's special service, and directed to our very loving friend, John Endicott, Esq., governor of his majesty's plantation in New England, and to the governor and council of the colony of Massachusetts, &c. respectively, and by order of the General Court at Boston recorded in the court records, it is particularly directed to the colony of New Haven, in which letters his majesty hath commanded this colony many matters of right very much respecting his majesty's service and the good of this county in general, expecting upon displeasure the strict observance thereof, which this court, his colony being situated by the sea side and so fully accommodated to fulfil his majesty's commands are resolved to their utmost to obey and fulfil; but in their consultation thereabouts, they find through the disloyal and seditious principles and practices of some men of inconsiderable interests, some of his majesty's good subjects in this colony have been seduced to send themselves from this colony, by which decision his majesty's affairs in these parts are like to suffer, the peace of this country to be endangered, and the heathen among us scandalized, in case some speedy course be not taken for the prevention thereof, the which, if we should connive at, especially at this time, his majesty having so particularly directed his royal commands, to this colony as aforesaid, we might justly incur his displeasure against us. This court doth, therefore, in his majesty's name, require all the members and inhabitants of this colony heartily to close in with the endeavors of the governor and assistants thereof for fulfilling his majesty's commands in the said letters expressed, and in order thereunto to return to their obedience, and paying their arrears and rates for defraying the necessary charges of the colony and other dues within six days after the publication hereof, unto such person or persons as are or shall be appointed to collect the same in accordance to the laws and order of this colony, all which being done, this court will forever pass by all former disobedience to this government; but if any shall presume to stand out against his majesty's pleasure so declared as aforesaid concerning this colony, at their peril be it. This court shall not fail to call the said persons to strict account and proceed against them as disloyal to his majesty and disturbers of the peace of this colony, according to law.

"This declaration being grounded in general upon his majesty's command, expressed in these letters, and in special in order to the prevention of his majesty's colonies, the letter of our governor requiring strict observance of the same under penalty of displeasure, of one thousand pounds fine, and therefore in case any difference should arise to his majesty on these accounts we must be enforced to lay the cause of it at your door, because when it was sent to the several towns of that colony and set up in public places to be seen and read of all that all might obey it, it was at Stamford violently plucked down by Brown, your constable, and with reproachful speeches rejected, though sent in his majesty's name and authority of our court of magistrates; and after it was published at Guilford, Bray Rossiter and his son hastened to Connecticut to require your aid against this government, which accordingly you too hastily granted, for on the 30th day of December 1663, two of your magistrates with sundry young men and your marshal came speedily to Guilford accompanied with Rossiter and his son, and countenancing them and their party against the authority of this General Court, that you knew to be obnoxious they were formerly to this jurisdiction for contempt of authority and seditious practices, and that they have been the ring-leaders of this rent, and that Bray Rossiter, the father, hath been long and still is a man of turbulent, restless, factious spirit, and whose design you have cause to suspect to be to cause a war between these two colonies or to ruin New Haven colony, without sending a writing before to our governor to be informed concerning the truth in this matter. Sundry horse, we are informed, accompanied them to Guilford, whither they came at an unseasonable time, about 10 o'clock in the night, those short days when you might rationally think that all people were gone to bed, and by shooting sundry guns, some of yours of their party in Guilford alarmed the town, which, when the governor took notice of, and of the unsatisfying answers given to such as inquired the reason of that disturbance, he suspected that, not without cause, hostile attempts were intended by their company; whereupon he sent a letter to New Haven to inform the magistrates there concerning matters at Guilford, that many were affrighted; and he desired that the magistrates at New Haven would presently come to their succor, and as many of the troopers as could be got, alleging for a reason his apprehensions of their desperate resolutions. The governor's messengers all excited to haste as apprehending danger, and reporting to them at Branford, they went up in arms, hastening to their relief at Guilford which the governor required with speed. Hereupon New Haven was also alarmed that night by beating the drum, &c. to warn the town militia to be ready. This fear was not causeless, for what else could be gathered from the preparations of pistols, bullets, swords, &c. which they brought with them, and by the threatening speeches given out by some of them, as is attested by the depositions of some, subscriptions of others, which we have by us to show when need require; and your two magistrates themselves, who ought to have the king's peace among their own party in their own speeches, threatened our governor that if any thing was done against these men, viz., Rossiter and his party, Connecticut would take it as done against themselves, for they were bound to protect them; and they rose high in threatenings. Yet they joined therewith their design of another conference with New Haven, pretending their purpose of granting to us what we should desire, so far as they could, if we would unite with them; but they held our members from us and upheld them in their animosities against us. Is this the way to union? And what can you grant us which we have not in our own right within ourselves, without you? Yea, it is the birthright of our posterity which we may not barter away from them by treaties with you. It is our purchased inheritance, which no wise man would part with upon a treaty to receive in lieu thereof a lease of the same upon your terms who have right thereunto. And why is our union with you by coming under your patent urged now as necessary for peace, seeing we have enjoyed peace mutually while we have been distinct colonies for about twenty years past? And why do you separate the things which God hath joined together in righteousness and peace—seeing you persist in your unrighteous dealing and persuade us to peace? It is true we all came to New England for the same ends, and that we all agree in some main things, but it doth not follow from thence we ought therefore to unite with you in the same jurisdiction, for the same may be said of all the united colonies which nevertheless are distinct colonies.

"20. That upon a more diligent search of your patent we find that New Haven colony is not included within the line of your patent, for we suppose that your bounds according to the expression of your patent may be, in a just grammatical construction, so cleared that this colony and every part of it, may be mathematically demonstrated to be exempted from it.

"21. That the premises being thoroughly weighed, it will be your wisdom and way to desist wholly from endeavoring to draw us into a union under your patent by any treaty for the future, and apply yourselves to your duty towards God, the king, and us. 1st. Towards God, that you fear him and therefore repent of your unrighteous dealings towards us and repair what you have done amiss by restoring our numbers without delay unto us again, that you may escape the wrath of God which is revealed from heaven against all unrighteousness and against all that despise his holy name, especially among the heathen, which you have done thereby. 2d. Towards the king, that you may honor him by looking at us as a distinct colony within ourselves as you see by the premises his majesty doth, and by restoring to us our former entire state and our numbers in obedience to his majesty, who hath commanded us a distinct colony to serve him in weighty affairs, and wherein if you hinder us, (as you will if you still withhold our members from us as much as in you lieth,) you will incur his majesty's just and high displeasure, who hath not given you in your patent the least appearance of just grounds for your laying claim to us. 3d. To us, your neighbors, your brethren, your confederates by virtue whereof it is your duty to preserve unto us our colony, state power, and privileges against all other that would oppose us, therein or would impose upon us. Is Rossiter and his party of such value with you, that what this jurisdiction doth against them your colony will take it as done to themselves? But if it be done as one of your committee is reported to have expressed it, that you must perform your promise to them as Joshua and the elders of Israel did to the Gibeonites, do you not see the sundry disparities between that vow and yours? or do you indeed make confidence of your *vow to Gibeonites if you term them so;* and without *regard to your* conscience break your promise and most solemn confederation to Israelites. Doubtless it will be safe for this colony to join in one government with persons of such principles and practices, and treaty will be able to bring us to it.

We believe that our righteous God to whom we have solemnly commended and committed our righteous cause, will protect us against all that shall do any wrong or oppress us, neither will he at all doubt the justice of his majesty *our* king as well as yours, and of his most honorable council, but that upon leaving the business open before them they will effectually relieve against your unjust encroachments as the matter shall require.

"We desire peace and love between us and that we may for the future live in love and peace together as distinct neighbor colonies, as we did about twenty years before you received and misunderstood and so abused your patent that your uncomfortable and afflictive exercises would issue herein. We have so long suffered for peace sake, now it is high time to bring that unbrotherly contest wherewith you have troubled us, to a peaceable issue. In order thereunto we do offer you this choice, either to return our members unto us voluntarily, which will be your honor and a confirmation of your mutual love, or to remove them to some other plantation within your own bounds and free us wholly from you for we may not bear it that such seditious, disorderly persons shall continue within the towns of this colony to disturb our peace, disperse our government and disquiet our members, and disable us to obey the king's command. But if they stay where they now are, we shall take our time to proceed according to justice, especially with Brown for his contempt of the declaration and [his disregard] of the king's commands and authority in this jurisdiction, and with Bray Rossiter and his son for all their seditious practices. Lastly, for preventing any misapprehension, we come here to explain our meaning in any passages in this writing which may seem to reflect censure of unrighteous dealing with us upon your act in General Assembly, that we may mean only such as have been active against us therein.

"For the commonwealth, by order of the General Court of New Haven Colony.

"JAMES BISHOP, Secretary.

"NEW HAVEN, March 9, 1663–4."

NOTE.—The above interesting document was transcribed from a *copy* of the original in possession of a gentleman of New Haven County. A comparison of this copy with the original, since made, shows that its language has in some instances been *modernized,* or otherwise altered by the copyist. The meaning of the writer, however, is generally well conveyed in the language as here given; consequently it has not been deemed advisable materially to alter the plates as cast for the first edition.

Connecticut made a spirited and pointed *answer* to this plea of New Haven, which is still preserved among our archives.

BIOGRAPHICAL SKETCHES.

ANDROSS, SIR EDMUND, the *only* royal governor of Connecticut, first came to America in 1674 bearing a commission from the Duke of York, as governor of the territory which had then recently been granted to him by the king. He commenced his administration in New York by the exercise of a liberal and lenient policy; which, however, was soon exchanged for the most tyrannical and unjust measures. In 1686, he was appointed "Governor of *New England*," and arrived in Boston on the 29th day of December of that year. On the following day he published his commission, and formally took the government into his own hands. As Connecticut still retained possession of king Charles' Charter, he saw the necessity of securing it before his commission could have a moral as well as legal force in that colony. He accordingly wrote to Governor Treat, notifying him of his appointment, and stating that he was authorized by the king to receive their charter. As this and subsequent applications failed, Andross at length visited Hartford in person, while the legislature was in session, and made a formal demand for the charter in the presence of the assembly. The summary manner in which the debate was terminated, and the charter secreted, has been so fully detailed in the body of this work as to require no repetition here. Though he failed in the accomplishment of the specific object of his mission, he proceeded to declare the old government of the colony dissolved and *his* administration established in its stead. With the aid of his secretary, Randolph, he now proceeded in the adoption of a series of oppressive and vindictive acts, which were particularly obnoxious to the people of Connecticut, as they had previously enjoyed the privilege of selecting their own rulers, and making their own laws. In 1688 the province of New York was added to his jurisdiction. But his triumph was of short duration. On the arrival of the intelligence that William and Mary had been proclaimed king and queen, in April 1689, the inhabitants of Boston and vicinity rose *en masse*, seized and imprisoned Andross, and re-instated the former officers of government. In Connecticut, the colonial government was also immediately re-established. Complaints were made against him through the agents of Massachusetts and Connecticut; and he retaliated by charging the colonies with rebellion, in treating with indignity the king's governor, &c. After a full hearing by the king in council, the complaints on both sides were dismissed. Andross was afterwards made Governor of Virginia, and arrived there in February 1692. Experience may have taught him wisdom, and age doubtless had softened the asperities of his nature. At all events, his administration appears to have been popular, and advantageous to the people. Agriculture, manufactures, and the arts, were encouraged, mills of various kinds were erected, and the cultivation of cotton was particularly recommended and fostered by him. He was succeeded by Francis Nicholson, Esq., in 1698. Sir Edmund Andross died in London, February 24, 1713-14.

Ashurst, Sir Henry, Agent of the colony at the court of Great Britain, was, as I have elsewhere stated, a son of Henry Ashurst, Esq., a member of parliament and distinguished for his zeal in establishing missions among the American Indians. Both father and son were dissenters, though the latter appears to have been a favorite of Charles II., and was created a baronet by him. Sir Henry married a daughter of Lord Paget. He possessed great influence at court, which was often employed in relieving dissenting clergymen when they were fined or imprisoned. Having always manifested a deep interest in the New England colonies, he was first chosen agent of Massachusetts, and subsequently of Connecticut. He rendered important services to both, and received various acknowledgments of their gratitude. In Massachusetts, however, a personal and partizan influence was at length brought to bear against him, and he was dismissed from the agency without receiving a just pecuniary reward. He died in 1710. His brother, Sir William Ashurst, was subsequently chosen agent of Massachusetts, but he declined the office, "being well acquainted with the slights put upon his brother." The latter became Lord Mayor of London and member of Parliament.

Backus, Rev. Charles, D.D., an eminent Congregational clergyman, was born in Norwich, in 1749, and graduated at Yale College in 1769. Three years from the last date, having in the meantime pursued the study of theology, he was ordained to the pastoral charge of the church in Somers, where he remained till his death, December 30, 1803. He opened a theological school, by means of which he assisted in the education of nearly fifty young men for the ministry. Dr. Backus, besides several occasional sermons, published "Five Discourses on the Truth of the Bible;" and a volume on Regeneration.

Backus, Rev. Isaac, the historian of the Baptist denomination, was born in Norwich in 1724, and became pastor of the Congregational church in Middleborough, Mass., in 1748. About eight years afterward, he became a convert to the sentiments of the Baptists, and succeeded in forming a church of that persuasion, of which he was installed pastor. He preached extempore, and with great power. The electors of Middleborough chose him a delegate to the convention which adopted the Constitution of the United States, in 1788. Besides a history of Middleborough, and various sermons and essays, he published a history of the Baptists, in three volumes. He died in the pastoral office in Middleborough, November 20, 1806.

Bayley, Richard, M.D., an eminent physician, and professor in Columbia College, N.Y., was born in Fairfield in 1745, and received his medical education in London. In the spring of 1776, he returned to this country in the capacity of Surgeon in the British army under Howe; but he soon relinquished his place, and settled in the city of New York in the practice of his profession. In 1792, he was elected professor of anatomy in Columbia College; and during the following year, he was transferred to the department of surgery, in which he particularly excelled. In 1795, Professor Bayley was appointed Health Officer of the port of New York. In August, 1801, in the exercise of his official duties, he boarded an Irish emigrant ship in which the fever prevailed. He was instantly seized with an intense pain in his head and a sickness at the stomach; and on the seventh day he expired, August 17, 1801, aged 56. He was a man of fiery temper, strong in his attachments, invincible in his dislikes, and of perfect integrity and chivalrous in his feelings. The state quarantine laws originated with him. He published an Essay on the Croup, in 1781; Essay on the Yellow Fever, in 1797; Letters on the Yellow Fever, in 1798.

Beach, Abraham, D.D., an Episcopal clergyman of high repute, was born in Cheshire, September 9, 1740, and graduated at Yale College in 1757. He was episcopally ordained by the Bishop of London in June 1767; and for seventeen years, including the period of the Revolution, he was rector of a church in New Brunswick, N. J. He was subsequently called to New York, as assistant minister of Trinity church, where he remained for about thirty years. He passed the evening of his days on a farm at Raritan, where he died September 11, 1828, aged 88 years. He published a Sermon on the Hearing of the Word; and a Funeral Sermon on Dr. Chandler.

Birdseye, Rev. Nathan, remarkable for longevity, was born August 19, 1714, graduated at Yale College in 1736, and was ordained the fourth pastor of the Congregational church in West Haven, October, 1742. In June 1758, he was dismissed, and took up his residence on his patrimonial estate in Stratford, where he spent sixty years. He died January 28, 1818, aged one hundred and three years and five months. The whole number of his descendants had been 258, of whom 206 were then living. In his latter years he occasionally preached, and once with great acceptance, at Stratford, after he was 100 years old. According to his account of the Indians near Stratford, there were sixty or eighty fighting men among them at the commencement of the eighteenth century; while in 1761, there were but three or four men left.

Bishop, James, was one of the most eminent men in the colony of New Haven, at the date of its union with Connecticut, he having there held the offices of magistrate, commissioner, and secretary. New Haven was for the first time represented in the General Court of Connecticut in May, 1665, on which occasion her deputies were James Bishop, and John Nash; and at the same session these gentlemen were chosen commissioners. To each of these offices, Mr. Bishop was often reelected, until 1668, he was chosen an assistant or magistrate. From 1683, until his death, June 22, 1691, he held the office of Deputy Governor of the colony. He was also clerk of the courts, and colonial auditor. A descendant of his, Samuel Bishop, Esq., was town clerk of New Haven for fifty-four years; a representative for twenty-six years; a member of the committee of correspondence and of the council of safety during the Revolution; besides being judge of probate, chief judge of the county court, and mayor of the city. He died in New Haven, in 1803, aged 80 years.

Bishop, Rev. John, successor of Mr. Denton as pastor of the church in Stamford, was a native of Great Britain, and came to New England in early manhood. Soon after the removal of Mr. Denton to Hampstead, in 1664, the people of Stamford, hearing of Mr. Bishop in the neighborhood of Boston, dispatched two of their number, Messrs. George Slauson and Francis Bell, to give him a call to settle among them in the gospel ministry. Although the country was filled with hostile Indians, they went on foot, carrying their provisions. They succeeded in finding Mr. Bishop " to the eastward of Boston." He accepted their call, and returned with them on foot to Stamford, bringing his Bible under his arm. This Bible is still preserved as an interesting relic by one of his descendants in Stamford. Mr. Bishop continued in the ministry for nearly fifty years, and died in Stamford in 1693. He was succeeded by the Rev. James Davenport, a grandson of the Rev. John Davenport of New Haven, and who became famous as a " revivalist " or itinerant.

Bissell, John, (says Farmer,) " came from England with the Rev. Ephraim Hewett, and settled at Windsor, as early as 1640." His name first appears upon our colonial records, July 2d, of that year, when he was a juror at a " Particular Court" in Hartford, in which honorable capacity he was often afterwards called to the seat of government. In May 1648, he attended the meeting of the General Court for the first time, as a representative from Windsor. To this office he was re-elected at fifteen times—but, including the terms specially called, he was present at forty-six sessions of the colonial legislature. In addition to these repeated tokens of the public confidence, he was frequently appointed by the town and colony, on important committees. In 1648, the General Court granted him the exclusive right to the Ferry over the Connecticut River at Windsor, on certain conditions. He died October 3d, 1677. He is believed to be the ancestor of all bearing the name of Bissell, in the United States.

Blinman, Rev. Richard, the first minister in New London, had previously been settled as pastor of a church in Chepstow, Monmouthshire, England. He came to New England in 1642, and after spending a few years at Gloucester, on Cape Ann, he removed to New London in 1648. In 1658, he left the latter place and became a resident of New Haven ; but soon after returned to England. The remainder of his life he spent in the city of Bristol, where he published a volume of 674 pages, entitled, " An Essay tending to issue the Controversy about Infant Baptism."

Bostwick, Rev. David, pastor of the first Presbyterian church in New York, was born in New Milford, January 8, 1721, and graduated at Yale College in 1740. He was settled in the ministry at Jamaica, Long Island, from 1745 to 1756, when he accepted a call from the first Presbyterian church in the city of New York. He died in the latter place, November 12, 1763, aged 42 years. Mr. Bostwick was an eloquent and instructive preacher, speaking without notes, and with great freedom and fluency. He published a sermon entitled, " Self Disclaimed, and Christ Exalted ;" and " An Account of the Life, Character, and Death of President Davies," in 1761. Soon after his death, a small volume was issued from the New York press entitled, "A Fair and Rational Vindication of the Right of Infants to the Ordinance of Baptism. By David Bostwick, A. M.," &c. An edition of this work was re-published in London in 1765, and another from the press of Robert Carter, New York, in 1837.

Brewster, Jonathan, an early settler of New London, was a son of Elder William Brewster, of the " May Flower," in which ship his wife Lucretia Brewster, also came passenger. Jonathan Brewster, came over in the Fortune, which arrived, November 10th, 1621. He first settled at Duxbury, and was several times a representative from that place. He commanded a coasting vessel, which plied between Plymouth and Virginia, and in this way probably became acquainted with Pequot Harbor (New London), of which place he became a resident, in 1648, and the first Town Clerk in 1649. He was often a representative and commissioner, and in 1657, was appointed an assistant; and during the same year, he was a commissioner on the subject of the difficulty between the Mohegan and Podunk Indians. He died in 1661. His children were, Lucretia, Mary, Benjamin, Elizabeth, Ruth, Grace, and Hannah. Benjamin Brewster was also often a representative.

Bruce, Rev. David, a Moravian Missionary, died in Sharon in 1749. He was a native of Scotland, and came to reside as a teacher and preacher among the Indians in the Housatonic valley, with whom he labored for many years. The Scaticokes at Kent, and the tribes residing at Stratfield, Derby, New Milford, Cornwall, and Sharon, were the objects of his especial care, and many were baptized and added to the church as the fruits of his ministry. As he was dying, he called his Indian brethren to him, and entreated them to remain faithful to the end. A stone with a suitable inscription still marks the place where his ashes repose, on the eastern border of "Indian Pond," in Sharon.

Buckingham, Rev. Thomas, was born in Milford, in 1646, was ordained pastor of the church in Saybrook in 1670, and died April 1, 1709, in his 63d year. His nephew of the same name was born in Milford, March 1, 1671, graduated at Harvard College in 1690, and became the pastor of the second church in Hartford. He was one of the most eminent ministers in Connecticut, being distinguished for his ability as a preacher, his pleasant temper, and his engaging manners. He published an election sermon in 1728; and died November 19, 1731. He was a son of Elder Daniel Buckingham, of Milford.

Buell, Rev. Samuel, D.D., was born at Coventry, September 1, 1716, and graduated at Yale College in 1741. On being licensed to preach, he officiated as an itinerant "revivalist," in different parts of New England, for about two years, with great ability and success. He was esteemed as a faithful co-laborer with Edwards and Whitefield in the great revivals of religion which characterized the middle of the eighteenth century. Mr. Buell was installed pastor of the church in East Hampton, Long Island, September 19, 1746; and died in that town, July 19, 1798, aged 81. His life was an eminently useful and laborious one. In 1776, when the British took possession of Long Island, he remained with his people, and did much toward administering to their temporal and spiritual wants. During this period, there was but one other minister within forty miles of him able to preach, and the care of all the churches in the vicinity fell upon him. He published a narrative of the religious revival among his people in 1764, and fourteen occasional discourses—all of which evince the vigor of his intellect and the ardor of his piety.

Bulkley, Rev. John, first minister in Colchester, was a son of the Rev. Gershom Bulkley, who had been pastor of the churches in New London and Wethersfield. His mother was a daughter of President Chauncey, of Harvard College. He graduated at Cambridge in 1699, was ordained in 1703, and died in June 1731. He was regarded as one of the ablest and most learned men in New England. Law, medicine, theology, and science, were studied and thoroughly investigated by him. He wrote a preface to Roger Wolcott's Meditations; and published an election Sermon in 1713, and a tract on Baptism in 1729. In 1724, he published "An Inquiry into the Right of the Aboriginal Natives to the Lands in America,"—in which he contended that the Indians had no just claims to any lands but such as they had subdued and cultivated, and that consequently the English were under no moral obligation to purchase the right of soil from them—but were at liberty to use it as their own.

Canfield, (or Campfield,) Matthew, one of the patentees named in the charter of King Charles II., was an early settler of Norwalk. He was often a representative and commissioner; was chosen an assistant in 1655, and custom-master in 1659. In 1654, he was deputized by the General Court, to assist the magistrates in the execution of justice, and was empowered to "examine misdemeanors, to grant out summons, or bind over delinquents to courts in this jurisdiction, to marry persons, and to press horses by warrant for the public welfare." In 1662, he was appointed with Messrs. Gold and Sherman, "to hold courts in Fairfield." He removed to Newark, N. J., previous to 1669.

Chaplin, Clement, whose name frequently occurs on our early records, was a ruling elder in the church at Wethersfield, a deputy in 1642, and is stated by the late Judge Goodwin to have been the first treasurer and secretary of the Colony in 1637. This, however, was before the colonial government was fully organized, and consequently his name is not included in the lists of colonial officers. He was an educated man, and came to New England in 1634. In 1636, he constituted one of Mr. Hooker's company, who traversed the wilderness from the vicinity of Boston to Hartford, and soon after settled in Wethersfield, where he continued to reside until his death. He left no children, and by his will, bequeathed his entire estate to his wife, Sarah Chaplin, who returned to England—where she executed a general power of attorney to William Parks, of Roxbury, Mass., in which she calls herself "of Edmondsbury, in the county of Suffolk, in the Kingdom of England, widow and relict of Clement Chaplin, late of Thetford, in the county of Norfolk, in said Kingdom, Clerk, deceased." By virtue of the power thus granted, Mr. Parks, on the 24th of September 1661, sold to Henry Wolcott, of Windsor, several tracts of land and buildings "situated in Wethersfield, and lately belonging to Mr. Clement Chaplin, deceased."

Chesebrough, William, the first permanent settler of Pawcatuck, (now Stonington), came to New England with Governor Winthrop's company, and first settled in Boston, where he was made a freeman in 1631. In 1632, he was chosen by the citizens of Boston to attend the next General Court, to advise with the Governor and assistants "about the raising of a public stock." He and his wife Anna, were members of the first church in Boston. After holding several offices of trust in that place, he removed to Braintree, (now Quincy,) in 1640, and thence to Reboboth, in 1644. In 1649, he settled in Stonington, where he spent the remainder of his eventful life. His controversy with the Connecticut government has been sufficiently detailed on pages 197 and 198 of this volume. A remarkable document exists in the Library of Yale College, in his hand-writing, headed—"The Asotiation of Poquatuck people—June 30, 1658." He was a man of energy and of the highest respectability, and enjoyed the confidence of his fellow-townsmen, and of the General Court of Connecticut, for a long series of years. He was often a representative, selectman, and commissioner; and in 1664, was appointed by the colonial legislature, (in connection with Messrs. Minor and and Stanton,) "to determine cases to the value of forty shillings, to grant summons according to law, to summon men to appear before him or before any court in the colony, to marry persons, and to punish for criminal matters to the value of forty shillings, or the stocks." He died, June 9, 1667. He had five sons, viz.: Nathaniel, Samuel, Elihu, Elisha, and Joseph. The two first named were born in Boston, Lincolnshire, England. Miss Caulkins informs us that Mr. Chesebrough, and all his sons were buried on the banks of the Wicketequack Creek, which flowed past their lonely residence.

Cheever, Ezekiel, "the Father of Connecticut Schoolmasters, and the Pioneer and Patriarch of classical culture in New England," was born in London on the 25th of January, 1614. He came to this country in June, 1637, landing at Boston, but proceeding in the same year with Theophilus Eaton and others to Quinnipiac, where he assisted in planting the colony and church of New Haven, his name appearing in the "Plantation Covenant," signed in "Mr. Newman's barn," on 4th of June, 1639, among the principal men of the colony. In 1646, he was elected a Deputy to the General Court, and there is reason to believe he was deacon of the Church from 1644 to 1650. In 1638, within the first year of the settlement of the town, he commenced his career as a schoolmaster in a Free or Grammar School, which he continued at New Haven till December, 1650, when he removed to Massachusetts, pursuing his vocation at Ipswich till November, 1661, at Charlestown till 1670, and at Boston in the Latin School till his death, on the 21st of August 1708, at the advanced age of 94 years—"venerable," says Gov. Hutchinson, "not only for his great age, but for having been the teacher of most of the principal men of Boston," and he might have added of other sections of New England. For further particulars see Barnard's *Life of Ezekiel Cheever*, with Notes on the early Free School of New England.

Clap, Rev. Thomas, President of Yale College, was born in Scituate, Mass., in 1703; graduated at Harvard College in 1722; was ordained as pastor of the church in Windham in 1726, where he continued for fourteen years. In 1740, he was chosen President of Yale College to succeed Mr. Williams, who resigned his place the preceding year. He was one of the most learned theologians of the new world, a rigid Calvinist in doctrine, and a firm adherent to the discipline and mode of church government then prevalent in New England. Regarding Whitefield and his itinerant followers as innovators and schismatics, he bore open testimony against them from the pulpit, and wrote several pamphlets on the subject. He afterwards published a book which he styled "A Defense of the New England Churches against the Arminians, who are spreading their doctrines over Connecticut." In 1752, he drew up the scheme of the "new divinity," as he termed it—in which he sums up the errors of several theological writers, controverts them with great ability, and then proceeds to expound the Calvinistic view of original sin, special grace, regeneration, and justification by faith. By the general association of ministers in 1755, this book was cordially approved and recommended. He published an Essay on the Nature and foundation of Moral virtue and obligation, in 1765; a History of Yale College, in 1766; conjectures upon the nature and motion of meteors which are above the atmosphere, in 1781; and several letters and sermons. President Clap constructed the first orrery, or planetarium, made in America; and had collected a mass of materials for a history of Connecticut, which were plundered or destroyed, with his other papers, in the expedition against New Haven under General Tryon. He resigned the office of President in 1766, and died January 7, 1767, aged 63.

Collins, Rev. Nathaniel, was born in Cambridge, Mass., and graduated at the college in that place in 1660. He pursued the study of theology, was ordained as pastor of the church in Middletown, and died December 28th, 1684. He united in his character all the qualities of exemplary piety, extraordinary ingenuity and obliging affability, and was a very excellent preacher. Cotton Mather, in his "Magnalia," says in reference to him—"There were more wounds given to Connecticut by his death, than Cæsar received in the Senate-house."

Cutler, Rev. Timothy, D.D., Rector of Yale College, was a son of Maj. John Cutler, of Charlestown, Mass., graduated at Harvard College in 1701, and was ordained January 11th, 1709, as minister of Stratford, where he remained ten years. He was the most celebrated preacher in the colony, and was highly esteemed for his learning. In 1719, he succeeded Mr. Pierson in the office of President of Yale College, and presided over that institution with dignity and reputation for about three years, when he conformed to the Episcopal Church. This defection from the established religion of the colony created much surprise and alarm. His high position, his wide spread reputation for talents, eloquence, and profound scholarship, and, above all, his acknowledged piety and zeal in the cause of his Divine Master, led the Congregational clergy to apprehend that serious consequences might follow to the denomination whose prosperity they had so much at heart. The trustees of the college passed a vote "excusing him from farther service" in his official capacity, and requiring of future rectors satisfactory evidence of the "soundness of their faith in opposition to Arminian and prelatical corruptions." He sailed for England with Mr. Johnson in November 1722, where he took orders, first as a deacon, and then as a priest. The University of Oxford conferred upon him the degree of doctor of divinity. Toward the close of the year 1723, he became rector of Christ Church, in Boston, where he continued until his death, August 17th, 1765, aged 82. Eliot describes him as haughty and overbearing in his manners; while others represent him as dignified and stately in his intercourse with strangers, but courteous and cordial to those who enjoyed his acquaintance or friendship. He spoke Latin with fluency, and Allen assures us that he was one of the best oriental scholars ever educated in this country.

Daggett, Rev. Napthali, D.D., President of Yale College, was a native of Attleborough, Mass., and a graduate of Yale in the class of 1748. He was first settled in the ministry at Smithtown, Long Island, whence he removed to New Haven in 1756, to fulfil the duties of his appointment as professor of divinity in the college, an office which he held during the remainder of his life. In connection with his professorship, he officiated as president from 1766 to April 1777, when he was succeeded in the latter office by Dr. Stiles. He died November 25th, 1780. He was a good classical scholar, and a sound divine. Dr. Wales was appointed his successor in the professorship.

DAVENPORT, REV. JOHN, the first pastor in New Haven, and afterwards minister of the first church in Boston, was born in Coventry, England, in 1597. We are told by Eliot that at the age of fourteen he was a student of Brazen Nose College, Oxford, where he received the degree of B. A., and though but a youth immediately began to preach, and at length became minister of St. Stephen's church, in Coleman street, London. He preached constantly in that city during the plague, and continued to visit his flock regularly when the pestilence was at its height. He subsequently received the degrees of master of arts and bachelor of divinity. About the year 1626, Mr. Davenport united with Dr. Sibs, Dr. Gouge, and several laymen, among whom was the lord mayor of London, in a plan devised to make a purchase of impropriations, and with the profits of the same to maintain a number of ministers who would assist in reforming abuses. Archbishop Laud condemned the proceeding as favoring non-conformity, and the money was confiscated to the king's use. Toward the close of the year 1633, he had become so much of a non-conformist, that his connection with the establishment was merely nominal, and he resigned his pastoral charge in Coleman street and retired to Holland that he might enjoy that liberty of conscience which he so much desired. In Amsterdam he was invited to become the colleague of the venerable Mr. Paget, pastor of the English church there, but as he differed with the Dutch divine, relative to the baptism of the children of unbelievers, he was, at the end of two years, compelled to desist from the public ministry, and returned to England. A letter from Mr. Cotton, induced him to embark for Boston, in New England, where he arrived June 26, 1637, in company with Mr. Eaton and Mr. Hopkins. In the following spring, he sailed with his company to Quinnipiack, or New Haven, and on the 18th of April preached the first Christian sermon ever heard in that then wilderness. He remained as pastor of the church in New Haven for a period of thirty years, and exerted an almost unbounded influence in the civil as well as ecclesiastical affairs of the colony. So high was his reputation as a preacher and theologian, that he was invited to become a member of the famous Westminster Assembly of Divines. For his humanity in harboring the Regicides, he was threatened with the vengeance of the crown. Disappointed and chagrined at what he deemed the annihilation of his little republic, by the union with Connecticut, he left New Haven in 1667, and succeeded Mr. Morton as pastor of the first church in Boston. He died of apoplexy, March 15, 1670, aged 72 years. Mr. Davenport published a Sermon on 2 Samuel i. 18, in 1629; a Letter to the Dutch Classes, directed "against the tyrannical government and corrupt doctrines of Mr. John Paget," in 1634; several pamphlets of a controversial character; a discourse about Civil Government in a new Plantation, whose design is Religion; The Saint's Anchor Hold; Demonstration of Jesus Christ to be the True Messiah; Election Sermon, in 1669; a Treatise on the Power of Congregational Churches; The Knowledge of Christ, wherein the Types, Prophecies, &c.,

are opened; God's call to his People to turn unto Him, in two fast-day sermons, 1670; and other sermons and pamphlets.

DAY, THOMAS, LL.D., the third son of Rev. Jeremiah Day, was born in New Preston Society, town of Washington, Conn., July 6th, 1777. He was a descendant, in the sixth generation, from Robert Day, who came to America among the first settlers in Massachusetts, and joined the company of one hundred persons, who, in 1638, under the lead of Rev. Thomas Hooker, first settled the town of Hartford, Conn.

Thomas Day graduated at Yale, in 1797, read law with Judge Reeve, at Litchfield, and afterwards with Judge Dewey, of the Supreme Court of Massachusetts, at Williamstown, where Mr. Day was a tutor in Williams College. In September, 1799, Mr. Day came to Hartford, read law with Theodore Dwight, Esq., was admitted to the bar in December 1799, and immediately entered on the practice of law in Hartford, where he continued to reside. In October, 1809, he was appointed Assistant Secretary of State, (George Wyllys being the Principal Secretary) and in 1810 he was elected Secretary of State by the people, and so continued for twenty-five successive years, by annual re-election, until May, 1835.

In May, 1815, he was appointed Associate Judge of the County Court, for the County of Hartford, and annually afterwards, except one year, until May 1825, in which year he was made Chief Judge of that Court, and was continued in that office by successive annual appointments, until June, 1833.

In 1818, as one of the senior aldermen of the city of Hartford, he became one of the Judges of the City Court, and continued such by successive annual elections, until March, 1831.

He was one of the Committee who prepared the Statutes of 1808, and by him the notes were compiled, the index made, and the introduction written. He was also one of the Committee who prepared the Statutes of 1821 and 1824.

In 1805 he commenced regularly reporting the Decisions of the Supreme Court of Errors; but he took notes of cases in the latter half of the 18th century, and his reports cover a period ranging through more than half a century. At the June Term, 1853, he declined a re-appointment, and the Supreme Court of Errors were pleased to express their high respect for his eminent services and exalted character, and to thank him for his advancement of juridical science, through his numerous reports, and other legal productions, and for his uniform kindness and courtesy in all his intercourse with the bench and the bar. He edited several English law works, in all about forty volumes, in which he introduced notices of American decisions, and made other improvements.

He was one of the Commissioners to distribute the stock, at the formation of the Phœnix Bank, and remained closely connected with that institution, as stockholder and director to the day of his death. He was for many years one of the Trustees of the Hartford Grammar School, of the Hartford Female Seminary, of the American Asylum for the Deaf and Dumb, and of the Retreat for the Insane. He was Director of the Connecticut Bible Society: President of the Hartford County Missionary Society, auxiliary to the Am. B. C. F. M.; President of the Connecticut Branch of the American Education Society;

President of the Goodrich Association, &c. He was an original member of the Connecticut Historical Society, and aided in its organization, in 1825, being at that time its Recording Secretary. On the revival of the Society in 1839, he became its President, and so continued till within a few months of his death. He was a liberal contributor to the funds of the Wadsworth Atheneum. and its first President.

Mr. Day was married on the 18th of March, 1813, to Sarah Coit, daughter of Wheeler Coit, of Preston, (now Griswold), who was a grandson of the Rev. Joseph Coit, of Plainfield, one of the first class that graduated at Yale College.

The Corporation of Yale College, in 1847, conferred on Judge Day, the honorary degree of LL. D.

It is not known that he ever made or left an enemy. He died at Hartford, 1st March, 1855.

The Superior Court held by Hon. Wm. W. Ellsworth, being in session, at the time of Judge Day's death, the members of the Hartford Bar, convened, and the Hon. Martin Welles, by request of the bar, moved the court to direct a complimentary resolution to be entered on the Records, and after speaking in high terms of Mr. Day's skill as a Reporter, grasping the precise point decided, and presenting that point clearly; as a Judge, upright, impartial, and fearless in the administration of justice; as a lawyer learned and accurate; he says:

Of him as a man, it is unnecessary for me to speak. Here in this city, where he resided so long, and discharged so many important public trusts; he was known and read of all men, and by all approved.

His has been a favored lot. Spared the exhausting and wearing contests which attend the active duties of the profession, he stood by, a calm intelligent spectator of the conflict, recording the result.

While others have been assailed in the ferocity of party spirit, or wounded by the shafts of calumny, he has passed smoothly on, "by gentle wings upborne."

Enjoying the consolations of friendship, and possessing an easy fortune and an extensive reputation, blest with all that is valuable in possession for earth, and all that is cheering in prospect for heaven, he has been kindly—calmly brought to the "consistent close of a consistent life,"—"content to live, yet not afraid to die."

And when the appointed hour came, he left us: to use the words of the just and beautiful eulogium of Dr. Hawes, at his funeral, as "one who had passed through life—without a cloud upon his sun, or a spot upon his character."

I move that these Resolutions now presented, be entered upon the Records of this Court.

Judge Ellsworth said—

"Gentlemen of the Bar:—I most cheerfully grant the motion. It is wholly unnecessary to say that I most heartily concur in the sentiments of these resolutions. They express nothing too much in eulogy of that respected man, whom we all reverenced—in whom we all placed the most unbounded confidence. His abilities and his judicial knowledge, were of the highest order. When I came into active life in this county, in 1813, there was already no superior guide, no one whom I could more freely and safely consult in relation to any question before the Court. He would have done honor to any judicial station that could have been assigned him in the State."

DENTON, REV. RICHARD, the first minister of Stamford, had been a minister in Halifax, Yorkshire, and came to New England previous to 1635. He was among the first settlers of Wethersfield, and occasionally exercised the duties of his profession while there. He removed with part of the church to Rippowams, (Stamford,) in 1641, where he remained for a few years in the pastoral office, and then, in connection with some of the principal men of that plantation, again removed, and commenced the town of Hampstead, on Long Island. He was the minister of that place until the year 1658. Cotton Mather, in his Magnalia, thus speaks of Mr. Denton—"First at Wethersfield, and then at Stamford, his doctrines dropped as the rain, his speech distilled as the dew, as the small rain upon the tender herb, as the showers upon the grass. Though he was a little man, yet he had a great soul; his well accomplished mind in his lesser body was an Iliad in a nut-shell. I think he was blind of an eye; nevertheless he was not the least among the *seers* of our Israel; he saw a very considerable portion of those things 'which eye hath not seen.' He was far from cloudy in his conceptions and principles of divinity; whereof he wrote a system entitled '*Soliliquia Sacra,*' so accurately considering the fourfold state of man—1st, in his Created Purity; 2d, Contracted Deformity; 3d, Restored Beauty; and 4th, Celestial Glory—that judicious persons who have seen it, very much lament the churches being so much deprived of it. At length he got beyond clouds, and so beyond storms; waiting the return of the Lord Jesus Christ, in the clouds of heaven, when he will have his reward among the saints."

It has generally been stated that Mr. Denton died in Hampstead. This is a mistake. He returned to England in 1658, and spent the remainder of his life in Essex. His epitaph is in Latin, of which the following is a free translation:

"Here sleeps the dust of RICHARD DENTON:
Over his low peaceful grave bends
The perennial cypress, fit emblem
Of his unfading fame.
On Earth—His bright example, religious light,
Shone forth over multitudes,
In Heaven—His pure-robed spirit shines
Like an effulgent star."

EATON, THEOPHILUS, first governor of the colony of New Haven, was born at Stony Stratford, in Oxfordshire, England, his father being at that time rector of the church there, but subsequently became the minister at Coventry. An intimacy was thus early formed between young Eaton and John Davenport, the father of the latter being mayor of the city—an intimacy which was never interrupted until they were separated by death. Eaton became a merchant, and his friend studied divinity. Says Eliot—"The one was diligent, and grew rich, and the other made a shining figure in his profession. This friendship, which began in the old country, was increased by the circumstances which led them both over to the American wilderness." Though he had been a patentee of Massachusetts, he determined, on reaching Boston, to assist in founding a distinct colony; and accordingly he accompanied Mr. Davenport in his first expedition to New Haven, where he remained until his death in 1657. For nineteen successive years he was chosen governor of the colony, and was honored and esteemed as an upright magistrate, a courteous and benevolent citizen, and as a practical christian. He was, perhaps, the wealthiest and most eminent personage that had then become a citizen of the new world. Aside from his success as a merchant, he had been governor of the East Land Company, and Ambassador from the King of England to the Court of Denmark. The arrival of such a man, with a determination of becoming a permanent resident in these western wilds, was hailed with gratitude by the people. The government of Massachusetts, desirous of retaining him and his company within their jurisdiction, immediately appointed him a magistrate. The various towns in the vicinty of Boston made them liberal offers of land as an inducement for them to settle there. But, as has been stated, he preferred to unite his fortunes with those of his friend Davenport. Though he had been reared in affluence, and was a favorite with the king, he endured with fortitude and dignity the perils and privations incident to the life of a pioneer. Whatever may be thought of the basis on which that colony was established, all historians agree in commending the wisdom and integrity of his administration.

Edwards, Rev. Timothy, first minister of East Windsor, was a son of Richard Edwards, a worthy merchant of Hartford, who was the only child of William Edwards, a first settler of the latter place. He graduated at Harvard College in 1691, and was ordained at East Windsor in May, 1694. After a ministry of sixty-three years, he died January 27, 1758, aged 88 years. The Rev. Joseph Perry was his colleague for the three years preceding his death. Mr. Edwards married a daughter of the Rev. Solomon Stoddard, of Northampton, and lived to see his son, Jonathan Edwards, the most distinguished divine in America. He was a faithful and successful preacher, and was universally esteemed by his cotemporaries for his exemplary life and genial manners. He published an Election Sermon in 1732.

Eliot, Rev. Jared, pastor of the church in Killingworth, was a son of the Rev. Joseph Eliot, of Guilford, and a grandson of the Rev. John Eliot, who was styled "the apostle to the Indians." He was born November 7, 1685; graduated at Yale College in 1706; was ordained October 26, 1709; and died April 22, 1763, aged 78. Like many other pastors of his day, he was a practitioner of medicine; and such was his fame in the treatment of chronic complaints, that he was sometimes called to Newport and Boston, and was more extensively consulted than any other physician in New England. Allen says of him—"Maniacs were managed by him with great skill. In the multitude of his pursuits his judgment seemed to be unfailing. His farms in different parts of the colony were well managed. Living on the main road from Boston to New York, he was visited by many gentlemen of distinction. Dr. Franklin always called upon him, when journeying to his native town." He was a skillful botanist at well as a scientific and practical agriculturalist. The white mulberry tree was introduced by him into Connecticut. He published a volume of "agricultural essays," which passed through several editions; also, Religion supported by Reason and Revelation, 1735; Election Sermon, 1738; Sermon on the taking of Louisbourg, 1745. Notwithstanding his labors in so many departments of usefulness, he did not neglect his duties as a minister of the gospel; and, for a period of forty years, preached *every Sabbath.*

FENWICK, COL. GEORGE, a native of England, became a joint proprietor of Saybrook, and the country adjacent thereto, in 1636, and erected a fort there. He went back to England; but came again to this country in 1639, bringing his family with him. As the agent of Lord Say and Seal, who claimed the territory by grant from Robert Earl of Warwick, he commenced the settlement at the mouth of the Connecticut river, and made extensive preparations for the reception of several gentlemen of wealth and distinction whom he expected would join with him in the establishment of a new colony. Being disappointed by their non-arrival, and saddened by the death of his wife, he sold out his rights to the Connecticut government in 1644, and returned to England, where he was chosen a member of parliament. He died in 1657.

FITCH, COL. ELEAZER, son of Joseph and grandson of the Rev. James Fitch, was born in Lebanon, August 29, 1726, and entered the public service at an early age as an officer in the French and Indian wars. He rose to the rank of colonel, and was particularly distinguished in the war with the French in Canada, gaining the love and admiration of his fellow-officers and soldiers, by his patriotic and honorable conduct and his noble bearing. He was an accomplished and remarkable man, and was very popular not only as an officer but as a citizen and neighbor. Unfortunately for his fame, he sided with the British in the Revolution, and of course lost his influence with his countrymen, and was persecuted, abused, and imprisoned. After the war, he received a grant of land in Canada, whither he went, and died there.

FITCH, REV. JAMES, first minister in Saybrook, and Norwich, was born in the county of Essex, England, December 24, 1622, and came to New England in 1638, at the age of 16 years. Though he had progressed far in his studies in England, he spent seven years under the instruction of Mr. Hooker and Mr. Stone in Hartford. In 1646, he was ordained at Saybrook, where he remained fourteen years, and then removed with a greater part of his church to Norwich. In his old age, he went to reside with his children at Lebanon, where he died November 18, 1702, aged 79. He was distinguished for the penetration of his mind, the energy of his preaching, and the sanctity of his life. He made himself perfectly familiar with the Mohegan language, and preached with success to the Indians in the vicinity of Norwich. To encourage them to abandon their savage life, he gave them land and taught them the arts of husbandry. The first wife of Mr. Fitch was Abigail Whitfield, daughter of the Rev. Henry Whitfield, of Guilford; his second wife was Priscilla, daughter of Major John Mason. He left a large family. His brother Thomas of Norwalk was the father of Governor Fitch.

FITCH, SAMUEL, brother of Colonel Eleazer Fitch, was born in 1723, graduated at Yale College in 1742, and settled as a lawyer in Boston. He was a very eminent man, and rose to the rank of Attorney-General of Massachusetts. In the contest which resulted in the revolutionary struggle, he sided with the mother country; and during the war he went to England to reside, where he died in 1784. He received the honorary degree of Master of Arts at Harvard College in 1766. Mr. Fitch married Elizabeth Lloyd, of Boston, and had three children, viz., William, Sally, and Ann. The daughters were pensioned by the British Government. Colonel Trumbull saw them in London, and described them as very beautiful and accomplished ladies. The son, William Fitch, was a colonel in the British Army, and was massacred by his own troops in the West Indies.

Gilbert, Matthew, an early and distinguished citizen of New Haven, accompanied Messrs. Eaton and Davenport, in their expedition to that place in 1638, and was constituted one of the "seven pillars" of the first church organized there. In October, 1639, he was chosen one of the magistrates of the colony, and continued to be reëlected until he was promoted to the office of deputy governor. Soon after the union of New Haven colony with Connecticut, by the charter of 1662, Mr. Gilbert was invested by the General Court "with magistratical powers to assist in the government of these plantations, and the people thereof, according to the laws of this corporation." In April, 1665, he was for the first time nominated as an assistant, or member of the upper house of the Connecticut legislature, but appears not to have been elected to that office by the people until 1677. He was a Commissioner of the United Colonies; and in May, 1673, he was one of the Committee appointed to define and establish the bounds of New Haven.

Goodyear, Stephen, an early magistrate of New Haven colony, and one of its wealthiest and most enterprising citizens, became a resident there in 1637. He was chosen deputy governor in 1641, and continued to hold the office until 1650. In 1653, he united with others in the purchase of a large tract of land on the Housatonic River, at a place called Paugasset, (now Derby). His wife embarked for England on board Mr. Lamberton's ship, in January, 1647, and was never heard of afterwards. Governor Goodyear died in London, in 1657.

Goodwin, William, was admitted a freeman at Cambridge, Massachusetts, in 1632; and was a representative from that town in the first General Court of Massachusetts. In 1636, he was associated with the Rev. Samuel Stone, in effecting the purchase of Hartford, (then known by the aboriginal name of Suckiage,) of Sunkquasson, the Indian sachem and proprietor of the soil. He was one of the wealthiest and most prominent men in the colony, and was long the ruling elder of the church in Hartford. In 1638, he was on the committee appointed by the General Court to negotiate a treaty of peace and amity with Sowheag, the Chief Sachem at Wethersfield. At the October session of the following year, the legislature of the colony designated him, in connection with Deputy Governor Ludlow, Capt. Mason, and others, to gather up "those passages of God's Providence which have been remarkable since the first undertakings of these plantations," and deliver them to the General Court, in April next ensuing, that they might be recorded. He was one of the executors of the Will of Governor Hopkins, who died in London in 1657, bequeathing large sums of money to purposes of education in New England. Elder Goodwin remained in Hartford until the celebrated controversy between him and Mr. Stone, in 1658, when he removed to Hadley, and was chosen ruling elder in the church there. He was subsequently a principal proprietor of Farmington, Connecticut, where he died in 1673. His wife, Susannah, died in 1676. He left but one child, Elizabeth, who married John Crow, of Hartford.

Graham, Rev. John, first minister of Southbury, a descendant of the Duke of Montrose, was born in Edinburgh, Scotland, in 1694, and graduated at Glasgow.

He came to America about the year 1725, and was settled at Southbury in 1733, where he died in 1773, aged 79 years. He was an eloquent preacher, and was much beloved as a pastor. Three of his sons were graduates and clergymen, and two others were physicians. His daughter, Love, married the Rev. Jonathan Lee, of Salisbury. Mr. Graham, in 1732, wrote a ballad against the church of England in Connecticut. He also published a tract on the same subject, and a rejoinder to Johnson's answer.

HAMLIN, GILES, was born in England in 1612, and was one of the early settlers and principal proprietors of Middletown. He was long engaged in foreign commerce, "partly by himself and partly with John Pyncheon, of Springfield, his brother-in-law John Crow, Jr., who dwelt in Fairfield, and elder Goodwin, of Hartford, afterwards of Farmington." Though we are informed by his epitaph that he was "near fifty years crossing the ocean wide," he was often honored by his fellow-townsmen. He was occasionally a commissioner of the United Colonies, was a representative at twenty-two sessions of the legislature, and from 1685 until his death he was a member of the Upper House. He died in 1689. The family retained a remarkable degree of influence in the town for a period of more than an hundred years. John Hamlin, a son of Giles Hamlin, was a representative at seven sessions and an assistant or member of the Upper House for thirty-six years. Col. Jabez Hamlin, son of John Hamlin, graduated at Yale College, and settled as a lawyer in his native town, where he died in 1791. He was a justice of the peace for about fifty years, a judge of the county court for nearly forty years, a representative at forty-three semi-annual sessions, and was repeatedly speaker of the House. He was a member of the Council of Safety in the Revolution; was judge of the court of probate for thirty-seven years, and mayor of the city of Middletown, from 1784, until his death. In this country, honors are not hereditary; and it is seldom indeed that three such men are found thus succeeding each other, in a single family. Jabez Hamlin, (a son of Col. Jabez Hamlin, graduated at Yale College in 1769, was a captain in the Revolutionary army, and died in the service of his country in September, 1776, aged 24 years. He was a young man of much promise, and was confidently looked to as one who, by his talents, acquirements, and ambition, seemed destined to succeed to all the honors of the family.

HEWETT, REV. EPHRAIM, minister at Windsor, came from England and was settled as colleague with Mr. Wareham in 1639. He was eminent for talents and usefulness, and was highly esteemed by his people and by his cotemporaries in the ministry. In 1643 he published, in a quarto form, "The Prophecy of Daniel explained." He died September 4, 1644, leaving a widow and four daughters, with a large estate.

HOOKE, REV. WILLIAM, minister at New Haven, had been a preacher at Taunton, England. In 1644, he was settled at New Haven as the colleague of Davenport, where he remained about twelve years. He returned to England in 1656, and was chaplain to Cromwell; and died March 21, 1677, aged 76. He published, among other works, "New England's tears for Old England's fears," a fast sermon at Taunton, July 23, 1640.

HOOKER, REV. THOMAS, one of the founders of the colony of Connecticut, was born in Leicestershire, England, in 1586, and was educated at Emanuel College, Cambridge, of which he was elected a fellow. After preaching for some time in London, he was chosen lecturer and assistant to Mr. Mitchell, at Chelmsford, in 1626. Though an eloquent and powerful expositor of the divine word, he was soon silenced for non-conformity, and became a teacher, having for his usher, John Eliot, who came to America and was a missionary among the Indians. As he was still harassed by the spiritual court, in 1630 Mr. Hooker went over to Holland, where he was an assistant to Dr. Ames, preaching sometimes at Rotterdam and sometimes at Delft. He arrived in Boston, September 4, 1633, in the Griffin—Governor Haynes, Mr. Cotton and Mr. Stone being among his fellow-passengers; and during the following month was ordained pastor of the church at Newtown, now Cambridge. In June, 1636, he made his famous journey through the wilderness to the Connecticut river, accompanied by his church and congregation, where he assisted in founding the settlement at Hartford. In this place he remained until his death—July 7, 1647, aged 61. He was one of the most eloquent men of the age in which he lived. Says Allen—"With a loud voice, an expressive countenance, and a most commanding presence, he delivered the truths of God with a zeal and energy seldom equalled. He appeared with such majesty in the pulpit, that it was pleasantly said of him, 'he could put a king in his pocket.' He has been called the Luther, and Mr. Cotton the Melancthon of New England." He preached without notes, and with remarkable fervency and fluency. Yet on one occasion, when preaching at Boston in the presence of Governor Winthrop, after proceeding for about fifteen minutes with his usual power of utterance and felicity of thought, he suddenly came to a pause and could think of nothing more to say. After several ineffectual attempts to proceed, he remarked that what he had intended to say was taken from him, and desired that a psalm might be sung. He withdrew for half an hour, and then resuming his discourse he proceeded for two hours in a strain remarkable for its pertinacity and eloquence. After the service, he remarked to his friends—"We daily confess that we can do nothing without Christ, and what if Christ should prove this to be the fact before the whole congregation?" He was noted for his benevolence, freely bestowing upon benevolent objects a large part of his income. On one occasion, when there was great scarcity of provisions at Southampton, on Long Island, he and a few friends fitted out a vessel loaded with corn and sent it to them. One day in every month he devoted to private prayer and fasting. A memoir of him in Dr. Mather's Magnalia, stiles him "the light of the western churches." The publications of Mr. Hooker are numerous. His most celebrated work, "A Survey of the Sum of Church Discipline," was published in London, in quarto form, in 1648. About one hundred of his discourses, which were transcribed by Mr. John Higginson, were published in London. Some of them have since gone through several editions.

Jarvis, Rt. Rev. Abraham, D.D., the second bishop of the Protestant Episcopal Church of Connecticut, was born in Norwalk, May 5, 1739, and graduated at Yale College in 1761. In November 1763, he sailed for England, where he was ordained deacon by the Bishop of Exeter, and priest by the Bishop of Carlisle. On his return, he became rector of Christ Church, Middletown, in the autumn of 1764; and was consecrated bishop in 1797, as the successor of Bishop Seabury. In 1799, Bishop Jarvis removed from Middletown to Cheshire; and from thence to New Haven in 1803. He died May 3, 1813, aged 73. He published a sermon on the death of Bishop Seabury, and another on the Witness of the Spirit. "The principal characteristics of Bishop Jarvis," says Dr. Blake, "were integrity and sincerity of purpose, and firmness and inflexibility of conduct." He received the degree of doctor of divinity from Bishop Seabury, who claimed the right to confer degrees in divinity as inherent in the episcopal office. The same honor was subsequently bestowed upon him by Yale College.

Johnson, Rev. Samuel, D.D., President of King's (now Columbia) College, was born in Guilford, October 14, 1696. Though I have given a somewhat extended sketch of him in the body of this work, there are some additional facts in his life which deserve a place here. As the "father of Episcopacy in Connecticut," he exerted an important influence upon the history of the colony during his life—an influence which did not die when he left the earth, but which has been diffusing and strengthening itself until the present time. As a student and tutor in college, as a preacher of the gospel, and finally as president of one of the oldest and most respectable institutions of learning in America, he fully sustained his reputation for profound learning, unwearied industry, superior talents and devoted piety. Having visited England and received Episcopal ordination as missionary at Stratford, in 1722, he devoted himself earnestly to the doctrines and forms of worship of the denomination with which he was connected. After the removal of his friend and predecessor, Mr. Pigot, to Rhode Island, he was the only Episcopal minister in Connecticut, and there were but few families in the colony that sympathized with him in his efforts. He was regarded as an innovator and as a disturber of that peace and unity that had so long prevailed among the established churches of New England. Amidst much opposition, he continued his missionary labors, and had the satisfaction in due time of knowing that his sacrifices had not been made in vain. According to Mr. Hobart, divers petty quarrels among the members of the Congregational churches in the vicinity, and the desire of some to escape the payment of their ecclesiastical taxes by joining a church whose minister received a salary from a foreign society, at first contributed not a little to swell the number of his congregation. Gradually, however, a class of intelligent, conscientious and zealous christians joined his communion, and his church became large and prosperous. Mr. Johnson was remarkable for the kindness and urbanity of his disposition, and the cheerfulness of his piety. Though he was often engaged in controversy with the clergy of his day, he never lost his temper or degraded himself by a resort to personalities. He was loved by his people and respected by all. In addition to the works referred to in the sketch of Mr. Johnson heretofore given, he published "Plain Reasons for conforming to the church;" two tracts in the controversy with Mr. Graham; a Letter from Aristocles to Authades; a defense of it in a letter to Mr. Dickinson; a demonstration of the reasonableness of prayer; a sermon on the beauties of holiness in the worship of the church of England; a short vindication of the society for the propagating of the gospel. He died in Stratford, January 6, 1772, aged 75. Mr. Leaming preached his funeral sermon, and Mr. Beach printed a discourse in which he attempted to do him justice. His son, the Hon. William Samuel Johnson, LL. D., was one of his successors as president of Columbia College.

JONES, WILLIAM, of New Haven, was a son of Colonel John Jones, one of the judges of Charles I., and was born, A. D., 1624. He was a magistrate and deputy governor of New Haven colony; and, after the union, was an assistant of Connecticut for *thirty-three years.* He died October 17, 1706, aged 82 years. Mrs. Hannah Jones, his widow, (a daughter of Governor Eaton,) died May 4, 1707, aged 74.

LEAMING, REV. JEREMIAH, D. D., a distinguished Episcopal minister, was born at Middletown in 1719, and graduated at Yale College in 1745. He was settled in the ministry in Newport, R. I., eight years, at Norwalk twenty-one years, and at Stratford eight years. He wrote and preached with great ability, and published several works of acknowledged merit—among which were, A Defense of the Episcopal Government of the Church, with remarks on some noted sermons on Presbyterian ordination, 1766; a Second Defense of the Episcopal Government of the Church, in answer to Rev. Noah Welles, 1770; Evidences of the Truth of Christianity, 1785; dissertations on various subjects, 1789.

LYMAN, GENERAL PHINEAS, was born in Durham in 1716; graduated at Yale College in 1738, and settled in Suffield as a lawyer, after having served as a college tutor for three years. He was chosen a representative for several years, and from 1752 to 1759 he was an assistant or member of the Upper House of the Connecticut Legislature. In 1755, he received from the General Assembly the appointment of major-general and commander-in-chief of the Connecticut forces in the northern expedition. When Sir William Johnson was wounded in the battle of Lake George, the entire command devolved on him; and for five hours, in the thickest of the fight, and in front of the breastwork, he issued his orders with wisdom and coolness. But Johnson, who was anxious for all the glory of the achievement, made no mention of General Lyman in his official account of the battle. It was for the victory achieved on this occasion that Johnson was knighted, and received from parliament 5,000*l.* In 1758 he served with Abercrombie and Howe, and was with the latter when he was slain. He was also with Amherst at the capture of Crown Point, and at the surrender of Montreal. In 1762 General Lyman commanded the provincial troops in the expedition against Havanna, and acquired a high reputation for his skill and courage. A company called "Military Adventurers," under the authority of Connecticut, had purchased of the Six Nations of Indians a large tract of land on the Susquehannah river. As the government of Pennsylvania claimed the same tract, General Lyman was sent to England in 1763, to obtain from the king a confirmation of the company's purchase. Another object of the company and their agent is stated by Dr. Dwight to have been, to obtain lands on the Mississippi and the Yazoo. Being deluded by idle promises, he remained in England for eleven years, until his mind sank down into imbecility. His second son went over in 1774 to solicit his return—a tract having about that time been granted to the petitioners. Soon after his arrival in this country, he embarked with his eldest son for the Mississippi. Both died soon after their arrival in West Florida in 1775. Mrs. Lyman, and all her family, except her eldest surviving son, accompanied by her only brother, Colonel Dwight, and others, proceeded to the vicinity of Natchez, in 1776, with a view of settling upon the lands purchased by her husband; but in a short time Mrs. Lyman, her two daughters, and Colonel Dwight, died; and the Spanish war completely broke up the settlement. The four sons of General Lyman joined the British in the Revolution.

MARSH, JOHN, was born in Hartford, in 1668, where he passed the principal part of his life. Through a long series of years he enjoyed, in a remarkable degree, the respect and confidence of his fellow-citizens. He was a representative from Hartford at about forty sessions of the General Assembly of the colony, and was an acting magistrate up to the date of his death. Being a man of wealth, he united with John Buel and others, in 1719, in the purchase of the township of Litchfield, then called Bantam, to which place he subsequently removed, though he remained there but a few years. While a resident of Litchfield, he was town clerk and selectman. Returning to Hartford, he died there in 1744, aged 76 years. His sons Ebenezer, William, and Isaac, settled in Litchfield. The first named of these, Colonel Ebenezer Marsh, was a representative from Litchfield, at *forty-eight* sessions; judge of the probate court for twenty-five years; and an associate judge of the county court for twenty-one. His descendants are numerous and highly respectable, embracing the names of Skinner, Seymour, Beebe, Pierpont, and other prominent and respectable families.

MASON, MAJOR JOHN, the military leader of our fathers in the early settlement of the colony, was born in England about the year 1600, and was bred to arms in the Netherlands under Sir Thomas Fairfax. His merit as an officer may be judged from the fact that during the civil disturbances in England in Cromwell's time, Fairfax addressed him a letter, requesting him to join his standard and give his assistance to those who were contending for the liberties of the people. Mason was one of the first settlers of Dorchester, Massachusetts, being a member of the company of the Rev. Mr. Wareham, in 1630. In 1635, he became an inhabitant of Windsor, Connecticut. The history of the part he acted in the Pequot War, which took place in 1637, I have given with a sufficient degree of minuteness in the early part of this volume. He was successively the commander-in-chief of the militia of Connecticut, a magistrate from 1642 to 1660, and Deputy Governor of the Colony from the latter date until he retired from public life in 1670. He had removed from Windsor to Saybrook in 1647, and thence to Norwich, where he died in 1672 aged 72 years. Major Mason was in person tall and portly, and in his manners dignified. He was wise and prompt in planning, and energetic in executing; and was equally distinguished for the purity of his morals and for his fearlessness in defending and maintaining the right. At the request of the General Court, he drew up and published a brief history of the Pequot War, which has since been frequently reprinted. An edition, with an introduction and explanatory notes, was published by Thomas Prince in 1736.

MINOR, COLONEL JOSEPH, a son of Captain John, and grandson of Thomas Minor, of Stonington, was born in Stratford, March 4, 1672–3, and accompanied his parents to Woodbury, when a child, where he spent the remainder of his long and useful life. He rose to the rank of colonel in the militia, and was very efficient in preparing men for service in the French and Indian wars. He was a representative from Woodbury, thirty-two sessions, town clerk twenty-eight years, justice of the quorum fourteen years, and judge of the probate court thirty years. He died October 20, 1774, at the advanced age of 102 years.

MINOR THOMAS, an early settler of New London and Stonington, was born in England, April 23, 1608; came to New England in 1630; married Grace, daughter of Walter Palmer, April 23, 1634; and was one of Winthrop's company who settled at Pequot, (now New London,) in 1647. In May, 1649, he was appointed by the General Court, in connection with John Winthrop and Samuel Lathrop, as justices of the court at New London, "to decide all differences among the inhabitants under the value of forty shillings." He was a representative in 1650, and was often reëlected. In 1653, he removed to that part of the plantation called Pawcatuck, (now Stonington,) where he spent the remainder of his days. He was one of the committee appointed in 1663, "to hear the case depending between Uncas and the inhabitants of New London, respecting lands, and to make report to the General Court." At the October session, he was again commissioned as a judge, with power, in addition to those before designated, "to grant summons according to law to any that might desire it, to summon men to appear before him or any court in the colony, to marry persons, and to punish for criminal matters to the value of forty shillings, or by stocks:" and was often afterwards appointed "to keep court at New London," in connection with Mr. Winthrop. During the war with the Dutch, in 1665, the northern colonies are greatly alarmed by the intelligence that De Ruyter, the Dutch Admiral, with a considerable force, was on his way to New England. The legislature of Connecticut appointed a committee, with ample powers, to take such measures as they might deem expedient, for "aid and relief." Of this committee Mr. Minor was a member. The Admiral, however, was diverted from his course, and never reached our coasts. In May, of the same year, Mr. Minor was appointed a commissioner; and was re-appointed for several years. Pawcatuck was long a "disputed territory," being claimed by the government of Rhode Island, as well as by Connecticut. In May, 1670, commissioners were appointed by the two colonies to negotiate a settlement of the question of jurisdiction They met in New London, according to agreement, in June following, but their deliberations resulted in nothing. The Connecticut commissioners then proceeded to Wickford, on the east side of the Pawcatuck river, and there read the King's charter; and, in compliance with the powers vested in them, they proceeded to appoint officers for Wickford and Pawcatuck. For the latter place, they appointed Thomas Minor, Thomas Stanton, and Tobias Saunders, commissioners, "invested with magistratical powers." Massachusetts had also, formerly laid claim to the same tract of country, and made a grant of land there to Harvard College. As that colony had surrendered her claim to jurisdiction, in May, 1674, the General Court of Connecticut, in compliance to an application from officers and friends of the college, confirmed to them certain lands; and appointed Captain Minor, and others, a committee to lay out the same. In October, 1676, Captain Minor was member of the committee appointed to treat with the Pequot, Narragansett, and Mohegan Indians;

and in next session, he was appointed to explore the Narragansett country with a view of ascertaining what localities were fit for plantations, to define and establish the boundaries between the several plantations, and to consult with such gentlemen as might be appointed by the government of Massachusetts on the subject of jurisdiction.

Captain Minor was also an efficient officer in the Indian wars. In February, 1676, when intelligence reached the Council of War, that the enemy were gathering in the Wabaquassett country, he, in conjunction with Captains Avery and Denison, was ordered to enlist as many soldiers as possible, and taking with him the Mohegans and Pequots, march forthwith against the enemy. In March, the council decreed that such soldiers as should go forth under the command of Captains Denison, and Avery, Leiutenant Minor, and Ensign Leffingwell, "shall have all such plunder as they shall sieze, both of persons or corn or other estate." In January, 1677, the council directed that all captives and plunder taken from the enemy, should be first tried and condemned by a court martial. The court marshal established for New London county, consisted of Major Palmes, Captain Avery, Lieutenant Samuel Mason, and Lieutenant Thomas Minor. Captain Minor was a son of Clement Minor, and grandson of William Minor, who died at Chew-Magna, England, February 23, 1585. The first of the name was Henry, who died at Mendippe Hills, Somersetshire, England, in 1359. The name, with armorial bearings, was given him by King Edward, in acknowledgement of his loyal service in providing an escort for his majesty on his way to embark for France. His business was that of a *miner*—hence the name. Captain Minor died in Stonington, October 23, 1690.

Mitchell, Matthew, a principal settler of Stamford, came from Halifax, England, to New England, in 1635, and spent his first winter in Charlestown, Mass. He removed to Saybrook in the summer of 1637, and thence to Wethersfield in the succeeding spring. He was a man of wealth, but suffered a series of losses, until he became comparatively reduced in his circumstances. Two or three times his property was destroyed by fire, the Indians killed his cattle, a shallop that he had sent to the river's mouth was captured and burned by the Pequots, and three men in charge of her, together with his son-in-law, were killed. Dr. Mather says, "The Pequot scourge fell more on this family than on any other in the land." "Afterwards," continues Dr. Mather, "there arose unhappy differences in the place where he lived, wherein he was an antagonist against some of the principal persons in the place ; and hereby *he that had lived in precious esteem with good men wherever he came*, now suffered much in his esteem among many such men, as is usual in such contentions." Mr. Mitchell was a member of the General Court in 1637 and 1638 ; but an influence was subsequently brought to bear against him in that body, so that when he was returned as "Recorder for Wethersfield," in April 1640, he was declared ineligible to the office in consequence of "lying under the censure of the court." He was fined twenty nobles for undertaking the office ; and those who had *voted for him* were fined five pounds. In July of that year, however, the censure of the court was remitted in the case of Mr. Mitchell, in consideration of the "extraordinary charges which he hath formerly borne for public service at the fort." In consequence of these disturbances, he removed to Stamford, where he died in 1645, in the 55th year of his age. He was the father of the Rev. Jonathan Mitchell, who graduated at Harvard College in 1647, succeeded the Rev. Thomas Shepard as pastor of the church in Cambridge in 1650, and died July 9, 1668, aged 42.

MIX, REV. STEPHEN, minister at Wethersfield, was ordained in 1694, and died August 28, 1738, aged 66 years. He was the youngest child of Thomas Mix, of New Haven, and of his wife Rebecca, a daughter of Captain Nathaniel Turner, who was lost at sea in the famous "Phantom Ship." Mr. Mix was born November 1st, 1672, and graduated at Harvard College, in 1690. He was remarkable for his wisdom, piety, and influence.

MULFORD, SAMUEL, son of John Mulford, Esq., a magistrate and commissioner at East Hampton, Long Island, (when that town was under the jurisdiction of Connecticut,) was born at East Hampton in 1645. "He was," says Mr. Hedges, in his centennial address, "attached to the government of Connecticut, and remonstrated against the annexation of the town to New York." For a period of twenty years—from 1700 to 1720—he represented the county in the Provincial Assembly of New York. He was a persevering opponent of the administration of Governor Hunter, watching the abuses of the government with a jealous eye, and no combatant ever maintained his post more unflinchingly than he. In 1716, the Assembly, subservient to the wishes of the governor, ordered a speech of Mr. Mulford's to be put into the hands of the speaker. Mulford thereupon boldly published the speech and circulated it. It denounced the corruption and governmental mismanagement of the finances, and the usurpations in collecting and disbursing the revenue. The governor commenced an oppressive and harassing suit against him in the supreme court, whose judges he himself had appointed. The suit, however, was suspended at the solicitation of the house. He now determined to petition the King in person, for redress. Among other grievances, the towns of East Hampton and Southampton complained bitterly of a duty of one-tenth on all the whale-oil brought into port by their enterprising mariners. Captain Mulford desired to obtain a bounty for the encouragement of the whaling business in place of this tax upon its industry. He crossed the Sound to Newport, walked thence to Boston, and there embarked for England—a self-constituted Envoy to the Court of St. James. He obtained access to the floor of the House of Commons, and was then permitted to read his memorial, which is said to have attracted much attention. The tax on oil was "ordered to be discontinued," and Captain Mulford returned home, triumphant, at the age of 71 years. He again took his seat, in the House of Representatives, and again the old question of his speech was called up. Perhaps his excellency was stung by his bold exposition, in England, of his cupidity and injustice. The compliant House called upon him for his reasons for printing the speech. He gave them, and withdrew. A vote of expulsion was immediately passed; but his constituency, true to themselves, reëlected him as their representative. In 1720, Hunter was succeeded in office by Governor Burnet. But as many of the evils complained of, still continued, the bold denunciations of Captain Mulford again drew down upon him the censure of the government officers. On the 26th of October, of that year, having refused to act with the old Assembly, then convened, on the ground that a new one should have been chosen, he was once more expelled from the House. Thus ended his public life. His advanced age deterred him from further service. He died August 21, 1725, aged 81 years.

Newman, Francis, second governor of New Haven colony, was a native of Great Britain, and one of the earliest settlers of the colony. In 1653, when the commissioners of the united colonies determined to make war upon the Dutch at Manhadoes, Mr. Newman was one of the agents appointed to examine the matters in dispute in a conference with Governor Stuyvesant, and to demand satisfaction. His colleagues were Capt. John Leverett, afterwards governor of Massachusetts, and Mr. William Davis. The Dutch governor avoided the examination, and the agents returned without obtaining the object of their mission. The next year, he was chosen a Commissioner to the New England Congress. Having been Secretary of the colony for several years, during the administration of Governor Eaton, when that gentleman died, in 1657, Mr. Newman was elected his successor. He continued in the office of governor until his death, in 1661.

Noyes, Rev. James, the first minister in Stonington, was a son of a distinguished clergyman of the same name in Newbury, Massachusetts, and was born March 11, 1640. Having graduated at Yale College in 1659, he prepared himself for the ministry and was ordained at Stonington, September 10, 1674. He died in the latter place, December 30, 1719, aged 80. He was a very fervent and zealous preacher, and in his daily walk and conversation breathed the spirit of his Divine Master. He was often consulted in civil affairs; was one of the first Trustees of Yale College; and was esteemed as a skillful physician. His brother, the Rev. Moses Noyes, was the first minister in Lyme, where he died November 10, 1729, aged 85. The Rev. Joseph Noyes, minister at New Haven from 1716 to 1761, was a son of the subject of this paragraph.

Occom, Samson, an Indian Preacher of the Mohegan tribe, was born near Norwich in 1723, and received his education from Mr. Wheelock, at Lebanon. From a roving, wild, and haughty savage, he became a humble christian, and for ten or eleven years was a teacher among the Indians on Long Island. He lived in a house covered with mats, changing his abode twice a year, to be near their planting grounds in summer, and the woods in winter. He was expert with his fish-hook and gun, and became an adept in many of the arts of civilized life. He bound old books for the people of East Hampton, made wooden spoons, cedar pails, churns, and gun-stocks. In August, 1759, he was ordained by the Suffolk Presbytery. In 1766, Mr. Wheelock sent him to England with Mr. Whitaker, the minister at Norwich, to promote the interests of Moor's Indian Charity School. As he was the first Indian preacher who had ever visited England, great curiosity was manifested to hear him, and immense throngs of people, of all classes, flocked to his meetings. Between February 16, 1766, and July 22, 1767, he preached in various parts of the kingdom between three hundred and four hundred sermons. Large contributions were made to the school, which was soon transplanted to Hanover, New Hampshire, and formed the germ of Dartmouth College. He was often employed as a Missionary among different tribes of Indians. In 1786, he removed to Brotherton, near Utica, New York, where the Oneidas gave him a tract of land, and where he died in July 1792, aged 69 years. His funeral was attended by upwards of three hundred Indians. An account of the Montauk Indians, written by Occum, is preserved in the Historical Collections of Massachusetts; and he published a Sermon preached at the execution of Moses Paul, an Indian, at New Haven, September 2, 1772. President Dwight says—"I heard Mr. Occum twice. His discourses, though not proofs of superior talents, were decent, and his utterance in some degree eloquent. His character at times labored under some imputations. Yet there is reason to believe, that most if not all of them, were unfounded; and there is satisfactory evidence that he was a man of piety."

PARSONS, REV. JONATHAN, minister in Lyme, graduated at Yale College in 1729, and soon after began to preach. He was settled in Lyme for several years, but spent the last thirty years of his life in Newburyport, Mass., where he had charge of one of the largest congregations in the country. He was a distinguished and successful preacher and an eminent scholar. His publications were numerous; among them were sixty-six sermons on various subjects in two octavo volumes. He died July 19, 1776, aged 66 years.

PARSONS, GEN. SAMUEL HOLDEN, son of the preceding, was born in Lyme and graduated at Harvard College in 1756. He soon after established himself as a lawyer in his native town, and was chosen a Representative for ten or twelve successive years. Having been appointed King's attorney for the county of New London, he removed to New London in 1774. This office his patriotism induced him to resign at the commencement of the Revolution. He early entered the service of his country, was appointed a colonel in 1775, and marched his regiment to Roxbury, where he remained until the enemy evacuated Boston. He was appointed a Brigadier-General in 1776, and was an efficient officer during the whole of the war. In 1780, he was one of the judges on the trial of Andre, and about that time received a commission as Major General. For his successful attack on the British troops at Morrisania, in 1781, Congress requested the commander-in-chief to express to him their thanks. Upon the establishment of peace, General Parsons opened a law office in Middletown, from which place he was sent to the Legislature at both the sessions of 1784, and again in 1785, and was more active and influential than any other man in the formation of the county of Middlesex. In the year last named, in fulfillment of his appointment as Indian Commissioner, he held a treaty with the Indians in Ohio, in connection with General Richard Butler and General George R. Clark, near the mouth of the Great Miami. By this treaty, the Indians ceded to the United States a large and valuable tract of country. In October, 1787, he was appointed one of the Judges of the territory north-west of the Ohio. Previous to entering upon the duties of this appointment he took part in the Convention of Connecticut, which in January 1788, adopted the Constitution of the United States. In 1789, the government of Connecticut appointed General Parsons, Oliver Wolcott, of Litchfield, and James Davenport, Jr., of Stamford, Commissioners to negotiate a treaty with the western Indians. But in that treaty he did not take a part; for, in returning to his residence in Marietta, he was drowned while descending the rapids of the Great Beaver Creek, Nov. 17, 1789, aged 52.

PHELPS, WILLIAM, an early settler at Windsor, came to New England in 1630, was admitted a freeman at Dorchester, Massachusetts, in 1631, and was a representative in the first General Court of that colony in 1634. He was also a member of the first court in Connecticut, holden April 26, 1636, and of the first board of magistrates in 1639. He was a deputy, or member of the lower house, at about twenty sessions. George Phelps, also of Windsor, was much in public life, and was chosen into the magistracy in 1658.

PIERPONT, REV. JAMES, fourth minister in New Haven, was born in Roxbury, Mass., in 1659, graduated at Harvard College in 1681, and was ordained at New Haven, July 2, 1685, as the successor of Mr. Street. On pages 458 and 459 of this volume, I have given a sketch of his character, together with a genealogy of the Pierpont family. He died in New Haven, November 22, 1714, aged 55, and was succeeded by the Rev. James Noyes. His daughter, Sarah, married the celebrated Jonathan Edwards. The articles of discipline, adopted with the Saybrook Platform, in 1708, were from the pen of Mr. Pierpont. He was one of the first trustees of Yale College, and was an efficient friend of education as well as of religion.

PIERSON, ABRAHAM, first President of Yale College, was the son of a distinguished clergyman of the same name, who came over from Yorkshire, England, previous to 1640, and was successively settled in the ministry in Southampton, Long Island, Branford, Connecticut, and Newark, New Jersey. The subject of this paragraph graduated at Harvard College in 1668, was ordained as colleague with his father at Newark, March 4, 1672, and was installed pastor of the church in Killingworth, Connecticut, in 1694. On the establishment of Yale College in 1701, he was chosen its first President, and continued to discharge the duties of the office with great ability and acceptance until his death, May 6, 1707, at the age of 60 years. He was a man of great learning and piety, an impressive preacher and a powerful writer. He wrote a system of natural philosophy, which was used as a text-book in the college for many years.

PRUDDEN, REV. PETER, was born in Yorkshire in 1601, and was a preacher in England before he came to this country. He arrived in Boston, July 26, 1637, and in the following spring sailed for New Haven, followed by many—" that they might enjoy his pious and fervent ministration." After exploring the country around New Haven, he finally decided to settle at Milford, with his followers. While negotiations for that place were going forward, Mr. Prudden supplied the pulpit in Wethersfield. He was installed pastor of the church in Milford, April 18, 1640, and died in that town in July 1656, in the 56th year of his age. He had made such an impression on the people of Wethersfield during his short stay there, that many of his hearers went with him to Milford and were among the principal settlers in the town. Mr. Prudden was greatly beloved and reverenced by his people. "His death" says Cotton Mather, "was felt by the colony as the fall of a pillar, which made the whole fabric shake."

PYNCHEON, WILLIAM, came to New England in 1630; settled in Roxbury, Massachusetts, and was chosen an assistant and treasurer of that colony. In 1636, he became a resident of Springfield, which was for a few years recognized as a part of Connecticut. He was a member of our General Court in November, 1636, and a member of the Upper House in March, 1637. In May, of the year last named, his vessel was pressed into the service of the colony, to transport men and munitions of war in the expedition against the Pequots. When famine threatened the towns upon the river, in 1637, he was deputed to purchase five hundred bushels of corn of the Indians, which he accomplished. "He was," says Mr. Hinman, "a thorough business man, and as a civilian, he ranked among the most prominent and efficient settlers." He at length refused to let the people of Springfield pay the Saybrook fort tax which had been laid by Connecticut, and in the controversy growing out of that subject, he espoused the cause of Massachusetts. He returned to England with the Rev. George Moxon, in 1652, and died at Wraisbury, on the Thames, in Buckinghamshire, in October, 1662, aged 74. His first wife died in New England; his second, died in Wraisbury, October 10, 1657. His children were—John, Joseph, William, Mary, and Mehitabel. The first of these, Colonel John Pyncheon, settled in Springfield; married Amy, daughter of Governor Wyllys, of Connecticut; was chosen a representative and assistant; and was a member of Sir Edmund Andross' council in 1687. He died in 1703, aged 77.

Richards, James, of Hartford, was admitted a freeman in October, 1664, and at the same time was declared by the General Court to be chosen an assistant in the place of Mr. Daniel Clarke, who refused to accept the place. This office he held, by annual reëlections, for fourteen years. In April, 1665, he was appointed, with Mr. Wyllys, to draw up an answer to the petition of the Duke of Hamilton, and present it to the next court; and was also placed upon the committee to go to New York for the purpose of congratulating His Majesty's honorable commissioners, and to treat with them concerning the claims of the Duke of York. He was a commissioner of the united colonies; colonial auditor; member of the governor's council; a commissioner at sundry times to treat with Rhode Island, Massachusetts, New Plymouth, with the commander of the Dutch fleet in New York, with the Mohawks, at Albany, &c., and agent of the colony in England. He died in Hartford, June 29, 1680, leaving a large estate, including lands and buildings in England. Among his bequests were—£10, in silver plate to the South Church in Hartford; £50 to the Latin School in Hartford; £20 to the Poor in Hartford; and £15 to his pastor, the Rev. John Whiting. His wife was Sarah, daughter of William Gibbons, of Hartford; his children were—Thomas, Mary, Jerusha, and Elizabeth. The last named, married Gurdon Saltonstall.

Sherman, Daniel, born in Woodbury, August 14, 1721, and spent his entire life in his native town. He was clerk of the probate court for sixteen years, judge of the probate court thirty-seven years, justice of the quorum twenty-five years, judge of the county court five years, and a representative at *sixty-five* sessions. He was also a delegate to the convention which adopted the Constitution of the United States, in 1788.

Stanton, Thomas, the "Indian interpreter," was long a useful and important man in the colony. The first mention made of him on our records is in April, 1638, when the General Court appointed him on a committee to treat with the Warronake Indians. At the same session he was appointed a "public officer" to attend upon all the meetings of the court and magistrates, "to interpret between them and the Indians," and his salary was fixed at £10 per annum. This salary was continued until April, 1646, when, "by reason of his long absence," it was suspended; but was restored to him in January, 1648. In February, 1649, liberty was granted him to erect a trading-house at Pawcatuck, and he was guaranteed the exclusive right to trade there for three years. In 1664, he was appointed by the General Court a commissioner at Pawcatuck and Mistick, and was often re-appointed; and was a representative at several sessions. The first county court ever held in New London, convened September 20, 1666; on which occasion the judges in attendance were Major Mason, Thomas Stanton, and Lieutenant Pratt. Mr. Stanton was also a commissioner to treat with the governor and council of Rhode Island, relative to the Narragansett country, in 1668. The Historian of New London, says—"On the Pawcatuck river, the first white inhabitant was Thomas Stanton. His trading establishment was probably coeval with the farming operations of Chesebrough, but as a fixed resident, with a fireside and a family, he was later upon the ground. He himself appears to have been always upon the wing, yet always within call. As interpreter to the colony, wherever a court, a conference or a treaty was to be held, or a sale made, in which the Indians were a party, he was required to be present. Never, perhaps did the acquisition of a barbarous language give a man such immediate, wide-spread and lasting importance. From the year 1636, when he was Winthrop's interpreter with the Nihantic Sachem, to 1670, when Uncas visited him with a train of warriors and captains to get him to write his Will, his name is connected with almost every Indian transaction on record." He died in Stonington, in 1678; Anna Stanton, his widow, died in 1688. He had nine children, viz.:—Thomas, John, Mary Hannah, Joseph, Daniel, Dorathy, Robert, and Sarah. His daughter, Dorathy, became the wife of the Rev. James Noyes.

In the list of passengers registered in England to sail for Virginia, in 1635, is found the name of Thomas Stanton, aged twenty. If this was the future interpreter, as there is little doubt, he was certainly an adept in acquiring the language of the aborigines, for he was Winthrop's interpreter at Saybrook in 1636. It may reasonably be doubted if he ever actually sailed for "Virginia" as that was a term often used to designate "America."

Steel, John, of Hartford, was a proprietor of Cambridge, Massachusetts, as early as 1632, and was a representative from that town in 1635. He was one of the board of magistrates appointed by the General Court of Massachusetts, March 3, 1636, "to govern the people of Connecticut for the space of a year (then) next ensuing;" and he was a member of the first General Court that ever convened in this colony, April 26, of the year last named. He was a member of the Upper House in 1636 and 1637; and was a deputy from Hartford and Farmington, at about forty regular semi-annual sessions, and was recorder of both of those towns. He died in Farmington, in 1665—leaving a son Samuel, who married Mary Boosy, and two daughters who married William and Thomas Judd.

Stone, Rev. Samuel, one of the first ministers of Hartford, was a native of England, and a graduate of the university of Cambridge. He came to New England with Mr. Cotton and Mr. Hooker, and was settled as an assistant to the latter in Cambridge, Massachusetts, October 11, 1633. When Mr. Hooker passed through the wilderness to Hartford, in 1636, Mr. Stone accompanied him, and was teacher of the church in the latter place until his death, July 20, 1663. He was one of the most brilliant and accomplished divines of the new world, and was alike distinguished for ability as a preacher and controversialist, his pleasing manners, and for his wit and eminent social qualities. He was a leader both in church and state. He was chaplain of the expedition against the Pequots in 1637, and was one of the three commissioners, appointed to negotiate a settlement of the difficulties between Sowheag, the Sachem of Pyquog, and the English settlers, in 1638. In October 1639, he was one of the persons designated by the General Court to collect and present to the assembly "those passages of God's providence which have been remarkable since the first undertaking these plantations." The colonial legislature, after his decease, granted to his widow and son five hundred and fifty acres of land. He published a volume relating to the congregational church in London, 1652; and left some valuable works in manuscript.

Treat, Richard, one of the patentees named in the Charter of Charles II., was a distinguished citizen of Wethersfield, where he was a resident as early as 1640. In 1642, he was appointed by the General Court, in connection with Governor Wyllys, Messrs. Haynes, Hopkins, Whiting, and others, to superintend building a ship, and to collect a revenue for that object. During the following year, he served as a colonial grand juror, and in 1644, he was for the first time a member of the General Court, a post of honor to which he was several times re-elected. From 1658, until 1665, he was an assistant or magistrate of the colony, and was one of the collectors of the Fenwick tax, and of the fund for the support of students in the College at Cambridge. He died in 1669. The following is a copy of his Will, viz.:

"The last Will and Testament of Richard Treat, Senr., of Wethersfield, in the Colony of Connecticut, in manner and forme as followeth.

Imprimis. I being weak and infirme of body, but of sound understanding and of competent memory, doe resigne my Soule to the Lord, hoping to be justified and saved by the merrit of Christ & my body to be buryed.

Item. I give and bequeath to my loving Wife, Mrs. Treat, after my deceasse, all the Lands of what kind soever I stand possessed of within the Bownds of Wethersfield, viz.: five Acres of Land lying in the dry swamp, which I have Improved and prepared for use, lyeing next my Sonn James his land.

Item. One peace of Meadow lyeing in the great Meadow, comonly called By the Name of send Home.

Item. The one half, or Eight Acres next Home of that peice of Meadow land comonly called fill barne.

Item. The Home lott, By the playne barn side.

Item. The dwelling housse that I formerly lived in, with convenient yard roome, and that end of the Barne on this side of the thrashing floore next the dwelling house with the one halfe of that Lott belongning to the said dwelling house lyeing next his Sonn Richards house & Lott, Except my wife and Son James shall agree other wise.

Item. All my pasture land fenced in beyownd my daughter Hollister's Lott.

Item. The use of two of my best Cowes which she shall chusse which is, they shall continue & stand longer than my loveing wife liveth, they shall be my eldest Sonne Richard Treats. I give to my loveing Wife, the standing bed, bedding, bedsted wth all the furniture thereto, belonging with the use of so much of the house hold Goods, during her life time, as she shall judg needfull for her comfort of what Sort Soever.

Item. I give and bequeath to my eldest Son Richard Treat, the full possession & comfirmation of the farme of Nayog, with all the respective priviledges thereto, belonging with Three of my youngest Heifers.

Item. I give to my seconn Sonn Robert Treate, Tenn pownds.

Item. I give to my youngest Sonn, James Treate, besides the Lands all ready made over to him, my Mill and grinding Stone, farm Timber, chaines, stillyards & my little Bible.

Item. I give unto my Sonn in law, Mathew Campfield, Twentie pownds for that which is remayneing of his portion.

Item. I give to my daughter Hollister, Forty Shillings.

Item. To my daughter Johnson, Tenn Shillings.

Item. My debts being payd, I give to my lovening Sons John Demon, and Robert Webster, equally, all the rest of my Goods and Chattles, what soever, except, Mr. Perkin's Booke, which I give to my Sonn John Demon, and my great Bible to my daughter Honour Demon, and that money in my Cousen Samuel Wells his hand unto my Cousen David Demon, Son of John Demon, Senr, & my desire is, that my Sonns in law, John Demon, Robert Webster, & Richard Treat, would be my overseers for their mutuall helpfullness to my loveing Wife, & endeavoure to see the accomplishment, this my last Will and Testament, & for the rattifycation hereof, I have this Thirteenth of February, 1668 set—to my hand & Seale.

RICHARD TREAT, SEN." { SEAL. }

UNDERHILL, CAPTAIN JOHN, of Stamford, a "soldier of fortune" was long conspicuous in the military affairs of the New Haven Colony. James I. sent him with the forces to aid the Dutch in the Low Countries in casting off the yoke of an oppressor, and he returned to England with the title of captain, bringing with him "a Dutch wife and a Dutch language." He subsequently came to Boston, where he was well received; and in a short time he took up his abode in Stamford, on the Sound. He soon became famous as an Indian fighter, and for years was engaged in war either in behalf of the English or Dutch. At one time he tells us that he received "a shot in the left hip through a sufficient buff-coat, and if he had not been supplied with such a garment, the arrow would have pierced through him," At another time he received an arrow between the neck and shoulder "hanging in the lining of his head-piece." According to his own account, he and his soldiers fought the Indians, armed with swords and muskets, and "clad in corslets, helmets, and bandoliers." He was in the Pequot war, and in the attack on the Indian fort at Mistick he was deputed to force the south entrance, and Mason the western. In describing the slaughter of that day he says—"Great and doleful was the sight to the view of young soldiers, who had never been in the war." But Underhill had been accustomed to such scenes, and though evidently conscience-stricken at the remembrance of the events described by him, he endeavors to justify himself by a resort to the Bible. "The Scriptures declareth," he says, "that women and children must perish with their parents;" and adds—"We had sufficient light from the Word of God for our proceedings; *we must contend valiently for the truth.*" He, however, rendered the colonies many important services. He was a man of untiring energy, activity, and courage, and such was the rapidity of his movements that his enemies were generally surprised and defeated. He died at Oyster Bay, on Long Island, in 1671. Captain Underhill was an author as well as soldier. The Massachusetts Historical collections contains a reprint of a work entitled—"News from America, or a new and experimental Discovery of New England, containing a true relation of the warlike proceedings these two years past, with a view of the Indian Fort or Palisado; by

Captain John Underhill, commander in the wars there. London, printed for Peter Cole, 1668." He took an active part in the civil affairs of Stamford, was a representative, and an assistant judge of the court established there.

Wadsworth, General James, a son of Colonel James Wadsworth, of Durham, graduated at Yale College in 1748, and settled in Durham as a lawyer. He rose to the rank of major-general in the Revolution, and was almost constantly in the public service, either in the field or as a member of the Council of Safety. In 1783, and again in 1785, he was elected a member of the Continental Congress; and was subsequently an assistant, comptroller of the state, and a delegate to the convention which adopted the Constitution of the United States. He died in September, 1816, aged 87.

Wadsworth, Colonel Jeremiah, a son of the Rev. Daniel Wadsworth, of Hartford, was born in 1743, and was early chosen a representative. At the commencement of the revolution he was appointed by the General Assembly of the state to the office of commissary of supplies; and in 1777, he received from Congress the appointment of commissary-general of purchases. He was elected a member of the Continental Congress in 1787; and was an assistant from 1795 to 1801. Colonel Wadsworth was a delegate from Hartford to the Convention which ratified the Constitution of the United States. He was an intimate friend of Washington, Lafayette, Rochambeau, and Putnam, all of whom he frequently entertained at his hospitable mansion. He died April 30, 1804, aged 61. The ate Daniel Wadsworth, Esq., of Hartford, the founder of the "Wadsworth Atheneum," was his only son. Catharine the only daughter of Colonel Wadsworth who lived to mature years, became the wife of General Nathaniel Terry, a lawyer and member of Congress.

Wadsworth, William, an early and prominent citizen of Hartford, was at Cambridge, Massachusetts, as early as 1632, and came to Hartford with Mr. Hooker in 1636, where he was appointed collector in the year following. He was often chosen a deputy, was a member of the colonial grand jury, and on a committee to treat with the Indians. He died in 1675. His wife was Elizabeth Stone, a sister of the Rev. Samuel Stone. His son John Wadsworth, Esq., of Farmington, was an assistant or magistrate from 1679, until his death in 1690. Another son, Captain Joseph Wadsworth, of Hartford, is famous in history for the part he took in preserving the charter from the grasp of Andross, and for silencing the attempt to read Colonel Fletcher's commission when that officer came to usurp the command of the Connecticut militia, in 1691. Captain Wadsworth was often a representative from Hartford, and seems to have retained his popularity to the last, notwithstanding the impetuosity and rashness of his nature. His acts above referred to, and more fully detailed in this volume, show him to have been ready for any emergency that might occur. On one occasion he was formally repremanded before the Assembly for declaring that certain acts of that body were inconsistent with the Charter; at another time he was fined ten pounds for "using reproachful words against Mr. Pitkin," one of the assistants. On still another occasion, he was brought before the court of assistants for having threatened, in a certain contingency, to "knock down Mr. Ichabod Wells, Sheriff of Hartford County." He died in 1729, at an advanced age.

WHITE, NATHANIEL, a son of John White, of Hartford, and Hadley, was a distinguished citizen of Middletown, where he died in 1711. He was one of the first magistrates in the town, and was elected a representative to the General Court at *eighty-five* semi-annual sessions.

WHITING, REV. JOHN, second son of William Whiting, sen., was born in 1635, graduated at Harvard College in 1653, and preached for three or four years in Salem, Massachusetts, where he was invited to settle, but declined the call. In 1660, he removed to Hartford, and became the pastor of the first church in that place. In 1670, a division occurred in his society, and a new church was formed of which Mr. Whiting was installed pastor, and continued such until his death, September 8, 1689. He married first, Sybel, daughter of Deac. Edward Collins, of Cambridge, Massachusetts, and had seven children, viz.: Sybel, John, William, Martha, Sarah, Abigail, and Samuel. His second wife was Phebe, daughter of Thomas Gregson, Esq., of New Haven, who was lost in the " Phantom Ship " in 1643, by whom he also had seven children, viz.: Thomas, Mary, Elizabeth, Joseph, Nathaniel, Thomas, and John.

WHITING, JOSEPH, youngest child of William Whiting, sen., was born in Hartford, October 2, 1645; married, August 6, 1670, Mary, daughter of John Pynchen, Esq., of Springfield, Massachusetts, and had Mary and John. His second wife was Anna, daughter of Colonel John Allyn, by whom he had seven children, viz.: Anna, John, Susannah, William, Anna, (2d,) Margaret, and John, (2d.) Mr. Whiting was Treasurer of Connecticut from 1679 until his death in 1718; and was succeeded in that office by his son, John Whiting, Esq., who was Treasurer for thirty-one years.

WHITING, JOSEPH, also a son of the Rev. John Whiting, was born in 1680, settled in New Haven, and became a leading man there. After having been frequently a representative, he was chosen a member of the Upper House in 1725. and was annually re-elected for twenty-one years. He married Hannah, daughter of Thomas Trowbridge, and had seven children. His eldest daughter, Hannah, married Jared Ingersoll, Esq.,the stamp-master; another daughter, Elizabeth, became the wife of the Rev. Chauncey Whittlesey, of New Haven.

WHITING, REV. SAMUEL, third son of the Rev. John Whiting, was born April 22, 1670, and was ordained and settled as the first pastor of the church in Windham, December 4, 1700. He married Elizabeth, daughter of the Rev. William Adams, of Dedham, Massachusetts, and great grand-daughter of Governor Bradford, of Plymouth. He was esteemed as a learned and eloquent divine. He was the father of Colonel William Whiting, (born January 22, 1704,) and of Colonel Nathan Whiting, (born May 4, 1724,) both of whom commanded regiments in the French war. His eldest daughter, Anna, (born January 2, 1698,) married Joseph Fitch, and was the mother of Colonel Eleazer Fitch, also an officer in the French War.

WHITING, WILLIAM, one of the most prominent and respectable of the Connecticut pioneers, first becomes known to us in 1632, at which date he was associated with Lords Say and Brooke, and George Wyllys, in the purchase of the Piscataqua country. He settled in Hartford, and was a member of the General Court in 1637. In 1642, he was elected a magistrate of the colony, and in

1643, he was chosen colonial treasurer—both of which offices he held until his death in July 1647. His children were—William, John, Samuel, Sarah, Mary, and Joseph. Among his bequests was one to Mr. Hooker, of £20, toward printing "his work on the 17th of John;" also the following—£10 to Mr Stone; £5 toward mending the highway between his house and the meeting-house; and £5 "to the godly poor in the town."

WHITING, WILLIAM, eldest son of the preceding, was for some years a resident of Hartford, and was sent to New Haven to urge upon that colony the expediency of uniting with Connecticut under the charter of 1662. He returned to England, and became a merchant in London; and in 1686, the assembly appointed him agent of the colony, to present their petition to the King relating to the writs of quo warranto that had been issued against the governor and company. He continued in the office of agent for several years, and received from the Assembly frequent expressions of thanks for his services. He died in London in 1699.

WHITING, COLONEL WILLIAM, second son of the Rev. John Whiting, was born in Cambridge, Massachusetts, in 1659; settled in Hartford, where he married Mary, daughter of Colonel John Allyn, and had three children. Colonel Whiting represented Hartford in the General Court at eleven sessions, and was speaker of the house in 1714. As early as 1693, he was appointed by the General Assembly to the command of the Connecticut troops sent to aid Sir William Phipps in protecting the eastern settlements of Massachusetts and Maine. In 1705, when Governor Dudley attempted to wrest from the jurisdiction of Connecticut the Mohegan country, and had induced the crown to appoint a court of commissioners, of which he was chief, to assist in carrying out his project, the legislature appointed Colonel Whiting one of the committee to attend the meeting of said Court, with instructions either to defend the interests of the colony, or to enter their protest against the action of the court, as the circumstances might require. In 1709, and again in 1711, he commanded the forces raised in Connecticut, to coöperate with General Nicholson in reducing the French in Canada, Acadia and Newfoundland. He was chosen sheriff of Hartford county in 1722, and acceptably performed the duties of various other civil offices until his death.

WHITTLESEY, REV. SAMUEL, minister at Wallingford, graduated at Yale College in 1705, was ordained as colleague with Mr. Street in May 1710, and died April 15, 1752, aged 66. "He was," says Dr. Allen, "one of the most distinguished preachers and faithful ministers of the colony. Such was the vigor and penetration of his mind that he easily comprehended subjects that presented great difficulties to others." He published a sermon on the death of John Hall, in 1730; an election sermon, 1731; a sermon on the awful condition of impenitent souls in their separate state, 1731; and a sermon preached at the ordination of his son, Samuel, at Milford, 1737. The Rev. Chauncey Whittlesey, an eminent scholar and pastor of the first church in New Haven from 1758 to 1787, was his son.

WOODBRIDGE, REV. TIMOTHY, minister at Hartford, son of the Rev. John Woodbridge, of Andover, Massachusetts, graduated at Harvard College in 1675 and was ordained as the successor of Mr. Haynes, November 18, 1685. In 1696 he introduced into Connecticut the practice of baptizing the children of those who "owned the covenant" without being received into full communion, a practice which led to a long and bitter controversy among the clergy of Connecticut. He was tall and of majestic aspect, and was one of the most famous men of his day. He preached the election sermon in 1727, which was published. Mr. Woodbridge died April 30, 1732, aged 80 years. His brother, Rev. John Woodbridge, (Jr.,) graduated at Harvard in 1664, was ordained as pastor of the church in Killingworth, in 1666, but subsequently removed to Wethersfield, where he was pastor from 1679 till his death in 1691.

WYLLYS, GEORGE, son of Hezekiah Wyllys, was born in 1710, graduated at Yale College in 1729, and succeeded his father as Secretary of State in 1735. To this important office he was annually elected by the people for a period of *sixty years.* During this whole time, he attended every session of the legislature and performed his official duties in a satisfactory manner. He died April 24, 1796, aged 85. His son, General Samuel Wyllys, graduated at Yale in 1758, and was a highly popular and meritorious officer during the whole of the revolution. After the war he was chosen to various civil offices in his native town, and, from the death of his father in 1796, was elected Secretary of State until 1809. He also rose to the rank of major-general of militia. The office of secretary was held by this family in uninterrupted succession for ninety-eight years.

WYLLYS, SAMUEL, son of Governor Wyllys, a sketch of whom I have given on pages 136—138 of this volume, was born in England in 1632, came to New England with his parents in childhood, and graduated at Harvard College in 1653. He was chosen an assistant, or magistrate, in 1654, and was annually re-elected for thirty-four years. He died May 30, 1709. The famous charter-oak, in which the charter of King Charles II, was secreted during the usurpation of Andross in 1678, stood and still stands in front of his house, in Hartford. His son, Hezekiah Wyllys, Esq., was secretary of the colony from1712 until his death in 1735.

STATE AND COLONIAL OFFICERS,

FROM 1639 TO 1818.

GOVERNORS.	First chos'n.	Last chos'n.	No. yrs.	DEP. OR LT.-GOVERNORS.	First chos'n.	Last chos'n.	No. yrs.
John Haynes,..........	1639	1653	8	Roger Ludlow,........	1639	1648	3
Edward Hopkins,......	1640	1654	7	John Haynes,.........	1640	1652	5
George Wyllys,........	1642		1	George Wyllys,.......	1641		1
Thomas Welles,.......	1655	1658	2	Edward Hopkins,......	1643	1653	6
John Webster,.........	1656		1	Thomas Welles,.......	1654	1659	4
John Winthrop,........	1657	1676	18	John Webster,.........	1655		1
William Leete,........	1676	1683	7	John Winthrop,........	1658		1
Robert Treat,..........	1683	1687	4	John Mason,...........	1660	1669	9
[*Sir Edmund Andross*,].	1687	1689	2	William Leete,........	1669	1676	7
Robert Treat,..........	1689	1698	9	Robert Treat,..........	1676	1708	17
Fitz John Winthrop,....	1698	1707	9	James Bishop,..........	1683	1692	7
Gurdon Saltonstall,.....	1707	1724	17	William Jones,.........	1692	1697	5
Joseph Talcott,.........	1724	1741	17	Nathan Gold,...........	1708	1724	16
Jonathan Law,.........	1741	1750	9	Joseph Talcott,........	1724	1724	
Roger Wolcott,.........	1750	1754	4	Jonathan Law,.........	1724	1741	17
Thomas Fitch,.........	1754	1766	12	Roger Wolcott,.........	1741	1750	9
William Pitkin,.........	1766	1769	3	Thomas Fitch,.........	1750	1754	4
Jonathan Trumbull,....	1769	1784	15	William Pitkin,........	1754	1766	12
Matthew Griswold,.....	1784	1786	2	Jonathan Trumbull,....	1766	1769	3
Samuel Huntington,....	1786	1796	10	Matthew Griswold,.....	1769	1784	15
Oliver Wolcott,.........	1796	1798	2	Samuel Huntington,....	1784	1786	2
Jonathan Trumbull,....	1798	1809	11	Oliver Wolcott,.........	1786	1796	10
John Treadwell,.......	1809	1811	2	Jonathan Trumbull,....	1796	1798	2
Roger Griswold,.......	1811	1812	1	John Treadwell,.......	1798	1809	11
John Cotton Smith *....	1813	1817	4	Roger Griswold,.......	1809	1811	2
				John Cotton Smith,....	1811	1813	2
				Chauncey Goodrich,....	1813	1815	2
				Jonathan Ingersoll,†...	1816	1818	2

SECRETARIES OF STATE.	First chos'n.	Last chos'n.	No. yrs.	TREASURERS.	First chos'n.	Last chos'n.	No. yrs.
Edward Hopkins,.......	1639	1640	1	Thomas Welles,.......	1639	1652	5
Thomas Welles,.......	1640	1648	8	William Whiting,......	1641	1648	7
John Cullick,..........	1648	1658	10	John Talcott,..........	1652	1659	7
Daniel Clark,..........	1658	1667	8	John Talcott,..........	1659	1678	19
John Allen,...........	1664	1696	28	William Pitkin,........	1678	1679	1
Eleazer Kimberly,......	1696	1709	13	Joseph Whiting,........	1679	1718	39
Caleb Stanley,.........	1709	1712	3	John Whiting,.........	1718	1749	31

* The successors of Governor Smith, under the Constitution, have been, Oliver Wolcott, Gideon Tomlinson, John S. Peters, Henry W. Edwards, Samuel A. Foote, William W. Ellsworth, Chauncey F. Cleveland, Roger S. Baldwin, Isaac Toucey, Clark Bissell, Joseph Trumbull, Thomas H Seymour, Charles H. Pond, Henry Dutton and William T. Minor.

† The Lieutenant-Governors under the Constitution have been—Jonathan Ingersoll, David Plant, John S. Peters, Thaddeus Betts, Ebenezer Stoddard, Charles Hawley, Wm. S. Holabird, Reuben Booth, Noyes Billings, Charles J. McCurdy, Thomas Backus, Green Kendrick, Charles H. Pond, Alexander H. Holley, William Field and Albert Day.

SECRETARIES OF STATE.	First chos'n.	Last chos'n.	No. yrs.	TREASURERS.	First chos'n.	Last chos'n.	No. yrs.
Hezekiah Wyllys,........	1712	1735	23	Nathaniel Stanley,......	1749	1755	6
George Wyllys,.........	1735	1796	61	Joseph Talcott,.........	1755	1769	14
Samuel Wyllys,.........	1796	1810	14	John Lawrence,.........	1769	1788	19
Thomas Day,*.........	1810	1818	8	Jedediah Huntington,...	1789	1789	
				Peter Colt,............	1789	1794	5
				Andrew Kingsbury,†....	1794	1818	24

COMPTROLLERS.	First chos'n.	Last chos'n.	No. yrs.	COMPTROLLERS.	First chos'n.	Last chos'n.	No. yrs.
James Wadsworth,.....	1786	1788	2	Andrew Kingsbury,.....	1791	1794	3
Oliver Wolcott,........	1788	1789	1	John Porter,...........	1794	1806	12
Ralph Pomroy,..........	1789	1791	2	Elisha Colt,†...........	1806	1818	12

ASSISTANTS.‡	Nom.	Elec.	Retired.
JOHN HAYNES, Hartford,..............	1639	1639	1653, died.
ROGER LUDLOW, Windsor and Fairfield,......	1639	1639	1654, to Va.
GEORGE WYLLYS, Hartford,...........	1639	1639	1644, died.
EDWARD HOPKINS, Hartford,...........	1639	1639	1657, to Eng.
THOMAS WELLES, Hartford,...........	1639	1639	1659, died.
JOHN WEBSTER, Hartford,..............	1639	1639	1659, to Mass.
William Phelps, Windsor,.................		1639	1643.
William Whiting, Hartford,................	1639	1641	1648.
Matthew Allen, Hartford,..................	1641		(below.)
William Hopkins, Stratford,................	1641	1641	1643.
JOHN MASON, Windsor, Saybrook, & Norwich,		1642	1671, died.
William Swaine, Wethersfield,.............	1643	1643	1645.
Henry Wolcott, Windsor,..................		1643	1655, died.
George Fenwick, Saybrook,................	1639	1644	1649.
John Cullick, Hartford,....................		1648	1658, to Bost.
JOHN WINTHROP, New London,........	1649	1651	1676, died.
Henry Clarke, Windsor,....................	1650	1650	1662.
John Talcott, Hartford,....................	1654	1654	1659, died.
Samuel Wyllys, Hartford,.................	1654	1654	1685, (below.)
Nathan Gold, Fairfield,....................	1657	1657	1658. (below.)
George Phelps, Windsor,..................	1658	1658	1663.
Matthew Allen, Windsor,..................	1658	1658	1668.
Richard Treat, Wethersfield,...............	1658	1658	1665.

* The Secretaries of State, since the adoption of the Constitution, have been the following, viz., Thomas Day, Royal R. Hinman, Noah A. Phelps, Daniel P. Tyler, Charles W. Bradley, John B. Robertson, Roger H. Mills, Hiram Weed, John P. C. Mather, Oliver H. Perry and Neh. D. Sperry.

† The successors of Mr. Kingsbury, in the office of State Treasurer, have been—Isaac Spencer, Jeremiah Brown, Hiram Rider, Jabez L. White, Joseph B. Gilbert, Alonzo W. Birge, Henry D. Smith, Thomas Clark, Edwin Stearns, Daniel W. Camp, Austin B. Calef and Frederick W. Coe.

‡ The Comptrollers since the adoption of the Constitution, have been—Elisha Colt, James Thomas, Elisha Phelps, Roger Huntington, Gideon Welles, William Field, Henry Kilbourn, Abijah Carrington, Mason Cleveland, Abijah Catlin, R. G. Pinney, John Dunham, Alex. Merrill and Ed. Prentis.

‡ List of magistrates, generally called Assistants, who constituted the Upper House of the Assembly; and in early times were the Supreme Court of the State. They were the leading men of their times. The list is copied from the Connecticut Annual Register, for 1848.

The CAPITALS indicate the Governors, and the SMALL CAPITALS the Deputy or Lieutenant-Governors. Those marked "died" deceased in office.

ASSISTANTS.	Nom.	Elec.	Retired.
John Wells, Stratford,	1658	1658	1660.
Alexander Knowles, Fairfield,	1658	1658	1659.
Nathan Gold, Fairfield,	(above)	1659	1694, died. ?
Thurston Rayner, Wethersfield,		1661	1662, (below.)
John Talcott, Hartford,	1661	1662	1688.
Daniel Clark, Windsor,	1661	1662	1664, resigned.
John Allyn, Hartford,	1661	1662	1696, died.
Henry Wolcott, Windsor,	1661	1662	1665, (below.)
Samuel Sherman, Fairfield,	1664	1662	1664, (below.)
Thurston Rayner, Wethersfield,	1664	1663	1664.
James Richards, Hartford,		1664	1666, (below.)
WILLIAM LEET, Guilford,	1665	1665	1683, died. ?
WILLIAM JONES, New Haven,	1665	1665	1698, died. ?
Benjamin Fenn, Milford,	1665	1665	1673.
Jasper Crane, Branford,	1665	1665	1668.
Henry Wolcott, Windsor,	(above)	1665	1681.
Samuel Sherman, Stratford,	(above)	1665	1668.
Daniel Clark, Windsor,	1666	1666	1668.
Alexander Bryant, Milford,	1665	1668	1679.
JAMES BISHOP, New Haven,	1667	1668	1692, died.
Anthony Howkins, Farmington,	1664	1668	1674, died.
Thomas Welles, Hartford,	1665	1668	1669.
James Richards, Hartford,	(above)	1669	1681.
John Nash, New Haven,	1670	1672	1688, died. ?
ROBERT TREAT, Milford,	1665	1673	1708.
Thomas Topping, Branford,	1670	1674	1685.
John Mason, Norwich,	1672	1676	1677.
Matthew Gilbert, New Haven,	1665	1677	1678.
Andrew Leet, Guilford,	1677	1678	1703.
John Wadsworth, Farmington,	1675	1679	1690, died.
Robert Chapman, Saybrook,	1669	1681	1685.
James Fitch, Norwich,	1678	1681	1698, (below.)
Samuel Mason, Stonington,	1681	1683	1703.
Benjamin Newbury, Windsor,	1664	1685	1690, died. ?
Samuel Talcott, Wethersfield,	1669	1685	1692, died. ?
Giles Hamlin, Middletown,	1667	1685	1690, died.
Samuel Willis, Hartford,	(above)	1689	1693, (below.)
[Fitz] John Winthrop, New London,	1689	1689	1690, (below.)
John Burr, Fairfield,	1685	1690	1695,
William Pitkin, Hartford,	1690	1690	1694, died.
Daniel Wetherell, New London,	1677	1690	1710.
Nathaniel Stanly, Hartford,	1690	1690	1713.
Caleb Stanly, Hartford,	1692	1692	1701.
Moses Mansfield, New Haven,	1683	1692	1704, died. ?
JOHN WINTHROP, New London,	(above)	1693	1707, died.
John Hamlin, Middletown,	1693	1694	1730.
Jonathan Sellick, Stamford,	1694	1695	1701.
NATHAN GOLD, Fairfield,	1694	1695	1723, died.
William Pitkin, Hartford,	1696	1697	1723, died.
Joseph Curtice, Stratford,	1696	1698	1722.
Samuel Willis, Hartford,	(above)	1698	1699.
Richard Christophers, New London,	1694	1699	1700, (below.)
James Fitch, Norwich,	(above)	1700	1709.
John Chester, Wethersfield,	1685	1701	1712.
Josiah Rossiter, Guilford,	1700	1701	1711.
Peter Burr, Fairfield,	1701	1703	1725.

ASSISTANTS.	Nom.	Elec.	Retired.
Richard Christophers, New London,.........	(above)	1703	1723.
John Alling, New Haven,..................	1703	1704	1717.
GURDON SALTONSTALL, New London,..	not nom.	1707	1724, died.
John Haynes, Hartford,..................	1696	1708	1714.
Samuel Eells. Milford,....................	1683	1709	1740, died. ?
Matthew Allyn, Windsor,..................	1706	1710	1734.
JOSEPH TALCOTT, Hartford,...........	1709	1711	1741, died.
Abraham Fowler, Guilford,...............	1705	1712	1720.
John Sherman, Woodbury,...............	1711	1713	1723.
Roger Wolcott, Windsor,.................	1712	1714	1718, (below.)
JONATHAN LAW, Milford,.............	1710	1717	1750, died.
James Wadsworth, Durham,...............	1716	1718	1752.
ROGER WOLCOTT, Windsor,...........	(above)	1720	1754.
John Hall, Wallingford,...................	1719	1722	1730.
Christopher Christophers, New London,......	1718	1723	1729.
Hezekiah Brainard, Haddam,..............	1720	1723	1727, died.
John Hooker, Farmington,.................	1709	1723	1734.
Josh. Wakeman, Fairfield,.................	1715	1724	1727.
Nathaniel Stanly, Hartford,................	1723	1725	1749.
Joseph Whiting, New Haven,..............	1722	1725	1746.
Ozias Pitkin, Hartford,....................	1725	1727	1747.
Timothy Pierce, Plainfield,................	1725	1728	1748.
John Burr, Fairfield,......................	1724	1729	1740.
Samuel Lynde, Saybrook,..................	1729	1730	1754, died.
Edmund Lewis, Stratford,..................	1729	1730	1739.
WILLIAM PITKIN, Hartford,............	1731	1734	1769, died.
Thomas Fitch, Norwalk,.....................	1730	1734	1736, (below.)
Roger Newton, Milford,....................	1729	1736	1740, (below.)
Ebenezer Silliman, Fairfield,................	1736	1739	1766.
THOMAS FITCH, Norwalk,..............	(above)	1740	1766.
Jonathan Trumbull, Lebanon,...............	1739	1740	1751, (below.)
Hezekiah Huntington, Norwich.............	1739	1740	1743, (below.)
John Bulkley, Colchester,..................	1735	1743	1753, died.
Andrew Burr, Fairfield,...................	1734	1746	1764.
Roger Newton, Milford,....................	(above)	1742	1762.
John Chester, Wethersfield,...............	1741	1747	1766.
Hezekiah Huntington, Norwich,............	(above)	1748	1773.
Gurdon Saltonstall, New London,...........	1746	1749	1754.
Thomas Welles, Glastenbury,..............	1749	1751	1761.
Benjamin Hall, Wallingford,................	1749	1751	1766.
Phineas Lyman, Suffield,...................	1751	1752	1759.
JONATHAN TRUMBULL, Lebanon,.....	(above)	1754	1784, declined.
Roger Wolcott, Windsor,..................	1747	1754	1760, died.
Jonathan Huntington, Windham,...........	1751	1754	1758.
Daniel Edwards, Hartford..................	1751	1755	1765, died.
Jabez Hamlin, Middletown,................	1754	1758	1766, (below.)
MATTHEW GRISWOLD, Lyme,.........	1755	1759	1786.
Shubael Conant, Mansfield,................	1754	1760	1775, died.
Elisha Sheldon, Litchfield,.................	1758	1762	1779, died.
Eliphalet Dyer, Windham,.................	1758	1762	1784, died.
Jabez Huntington, Windham,...............	1761	1764	1781, died.
William Pitkin, East Hartford,.............	1763	1766	1785, resigned.
Roger Sherman, New Haven,...............	1761	1766	1785, resigned.
Robert Walker, Stratford,..................	1760	1766	1772, died.
Abraham Davenport, Stamford,............	1764	1766	1784.
Wm. Samuel Johnson, Stratford,............	1765	1766	1776, (below.)

ASSISTANTS.	Nom.	Elec.	Retired.
Joseph Spencer, East Haddam,.............	1765	1766	1778, (below.)
Zebulon West, Tolland,....................	1766	1770	1771.
OLIVER WOLCOTT, Litchfield,..........	1768	1771	1797. died.
Jabez Hamlin, Middletown,................	(above)	1773	1785.
James A. Hillhouse, New Haven,...........	1771	1773	1775.
SAMUEL HUNTINGTON, Norwich,......	1773	1775	1796.
Richard Law, New London,.................	1774	1776	1784, Judge.
William Williams, Lebanon,................	1774	1776	1780, (below.)
Titus Hosmer, Middletown,.................	1775	1778	1780, died.
Oliver Ellsworth, Windsor,...........(below,)	1778	1780	1785, Judge.
Joseph Spencer, East Haddam,..............	(above)	1779	1789.
Adams, Andrew, Litchfield,................	1779	1781	1790.
Benjamin Huntington, Norwich,............	1779	1781	1790, (below.)
Joseph Platt Cooke, Danbury,..............	1783	1784	1803.
Stephen Mix Mitchell, Wethersfield,.........	1783	1784	1793.
William Williams, Lebanon,................	(above)	1784	1803.
William Hillhouse, New London,............	1783	1785	1809.
Erastus Wolcott, East Windsor,.............	1772	1785	1790.
JOHN TREADWELL, Farmington,.......	1783	1785	1811.
Jonathan Sturges, Fairfield,................	1784	1785	1789.
James Wadsworth, Durham,.................	1776	1785	1788.
Wm. Samuel Johnson, Stratford,............	(above)	1786	1789.
John Chester, Wethersfield,................	1786	1788	1792, (below.)
James Hillhouse, New Haven,..............	1785	1789	1791.
Jedediah Strong, Litchfield,................	1786	1789	1791.
Jesse Root, Coventry,......................	1780	1789	1789, Judge.
James Davenport, Stamford,................	1789	1790	1797, died.
Roger Newberry, Windsor,.................	1789	1790	1809.
Heman Swift, Cornwall,...................	1789	1790	1802.
John Chandler, Newtown,.............	1789	1790	1795, died.
Benjamin Huntington, Norwich,............	(above)	1791	1793, Judge.
Amasa Learned, New London,.............	1790	1791	1792.
Jonathan Ingersoll, New Haven,............	1790	1792	1798, (below.)
Tapping Reeve, Litchfield,.................	1789	1792	1793.
Asher Miller, Middletown,.................	1791	1793	1793, Judge.
Thomas Grosvenor, Pomfret,...............	1789	1793	1802.
Thomas Seymour, Hartford,................	1791	1793	1803.
Aaron Austin, New Hartford,..............	1792	1794	1818.
Jeremiah Wadsworth, Hartford,.............	1787	1795	1801.
JONATHAN TRUMBULL, Lebanon,.....	1788	1796	1809, died.
David Daggett, New Haven,...............	1794	1797	1814, Sen. C.
Jonathan Brace, Hartford,..................	1797	1798	1799, (below,)
Zephaniah Swift, Windham,...............	1791	1799	1800, (below.)
Nathaniel Smith, Woodbury,...............	1798	1799	1805, Judge.
John Allen, Litchfield,....................	1794	1800	1806.
Zephaniah Swift, Windham,...............	(above)	1801	1801, Judge.
Oliver Ellsworth, Windsor,................	(above)	1802	1808.
Jonathan Brace, Hartford,.................	(above)	1802	1819.
Chauncey Goodrich, Hartford,.............	1793	1902	1808, (below.)
John Chester, Wethersfield,................	(above)	1803	1809. died.
William Edmund, Newtown,................	1793	1803	1806, Judge.
Elizur Goodrich, New Haven,..............	1801	1803	1818.
Matthew Griswold, Lyme,.................	1802	1805	1818.
Stephen T. Hosmer, Middletown,............	1798	1805	1815, Judge.
Asher Miller, Middletown,.................	(above)	1806	1817.
Henry Champion, Colchester,...............	1803	1806	1818.

ASSISTANTS.	Nom.	Elec.	Retired.
Calvin Goddard, Norwich,..................	1806	1808	1815, Judge.
Isaac Beers, New Haven,..................	1804	1808	1809.
John Cotton Smith, Sharon,.................	1807	1809	1810, Judge.
Judson Canfield, Sharon,..................	1804	1809	1815.
Theodore Dwight, Hartford,.................	1808	1809	1816.
ROGER GRISWOLD, Lyme,.............	1793	1809	1812, died.
Frederick Wolcott, Litchfield,..............	1808	1810	1819.
JOHN COTTON SMITH, Sharon,.........	(above)	1811	1817.
Chauncey Goodrich, Hartford,.............	(above)	1813	1815, died.
Roger M. Sherman, Fairfield,...............	1808	1814	1818.
Samuel W. Johnson, Stratford,.............	1810	1815	1818.
Noah B. Benedict, Woodbury,..............	1810	1816	1818.
William Perkins, Ashford,.................	1810	1816	1818.
Samuel B. Sherwood, Fairfield,.............	1815	1816	1817.
Jonathan Ingersoll, New Haven,..........	(above)	1816	1819.
Asa Chapman, Newtown,..................	1809	1817	1819.
Elias Perkins, New London,................	1813	1817	1819.
OLIVER WOLCOTT, Litchfield,............		1817	1819.
William Bristol, New Haven,...............	1817	1818	1819.
Elijah Boardman, New Milford,.............	1817	1818	1819.
David Tomlinson, Oxford,..................	1817	1818	1819.
Sylvester Wells, Hartford,..................	1817	1818	1819.
JOHN S. PETERS, Hebron,..............	1817	1818	1819.
James Lanman, Norwich,..................	1817	1818	1819.
Enoch Burrows, Stonington,................	1817	1818	1819.
Peter Webb, Windham....................	1817	1818	1819.

ROLL OF DEPUTIES

TO THE GENERAL COURT OF CONNECTICUT

FROM APRIL 1640, TO THE UNION WITH NEW HAVEN COLONY, APRIL 1665.

NAMES OF DEPUTIES.	First elected.	No. ses.	NAMES OF DEPUTIES.	First elected.	No. ses.
Mr. Allyn,................	1648	14	Mr. Jonathan Brewster,....	1650	7
Lieut. John Allyn,.........	1661	1	John Burr,...............	1641	1
Thomas Allyn,............	1656	1	Mr. Jehu Burr,...........	1645	7
Ensign James Avery,......	1659	6	Lieut. John Budd,.........	1664	1
			Richard Butler,...........	1656	8
Andrew Bacon,...........	1642	25			
Mr. John Banks,..........	1651	6	Mr. Matthew Canfield,.....	1654	12
Joshua Barnes,............	1663	1	Nath. Canfield,...........	1655	1
William Beardsley,........	1645	7	Hugh Caulkins,...........	1652	11
Mr. James Bishop,........	1665	1	Mr. Robert Chapman,.....	1652	17
Thomas Birchard,..........	1650	2	Thomas Chapman,........	1652	2
Samuel Boardman,........	1657	17	Mr. Chaplin,.............	1642	2
Mr. John Bissell,..........	1648	16	Mr. William Chesebrough,..	1653	5
Lieut. James Boozey,......	1640	14	William Cheeney,.........	1660	5
John Bronson,............	1651	4	Mr. George Clark,........	1665	1

NAMES OF DEPUTIES.	First elected.	No. ses.
Mr. Daniel Clark,	1653	5
Henry Clark,	1642	2
Mr. John Clark,	1649	21
Mr. Clarke,	1641	9
John Cooper,	1665	1
Thomas Coleman,	1651	9
Sergt. William Cornwell,	1654	3
Thomas Cook,	1665	1
Richard Crabb,	1640	2
Mr. Cullick,	1644	3
John Cowles,	1653	2
Mr. John Deming,	1646	19
Capt. Denison,	1653	3
Nathaniel Dickerson,	1646	19
Samuel Drake,	1662	1
John Edwards,	1643	2
Nath. Ely,	1656	1
Mr. Thomas Fairchild,	1646	11
Mr. Joseph Fitch,	1654	10
Nathaniel Foot,	1641	2
Thomas Ford,	1640	4
John Fowler,	1665	1
Lieut. Walter Fyler,	1661	3
Mr. William Gaylord,	1640	36
George Graves,	1656	4
William Goodrich,	1660	3
John Gregory,	1659	3
Francis Griswold,	1664	1
Edward Griswold,	1656	9
Matthew Griswold,	1649	3
Nath. Griswold,	1650	1
Philip Graves,	1642	14
Henry Gray,	1642	2
Samuel Hale,	1656	3
John Hall, Jr.,	1653	1
Samuel Hall,	1660	1
Mr. Hall,	1661	1
Thomas Halsey, Jr.,	1664	1
Joseph Hawley,	1658	1
John Hart,	1659	2
Stephen Hart,	1646	13
Ed. Harvey,	1646	1
Mr. Hill,	1641	10
William Hill,	1651	3
Mr. John Hollister,	1644	14
Mr. Hosford,	1652	1
Mr. Anthony Hawkins,	1657	13
Mr. John Howell,	1662	2
Walter Hoyt,	1658	3
George Hubbard,	1640	3
Mr. Cornelius Hull,	1656	9
Mr. George Hull,	1649	1
Josias Hull,	1659	4
Mr. Hull,	1640	15
Thomas Hunt,	1664	1
John Hurd,	1649	4
John Jessop,	1664	1
Thomas Judd,	1646	14
Ensign Joseph Judson,	1658	9
William Kenney,	1662	1
John Ketchum,	1664	1
Sergt. John Kilbourn,	1660	4
John Lattimer,	1654	1
Cary Latham,	1664	1
Thomas Leffingwell,	1662	1
Mr. Lord,	1656	8
Matthew Marvin,	1654	1
Captain Mason,	1641	2
Good. Meads,	1653	1
Mr. Thomas Minor,	1650	3
Thomas Morehouse,	1653	1
Isaac Moore,	1657	1
Mr. John Moore,	1653	6
James Morgan,	1657	5
Joseph Mygatt,	1656	11
Capt. Benjamin Newbery,	1656	7
Thomas Newton,	1645	1
Mr. Isaac Nichols,	1662	3
Sergt. John Nott,	1662	7
Lieut. Richard Olmsted,	1653	9
William Parker,	1652	1
Mr. Parks,	1642	2
Mr. Phelps,	1645	20
Mr. Plumb,	1642	1
John Pratt,	1641	3
Mr. Porter,	1646	2
Mr. Thomas Pell,	1664	1
Thomas Rayner,	1640	1
Nath. Richards,	1658	1
John Robbins,	1643	2
Mr. Robbins,	1656	3
Mr. James Rogers,	1661	7
Robert Rose,	1641	2
Mr. Rossiter,	1643	2
Robert Royce,	1661	1
Captain Seely,	1664	1
Samuel Sherman,	1660	1
Thomas Sherrat,	1649	2
Thomas Sherwood,	1645	3

NAMES OF DEPUTIES.	First elected.	No. ses.	NAMES OF DEPUTIES.	First elected.	No. ses.
William Smith,...........	1652	4	Mr. William Wadsworth,...	1652	17
Samuel Smith,............	1641	21	Ens. William Waller,......	1663	2
Mr. Spencer,..............	1640	1	Mr. Andrew Ward,.......	1648	13
Sergt. John Stanley,.......	1659	4	Nath. Ward,............	1656	1
Ed. Stebbing,.............	1640	16	Robert Warner,..........	1660	7
Thomas Staunton,.........	1651	1	Robert Webster,..........	1653	9
Thomas Staples,..........	1649	3	Richard Webb,...........	1655	1
John Sticklin,............	1641	1	John Welles,............	1656	4
Mr. Steele,..............	1640	34	Mr. Samuel Wells,........	1657	8
Samuel Stocking,.........	1658	3	Mr. Thomas Wells,........	1662	1
Mr. Stoughton,...........	1640	8	John Wheeler,...........	1657	4
Mr. Swayne,............	1641	3	Mr. Westwood,...........	1642	21
Lieut. Samuel Swayne,.....	1665	1	Nathaniel White,.........	1659	8
			Thomas Whitmore,........	1654	1
Mr. Taintor,.............	1646	2	William Wilcoxson,.......	1646	1
Mr. Talcott,.............	1640	30	Anthony Wilson,..........	1646	1
John Tinker,.............	1660	2	David Wilton,............	1646	11
Daniel Titterton,..........	1646	4	Andrew Winard,..........	1653	1
Thomas Thomson,.........	1650	1	Barnabas Wines,..........	1664	1
Thomas Thornton,........	1651	1	Mr. Henry Wolcott,.......	1655	3
Thomas Tracy,...........	1662	23	John Wilford, ...	1664	1
Mr. Treat,...............	1644	5	Mr. Richard Woodhull,*...	1664	1
Michael Try,............	1657	1			

CATALOGUE

OF THE CONGREGATIONAL CLERGYMEN IN CONNECTICUT AND NEW HAVEN COLONIES,

DOWN TO 1665, VIZ.

NAMES.	From.	To.	NAMES.	From.	To.
Thomas Hooker, Hartford,	1633	1647	John Higginson, Guilford,.	1650	1659
Samuel Stone, Hartford,...	1633	1663	Joseph Elliott, Guilford,..	1660	
Ephraim Hewett, Windsor,	1639	1644	Samuel Russell, Branford,.	1644	1665
Sam'l Hooker, Farmington,	1661	1697	Rd. Blynman, N. London,.	1650	1658
John Davenport, N. Haven,	1639	1668	N. Russell, Middletown.	1658	1713
Wm. Hook, New Haven,.	1644	1656	Henry Smith, Wethersfield	1641	1648
Nicholas Street, N. Haven,	1659	1674	Jona. Russell, "	1648	
Peter Prudden, Milford,...	1640	1656	Joseph Haynes, Hartford.		1679
Roger Newton, Milford,..	1660	1683	Samuel Whiting,........		
Henry Whitfield, Guilford,	1639	1650	Thos. Buckingham, Sayb'k	1660	

* From May, 1637, to April, 1640, the popular branch of the General Court or General Assembly, as it was afterwards called, was composed of "*Committees*." The following gentlemen served in that capacity between these dates, viz.:—Mr. Whiting, Mr. Webster, Mr. Williams, Mr. Hull, Mr. Chaplin, Mr. Talcott, Mr. Hosford, Mr. Mitchell, Mr. Sherman, Capt. Mason, Mr. Hopkins, Mr. Steel, Mr. Ford, Thomas Marshall, Mr. Andrew Ward, George Hubbard, John Gibbs, Thurston Rayner, Mr. Moxam, Mr. Burr, Mr. Spencer, John Pratt, Edward Stebbing, Mr. Gaylord, Mr. Henry Wolcott, Mr. Stoughton, James Boosey, Richard Crabb, Mr. Porter, Mr. Tappan, and Mr. Hill. Many of the deputies above named, were frequently elected *after* the union.

NAMES.	From.	To.	NAMES.	From.	To.
Gershom Bulkley, "	1661	1666	Richard Denton, Stamford,	1641	1644
James Fitch, Norwich,...	1660	1694	John Bishop, Stamford,...	1644	1694
Mr. Jones, Fairfield,.....			Adam Blackman, Stratford,	1640	1665
Samuel Wakeman, do....	1665	1692	Israel Chauncey, Stratford,	1665	1722
Zechariah Walker, Stratford		1670	Thomas Hanford, Norwalk,	1654	

MASTERS.

List of gentlemen who are designated upon the Colonial Records of Connecticut, with the prefix of *Master* (or "Mr.") previous to the union of that colony with New Haven, 1665—including those who bore military titles of a nearly equal rank, viz:

NAMES.	Year.	NAMES.	Year.
Mr. Ludlow,.................	1636	Mr. Holmes,.................	1638
Mr. John Steele,..............	1636	Mr. Moxam,.................	1638
Mr. Wm. Swayne,............	1636	Mr. Burr,..................	1638
Mr. Wm. Westwood,..........	1636	Mr. Stephen Terry,...........	1638
Mr. Andrew Ward,...........	1636	Mr. Samuel Stone,............	1638
Mr. Wm. Phelps,.............	1636	Mr. William Goodwin,.........	1638
Mr. Wm. Pyncheon,..........	1636	Mr. George Wyllys,...........	1639
Mr. Thomas Allen,............	1636	Mr. William Gaylord,..........	1639
Mr. John Oldham,............	1636	Mr. Spencer,.................	1639
Mr. John Plumb,.............	1636	Mr. Stoughton,...............	1639
Mr. Francis Stiles,............	1636	Mr. Henry Wolcott,...........	1639
Mr. Seely,....................	1636	Mr. Moore,..................	1639
Mr. Strickland,...............	1636	Mr. Weed,..................	1639
Mr. Mitchell,.................	1636	Mr. Skinner,................	1639
Mr. Clement Chaplin,.........	1636	Mr. Porter,.................	1639
Mr. Thomas Welles,...........	1637	Mr. Tappan,................	1639
Mr. William Whiting,.........	1637	Mr. Hill,...................	1639
Mr. John Webster,............	1637	Mr. Fenwick,...............	1639
Mr. Williams,...	1637	Mr. Hooker,................	1639
Mr. Hull,....................	1637	Mr. John Woodcock,..........	1639
Mr. Talcott,..................	1637	Mr. Prudden,...............	1639
Mr. John Sherman,...........	1637	Mr. Matthew Allen,...........	1639
Mr. Hosford,.................	1637	Mr. Ephraim Hewett,..........	1640
Mr. John Mason,.............	1637	Mr. Arthur Williams,.........	1640
Mr. John Haynes,............	1637	Mr. Parks,..................	1640
Mr. Smith,...................	1638	Mr. Moody,.................	1640
Mr. Edward Hopkins,.........	1638	Mr. Edward Hopkins,.........	1640
Mr. Thomas Ford,............	1638	Mr. Rossiter,...............	1640

* These names are gathered mainly from J. Hammond Trumbull's "Colonial Records." It will be observed that many eminent names in our Colonial history, are not found in the roll here given. The reasons are obvious. The period covers only the first thirty years of our existence as a colony. Many gentlemen who were in Connecticut during that time, afterwards became prominent; others did not arrive from England until a later date. I have not been able to obtain anything like a complete list of those who bore this title in New Haven Colony. A very few only of the names here given, belonged to other jurisdictions.

NAMES.	Year.	NAMES.	Year.
Mr. Robert Saltonstall,	1641	Mr. John Wells,	1658
Mr. Deynton,	1641	Mr. Alexander Knowles,	1658
Mr. Clark,	1641	Mr. Baker,	1658
Mr. Coggen,	1641	Mr. Mulford,	1658
Mr. Fowler,	1641	Mr. Cobbett,	1658
Mr. Astwood,	1641	Mr. Danforth,	1658
Mr. Tapp,	1641	Mr. Brown,	1658
Mr. Phœnix,	1642	Mr. Norton,	1658
Mr. Cullick,	1642	Mr. Matthew Canfield,	1659
Mr. Tyler,	1642	Mr. Walter Hoyt,	1659
Mr. Eldridge,	1642	Mr. Samuel Wells,	1659
Mr. Chester,	1642	Mr. Thomas Fairchild,	1659
Mr. Treat,	1642	Mr. Wilton,	1659
Mr. Robbins,	1643	Mr. Barrett,	1659
Mr. Branker,	1643	Mr. Josiah Stanborough,	1659
Mr. John Hollister,	1643	Mr. Bruen,	1660
Mr. Andrews,	1644	Mr. John Cotton,	1660
Mr. Gilbert,	1646	Mr. Varlet,	1660
Mr. Graves,	1646	Mr. Stow,	1660
Mr. Cosmore,	1647	Mr. Rayner,	1660
Mr. Taintor,	1647	Mr. Bond,	1661
Mr. Boozey,	1647	Mr. Baker,	1661
Mr. Howell,	1647	Mr. Hall,	1661
Mr. Pinney,	1648	Mr. Richard Woodhull,	1661
Mr. Olcott,	1648	Mr. Thomas Pierce,	1661
Mr. Blackleach,	1649	Mr. Halsey,	1661
Mr. Blackman,	1649	Mr. Palms,	1661
Mr. Jonathan Brewster,	1650	Mr. Thomas Bull,	1661
Mr. Blinman,	1651	Mr. Joseph Willard,	1661
Mr. Augustine,	1651	Mr. Wm. Pratt,	1661
Mr. Wm. Lewis,	1651	Mr. Wm. Waller,	1661
Mr. Wheeler,	1651	Mr. Wm. Bushnell,	1661
Mr. John Steele, Jr.,	1651	Mr. Reynold Marvin,	1661
Mr. Thomas Barnes,	1651	Mr. Jonas Wood,	1662
Mr. Richard Olmsted,	1651	Mr. Wadsworth,	1662
Mr. Daniel Clark,	1653	Mr. Thomson,	1662
Mr. Denison,	1653	Mr. Joseph Haynes,	1662
Mr. Cook,	1653	Mr. James Rogers,	1662
Mr. Samuel Wyllys,	1654	Mr. Samuel Smith,	1662
Mr. Samuel Mayo,	1654	Mr. James Avery,	1662
Mr. Bryant,	1654	Mr. John Young,	1662
Mr. Fitch,	1654	Mr. Glover,	1662
Mr. John Whiting,	1654	Mr. Elton,	1662
Mr. Wm. Whiting, Jr.,	1654	Mr. Tucker,	1662
Mr. Baxter,	1654	Mr. William Pitkin,	1662
Mr. John Russell,	1654	Mr. Samuel Talcott,	1662
Mr. Ogden,	1656	Mr. Rickball,	1662
Mr. Benjamin Newbury,	1656	Mr. Sylvester,	1662
Mr. Nathan Gold,	1656	Mr. Gardiner,	1662
Mr. Wareham,	1656	Mr. Tyler,	1663
Mr. Thomas Pell,	1656	Mr. Anthony Howkins,	1663
Mr. Lord,	1656	Mr. Robert Chapman,	1663
Mr. Kilbourn,	1657	Mr. Burr,	1663
Mr. John Betts,	1657	Mr. Thomas Minor,	1663
Mr. Dickerson,	1657	Mr. Jones,	1663
Mr. Nott,	1657	Mr. Samuel Sherman,	1663

NAMES.	Year.	NAMES.	Year.
Mr. Hanford,................	1663	Mr. Wood,..................	1664
Mr. Wakeman,...............	1663	Mr. Barton,.................	1664
Mr. Richard Mills,............	1663	Mr. Thomas Benedict,.........	1664
Mr. John Budd,..............	1663	Mr. Richard Betts,............	1664
Mr. Richard Smith, Sr.........	1663	Mr. William Noble,...........	1664
Mr. Joseph Hews,............	1663	Mr. William Hallett,..........	1664
Mr. Edw. Hutchinson,.........	1663	Mr. James Hubbard,..........	1664
Mr. Richard Smith, Jr.........	1663	Mr. William Wilkins, ...	1664
Mr. Bourne,.................	1663	Mr. James Richards,..........	1664
Mr. Dallye,..................	1663	Mr. Fordham,...............	1664
Mr. Tracy,..................	1663	Mr. Walker,.................	1664
Mr. John Scott,..............	1664	Mr. Loveridge,...............	1664
Mr. Bissell,..................	1664	Mr. Hagborn,................	1664
Mr. Hamlin,.................	1664	Mr. Douglass,................	1664
Mr. John Hicks,.............	1664	Mr. John Moore,.............	1664
Mr. Robert Coe,.............	1664	Mr. John Stanley,............	1664
Mr. John Coe,...............	1664	Mr. Cornelius Hull,...........	1664
Mr. William Clark,...........	1664	Mr. John Banks,.............	1664
Mr. Jessup,.................	1664	Mr. Robert Treat,.............	1664

FAMILY NAMES

OF SOME OF THE PLANTERS OF THE COLONIES OF CONNECTICUT AND NEW HAVEN,

PREVIOUS TO THEIR UNION IN 1665.

Abbe,
Abbott,
Abel,
Abernethy,
Ackley,
Adams,
Addis,
Adgate,
Adkins,
Aiken,
Alcock,
Alexander,
Allen,
Alsop,
Alvord,
Andrews,
Andrus,
Armstrong,
Arnold,
Ashley,
Astwood,
Atkins,

Atkinson,
Atwater,
Atwood,
Austin,
Avery,
Axtell,
Ayres,

Backus,
Bacon,
Bailey,
Baker,
Baldwin,
Bamster,
Bancroft,
Banks,
Barber,
Barden,
Barker,
Bailey,
Barlow,
Barnard,

Barnes,
Barnum,
Barrett,
Barrows,
Bartlett,
Bateman,
Bates,
Bascomb,
Bassett,
Baxter,
Beach,
Beacham,
Beale,
Beard,
Beardsley,
Beaucamp,
Beebe,
Beecher,
Beers,
Beckley,
Beckwith,
Belcher,

Belden,
Bell,
Bellingham,
Beaumont,
Bement,
Benedict,
Benham,
Benjamin,
Bennett,
Benton,
Benson,
Betts,
Bidwell,
Bigelow,
Birchard,
Biggs,
Billings,
Bingham,
Bird,
Birdseye,
Birge,
Bishop,

Bissell,
Buckland,
Blachford,
Blackleach,
Blackman,
Blakesley,
Blinman,
Bliss,
Bloomer,
Blomfield,
Boardman,
Bolles,
Boltwood,
Bolt,
Bond,
Boosy,
Bordain,
Booth,
Bostwick,
Boswell,
Botsford,
Bowe,
Bowers,
Boughton,
Boyd,
Boyes,
Boykin,
Brackett,
Bratfield,
Brace,
Brawley,
Bradley,
Bradstreet,
Brainerd,
Bramfield,
Branker,
Brattle,
Breed,
Brewster,
Bruen,
Bridgeman,
Brigden,
Briggs,
Brinsmade,
Bristol,
Brockett,
Brodwell,
Brockway,
Bronson,
Brooke,
Brooks,
Brown,
Browning,
Brundish,
Brush,
Bryan,
Budd,
Buck,
Buckingham,
Buel,
Bulkley,
Bull,
Bunce,
Bunnell,
Burden,
Burgess,
Burnham,
Burroughs,
Burr,
Burrett,
Burwell,
Bush,
Bushnell,
Butler,
Butterfield,

Cabell,
Cadwell,
Calder,
Camp,
Canfield,
Carr,
Carrington,
Carrier,
Carter,
Case,
Castle,
Catlin,
Cattell,
Caulkins,
Chalker,
Chalkwell,
Champion,
Chauncey,
Chappell,
Chapin,
Chaplin,
Chapman,
Charles,
Charwell,
Chalfield,
Chatterton,
Chidsey,
Cheeney,
Chapperfield,
Cherry,
Cheener,
Chester,
Cheseborough.
Chichester,
Chittenden,
Christophers,
Church,
Churchill,
Clark,
Clemons,
Clough,
Carbitt,
Cadman,
Cadner,
Coe,
Cogswell,
Coit,
Cole,
Cone,
Constable,
Cowles,
Colfaxe,
Coleman,
Collier,
Collins,
Coltman,
Colt,
Colton,
Comstock,
Conklin,
Coker,
Cooke,
Cooley,
Cooper,
Cornelius,
Cornwell,
Cary,
Cosmore,
Colton,
Crane,
Craddock,
Cross,
Crowell,
Crumb,
Cullick,
Curtis,
Curwin

Daniels,
Davenport,
Davis,
Davies,
Dawes,
Day,
Deming,
Denison,
Denslow
Desborough,
Dewey,
Dibble,
Dickinson,
Douglass
Dowd,
Drake,
Dyer,
Dixon,
Dix,
Dudley,
Dummer,

East,
Eaton,
Edwards,
Edmunds,
Eggleston,
Elderkin,
Eldred,
Eldridge,
Ellis,
Ellison,
Elliott,
Elmore,
Elsing,
Ellsworth,
Elton,
Ely,
Everts,
Evans,

Fairchild,
Farrand,
Fellowes,
Fenn,
Fenner,
Fenwick,
Ferman,
Ferris,
Filley,
Finch,
Fish,
Fisher,
Fitch,
Fletcher,
Foote,
Ford,
Foster,
Fowler,
Franklin,
Frost,
Fugill,
Freeman,
Fuller,
Fyler,

Gager,
Gaines,
Gaylord,
Galpin,
Gardner,
Garrett,
Gibbons,
Gibbs,
Gibbud,
Gilbert,
Gildersleeve,
Gillett,

Glover,
Gold,
Goodman,
Goodrich,
Goodwin,
Goodyear,
Grannis,
Grant,
Graves,
Gray,
Green,
Gregson,
Gridley,
Griffin,
Griswold.
Gunn.

Hale,
Hall,
Hallett,
Halsey,
Hamlin,
Hanford,
Hardy,
Harrison,
Harris,
Hart,
Hartley,
Harvey,
Hazard,
Hawkins,
Hawkes,
Haynes,
Hayward,
Hayes,
Heaton,
Hewett,
Hicks,
Higginson,
Higley,
Hill,
Hills,
Hillyar,
Hine,
Hitchcock,
Hickok,
Hoadley,
Houghton,
Holbrook,
Holbridge,
Holcomb,
Hollister,
Holt,
Hopkins,
Hook,
Hooker,
Hoskins,
Hosford,
Horton,
Hosmer,
Hoyt,
Howard,
Hubbard,
Hubbell,
Hudson,
Husted,
Humphrey,
Hull,
Hungerford,
Hurd,
Hutchinson

Ireland,
Ives.

Jackson,
Jacox,
James,
Jenner,
Jennings,
Jessup,
Johnson,
Jones,
Jordan,
Judd,
Judson.

Keeler,
Kellogg,
Kelsey,
Kenney,
Kirby,
Kitchell,
Ketchum,
Kilbourn,
Kimberly
King,
Kirkham,
Knowles.

Langdon,
Larribee,
Lamberton,
Lathrop,
Latham,
Latimer,
Lane,
Lay,
Law,
Lawrence,
Lee,
Leete,
Leffingwell,
Leonard,
Leverett,
Lewis,
Lines,
Livermore,
Lobdell,
Lockwood,
Loomis,
Lowe,
Lord,
Lucas,
Ludlow
Lupton,
Lyman,
Lyon.

Mygatt,
Mapes,
Marsh,
Marshall,
Marshfield,
Martin,
Marvin,
Mason,
Maynard,
May,
Mayo,
Mead,
Meigs,
Mercer,
Merrick,
Merwin,
Merrill,
Miles,
Mills,
Minor,
Mitchell,
Moody,
Moore,
Morehouse,
Morgan,
Morton,
Moses,
Moulthrop,
Mudge,
Mulford,
Munson.

Nash,
Newbury,
Nettleton,
Newman,
Newton,
Nichols,
Noble,
North,
Northam,
Northrop,
Norton,
Nott.

Odell,
Ogden,
Olcott,
Oldham,
Oldridge,
Olmsted,
Orton,
Orvis,
Osborne.

Packer,
Paine,
Palmer
Palmes,
Pantry,
Parker,
Parks,
Parkman,
Parsons,
Partridge,
Patterson,
Patton,
Peck,
Peacock,
Pell,
Perkins,
Perry,
Pettibone,
Phelps,
Phillips,
Pierce,
Pinney,
Pinckney,
Pitkin,
Pincheon,
Platt,
Plumb,
Pomeroy
Pond,
Potter,
Porter,
Post,
Powell,
Pratt,
Prentice,
Pritchard,
Preston,
Prindle,
Prime,
Provost,
Prudden,
Pierson,
Pine,
Putnam,
Purdy,
Punderson,

Quicke,

Quinly.

Randall,
Rayner,
Read,
Reeder,
Reeves,
Reynolds,
Riggs,
Rice,
Richards,
Riley,
Risley,
Robbins,
Roberts,
Robinson,
Rogers,
Rossiter,
Rowland,
Royce,
Rudd,
Russell.

Sadler,
Salter,
Saltonstall,
Sanford,
Sawyer,
Savage,
Scott,
Scranton,
Scudder,
Seager,
Seldon,
Selleck,
Sension,
Seymour,
Shepard,
Sherman,
Sedgwick,
Seeley,
Shute,
Sherwood,
Sill,
Simpson,
Skidmore,
Skinner,
Smith,
Southmayd,
Spencer,
Stillson,
Stoddard,
Stanton,
Staples,
Starks,
Stebbing,
Stedman,
Steele,
Stephens,
Stephenson,
Stillwell,
Strickland,
Stocking,
Stone,
Stoughton,
Stowe,
Strong
Stiles,
Sultan.

Tallcott,
Tallman,
Tallmadge,
Tapp,
Tapping,
Taylor,
Tench,
Terry,
Thorp,
Thompson
Thornton,
Thrall,
Tibballs,
Tillton,
Tinker,
Titterton,
Titus,
Tomlinson,
Tompkins,
Torrey,
Tong,
Tracy,
Treat,
Trowbridge,
Trumbull,
Try,
Tucker,
Tudor,
Turner,
Turney,
Turrell.

Uffoot,
Underhill,
Upson,
Usher.

Vaill,
Vincent,
Veare.

Wade,
Wadhams,
Wadsworth,
Wakely,
Wakeman,
Waller,
Waples,
Ward,
Wareham,
Warner,
Warren,
Waterhouse,
Waters,
Watson,
Watts,
Wainwright,
Webb,
Webster,
Weed,
Welch,
Wellman,
Welles,
West,
Westall,
Westcott,
Wesley,
Weston,
Westwood,
Wetmore,
Wheeler,
White,
Whitehead,
Whitfield,
Whiting,
Whitman,
Whitmore,
Wyatt,
Wicks,
Wickham,
Wilcox,
Wilcoxson,
Wilkinson,
Wilkins,
Willard,
Willis,
Williams,
Willett,
Willey,
Wilson,
Wilton,
Winchell,
Wines,
Winthrop,
Wolcott,
Wood,
Woodruff,
Woodford,
Wooster,
Woodcock,
Works,
Wright.

Yale,
Yates,
Young,
Youngs.

INDEX OF NAMES.

VOL. I.

ALPHABETICAL INDEX OF SUBJECTS.

VOL. I.

INDEX OF QUESTIONS.

VOL. I.

NOTE.—[The figures in the margin denote the pages in the history to which the questions refer.]

QUESTIONS.

CHAPTER I.

(17.) When did Wah-qui-ma-cut visit the Governors of Massachusetts and Plymouth?

What was his object?

What inducement did he hold out to settlers?

How was he received?

Who visited the Valley of the Connecticut?

(18.) What report did Winslow make?

Where was the first English trading-house in the valley established?

By whom was it erected?

Who opposed his passage up the river?

(19.) From whom did Holmes purchase the land at Windsor?

Who were enraged at the conduct of Holmes?

Who attempted to drive the English from the river?

What was the result of the attempt?

(20.) To whom and how did the Plymouth Company convey the territory of Connecticut?

To whom and when did Warwick convey it?

What was the character of the new proprietors?

(21.) What did Milton say of one of them?

By whom was the soil pre-occupied?

Why did the settlers in Massachusetts seek for new quarters?

By whom was their removal to Connecticut opposed?

(22.) Who was the principal advocate for removal?

Where had Hooker been settled in England?

Why was he silenced?

Who petitioned the Bishop in his behalf, and with what result?

With what expectation did his parishioners embark for America?

Where did they settle?

When did Messrs. Hooker and Stone, arrive in Massachusetts?

(23.) Who was the chief opponent of removing to Connecticut?

What were the arguments of Hooker?

What were Mr. Cotton's arguments?

(24.) What was the result of the discussion?

What is said of Hooker's views?

By whom and when was the order of the General Court of Massachusetts set at defiance?

Where did they settle?

When did Massachusetts grant the application to remove, and with what proviso?

(25.) Who next removed from Massachusetts?

Where did they settle?

By whom were they followed?

How many persons passed through the wilderness in October, 1635?

With what obstacles did they meet?

Where did they settle?
What distinguished man came to New England this year?
What were his instructions?
(26.) What was the title given him in his commission?
Who were preparing to anticipate him?
Who erected a fortification at the mouth of the river?
What did the Dutch do when they saw the new fortress?
How had the settlers on the river for warded their effects from Massachusetts?
(27.) What became of them?
How did they procure corn?
What other misfortunes attended them?
Where did many of the settlers go?
How did those who remained provide for themselves?
How did the cattle fare?
(28.) What was the government of the colony?
When were the General Courts to meet?
How many magistrates were to be chosen?
How many deputies were to be elected from each town?
How were the special courts to be constituted?
What were the powers of the General Court?
(29.) When and where was the first court held?
What prominent statesman was present?
What act was passed?
Who started for Connecticut?
What number of persons was there in the company?
How did they proceed on their journey?
How was Mrs. Hooker borne?
What was the character of the emigrants?
(30.) What were the characteristics of the route?
How long were they on the journey?
How did their new home appear to them?
How is the scene described?
(31.) What results are to follow?

CHAPTER II.

(32.) How does the present age differ from that of which we are speaking?
What is said of our woodlands?
What were the peculiarities of the original forests?
(33.) What were some of the animals sheltered by them?
What depredations did they commit?
What measures were taken against these offenders?
What is said of the varieties of wild fowl?
(34.) What kinds of fish abounded?
What number of Indians inhabited Connecticut?
What peculiarities indicated a common origin?
In what towns did the "river Indians" live?
How many sovereignties and bondmen were there in Windsor?
(35.) What was the extent of the Mohegan and Pequot country?
Were they distinct tribes?
What was the position and character of Uncas?
What was the character and power of Sassacus?
(36.) What were his familiar haunts?
Where was his principal fort?
What was the extent of his power and wealth?
How and where was his other fort situated?
What were the peculiarities of form and feature in the red man?
(37.) How were the Indians dressed?
What were some of their peculiar traits?
(38.) What is said of their power of endurance?

How were the males accustomed to spend their time?
What were the usual labors of the females?
What were their physical characteristics?
(39.) What were the principal manufactures of the aborigines?
How was the tomahawk constructed?
What was their mode of making canoes?
(40.) What were their objects of worship?
What was the name of their "Good Spirit?"
What was the name of their spirit of evil?
Which did they worship most?
(41.) What was their priesthood called?
What was their civil government?
How were the aristocracy bred?
How did they contrive to exalt themselves?
What motives induced Massasoit to welcome the English?
(42.) What were the plans and motives of Uncas?
What were the purposes of Sassacus?
What was the speed of an Indian runner?
What representations did the couriers make?
What depredations did the agents of Sassacus commit?
(43.) What Englishmen were murdered by Indians?
What were the particulars of these murders?
What events immediately followed?
(44.) Who began to be alarmed?
To whom did the Pequots send a message, and for what object?
What reception did he meet with?
Who were afterward sent?
What charges did the Governor make against the Pequots?
What defence did the agents make?
What requests did they make?
(45.) What were the terms of the treaty established?
Did the Indians abide by it?
Who was murdered by the Indians?
Who rescued Oldham's vessel from the murderers?
What were the circumstances of the rescue?
(46.) In what condition was Oldham's body found?
Who committed the body to the sea?
What was done with Oldham's vessel?
Who were concerned in the murder?
By whom was the murder disclaimed?
What measures were devised to avenge the death of Oldham?
(47.) Who commanded the expedition against Block Island?
What was the Island called by the savages?
What did Endicott accomplish?
Whence did he sail from Block Island?
What did Gardiner tell him?
(48.) Where did Endicott next land?
What did he tell the Indians?
With whom did he demand an interview?
What was the object of the Indians in keeping him in parley?
How was Endicott outwitted?
What did he accomplish?
(49.) Where did he land the next day?
What did he do there?
Whence did he then sail?
What was Gardiner's advice to him and his men?
With what were they loading their shallops?
What reception did the Indians give them?
What were the results of the expedition?
Where was the next attack of the Indians?
(50.) What was done with Butterfield?
Who was the next victim?

What was the result of their tortures?
How were the Indians employed?
What further depredations did they commit?
(51.) Where was Mason sent?
What murders were committed at Saybrook?
How did the Indians attempt to insult the English?
What murders and mutilations are mentioned?
What efforts were made to terrify the English?
How was the sarcasm of the English manifested?
(52.) Who was the Indian interpreter?
What conversation passed between him and the savages?
Who did the Indians acknowledge themselves to be?
What threats did they make?
What reply did Gardiner make?
(53.) What did the Indians do at Wethersfield?
To whom did the captive maidens owe their lives?
Who was sent from Massachusetts to reinforce the garrison at Saybrook?
How many English people did the colony contain?
(54.) How was the General Court constituted?
What important act was passed?
What is said of its phraseology?
How many troops was each town to furnish?
How soon were the troops ready to sail?
Where and when did they embark?
How many English and Indians were embraced in the army?
Who was the commander?
Who was the chaplain?
(55.) How long were they in reaching Saybrook?
Who joined with Mason?
What had Uncas accomplished?
How was the Indian spy executed?
How long was Mason wind-bound at Saybrook?
(56.) What were Mason's instructions?
Why did he conclude it best to disobey these instructions?
What did he urge upon the Council of War?
(57.) Why did his men hesitate?
What was to be done?
Who was desired "to commend their condition to the Lord?"
What was the result?
To whose residence did they march?
What was Miantinomoh's opinion?
(58.) What was Capt. Patrick's request?
Why was it not complied with?
When did the army begin their march for the Pequot forts?
With what reception did he meet from a Narragansett sachem?
What did Mason do?
To what was the conduct of the Nihanticks attributable?
How many Indians had joined Mason?
(59.) How did they behave as they approached the seat of Sassacus?
What did Uncas say?
What intelligence did Mason now receive?
(60.) How was the prediction of Uncas verified?
Who was Mason's guide?
Where and how did the English pass the night?
How did the enemy pass the night?
When did they re-commence their march?
How far did the fort prove to be from their place of encampment?
(61.) What passed between Mason and the chiefs?
What was the order of attack?
How did the assailants succeed in entering the fort?
What incidents occurred?

(62.) How many acres did the palisades embrace?
How many houses did they enclose?
What exclamation did Capt. Mason make?
What followed?
(63.) What did the savages do?
How is the scene described?
What number of wigwams were burnt?
Now many of the enemy were destroyed?
What treasures were consumed?
How many escaped?
How many were taken prisoners?
How many of the English were among the killed and wounded?
(64.) What was the situation of the victors?
What circumstance did they hail with joy?
What followed when the tidings reached the fort of Sassacus?
Why did Mason commence his march toward Pequot harbor?
How many men had he to engage in battle?
What point did the Pequots reach?
(65.) How did they manifest their grief?
Who defended the rear during Mason's return?
How did the Pequots seek revenge?
Were any slain during the return march?
How long was Mason absent from Hartford?

CHAPTER III.

(66.) How was Sassacus treated by his people?
What charges and threats did they make?
What were the results of their consultations?
(67.) Who fled to the westward?
What did Roger Williams do?
What did the Governor and Council of Massachusetts do?
Who commanded the new expedition?
Who was its chaplain?
What was its object?
What did it accomplish at Pequot harbor?
What did Connecticut do?
Who commanded the Connecticut troops?
Who went with the army as advisers?
What did the Council of War determine upon?
(68.) What traces did they discover of the fugitives?
What was done with the Sachems taken by Stoughton?
Where did their execution take place?
What is the place still called?
Why did the English prolong their stay at New Haven?
What tidings did the Pequot spy bring?
(69.) Where was the swamp situated?
How many Pequots were there concealed?
What was the result of the skirmish?
What did the Fairfield Indians say?
What Indians were offered life?
Who accepted the terms?
Who continued the fight?
(70.) What plan was finally agreed upon by the English?
How did they pass the night?
Whose quarters did the enemy first attack?
Who relieved Capt. Patrick?
How many Pequot warriors fled?
How many were killed?
How many were taken prisoners?
(71) What became the property of the conquerors?
What became of the captives and booty?
Who were among the captives?
What was done in their behalf?
How did those captives fare that fell to Connecticut?
What was the fate of Sassacus?
What was done with his scalp?

Who met the magistrates of Connecticut?
How many of the Pequots survived?
What were the terms of the treaty entered into?
(72.) What was done with the survivors?
What was the primary cause of the war?
What can be said in its justification?
(73.) How may the reader come to a just conclusion?

CHAPTER IV.

(74.) What had England borrowed from feudalism?
What kept her in a state of unrest?
What sentiment prevailed?
What is said of the progress of liberty?
What was the character of Henry VIII.?
(75.) What were his religious sentiments?
What were some of his cruel acts?
What was the result of his alliance with Catharine Howard?
What is said of Catharine Parr?
(76.) What were the King and his subjects doing?
Was the spirit of the reformation progressing?
Who composed the reformation party?
What was accomplished during the reign of Edward?
(77.) What were the position and policy of Elizabeth?
What was her character?
(78.) Who were her counselors?
For what was she solicitous?
What did she accomplish?
How might she have avoided many evils?
What was required in religious belief?
What was the result among the clergy?
What were the objects and powers of the Court of High Commission?
(79.) For what were men hanged?
What was the result of these harsh measures?
How was the accession of James, I., recieved by the puritans?
Had they cause to be disappointed?
How many clergymen were silenced in a single year?
What was the conduct of the king toward the puritans?
Who were the progressive party?
Wherein were they like the members of the established church under Elizabeth?
(80.) What is said of those who were in power?
What was the nature of the struggle?
What did the extreme measures of the two parties evince?
In what respects were they alike?
To what alternatives were the puritans driven?
(81.) Whither did they fly?
What was their leading motive?
What secular motives had they?
Why did the fathers of Connecticut leave Massachusetts?
(82.) What was the origin of human government?
What were the characteristics of the powers of the government of Connecticut?
How shall we judge of them impartially?
(83.) What may be said of the mirror provided for us?
How does the preamble of the Constitution begin?
What is further stated in it?
What were the objects arrived at?
When were the General Assemblies to be held?
What was the April Court to be called?
(84.) When were the officers of the colony to be chosen?
By whom were the officers to be chosen?
In what order were they to be elected?

In what manner was the Governor to be chosen?
How were the other officers to be nominated and chosen?
How many magistrates were to be elected?
(85.) How and when were the nominees to be propounded?
How often could the same person be elected governor?
What qualifications were requisite in the candidate for governor?
How was the court of election to be constituted?
How was it to proceed?
How were the regular courts to be convened?
In what contingencies and how were the special courts to be called?
In case of neglect of the proper officers to call the courts, how were they to be convened?
(86.) How were meetings for the choice of deputies to be called?
By whom were the deputies to be chosen?
Who were eligible to the office of deputy?
How were deputies to be chosen?
How many deputies might each town send?
What were their powers?
What course was to be pursued when deputies were not legally elected?
How was the General Court to be constituted?
If called by the people, of whom was it to consist?
(87.) With whom was lodged "the Supreme power of the Commonwealth?"
What power had the Governor or Moderator?
How were taxes to be raised?
What is said of our Constitution?
What are the characteristics of the British Constitution?
(88.) What are some of the features of the Constitution of Connecticut
(89.) What is said of our towns?
Did our Constitution recognize the king?
What is said of it in connection with other American Constitutions?
(90.) What laws were passed under it?
What does Brancroft say of it?

CHAPTER V.

(91.) What calamity threatened the settlers?
How did Mr. Pyncheon relieve them?
What other means of relief was resorted to?
How much corn was procured of the Deerfield Indians?
Why was the Colony in debt?
What was the amount of the tax laid?
(92.) Who was appointed commander-in-chief of the Militia?
What were his instructions?
What was the amount of his salary?
Who delivered to him the staff of office?
How is the scene described by Dr. Bushnell?
(93.)What distinguished men arrived in Boston?
How were they received?
What efforts were made to retain them in Massachusetts?
What led them to explore the coast of Connecticut?
What place did they finally select for a settlement?
(94.) What had the Dutch named the place?
When did the company sail for Quinnipiack?
Where did they spend their first Sabbath?
How is the scene described?
Who were some of the principal gentlemen present?
(95.) What was the subject of Mr. Davenport's discourse?

What was Mr. Prudden's text?
What was the peculiarity of their "plantation covenant?"
What was the condition of their first crops?
What phenomena occurred?
(96.) What were some of its effects?
Of whom was the land purchased?
What were the peculiarities of the deed of sale?
Who acted as interpreter?
What was the extent of the second purchase?
Of whom was this purchase made?
What towns did it embrace?
What was the consideration for the deed?
(97.) What emigrants arrived from England?
Where did the people of New Haven meet to organize their government?
From what text did Mr. Davenport preach?
What was the character of his sermon?
(98.) What resolutions were adopted?
By what were they to be guided?
What were the desires and wishes of the free planters?
Who were to be free burgesses?
What were their powers?
How did they commence their church organization?
(99.) Who were the seven pillars of the church in New Haven?
Was the government a "theocracy?"
How was their civil government organized?
(100.) How long were they deliberating?
Why did they adopt the laws of Moses?
What was the practical workings of their system?
Were not its results good?
(101.) When were Milford and Guilford settled?
Who were the principal settlers of Milford?
When was Milford annexed to the Colony of New Haven?
Whence did the settlers come?
What is said of Robert Treat?
How many composed the first company?
Who was their guide?
What is said of the Paugasset Indians?
(102.) What is said of the early settlers of Guilford?
Who was their clergyman?
What is said of him?
What was the history of Samuel Desborough?
(103.) What high office did he hold?
When did he sign his submission to Charles II.?
How was he treated by the King?
Where and when did he die?
What memorial exists of him and of his wife?
How does his miniature represent him?
(104.) What was the history of William Leete?
Was Guilford ever independent of New Haven Colony?
What characterized the year 1639?
What were the characteristics of Ludlow?
To what place did he remove?
Where had he previously lived?
(105.) Who soon joined his party?
To what Colony did the town belong?
Of whom was the land purchased?
What town was next purchased and settled?
Who was the first magistrate of the town?
Who were some of the principal settlers?
Who was the first clergyman?
What is said of him?
What is said of Stratford?

CHAPTER VI.

(106.) Where had a new Commonwealth sprung up?

Who were some of its proprietors?
What was its nominal extent?
By whom was it established?
When did he and his household arrive?
What did they name their settlement?
How long had there been a garrison at Saybrook?
Who were the original proprietors of the town?
Who was the first clergyman?
What other names appear upon the early records?
(107.) What was the Government, and by whom administered?
When was it annexed to Connecticut?
What threatened another Indian war?
What was the extent of Sowheag's jurisdiction?
What was the cause of the quarrel between him and the people of Wethersfield?
What did the Court decide?
Who were appointed as arbitrators?
What was the result?
What did the Court then determine?
(108.) How was the project regarded in New Haven?
What did Connecticut do?
Wherein had the Pequots offended?
Who were sent to punish the transgressors?
What did they accomplish?
(109.) Where did Mason and his men spend the night?
At what were they surprised?
What conversation took place between Mason and the Indians?
What did the English accomplish?
What plan for the public safety was proposed?
Who were appointed to consult with Col. Fenwick?
What was the object of the proposed union?
(110.) Of what was it the forerunners?
What did the General Court do?
What did its action amount to?
How was the tribunal in each town constituted?
How were its members elected?
What were its powers?
How often did it meet?
What provision was made for a land record?
(111.) What was the duty of land-holders?
What is said of the utility of the object?
What are the requisites of a legal provision?
What provision was made for settling estates?
(112.) What is said of the difficulty of purchasing lands of the Indians?
What purchases were made, and settlements commenced?
What troubles attended the settlement of Greenwich?
How did Connecticut extend her limits?
What was the extent of the purchase?
(113.) What township was next purchased?
Who was the first minister there?
Where was Capt. Turner sent to buy lands?
How many families were sent to take possession?
What other purchase was made on Long Island?
Under whose auspices was the settlement begun?
Who were some of the leading planters there?
What is said of Wethersfield?
What was the character of her people?
(114.) What remark had their conduct elicited?
To what was their conduct attributable?
Under whose direction was Windsor settled?
What is said of him?
Who were the other principal settlers?

What were some of the names of other settlers?

(115.) What was one of the results of the troubles in Wethersfield?

Who attempted to tranquilize the differences?

Who removed to Stamford?

Who remained in Wethersfield?

Where did most of the proprietors own land?

(116.) What is said of the intermarriages of the Wethersfield families?

Why was the project for a confederation revived?

For what purpose had delegates been annually appointed?

Why did Massachusetts feel indifferent on the subject?

How did Connecticut and New Haven differ from Massachusetts?

What did Massachusetts claim?

What object had she for delay?

What colonies sent commissioners to Boston?

Who did Connecticut send?

(117.) Who were the commissioners of New Haven?

Who represented Plymouth?

Who went in behalf of Saybrook?

Who were the Massachusetts delegates?

Who did these men prefigure?

What name was given to the confederation?

What do they declare?

What is stated in regard to the jurisdiction of each colony?

How many Commissioners may each colony send?

How often are they to meet?

What are their powers?

In case of war how are the expenses to be borne?

(118.) In case of an invasion, what number of troops was each colony to furnish?

In this Congress, how many votes were necessary to bind the whole body?

If a majority voted for any measure, and yet not the requisite number, what was to be done?

What law was passed in regard to fugitives?

What trouble arose among the Indian tribes?

Who represented the Narragansetts, and who the Mohegans?

(119.) What had Uncas done?

How had Miantinomoh violated his pledges?

What were the suspicions against him?

What request was made of Massachusetts, and with what success?

What course did Miantinomoh take?

(120.) What did he intend?

What is said of Uncas and his spies?

Where did they discover the Narragansetts?

How is the spot described by Miss Caulkins?

What course did Uncas persue?

What did he demand of Miantinomoh?

Did the parley take place?

(121.) What was the substance of it?

What was Uncas' stratagem, and what its result?

Whither were the invaders pursued?

How were some of them killed?

What impeded the speed of Miantinomoh?

(122.) When he was overtaken by Uncas, what followed?

How many Narragansett's had been slain?

Who were among the captives?

What did Uncas say to his prisoner?

What did Uncas do with him?

What did the Mohegan chief agree to do?

(123.) What charges were brought against Miantinomoh?

Were the charges probably true?

Who were made judges in the case?
What was their decision?
Where was he taken for execution?
Who was the executioner?
(124.) How was he killed?
What did Uncas then do?
Where was he buried?
How did his people commemorate his death?
What is said of the sentence and character of Miantinomoh?

CHAPTER VII.

(126.) What were the relations existing between the English and Dutch colonies?
Who first sailed along our coast?
What was the name of his yacht?
Where and when was it built?
What point did he probably discover?
What name did he give it?
What other discoveries did he make?
What island is named from him?
(127.) What did he enter and explore?
Who soon followed him?
What trade did they carry on?
When did they purchase the land at Saybrook?
What name did they give it?
When did they purchase Dutch Point?
What prior claims did the English set up?
Why should the respective claims be suffered to rest?
When did the war break out between the Dutch and Indians?
How did it originate?
(128.) What wrong did the Mohawks commit?
What commission was granted to Marine?
How did he act under it?
To whom did the Dutch governor apply for assistance?
What resulted from the application?
How did the Dutch like the war?
What was the Dutch governor compelled to do?
How many Dutchmen did the Indians kill?
(129.) What settlements were broken up?
When did Mrs. Hutchinson leave Rhode Island?
To what place did she and her family retire?
What may have been her object?
Did the Indians understand her mission?
What did they do?
How many shared her fate?
(130.) What did the Indians continue to do?
To whom, and with what result, did the Dutch governor apply?
How long did the war last?
What is said of Underhill?
How many Indians did he kill?
How were the people of Stamford affected by the war?
What is said of the year 1644?
How did the colonists attempt to avert the threatened calamities?
What did the Indians of western Connecticut do?
(131.) What took place between Ludlow and the Indians?
What advice did the New Haven court give?
On what condition were the Indian prisoners liberated?
What outrage did an Indian commit at Stamford?
To what other warlike measures did the Indians resort?
What towns applied for assistance?
(132.) What was done with the savage who had made the assault at Stamford?
By whom and when had Totoket been purchased?
Why was the same territory conveyed to Mr. Swaine?

Who joined Mr. Swaine's party?
What name was given to the town?
When did the Commissioners meet at Hartford?
What claim was set up by Massachusetts?
What was done in regard to it?
(133.) What depredations were committed in Virginia?
What object was it believed the Indians had in view?
What is said of the Narragansetts and Mohegans?
Who were sent to visit the Sachems?
What offers and promises were they to make?
What charges were made against Uncas?
In whose favor was the decision?
What did the Narragansetts agree to?
(134.) Who now waited upon the Commissioners?
What did they want?
Did they receive it?
What claim was renewed by Massachusetts?
In whose behalf did Fenwick interpose?
What did the Commissioners decide?
What other claim was renewed by Massachusetts?
What was finally decreed?
What is said of Southampton?
(135.) What committee was appointed by the General Court?
When were the articles of agreement signed?
What lands, &c., were made over to Connecticut?
What other items did the articles contain?
When was the agreement ratified?
What specifications were embraced in the tariff?
(136.) What amount was thus paid for the purchase?
What measures were taken to put the fort in repair?
Whose death is mentioned?
Where did he leave an estate?
(137.) What is said of his character?
When and for what purpose did he send over his steward?
(138.) When did he arrive in Connecticut?
When was he chosen deputy governor and governor?
What kind of a life did he lead?
Where sleeps his dust?
What is said of the Charter Oak Place?
When and how did the Narragansetts violate their treaty?
What measures were taken to protect the Mohegans?
When did the commissioners convene in Boston?
(139.) What proposals were made to the Indians?
What threats were made by a Narragansett?
What did Roger Williams write to the commissioners?
What did the commissioners do?
Who had command of the Connecticut and New Haven forces?
Why was Atherton sent in advance?
What instructions were given to Gibbons?
(140.) What request did the Narragansetts make of Winslow?
What did the commissioners do with the present sent to Winslow?
What tidings did the messengers bring back with them?
Who soon arrived in Boston?
What did they deny and urge?
What did they offer to do?
What did the commissioners say?
What did the Indians acknowledge?
What token of submission did they offer?

(141.) What were the terms of the new treaty?
What impelled them to submit to its terms?
When was a settlement commenced upon the Tunixs river?
When was the town incorporated, and what was it named?
What was the size of the township?
What towns have set off from it?
What is said of the first settlers?
What subject was laid before the commissioners in 1646?
(142.) What claims were re-asserted by the Dutch governor?
What charges did he make against the English?
What answer did Gov. Eaton make?
What complaints were made against the Dutch?
What did the commissioners write to Gov. Kieft?
(143.) What other complaint was made against the Dutch?
What effect had these letters upon Kieft?
What defense did he make?
What denial and protest did he make?
What was the substance of the reply of the commissioners?
(144.) What was the design of Sequasson?
Who did he hire to execute the plot?
What did he do, after receiving the rewards?
What did the Windsor Indians do?
Whom did the commissioners cite to appear before them?
What did he do?
To what are the savages likened?
How did the Mohawks spend their time?
What is said of their tax-gatherers?
(145.) What towns did the Mohawks visit?
How were they surprised and captured?
How did the captors attempt to torture one of the prisoners?
By whom was he liberated?
What effect had this act upon the Mohawks?
In what business had the people of New Haven been engaged?
What is said of their estates?
For whom had they long waited in vain?
What did they at length do?
(146.) With what was their ship freighted?
How many souls embarked in her?
How was she got out of the harbor?
What were the farewell words of Mr. Davenport?
Was she ever heard from?
When were those who embarked in her treated as dead?
What is said of the "Phantom Ship?"
(147.) What was the position of the "spectre" on board?
How did the "Phantom Ship" disappear?
When were the chiefs again cited to appear before the commissioners?
Who disobeyed the summons?
What excuse and defense did Pessacus make?
What was the result of the conference?
(148.) What town neglected to raise the Saybrook fort tax?
On what ground?
What was the decision of the commissioners?
What did John Winthrop claim?
On what ground did Connecticut oppose his claim?
Was the claim abandoned?
Whose death is referred to?
(149.) What is said of her history?
Where and in what condition is her monument?
Of what does it speak?
(150.) What reflections and suggestions are made?

CHAPTER VIII.

(151.) When was the settlement commenced at Pequot Harbor?
Who were the principal settlers?
With what were they intrusted?
By what colonies was the territory claimed?
When did Mr. Peters embark for England?
When did Mr. Winthrop remove his family from Boston?
Who accompanied him?
Where did they spend the first winter?
When did he remove his family to Pequot Harbor?
What is the place now called?
Under the protection of what colony was the plantation commenced?
When was the jurisdiction conceded to Connecticut?
(152.) Who were appointed to hold court there?
What encouragement was offered to such as should settle there?
What name did the court suggest?
What name was selected by the planters?
What did the Narragansetts and Nihanticks resolve upon?
Who did they hire to assist them?
How many warriors did they raise?
To what place was a deputation sent?
How did they find the Indians there?
What representation was made to Stanton?
(153.) What did Stanton tell them?
What effect did his threat have?
What depredations did the Narragansetts commit?
What request did Rhode Island make?
What answer did she receive?
What further complaint and warning were made?
What question again came up for dis-
Of what did Massachusetts complain?
(154.) What is said of her answer to Gov. Hopkins?
What were some of its arguments?
What did her committee further intimate and say?
Who replied in behalf of Connecticut?
(155.) What defensive arguments did they advance?
How did they respond to the threats of Massachusetts?
(156.) In whose favor was the decision?
When did Gov. Stuyvesant arrive in New York?
How was he welcomed by the commissioners?
What complaints did they make?
Did he make answer to their complaints?
Whose vessel did he cause to be seized?
To whom did Westerhouse state his grievance?
What did the commissioners do?
What further protest did they make?
(157.) How did they regard the seizure of the ship?
What suggestions and threats did they make?
How did their epistle to him close?
What murders were committed by the Indians?
What occurred in the year 1647?
What order did the General Court make?
(158.) Where were murders committed by the Indians?
How did the hatred of the Narragansetts manifest itself toward Uncas?
With whom did they confide their secrets?
What did the assassin do?
Did Uncas at last recover?
For what purpose did he appear before the commissioners?
Wherein did he tell the truth?

For what purpose was Ninigret cited to appear before the commissioners ?
What was thought of his defense ?
How was he dismissed ?
(159.) What rumor alarmed the colonies ?
Who probably fabricated the story ?
What motive had he to do it ?
(160.) What charges did the Pequots bring against him ?
What had he promised them ?
Had he kept his word ?
What did a Pequot sachem charge him with ?
To what did others testify ?
Did the commissioners believe the testimony of the Pequots ?
What was he ordered to do ?
What was the substance of their petitions and statements ?
(161.) What effect had these repeated supplications ?
What subject was again considered ?
How did Massachusetts retaliate ?
When did the commissioners meet at Hartford ?
Who presided ?
What had the Narragansetts neglected to do ?
Who was sent to enforce the payment ?
What were his instructions ?
With whom did he have an interview ?
(162.) What did Pessacus do ?
How did Atherton proceed ?
What was the effect of this summary proceeding ?
Whom did Atherton next visit ?
What charge did he bring against Ninigret ?
What did he insist upon ?
(163.) What is said of Atherton's expedition ?
What did Stuyvesant conclude to do ?
When did he arrive in Hartford ?
What invitation was given him ?
How did he desire the business should be conducted ?
Was his request granted ?
What did he complain of, and assert ?
(164.) What did he demand, and protest against ?
Where had he dated his letter ?
What did the commissioners say ?
What further passed between them ?
Who was compelled to yield ?
How did the commissioners state their title to Connecticut ?
What did they say in regard to the claims of the Dutch ?
(165.) How was the boundary question to be settled ?
Who were appointed arbitrators ?
When did they make their report ?
What did they say in regard to the grievances of Connecticut and New Haven ?
What did they say about the seizure of Westerhouse's vessel ?
(166.) What bounds were established ?
What lands were the Dutch to hold ?
How long were the bounds designated to be observed ?
When was the report signed ?
When was liberty granted to settle Norwalk ?
(167.) Who had previously purchased parts of this town ?
When did the petitioners settle there ?
When and by whom was the western part of the town deeded to them ?
What were the names of the first settlers ?
What did they bind themselves to do ?
What was the nature of Ludlow's contract ?
(168.) From what was the name derived ?
Who was the first clergyman of the place ?
When did the settlement at Mattabesett begin ?

What previous record is referred to?
What probabilities are suggested?
When was the town incorporated?
When was it first represented?
When was it named Middletown?
(169.) How did the scene appear to the pioneers?
What is said of the Narrows below the city?
What is said of the Indians at Mattabesset?
Where had they a reservation?
(170.) What is said of the Indian burial ground?
What is said of the graveyard at Indian Hill?
What reinforcement of the settlement on Delaware Bay was attempted?
To whom had they letters?
What did Stuyvesant do?
(171.) What threats did he make?
When did the commissioners meet?
Who presented their petition?
What was its character?
What did the commissioners say to Stuyvesant?
What did they resolve?
What deputation waited upon them?
What commissions had these agents?
(172.) What did they want of the colonies?
What inducement did they hold out?
What did the General Court do?
What nations were at war?
What orders for defense were given?
What were the Indians required to do?
What rumors had gone abroad?
(173.) On what were they founded?
When was a meeting of Congress called?
What was the result of the investigation?
How was Stuyvesant affected by the charges against him?
What did he offer to do?
What course was adopted by Congress?
(174.) Who composed the committee?
How were they received?
What did he refuse to do?
What is said of both parties?
How did the conference close?
What did the agents do on their way home?
What other charge was preferred against Stuyvesant?
What did Stuyvesant do?
What was Congress in favor of?
What is said of the opposition of Bradstreet?
(175.) What was the result of the conference?
What was the purport of Mr. Norris' memorial?
To what did the continued dissent of Massachusetts lead?
Why was Massachusetts compelled to yield?
For what purpose were the ships of Cromwell coming?
What is said of the alleged plot against the English?
(176.) Was the conduct of Massachusetts justifiable?

CHAPTER IX.

(177.) In what did the charges against the Dutch result?
Of what did Stamford and Fairfield complain?
Why had they reason to be anxious?
What threat did Stamford make?
What induced her people to yield?
What did Fairfield resolve to do?
Who was appointed commander-in-chief?
(178.) Where had Ludlow resided?
When was he chosen an Assistant?
When did he sail for America?
When was he chosen deputy governor of Massachusetts?
Against whose election did he protest?

How did the people requite his opposition to Haynes?
When and to what place did he remove?
On what mission was he sent in 1637?
(179.) What is said of his profession and talents?
What is said of the Constitution of 1639?
How does it compare with the writings of Milton?
When was Ludlow chosen deputy governor of Connecticut?
Who was elected governor at the same time?
How must the coincidence have affected Ludlow?
(180.) What characteristic is alluded to?
When was he appointed to revise the laws?
When was the code published?
What remote cause of his voluntary exile is referred to?
What reference is made to the conduct of Fairfield?
(181.) Why did her people take up arms?
How was their conduct treated?
Who were charged with fomenting insurrections?
What must Ludlow have known and felt?
What was quite evident?
When did he embark for Virginia?
Why have I been thus minute in regard to him?
What further is said of him?
(182.) Who died just previous to Ludlow's departure?
Where was Haynes born?
Of what was he the owner?
What income did he derive from it?
Whom did he accompany to America?
When was he made governor of Mass.?
By whom was he succeeded?
When and how often was he governor of Connecticut?
How did he compare with Ludlow?
Of what was he a representative?
(183.) Of what was Ludlow the prototype?
What question still agitated the colonies?
Why and by whom was Manning arrested?
What occurred during his trial?
What did the people of Milford do?
Who arrived in Boston?
By whom and for what purpose were they sent?
Who wrote to Gov. Eaton on the subject?
What did Connecticut authorize her agents to do?
What was the feeling in Massachusetts?
(184.) What did they authorize Sedgwick and Leverett to do?
What did the commissioners decide?
What put a stop to these preparations?
How were the fleet and volunteers employed?
(185.) Why had not the war against Ninigret been pursued?
(186.) On what mission was Capt. Mason sent?
Where was Lieut. Seely sent?
What message did Congress send to Ninigret?
What answer did Ninigret send back?
What did the commissioners order?
What officers did they nominate?
(187.) Who did Massachusetts select to to take the command?
What orders did Willard receive from Congress?
What did he find on arriving at the Nihantick village?
What had become of Ninigret?
What did Willard do?
What did certain Pequots do?
How did Congress receive Maj. Willard?
What reply did they make to his excuses?
(188.) What is said about his acting under private instructions?

What is said of the attempt to defend the Long Island Indians?
Was it right and politic to let Ninigret wage war against them?
What was a cause for alarm?
What Indians were taken under the protection of the English?
Where were lands assigned them?
What privileges were allowed them?
What was the conduct of Ninigret?
Who complained against him?
Who was sent to watch his movements?
(189.) What were the instructions of Capt. Young?
What effect had this measure?
How long was this armed vessel kept cruising?
What is said about calamities not journeying alone?
Whose death is referred to?
What was his age?
(190.) Where had he owned a large estate?
Where and when was he born?
Whose son was he?
What is said of the manor-house?
What is said of the motto on the family arms?
(191.) How had he lived in early life?
What change took place?
Who was his religious teacher?
With what party did he become identified?
For how much did he sell his estates?
When did he first visit New England?
(192.) When did he arrive in Massachusetts a second time?
Who came with him?
When did he remove to Windsor?
When was he first a member of the General Court?
When was he chosen a magistrate?
When did he die?
What is said of his monument and its inscription?
How did Cromwell regard New Haven?
What project had he formed for settling Jamaica?
When and how did he address his New Haven friends on the subject?
What did the court resolve?
(193.) What complaints were made against Greenwich?
What did the General Court do?
What answer did the people of Greenwich make?
What did the court further resolve?
What was the result?
How had Uncas behaved?
Upon whom did he now make an attack?
(194.) What other misdeeds of his are referred to?
What did Congress compel him to do?
What trial of his is referred to?
When and where did Gov. Eaton die?
Where was he born?
Of what company had he been the agent?
What high office had he held abroad?
When did he remove to America?
(195.) What were his characteristics as a judge?
What is said of his appearance and abilities?
What were his social and religious habits?
What was his last conversation with his wife?
What were the circumstances of his death?
(196.) What is said of his funeral, and of the public loss?
Who died about the same time?
Where had he been a merchant?
Where was he chosen a magistrate?
How often was he chosen governor?
When did he return to England?
What offices did he hold there?
What evidence did he give of his regard for Connecticut?
(197.) What other bequest did he make?

When and where did Chesebrough and Stanton settle?
What was the place called?
What was Chesebrough's business?
Under what authority did he settle there?
Why was the jealousy of Connecticut excited?
By whom was he interrupted?
Why did he refuse to comply?
What was he further ordered to do?
When did he present himself before the court?
(198.) What defense did he make?
What was the result?
When did Thomas Minor settle at Pawcatuck?
On what committee was he placed?
What other persons were there soon after?
What did the boundary commissioners decide?
When did the town become a part of Connecticut?
(199.) When and why was the place called Mistick?
When was the name changed to Stonington?
What is said of the history of the town?
When and why did the names of Welles and Webster, disappear from our records?
Where was Welles buried?
Who seized and imprisoned Uncas?
What word did Uncas send to the English?
Who went to his relief?
(200.) What followed this timely succor?
How is Uncas said to have rewarded Leffingwell?
How large a tract did he sell the company at Saybrook?
What did they pay him for it?
Who was at the head of this company?
How many members were embraced in the company?
What additions were made to the settlement in the Spring of 1660?
What was the character of the first settlers?
(201.) What were their names?
What is said of the hills of Norwich?

CHAPTER X.

(202.) When did the reign of Elizabeth close?
Who succeeded her?
What signalized the next quarter of a century?
What is said of Cromwell's reign?
To what event does this bring us?
(203.) Why were the colonies lost sight of?
Why might the colonists have imagined themselves beyond the reach of British rule?
Why was the king not recognized in their Constitution?
What effect did the restoration have?
(204.) By what dangers were the colonists surrounded?
What was the position of the king?
What did the colonists determine to do?
What did they avow themselves to be?
What sum did they appropriate?
Who were appointed to perfect the petition?
What were they further authorized to do?
(205.) Who was appointed agent of the colony?
What were his instructions?
What was the purport of the petition?
To whom was a letter addressed?
What was its purport?
(206.) After Winthrop's arrival in England, to whom did he apply?
How did he further the object of the petitioners?

Where and how had Say and Seal lived during the protectorate?
(207.) What did he assist in doing?
How was he rewarded?
What is said of his interposition in behalf of Connecticut?
What is said of Winthrop?
How may he have interested the king?
(208.) Who would have failed in the object?
What did Winthrop present to the king?
What effect had it?
(209.) What did the king do?
When did the letters patent receive the royal signature?
What was thereby confirmed to the patentees?
What are the names of the patentees?
What privileges were given to them?
When were they to hold their general assemblies?
Of whom were these assemblies to consist?
What might the corporation do?
(210.) For what did it especially provide?
Who were named as governor, deputy governor and magistrates?
What was done by the freemen and by the General Court?
What is said of the court held July 22nd?
(211.) When and where was the Charter first publicly shown?
When was it read in Connecticut?
What was done with it?
What was done at this session of the Assembly?
What notice was given to the people of Westchester?
What resolve was passed respecting Mistick and Pawcatuck?
(212.) What special importance did it give to Connecticut?
What deputations came to Hartford?
What other similar applications were made?
Who were sent to treat with New Haven?
What did this Committee do?
(213.) What did they present to the authorities there?
What did their declaration inform New Haven?
By whom was the reply probably framed?
When did the freemen of New Haven meet?
(214.) What was done in regard to the charter?
Who appeared in behalf of New Haven?
How did he "discharge the duty of his place?"
What is said of the debate?
Who were appointed to draw up an answer to Connecticut?
What propositions were to be embraced in the answer?
(215.) What were the committee directed to do?
Who was probably the author of this reply?
What is said of it?
What do the committee say?
(216.) What urgent request did they make?
What charge is implied in the extract given?
When did the Assembly of Connecticut meet?
What committee was appointed?
What did the committee do?
What acts of Connecticut had offended New Haven?
(217.) When did the Court meet in New Haven?
What proposition was laid before it?
What answer was given?
What remonstrance was made?
When did the agent of New Haven arrive in England?

What did Winthrop undertake to guarantee?
What did Winthrop write to the Deputy Governor?
(218.) What did he intimate?
What towns did Connecticut attempt to embrace within her jurisdiction?
What new committee was appointed at the August session?
What were they instructed to do?
What did this committee effect?
(219.) What complaint did New Haven make to the Congress?
Who defended Connecticut, and how?
What is said of Winthrop's course?
Who spoke in behalf of New Haven?
What decree did they procure?
(220.) What is said of the jealousy of Massachusetts?
Of what did Stuyvesant complain?
What was done with the matter complained of?
When did the Assembly of Connecticut again meet?
What act was passed?
What committee was appointed?
(221.) What was Thomas Pell authorized to do?
To what petitions did the Assembly listen?
What town was settled and named?
What was done by the New Haven Court?
(222.) Whom did they resolve to petition?
What measure did they adopt to collect the taxes?
What was the condition of New Haven?
What was the effect of the tax-law?
What particular case is referred to?
What did these men do?
(223.) What did Gov. Leete do?
How did these towns respond?
How did the affair terminate?
When did the New Haven Court meet?
What did Gov. Leete state?
What did the court answer?
Who were appointed to make a statement of grievances?
What was their report called?
(224.) What was its character?
For what towns did the Assembly of Connecticut appoint officers?
What officers were appointed in New Haven?
Who declined to accept?
What is said of the Duke of York?
(225.) What islands were embraced in his patent?
What was a main object of this patent?
For what did a fleet sail for America?
Who was the commander?
What was he further authorized to do?
Who were to be associated with him?
When did Col. Nichols arrive in Boston?
What did he do?
Who did he invite to consult with him?
What accompanied the commission of Nichols?
(226.) What was the purport of the letter?
What did Winthrop do?
When did Nichols demand the surrender of the fort?
In what way did Stuyvesant respond to the summons?
(227.) What did he say?
What offer did Nichols make?
What occurred in regard to this offer?
What was the purport of Nichols' second letter?
What did Winthrop do?
What course did Stuyvesant take?
How did the Burgomasters behave?
What was Stuyvesant obliged to do?
(228.) What solicitations reached him?
What order did Nichols give?
How did Stuyvesant behave?
What was his last resort?
What passed between his ambassadors and Nichols?

What was he compelled to do?
What was the result of his capitulations?
(229.) What course did Mr. Whiting take?
When was the General Court called at New Haven?
What ensued?
What was obvious?
What was finally resolved?
When was another Court called?
Whence proceeded the chief opposition to the Union?
(230.) What is said of Davenport?
What is said of the claims of the Dukes of York and Hamilton?
What present did the Assembly make to the King's commissioners?
(231.) What committees were appointed?
Who was at the head of the last committee?
What was the last committee ordered to do?
Who were clothed with the authority of magistrates?
What is said of Winthrop?
(232.) What was he aware of?
What was decided to be the Southern bounds of Connecticut?
Under what government was Rhode Island decided to be?
What were the Western bounds of the Colony?
To what did this put an end?
When was the last General Court of New Haven held?
What resolutions were adopted?

CHAPTER XI.

(234.) What is said of the restoration of Charles II.?
What had Charles promised?
What is said of the Presbyterians?
Who were some of his principal officers?
(235.) What is said of the commons and lords?
To whom were the lords especially intolerant?
What proclamation did the king make?
How many of the judges surrendered themselves?
What is said of others?
How many were executed?
Which of the judges arrived in Boston, and when?
(236.) How were they treated there?
Where did they go on leaving Boston?
How were they treated when the king's opinion of them was known?
What did Gov. Endicott do?
Where did the judges then go?
When did they reach there?
How did Davenport treat them?
(237.) Of what did they discourse?
How did they appear and conduct?
What came with the mandate for their arrest?
What did the authorities of Massachusetts do?
Who were commissioned to arrest them?
(238.) How did the pursuers proceed?
What did Winthrop do and say?
At what place did they next stop?
What did they request Gov. Leete to do?
What did Leete do?
(239.) What did the pursuers say to him?
How long did they remain in Guilford?
Who were sent to New Haven in advance of them?
Why did he refuse to issue the desired warrant?
What is probable in regard to the Indians?
(240.) What effect had the news in New Haven?
What was the text of Davenport on that Sabbath morning?
When did Kellond and Kirk proceed to New Haven?
How long did they wait for Gov. Leete?

What reply did Leete make to their request?
(241.) How did he again tell them?
What response did they make?
How long was he in consultation with the magistrates?
What did they decide was necessary to be done?
How did the pursuers remonstrate?
What further took place between them and the governor?
(242.) To what place did they now proceed?
How did Stuyvesant receive them?
Where were the judges concealed at this time?
Whence did they proceed from Sperry's house?
Where did they go on the 15th?
What has their cave since been called?
What is said of the cave?
(243.) How long did they remain there?
How were they provided with food?
What caused them to leave their shelter?
(244.) For what did they go to Guilford?
What relic of them still remains there?
How did Endicott and Davenport differ?
To whose house did they next resort?
How long did they remain there?
Who often visited them?
How did they behave while there?
(245.) What incident occurred there?
What induced them to leave Milford?
For what town did they set out?
How did they proceed?
Where is one of their stopping places?
At whose house were they secreted?
(246.) What is said of Whalley?
What was the standing and position of the family?
What is said of his military career?
By whom, and why was he hated?
What charge did Peters make against him?
Who was committed to his keeping?
What charge against him was decreed by the king?
What occurred at Hampton Court?
(247.) What occurred at the battle of Dunbar?
When was he created a lord?
How was he insulted by Ashfield?
What threat did he make?
What is said of his character and talents?
Who did he marry?
Who did his daughter marry?
Whose son was Gen. Goffe?
How was he promoted?
What is said of him at the battle of Dunbar?
(248.) What were his honors and services as a civilian?
What was his crowning honor?
What were his characteristics?
What is said of his letters to Mrs Goffe?
By what assumed name did he address her?
What extract from his correspondence is given?
What is said of it?
(249.) What further extracts are given?
What reference is made to the Middletons and Cromwells?
Why do we regard Mrs. Goffe and Mrs. Godolphin with reverence?
(250.) Where and to what class did Col. Dixwell belong?
To whom was he uncle?
To what military rank did he attain?
What civil offices did he hold?
When did he visit Hadley?
How long did he remain there?
By what name was he known in New Haven?
Previous to what date did he arrive there?
To whom was he known?
(251.) Who was his most intimate friend?
What was their local position?

What reply did Mr. Pierpont make to the inquiry of his wife?
What incident is related of Andros' visit to New Haven?
(252.) When did he die?
Where was he buried?
Where were Goffe and Whalley buried?

CHAPTER XII.

(253.) Where did Col. Nichols take up his abode?
Where did the other commissioners go?
On what did they insist?
What did they do in regard to titles derived from the Indians?
Where did they hold courts?
What did they attempt to make?
What was the extent of the proposed province?
(254.) What did they next do?
What is said of Connecticut?
What counties were organized in 1666?
What bounds were affixed to each?
When was Lyme incorporated?
Of what family has it been the seat?
What tract had been purchased in 1662?
(255.) How many original proprietors were there?
When was the town incorporated?
What name was given to it?
From what places were the first settlers?
What was the nature of the soil?
When was Simsbury incorporated?
When was Wallingford settled?
(256.) Who was the first minister there?
From what text did Mr. Davenport preach?
When was the land at Paugasset purchased?
What applications were made to the General Court?
What response was made by the court?
How were the people affected by the proceedings?
Of whom was a further purchase made?
(257.) Who were some of the principal settlers?
When and with what success did they renew their petition?
What decision was given?
What further representation did they make?
What did the Assembly do?
What is said of the Naugatuck valley?
What dispute broke out in Stratford?
Who were the leaders of the parties?
(258.) What plan was proposed?
Who were permitted to settle in Pomperaug?
What did they do with the corn?
When did they sail for Pomperaug?
What had they been told?
(259.) What incident occurred by the way?
What did they do when they came in sight of their land?
What did they next proceed to do?
Where did they encamp?
What is said of the purchase?
What was the extent of the township?
(260.) What did they do soon after their arrival?
When was the town incorporated?
What name was given it?
What towns have been set off from it?
What was thought of Philip?
What did the Governor of Massachusetts do?
(261.) What did they request of Philip?
What reply did he make?
What efforts had been made by Massachusetts?
What is said of Eliot and Mayhew?
What results followed the efforts of these missionaries?
(262.) How did Philip treat the Gospel?
What instructions had Massasoit given to his sons?
What changes had taken place in the condition of the Wampanoags?

(263.) How were the Indians treated by the English?
What had Philip been ordered to do?
What was he also obliged to do?
What act of violence was committed?
What was done with the offenders?
(264.) What was done at Swansey?
Was this recrimination the act of Philip?
How did he regard it?
What Indians were the allies of the English?
What motives led them to be friendly?
How must Canonchet have contrasted the power of the two races?
(265.) How did the English regard the Indians?
What superstitions are referred to?
What cause had the English for alarm?
In what way were Philip and his allies employed?
(266.) What villages were destroyed by the Indians?
To what places was the alarm sent?
Who went to the relief of the sufferers?
What accompanied the expedition?
What assistance went from Boston?
To whose camp did the English proceed?
What incidents occurred?
What trophies were sent to Boston?
Who marched to Pocasset-neck?
(267.) What inquiry did Church make?
What did he advise?
If his advice had been followed, what might have resulted?
What is said of the fight at Pocasset?
What took place at Mendon?
What occurred to Captains Hutchinson and Wheeler?
What occurred to Capt. Beers and his party?
(268.) What was the place called?
How did the Indians attempt to terrify the English?
What service did Major Treat render?
What is said of Connecticut?
How did the Narragansetts behave?
(269.) What was once their condition?
What reference is made to the pestilence?
Where did they live?
To whom was Massasoit subject?
How had the Narragansetts been enabled to subdue the Wampanoags?
What alliance is referred to?
How was the independence of the Wampanoags regarded by Sassacus?
Why did Sassacus court an alliance with the Narragansetts?
What was the condition of the Narragansett warriors?
(270.) What is said of the tribe?
What did the commissioners conclude?
When had this taken place?
Between whom was a treaty concluded?
What were its stipulations?
To what did the English agree?
(271.) What had been done at Hadley?
What was stored at Deerfield?
What did Capt. Lathrop attempt to do?
How many men had he with him?
What was their fate?
Who came to the rescue?
What did the Indians say to Mosely?
How long did the fight continue?
Who were compelled to retreat?
What did the Indians do?
(272.) Who came to the rescue?
What effect had his arrival?
How many Indians had been slain?
What name was given to the stream near which the battle was fought?
What orders were given by the Congress?
How was Maj. Treat's command employed?
What is said of the Springfield Indians?
What had Philip resolved to do?
Who discovered the plot?
To whom were messages sent?

(273.) What occurred to Lieut. Cooper?
What did Philip and his allies do?
In what condition were the people?
What delayed Maj. Treat?
How many dwellings had been destroyed?
Who were the principal sufferers?
What did the assembly do?
What word was received from Mr. Fitch?
(274.) Where was Maj. Treat sent?
How many warriors had he with him?
What place did he attack?
What part did Maj. Treat take?
What became of Philip's warriors?
What resulted from the news received from Mr. Fitch?
What was each county required to do?
What orders were given to Capt. Avery?
(275.) What was Capt. Mason to do?
What other measures were adopted?
How had the arts of Philip prevailed?
Of what was the Congress satisfied?
What fears were entertained?
How many warriors and muskets had the Narragansetts?
What did the English apprehend?
(276.) What did Congress decide?
How many men did each colony furnish?
Who commanded the Connecticut companies?
Who was the commander-in-chief?
What was done besides providing for the wants of the troops?
When did Treat arrive at Pattyquamscot?
What had the Indians done?
What took place the next day?
What is said of the succeeding night?
(277.) What was the order of march?
What was the position of the enemy's town?
How had it been fortified?
How was the fort discovered?
How was it constructed?
What is said of the area?
How must the fort be entered?
(278.) Who first entered it?
What was their fate?
What is said of the prudence of the attack?
What Captains were among the slain?
How did the Connecticut troops proceed?
How many Connecticut Captains were killed?
(279.) Who attacked the enemy in the rear?
What effect had this manœuvre?
What other captains were killed?
Which party triumphed?
How many wigwams were within the fort?
What other property fell into the hands of the victors?
How many Indian warriors were slain?
How many were taken prisoners?
What request did Capt. Church make?
(280.) What was done with the village?
How is the scene described?
How many officers and soldiers were killed or wounded?
What was the situation of the captors?
What did they do?
(281.) When did they reach their destination?
What is said of the wounded soldiers?
What proportion of the army were unfit for duty?
Why were the Connecticut troops most disabled?
How many Connecticut soldiers had been slain?
What is said of Major Treat?
What reference is made to the thanksgivings of our people?
(282.) What did Maj. Treat find it necessary to do?
How did Philip respond to overtures of peace?

Where and for what were volunteer raised?

Who commanded them?

What Indians were associated with them?

What did they do?

What is said of Canonchet?

Who came upon his trail?

(283.) How did he attempt to escape?

Who pursued him?

What garments did he throw off?

How and by whom was he seized?

What did he scorn to do?

What reply did he make to Robert Staunton?

When life was offered him what did he do?

(284.) With what did they taunt him?

What response did he make?

What sentence was pronounced upon him?

When told of his sentence, what answer did he make?

Who superintended his execution?

What civil officers were chosen?

What measures were taken to carry on the war?

What officers were appointed for these forces?

(285.) Whence did Talcott march?

What did he accomplish?

What did he do in the country of the Nipmucks?

To what places did he then march?

From what did the army suffer?

What was next accomplished?

Where did he surprise the main body of the enemy?

(286.) How many Indians were killed and captured?

What was done with the captives?

What did Talcott do at Providence and Norwich?

What was the aggregate killed and captured by him?

How many did he capture on his return march?

What had been accomplished within three months?

After recruiting, where was Talcott next stationed?

Where did he overtake the enemy?

(287.) What orders did he give?

What defeated this stratagem?

What prevented the destruction of the enemy?

What sachem was killed?

How many warriors were killed or captured?

CHAPTER XIII.

(288.) What had prevented England from interfering with our affairs?

When did her jealousies revive?

What did the Duke of York do?

What was Andross commissioned to be?

What claim and threat did Andross make?

(289.) What were Andross' plans?

What measures of defense were taken?

Who commanded at Saybrook?

When was Andross seen approaching Saybrook?

What did the people there resolve to do?

What did the militia do?

(290.) What is said of the letter issued by the council?

To whom was it addressed?

How did it commence?

What instructions did it contain?

(291.) What further instructions are given?

What particular acts are specified?

If attacked what were they to do?

(292.) What is contained in the postscript?

When and where did the Assembly meet?

What protest did they make?

What were the people commanded to do?
(293.) What was done with the protest?
When did he land at Saybrook?
By whom, and with what message was he met?
What was Andross' object in landing?
How did he proceed?
How was he received by Capt. Bull?
(294.) What further passed between Andross and Bull?
In what manner did Andross leave?
What action did the Assembly take?
What is the language of its declaration?
Who were to act as agents of the Colony?
(295.) When and where did Winthrop die?
What were the characteristics of his mind?
(296.) Where and when was he born?
(297.) Where was he educated?
What were the peculiarities of his father's letters?
What extract is given?
(298.) What directions are given to the son?
Where did he travel?
(299.) When and with whom did he sail for America?
Did he return to England?
What commission did he receive?
When was he chosen a magistrate?
When was he elected Governor and Deputy Governor?
What further is said of him?

CHAPTER XIV.

(300.) What was the financial condition of Connecticut?
What services had she rendered?
What amount of taxes were levied?
How did she determine to remunerate herself?
(301.) How were former decisions and claims set aside?
What charges were made against the people of Rhode Island?
What is said of the conduct of Connecticut?
What application was made for redress?
What reference is made to boundary questions?
How had Connecticut succeeded in the Andross affair?
(302.) What enemy of the colonies is referred to?
When did he arrive in Boston?
How was he employed?
What was his ruling motive?
What did Congress recommend?
What day was set apart in Connecticut?
What act was passed by the Assembly?
What is said of the question of jurisdiction?
What commissioners were appointed?
(303.) For what were they appointed?
Where did they meet?
What decision did they make?
What new claim was set up?
Who was the agent of the claimants?
What is said of the defense of Connecticut?
(304.) What intelligence was received from the King?
What response did the assembly make?
What new charge was brought against the colonies?
What law was passed at the requisition of the King?
For what did the citizens of Farmington petition?
What report did the committee make?
(305.) When was the town incorporated?
What name did it receive?
What calamity occurred in 1691?
What occurred in 1712?
What is said of the change in the town?

(306.) What is said of the Naugatuck Valley ?
What was the conduct of King Charles II. ?
Why had Connecticut been favored by him ?
Who succeeded him ?
For what was Connecticut obliged to contend ?
When was the new King crowned ?
(307.) What was one of his first acts ?
When did the Assembly meet ?
What did the Assembly do ?
What next occurred ?
What did Gov. Treat do on receiving these documents ?
Who was sent to England as agent of the Colony ?
What were his instructions ?
(308.) When was another writ of quo warranto served ?
What did it require ?
What is said of the day therein named ?
What is said of the King's conduct ?
For what was his reign characterized ?
(309.) How many charters had been annulled by him ?
What particular charters are named ?
What government had been established in New England ?
What was done in regard to the Narragansett country ?
What had Connecticut cause to fear ?
(310.) When was an Assembly called ?
What was accomplished ?
What was done by the Assembly in March ?
What was done at the session in May ?
What would be the result if they surrendered their charter ?
(311.) What might follow resistance ?
With whom did they leave their affairs ?
What did our agent in England do ?
What did he write to Gov. Treat ?
What was done by the Assembly in June ?
What were the Governor and his assistants directed to do ?
What advice did President Dudley give ?
Was it followed ?
By whom was Dudley superseded ?
When did Andross arrive in Boston ?
(312.) What was the purport of his letter to Connecticut ?
What was the purport of his second letter ?
What did the Assembly decide ?
What was the substance of their address to the king ?
What alternative request did they make ?
Into what was it construed ?
(313.) What is said of this construction ?
Did the colony surrender its charter ?
When did Andross arrive in Hartford ?
How was he attended ?
What was the object of his visit ?
How was he received ?
(314.) What did he demand and declare ?
What did the Assembly do ?
What was the substance of Gov. Treat's remarks ?
Did Andross reply ?
What is probable in regard to Treat's motive ?
(315.) What was done as evening drew on ?
What was first done with the charter ?
What was done with the lights ?
When the candles were re-lighted, what had disappeared ?
What is said of the search for it ?
How did Andross behave ?
(316.) In what words did he answer the government ?
What did he next do ?
Who of his Council was from Connecticut ?
(317.) What instructions did he give ?
What was the object of these instructions ?

What may have induced him to take a different course?
What was one of his first acts of tyranny?
What regulations did he make in regard to marriages?
(318.) What had been the position of the clergy?
How were they regarded by the people?
What was the nature of the sentiment?
What idea had the people brought with them?
What laws did Andross repeal?
What motives induced him to do it?
What threats did he make?
(319.) What laws did he make relative to settling estates?
How was this regulation burdensome?
How were the colonies taxed?
What other province was added to Andross' government?
What did he declare?
What did he say of an Indian deed?
What did he compel the planters to do?
(320.) What was done to those who refused to submit?
What acts of tyranny were practiced by him in Massachusetts?
What did Randolph say of the government?
How did Andross treat the petitions of the people?
What served to shield Connecticut?
(321.) What further is said of Treat?
What was the situation of Connecticut?
What great event occurred?
What did Andross do?
What did the people of Boston do?
When was the charter government of Connecticut resumed?
What tidings soon reached Connecticut?
(322.) How did the Assembly hail the new king?
Who had been sent to America by Wyllys?
What deputation came to Gibbons?
(323.) What request and statement did they make?
Was their solicitation heeded?
Who seized the charter from the midst of the Assembly?
What did he do with it?
What parallel is here drawn?
What is said of the *Charter Oak?*

CHAPTER XV.

(324.) Who had assumed the government of New York?
In whose behalf did he hold the fort and city?
What request did Leisler make?
Who were appointed to confer with him?
For what purpose was Capt. Bull sent to Albany?
What other aid did Connecticut render?
What did the New England Indians do?
(326.) What was supposed to have excited them?
Why was a special assembly called?
What did the Revolution of 1668 bring with it?
What great object was contemplated?
How was it foiled?
What did Frontenac do?
What was the object of the detachment under D'Aillebout and others?
When did they arrive in Schenectady?
(327.) What intelligence did the scouts bring?
When and how did the work of death begin?
What details are given?
How many captives were secured?
What became of the rest of the survivors?
(328.) How many of Capt. Bull's men were killed and captured?
How were the tidings received in Albany?
How did the people there behave?

How might the people of Schenectady have repelled the attack?
What took place at Salmon Falls?
How many were killed or captured?
(329.) What aid was asked of Connecticut?
What has been one of the attributes of Connecticut?
How did she respond to the calls?
What regulations were made for her own towns and people?
What town was incorporated at the same session?
(330.) When and where did the Congress meet?
What was the object of the meeting?
What was done?
Did England render the desired assistance?
What did New York and New England determine to do?
What plan was agreed upon?
Who acted as commissary?
What was expected of New York?
(331.) Who commanded the army?
When did he arrive at Wood Creek?
How was he disappointed?
What reply did he receive from the Indians?
How was he again disappointed?
What did the Indians tell him?
(332.) What else had Milborn neglected to do?
What did the council of war decide?
When did Sir William Phipps reach Quebec?
When did he commence the attack, and with what success?
Who defended the city, and with what success?
What other disaster befell Sir William?
(333.) Had he arrived a week earlier, how would he have found Quebec?
What might have been the result had Milborn been faithful?
What is said of Leisler's abuse of Winthrop?
Who were compelled to take refuge in Hartford?
What arbitrary act did Leisler commit?
(334.) Who rescued Winthrop?
What reference is made to Leisler conduct?
How did the authorities of Connecticut regard it?
What action did the Assembly take on the subject?
(335.) What resolve did they pass?
How else did they testify their gratitude?
When was Windham incorporated?
By whom and to whom had it been divided?
What other towns did it originally embrace?
When did the settlement commence there?
What did Frontenac determine to do?
How large an army did he raise?
(336.) When did he start for the Mohawk country?
What did he accomplish?
Who pursued the French army?
When did he reach their encampment?
Did he attack the enemy?
Under what circumstances did the French desert their camp?
Who joined Schuyler the next day?
Was the pursuit resumed?
How did they effect their escape?
(337.) What call was made upon Connecticut?
How was the call responded to?
For what did Sir William Phipps ask?
How was his request answered?
When did Gov. Fletcher arrive from England?
With what powers was he invested?
(338.) What did this commissioner take for granted?

When did the Assembly meet?
What did they order?
Who was appointed to present it to the King?
What were his instructions?
(339.) What further was he to inform the King?
What was left discretionary with him?
(340.) Who was appointed to counsel with Fletcher?
What resulted from his mission?
When did Fletcher visit Hartford?
What demand did he make?
How did he subscribe himself?
What did he further command?
How were his wishes complied with?
What effect had his remonstrances?
(341.) What did Col. Bayard do?
What was the purport of his letter?
What effect had it?
What did the Assembly and the Governor say?
What order did Fletcher give in presence of the train-bands?
How was Bayard interrupted?
(342.) What did Wadsworth say to Fletcher?
What effect had this speech?

CHAPTER XVI.

(343.) When and why was a special Assembly convened?
How much money was raised?
To whom was it paid?
What provisions were made for the soldiers?
What did Winthrop do in England?
(344.) What decision was given?
What amount of taxes was paid?
How much did Connecticut pay for the defense of Massachusetts and New York?
How many ratable polls were there in the colony?
What was the amount of the Grand list?
How much did Connecticut pay for the expedition to Canada?
How did Fletcher harass the colony?
(345.) How much had been paid in the aggregate?
When was Bellamont commissioned?
What provinces did his commission embrace?
Who were sent to wait upon him?
When did he arrive in America?
What did he say of Mr. Saltonstall?
(346.) Who was elected to succeed Gov. Treat?
To what office was Treat elected?
What important change took place in the legislature?
When did this organization go into effect?
Who was chosen Speaker, and who the first Clerk of the House?
What permission was granted to Gov. Winthrop?
What other purchase had he made?
(347.) When did the settlement on it commence?
When was it incorporated and named?
When was Colchester settled and incorporated?
Who were among the principal proprietors?
Who were the first settlers of Durham?
When was it incorporated?
(348.) When were boundary commissioners appointed by New York?
When and where did the commissioners meet?
What was done by them?
When was the boundary agreed upon?
What tract of land was ceded to New York?
What is it still called?
What did Connecticut receive in place of it?
To whom had Voluntown been granted?
What was the size of the township?
(349.) When was it incorporated?

From what town was Mansfield set off?
When was it incorporated?
What were the names of some of the early settlers?
When was Danbury settled and incorporated?
Who were the principal proprietors?
From what town was Canterbury taken?
Who were the principal settlers?
What war is referred to?
What requisition was made upon Connecticut?
(350.) What committee was appointed?
With what powers were they invested?
When was an Assembly called?
What was done in regard to the Indians?
How many troops were sent into Massachusetts?
What is said of Dudley and Cornbury?
(351.) How was Dudley useful to Cornbury?
To what place did Dudley aspire?
How had he endeavored to prepare the way?
What did he do in regard to the New England charters?
What office did Dudley now hold?
(352.) Why did he wish to add Connecticut to his domains?
What bill did he propose?
What did the bill aim at?
What charges and enactments did it contain?
(353.)How did Ashurst regard it?
What was the purport of his petition?
Did it obtain a hearing?
What other considerations were presented in it?
(354.) What was the fate of the bill?
What course did Dudley now take?
What is said of Cornbury?
What reference is made to certain sons of Connecticut?
(355.) What was now decided upon?
Who filed complaints against the colony?
What work was brought to bear upon the subject?
(356.) When was the book written?
When was it received in England?
What did the complaint alledge?
(357) For what did he thank the Assembly?
What story was now circulated?
What motives had the malcontents?
What charge might have been made against the colony?
(358.) How was the queen affected by the petition?
What did she do?
When and by whom was the survey commenced?
Having completed the survey, what did they do?
How are the lines defined?
(359.) To what place did Dudley remove his Court?
Was Connecticut notified of the Court?
Why did she send a committee to the Court?
What were their instructions?
Who were the committee?
(360.) What did the committee do?
What did they say in their protest?
What decision was given in the case?
How is the transaction characterized?
(361.) What was Dudley's object in the affair?
What effect had the charge?
When did the trial of Connecticut come on?
What had Dudley and Cornbury done?
(362.) What decision had the Attorney General given?
What is said of the opinion?
How did Ashurst feel and act in the premises?
How was he connected?
What service did his lordship render?

(363.) What arguments were used in behalf of Connecticut?

(364.) What further arguments and requests were made?

What order was given by the Council?

How was this decision received by Dudley and Cornbury?

(365.) What did he know the Assembly could prove?

What letter had they in their keeping?

What reference is made to the charge of piracy?

Was the suit prosecuted?

(366.) What letter was received in the colony?

CHAPTER XVII.

(367.) By what were the colonies alarmed?

When and where was the council of war convened?

Of whom did it consist?

What did Gov. Treat and Maj. Schuyler do?

What Indians were suspected?

What towns were to be fortified?

What was done in regard to Waterbury?

Who were appointed to remove the suspected Indians?

To what places were they to be removed?

What further order was given?

(368.) What request was received from Dudley?

What response did Connecticut make?

When and at what age did Gov. Winthrop die?

What is said of him?

When was a special Assembly called?

Who was elected Governor?

(369.) What was done at the regular election?

How old was deputy Governor Treat?

Who was elected to succeed him?

Where and when was Gov. Treat born?

What is said of Richard Treat?

When was Robert Treat chosen a magistrate?

How long did he hold the office?

(370.) What part did he take in the controversy between New Haven and Connecticut?

What is said of his military services?

When was he elected deputy Governor?

When was he elected Governor?

How long was he Governor?

What is said of Treat and Winthrop?

(371.) What was his character as a military leader?

How did he excel as a civilian and citizen?

Where and when did he die?

(372.) What effect had the conduct of Connecticut on the Canadian expedition?

Of what did the queen advise the colony?

What was it resolved to do?

How many men was Connecticut to furnish?

How many men were the other colonies to furnish?

What did the Earl of Sunderland acquaint the colonies?

What was the object of the armament?

What other project was contemplated?

Who commanded the Connecticut quota of troops?

For what did the Assembly thank the queen?

When was the armament ready to sail for Quebec?

Who commanded the army?

(373.) What was he directed to do?

What did the colonies do?

What was done to protect the army and frontier?

Was the expedition successful?

What proportion of the troops died?
How many men did Connecticut lose?
What amount of Bills of Credit were issued?
What is said about the issue of paper money?
(374.) What efforts were the French making?
If they could accomplish this, what might follow?
Where and when did the governors meet?
For what object did they meet?
Who were invited to meet with them?
What was the result of their deliberations?
What did the Assembly do?
When and of whom was Ridgefield purchased?
(375.) When was the town incorporated and named?
Who were the principal proprietors?
What did Col. Schuyler do?
What address did he carry with him?
How were he and the sachems received?
What was the substance of their remarks to the queen?
(376.) What were they led to hope?
What advices arrived in New England?
What did Nicholson do?
What proved to be the object of the fleet?
When and why was an Assembly called?
How did Connecticut respond?
How soon were her troops in Boston?
When was the provincial fleet ready to sail?
Of what did it consist?
Who commanded it?
When did it reach Port Royal?
When and by what was the attack commenced?
(377.) When did the fort capitulate?
How many of the provincials were lost?
What did Nicholson next do?
What orders and promises did he bring from the queen?
Where did the governors meet?
When did the fleet arrive from England?
Of what was it destitute?
What suspicions were excited?
What did the colonies do?
What did the Assembly of Connecticut do?
What was the purport of their letter to the queen?
(378.) How soon were the army and fleet ready?
Of what was the fleet composed?
How many land forces were there?
Who commanded the fleet?
Who commanded the land forces?
How many troops had Nicholson?
Who commanded the Connecticut forces?
Who commanded those of New York and New Jersey?
When did Walker reach the St. Lawrence?
Where and how long did he remain?
What was his condition on the 22d?
What did the pilots advise?
What was the Admiral told?
What order did he give?
(379.) What further passed between Goddard and Walker?
How many transports were wrecked?
How many English officers and soldiers were lost?
For what place did the fleet sail?
How long before they arrived there?
What resulted from the council of war?
Upon whom was the failure of this expedition charged?
(380.) When was Hebron incorporated?
Who were the first settlers of the town?
When was Killingly incorporated and named?

Who were among the first settlers?
When was Newtown incorporated?
When was Coventry incorporated?
What is its situation?
When was the settlement at *Weatinoge* commenced?
What early families still retain an honorable position there?
(381.) When was the town incorporated?
What was it named?
When was Pomfret incorporated?
Who were among the early settlers?
What distinguished officer resided there?

CHAPTER XVIII.

(382.) When was the Treaty of Utrecht dated?
What had resulted from it?
What did the French Jesuits do?
What effect had the conduct of the English?
What charge was brought against Sebastian Ralle?
What course did Gov. Shute take?
What did he succeed in doing?
What was thought in regard to Father Ralle?
(383.) How did the Indians behave?
What specific act is referred to?
What was the supposed loss of the English?
Why did the government at Louisbourg refuse to pay it?
Who was sent to protect Eastern Massachusetts?
What was he ordered to inform the Indians?
What was resolved upon by Massachusetts?
What was further determined?
(384.) Did the governor and council concur?
What occurred the next year?
What is said of Father Ralle?
What occurred among the Norridgewocks?
What was done by the General Court of Massachusetts?
What is said in regard to the hostages?
(385.) What did the Council consent to?
What was accomplished by the expedition?
How did the Indians take their revenge?
To what did these depredations lead?
What tribes united with the Norridgewocks?
What depredations did they commit?
(386.) What effect had the war?
What request did Gov. Shute make?
What threat accompanied the request?
What did the Assembly of Connecticut do?
For what were commissioners appointed by Massachusetts?
What were they instructed to do?
What reference is made to Gov. Shute?
(387.) What expeditions are referred to?
How did Connecticut regard the war?
What part did she take in it?
(388.) When was Ashford settled and incorporated?
What officer was born there?
When was Tolland incorporated?
What served to retard the growth of the settlement?
What were the names of some of the settlers?
When was Stafford surveyed and settled?
What was ordered to be done with the proceeds of the unsold lands?
Who were the principal settlers?
When was Bolton settled and incorporated?
What names did the first settlers bear?
When was Bantam first settled?
Into how many rights was the town surveyed?

(389.) When was the town incorporated?

What were some of the names of the first settlers?

What name was given to the town?

CHAPTER XIX.

(390.) What is said of George II.?

Why did the Assembly take measures of defense?

What were those measures?

How were the regiments to be officered?

Why was Admiral Vernon sent abroad?

What were the principal objects aimed at?

(391.) What was the design of the English Government?

What were the colonies to do?

To what was the zeal of England in part owing?

When was the Assembly called?

What did the governor do when the requisition reached him?

What measures did the Assembly take?

What were the governor and committee of war authorized to do?

(392.) What was done for the protection of the coast?

To what amount were bills of credit issued?

What was done in England?

When did the armament sail from England?

Who was the commander of it?

Of what did it consist?

What was the extent of the united fleet of Cathcart and Vernon?

How many seamen were on board?

What was the extent of the land army?

(393.) When did Cathcart die?

On whom did the command of the army devolve?

What course did Vernon take?

How did his search end?

What had become of the French fleet?

What had taken place at Carthegena?

What did Vernon and Wentworth finally do?

What was the result of the attack?

When did the army and fleet withdraw?

How many Spanish vessels were captured?

(394.) What success did they meet with at Cuba?

What great misfortune followed?

How many died daily?

How many died in forty-eight hours?

What was the extent of the mortality among the New England troops?

What was resolved by the British government?

What is said of Oglethorpe?

(395.) Did France maintain her neutrality?

When did France declare war against England?

When and by whom was Canso captured?

What other place was attacked by Duvivoir?

What is said of Louisbourg?

What did the people of New England resolve?

(396.) What plan was suggested?

What did Gov. Shirley do?

What might be expected of Com. Warren?

What had been determined upon?

(397.) What was the naval force of New England?

When did Gov. Shirley reveal the plan to the General Court?

What was enjoined upon the members?

How was the plan regarded by the country members?

What arguments were used in favor of the measure?

(398.) What further arguments were urged?

What arguments were urged *against* the expedition?

(399.) What was the fate of the measure?

What course did Gov. Shirley now take?

Who petitioned that the measure might be revised and passed?

By what majority was it finally carried?

(400.) How was it received by the colonies?

What was the quota assigned to each New England colony?

When did the Assembly of Connecticut convene?

How many men did they vote to raise?

What bounty was offered?

Who was appointed commander-in-chief?

What other officers were appointed?

At what place were they to embark?

Who were appointed to proceed to Boston?

What was the object of their mission?

(401.) Who was commander-in-chief of the expedition?

Who was second in command?

What was the character of the soldiery?

What was the naval power of New England?

What naval captains are named?

Who commanded the whole naval force?

What did New York do?

What other captains were appointed in March?

Who was chaplain of the Connecticut troops?

What word was received from Com. Warren?

(402.) When did the troops arrive at Canso?

Of what did the land army consist?

What induced Com. Warren to sail for our coast?

With what ships did he reach Canso?

For what place did he sail thence?

(403.) What is said of the Renomme?

When did the fleet and army arrive at Chapeaurogue bay?

When did the enemy first learn the object of the expedition?

Who was sent to prevent the invaders from landing?

What was the result?

What was done on the following morning?

(404.) What further was accomplished by the advance corps?

What labor was now to be accomplished?

How were the difficulties surmounted?

(405.) How many fascine batteries were erected?

How was the Vigilant captured?

Who commanded her?

How many men, and what stores, were on board?

What might have changed the fortune of the expedition?

How was the British fleet augmented?

(406.) In what condition were the defenses of the town?

When did the enemy beg for a cessation of hostilities?

What took place on the 17th of June, 1745?

What was the condition of the provincial army?

How had the request for supplies and recruits been answered?

What did Connecticut vote to do?

(407.) When did the storm commence?

How long did it continue?

How were the soldiers sheltered?

What is said of their behavior?

How was the intelligence of the victory received in Boston?

What did Pennsylvania, New Jersey, and New York do?

(408.) What is said of the strength of Louisbourg?

How many men composed the garrison?

How did the French regard the capture?
What was the value of the prizes taken?
What added to the chagrin of the French?
(409.) What part had New England in the glory?
How many men did Connecticut furnish?
For what did Connecticut petition?
Was her prayer regarded?
What is said of England?
What did France resolve to do?
(410.) What plan was decided upon?
How many men were to be raised by the provinces?
How many men did New England raise?
How many were furnished by the other colonies?
How many were furnished by Connecticut?
What did the Assembly of Connecticut do?
(411.) How soon were our troops ready to embark?
Under whose command was a fleet being fitted out at Portsmouth?
How long was it delayed?
What did it accomplish?
What was done by France?
Of what did D'Anville's fleet consist?
How many land forces were on board?
Who were they to meet at Nova Scotia?
When did the fleet and armament leave France?
By what was D'Anville delayed?
What was done with one of his largest ships?
What became of the Mars and the Alcide?
Why did the Ardent put back?
(412.) When did D'Anville reach Chebucto?
What had become of his fleet?
What had become of Conflans?
What rumors prevailed?
Of what was it said to consist?
What effect had the news upon the colonies?
What defensive measures were taken?
(413.) What did D'Anville do?
Who succeeded him?
What did D'Estournelle propose?
What did the governor of Canada do?
What was decided upon?
What effect did this have upon D'Estournelle?
What course did Jonquiere take?
What is said of the fatality of the dysentery?
(414.) What incident defeated the plan of Jonquiere?
What effect had the storm in October?
What prepared the way for the peace of Aix la Chapelle?
To what amount were bills of credit issued by Connecticut?

CHAPTER XX.

(415.) To what are we apt to attribute too much importance?
What is said of Shakspeare and Bacon?
What is said of Milton and Cromwell?
(416.) To whom should we turn our attention?
What reference is made to English women?
For what are we to look in the undistinguished pioneers?
What has been thought of the origin of the people of Connecticut?
What has led to such an opinion?
(417.) Is such an idea correct?
What is said of their descent?
What does investigation show?
(418.) What prevented the pioneers from dwelling upon the past?
How did the puritan regard life?

How did he differ from others?
Were *all* the settlers thus forgetful of the past?
(419.) What is said of the most illustrious names in our history?
From what class did our first land-holders spring?
How is this proved?
What is said of the servants of the planters.
What might be explained by investigating this subject?
(420.) Why did the settlers engage in such humble employments?
(421.) What is said of Henry Wolcott?
In what occupations did Roger Wolcott engage?
What was the business of Webster and Welles?
What was Gov. Leete's business?
What is said of Gov. and Richard Treat?
To what hardships did Winthrop submit?
(422.) How was labor regarded?
How were idleness and vice looked upon?
What were our fathers unconsciously doing?
What is said of those who hold labor in derision?
Are we to infer that there were no grades in society?
What is said of the title of "*Honorable?*"
(423.) Who bore the title of "*Esquire?*"
When was Gov. Welles dignified with the title?
How was the title of "*Gentlemen*" used?
(424.) To whom did the prefix of "*Mr.*" (or *Master*) belong?
What classes did it embrace in Connecticut?
Of what was it an index?
What is said of the appellation of "*Sir!*"
To whom was the title of "*Goodman*" given?
(425.) What was the corresponding term applied to the other sex?
How were military titles regarded?
What was the highest military office in the colony?
Who bore that title first?
How was Mason regarded?
How were ecclesiastical titles held?
What titles of this class were in use?
(426.) When did society begin to assume its old English features?
By what terms were the different classes distinguished?
To whom was the term *Yeoman* applied?
What other title did they sometimes bear?
What changes took place in these classes?
What farther is said of Yeoman?
(427.) What is said of the educated class?
Who subsequently became the pillars of the aristocracy?
What was the position of the clergy?
What further is said of the aristocracy and yeomanry?
To whom was this respect for orders owing?
How were they compelled to live?
How did the planters pass their first winter on the Connecticut river?
(428.) What houses were soon erected?
What distinguished the houses of the clergy, governor and magistrates?
What is said of Mr. Whitfield's house?
In what kind of houses did the better classes live?
Of what were these frames made?
What is said of the rafters?
How was the building covered?
How were the rooms finished?
How were the windows constructed?

(429.) What is said of the doors?
What was the usual height of the rooms?
What were the peculiarities of the chimnies and fire-places?
How were the fires built?
(430.) What is said of the fire-side?
What superstitions are referred to?
What reference is made to King James I., Sir Water Raleigh, and others?
(431.) What were the peculiarities of Gov. Eaton's house?
Of what did breakfast consist among the planters?
What constituted their dinner?
(432.) Of what did their supper consist?
Of what was their table furniture made?
What is said of the tables of the clergy and magistrates?
What is said of food and furniture in after times?
What was the usual mode of traveling?
What was the character of the planters?
(433.) Of what have they been accused?
Of what kind was their bigotry?
What is a characteristic of reformers?
What extremes are referred to?
How did the bigotry of puritanism differ from that of the church of England?
In what respects did they both go to extremes?
(434.) How did the puritans and cavaliers behave toward each other?
What should be shunned in both?
How were the people of Connecticut taught to differ from those of Massachusetts?
Why had the puritans left England?
Upon what did they look with jealousy?
(435.) What did they resolve to do?
What were the public days of Connecticut?
How was fast day observed?
What was their great festival?
When was it appointed?
(436.) Where was it usually celebrated?
What preparations were made?
What is said of the gathering of families?
How was the day spent?
(437.) What took place after the repast?
What may have been their topics of conversation?
How was the evening closed?
How is the day still regarded?
(438.) What other occasions of festivity and rejoicing were there?
How are ancient and modern weddings contrasted?
What is said of balls in early times?
What was the comparative expense attending them?
(439.) What was the occasion and character of ordination balls?
What customs at funerals are referred to?
What particular funeral is referred to?
What reference to this custom was made by the Continental Congress?
(440.) How must the early planters have dressed?
What measures were adopted to provide themselves with clothing?
What part did the females perform in this work?
What costly articles of dress are referred to?
Of what were small-clothes made?
How were they fashioned?
(441.) What buckles were worn?
How was the coat made?
What variations in the style are referred to?
Of what colors were cloaks?
What was the usual shape of the hat?
What other styles are referred to?
(442.) When were watches and rings first worn in New England?
What is said of the hair and beard?
When were wigs worn in New England?
By what classes were they worn?

How did they effect the appearance of the wearer?
Of what, and how were they made?
When did they cease to be worn?
What reference is made to the women of New England?
What changes ultimately took place?
What articles were imported?
How are *Trailing Gowns* described?
What is said of *Hooped Skirts?*
(445.) What account is given of the *Towering Head Dresses*?

CHAPTER XXI.

(446.) What has been said in regard to the motives of the emigrants?
What is said of the doctrines of the Church of England?
What were the great points in dispute?
What must those do who could not conform?
(447.) Under what circumstances did many of the clergy come hither?
What was the character of the clergy?
What is said of the faithful scholar?
What is said of Davenport, Hooker and Wareham?
(448.) What reference is made to Blackman, Whitfield and Stone?
What were the usual church officers?
What exceptions were there?
How were the officers set apart?
What was the specific duty of the pastor?
(449.) What was the duty of the teacher?
What was the duty of the ruling elder?
What is said of the office of deacon?
What were his duties?
(450.) What were the qualifications of a deacon?
What was the number of deacons required?
What were the requisites of church-membership?
When did an opposing party manifest itself?
What were the peculiarities of this new party?
When and where did a General Council assemble?
What were the principal matters brought before them?
What was the substance of their decision?
Did this decision end the controversy?
What further was done?
Of what was this decision the origin?
Upon what belief did the churches act?
To what did they hold?
(452.) What was regarded as irregular?
How did the churches regard ordination?
What was the form of ordination?
By what authority were these views sustained?
How were the churches of Connecticut governed?
(453.) What is said of each individual church?
How was the Bible regarded?
What was the population of the colony at the date of the union?
How many clergymen were there?
How many families were there to each preacher?
How many families sometimes supported a minister?
(454.) What was the character of the clergy?
What is said of our ecclesiastical quarrels?
(455.) Where did the first of these quarrels originate?
In what condition were the people of Wethersfield?
To what did the controversy lead?
Who was the first pastor of Wethersfield?
When did he enter upon his duties there?
What is said of him?
When did he probably arrive in Boston?

When is he first known to have been a resident at Wethersfield?
(456.) How was he treated there?
What was the result of an investigation of the charges?
When did he die?
Who died shortly before?
Where and when was he born?
Where did he graduate?
What was he called?
What was the nature of his preaching?
With whom is he compared?
(457.) What is said of Davenport?
What is said of Cotton?
What is said of Hooker?
How was he regarded as an orator?
What is said of his prayers?
In what was he skilled?
What was his chief conflict?
What was his appearance?
Under what circumstances was Mason overawed by him?
(458.) Where and when did he die?
Who were the principal clergy of New Haven?
Where and when was James Pierpont born?
Where and when did he graduate?
When was he ordained at New Haven?
What farther is said of him?
How is he compared with Davenport, Wareham and Hooker?
What is said of his moral nature?
(460.) What was the character of the next great controversy?
How did it originate?
What was claimed?
What effect had the dispute throughout the commonwealth?
When and why did it terminate?
Who sided with Elder Goodwin?
(461.) Who succeeded Mr. Smith at Wethersfield?
In what way did Mr. Russell testify?
What views did he hold?
What act did he perform?
What was the character and position of Lieut. Hollister?
By whom was a petition signed?
(462, 463.) What was the prayer of the petitioners?
(464.) When did Hollister present the petition?
What order was obtained?
What was to be done with the reasons?
In case the order was not complied with, what course was to be taken?
(465.) When the Court met in October, what did it find?
What did the Court desire?
How did the quarrel end?
Who was at fault?
(466.) What took place in 1659?
What did the Court order in October, 1666?
To what did the ministers object?
What was done on that account?
What farther was done in the premises?
What was the great point at issue?
What had occasioned trouble in Windsor?
(467.) What did the General Court do?
What was the result of the ballot?
What did the legislature then devise?
What farther took place on the subject?
When was Mr. Mather settled in Windsor?
What is said of his ministry?
Where did a controversy now spring up?
To what did Mr. Whiting adhere?
(468.) What is said of Mr. Haynes?
What was the result of the controversy?
How did the controversy at Stratford result?
What is said of the Cambridge Platform?
What did the Assembly do?
When and where did the clergy meet?
What did they adopt?
What next disturbance is noted?
How did it originate?
How did it progress?

(469.) What did Mr. Ward and his friends do?
Did the legislature grant their request?
What did the church under Mr. Ruggles do?
When and how was the contest ended?
When did the "great revival" commence?
Where and under whose preaching did it begin?
Where did it spread?
What succeeded it?
When did it re-commence?
Who were its subjects?
(470.) Who were its advocates and co-workers?
By whom was it opposed?
What laws were passed?
What were some of its abuses?
(471.) What course was taken by ecclesiastical bodies?
What pretexts were there for this course?
What is said of the trial of Mr. Robbins?
What is said of the controversy in Milford?
How did it result?
What course did Mr. Noyes take?
What resulted from this?
When was Mr. Bird installed over the new church?
When did the "Wallingford Controversy" prevail?
How did it commence?
What charges were made against Mr. Dana?
How were the ordaining council treated?
(473.) When was the new Society incorporated?
Who became their Pastor?
What is said of the religion of the colony?
What was done by the General Court in October, 1644?
What was the nature of the proposition?
From what was this principle in part borrowed?
How did the plan differ from that of England?
What were the whole population obliged to do?
What provision was made for dissenters?
What was the operation of the system?
(474.) What is said of these ecclesiastical difficulties?

www.ingramcontent.com/pod-product-compliance
Lightning Source LLC
LaVergne TN
LVHW021100110826
845150LV00001B/136